ESSAYS ON
MODERNIZATION OF
UNDERDEVELOPED SOCIETIES

VOLUME TWO

Essays on Modernization of Underdeveloped Societies

VOLUME TWO

Editor

A. R. DESAI

Department of Sociology
University of Bombay

HUMANITIES PRESS

New York   1972

First published
in the United States of America 1972
by Humanities Press Inc.,
303 Park Avenue South
New York, N.Y. 10010

SBN 391-00214-7

PRINTED IN INDIA
PRINTED AT MOHAN MUDRANALAYA, BOMBAY 15 DD (INDIA)

CONTENTS

VOLUME TWO

1

THE SELF-CONTRADICTORY CHARACTER OF INTROSPECTIVE PSYCHOLOGICAL AND NON-COGNITIVE META-ETHICAL SOCIAL THEORIES

F. S. C. NORTHROP

By AN introspective psychological ethical or normative social theory will be meant one that identifies the whole or a part of the meaning of the word "good" with introspective psychological data such as a pleasure, pain, approval, disapproval, preference or interest. When the whole of the meaning is so identified, the introspective psychological ethical theory is cognitive; when this is true only of part of the meaning of any normative word and the remaining part refers to a sentence of a non-indicative type of which it is meaningless to predicate truth or falsity, the theory is to that extent non-cognitive. Irreducible command theory, or decision-making law and politics, is one example. When the entire meaning of normative words is of the latter type, the ethical or social theory is completely non-cognitive. These distinctions will be given analytic clarification and precision in the sequel. We shall examine cognitive introspective psychological ethical theories first.

The meta-ethical Postulate 1E of the version which identifies the meaning of the word "good" with an introspected approval of the object being judged is:

1E For any person p and for any object of ethical judgment x to say

1

that x is good as judged by p is equivalent to saying that x or its causal effect is approved by p.

Substitute the expressions "pleasant to", "preferred by" or "an object of interest of" for "approved by" in the foregoing postulate and one has the hedonistic, preference or interest version of an introspective psychological ethical theory. This substitutability means that the theories are formally equivalent. Hence, what holds formally for one of them holds for all the others. In what follows we shall use the approval version and occasionally the hedonistic.

Once Postulate 1E above, or any formal equivalent, is assumed, ethical judgments become cognitive. To say that a judgment is cognitive is to affirm that it is meaningful to predicate truth or falsity of propositions expressing the judgment. The cognitive character of introspective psychological theories of ethics follows from 1E. It tells us that in order to determine the truth or falsity of one's ethical judgment one has merely to introspect whether the object of the judgment is associated in one's radically empirical experience with one's approval, preference, interest or a sensation of pleasure.

An interesting question arises when one applies such a criterion of the truth or falsity of ethical judgments to any introspective psychological theory of ethics itself. Such an application occurs in Lord Russell's essay, "Is There Ethical Knowledge?" Here he writes: "I, for one, find it intolerable to suppose that when I say 'Cruelty is bad' I am merely saying, 'I dislike cruelty,' or something equally subjective." [1] Stated in terms of the approval theory, this sentence is "I, for one, find it something I must disapprove to suppose that when I say 'Cruelty is bad' I am merely saying 'I disapprove of cruelty' or something equally subjective." In this statement Lord Russell is disapproving of an introspective psychological theory of the meaning of ethical words if it has the consequence indicated. In short, he is making the introspective psychological theory of ethics itself an object of ethical judgment. His statement also assumes it to be a meaningful possibility that the approval theory is disapproved. Isn't there something paradoxical about such a theory?

It will help us to answer this question if we consider the remainder of Lord Russell's article. It attempts to show that the approval theory, or its formal equivalent psychological hedonism, does not have the intolerable consequence to which he refers. His procedure consists in distinguishing between "good" as equated with "x is approved by me" and "objectively good or bad" as equated with "x is what the majority approve or disapprove" and then adding the empirical assumption that what the majority

---

[1] Russell, Bertrand, *Human Society in Ethics and Politics*, Simon & Schuster, New York, 1955, Chapter IX, p. 92.

approve possesses three common qualities of which pleasantness is the most important and "intelligence and aesthetic sensibility" are also requisite.

Does this proposal escape the "intolerable"? The following considerations throw light on this question.

The proposal entails operationally that before one can make a personal normative judgment with any objective validity he must first carry through an empirical sociological and anthropological survey to determine two things: (a) What the majority approve, and (b) whether what they approve is characterized by pleasant consequences, intelligence and aesthetic sensibility. I find it difficult to reconcile this consequence of Lord Russell's proposal with his own moral judgments. My high respect for his moral courage and integrity does not arise from observing in him the habit of catering and pandering to what the majority approve before stating his own moral convictions not merely about what he, but also about what they, should do. Instead, I respect his moral courage and integrity, even in some instances when I may not agree with his judgment, because he utters his judgments forthrightly and publicly, frequently drawing down upon himself the bitter criticism and disapproval of public opinion, going to jail if necessary for his convictions. Must not any theory of personal ethics have consequences such as this for its adherents if the expression "moral courage and moral integrity" is to have any meaning?

Consider now the empirical assumption in his theory—the thesis namely that what the majority approve does in fact have the three common qualities listed above. Viewed from a purely theoretical standpoint, this version of the approval theory is far less likely to be true than the approval theory without this empirical assumption. It has often been noted by mathematical physicists that the theory that planets move in an orbit which is an eclipse is far more likely to be true than the earlier thesis that their orbits are perfect circles, the reason being that of any two theories, one of which is a special case of the other, the more general case is theoretically the more probable.

Even so, what is theoretically less probable may be the case empirically. Unfortunately, however, Lord Russell presents no empirical evidence supporting the empirical assumption that conduct which the majority approve possesses the three common qualities which he specifies. Clearly, to give such evidence would require that he be a social anthropologist or that he present the findings of social anthropologists, and this he has not done. This suggests that these three qualities refer in his case not to what the majority do in fact approve, but to what they ought to approve if Lord Russell is not to find their approvals intolerable. Note the words with which he prefaces his empirical assumption that majority-approved conduct possesses the common properties of "intelligence and aesthetic sensibility"

as well as pleasantness. These prefatory words are "I think we must include such things etc.".[2] Clearly his "I think we must" is not a cognitive
statement of fact that the majority approve only of conduct characterized
by these three qualities; it is instead an evaluative statement of what ought
to characterize the conduct approved by the majority. The cognitivism of
this attempt to save the approval theory of ethics from the intolerable is,
therefore, spurious. One is able to accept the approval theory, retain ethical
cognitivism and escape the intolerable only by shifting from what the
majority approve in fact to what they ought to approve.

The adherent of the approval theory or of any other psychological
theory of ethics and law is left, therefore, on the horns of the following
dilemma: If he saves the cognitivism of his normative judgments, which
he affirms to be the major merit of his theory, he is forced to implications
which he finds intolerable and must disapprove of most vehemently. If, on
the other hand, he amends the theory after the manner of Lord Russell by
requiring that what the majority approve exhibits certain specified common properties, then he loses his cognitivism.

Of the two horns of this dilemma, it is the former which any adherent
of the approval theory must choose—for he can accept the alternative non-
cognitive version of the approval theory only by committing the logical
fallacy of shifting surreptitiously from what in fact the majority do approve
to what they ought to approve. But to accept the former alternative leaves
the cognitive approvalist in the paradoxical position of affirming a theory
which (*i*) identifies the word "good" with what he approves, and (*ii*) implies consequences which are for him intolerable and hence to be disapproved. Such a predicament raises the question whether the approval,
or any other cognitive psychological, theory of ethics is not a self-
contradictory theory.

The following considerations suggest an affirmative answer. As noted
above, the approval version of the introspective psychological theory of
ethics is:

1E For any person p and for any object of ethical judgment x, the expression "x is good as judged by p" is equivalent to the expression
   "x is approved by p."

The phrase at the beginning of this postulate expresses the fact that p and
x are universally quantified variables.

This phrase is necessary for very important reasons. No ethical theorist
is affirming that his theory of what the word "good" means is the case
only for one or some objects of ethical judgment. It would be a poverty-

---

[2] *Ibid.*, p. 99.

stricken theory indeed that would not be plausible for at least one object of normative judgment. Similarly, when the adherent of any ethical theory specifies what he believes the meaning of the word "good" to be, he is not asserting the singular proposition "This is the case, merely for me"; nor is he affirming the particular proposition "This is the case, merely for some p, namely those who happen to agree with me." Otherwise his theory would be trivial and of interest only to the members of his intimate family and to his biographer. Instead, he is making the universal, rather than merely an autobiographical, statement that the meaning of normative words in anyone's experience and in anyone's linguistic usage turns out under careful analysis, even when some people may suppose the contrary, to be what the elemental postulate of his ethical theory affirms. One method for determining which theory of the meaning of normative words is correct is that, therefore, of pressing the elemental universally quantified ethical postulate of each theory to its logical consequences to determine whether it leaves meaningless ethical statements which even the adherent of the theory must admit to be meaningless. Another method is to determine whether the logical consequences of a particular ethical theory are self-contradictory. This is the method we are pursuing here.

But if any theory is to be tested in either of these two ways, its elemental ethical postulate must be fully and accurately stated. This will not be the case unless it is realized that what is being affirmed concerning the meaning of ethical words is being affirmed not merely for all objects of ethical judgment but also for all people making such judgments. Hence, the importance of the universally quantified variables p and x in the phrase, "For any person p and for any object of ethical judgment x" in Postulate 1E above.

Since ordinary prose is frequently ambiguous concerning the quantification of its variables, such as "person" or "object of ethical judgment", leaving it uncertain whether what is affirmed of them holds for all or merely some instances, and also for reasons of brevity in establishing a proof, it is advisoble to state postulate 1E in the symbolism of *Principia Mathematica*: Let (p) (x) mean "For any person p and any object x"; $\exists p$ and $\exists x$ mean "There exists at least one p" and "There exists at least one x"; the symbol $\therefore$ mean that all to its right holds for the preceding quantified variables; the symbol $=$ mean the relation of equivalence between sentences; and the symbol $:=:$ mean that the sentence to its right is equivalent merely to the portion to its left that follows the symbol $\therefore$. The elemental assumption of the approval theory, where x means any object of ethical judgment, then is:

1E $\quad (p)$ (x) $\therefore$ x is good as judged by p $:=:$ x is approved by p.
2E $\quad (p)$ (x) $\therefore$ x is bad as judged by p $:=:$ x is disapproved by p.

M-2

The symbol (x) in $1E$ tells us that any object of ethical judgment whatever may be substituted for x. To consider whether the approval theory of ethics is intolerable is equivalent to considering whether it is to be disapproved most vehemently and is, therefore, to treat it as a proper object of ethical judgment. Postulate $1E$, therefore, permits us to substitute the approval theory itself for x in $1E$. Since the expression "x is approved by p" to the right of the $:=:$ in $1E$ leaves it a purely empirical question as to whether the object of ethical judgment is approved or disapproved, $1E$ entails the theoretical possibility that the approval theory is disapproved by at least one person. But by $2E$, to say that an object of ethical judgment is disapproved is equivalent to saying that it is bad. It follows that the approval theory of the meaning of the word "good" entails as meaningful the theoretical possibility that its meaning of the word "good" is bad. In short, the approval theory, or any other formally equivalent, introspective psychological theory of the meaning of normative words is an ethically self-contradictory theory.

We do not have to restrict ourselves, however, to a mere theoretical possibility. There exists at least one person, the writer if not Lord Russell, who disapproves of the approval theory because he finds the theory to be intolerable in its consequences with respect to the objectivity of moral judgments. The following proposition is, therefore, empirically true.

There exists at least one person such that the approval theory of what the word "good" means is disapproved and, therefore, by its own criterion, bad.

It follows not merely as a theoretically entailed *possibility* but also in empirical actuality that this or any other formally equivalent introspective psychologically theory of ethics is ethically self-contradictory.

To be ethically self-contradictory is also to be logically self-contradictory. It follows that the foregoing proof can be put in a purely logical form, *i.e.*, the form of a non-normatively worded contradiction. To show this let us begin again with

$1E$ $(p) \cdot (x) \therefore x$ is good as judged by $p :=: p$ approves of x.

Substituting the approval theory itself in $1E$, thereby eliminating x, gives

THEOREM 1 (p) The approval theory is good as judged by $p :=:$
p approves of the approval theory.

Consider first the sentence to the left of the equivalence sign in this theorem. It is
S The approval theory is good as judged by p.

Assuming the approval theory, is it possible to say anything concerning its truth or falsity when considered thus by itself?

It is to be noted first that S is a metameta-ethical sentence. Its subject, "The approval theory", is equivalent to the meta-ethical sentence $1E$ which has as its subject the ethical sentence "x is good as judged by p". Conversely, since a sentence is ethical if it asserts a normative word such as "good" of something x, and since a meta-ethical sentence is a sentence such as $1E$ which makes an assertion about the ethical sentence "x is good as judged by p", so sentence S which makes an assertion about the meta-ethical assertion $1E$ is a metameta-ethical sentence.

Consider the meaning of (a) the subject and (b) the predicate of the metameta-ethical sentence S. Analysis exhibits

Three Laws of Metameta-Ethics

The subject term of S is "the approval theory". Since this theory is the meta-ethical theory of the meaning of the ethical predicate "good" specified in $1E$, the meaning of the subject term of the metameta-ethical assertion S is $1E$. But there are many different meta-ethical theories of the meaning of the ethical word "good", of which the word "good" may be metameta-ethically predicated after the manner of sentence S. Whatever the meta-ethical theory T, however, of which the word "good" is thus metameta-ethically predicated, the following metameta-ethical law I^{mm} will hold concerning the meaning of the subject term:

I^{mm} (T^m) (p) $\therefore$ The meaning of T^m in "T^m is good" $:=:$ The meta-ethical postulate of T^m.

Consider now the meaning of the predicate term in any metameta-ethical statement, such as S, of the form "T^m is good". Since whatever T^m may be, the meaning of "good" is given by the meta-ethical postulate of T^m, it follows that the second law of metameta-ethics holds.

II^{mm} (T^m) (p) $\therefore$ The meaning of "good" in "T^m $:=:$ The meta-ethical postulate of T^m.

Since by I^{mm} and II^m, the subject term (a) and the predicate term (b) of any metameta-ethical statement of the form "T^m is good" have the same meaning, the following metameta-ethical law is true tautologically and hence true for any p.

III^{mm} (T^m) (p) "T^m is good." Taut,

Substituting the approval theory for T^m in III^{mm}, gives the following tautologically true proposition concerning the approval theory. Let us call it

THEOREM 2. (p) The approval theory is good.   Taut.

By the meta-ethical postulate $1E$ of this theory, this is equivalent to

THEOREM 3. (p) The approval theory is approved by p.

But by $1E$, because of the sentence to the right of its equivalence sign, the approval theory entails the theoretically meaningful possibility that whatever x may be, at least one person p may disapprove of x. In other words, whether x, whatever it be, is approved or disapproved is an empirical question. Hence the approval theory entails the following theoretically meaningful possibility, which in the case of the approval theory for the writer, if not for Lord Russell, is an actuality.

THEOREM 4. $(x) \exists p \therefore p$ disapproves of x.

Substituting the approval theory for x, thereby eliminating x, gives

THEOREM 5. $\exists p \therefore p$ disapproves of the approval theory.

But Theorem 5 is the contradictory of Theorem 3. The approval theory is, therefore, a logically as well as an ethically self-contradictory theory and therefore false on purely logical as well as moral grounds.

Examination of the two proofs exhibits this difference between them: The proof that the theory is ethically self-contradictory consists of the demonstration that its own specification of what the words "good" and "bad" mean entails the theoretically meaningful possibility that good is bad. The direct proof that the theory is logically self-contradictory consists in showing that it entails in Theorem 3 a universal affirmative proposition and in Theorem 5 the substantively identical particular negative proposition.

It has been suggested that these proofs are invalid because to say of any proposition that it is disapproved does not entail that it is false. This suggestion is erroneous for two reasons.

First, the foregoing proofs do not rest on the false assumption that to disapprove of *any* proposition entails its falsity. The falsity of the postulate that states the approval theory of ethics is the by-product of its self-contradictory character; falsity is not a part of the proof that it is self-contradictory.

Second, the suggestion requires for its validity the assumption that for *no* proposition is it the case that disapproval entails falsity. In other words, the suggestion assumes that because it is the case with most propositions that to disapprove of them does not entail their falsity, therefore this is the case with all propositions. This assumption is both a logical *non sequitur* and empirically false. Two concrete examples will show why.

Consider the proposition, "The earth is spherical in shape." Obviously, to disapprove of this proposition is irrelevant to its truth or falsity, since neither the meaning of the word "earth" nor that of the word "sperical" makes any reference to a person's approvals or disapprovals. The same is true of G. E. Moore's meta-ethical theory that "good" is a non-empirical primitive ethical predicate.

(*p*) (*x*) ∴ *x* is good := : ϕ *x*, where ϕ is a primitive non-empirical ethical predicate.[3]

Hence, to approve or disapprove of such propositions throws no light on the truth or falsity of what the proposition affirms. But such is not the case when the substantive content of the proposition refers to approvals or disapprovals. Then to disapprove or approve of what the proposition affirms is relevant to the truth or falsity of what it affirms. Consequently, if the proposition contains also an ethical word such as "good", then to disapprove of the proposition may entail that it is ethically and logically self-contradictory. The assumption upon which the critic's suggestion rests (the assumption, namely, that for *all* propositions, disapproval does not entail falsity) is, therefore, erroneous.

There is, however, a more weighty objection that may be brought against the foregoing proofs. This objection appeals to the theory of types and its thesis that a function cannot take itself as a value of one of its variables. Our proofs violate this restriction when they substitute the approval theory itself for the variable *x* in the basic meta-ethical postulate of this theory.

What is to be said of this objection? First, it is a formal one; and, as mathematicians have noted of the theory of types in Russell and Whitehead's logical theory of mathematics, it seems to be an *ad hoc* assumption not justified on purely logical grounds. Moreover, when appealed to in mathematics, the result is the ruling out of theorems which the science requires. To avoid this consequence, the theory had to be restricted, thereby becoming even more *ad hoc* and artificial. Second, Professor Paul Weiss and the mathematical logician, Professor F. B. Fitch have noted that the theory of types rules out all self-referential statements, whereas it is neces-

---

[3] Moore, G. E., *Principia Ethica*, Cambridge Press, London, 1922, pp. 6-16.

sary to have such statements.[4] Moreover, Professor Fitch has developed a
logic in which such self-referential statements can be made. Hence, the
rejection of our proof on logical grounds is not warranted. Third, we are
concerned with ethical and legal theory. The elemental ethical postulates
of such theory define the most basic beliefs and institutions of men. For
example, as Sir Henry Maine has shown,[5] "law of status" societies (still
persisting throughout Africa, Asia and the Old South in the United States)
identify the meaning of ethical words not with introspective psychological
data, but with data of natural history and biology such as sex, primogeni-
ture of birth, color of skin and tribal origin of one's ancestors. To apply
the theory of types to such theories is, therefore, to prevent one from
evaluating these beliefs and institutions as good or bad.   Nevertheless,
it is precisely of people's normative beliefs that it is most appropriate
to predicate goodness and badness or justice and injustice. Another unfortunate consequence of applying the theory of types to meta-ethical
statements, therefore, is that G. E. Moore's "open question argument"[6]
becomes invalid for such objects of ethical judgment. Similarly, Lord Russell's evaluative reference to the approval theory as "intolerable" should
it have certain consequences also becomes meaningless. It appears, therefore, that the appeal to the theory of types in order to avoid our proofs of
a contradiction in the approval theory of ethics is not justified on either
logical or ethical grounds.

It was noted in the first paragraph of this inquiry that psychological
hedonism, the preference theory or the theory of interests are formally
equivalent to the approval theory. Hence the proof of a formal contradiction in any one of them is a proof of such a contradiction in all of them.
To demonstrate this in each case, substitute the expressions "pleasant to",
"preferred by" or "object of interest of" for "approved by" in Postulate
$1E$; substitute the resultant postulate for the variable x in itself, and then
predicate for at least one person the respective "painful", "not preferred"
or "not interesting" of this statement. We conclude, therefore, that all
cognitive introspective psychological theories of the meaning of the words
"good", "objectively good" or "legally just" are ethically and logically self-
contradictory theories.

The dilemma in which the adherent of any introspective psychological
theory of ethics finds himself was described above. It was noted that the
intolerable type of subjectivity to which the theory leads can be escaped

[4] Fitch, F. B., *Symbolic Logic*, Ronald Press, New York, 1952, and "Self-Reference
in Philosophy", *Mind*, Vol. 55, n.s., 1946, pp. 64-73; Weiss, Paul, "The Theory of
Types", *Mind*, n.s., Vol. 37, 1928, pp. 338-48. See also Urban, W. M., *Humanity and
Deity*, Allen & Unwin, London, 1959, p. 209n.

[5] Maine, Sir Henry S., *Ancient Law*, John Murray, London, 1908, p. 151.

[6] Moore, *op. cit.*, p. 43.

by rejecting the theory's claim to being a cognitive theory and by identifying the meaning of "objectively good" not with what the majority of mankind do in fact approve or find pleasant, but with what they ought to approve or find pleasant. Is this non-cognitive version any the less self-contradictory? The following considerations show that it is not.

By normative non-cognitivism we mean any theory of the meaning of ethical words such as those formulated by Professors Charles Stevenson and A. J. Ayer in Anglo-American analytic philosophy and by Professor Alf Ross of Copenhagen in value theory and jurisprudence.[7] Professors Stevenson and Ayer often call this type of theory an "emotive theory". Professor Ross has described it as "the non-logical character of value propositions". Both terminologies are unfortunate.

The word "emotive" is likely to be misleading because of its ambiguity. This becomes evident when it is noted that the introspection of an emotion or passion is as much a cognitive item of meaning as is the introspection of pleasantness, an interest, an approval or a preference. Were "the emotivists" using the word "emotive" in this sense, their theory would be cognitive and formally equivalent to any of the cognitive introspective psychological theories considered above. Also they would be open to Moore's "naturalistic fallacy" which they affirm to be a fallacy. Then to say "this introspected emotion is good" would be equivalent to uttering the trivial tautology, "this introspected emotion is this introspected emotion." Clearly this is not what Professors Stevenson and Ayer mean. Instead, they are using the word "emotive" not in the sense of a cognitively knowable introspective psychological datum, but in the quite different sense of the assertion about some object x, of a statement of a non-indicative kind, of which it is meaningless to say that it is true or false.

The "emotivists" Ayer and Stevenson, therefore, agree with Moore that when one says, "My introspected passion is good", one is not uttering the trivial tautology, "My introspected passion is my introspected passion"; instead, one is asserting a synthetic statement, i.e., one in which the predicate term adds a meaning not given in the meaning of the subject term. Their difference from Moore and all other ethical cognitivists consists in the rejection of the thesis that the predication of the non-tautological ethical predicate of any object x of ethical judgment is a proposition, i.e., an indicative sentence of which it is meaningful to affirm that it is true or

[7] For complex examples of such theories, see Charles L. Stevenson's "The Emotive Meaning of Ethical Terms", *Mind*, Vol. 46, 1937, pp. 14-31; "Ethical Judgments and Avoidability", *ibid.*, Vol. 47, 1938, pp. 45-57; "Persuasive Definitions", *ibid.*, Vol. 47, pp. 331-50; and *Ethics and Language*, Yale Univ. Press, New Haven, 1944; Ayer, A. J., *Language, Truth and Logic*, Gollancz, London, 1948; Alf Ross, *Towards a Realistic Jurisprudence*, Munksgaard, Copenhagen, 1946, and "On the Logical Nature of Propositions of Value", *Theoria*, Vol. 11, pp. 172-210.

false; instead such synthetic sentences are not propositions but exclamatory, hortatory, imperative or ejaculatory assertions. This thesis, applied to a part of or the whole meaning of any normative word, is what we mean by normative non-cognitivism.

Alf Ross's statement of this theory as "the non-logical character of value propositions" is even more unfortunate. A proposition is by definition a sentence of which it is meaningful to say that it is true or false. By "non-logical" Ross means a sentence of which it is meaningless to affirm truth or falsity. Hence to talk about "non-logical propositions" in value theory is to talk about the self-contradictory. What Professor Alf Ross means clearly is instead the thesis, identical with that of Professors Ayer and Stevenson, that synthetic *sentences* which predicate a normative word of an object x of ethical judgment are in part at least non-indicative sentences of which it is meaningless to affirm that they are true or false. In short, the meaning in the predicate term of the assertion that is not contained in the meaning of the subject term of the sentence refers in part at least to a non-indicative sentence about the object of normative judgment x and is in this sense non-cognitive in meaning.

Expressed more concretely, it affirms that the meaning of any sentence containing a normative word such as "good", "bad", "just" or "unjust" entails, when correctly analyzed, the reference to at least one non-indicative sentence such as "Cheers!" "Boo!" "Shoulder arms" or "You like x also." The simplest and usual analytic statement of normative non-cognitivism then becomes the following, where $N-C$ means a meta-ethical postulate of normative non-cognitivism.

$1E^{N-C}$ (p) (x) $\therefore$ x is good as judged by p
  $:=:$ (a) p approves of x and
   (b) p utters of x "Cheers!"
$2E^{N-C}$ (p) (x) $\therefore$ x is bad as judged by p
  $:=:$ (a) p disapproves of x and
   (b) p utters of x "Boo!" [8]

Note that sentence (a) to the right of the equivalence sign insures that $1E^{N-C}$ is an introspective psychological theory of ethics, whereas sentence (b) specifies that it is the non-cognitive version of such a theory. Our final question now becomes: Is this theory specified by Postulates $1E^{N-C}$ and $2E^{N-C}$ any the less self-contradictory than the cognitive introspective psychological theory of ethics that was analytically stated in Postulates $1E$ and $2E$?

---

[8] For much more complex and subtle examples of such a theory, see Stevenson, Charles L., *Ethics and Language, op. cit.* note 7.

To answer this question, let us make the following substitutions in the proofs, given above, that the latter theory is ethically and logically self-contradictory: (*i*) Replace the original Postulates 1E and 2E with Postulates $1E^{N-C}$ and $2E^{N-C}$. (*ii*) Substitute the latter non-cognitive theory itself for x in Postulate $1E^{N-C}$. (*iii*) Assert for at least one person p the non-indicative sentence "Boo!" of this non-cognitive theory, after the manner in which, in the original proof, "disapproves of" was asserted of the cognitive approval theory. Since, throughout these substitutions, the form of the proof remains invariant, it follows that non-cognitive as well as cognitive introspective psychological theories of ethics are self-contradictory.

This proof that any non-cognitive introspective psychological theory of ethics is self-contradictory is due not to its introspective psychological assumption (a) but to its non-cognitive assumption (b). In short, the non-cognitivism alone is self-contradictory. It follows (as Professor Fitch suggested in his article on self-referential statements) [9] that any non-cognitive theory of the meaning of normative words [whether it be asociated with cognitive assumptions as in $1E^{N-C}$ (a) or not] is a self-contradictory theory.

The following ethical or other normative theories, being self-contradictory, are, therefore, false. (1) Any introspective psychological theory. (2) Any non-cognitive theory. (3) Any combination of (1) and (2). These results are not however purely negative. They suggest

Several Positive Conclusions

The proof that any non-cognitive metanormative theory is self-contradictory entails that the meaning of normative words is cognitive. There are reasons, however, for believing that at least some traditional cognitive normative theories are also self-contradictory or else fail to give meaning to what is clearly meaningful and even required, especially in legal science. Hence, the articulation of a consistent and adequate normative cognitivism must await another occasion.

Nevertheless, an examination of the source of the contradiction in the two proofs given above indicates specific conditions which must be met if such a theory is to be achieved. Since the contradiction shows itself in slightly different ways in two proofs, the analysis of each helps to narrow the range of possibilities within which the correct cognitive normative theory is to be found.

The proof that any introspective psychological or non-cognitive metanormative theory of the meaning of the word "good" is ethically self-

[9] Fitch, F. B. *Symbolic Logic, op. cit.,* p. 221 and "Self-Reference in Philosophy", *Mind, op. cit.,* note 4.

contradictory arises in major part from the theory's intolerable consequences with respect to the objectivity of moral judgments. This intoler-
ability is especially serious in law where the normative judgment is assumed to be prescriptive for the accused and not merely for the judge or
the majority in the legislature who approved of the statute under which
the defendant is declared to be guilty. What is it in any introspective psychological or non-cognitive theory of the meaning of normative words that
leads to such morally and legally intolerable and inadequate consequences?
Clearly it is the relativity to the perceiver or to the evaluator of the item
of knowledge or the non-indicative statements with which the meaning of
such normative words as "good", "just" or "legally obligatory" are identified. What is one person's pleasure is another person's pain. What one
person cheers, another person may boo.

A question arises immediately: Why identify the meaning of normative
words with such factors? To ask this question is to become aware that
introspective psychological and non-cognitive theories of ethics, law and
politics are not the primitive meta-ethical theories they frequently pur-
port to be. Instead, they assume also as unqualifiedly true a cognitive
epistemological premise—that is called radical empiricism. For it is only
if one restricts all meaningful words to determine, denotatively presented
or ostensibly defined factors, given radically empirically through the so-
called outer senses or introspectively, that it becomes necessary, as in the
meta-ethical affirmations $1E$ or $1E^{N-C}$ above, to identify the meaning of
all normative words with nothing but such radically empirical factors which
are thus relative to the particular percipient or evaluator. It follows positively that if an ethically consistent and legally adequate theory of the
cognitive meaning of normative words is to be achieved, there must be
at least one normative word and sentence, the meaning of which refers
to an item of knowledge that is not relative to the percipient and the
evaluator, applying to the person being judged, the judge and the majority-
approved norms of the legal system alike. In other words, a consistent
normative cognitivism entails that the meaning of at least one normative
word and sentence be identified with an item of cognitive meaning the
same for everyone of (1) a naive realistic or (2) a Kantian or (3) a neo-
Kantian or (4) a logically realistic epistemology. By (4) is meant a theory
of conceptual meaning in which, as in the epistemology resulting from the
philosophical analysis of the theories and methods of contemporary mathematical physics, there are irreducible axiomatized "constructs", of what
the writer has called "concepts by postulation that are concepts by intel-
lection" designating entities and laws which are the same for all percipients, related by "epistemic correlations" or "rules of correspondence" to

the "concept by intuition" of a radically empirical epistemology.[10] The specification of which of these four possibilities is the correct one must also await another occasion.

Possibility (1), however, can be dismissed immediately. A naive realistic epistemology identifies the meaning of any word with an item of knowledge purporting to be the same in its defining properties for all percipients, yet identifies these defining properties with naively given, i.e., radically empirically inspected, qualities. Experts in naively known or radically empirical objects of knowledge—radical empiricists such as Berkeley and Hume—have shown, however, that all such radically empirical qualities or relations, whether primary, secondary or tertiary qualities, are relative to the percipient. The objectivity, the same for everybody, which naive realism purports to give, is, therefore, spurious. Also when the meaning of normative words is identified with such naive realistic notions, Moore's naturalistic fallacy occurs. It follows positively that a consistent normative cognitivism must restrict itself to epistemological possibility (2) or (3) or (4) above.

Do our two proofs, that introspective psychological or non-cognitive meta-normative theories are self-contradictory, throw any light on which of these three possibilities is the correct one? Let us call these two proofs the "ethically self-contradictory" and the "logically self-contradictory" versions.

With respect to the former, it is to be noted that a radically empirical introspective psychological ethical cognitivism does not become ethically self-contradictory if, remaining consistently and completely radically empirical, one keeps the theory purely autobiographical, never universalizing it meta-ethically and never attempting to find any meaning for the goodness or badness of the object being judged so far as the object itself or other people are concerned. What this ethically consistent introspective psychological cognitivism amounts to is the merely singular autobiographical meta-ethical proposition holding only for the evaluator. Then, when I affirm another person's conduct to be good or bad, I am making a meta-ethical identification of the word "good" with my private, introspected psychological approval of the object of ethical judgment x and this meta-ethical identification is known to be cognitively true only for me.

Let us call this ethically consistent introspective psychological ethical cognitivism "autobiographical cognitivism". It permits of two possibilities: (a) One can leave this private meta-ethical theory unrestrictedly radical empirical and unrestrictedly autobiographical, or (b) one can restrict it by identifying the meaning of non-autobiographical goodness or badness which

---

[10] Northrop, F. S. C., *The Logic of the Sciences and the Humanities*, Macmillan, New York, 1947, Chapters V and VII.

is the same for all evaluators, with an item of cognitive knowledge of epistemological type (2) or (3) or (4) above. Possibility (*a*) we shall call "unrestricted autobiographical normative cognitivism", possibility (*b*) "restricted autobiographical normative cognitivism".

In the case of (*a*), an ethical contradiction of the form exhibited in our first proof cannot arise because of intolerable consequences with regard to the objectivity of normative judgments, since on this unrestricted radically empirical autobiographical theory, objectivity is meaningless. At most a contradiction might seem to arise only under the empirical circumstance that, speaking purely autobiographically, I disapprove of what I approve. Because, however, this unrestricted autobiographical cognitivism affirms no universal meta-ethical proposition about all persons and all objects of ethical judgment, or even about the same object at different times, my disapproving of what I approved a moment ago means merely that I have changed my mind or that a sensation of pleasantness associated with the object *x* has been succeeded by a sensation of pain. To say the same thing legally, one autobiographical judgment sets, even for the same judge and two completely similar objects of his judgment, no *stare decisis* precedent for the next autobiographical judgment. Hence to apply unrestricted autobiographical normative cognitivism consistently is to reject both a personal morality of principle and litigational dispute-settling under codified or codifiable laws prescriptive for everybody, for a purely existential, nominalistically particular operational procedure such as mediation in which the mediator conveys the autobiographical assertions of each disputant to the other and the disputants reach a common autobiographical judgment which is approved by both of them.

This unrestrictedly autobiographical normative cognitivism is not merely of theoretical interest. It is the "first-best" theory of good and just behavior in a classical Confucian, Buddhist or Gandhian Hindu Asian society and in one version of American legal realism. For a more complete description and the radically empirical root of its classical Asian effectiveness, see the writer's "The Mediational Approval Theory of Law in American Legal Realism".[11]

Since unrestricted autobiographical normative cognitivism, because of its unrestricted radical empiricism, leaves rule morality and litigational dispute-settling meaningless, it follows positively that if the latter kind of morality and legal science are to be meaningful, then at least restricted autobiographical normative cognitivism must be accepted. This amounts to the restriction and subjection of (*i*) autobiographical cognitivism to per-

[11] Northrop, F. S. C., "The Mediational Approval Theory of Law in American Legal Realism", in *Virginia Law Review*, Vol. 44, 1958, pp. 347-63. For similar classical Asian dispute-settling see also "The Epistemology of Legal Judgments" in *Northwestern University Law Review* (1964), Vol. 58, pp. 732-49.

sonal moral and official judicial review as measured by (ii) a non-autobiographical meaning of personally good and legally just which is the same for everyone and is made cognitively meaningful by epistemological possibility (2) or (3) or (4) above.

The preservation of autobiographical normative cognitivism in (i) is equivalent to identifying "the good and just so far as the evaluator alone is concerned" with unrestricted autobiographical cognitivism. This does justice to the unique value and the primacy of the contribution and judgment of each particular person. Requirement (ii) is equivalent to adding that before I can regard what I autobiographically affirm to be good or just in any more than an autobiographical sense, I must take into consideration all other evaluators by measuring what I autobiographically approve with a non-autobiographical meaning of good and just that is cognitively true for the person being judged and everybody else as well as for myself. This restricted autobiographical normative cognitivism is also of more than theoretical interest. An example is the unique legal and political system called the United States of America. In it majority-approved legislative statutes are in judicial review measured against a Jefferson-demanded Bill of Rights which Jefferson explicitly said was to be interpreted by the courts as law.[12]

A clue to the content of requirement (ii) in restricted autobiographical cognitivism becomes evident when we examine our proof that introspective psychological or non-cognitive meta-ethical theories (as distinct from unrestricted autobiographical ethical judgments) are logically self-contradictory. This proof consisted in deducing from the non-autobiographically trivial meta-ethical assertion $1E$ of $1E^{N-C}$ above the two following theorems.

THEOREM 3 (p) : the approval theory is approved.

THEOREM 5 $\exists p$: the approval theory is not approved.

Theorem 3 arises, by the meta-ethical law III above, from the universally lawful character of any meta-ethical theory whatever if it is not to be autobiographically trivial. Theorem 5 arises because the radical empiricism of the unrestricted approval theory entails the relativity to the percipient and the evaluator of that with which the theory identifies the meaning of any normative word *whatever the objejct* x *of normative judgment may be.* When, however, the ethical sentence in $1E$ is not universalized metaethically, by being kept an autobiographical singular meta-ethical pro-

---

[12] Jefferson, Thomas, *The Life and Selected Writings of Thomas Jefferson,* edited and with an Introduction by Adrienne Koch and William Peden, Modern Library, New York, 1954, p. 609. Also Northrop, F. S. C., *Philosophical Anthropology and Practical Politics,* Macmillan, New York, 1960, p. 307.

position, and the universal meta-ethical law rooted in epistemological possibility (2), (3) or (4) is added, then Theorem 3 above just does not follow
for any x whatever, even after moral or judicial review of the ethical or
legislative judgment. Thus the logical contradiction is avoided. Also the
empirical reason for disapproving of the approval theory because of its
intolerable consequences with respect to the objectivity of one's ethical
judgment is removed. Restricted autobiographical introspective psychological normative cognitivism is, therefore, both formally and empirically
a consistent theory.

Can anything more be inferred from our two proofs concerning the
content of the non-autobiographical norm which measures any autobiographical ethical judgment or majority-approved legislative statute? Two
considerations suggest a positive answer.

It was noted above that the unrestricted autobiographical version of
radical empirical introspective psychological normative cognitivism also
escapes the contradiction exhibited in our two proofs. But how can this
be true if, as required by the metameta-ethical laws I, II and III, any
meta-ethical theory whatever of the meaning of normative words is autobiographically trivial unless it universally quantifies itself for any person
and any object of normative judgment? The answer is that, staying strictly
with its radical empiricism, unrestricted autobiographical cognitivism
affirms, with the radical empiricist Hume, that radically empirical knowledge does not give one the relation of necessary connection or the idea
of universal lawfulness in either natural or normative science. Hence, assuming that only radical empirical concepts are meaningful, universally
quantified meta-ethical theories are meaningless; and, as described above,
in place of the universally lawful meta-ethical rule $1E$ or $1E^{N-C}$ it substitutes a purely existential non-theoretically meaningful operation of mediation which carries no *stare decisis* implications whatever for any future
normative judgment or dispute. This leaves meaningless, however, the many
religions and moralities of principles and the countless litigational legal
systems with their universal prescriptive laws—systems existing in the
Confucian, Buddhist and Hindu Orient as well as throughout the Occident.
It follows positively, therefore, that if this kind of morality and legal
system is to be meaningful, the meta-ethical and meta-legal postulate (*ii*)
which defines its meaning must express the idea of universal law for all
persons and all objects of normative judgment together with, as Kelsen
has recently re-emphasized,[13] its ought-to-be-ness. This, moreover, is precisely what an epistemological theory of the meaning of normative words
of type (2) or (3) or (4) provides.

[13] Kelsen, Hans, *General Theory of Law and State*, Harvard University Press, Cambridge, 1945, pp. 29-93, 115 ff. Also "Causality and Imputation" in *What Is Justice?*,
University of California Press, Berkeley, 1957, pp. 324-49.

Even so, normative cognitivism is not yet established. Two questions still remain. First, which of the three epistemological theories of universal lawfulness and its ought-to-be-ness is the correct one? Second, since there are many consistent universal normative laws and legal systems with diverse and even incompatible contents, what possible meaning can there be for calling any one of them cognitively meaningful, i.e., true or false? These two questions, because of the three epistemological possibilities, break into the following three questions: (A) Is every universal normative law a merely hypothetical imperative relative to the First Constitution or the customary "living law" of the particular moral community and legal system, as Professors Kelsen, Toulman and other moral legal and cultural relativists maintain? Neo-Kantianism, i.e., epistemological possibility (3) above, answers this question in the affirmative. Or (B), Is there at least one universal law which is a categorical imperative and hence not relative to the particular First Constitution and culture? If so, (C) Is this categorical imperative cognitively true because (a) it is a synthetic a priori proposition as Kant's epistemological possibility (2) affirms, or because (b) it is an analytic proposition and hence true tautologically as epistemological possibility (4) entails? [14]

In a work now in preparation, the writer will attempt to show that the answers are to (A), No; to (B), Yes; and to (C), epistemological possibility (4) rather than (2).[15] In any event, the analysis of our two proofs that any introspective psychological or non-cognitive meta-ethical social theory of the form $1E$ or $1E^{N-C}$ above is both ethically and legally self-contradictory, has established at least two positive conclusions: First, if normative words are meaningful, then their meaning is cognitive; second, if rule ethics or any litigational legal and political system is meaningful, then universal lawfulness together with its ought-to-be-ness is present and this requires (2) a Kantian or (3) a neo-Kantian or (4) a logically realistic epistemology in epistemic correlation with a radically empirical theory of the meaningful. For the interdependence of (4) and the Nihilistic Mahayana or the Unqualified Non-dualistic Vedantic concept of the self see the present writer's contribution in *East-West Studies of the Self*, edited by P. T. Raju and Albury Castell.[16]

[14] *Yale Law Journal*, Vol. 71 (1962), 1043-48; also *The Complexity of Ethical and Legal Experience*, Little Brown, Boston, Mass., 1959, Ch. 22, and *Philosophical Anthropology and Practical Politics, op. cit.*, note 12, pp. 316-38.

[15] "The Relation between Scientific Natural Knowledge and Intrinsic Humanistic Values in Western Culture" in a volume edited by John E. Smith to be published by George Allen and Unwin in London.

[16] Martinus Nijhoff, The Hague, 1968, Ch. I.

2

FIELDWORK PROBLEMS IN COMPARATIVE RESEARCH ON MODERNIZATION

ALEX INKELES

THE COMPARISION of *societies* is an intellectual pursuit as old as sociology; indeed it goes back to Greece and Rome. As a systematic discipline, however, it is quite young, although it certainly was well launched by the 1930's as reflected in the work of men such as Kroeber in anthropology and Sorokin in sociology. The sytematic comparative sociological study of *populations,* however, is much more recent; indeed it was not well launched until the 1950's. Pioneering efforts in this new mode of analysis were made by Daniel Lerner in his study of six nations in the Middle East published as *The Passing of Traditional Society* in 1958 and by G. Almond and S. Verba in *The Civic Culture* published in 1963. In these studies public opinion data were collected by simply "contracting out" to a professional polling agency the task of translating a standard questionnaire and using it to interview a sample of the local population such as might be used for any ordinary purpose.

Attractive as such procedures may be for their simplicity and ease, they are increasingly considered unacceptable by sociologists committed to the systematic comparison of national and sub-national populations. For one thing, it no longer seems acceptable to farm out responsibility for the local fieldwork. Too many of the presumably "routine" decisions which must be made prove on experience not to have been routine, and the resultant misunderstandings have severe consequences when one comes to analyze the

20

data. For another, we have come increasingly to feel that following such a mechanical procedure may yield either trivial or misleading outcomes. For maximum richness and relevance the local culture must be reflected in the research design, and local wisdom utilized in the collection and analysis of the results. Third, there are considerations of justice, and goals for the development of social science which transcend the interests of any particular research. A survey farmed to a professional agency and then shipped off to another country for analysis leaves behind no residue of training for the local social scientists, either in designing and conducting fieldwork or in the systematic analysis of collected data.

Considerations such as these have persuaded at least some students of comparative societal analysis that all studies involving the simultaneous comparison of several different national or sub-national populations should be undertaken only on the basis of *fieldwork*. I was among those convinced of this principle. Therefore on organizing the Harvard Project on the Social and Cultural Aspects of Economic Development in 1961, I decided that in any country in which my project collected data it would work through ond with some local scientific organization which would serve as consultant to and collaborator in the research. Either the field director or the associate field director was to be a social scientist native to the country in which we worked. I expected that the native social scientist would serve not only as a technical expert, but would make an independent intellectual contribution in the course of the fieldwork, and would later take major responsibility for writing a separate "national" report on the phase of our project conducted in his country. In addition, the interviewers, insofar as possible, were to be students of social science for whom their work should be learning and training experience and not merely a job.

This paper tells how we elaborated these and related objectives, and describes our experiences in attempting to implement them in practice in a multi-nation comparative study of individual modernization. By sharing our experiences we hope to make it easier for those who come after us to avoid some of our mistakes, to test our conclusions, and to achieve further advances on the basis of such progress as we may have made in developing sound theory and sensible practice for the conduct of comparative research. We also view our experience as a venture in international understanding and misunderstanding, and a case-study for analysis of the problems of international co-operation in the development process. We therefore present our experience in some detail.

To fully understand and evaluate our experience one must, of course, see it in the context of the programme of research whose objectives the fieldwork was meant to advance. The Harvard Project on the Social and Cultural Aspects of Economic Development is an investigation of the forms

and sources of modernization *in individuals*.[1] Its focus is on the person
rather than the society or the institution, and its emphasis is socio-psychological rather than purely sociological or structural. Six countries are represented: Argentina and Chile, East Pakistan and India, Nigeria and
Israel.

The study is based on an extensive interview, up to four hours duration,
administered to a highly purposive sample including sub-groups of: cultivators still working the land in rural villages; "new workers", that is, migrants to the city newly arrived and with only limited experience in industrial employment; urban non-industrial workers (UNI's), earning their living outside large-scale productive enterprises; and experienced workers in
industry with between three and twelve years of experience on the job.
Industrial workers are the largest group in each country, some 600 to 700,
whereas the other sub-groups were to be 100 each. The selection of cases
was on the basis of the respondent's meeting certain common characteristics as to sex (all male), age (18-32), education (usually 0-8 years), religion,
enthnicity, rural or urban origin, residence, and, of course, the occupational
characteristics already mentioned.

Respondents were chosen within "sites", the most important being the
factory. Up to 100 factories were included in each country. In practice,
virtually everyone meeting the sample criteria was selected from each factory, except the very largest. In those, up to 20 men were selected at random from among the pool of eligible subjects. Factories were selected on
the basis of differentiation by size (5 categories), product (7 categories) and
relative "modernity" (2 categories). Village were chosen as "sites" on the
basis of being either the same as those from which the migrant industrial
workers had come originally, or as being precisely equivalent in region,
culture, crop and the like. Urban non-industrials (UNI's) had to work outside large-scale production organizations in the same cities as the workers
and otherwise meet the general sampling criteria. Since we are not making
generalizations as to the national populations, we emphasized more the
keeping of the sub-samples like each other in all respects except occupation,
rather than selecting them to be representative of any "parent" population.
Nevertheless, our industrial samples prove to be very similar to their defined parent populations, although more so in some countries than others.

    [1] In its different aspects, stages, and settings the research has been supported by the
Rockefeller Foundation, the Ford Foundation, the National Science Foundation, and
the National Institutes of Mental Health. The Cultural Affairs Division of the Department of State provided local currencies to support our fieldwork in India, Israel and
Pakistan, and the office of Scientific Research of the US Air Force supported technical
exploration in problems of translation and computer analysis undertaken in Cambridge
(Mass). All of these organizations gave their support through the Center for the International Affairs of Harvard University, which is the sponsor and institutional home of
our project.

The main objective of the larger research programme is to test a theory concerning psycho-social modernity. Individual modernity is here conceived of as a complex set of inter-related attitudes, values, and behaviours fitting a theoretically derived model of the modern man, at least as he may appear among the common men in developing countries.[2] Whether this syndrome actually exists in nature, and is the same from country to country, is one of the prime question to which the Project addresses itself.[3] The second major objective of the Project is to assess the determinants of individual modernity. We are asking: What makes a man modern? What is the differential impact of varying modernizing settings on attitudes and values?

Sustained development seems to depend on the wide diffusion through the popuation of certain attitudes, values, dispositions to act, and habits of doing things which, in combination, characterize the "industrial man" and differentiate him from the man of tradition who makes up the bulk of the population in most underdeveloped countries. This idea was an extension of one I orginally developed after undertaking a review of data about modern large-scale industrial societies, reported in my paper "Industrial Man".[4] There I sought to show that "the standard institutional environments of modern society induce standard patterns of response, despite the countervailing randomizing effects of persistent traditional patterns of culture". But in preparing "Industrial Man" I was obliged to rely on bits and patches of evidence drawn from studies not sytematically designed to test a coherent theoretical formulation. In undertaking the Project on the Social and Cultural Aspects of Development, therefore, I resolved to test my ideas sytematically and vigorously, specifying the relevant theory and the measures most appropriate to ascertain precisely what features of social structure produce changes in the incumbents of particular organizational roles.

In my current research I take as a working assumption that experience in a modern industrial enterprise will induce changed attitudes which, on the whole, will make men better adapted and more effective citizens of a modern society. I see the factory not only as a productive enterprise, but also a school, imparting certain more general lessons whose significance will be felt far beyond the confines of the factory. The general objective of the Project, therefore, was to find out whether and how work in factories

[2] A brief description of this model appears in Alex Inkeles, "The Modernization of of Man". A full account is contained in Alex Inkeles, "A Model of the Modern Man".

[3] We already have an answer to this first question: the syndrome does indeed exist in nature. Furthermore, the psychological "structure" of individual modernity is basically very much the same in all six of the very different countries we studied. A preliminary report of these findings may be found in David H. Smith and A. Inkeles, "The OM Scale: A Comparative Socio-Psychological Measure of Individual Modernity".

[4] Alex Inkeles, "Industrial Man: The Relation of status to Experience, Perception, and value",

or similiar enterprises changes attitudes, values and habits in the ways which are relevant to the individual's adjustment in and contribution to a modern or modernizing society. At the same time we were testing the role of other "modernizing" experiences such as education, contact with urban living and exposure to the media of mass communication.

On the dependent variable side, the matters investigated include: orientations to time, technical competence, efficacy (mastery), trust, dignity, planing, particularism-universalism, new experience, and opinion; educational aspirations and attitudes toward education; aspirations for advancement for self, children, community and nation; readiness for change and mobility; political orientations, attitudes, and activities; use of modern and traditional information media; attitudes about family-size and planning; women's rights and kinship obligations; religious orientations and behaviour; social class attitudes and consumption behaviour.

I was eager that the theory have a thorough test, one which would leave minimum doubt as to whether it applied only under unusual circumstances or indeed had rather general validity. This required that it be tested not in one, but in several countries, each to be treated as another "replication" of the same basic experimental design. My pursuit of a thorough test of this social scientific theory had to be co-ordinated, however with general commitment of my project and the Center for International Affairs to contribute to our understanding of the problems of economic development and to make such practical contributions as we could manage along the way. Hence the distinctive character of our experience in fieldwork in six developing countries, which we now propose to share.

For our presentation we have used seven headings. These permit a more or less chronological account of our experience as we discuss, in turn, the issues raised by: selecting the countries; establishing our field stations; finding and training a staff; constructing and translating the questionnaire; the conduct of the interview; response bias and its challenge; and problems of maintaining communication amongst the several national research teams.

1. SELECTING THE COUNTRIES

The sample design described above was applied with numerous adaptations, in six countries: Argentina, Chile, India, Israel, Nigeria and Pakistan. The question inevitably put to us about this array is: "How did you decide on the number six, and why these particular six?" The answer cannot be given in a word, or even a sentence. Both the number and identity of the countries selected was determined by the interaction of forces and considerations practical and romantic, ambitious and conservative, personal and impersonal, planned and accidental, scientific and impulsive.

To achieve our scientific objective, it was clear that we had to work in more than one country. That was the only way to be reasonably certain that our findings, whether they supported or contradicted our hypotheses, were not determined by some accidental concentration of circumstances in the *one* country we might decide to study. Since there were initially three senior members of the project staff,[5] it seemed sensible to strive for at least three countries. That meant that each senior member had to attempt one country entirely on his own, without the support of a co-director; but we decided to accept that burden for the advantage of scope and the appeal of allowing each man his "own" country. Yet we were ambitious to establish our propositions on as general a level as possible. The greater the range and number of countries in which our theory worked—should it so turn out—the more we could assume it would equally work in other lands as yet unstudied. On the other hand, should the theory fail in some cases, we could collect on our scientific insurance policy by turning our attention to the new problem of why the theory worked in certain countries and not others. In addition each new country, according to its special characteristics, offered the possibility of interesting variations in the basic design which could enrich the study as a whole.

There was, however, no obvious scientifically determined upper limit on the number of countries we might study. That upper boundary was, therefore, settled by the limits on our resources and personnel. Our budget was not unlimited. Even if we could find more senior personnel qualified and motivated to undertake the ardous fieldwork we planned, each addition to the senior staff required the accomodation of new interests. Such new interests could be accommodated only at some risk of diffusion of our original clear purpose, and meant an almost certain increase in the burden of the fieldwork as we stretched ourselves to cover more and more. We therefore resolved on a simple formula. Each senior staff member agreed to accept the prime responsibility of conducting the study in only one country. But each also undertook conscientiously to explore the prospects of working simultaneously in a neighbouring country, and to initiate work there if progress in the primary setting permitted. Since we were three seniors—Inkeles, Schuman, and Ryan—this formula established six as the maximum number of countries the project would attempt to study. That also represented a sensible upper limit so far as our budget was concerned. It seemed, as well, to be the point beyond which the sheer bulk of the data we might collect would exceed our capacity to process and analyze it. We settled then on the goal of not less than three nor more than six countries.

We recognized then, and emphasize now, that the ideas we wished to test could be explored in a relatively advanced industrial country. Even

---

[5] These were Alex Inkeles, as Project Director; Dr. Howard Schuman and Dr. Edward Ryan, as Research Associates of the Center for International Affairs.

in the United States, for example, our basic design could be applied by studying the flow of migrants from the agricultural South or Appalachia into urban industrial centres such as Atlanta or Detroit. Certainly, if we had settled on such advanced countries, the task of gathering our basic data would have been greatly eased. But the problem we had selected to study seemed much more germane to the developing countries, and for numerous other reasons we were committed to working there.

The Harvard Project on the Social and Cultural Aspects of Development had been launched on the assumption that we needed to understand better the role of socio-psychological and cultural forces in accelerating or impeding economic development and the broader process of nation-building and modernization. This choice was in line with the main thrust of the general research programme at the Center for International Affairs, whose research efforts in economics, and to a lesser degree in political science, were overwhelmingly concentrated on the problems of development and growth. The basic operating grant our project had accepted from the Rockefeller Foundation carried the understanding that we would concentrate our efforts in the study of development. All the members of the staff were personally deeply convinced of the importance of greater understanding of the social problems of developing countries.

Although we wanted to do basic research, we hoped that the results would have some practical consequences. If we studied the more developed countries our effort might still be of general scientific interest, but the resources and new information added by our project would be essentially redundant from the point of view of the host country. By conducting our investigation in underdeveloped nations we felt our descriptive data in itself would provide a useful pay-off for our hosts. In addition, by training local staffs in the course of our fieldwork, we could add significantly to the pool of trained manpower and research know-how available in the less developed countries. Indeed, we realized that in some cases our fieldwork would be the first major social survey ever conducted there. The people we would train and give experience to even if few in number, might play a crucial role in the future development of social science in their country. There was, therefore, no hesitation on our part that we should concentrate our efforts in developing countries. But which?

Given our research design, there were certain objective factors which greatly reduced the number of countries from amongst which we might select our field sites. Only those nations could qualify which had already experienced a substantial amount of industrialization, and in which there was sufficient current industrial activity and growth to ensure some flow of labour from the countryside to the city-based factory. This requirement immediately ruled out large parts of Africa, Asia and, indeed, Latin America.

A second indispensable requirement was that any country we worked in should be a reasonably open society with at least moderate political stability. A society in political turmoil is not an appropriate setting for protracted interviews on delicate social and political issues. Indeed, in developing countries such turmoil is particularly likely to centre on the industrial sector, the very one we planned to work in most intensively. Furthermore, we recognized that in such settings a team of interviewers is itself likely to become not only an object of unusual attention but also of suspicion and even protest. Clearly the Congo or the Dominican Republic would not have been suitabe settings for our work. But political stability would afford us no advantage if it was the end product of political repression. Haiti, for example, would have been something less than an ideal setting. Even if one could imagine the Haitian dictator permitting a social research team to enter the country—indeed even if he delivered the interviewees according to our request—what meaning could the results have?

The third requirement was that the general level of modernization, and particularly the level of development in the nation's universities, have risen high enough to offer some promise of local facilitation of our work. Since we were to be outsiders, we needed the guidance and assistance of men in the countries who could supplement our research skills with their intimate knowledge of the local setting and its culture. For such collaboration to be effective the local community had to have had enough experience with social research to comprehend our purpose, and to provide at least some part of our staff needs. To permit us to sample the factories intelligently we had collected certain census data on industrial plants, labour force statistics, and the like. Thus, the range of eligible nations narrowed still further.

Within these objective limits, however, we allowed personal preference and accidental factors—fortunately mostly happy accidents—to play a part. We were fairly well agreed that the three great continental areas other than Europe and North America should, if possible, all be represented. Fortunately Howard Schuman had always had an interest in Asia and was eager to go there. Edward Ryan had previously done extensive fieldwork in Indonesia and already knew Chinese very well. Like most anthropologists he wanted to know intimately as many of the major culture areas of the world as he could. He opted for Africa. That left me with no choice other than what I would have chosen anyway— Latin America. So the first wave of choices was amicably settled.

In Asia both Pakistan and India were obvious candidates by our objective criteria. Dr. Schuman settled on Pakistan for a number of reasons. Pakistan, especially East Pakistan, had since the early 1950's been experiencing a substantial spurt in industrial growth, thus holding out the prospect that could easily find men who met our sampling criteria. It was much more

compact and homogeneous than India, which meant that the fieldwork
would be more efficiently executed with modest resources. Pakistan was
one of the countries in which the Economic Development Advisory Service
of our parent Center for International Affairs had for some years maintained a group of economic advisers to the government planning board.
One "wing" of the advisory service was located in East Pakistan. They had
accumulated extensive knowledge of the nation's economy, as well as practical experience in dealing both with problems of doing research and of
living in the country. Indeed, the success of their work largely assured
that any additional groups coming from Harvard, and especially from our
Center, would find their path smoothed by the substantial goodwill generated by these earlier efforts. Dr A. F. A. Husain, who was a leading professor of economics at the Dacca University, had earlier spent a year at
our Center, and had become well known to us. Indeed, he had done a
pioneering study under UNESCO sponsorship of the values and adjustment of Pakistani workers, so he was sympathetic to our objectives and
well understood our problems.[6]

Professor Husain kindly agreed to serve as sponsor and adviser of our
research, and encouraged his younger colleague Dr. Farouk to serve with
the project on a more regular basis. Financial support for our expenses in
local currency could be met by a grant from the Bureau of Cultural Affairs
of the Department of State. The Pakistani government evidently saw no
obstacle to our conducting the research under the auspices we had arranged.
So for many reasons, large and small, we decided to initiate our work in
Dacca.

We did, however, have doubts as to whether the level of industrial
development in East Pakistan would prove great enough to supply all the
interviews we needed, and it was not clear whether social research was
sufficiently developed at the University of Dacca to provide enough individuals having the necessary experience to staff our fieldwork. Our plan,
therefore, was to treat the first phase of work in Dacca as in part a feasibility study. Dr. Schuman agreed that while in Dacca he would explore
various possibilities in India. Should the Dacca situation prove unsuitable
he might move to India. On the other hand, should East Pakistan prove
adequate to our purpose, the explorations in India might yet provide the
basis for our later setting up a separate programme there.

The decision to initiate our American programme in Nigeria was governed by considerations very much like those operating in the case of Pakistan
and was approached cautiously because we had similar reservations. In
1962 Nigeria was considered the most promising country in Africa in eco-

[6] A. F. A. Husain, *Human and Social Impact of Technological Change in Pakistan*.
Also see A. F. A. Husain & A. Farouk, *Social Integration of Industrial Workers in
Khulna*.

nomic prospects and in potential for democratic political development. Its size and resources, and its political appeal attracted to it a good deal of foreign industrial capital. But we were most influenced in our choice by the encouragement of K. O. Dike, who was then Vice-Chancellor of the Federal University of Ibadan, in the capital of the Western Region.

In 1962 Dr. Dike was a guest speaker at a meeting in Boston sponsored by the United States Commission for the United Nations, at which I was a delegate sent by the Eastern Sociological Association. When I sought Dike out during a break in the Conference proceedings, our mutual interest became quickly apparent. Dr. Dike was eager to strengthen the capacity of the University at Ibadan to teach modern social science, and he recognized that his purpose could be advanced by having as much quality research as possible conducted at the Nigerian Institute of Social and Economic Research affiliated with the University. He was particularly eager to have represented in the Institute's programme the type of large-scale empirical field study so well developed in the United States. Our research, and especially the presence of so experienced a social scientist as Edward Ryan, held every promise of simultaneously advancing both of the Vice-Chancellor's objectives. We felt fortunate indeed, therefore, to have Dr. Dike's invitation to come to Ibadan, and to conduct our research as an integral and official activity of the Nigerian Institute for Social and Economic Research. Nevertheless, we considered the commitment tentative until we could ascertain, on the spot, whether the extent of industrial development and the composition of the labour force could yield the samples required by our research design. It was also unclear, given the insufficient development of certain kinds of social research facilities and experience at the University, whether we could find suitable men in sufficient numbers to staff the fieldwork.

The decision to launch our South American venture in Chile depended less on a chance encounter, but was no more the outcome of a precise scientific judgment. Having been elected "our man in South America", I wrote to various knowledgeable leading social scientists in the United States and elsewhere for advice. Many sources suggested that Dr. Peter Heintz, Director of the UNESCO-sponsored Latin American School of Science (FLACSO) in Santiago, Chile, was one of the best informed about appropriate settings for social research throughout Latin America. He replied to our inquiry quite conscientiously by frankly reviewing the advantages and disadvantages of the few centres in Latin America which, in 1962, could reasonably be considered an appropriate base for our research. FLACSO was itself among them. Happily, Dr. Heintz went on to offer us his personal collaboration and the hospitality of FLACSO if we wished to come to Santiago. Since Chile was otherwise so eminently qualified to be in our sample of nations, and we had heard such fine things both about

FLACSO and Dr. Heintz, his invitation was soon warmly accepted.

Thus, we selected the three initial field stations. Our plan for choosing the additional countries was very simple. We resolved that, if it was at all possible, given the conditions he might meet when he got into the field, each of the three field directors would attempt to launch the study in a nearby country. Our main objective was to capitalize on scarce manpower and resources. In effect, each of the three senior staff members was being asked to do double duty. That way we could save the cost of sending another American into the field on the same continent. The field director would become, in effect, a regional rather than merely a national representative. But the plan suffered from obvious limitations on the time and energy of the field directors who would be otherwise absorbed in launching the study in the country of their prime interest. Since our financial resources were limited, and we had to protect our investment in the first set of countries, we viewed each effort at expansion most cautiously. Beyond a certain point not much of scientific value would be gained by just adding more and more countries. We resolved, therefore, that each of the countries in the second set should contribute something of special interest to our overall design.

The advantages of working in India as the match to Pakistan did not require much elaboration. The contrasts between India and Pakistan represented a kind of natural experiment. In politics, the one was developing under the highly centralized control of a military leader practicing what he called "guided democracy", whereas the other had leapt unabashedly into the whirlpool of multi-party democratic parliamentarianism. In economics Pakistan was predominantly devoted to private enterprise, whereas India talked socialism and the State played a massive role in the creation and operation of industry. India was Hindu (among other things); and Pakistan, Muslim. The prospects for interesting comparisons were, therefore, very attractive from a social scientist's point of view.

The decisive reason for including India, however, was our discovery of Dr. Amar Kumar Singh. Dr. Singh was Chairman of the Department of Psychology at Ranchi Unversity. Ranchi is of the newer and less-well-known of the Indian Universities. It had the advantage, however, of being in the centre of the State of Bihar, which is often called the Ruhr of India and which had been undergoing a period of extraordinary industrial expansion. Even more important to us, Dr. Singh was well-versed in the methods of contemporary social research, having obtained his doctorate at the London School of Economics with a survey of the opinions and adjustment of Indian students in England.[7] This meant he could conduct the research with a minimum of assistance from Dr. Schuman, a condition

[7] Amar K. Singh, *Indian Students in Britain.*

we knew we must accept both because of Dr. Schuman's burdens in Pakistan and the difficulties of travel between Pakistan and India. These difficulties were not mechanical, but political. It was simple to make airplane connections from Dacca to Ranchi. Political tension between India and Pakistan was at the time very high, however, and Dr. Schuman could not obtain unlimited re-entry permits to get back into India. Indeed, his visa permitted only three. It is one of the anomalies of this sort of experience that if Dr. Schuman had been even thousands of miles away but in another political unit he might have found it easier to see Dr. Singh regularly than he did being only a few hundred miles away in East Pakistan.

The choice of Bihar had the further advantage that it contained several factories which were located out in the country, far from any urban conglomeration. This permitted us to test the influence of urban residence. An additional advantage of Bihar was the presence of large numbers of so called "tribal" groups, not part of the mainstream of Hindu culture, who, alongside the latter were also entering in large numbers.

Argentina entered the sample as the second unit of the South American pair on much the same basis as did India. Chile is one of the more industralized countries of South America. It had experienced some modernization, and it had a modest but almost fully absorbed indigenous American Indian population. For an interesting comparison we might have moved either in the direction of one of the countries with a large Indian population, such as Bolivia or Peru, or toward one of the even more industrialized and cosmopolitan countries such as Argentina, Brazil or Uruguay. The decisive factor in our choice was the interest of, and offer of assistance from, Professor Gino Germani then Director of the Institute of Sociology at the University of Buenos Aires.[8] Prof. Germani was able to offer valuable encouragement and guidance; the facilities of his school and of the DiTella Foundation, at which he directed a social research programme; some financial assistance and, most important, an introduction to the young professor of methodology in his Department, Perla Gibaja. Professor Gibaja was interested in adapting our research plan to, and conducting it in, Argentina; and with Professor Germani's co-operation we were able to arrange to free part of her time from teaching. There were no restrictions on movement between Santiago and Buenos Aires, so that I could visit regularly to consult. Since in all other respects Argentina met our general requirements, we gratefully accepted the opportunity to work there offered by Germani and Gibaja.

In Africa we failed to follow the pattern established for Asia and South

[8] Gino Germani is now Monroe Guttman Professor of Latin American Studies at Harvard University.

America. The difficulty Dr. Ryan experienced in completing our design in Nigeria did not leave him the time or resources to launch a parellel study in a neighbouring country. We had considered Ghana because it then offered a more "mobilized", indeed dictatorial, political setting in contrast to the open democratic system in Nigeria. But the very fact which gave it interest also promised to be a major obstacle to the free conduct of our kind of social research. What was decisive, however, was our failure to hear of anyone in Ghana to the level of competence of Professors Singh and Gibaja, at least not in a situation which would permit them success- fully to undertake the research. We therefore abandoned any hope of finding a truly African match for Nigeria, and instead accepted an oppor- tunity to conduct our study in Israel.

Israel certainly qualified as one of the young "emerging" nations, and it was decidedly a "developing" country even if not necessarily an "under- developed" one. But it seemed very much an extension of Europe, despite its location in the Middle East. Since we lacked a European or North American standard of comparison, however, we concluded we might capi- talize on this very quality of the country. We could thus test whether our underlying ideas applied equally well to a European population, albeit one living in a "new nation". Our decision to make the additional effort for this marginal purpose was influenced by two factors. First, ample funds in Israeli currency were available to cover the cost of fieldwork there, since Israel was one of the countries which had been receiving large shipments of surplus food from the United States, paid for in "blocked" local currency. Second, we could count on the co-operation of the Israel Institute of Applied Social Research, headed by Professor Louis Guttman of Jerusalem Univer- sity. The Institute was an experienced and highly competent research centre which regularly undertook surveys of the Israeli population and had previously conducted several researches in co-operation with American groups. Furthermore, the Institute was prepared to assign Uzi Peled, who was a knowledgeable and experienced member of the staff, to work full time with our project. Since these advantages meant a mini- mum additional strain on our financial and personnel resources, we decided to put aside our reservations as to Israel's strict comparability with the other countries.

As it turned out, our reservations proved to be beside the point. From our earliest discussions with the advisory board in Israel, and from data available to the Israeli Institute, we quickly discovered that among the social strata we wished to sample—namely young men of relatively low education working on the production line in industry—there were very few Jews of European origin. Those who met our sampling requirements proved to be overwhelmingly from the later waves of immigration, who came to Israel from the countries of the Middle East, Asia, and Africa.

Although they were Jews by religion, their culture was not that of Europe. Broadly speaking, they could quite reasonably be considered the equivalent of the groups entering our sample in the other countries, at least in the sense that all had a distinctively non-European culture. The presence of these "Oriental Jews" in our sample added still another interesting dimension, by permitting us to study the modernization process among a people of markedly traditional cuture who were suddenly removed into a quite modern and predominantly European setting.

With the selection of Israel we closed the books so far as permitting additional nations to enter the lists. There was briefly some chance that we might work out an arrangement with a sociological group in one of the Communist bloc countries but, for various reasons easily surmised, that plan failed to materialize. We entertained overtures from other countries which might have extended our reach in South America, but it was apparent that we had come to the limits of our funds, our capacity to staff new ventures, and our ability to administer anything more complex than that on which we were already launched.

What then was true of the set of countries we had finally settled on, and what might be the implications of their national characteristics for the set of hypotheses we were trying to test? We noted above some characteristics of each country which was of particular interest to us. Now we should look at some of the more objective facts, giving attention to our set of nations as a group. Before we examine the relevant statistics, we wish to emphasize that ours were not representative national samples and therefore the conditions which prevailed for each of these nations as a whole did not necessarily apply in the particular regions from which we drew samples, nor to the specific groups we reached with our interviews.

In assessing the development of our set of countries our standard need not be one of the most industrialized nations of Europe, such as the United Kingdom, but may rather be one of the less developed, such as Greece. Table 1 shows that in the period just prior to our study all six countries manifested most or all of the distinguishing marks of an underdeveloped nation, although Israel did fairly consistently get up to or even out-perform Greece on a number of the indices. Our six countries had low per capita income, and their economies showed long periods of relative stagnation with little or no growth year by year; the population increases they experienced were high enough to qualify as examples of the population "explosion", and their urban centres were expanding at an abnormally high rate; education reached only a modest part of the population, and mass communications were only weakly developed; and health facilities were often spread very thinly indeed.

For our purposes the most important indicators are those which reflect the level of industrial development. Whereas in the United Kingdom and

SELECTED INDICATORS OF ECONOMIC DEVELOPMENT

TABLE 1

	Argentina	Chile	India	Israel	Nigeria	Pakistan	Greece	U.K.
1. Gross National Product Per Capita (1957 $US)*	$490	$379	$73	$726	$78	$70	$340	$1,189
2. Economic Growth Per Capita Increase (1950-60)*	-0.4	+1.3	+1.0	+5.8	+1.2	+0.3	+5.3	+2.3
3. Industrial Employment as % Working-age Population (1960)*†	18	17	8	18	nda	7	12	35
4. Wage and Salary Earners as % Working-age Population (1955)*	43	43	19	38	3	22	21	61
5. Manufacturing as % Gross Domestic Product (1960)†	22	20	17	23	3	13	nda	35
6. % labor Force in Agriculture (1955)*	25	30	71	15	59	65	48	5
7. Population Increase (Annual Rate 1958-61)*	1.7	2.4	2.2	3.0	1.9	2.1	0.9	0.7
8. Crude Birth Rates per 1000 Population (Average 1955-59)*†	24	36	39	28	50	20	19	16
9. Inhabitants per Physician (1960)†	670	1,600	5,800	400	27,000	11,000	790	960
10. Infant Mortality per 1000 live births (Average 1955-59)*†	60	118	146	36	78	nda	41	24

11. % Illiterate in Population 15 years and over (1950)†	14	20	81	89	6	81	26	1
12. Primary and Secondary School Pupils as % aged 5-19 (1960)*	57	58	29	25	69	20	53	80
13. Radio Receivers per 1000 populaton (1960)*†	175	130	5	4	194	3	94	289
14. Daily Newspaper Circulation per 1000 population (1960)*	155	134	11	8	210	7	125	506
15. Domestic Mail per Capita (1960)†	65	13	8	3	56	6	23	191
16. % Urban Population in cities 20,000+ (1955)*	48	46	12	11	61	8	38	67
17. % Increase in Urban Population (20,000+) (Annual Rate 1950-60)*	nda	.47	.18	nda	.39	.28	.61	.10

nda = no data readily available.

All the figures given should be regarded as only approximate. This applies particularly to the years indicated. They were selected to represent the period just prior to our field work, but for particular measures the original sources often were forced to rely on different years as the figures happened to be available for any given country. Different census periods, different conventions for arriving at national statistics and differential accuracy in national record keeping and reporting all affect the precision with which these figures represent the true values for the measures cited. These considerations are too refined for our purposes, but interested readers should consult the original sources, indicated below in the footnotes.

* Bruce M. Russett, Howard R. Alker, Karl W. Deutsch and Harold D. Lasswell, *World Handbook of Political and Social Indicators*, New Haven: Yale University Press, 1964.

† *United Nations Statistical Yearbook, 1964*, 16th Issue, New York: United Nations, 1965.

Japan, and even Italy, the proportion of gross national product having its origin in industry is 30 per cent or more, in our countries it ranges from a low of 3 per cent in Nigeria to a high of 22 per cent in Argentina. The proportion of the labour force in industry, the per capita energy consumption, rates of growth per capita in GNP, and other measures point in the same direction. This is a set of countries at best only moderately industrialized. They are well suited to the purposes of our study because they permit us to examine the impact of industry in a setting in which it has not customarily been the predominant mode of economic activity but is, rather, a new and relatively alien infusion into a more traditional agricultural, craft, or trading economy. This holds even for Israel despite its relatively high standing on many of the economic indicators.

Beyond this common characteristic, however, the six nations display very marked diversity. On almost every measure, be it one relating to education, health, mass communication, or wealth, our countries cover an exceedingly wide range. We included representatives of the poorest in the world, and others which equal or exceed the less advanced countries of Europe on indices of modernization and development. Within this array, however, we may discern some broad strata, their number depending on the criteria used.

If wealth be the criterion, especially as measured by per capita GNP, then our set of countries may be divided into two main strata. The poorest —Pakistan, India, and Nigeria—are homogeneous, clustering around $75 per capita GNP. There is a sharp break before we come to Chile at close to $400 with Argentina and especially Israel, going substantially higher. The other indicators generally taken to reflect the wealth of a country suggest a similar division into two strata.

Although the two-strata division on economic grounds holds promise of facilitating some interesting data analysis, it is unfortunate that the economic categories are co-extensive with certain cultural distinctions, rather than being cross-cut by them. The three countries more European in their origins, contemporary culture, and current ties are all in the upper stratum economically. The three with more distinctive cultures are all in the lower stratum economically. This means, unfortunately, that should our theory work much better in the economically more advanced nations we will be unable to say whether it does so because those countries are more developed or because they are more European. Our situation is improved, on the "advanced" side, by the fact that our Israeli subjects were overwhelmingly non-European, having rather an "oriental" or "near-Eastern" culture. Nevertheless, we would clearly be better off if our Asian set had included Japan, since it is so highly industrialized and relatively developed while being so unambiguously non-Western in cultural origin, and, to a degree, in contemporary social structure.

On a number of measures, however, Chile falls more with India and even Pakistan as, for example, in per capita circculation of domestic mail and in infant mortality. This would suggest a division into three strata. A case could also be made for a four-tier arrangement with Nigeria on the lowest step, India and Pakistan on the second, Argentina and Chile on the third, and Israel on the fourth.

In any event, we were not attempting to "represent" the developing nations of the world in any systematic way. Clearly our approach to selecting countries yielded a wide range of economic, social, and political conditions. This range permits us the most stringent and varied test of our theory. We argue that the factory will have a substantial modernizing effect in very traditional settings which might otherwise act to dampen or even smother its influence. Because the instrument and sample design were everywhere so fundamentally alike, the study done in each country represents an independent simultaneous duplication or replication of the "experiment". If factory experience can be shown to have a modernizing influence in all six countries, despite the great variation in the local culture of the workers, and in the geographical, political, and social setting of industry, then the factory emerges as indeed a powerful and autonomous school for modernity.

The same array of countries permits us to test different predictions as well. The factory could have its modernizing effect mainly in the least developed countries. This forecast rests on the assumption that it is the contrast between the inherent rationality and high efficacy of the factory, on the one hand, as against the surrounding traditional culture, on the other, which enables the factory to serve as a school in modernity. According to the theory, in an environment already generally modernized, such as that in the U.K. or the United States, the factory as such would be able to add little to the modernizing influences the individual had already received from other sources. This reasoning leads to the prediction that in our study the highest correlations between factory experience and individual modernity should be found in Nigeria, Pakistan and India.

Yet exactly the opposite conclusion is equally plausible. It may be argued that in a setting generally steeped in tradition, the influence of the factory will be muted or even totally nullified by the large number of countervailing pressures in the individual's daily life. Manning Nash's study, *Machine Age Maya*, well illustrates the point. In this view, only in a society in which substantial development has already taken place, and people are more open to change, can the socializing influence of the factory be expected to manifest its effects. This reasoning leads to the prediction that the correlation between factory experience and individual modernity should be substantial in Israel, Argentina and Chile, and weak or insignificant in Pakistan, India, and Nigeria. The project's official position was limited to predicting that the influence of factory experience would be significant in all our six countries, despite the great variation in their relative degree of modernization. Although we formulated the other two predictions, we did not, in advance, take a stand as to whether the impact of factory experience would be *greater* in the more or in the less advanced countries. Nevertheless, it was clearly advantageous that our procedure for selecting countries yielded an array whose diversity would permit us to test these more complex theories.

2. ESTABLISHING THE FIELD STATIONS

As the project director, I can now acknowledge that I took a very sanguine view of the world indeed and expressed enormous confidence in myself and my two younger colleagues, when I sent each of us alone to a distant and unknown underdeveloped country, equipped—beyond what was in his head or built into his character and experience—with no more than could fit in two suitcases, armed only with a beribboned letter of introduction under the seal of Harvard University and a modest supply of travellers cheques, and carrying the following instructions: Establish yourself in the community; locate and train a staff; translate, pre-test and adapt our questionnaire; arrange to draw the complex sample required by our research design; complete between 700 and 1,000 four-hour interviews; translate or code such parts as require local language, knowledge or skills; while you are over there arrange for the study to be conducted in a neighbouring country; and be back with the job completed in something between 12 and 18 months.

Now that the fieldwork is well behind us we can admit not only to having been optimistic, but also to having been extraordinarily lucky to have so well succeeded in our objectives. Of course, our luck required something more tangible to work with. Foremost among the ingredients which insured our success was the splendid co-operation we received from groups and individuals in the countries we studied—government officers, university officials, factory directors, trade union leaders, village chiefs, and the farmers and workers whom we interviewed. We were sometimes rebuffed, there were some misunderstandings, and even a few definitely unpleasant incidents. But it was heartening to us to discover how much goodwill there is in the world—at least for University researchers. Indeed, at the end we were a bit startled to realize that in more than six thousand quite substantial and extended encounters with other human beings, not more than a few dozen proved to be decidedly unsatisfactorily to one or both parties.

Our success also depended heavily on the superior qualities, the skill, knowledge, devotion, and intergrity, of our chief collaborator in each country, as well as the staffs they assembled to work with them. But in all this something must surely have been owed to the rules and procedures we adopted to guide our fieldwork. As a successful advertisement runs: "We must be doing something right." We believe we were. Knowing what and how we did things is important in assessing the reliability of our materials, and hence essential to the analysis which will follow. It may have additional interest, however, as a case-study: Our experiences may guide others, and our rules of procedure may have relevance for subsequent ventures in comparative analysis of social stucture.

Although we perfectly well understood that neglect of the practical exigencies could be costly of time and money, the three men of the original team were in solemn agreement that considerations of technical efficiency were at all times to be kept subordinate to the broader aims of the project and to our larger responsibilities as representatives of Harvard University and as members of the community of scholars. As we defined our project, it was designed not only as a scientific investigation, but also as a training programme for the local staff and as a source of potentially useful practical information for the host community. This meant that in selecting our staff we gave preference to individuals we believed might play some role in future programme of social research in the given country even when others were available who could be hired for less or who already had greater practical skills but had little stake in their country's future social research.

To fulfil the interests of the local community we resolved in advance that a set of the materials collected in each country should be at the complete disposal of our co-directors. The facilities of the project in Cambridge were to be made available to support the co-directors' preparation of reports based on our data, but analyzed in such a way as to make them maximally relevant and useful in the local setting. We authorized and encouraged each of the field directors and co-directors to add additional questions and sample groups within limits appropriate to our study. Through fellowship offered directly by the project or arranged by it, we were able to bring all of our major co-directors to Harvard for periods of from one to three years to work on their respective national reports. Appointed as research associates of the Center for International Affairs, they were able to undertake further training, to secure technical guidance, to utilize the excellent computer facilities at Harvard and to be entirely free from their usual duties in order to devote themselves exclusively to the preparation of their respective national reports.

To protect the reputation of our institution, and to secure the friendly reception of social research projects which might later come on the scene, the field staff all agreed to observe the following principles: full and frank disclosure of nature of our work, including our sources of support; absolute respect for the confidentiality of all information we collected both from managers, cultivators and workers, with particular emphasis on the absolute anonymity of all interviews; strict neutrality and non-interference with regard to issues of policy which might be agitating the people of the factories and farms in the country in which we were working, combined with a willingness to offer freely such technical competence as we might have to all entitled to call upon it whether from management or labour; and scrupulous observance of local laws and customs, to be maintained even if nationals and other segments of the foreign colony might be quite casually flouting them. This last, for example, was applied particularly to such matters as currency regulations.

Establishing our field stations meant securing permission to enter and conduct research in a given country and area; establishing an appropriate and legitimate corporate identity in the community; locating and securing the participation of a local co-director; creating the material and staff base for the actual conduct of interviews; and collecting descriptive materials, census data, and the like necessary to the intelligent execution of the research design. Athough these problems had to be faced in some degree in all the countries, they were naturally more imposing in the three in which we assigned chief responsibility to one of the staff members from Harvard.

The most critical task was finding the right co-director, or some equivalent form of local collaboration. At first glance our prospects of success seemed poor. In some of the countries we had chosen, social research was little established, or even unknown, in the form we planned to conduct it. We could expect that individuals with the requisite qualifications would be not only scarce, but also deeply engaged for the present and heavily committed for the immediate future. In some cases, those with the qualifications and talents we demanded would have good chances to secure positions much more prestigeful, powerful, and rewarding than those we could offer. It was not clear how we could effectively save our collaborators the penalty of time lost in seniority systems, if they took leave to come with us. Heavy demands for teaching, and the often low priority assigned to research, made it unlikely that local university administrations would readily release men from their responsibilities in the classroom. Burgeoning nationalism and continuing anti-colonialism, even in the era before project Camelot and the CIA scandals, sometimes made intimate collaboration with a research group from the United States suspect and could possibly be a "taint" detrimental to a young person's career. Beyond all this, the service we offered was one arduous in the extreme, far more demanding than the usual routines of teaching, individual scholarship, or research in a large organization. In most cases we were asking our collaborators to help us build "from scratch" a complete staff and administration for a large-scale survey, while offering them very limited resources in an environment often indifferent and possibly hostile to the venture.

Yet powerful factors promised to work to our advantage. If there were serious and promising young social scientists in the country, we could offer them a unique oppurtunity. To associate oneself with international comparative research on such a scale was itself inherently exciting. Our plan for conducting the study offered training and experience in research on a scale not ordinarily available in underdeveloped countries and certainly not to such young people. The offer of later study at Harvard, and period for writing free from other responsibilities, were additional components of our appeal. Limits on responsibility, and the minimization of risk, were necessarily attractions to inexperienced young researchers in the early stages of their career. Were it not for our initiative and financial resources we brought, there was, in most cases, little immediate prospect that this kind of data, or anything on a comparable scale, could be collected at all. Those who were primarily teachers could see the advantage of the training opportunities we offered, not only for themselves but for their students. It seemed reasonable that this effort would leave behind it a corps of young people trained and experienced in interviewing and other aspects of research which could be drawn on in the country's future.

Perla Gibaja in Argentina, Amar Singh in India, and Uzi Peled in Israel, already had an appropriate institutional base. In Chile, Professor Heintz defined our research as an integral part of the training programme of the Latin American School of Social Sciences, and kindly arranged an appointment for me as Visiting Professor, without stipend. Professor Heintz proposed one of the young professors of his staff, Professor Juan Cesar Garcia, and generously agreed to release him from part of his teaching obligations. This seemed justified on the grounds that the staff, and especially the students, would be extensively engaged in the research, thus providing them with training and experience in accord with general objectives of FLACSO. Since Dr. García had to continue with the major part of his formal teaching duties, however, we asked his wife, Carlota Rios, to join us as administrative officer of the project. She was not only a specialist in administration, but in her own right a well-trained sociologist with some experience in survey research. Her knowledge of administrative procedures in the Chilean context proved an invaluable resource.

The Vice-Chancellor's interest in our work in Nigeria yielded Dr. Ryan an appointment as Research Associate in the Nigerian Institute for Social and Economic Research. Despite the existence of the Institute, the sort of field study we envisaged, was little known and not well institutionalized in Nigeria. Men with university experience, let alone professional graduate training, were rare, and the few with qualifications and talent usually had enormously alluring opportunities open to them either in politics or in government. We therefore considered ourselves exceptionally fortunate to secure the collaboration of Olatunde Oloko, who was then a Research Fellow of the Institute. He had extensive knowledge of Nigerian affairs relevant to our project, as well as some familarity with survey research and a keen desire to learn more.

Here again a happy accident seemed to favour our work. Although Oloko had been mentioned as one of the most obviously qualified men in Nigeria, Dr. Ryan had been told he had already left for the United States. They chanced not to meet anywhere in Ibadan. Discouraged by the poor prospects of finding a collaborator, and yet deeply convinced as to the indispensability of such a man in the African context, Dr. Ryan decided to explore the other sites we had considered as in the "reserve" category. He actually applied for a visa to Ghana. But for the usual reasons it was long delayed in arriving—long enough to allow for a chance meeting with Oloko, which shortly led to his joining the project as co-director for Nigeria.

In Pakistan Professor Husain was instrumental in securing for Dr. Schuman an appointment as Visiting Lecturer in the newly established College of Social Welfare at the Dacca University. Unfortunately Professor Husain's other duties in teaching and consulting with the government obliged him to severly limit the time he could devote to advising our project, and he recommended one of his younger associates, Dr. A. Farouk, who had worked with him on his earlier survey of Pakistani factory workers. Our initial contacts indicated this would be a fruitful collaboration, but just as we were about to begin our fieldwork Dr. Farouk secured a fellowship he had long sought for advanced training in Germany. No suitable substitute could be found in East Pakistan. But it appeared that several of the graduate students from the Welfare College who joined the staff could, collectively, play the role. Since all seemed comfortable with this arrangement, Dr. Schuman proceeded without a senior local co-director, and worked with his staff serving collectively in guiding the fieldwork in collaboration with him.

Our connection with well-established national institutions, our sponsors in them, and our local co-directors were essential elements in establishing our place in the community and legitimating our enterprise. We could thus present our work—as it honestly was—as a co-operative venture between Harvard University and the local university or research institute. Henceforth when we asked individuals to co-operate we did not need to appeal in the name of something so abstract and remote as science, or so distant as a great university from a very foreign country. Rather we could ask for co-operation on behalf of a national institution represented by local people who planned to do a job they saw as of potential benefit to their own community.

It may have been possible to proceed in a less cumbersome or technically more rational way. We might, for example, have chosen to work only where there were commercial agencies of the sort established by the international Gallup and Roper organizations, simply paying for a service, having our data collected for us by people with whom we had very little contact and who had no particular intellectual investment in our effort. Apart from the issue of confidence in the results, we could not accept this approach as in accord with our principles.

Scholars in underdeveloped countries often protest against such procedure which they see as a new wave of colonialism. Social researchers who follow this procedure are often depicted as latter-day conquistadors exploiting local resources—taking back the social science equivalent of gold, or copper, or oil, to their home country for processing and for personal enrichment—without any real benefit to the country and the people from which these riches are extracted.[9] A strict analysis of this analogy can certainly find flaws in the reasoning, but we were as interested in rights and feelings as in logic. We decided to proceed otherwise.

The field stations shared some features rather widely. Of course, the flow of work also varied considerably according to the administrative style of the director, the influence of the local culture, and the distinctive requirements of the local situation. We must leave the more detailed description of distinctive features of the several field stations to the individual country reports, and here restrict ourselves to the most common features.

A local advisory board, formal or informal, was generally constituted for the project, usually including such men as leading academicians with special competence to advise our group; owners and managers of industry, and trade union leaders, drawn either from their official associations or from among qualified and interested individuals; and, on occasion, from government agencies, such as the ministry of industry or labour, who were in a position to facilitate our work.[10] The advisory board served to introduce us to the community, to give legitimacy to our effort, and to help us to avoid the gross errors our lack of familiarity with the local scene might produce. They also pointed out the most promising direction and the most efficient paths for reaching our objectives.

The ultimate responsibility for decisions, however, rested with the field director, and in no case did any board or any member of it seek to interfere in strictly scientific matters. Yet their service was at some points of inestimable value. For example, knowledge held by the board members enabled us, at the very outset, to confront the fact that in Israeli industry the men working on the production line, especially in the younger and lower-educa-

[9] For a spirited exchange bearing on this issue as it applies to India, see Marshall B. Clinard and Joseph W. Elder, "Sociology in India: A Study in the Sociology of Knowledge" and Ahmed Imtiaz, "Note on Sociology of India".

[10] For example, in Israel, where the advisory board was most active, it included: an industrial sociologist from one university; another from a department of industrial engineering and administration; the manager of the efficiency section, and the chairman of the labour committee, of the Manufacturer's Association; two representatives from the Israel Management Centre; and senior staff members of the Israel Institute of Applied Social Research.

ted categories, would be overwhelmingly of Asian or African rather than of European origin. This permitted an early and essential adaptation of our research design. We might otherwise have spent innumerable unproductive hours in a fruitless search for interviewees of European origin who met our sampling criteria.

So as not to burst unannounced upon an unprepared industrial community which might therefore respond overly timidly or defensively, we sought wherever feasible, to place in local newspapers or magazines an account of our research objectives and plans, including a plea for co-operation. This generally came about through granting, or inviting, an interview with a young journalist for use either in print or on the radio. Whether this was a sound procedure could not easily be decided in advance. We ran the risk, of course, that either the attitude taken toward us by the journalist, or the political sensitivities of the local community, might cause this publicity to generate resistance to our work even in advance of our having done anything at all.

Apparently, in all cases where such stories were printed, they did no harm that we know of. Indeed, we generally felt the stories received much less attention than we had hoped. In at least one case, however, our co-director was convinced a newspaper story about our work played a substantial and positive role. An early report on our research was printed in the *West African Pilot*. This newspaper was very important in shaping opinion in the Ibo community, and the NCNC Party. Mr. Oloko believes that the news-story played a significant role in winning the approval of certain trade unions connected with the NCNC Party for our work in highly unionized places such as the Nigerian Railways Corporation and the Port Authority Establishments at Apapa and Victoria Island.

Advance publicity in the press and on the radio was supplemented by more direct efforts to explain our objectives and mode of working to key individuals and groups. These efforts included consultation with appropriate government organizations, such as the ministries of labour and industry, the ministry of public health or safety, and the census bureau, and visits or lectures to chambers of commerce, associations of managers and trade unions. By face-to-face contact in a friendly atmosphere in these informal meetings we were able to do a great deal not only to explain our mission and describe our work, but to allay suspicion, satisfy curiosity, and relive anxiety.

The meetings not only helped to make clear what we needed *to avoid* in order not to create tensions or resentment, but also often made clear what we needed to do in order to satisfy the local community. In one case, for example, the trade union leaders wanted special assurances that the anonymity of the interview would be absolutely secure. In another, the representatives of a particular industry requested that they would like eventually

to see the summary figures for certain questions as they were answered by
workers in that industry. In a third, we were cautioned against asking anyone's precise party affiliation because of the tensions arising from an im-
pending election. Virtually all of the requests were quite reasonable, and
almost without exception could be acceded to without compromising our
basic principles or procedures. Where difficult issues arose we reaffirmed
our position, begged indulgence, and promised to make such adjustments
as we possibly could. Almost no one insisted on, or even attempted,
censoring or editing our questionnaire. Indeed, the number of instances
in which people insisted on examining the questionnaire was quite small.
Most people seemed quite satisfied with our explanation of the research
and the examples of our questions we routinely included in that description.

Valuable as all this advance work in public relations may have been
in guaranteeing our general freedom to work in the community, the critical
contacts were those with the factory managers. Without their permission
we could not enter the plant to sample. Since we hoped to do most of the
interviewing in the factory, and if possible during working hours, their
co-operation was most essential.

The pattern of contact varied with the field director's sense of what was
appropriate in the given country. In some case a letter was sent in advance
to the management of those factories which had been drawn for the sample,
briefly explaining the project and announcing our intention to call on them.
This was followed by a personal visit, usually by the field director or his
personal deputy. Where the local culture gave heavy importance to approaching people through intermediaries or personal introductions, we sought
out the appropriate sources. In Nigeria, Dr. Ryan neither wrote nor phoned
ahead, having found it hard to get much understanding or help from the
secretaries he thus invariably reached. Instead he called personally on each
factory, his impression, as stated in his field report, "in Nigeria managers
are accustomed to handling personally matters which in the United States
and Europe would be dealt with, or at least screened by, subordinates;
hence business is conducted informally and personally." This impression
was apparently correct, since in only 1 factory of 119 he visited was Dr.
Ryan refused permission to conduct the interviews in or around the plant.

Once the manager was reached we explained our research in much the
same language we had used for more public presentations. We admitted
we could offer him no immediate concrete benefit, but only the possibility
that in the long term what we learned might be useful to management in
guiding its labour relations. In the short run we were asking him simply to
support an international co-operative venture which we believed had significance for developing countries and might contribute to the advancement
of knowledge and to the development of his country.

The response of management, and the motivation for participation, was very diverse. Some understood our purpose very well, and even became absorbed in lively discussions of underlying ideas. Others apparently thought it all very bizarre, abstract, or impractical, but were unwilling to seem to be Philistines or to be left out of something undertaken by an apparently prestigious organization enjoying the co-operation of the leading industrial firms. For many managers the chief motivation to co-operate arose from a feeling that they did not well understand their workers, that turnover was excessive or disgruntlement endemic, and so they were interested in assisting a research which might throw light on those problems. Indeed, some drew us into long discussions of those issues before, during and after our interviews.

In plants in which there were trade unions, we could not approach the workers without approval of the trade union any more than we could enter the factory grounds without permission of the factory manager. Our methods for approaching trade union leaders were similar to those for managers, and seemed about as successful. We had the impression many of the trade union leaders hoped that our listing of the workers' grievances during the course of the interview and our general inquiry into the factory as a *social* environment might stimulate personnel policies more favourable to the workers.

In one way or another, all the field directors echoed the sentiment of Dr. Schuman when he wrote about his experience in Pakistan that: "Cooperation from factory officials was generally excellent—much better than I had anticipated. This was due to the right mixture of support from the government, local and foreign university sponsorship combined and other factors in our general procedure."

The impression any organization makes on the community and the response to it are in part shaped by the physical setting from which it conducts its work. Since ours was an academic project, we would have preferred to work from offices at the university or the research institutes connected with it. This proved possible in Israel, where we could use the facilities of the Israel Institute of Applied Social Research and in India where the Ranchi University provided the necessary office space. By force of circumstance, Professor Gibaja ran the Argentinian project from her own tiny office and a nearby room the department of sociology made available to her. In the other cases, however, it was necessary to utilize space outside the university, although FLACSO kindly provided me with an office but could do little more.[11] Dr. Garcia found a semi-detached house for rent in

---

[11] This limitation applied to office space, almost everywhere in short supply. FLACSO otherwise contributed substantially, releasing Dr. Garcia from some of his regular teaching duties to conduct project work, providing administrative support without charge, and facilitating our effort in numerous other ways. Similarly, the University of Ranchi, through the good offices of the Vice-Chancellor, Mr. S. Sinha, arranged for Dr. Singh

a new housing development near the university campus, and the project established its headquarters there. Dr. Schuman rented a large house and used part of it as project office while maintaining his personal residence in the other part. Much the same thing was done by Dr. Ryan in Apapa near Lagos. Since the interviewers had joined the project in Ibadan and were hence unable to live at home while we worked in Lagos, a house was found for them to share, where the project also employed a cook to prepare meals for the staff.

The overwhelming majority of interviews with factory managers[12] and workers took place in the factory, so that our rather special office arrangements were not directly confronted by most people we dealt with. Those managers who did not come to conferences at our offices or who were interviewed there seemed not to be put off by our special arrangements. Indeed, we believe the workers interviewed there rather enjoyed the chance to visit in places they ordinarily did not get to see. More serious was the fact that unwittingly each of the field directors became not only a research scientist but an office manager, and even the head of what was in effect a large household. It was a good way to learn more about the local culture, but also inevitably very costly in scarce professional time and human energy. If we had larger resources we would have been well advised to assign each field director a full time administrative assistant.

3. SELECTING AND TRAINING A STAFF

Both our mandate and our plan of work required us to find and train a local interviewing staff. The elaboration of training and the regularity and intimacy of contact between field director and staff varied considerably.

The procedure used in Israel was probably the most routine. The Israel Institute regularly conducted survey interviews, although generally only a fraction of the length of ours, and so could draw on a pool of experienced interviewers. They were organized in teams of eight to twelve in each of the three main cities. Once selected, the Israeli interviewers were asked to study the questionnaire and a file of materials describing the project. A series of intensive briefing sessions were held to clarify general issues and to call attention to special features of the interview. Before the first interviews there was a two-day training session in which practice was

to be freed from administrative duties as Chairman of the Psychology Department, and assigned other members of the Department to assist in project work. This spirit of co-operation backed up by generous support was the norm in the other settings as well.

[12] In addition to our standard questionnaire for the workers, we developed a special questionnaire for factory managers designed to assess the philosophy of management they espoused, especially with reference to human relations in the plant.

obtained by having the interviewers interview each other. Superiors reviewed each questionnaire as completed and called to the attention of both the individual interviewer and his team any general and specific shortcomings. The field director held weekly meetings with the several teams to review progress and resolve problems. Since the interviewers worked full time over a period of several months, they became quite adept at conducting the interviews.

While all this suggests good procedure and may give confidence in the quality of the interviews, we cannot claim to have made a distinctive contribution to research training in Israel. Our main claim to innovation there lay in introducing the long and thorough life-history interview, something they had not previously attempted, and in demonstrating that an Israeli Arab could not only capably but amicably act as interviewing supervisor for a team of Israeli Jews.[13] In several of the other countries, however, most notably in East Pakistan and Nigeria, the training and experience our staff received was unique to the country.

Both Dr. Schuman and Dr. Ryan elected to work intensively with a small group of men, mostly drawn from among advanced students in the university, with whom they established a very long-term relationship of great intimacy and frequency of contact. Basically, the same set of men worked as a team on the translation and adaptation of the questionnaire, its initial and subsequent testing, and the entire programme of interviewing both in the city and the countryside. Thus we offered interviewers an experience we hoped would be rewarding, not only in material terms, but in terms of personal growth, professional training, and national development. For Nigeria, in which our effort was perhaps most foreign to the culture and its experience, Ryan reported:

> Work on the project to be closely related to larger and longer range goals in the lives of individual members. Stability of staff could be fairly well assured by paying an attractive salary, and undertaking, as far as possible, seriously to help staff members move to attractive or secure positions when the project was completed. Stated in this way, however, there is serious de-emphasis of the genuine ethical commitment which most of the personnel had to completing the work. It would be easy to underestimate the importance of this factor. Thus, the project lost no personnel during the course of the fieldwork. This, in spite of the fact that the

---

[13] The latter came about through my initiative in urging the Institute to take advantage of the services of Subkhi Abu-Gosh, trained at Princeton University as an exchange scholar, and just completing his doctoral dissertation in political science at the time the project got under way in Israel. The suggestion was warmly seconded by Mr. Peled and graciously approved by Professor Guttman. Dr. Abu-Gosh subsequently became a study director within the Israel Institute of Applied Social Research.

conditions of work were at times trying and exceedingly demanding, and that, particularly in times of unusual stress, I was far from jovial and in other ways quite difficult to work for.

We were naturally delighted by the commitment we feel we had from our staffs. Our opinion is that this was generated mainly by the quality of the people we recruited and by the personal relations we maintained with them. Nevertheless, we also took more formal precautions to insure the interests of the project where local conditions seemed to require them. In Pakistan, for example, Dr. Schuman was advised that he ran the danger that the staff, after much training, might begin to drift away just before the project ended its work, a not uncommon event in Pakistan where jobs are scarce and a man must attempt to find other work well before his present job ends. To insure against such premature separation, a bonus payment of half the regular salary was set aside each month, with the understanding the interviewer would receive it at the end of the fieldwork *only* if he fulfilled two conditions. One was that he remain with the project until its completion, except in so far as excused earlier. The other was that his interviews be carried out honestly over the whole term of the work.

The possibility that interviewers may dishonestly conduct and record their interviews is a nightmare vision haunting all opinion surveys, no less in the developed countries than elsewhere. To insure complete honesty in the conduct of the interviews we asked each field director to set up procedures appropriate to the local situation. Perhaps the most elaborate and stringent were those established by Dr. Singh in India. In evaluating these measures as described by Dr. Singh below—it should be kept in mind that these rules were not the solution adopted by a suspicious and mistrustful foreigner blundering around in an alien culture. They represent the considered judgment of a native who knew his own culture and students, and whom we can certify from long experience to be a man of firm but gentle disposition. Dr. Singh wrote in his field report as follows:

The problem of ensuring honest fieldwork is an extremely important, though delicate issue. The interview was a difficult one, the actual time taken was about four hours. In such situations one is likely to get what may be described as the "tea-shop bias", that is, the filling-in of the questionnaires in a tea shop. I had devised several checks to minimize the possibiity of such hazards. First, I was careful in selecting the interviewers. And I have a feeling, after the fieldwork has been over, that perhaps the best possible precaution against dishonesty is proper screening in selection. I had even preferred some less academically brilliant interviews to those who could face the strains of the interviews without impatience and grudge. Secondly, every interviewer was required to give sureties from two responsible persons that he will refund all the money spent on him if it was found that he had dishonestly filled in the questionnaires. Thirdly, we had obtained some information from independent sources. These were factual information regarding age, father's occupation, salary, overtime, name of the native village etc. The interviewers did not know about these. As soon as the questionnaires were returned we checked this information. Fourth, we used a quick check with a large number of respondents to find out if the interview was done, where it was done, who did it, how long it lasted etc. And finally, we tried to give as many facilities to the interviewers as possible.

The measures adopted elsewhere were generally not so extensive nor so rigorous as those taken by Dr. Singh, but serious attention was everywhere given to the issue. All the field directors agree with Dr. Singh that the best assurance of strict integrity was the careful selection of interviewers and the intimacy of association with them in the course of the work. We believe this to be demonstrated by the extraordinary correspondence between what our interviewers reported and what we found when we did our spot checks to verify the integrity of the interviewing.

We may take as one illustration among many the Nigerian programme for locating and interviewing urban non-industrial workers. Dr. Ryan divided each city into sampling areas, and then assigned each interviewer the task of combing a single street, checking with all those in certain specified occupations to ascertain whether they fitted our sampling criteria.[14] This was a very different matter from sitting in a comfortable, possibly air-conditioned, room in a factory and having workers brought to you to be inteviewed. It was hot, exhausting, unattractive, discouraging work. The probability was, therefore, great that any interviewers who lacked integrity would either sit out the afternoon in a bar and later report there were no eligibles on their street, or weaken and bring in cases which in fact did not qualify. The actual outcome was quite different.

Because several days went by without a single eligible respondent being found, Dr. Ryan decided to visit certain areas himself, accompanied by a member of the staff in whom he had highest confidence, with the intention of "recombing the territory, building by building". He was not able to find a single respondent who had been missed! Granting, as he himself acknowledges, that he personally "would miss many clues from the environment to which the interviewers had been sensitive, and that therefore he (Ryan) would miss a great deal," the outcome still must count heavily on

[14] This was when we were interviewing "urban non-industrial workers". These were men who pursued traditional crafts in the city—barbers, furniture-makers, small retail tradesmen. There was, therefore, no great problem in identifying one of the "specified" occupations.

the side of the conscientiousness of the Nigerian staff in search for eligible interviewees. Neither was there any evidence that out of discouragement the interviewers lowered their standards and compromised by bringing in cases who really did not fit our sampling criteria. Dr. Ryan later personally contacted 75 per cent of the men eventually selected to enter the sample as urban non-industrial (UNI) cases. All had in fact been interviewed; their background characteristics accorded with the face-sheet, and they seemed to hold the views they were recorded as holding. It seems almost certain there was not a single fraudulent interview in this sample.

Unfortunately, there were instances in which we could not so carefully select our interviewers nor maintain appropriately close supervision. In this respect Professor Gibaja was most disadvantaged, since she had less money and fewer staff, and was only partly free of her regular teaching obligations. Thus for the work in the countryside she was obliged to subcontract the interviewing to a team from the University of Córdoba with which she maintained cordial relations. This was also required in Chile for the interviewing done in the city of Concepcion, because of its distance from Santiago. We cannot with the same confidence certify the security of those interviews, not because we have the least doubt as to the integrity of the staff there, but only because we were not on the scene to check in the same way as we did elsewhere.

After our verification procedures were completed, a few interviews were discarded either because we were not confident about the conditions under which they were done, or evidence internal to the questionnaires threw doubt on their veracity. The largest block was accounted for by two interviewers we discarded. Since these were almost all in the scarce UNI category, and our quotas were in general severely underfilled in Argentina, this was a very painful decision to make. It was made on the initiative of Professor Gibaja herself, who thus made a substantial sacrifice for the sake of reliability. Dr. Singh also discovered one interviewer who came to attention because he seemed to discharge his duties with exceptional speed. A careful check revealed that he had indeed contacted all his interviewees and conducted an interview of sorts. But he had skipped large segments of the questionnaire, checking those items at random. This man was discharged, and all his interviews withdrawn—a less traumatic gesture in a sample of over 1300 cases.

Such incidents seem unavoidable, and they certainly reduce the reliability of survey results. All in all, however, we feel we maintained a standard of integrity for our interviews which was at least the equivalent of that in any study done in the most advanced countries. For the conditions which prevail in the developing countries we believe it to have been unprecedented. We are proud of our record, and grateful to the vast majority of interviewers. But we are also glad we adopted strict verification procedures, follow-in the adage of the American Revolution: "Trust in God, but keep your powder dry."

4. CONSTRUCTING AND TRANSLATING THE QUESTIONNAIRE

When the three field directors left Cambridge in the first months of 1963, they did not carry with them a fixed questionnaire. Insofar as possible we wished our final questionnaire to reflect the special emphases of the cultures we were to study. Similarly, we kept open-ended the definitive specification of our sampling requirements, so that when we wrote the final guidelines they could reflect the concrete social reality of the settings in which our fieldwork was done. The guiding ideas of the project had, of course, already been formulated by the project director. One does not develop sociological theories in a committee. And the main strategy for the fieldwork had already been broadly outlined. Otherwise ours would have been only a fishing expedition, and one proceeding without compass or chart. Nevertheless, we kept many of critical decisions open. We treated our plans as tentative and our questions as experimental. We hoped to learn a great deal of special relevance from our local collaborators, and anticipated we would broaden our thinking, sharpen our design, and improve our questions by elaborating them in the settings in which they would be eventually applied.

In Cambridge we had prepared a set of memoranda outlining the main themes which defined, in theoretical terms, the concept of individual modernity and the related topics we hoped to study. For many of these we had prepared a well-elaborated set of pre-coded questions. For others we had not yet formulated questions, but had general guidelines for conducting exploratory open-ended interviews which we hoped would suggest appropriate questions. And for a few themes we had only sets of general specifications, which could be given substance as interview material only after being re-worked in consultation with our local collaborators.

To test our initial ideas, each of the Harvard field directors committed himself to putting each of our tentative questions to, and to exploring each of our themes with, at least thirty individuals, half of them experienced industrial workers and half cultivators living in rural villages. By conservative estimate it took at least sixteen hours to put the questions and explore all the topical themes called for by our preliminary interview. We allowed each field director three months from the time of his arrival for this phase of the operation.

Obviously, the work could not even begin until a local collaborator and staff had been recruited. Once they were found, the director had to explain the basic objectives of the research, to elaborate and discuss the concepts underlying each theme in the study, and achieve some preliminary translation of each question and interview guideline. The interviewers had to be given some initial training. Subjects willing to be interviewed had to be located, the test interviews conducted, the responses recorded, translated, discussed and evaluated by the local staff. The only compromise we had allowed in this plan was that the thirty persons answering each question or commenting on each theme need not be the same set of individuals. This made it easier to find people willing to undergo the experiment, but it also meant finding more than thirty willing subjects. All this was to be going on while the director also gave his attention to the many difficult routines attendant upon setting up an office in a foreign country.

It will not be a surprise that we did not all complete this phase in three months. Nevertheless, by August 1963 the three field directors were able to meet in Dacca, each having more or less completed his initial task.[15] There, in a month-long conference of great intensity, we shared our initial experiences. We covered the ground question by question and theme by theme. Each reported what he had learned about the nature of the problem as seen in the perspective of his field setting. We discussed the ambiguities of our concepts when they were measured against the peculiarities of the local culture, the strengths and weaknesses of the questions when rendered in different ways in the various languages, and the ease or difficulty of finding different sorts of respondents.

One striking feature of this conference we did not become aware of until it was well along. In some subtle way each of the field directors had become much less a member of the Harvard team and somehow more a representative of the cultural perspective of the people with whom he had been working. Although this complicated our relationship, and slowed down our work, it undoubtedly contributed the richness and relevance of the definitive questionnaire which we finally hammered out. At the end of the month we all moved on to Calcutta, to meet with Amar Singh, who added the perspective of still a fourth culture to our deliberations.

The questionnaire, and the sampling plan also finalized at the Dacca conference, were carried back to our respective field stations for the examination and evaluation of our local collaborators, and then passed on to the stage of translation.

We were attempting to measure subtle and elusive psycho-social properties of the person and his mental functioning, tapping such dimensions as his sense of efficacy, openness to new experience, and time orientation. Yet the people to whom we would talk were mainly very simple, possessed of little or no formal education, occupationally engaged in highly concrete manual operations. We therefore faced a massive challenge to develop ques-

[15] David Smith also attended the conference, and participated fully in all phases of the discussion.

tions which, while comprehensible and meaningful to the men we would interview, would yet permit us to score them on the more abstract dimensions of our conceptual scheme. The problem was enormously complicated by the necessity to use questions which would be meaningful in six different societies and in as many or more additional cultural sub-groups.

We sought to resolve the problem by restricting ourselves to situations and relationships which are more or less universal, and which, we reasoned, should have meaning to almost anyone, anywhere. Does a boy learn more of the truth from old people or books? Would you prefer your son to have a job running a machine at 150 rupees per month or to be a clerk in an office at only 100 rupees? Can you usually count on the others working with you to do their share of the work? Can a man be really good even though he does not believe in religion? If a boy is poor but ambitious and hard-working, can he still expect to get ahead in life? Even these questions assume familiarity with such things as machines and offices in which people may clerk. And there is no shortage of ambiguities concerning matters such as the referrent of "religion" or the different meanings people can read into the idea of "getting ahead in life".

Despite our best efforts we clearly made many mistakes, so that our interviewees were sometimes sorely tried. Take the matter of reporting your pay. Dr. Singh followed the Pakistan version of the questionnaire because of his close association with Dr. Schuman. In Pakistan, people reckoned their pay by the day, in India, by the month. When we asked the Indian workers, to keep in mind the daily wage of an ordinary worker and then to estimate how much one should pay the engineer per day, we simply overwhelmed many of them. It was enough of a task to decide how much an engineer should properly get per month. When we inadvertently required them to convert from the usual monthly rate to the daily rate in terms of which we were asking the question, we simply left many of our subjects in an arithmetic confusion.

This example represents a technical failing we might have avoided. But in numerous other instances the difficulty was more deeply rooted in irremedial cultural differences. Consider, for example, the idea of "influencing" someone. A number of our questions about politics and the realm of opinion required our interviewees to say whether they had ever tried to "influence" a politician, or whether people like them could "influence" the course of government action. It proves almost impossible to render the concept of influence, as we meant it, in Yoruba. The Yoruba seem to be quite familiar with the idea of commanding someone, or forcing him, or begging him, or pleading with him, but not of "influencing" in the sense in which we commonly use the word in English; that is, of changing another's view or his action by presenting effective arguments, by insisting clearly and forcefully on your rights, or by making clear how it is in his long-term interest to accommodate you. The idea could be expressed only by a substantial circumlocution, and then only very inexactly. Similar problems existed in the other societies in rendering concepts such as skill, equality, dignity, human nature, responsibility, and numerous others.

Our general procedure for guaranteeing the maximum uniformity in rendering our questions in terms readily comprehended by individuals from other cultures was simple even if tedious. Our questionnaire included "field director's notes" for many questions which we felt were so cryptic or colloquial in English as to leave doubt as to our intentions. These notes elaborated on the concepts involved in the question. Beyond that, we relied on protracted discussion in which we explained each of our main concepts in detail to make clear its relation to our general objectives. This explanation was followed by a discussion of each question, in which we expounded the role it was expected to play in measuring some more general orientation or attitude, and explained the particular choice of ideas, situations, and even words used. This deep sharing of a common understanding of our underlying ideas and their concrete embodiment in questions, we considered the best insurance against a process of "drift". Such drift might, in the end, have left us with only minimally comparable questionnaires in the several countries. Our procedure assumed that we all had roughly the same apperceptive mass and could converse equally well in English. For both Professor Gibaja and García this was not the case so far as English was concerned, and their briefing was in part conducted in Spanish by myself and David Smith.[16]

In the end there were clearly some instances in which we had not understood each other, and the question as it was rendered in different countries did not consistently get at what those who wrote it intended. An example is provided by our effort to measure the worker's response to patriarchal and diffuse, as against more precise and contractual, relations between superior and subordinate. Our conception of the more modern worker was that he will insist that his boss not ask things of him which go beyond formal lines of duty in production. We therefore put the question: "Do you think it is right or wrong for a boss to require his workers to do personal services for him such as washing his car outside of working hours?" In this formulation everything hinges on emphasizing the *personal* aspect of the service and its performance *outside working hours*. When this theme was investigated in Chile and Argentina, however, these distinctions were blurred, and the Spanish question spoke only of the foreman "asking a favour", without

[16] David Smith was connected with the project from its early period. As a graduate student he served as a research assistant to the field director in Chile. After receiving his doctorate on the basis of research done in Chile he became Associate Director of the project in Cambridge. He will, with me be co-author of the main report of the project to be published under the title *Becoming Modern*.

making it explicit that the request was somehow "out-of-bounds". This was not a problem in translation. The idea could have been easily rendered in Spanish. The failure was one of communication, of making clear to our Latin American colleagues exactly what kind of favour we had in mind. Inevitably, in the form in which it was used, the question had a different meaning for our interviewees than we had intended, and was responded to accordingly.

Despite such incidents, we are satisfied that conceptual misunderstandings, at least of a more serious variety, were not numerous. Admittedly, the cumulative effect of a substantial number of less serious misunderstandings did act to reduce the strict comparability of the interview, but not so consistently as to give it a basically distinctive structure or style in any country. The process of drift at the level of conceptual equivalence was, we belive, modest, if not minimal. Almost all of our concepts were eventually fairly well rendered in the thought system of the several cultures involved, even though there were times when this could be done only by awkward or wordy constructions and circumlocutions.

However good our mutual understanding of the questions, we might still greatly reduce their comparability in the process of the translation. In the example of the boss asking for favours outside hours and beyond the line of duty, the Chilean and Argentinian version used the word "servicio", which can quite reasonably be interpreted not as a personal favour but as an action performed in the line of duty. This further added to the difference separating the Latin American version of the question from that used elsewhere.

No doubt the best insurance against the "drift" resulting from the process of translation would have been to find a single field director who was simultaneously absolutely fluent in all the languages we used. Barring that unlikely event, we could at least hope for field directors who at least knew both English and the local language. That condition was met in India and in Nigeria, since Dr. Singh and Mr. Oloko both had colloquial and near-perfect English. García and Gibaja commanded only very limited English, and my Spanish, in turn, was far from fluent. Dr. Schuman knew no Bengali at all on his arrival in East Pakistan. In these cases, therefore, junior members of the staff who were more truly bilingual were drawn more into the translation process. Only in Israel was the translation contracted out to individuals who specialized in such work.

In those cases in which the field director was not fluent in both languages, and to a lesser degree elsewhere, we attempted to control the quality of the translation by having various third parties re-translate the questionnaire back into English. This device, now widely utilized, in cross-national research, proved highly effective. It served not only to locate simple mistranslations and to identify which could not accurately be rendered in the local language, but also to expose instances in which the local staff clearly had not understood the original concept in English or had incorrectly interpreted the purpose behind a question.

The range of problems involved may be illustrated by our experience with the translation into Hebrew. The process of re-translation into English is itself a translation like any other. Words and ideas which were in fact translated into Hebrew well could appear in the re-translation as if they had been rendered badly. In question GO-7,[17] for example, the original described a boy resisting the pressure of opinion even when his "whole group" was against him, meaning to emphasize *unanimity* in the opposition. The re-translation spoke only of his group being in opposition—without conveying the sense of uniform disagreement. Examination of the Hebrew, however, indicated it had indeed correctly conveyed the idea of unanimity. In other words, it was not the translation into Hebrew that was misleading, but rather the re-translation into English. The question: "What good is an education for an ordinary man?" uses the word education to mean formal schooling. In the re-translation into English the word "enlightenment" appeared to have been substituted for education. In fact, it had not. The Hebrew version apparently used the common word for education just as we had intended. The re-translation of CH-1 gave the impression we wanted to know a man's "conviction" as a factory worker, whereas we wanted to know about his "experience" as a factory worker. The original translator had clearly understood it as we said it, and the distortion was in the re-translation.

In other cases the re-translation was not inaccurate, but different enough to have stimulated a check and discussion of the original, which often increased our confidence in the Hebrew version. In DI-4 for example, we ask the interviewee whether his parents had made him feel humiliated The re-translation used the English "embarrassed", close enough but also different enough to warrant a check. The Hebrew word was, upon discussion, confirmed as being close in meaning to the English standard. In another case, the original asked about sources of information one would "trust" (M-6), but the re-translation used the English "rely on". Again this was close, but open to question. Apparently the Hebrew had tapped the same dimension we had in mind.

So far so good. But the re-translation back into English also exposed a substantial number of outright errors which had crept into the Hebrew translation. For example, in WR-12 we wanted to convey the idea of man

---

[17] Each question in our questionnaire is identified by letters and a number. The letters stand for the topic with which the question deals. Thus GO designates a question on the theme "Growth of Opinion" and DI a question on the theme of human. "Dignity". The number indicates which, in the total set of questions on that theme, the particular item represents.

helping his wife by doing only the "heavy" or "hard" work around the house. In Hebrew it came out with him doing the "thorough", i.e. "the general", housekeeping. In a question on the acceptance of new methods in agriculture (CH-3), we describe two boys working in the fields who "pause" in their work and then "discuss" the methods of raising rice or corn. The boys came out of the translation "neglecting" their work and "arguing" about the new techniques. Quite a different matter. In CI-14 we offered a choice between three petitioners, one of whom had "the most right under the law" to have his petition granted. The Hebrew had him basing his case on having greater "privilege". In assessing political aliena-tion we asked whether government "officials" took seriously their obligation to serve the public (CI-14). The translator had downgraded the *officials* to governments *clerks*. To test the willingness to yield to pressure we asked in KO-6, whether, in helping out a friend or relative, a boy should "break a rule". The Hebrew translator had escalated the barrier, asking whether the boy should for this purpose "act contrary to law".

We believe all of these simple mis-translations were effectively corrected. They would not even have been identified—in any event not until it was too late—except for our use of the re-translation technique.

One of the most useful functions of the re-translation was to highlight conceptual problems which escaped notice so long as the field staff's mutual exchange was exclusively in English. There seems to be no Hebrew word for "dignity," nor for "authority" either. Both are central concepts in our research, and had been discussed with Mr. Peled many times. So long as he was conversing in English, however, Mr. Peled was never obliged to con-front the problem. He freely used both "dignity" and "authority" in English, heedless of the lack of a Hebrew equivalent. Fortunately, the translator had managed to render "authority" reasonably well by reference to "men who give orders and instructions". One translator had simply left a blank whenever dignity was used. Another[18] had rendered it in Hebrew as "honour"—a definite mis-translation. We finally rendered it as "treatment which is respectful and considerate of your feelings".

We never found a completely successful way to say in Hebrew "a boy was *fated* to fail". We could, however, easily accept the substitution of a "horoscope" for the idea that "it was written in the stars". We even more approved the translators' spontaneous and perhaps unconscious substitution of an "old man" for the "poor man" in the story (AS-9) of the farmer who desperately needed the help of his only son on the farm. The son, while lov-ing his parents, nevertheless felt he should continue his schooling. We had

[18] Wherever possible we made it a practice to have two independent translations of the questionnaire prepared. This not only offered a choice, it also served to call to attention instances in which the original English language word was unclear or diffi-cult to render in the local language.

meant the question to create the greatest possible conflict between the alternatives of schooling for a bright boy and the obligations to a parent. The translator apparently sensed that in the Israeli context the father who was *old* and without help would arouse more sympathy than one equally without help but suffering only *poverty*.

Translators are generally educated men. They find it hard to render something in the common speech, even if it is so in the original. It is also easier to maintain reasonable equivalence from one language to another if one sticks to somewhat more standard educated speech. Since we were everywhere dealing mainly with people of very low education, and men often living in very isolated conditions, our questions had to be couched in the simplest possible language.

Even if it upset the local staff's sense of propriety, we had to find and use the words of the common people, no matter how bizarre, ungrammatical, or even vulgar. Our questionnaire, therefore, everywhere underwent a second process of translation in the effort to render it in the common speech. This was often difficult, because the local language experts seemed almost invariably too sanguine in their assumptions about the words people knew. In some cases our interviewers, who themselves came from the same background as our interviewees, were able to render great service in this process of simplification. Dr. Singh's field report describes the process thus:

> The problem of translation was even greater in India because of the heterogenous nature of our sample, which included tribal and non-tribal persons from villages and cities. We tried to make the language as simple as we could so that the uneducated farmers could understand it. We used a very low level Hindi which is spoken by both tribal and non-tribal persons, and sacrificed the sense of grammar for the sake of proper communication. We used words which, strictly speaking, are not grammatically correct from the academic point of view, but nonetheless are used in day-to-day conversation. The correct Hindi word for religion is "dharma". People of low education speak it as "dharam". We preferred the word which people use. For husband the correct word is "pati", but the people from lower strata, particularly tribals, use the word "adami" for it, which literally means "any man". We used both, keeping "adami" under bracket to be used in tribal cases.

5. CONDUCT OF THE INTERVIEW

Our questionnaire was very long and complex in the range of issues with which it dealt. The larger versions contained over 300 questions, and required four hours of interviewing time. The majority of our interviewees were not accustomed to long verbal exchanges. The issues raised by our questions were often ones they had never had presented to them before. Even in the case of those problems they had previously encountered, no one had ever before asked them to *express* their opinion. The whole idea of an interview was something new in many of the countries, and in any event those in our sample had never heard of the idea, let alone met anyone who had had the experience.

In some places our interviewees easily confused our purposes with that of quite different people who came around "just to talk". In Nigeria we were often welcomed because there was a widespread belief that being interviewed could lead to getting a good job, or even a scholarship for study abroad. Since we selected only Yoruba-speaking men, it was logical for the others, especially the Ibo who were a major component of the industrial labour force, to believe that we were discriminating against their tribe. In many Israeli villages it was quickly concluded that we must be connected with the tax authorities, because the early section of our questionnaire inquired into individual and total family earnings and expenditures. In Argentina we were caught in "planes de lucha", a series of strikes mounted by the trade unions in protest against the anticipated return of Peron. The strikes involved the tactic of locking management personnel up in their offices for hours at a time. An interviewer wandering about the plant in that heated atmosphere could easily be mistaken for a member of the administrative staff and be locked up with them.

Despite the occasional dramatic incident which these mistaken images of our role generated, we feel we succeeded in conducting all but a very few of interviews in a setting and style maximally conducive to a frank and thoughtful, rather than an evasive and mindless, response. After a man was selected for our sample we explained the general scientific purpose of the interview, speaking sometimes first through the personnel officer but always adding a statement of our own in face-to-face contact at the start of the interview. The absolute integrity of the interview was explained, in order to allay any fears that whatever was said would be known by any-one else outside the room in a way that could directly identify it with the interviewee. Every effort was made to insure that the interview was con-ducted in relatively complete privacy. Usually we secured a private room in each factory. Where interviews had to be conducted in the open at the bench, we took pains to see no one was loitering about or looking on, at least not within earshot. When these conditions could not be satisfied at the plant, we brought the man back to our project headquarters.

These ideal conditions less often prevailed in the inteviews with urban non-industrials. Kiosk operators and taxi drivers often refused to interrupt their work—indeed often they could not do so without irreparable econo-mic loss. Sometimes they had to be interviewed as they went about their business. Since they generally worked in very public places, it was difficult to find a quiet private corner, although a nearby restaurant might serve. In Nigeria it proved impossible to do even screening interviews in the markets, although the largest number of urban non-industrial workers could be found there. Huge crowds were drawn to the spot as soon as we began.

In India, Dr. Singh found less trouble in locating people and conducting the interview in the villages than in the towns. In general, however, conditions were often far from ideal in the villages. Workers were generally released from their duties by management. They lost no time or money, and often appreciated the escape from their machine and the freedom to talk and smoke—sometimes even in an air-conditioned office. Farmers could not so easily spare the time from work, and had to be interviewed after a hard day's effort in the fields. They would not only be tired, but also were often surrounded by barnyard animals, a wife, screaming children, and other relatives who crowd in and try to help provide the answers. Nevertheless, more than 90 per cent of the interviews in all countries were judged by the interviewees to have been conducted either in "absolute privacy" or under conditions in which there may have been onlookers, but they did not interfere. Less than 1 per cent of the interviews were conducted under conditions such that onlookers were "a serious problem", and those mostly in the countryside or with urban non-industrials.

The critical factor in the success of the interview, however, was its intrinsic interest and the way in which it was conducted. The simple natural problems of everyday life with which our questions dealt seemed successfully to engage the attention of almost everyone. Although so much thinking was hard work for them, as not a few pointed out, the interviewees enjoyed the opportunity to have so many votes to cast on such basic questions of life. We eased their task by offering nicely balanced alternatives from which a man might choose, thus freeing him of the necessity of formulating the matter entirely for himself. At the same time we gladly accepted any comments and amendations, which were carefully written down by the interviewer. This impressed the interviewee with the seriousness of the enterprise and the importance of his answers. It also provided us with a large body of qualitative material we could use to interpret the pre-coded answers.

Our interviewers were instructed and trained not to impose any point of view, not to lead the interviewee, nor in any way to seem to judge him either for the content of his answers, the language he used, the ideas he expressed, or the ease or difficulty with which he handled the questions. There were, of course, cases in which the individual, the situation, or the culture, one or all, produced tensions and even conflict. In Nigeria we discovered that using an "X" to mark on the printed questionnaire form the alternative chosen by the interviewees seemed to disturb them. Apparently an "X" meant to them not a neutral check mark, but suggested they were being put down for the "wrong" answer. Seemingly getting one answer after another "wrong" would clearly be potentially disturbing to anyone. We switched to a more neutral kind of check mark vaguely like a "C".

During the early stages of interviewer training in Nigeria one interviewer was assigned a respondent who was confused by the questions, kept changing his mind, and took very long to answer. It was late at night, and getting later, and in a fit of exasperation the interviewer said: "For Christ's sake, answer the question. If you don't, we'll be here until midnight." As Ryan reports the incident: "Not surprisingly the interview blew apart. The respondent rushed into the lounge area, greatly agitated, and declared he would not continue. The interviewer followed, also a bit agitated, speaking in Yoruba to the man." The insult was patched up by Dr. Ryan who drove the man home. More important it formed the basis for new training sessions designed to change the behaviour of the interviewer at fault and to help the others learn a valuable lesson.

In the overwhelming majority of cases the interview turned into a pleasant personal exchange satisfying to both interviewer and interviewee. Despite our fears, fatigue was generally not an issue. The interviewers got much more tired than the interviewees. Professor Gibaja speaks for all the field directors when she says:

Despite previous fears and expectations, experience seems to show that this type of interview can be done without major opposition of the respondents. On the contrary, we got a high degree of cooperation and sincerity from the respondents who, in general, established very good relations with the interviewers, and could overcome with goodwill the difficulties that no doubt many of them encountered in the experience. Making the interview during working hours had its positive side. The worker was free from his work for three or four hours; almost always he was taken into a comfortable place where he could smoke or have coffee; and above all he experienced a new situation. Most of the interviewers were young students with a positive attitude toward the respondent, who were desirous not only to obtain answers, but probably to live out a personal experience in an environment completely different from their own. This attitude of the interviewers tended to decrease the anxiety which being interviewed produced in certain workers, and their personal approach eased the strain and made the interview a pleasant experience.

These personal impressions are strongly supported by some of the statistics we collected. Interviewers overwhelmingly rated the interviewees as "generally" or "very" co-operative, the range going from 85 per cent in India to 98 per cent in Pakistan. There is little reason to believe these estimates inflated. We neither criticized interviewers for having unco-operative subjects, nor praised them having co-operative ones. If the interviewer wanted to protect himself against complaints he would have been much better advised to shift the blame on to the interviewee by saying the latter was "unco-operative". Moreover, these positive images of co-operation by the interviewee were evidently *not* influenced by some "halo effect" which bathed the whole exchange in a glow of indiscriminate goodwill. Interviewers clearly could take a critical view of the interviewee. For example, 65 per cent of the interviewees in Pakistan were rated as "very co-operative", but only 4 per cent were rated as being "flexible" and only 18 per cent as being "very intelligent".

The statements and actions of the interviewees support the judgment of the interviewers. In Nigeria, for example, Dr. Ryan often drove men home after they had stayed late to be interviewed at our headquarters. This was a gesture greatly appreciated, and generally put the interviewee in an expansive mood. Both by word and sign Dr. Ryan indicated he would appreciate a frank assessment of whether the interview had been as they thought it would be, or might wish it to have been. The expressions of satisfaction were markedly regular and warm. In Nigeria only 3 interviews were broken off, out of a total of 723 which were begun. Of the three, two men later agreed to continue, and completed the interview. The record was about the same in all the other countries, except Israel, in which the number broken was above 50. The majority of these were relocated, however, and the interview completed, admittedly in some cases only when the local rabbi interceded to plead our cause.

We had no power over anyone except for that which derived from a personal appeal. We in no way restrained any one. We had nothing to offer as reward other than the interview itself. We began a total of about 5,600 interviews in the six countries. Of these less than 30 broke off the interview *and* failed to continue later. Thus, some 99½ per cent found either us or the interview attractive enough to stay with it for up to four hours. This is, we believe, an exceptional record. We point to it not only out of understandable pride, nor only to persuade others that detailed life-history interviews by the survey method are feasible even in developing countries. The low proportion of disrupted interviews has implications for the interpretation of our results. It insures that whatever difference we find between and within groups cannot be an artifact of selection or screening within the interviewing process itself. Our procedure clearly did not squeeze men of lesser modernity out, nor lock in those of higher modernity among the men initially and objectively selected for inclusion in our sample.

6. RESPONSE BIAS AND THE COMPREHENSION OF OUR QUESTIONNAIRE

It required goodwill to sit through a four-hour interview. We evidently generated enough of that. Yet that goodwill could be our undoing if it motivated men benignly to say just anything which came into their heads in order to able to offer *something* in answer to our questions, whether understood or not. This tendency toward genial agreement with whatever the interviewer may ask is known as response set or response bias. It can produce seriously misleading, indeed even totally spurious results, especially in samples such as ours. The problem arises because individuals of lower education, at least when confronted with an interviewer, almost inevitably of higher status, tend to say they agree to almost anything reasonable they are asked. If the questions in a study all use the agree-disagree format for the answers, a significant segment of the low educated respondents will end up being scored for a disproportionately large number of "agree" answers.

In certain cases this tendency to agree, or "acquiescence set" as it is technically called will not given a simply *false* picture, but rather will *obscure* the real attitudes of the men interviewed. This will come about if the content of the questions regularly shifts from one position to another on some continuum, such as traditional-modern. In that case always agreeing produces what in scholarly language is called a randomizing effect or, in the vernacular, a hash. Under those circumstances one does not know what was really going on, but one is at least not led to make false assertions. However, in the unhappy case where the content of all the questions has the same thrust or emphasis, then the effect of the "acquiescence set" may be to make men *seem* to hold a position which in fact they do not, or seeming to hold it much more strongly than they actually do.

The combination of the resarcher's lack of awareness of what he is doing, plus the response bias of some of his subjects, can thus produce highly spurious results. This has been dramatically illustrated in the study of authoritarianism, using the well known "F" scale. The scale presents statements such as: "Obedience and respect for authority are the most important virtues a child should learn", and "Homosexuals are hardly better than criminals, and ought to be severely punished". The respondent is asked to select his answer on a fixed range for all questions, from "strongly disagree" to "strongly agree". All the statements in the scale are arranged so that agreeing leads to being scored as more authoritarian. If the questions were all turned around somehow, a person who manifested the agreeing tendency could almost as easily be made out to be anti-authoritarian.

Henry Landsberger has given a dramatic demonstration of this outcome using the "F" scale with a Chilean sample of housemaids attending an adult education class at their trade union centre. They took the "F" scale in the usual way, and then shortly after were given the scale again with the questions now "reversed" in emphasis. In both instances the maids were required to agree or disagree with the statements. Since some maids were extremely prone to acquiescence, and all showed this response propensity to some degree, the second time around they often agreed with statements which were the opposite of those they had agreed to earlier. For example, in the first form they agree with the statement "One cannot trust people". Half an hour later they were agreeing with the opposite: "One can trust people". Consequently, some of the same individuals were classified as "authoritarian" on the basis of the first scoring and as "democratic" on the second. The results were statistically significant.[19]

The problem is compounded by the fact that people of higher education do not manifest response set to anything like the same degree as do less educated groups, and university trained people manifest it not at all.[20] The combination of these elements may produce spurious confirmation of a hypothesis. For example, if your hypothesis were that authoritarianism decreases with rising education, and used the "F" scale as above, proof of your hypothesis could be assured regardless of the actual situation. Let us assume, for example, that in fact—without the effect of the "acquiscence set"—the average score of high and low-educated people on authoritarianism were equal. However, if the test used was susceptible to the influence of response bias, then the low-educated, merely by virtue of their tendency to agree, would, on the average, get high scores on authoritarianism. The well-educated without a marked response set, would presumably get only average scores. The resultant difference between the two groups, even if statistically significant, would be largely an artifact of the method of measuring "authoritarianism".

We believe that in the otherwise outstanding study of Joseph Kahl on modernization in Brazil and Mexico, a significant part of the correlation he found between socio-economic status and attitudinal modernity in individuals results from "acquiescence set".[21] Virtually all of his questions used the agree-disagree format. The statements in his questionnaire were almost all phrased to express a traditional viewpoint. If a respondent agreed with the statements he was scored as more traditional. Because of the well-

[19] The correlation between their first and second was −.39, significant at the −.05 level. A week later the correlation was −.39 and a month later −.56. See Henry Landsberger and Antonio Saavedra, "Response Set in Developing Countries".

[20] Thus, Landsberger and Saavedra (op cit.) put a group of university students in Chile through the same procedure as the maids already described. Despite the reversal of the items, the university people scored the same either way. The correlations of their scores in two trials were .70 and .79, both significant at the .01 level, and positive, whereas the correlation for the maids was negative.

[21] Joseph A. Kahl, The Measurement of Modernism.

estabished response set toward agreement among the less-educated, we must assume that those of Kahl's groups lower in the socio-economic strata therefore received scores inflated in the direction of greater traditionality. This advantage did not afflict the better-educated. The outcome, therefore, would be to exaggerate, perhaps greatly exaggerate, the relative modernity of the well-educated in comparison with the less-well-educated taking the same test.

If one does make this mistake there are methods for later making a technical correction which adjusts the individual score to make allowance for each person's property to agree or disagree, as the case may be.[22] While acknowledging that response bias was "a disturbing element" in his study, Professor Kahl did not attempt such an adjustment. There remained therefore, some ambiguity as to how far the differences he found were real, and how far merely an artifact of method of asking questions with his particular sample groups.[23]

There is another type of response set almost as powerful as the agreeing tendency, known as the social desirability set. This tendency is also believed to be more common among the less-educated but is assumed as well to represent a certain personal psycho-social disposition. Persons with this set tend to select that answer to a question which they believe will make the best impression on others, regardless of what they actually believe.

To avoid difficulties with response set we adopted a firm rule at the outset not to use the agree-disagree format, or indeed, any other invariant pattern of responses. Some few of our questions requested an answer in terms of agree-disagree, or "yes-no". Some others presented a small scale, from very important to not-important, or the like. In content, however, these were highly varied, and we took pains to insure that the "direction" of the modern and traditional answer was not always the same. Equally important, we cast the great majority of our questions in such form that the individual was presented a set of complete alternatives or positions on some issue. These alternatives were couched in such terms as to make them all have the quality of the socially acceptable or desirable. For example, in inquiring into job choices, we asked which of these two jobs would you prefer your son to take: A machinist's job at 400 per month *or* a white collar desk job at 300 per month? And in testing the sense of efficacy we put

---

[22] See David H. Smith, "Correcting for Social Desirability Response Sets in Opinion-Attitude Survey Research".

[23] Professor Kahl (*op. cit.*, p. 29) concluded that the effects of "acquiescence set", while substantial, were not large enough to render his results "spurious". Our examination of his data leads us strongly to support his conclusion. But we do believe the correlations he reports between education and modernism are inflated by response bias, and that this gives an inaccurate impression of the actual sensitivity of his scale of modernism.

the balanced alternatives as follows: "Some say that accidents are due mainly to bad luck. Others say accidents can be prevented by care. What do you say?"

In addition to varying our question style and format, and offering balanced alternatives, we sought to offset the effects of response set by the organization of our questionnaire. If at one time and place you ask a whole string of questions about the same theme, the chances are an intelligent interviewee will perceive your purpose, and may then slant his answers so that he will appear in what he assumes is "the best light" from the interviewer's point of view. This can be especially germane if you are trying to find out whether men are responsible or careless, superstitious or scientific, kind or cruel, and, of course, modern or traditional.

We felt that the form and content of our questions did a good job of concealing our purpose and kept hints as to the "right" answer to a minimum. Nevertheless, we also arranged our questionnaire so that it did not call too much attention to the analytic variables which were our chief scientific concern. The interview was, therefore, not organized in sections dealing with our main themes such as efficacy, dignity, time, or openness to new experience. Instead, it was arranged, and described to the interviewee, under broad topical headings such as: family life, raising children, work experience, community life, friendship and so on. The questions relating to our analytic themes were then scattered, as appropriate, throughout these more topically organized sections of the interview. It would have taken a very perceptive and alert person indeed to discern that we were really most interested in analytic variables like dignity. It would have been even harder to identify which particular question was meant to tap one or another dimension, and a man deserved the prize if he could go still further and guess which was the "right" alternative.

By these means we believe we reduced to an absolute minimum the danger that any pattern which might emerge from our data could be the result of response set. Indeed, we may have carried our efforts too far. To some degree everyone thinks in sets and categories. It helps a man to clarify his position on an issue if at one time, he must deal with a variety of questions all on the same topic. By varying the pattern of our questions as much as we did, and by scattering them so throughout the interview, we probably inadvertently lowered the correlation between questions which are related to each other, and lowered the resultant reliability of our attitude scales. This was especially likely to happen in our research because people of low education have a difficult time expressing their ideas as consistently as they may feel or believe them, unless they are helped out by a good deal of structure brought into the discussion from outside.

Given the level of education of our samples and the limited worldly sophistication of the milieus in which they grew up and now lived, it might be argued that response set should have less concerned us than taking care to insure that our respondents really understood us, and we them. The efforts we made to render our concepts in simple terms, to control distortion in the translation, and to couch our questions in the common language, all reflected this concern to evoke personally meaningful responses. How well we succeeded, in the end, effectively to communicate with our inteviewees, and they with us, is a matter inherently difficult to say because what is a reasonable standard is ambiguous. There are, however, a number of measures we adopted whose evidence is relevant for judging how well respondents understood both what we asked them and what they themselves were saying in reply.

At the end of the interview, the interviewer rated each subject's comprehension and understanding of the questionnaire. The proportions whose understanding was rated as "very poor", i.e. in the lowest category, ranged from less than 1 per cent in Nigeria to a maximum of only 9 per cent in Argentina and in India.

A check on the interviewers' impressions may be derived from the distribution of our "R" or repetition scores. To the left of each question there were 3 blanks, one to be checked by the interviewer every time it proved necessary to repeat a question for the interviewee. After three repetitions the interviewer was supposed to pass on to the next question and the person was scored DK/NA (doesn't know; no answer). There was, as one might expect, enormous individual variation in the number of times questions had to be repeated.[24]

One poor soul in Chile and another in Argentina racked up 577 repetitions, an average of more than one per question.[25] The media number of repetitions per interview was, however, quite modest, ranging from 6 in Argentina to 30 in Pakistan. Taking into account the base number of questions to which the "R" score was applied in different countries, that works out in the Pakistani case as one repetition for every 9 questions, and in Argentinian one for every 73. To our knowledge, this technique of scoring repetitions was never before tried; therefore we have no comparative basis for judging performance. Considering the typically low education of our respondents, however, we interpret the results as indicating our interviewees understood us quite well. Moreover, in the typical study these events would have been classified as "Doesn't Know" or "No Answer", and that would have been the end of it. A little patience on our inter-

[24] We are not unaware that this seeming individual variation could be significantly contributed to by variation in the conscientiousness the interviewer displayed in noting whether questions had to be repeated.

[25] There were some 440 items to which the "R" score applied in Chile and Argentina, yielding an average, for these men, of 1.3 repetitions per question. In Pakistan the "R" score was applied to only 258 questions.

viewer's part often indicated that these people really did have something to say.

The repetition score data is supported by the frequency of DK/NA (Don't Know—No Answer) responses. We have the information for three countries, and only as applying to the approximately 180 attitude questions in the core questtionnaire. The average number of DK/NA responses per subject, available for three countries only, was: Chile 0.4; Israel 4.2; Nigeria 1.6. The number of DK/NA responses, of course, reflects not only the understanding of the questionnaire by the respondent, but the diligence of the interviewer in pursuing an answer. Nevertheless, the fact that failure to answer was limited to about one question per 100 for the average respondent is decidedly encouraging. Indeed, it is a standard of performance rarely attained in regular national surveys in even the most highly developed countries.[26]

All efforts to repeat questions and keep down the number of DK/NA responses may be challenged by saying that our technique probably encouraged people to say anything which came into their heads, whether they understood the question or not. We have powerful evidence that this was not the case. In Pakistan we undertook a special test of the understanding of our questionnaire. The technique, which we call the "random probe", involved following the interviewee's choice of one of our fixed alternatives with some further query such as: "And why do you think (or say) that?"[27] The answers were scored on a scale from 1, for complete understanding, to 5 indicating serious misunderstanding. The low score was given even when the respondent's explanation of his reply was quite clear in itself, but was not in accord with the choice he had made among the fixed alternative answers to the question. The scoring, in short, was very stringent indeed.

The scoring system may be illustrated by considering two questions on religion, one on which was poorly understood, the other well. The first of these, rather complex, asked:

Do you think that whether a man works diligently every day is:
1. an absolutely essential part of religion,
2. an important but not essential part of religion, or
3. of little importance to religion.

[26] In all fairness we must acknowledge this is not necessarily a serious defect in most public opinion polls. Their purpose is mainly to estimate the distribution of opinion, and on most issues having 5 or even 10 per cent of the population DK/NA will not much affect the outcome. In our study, however, the type of intensive analysis we planned to undertake made it important not to lose cases in this way.

[27] The random probe technique was developed by Dr. Schuman and is more fully described in: Howard Schuman, "The Random Probe: A Technique for Evaluating the Validity of Closed Questions".

A typical response to the "random probe" from a man who had chosen the first alternative was: "My family depends on me. If there is no food and empty stomachs (due to laziness), then I cannot give attention to prayer." Respondents who chose alternative three gave even more seemingly irrelevant explanations, for example: "It is not good to work hard every day. It will ruin the health." Both these men were scored as not having understood the question well.

Only a minority of probed respondents (about two-fifths) understood the question in the intended frame of reference. An example of a reply scored 1 for complete understanding was: "Allah has written in the Koran that men should work hard each day." Altogether this question proved to be one of those creating the most confusion. Its average score on the scale was 2.3, less than a B average.

Quite the opposite experience is provided by the following yes-or-no question, intended to determine whether ethical and religious actions are conceived as separable: "Do you think a man can be truly good who has no religion at all?" When this question was first presented to local translators and interviewers, their reaction was unanimously negative. They felt no ordinary man would understand the point of the question. Whatever might be the case among Westerners or among the university-educated, they said, the average Pakistan Muslim would certainly see a non-religious man as "by definition" devoid of goodness. All agreed that the question could not lead to meaningful responses and should not be included.

It was included, however, and in fact produced about one-third "yes" and two-thirds "no" choices. But was the question perhaps misinterpreted in some way? The random probes indicate that understanding was very good indeed. A typical probe explanation for a "yes" response was: "He may not believe any religion, yet he can render good offices to the people of the land." Another man who chose the "yes" alternative said in response to the probe: "He may be good and his heart may be very pure, and he can help people anyway." The probe answer to the "no" responses were also to the point: "The man who has no faith has no idea of good and bad, so he cannot be good." "The person who has no religion, what good thing may be in him? He is wretched." Of the 52 men probed on this question, only one was coded as confused, and the question earned a mean "understanding score" of 1.1.

The random probe was applied to only 10 questions during the course of any one interview. It might, therefore, be unreliable as a way of rating the understanding of any one person. But it was used in all the thousand interviews we conducted in Pakistan. Each of the approximately 200 questions in the Pakistani questionnaire was, by this procedure, "probed" 50 times. There were altogether, therefore, 10,000 different "probes", providing a much more stable basis for judgment. The median score for the entire set of questions was 1.4, between an A and a B. Of the 200 questions, 87 per cent were rated as having been understood well or very well. This was not only cheering news about our success in writing intelligible questions; it also indicated unmistakably that in all but a few cases our interviewees understood not only what *we were asking,* but understood and could explain and justify *what they were answering.*

Checking this impression on an individual basis, we found almost 90 per cent of the individuals were scored as having understood our questions at the B level or better. Only 22 out of a 1,000 men had a mean score of 3 or worse. These were the C and D men, who failed substantially to understand our questions. When we consider that almost 40 per cent of the Pakistan sample had *never* been to school and only 12 per cent had completed six or more years, the level of understanding of our questionnaire which they manifested was very reassuring not only with regard to Pakistan, but also for the other countries in which the average level of education of our respondents was much higher.

7. COMMUNICATION AND DRIFT

All the problems of conducting the fieldwork were influenced not only by the local conditions in each country but by the requirements inherent in a comparative study. No matter how firm their common understanding and joint commitment to a group goal, men who are not in regular face-to-face contact begin to drift apart. The chances that we would see and do things differently were increased by the inevitabe pressures created by the distinctive environments in which we found ourselves. Dr. Schuman was convinced the proportion of men in Pakistan with no schooling at all rendered many of our questions too difficult for use there. Was he free to change the questions with four alternative answers by reducing the number of choices to two? Our standard sampling procedure defined a "new worker" as one with less than three months of experience. Dr. Ryan could not locate enough men in Nigeria with less than three months of industrial experience —would it spoil the design to accept men with up to nine months of experience as "new" workers? Plant managers in Chile asked Dr Garcia not to inquire into certain aspects of their workers' political affiliation. Would it destroy the usefulness of the set of political questions if in Chile we omitted questions on the party preference? People in Argentina, for some inexplicable reason, laughed when we suggested a little pill given by a doctor might prevent conception. Could the situation be changed to suggest "a minor and painless operation"? So it went, through dozens and even hundreds of queries regarding public relations, staff, questionnaire, and sample.

If each field director dealt with every issue according to his own lights, the drift away from a common design could go so far that the individual country studies would no longer serve their scientific purpose of being each a more or less exact replication of the other. Comparisons of the results among the countries within the set would be rendered difficult or impossible. On the other hand, to insist on rigid adherence to a set of fixed criteria was to face the field director with the prospect of squandering his resources in, what would seem to him, obviously futile searches for scarce informants. Or, it might oblige him to collect clearly misleading or inappropriate informaiton.

What was needed was constant and full discussion and review of issues and mutual interaction on a more or less daily basis. But that was impossible with the distances separating us. If we had it to do over again we would seriously consider equipping each field director with a short-wave radio or of investing in admittedly expensive regular long-distance telephone conferences. The measures we did adopt were more modest. We relied primarily on the depth of each field director's understanding of our general purpose and his commitment to our ultimate joint effort in analysis. This understanding provided each field director with a standard which, we hoped, would permit him to recognize those decisions which clearly fell in the range of the optional, and those which were more fundamental and required consultation and joint agreement. The three founding members developed their shared perspective during many months of joint effort in Cambridge. Each tried in shorter intervals of collaborative work to communicate this common "culture" of the project to the three field directors who joined us later.

Our entire approach was given a thorough review and complete overhaul during the month-long meeting in Dacca in August 1963. This came after the three field directors had each had between three and six months of experience pre-testing questions, locating and training staff, and assessing the feasibility of our research design. Some of the sessions were held in Calcutta, where we could be joined by Dr. Singh, thus adding the perspective of a fourth country. In addition, as the project director I took to the road, and spent at least one month in each of the field stations other than my own Chilean base. This gave me a sense of the special conditions of the several different field teams, thus facilitating more sound decisions concerning the adaptation of our design in each country. These trips also permitted me to bring to the others news of the problems encountered elsewhere and of the adjustments made by the several field directors. These face-to-face conferences were supplemented by a constant flow of letters, so that I spent most of my time in Chile glued to my typewriter answering the queries of the field directors, and trying to keep the rest informed as to what the others were doing.

Under even ordinary circumstances, there would be a substantial probability of serious communication problems in such a complex enterprise. Under the conditions prevailing in some of the developing countries the prospect loomed large indeed. Poverty in Pakistan is so great that an airmail stamp on a heavy registered letter could easily exceed a week's wages for the messenger who carried it or the postal clerk who handled it. The temptation to lift and sell the stamp was often more than some men could bear. In the face of the political tensions between India and Pakistan, the local authorities there naturally became alarmed when telegrams went between Ranchi, Dacca, and Cambridge bearing such mysterious cryptic messages as: "Suggest you eliminate DI-2 and EF-7. Stop. Replace ST-5 with GO-4. Stop. Confirm action taken." These references to the code numbers of our questions conjured up the vision of secret agents being done away with, and led to an inquiry from the local police authorities in Ranchi. It was politely suggested to Dr. Singh that it might save future embarrassment if I stopped sending these seemingly compromising cables. A strike of postal workers in Agentina cut off all communication with Professor Gibaja for several weeks, and Dr. Ryan was for a number of weeks totally unaware of a number of important changes in our plan adopted everywhere else because of a misunderstanding about what his postal box number was when he transferred his office from Ibadan to Lagos.

Such mechanical failures in the communication system, coupled with the inevitable misunderstandings and inadequacies of human communication itself, meant local decisions were taken without adequate consultation, or on the basis of mistaken impressions and wrong information. Some of the incidents were very painful, and we paid dearly for them. For example, the sheet describing the ratings to be made by the interviewer of each interviewee somehow got detached from the end of the master questionnaire, and so was never used in either Chile or Israel. Since he was in contact mainly with Schuman in Pakistan, Dr. Singh assumed the version of the questionnaire used there was a Bengali translation of the true "master". In fact the Bengali version was much reduced from that used in Chile, Argentina and Israel. Dr. Singh later declared that had he known of the fuller version he would have included many of the questions contained in it even though they were not used in Pakistan.

Quite apart from such outright misunderstanding, the field directors were simply forced to make many decisions without any consultation, merely because of the pressure of local circumstances, limited resources, and dwindling time. Many of these decisions were creative and contributed greatly to fulfilling the project's objectives. Dr. Schuman's use of the random probe may have slightly disrupted the flow of the interview, and made it a somewhat different experience in Pakistan as compared with the other countries, but the price was surely small compared to the substantial scientific yield. By contrast, the decision to reduce most of the fixed alternatives from four to two in Pakistan was apparently unnecessary. Later anaysis showed that questions with three or four alternatives were as well understood as those requiring a choice among only two. Yet this change made it much more difficult to compare the distribution of responses in Pakistan with that in other countries.

All this inevitably and inexorably contributed to the drift which progressively pulled each national project away from the standard of strict comparability with the others, and thus away from the fulfilment of its distinctive mission in the overall design. There are, therefore, some points in the analysis at which we lose one or two countries from our six-country set. On the whole, however, we feel this drift was kept to a quite reasonable minimum. The study design, the array of the questions and their form, were sufficiently close in all the countries to permit using each national study as a more or less exact replication of the others, granting some modest compromise and many minor adjustments.

Bibliography

Almond, Gabriel A. and Sidney Verba, *The Civic Culture: Political Attitudes and Democracy in Five Nations*, Princeton New Jersey: Princeton University Press, 1963.

Clinard, Marshall B. and Joseph W. Elder, "Sociology in India: A Study in the Sociology of Knowledge", *American Sociological Review* (30:4) 1965, pp. 581-587.

Husain, A. F. A., *Human and Social Impact of Technological Change in Pakistan*, a report on a survey conducted by the University of Dacca and published with the assistance of UNESCO, Dacca: Oxford University Press, 1956.

――――― and A. Farouk, *Social Integration of Industrial Workers in Khulna*, Dacca: Bureau of Economic Reseach, University of Dacca, 1963.

Imtiaz Ahmed, "Note on Sociology of India", *The American Sociologist* (1:5) 1966, pp. 244-247.

Inkles, Alex, "Industrial Man: The Relation of Status to Experience, Perception, and Value", *American Journal of Sociology* (66:1) 1960, 1-31.

――――― "The Modernization of Man", in M. Weiner, ed., *Modernization*, New York: Basic Books, 1966.

――――― "A Model of the Modern Man", in Wm. A. Faunce and H. Garfinkel, eds., *Cross Cultural Research in Developing Areas*, East Lansing, Michigan and New York: Social Science Research Bureau and Free Press.

Kahl, Joseph A., *The Measurement of Modernism*, Austin, Texas and London: University of Texas Press, 1968.

Landsberger, Henry and Antonio Saavedra, "Response Set in Developing Countries", *Public Opinion Quarterly* (31:2) 1967, pp. 214-229.

Lerner, Daniel, *The Passing of Traditional Society*, Glencoe, Ill: The Free Press of Glencoe, 1958.

Nash, Manning, *Machine Age Maya*, Glencoe, Illinios: The Free Press, 1968.

Russet, Bruce M., *et al.*, *World Handbook of Political and Social Indicators*, New Haven: Yale University Press, 1964.

Schuman, Howard, "The Random Probe: A Technique for Evaluating the Validity of Closed Questions", *American Sociological Review* (31:2) 1966, pp. 218-223.

Singh, Amar K., *Indian Students in Britian*, Bombay: Asia Publishing House, 1963.

Smith, David H., "Correcting for Social Desirability Response Sets in Opinion-Attitude Survey Research", *Public Opinion Quarterly* (31:1) 1967, pp. 87-94.

—— and Alex Inkles, "The OM Scale: A Comparative Socio-Psychological Measure of Individual Modernity", *Sociometry* (29:4) 1966, pp. 353-377.

United Nations Statistical Yearbook, 1964, 16th Issue, New York: United Nations, 1965.

3

FEDERALISM AND THE INDIAN ADMINISTRATIVE SERVICE

D A V I D   C.   P O T T E R

THIS ESSAY explores relationships between the Indian Administrative Service, or IAS, and India's federalism. It divides into three parts: first, I say something briefly about the nature of India's federalism; next, I discuss some structural and functional features of the IAS in that federalism; and finally, I suggest the hypothesis that the IAS straddles and supports India's federalism without violating it. The hypothesis, if accepted, may be of more than passing interest for two reasons. First, it may force social scientists to amend William H. Riker's important theory of federalism.[1] He maintains that the federal bargain is controlled by one institutional condition—the party system. The hypothesis stated in this essay suggests that India's federalism is controlled also by an administrative institution—the IAS. Secondly, a series of hypotheses like this one, if confirmed, may enable social scientists eventually to locate critical controls which allow the existing governmental structure in India to persist over time. Social scientists of behavioural persuasion may then be able to predict more accurately than they do now the future direction of Indian politics within that structure. Likewise, those social scientists who believe that sustained development is not possible within the existing political structure will be able to

[1] William H. Riker, *Federalism* (Boston, 1964).

identify those institutions which maintain the status quo and thus act as obstacles to the development process.

FEDERALISM

The Indian constitution is federal, according to Riker's working definition, if three conditions are satisfied: "(1) two levels of government rule the same land and people; (2) each level has at least one area of action in which it is autonomous; and (3) there is some guarantee (even though merely a statement in the constitution) of the autonomy of each government in its own sphere." [2] Article 245 of the Constitution of India satisfies condition (1). Article 246(3), read with the State List in the Seventh Schedule, satisfies ordinarily conditions (2) and (3), although there the position is rather complex, e.g., the provisions of Article 250 regarding Proclamations of Emergency, and the provisions of Article 249 where the Rajya Sabha by resolution of two-thirds of the membership can allow the national Parliament to make laws for one year regarding matters on the State List.

The actual working of India's federalism corresponds generally with the formal constitutional guarantees. Two points can be made here. One concerns the results of a study of union-state administrative relations with special reference to Rajasthan. The major finding of the study is that co-operative federalism best characterizes union-state relations, in which "the personality of the states and their operative freedom may at times be compromised but it is certainly not crushed and denied altogether".[3] The study cities, for example, the fact that the central government "has no device to ensure that its general directives [in the Five-Year Plans] will be complied with".[4] The study instances the Third Plan directive that beneficiaries of irrigation projects be required to dig field-channels which has remained inoperative in Rajasthan because "the necessary amendment in the [Rajasthan] Panchayat Samitis and Zila Parishads Act has not yet been made".[5] This experience, which is possible only in federalism, leads us to the second point regarding the working of India's federalism. This concerns the Congress Party. In the field-channels case, cited above, the Congress government in New Delhi made a law affecting diggers of field-channels in the states but the Rajasthan Congress government rendered the law inoperative by failing to make the necessary state law. The Rajasthan

[2] Ibid., p. 11.

[3] Iqbal Narain and P. C. Mathur, "Union-State Relations in India: A Case Study in Rajasthan", Journal of Commonwealth Political Studies, Vol. II, No. 2 (May, 1964), p. 138. Another study which reaches a similar conclusion is Marcus Franda, West Bengal and the Federalizing Process in India (Princeton University Press, 1968).

[4] Ibid., p. 129.

[5] Ibid., pp. 131-32.

Congress thereby demonstrates its autonomy by failing in this case to act in concert with the national Congress. The Congress Party has been, of course, a vital controlling mechanism holding the Indian union together. Nevertheless, it must be stressed that a federal relationship does exist between state Congress governments and the national Congress government. A federal relationship also exists between the national government and those state governments not controlled by the Congress Party.

Having established that India's federalism exists, we now turn to our central concern, the IAS in that federalism.

THE IAS

The IAS is the successor to the Indian Civil Service (ICS), that well-known bureaucratic institution which effectively served in a crucial way to maintain British colonial rule in India for more than a century. The structural features of the IAS are basically the same as those of its predecessor.

Three structural features of the IAS are relevant to the analysis in this essay. Baldly stated they are that the IAS is (1) select, (2) all-India, and (3) elite.

First, the IAS is select. It came into existence in 1947 as successor to the ICS, with Indian ICS officers comprising its first and most senior recruits. Rapid recruitment to the IAS was essential as the bulk of the British ICS officers retired immediately after independence and virtually all Muslim ICS officers moved to Pakistan. Although the Union Public Service Commision has held regularly since 1948 annual competitive examinations for recruitment to the IAS, only fifty-six per cent of the IAS at the present time have been recruited in this way, the remaining forty-four per cent consisting of emergency recruits, officers promoted to the IAS from state services, and those remaining ICS officers (only two of whom are British) who now form part of the IAS.[6] Despite its rapid growth by emergency recruitment, examination and promotion, the IAS today numbers about 2,500 men and women and therefore comprises ony .0002 per cent of the more than nine million government employees in India. It is, therefore, very select indeed.

The IAS is an all-India service, its members serving in bureaucratic posts in national, state and local governments. The IAS as a whole is made up of sixteen state cadres, plus one more for the Union Territories. There is no central government cadre of the IAS. When each new recruit is confirmed in the Service, he is allocated permanently by the central government to a particular state cadre. What makes the IAS all-India is that, during the course of an officer's career, he may, and many of his colleagues certainly

---

[6] Ministry of Home Affairs, *The Civil List of the Indian Administrative Service* (as of 1st January 1968) (New Delhi, 1968). The figures are compiled by the author from this source.

will, work from time to time for the central government; and, if so, then
he is placed on deputation to it for a period of not more than five years
and, except in very unusual circumstances, he reverts at the end of his
deputation period to the state of his cadre. Approximately seventy per cent
of the members of the IAS at any time are working for a state government,
not the central government.[7] While serving under a state government, an
IAS officer is formally under its administrative control. However, and this
is another aspect of the all-India arrangement, he is governed by service
rules made by the central government and these cannot be altered or inter
preted to his disadvantage except by, or with the approval of, that government. And he can appeal to the central government where he considers
that his service rights have been infringed by an order of the state
government.

The IAS is also an elite service in the sense that most of the top generalist posts in central, state and local governments throughout the country
are in practice reserved for, and are held by, its members. For example,
in 1964, IAS officers held the post of secretary (top bureaucratic post in a
ministry) in nineteen of the twenty three ministries in the central government as well as the post of Secretary to the President and to the Prime
Minister.[8] Eighty-six per cent of the secretaries of the major departments
in each state government and eighty per cent of the district collectors
throughout India were also IAS officers.[9] Furthermore, if special conditions
did not obtain in two or three states, the percentages reflecting this IAS
dominance of key posts in state and local governments would have been
even higher. IAS officers also held important policy-making positions in
many public enterprises in the country.

The functional characteristics of the IAS are rather more difficult to be
precise about. Nevertheless, for the purpose of the analysis in this essay,
I think at least two important orientations which determine IAS behaviour
today can be identified. These are (1) a sense of the primacy of law and
order, and (2) a predisposition to act in accord with national policy, when
national policy and regional policy are in conflict.

The "law-and-order orientation" applies particularly to the IAS district
collector although it spills over into IAS behaviour in state secretariats
and in the Ministry of Home Affairs in New Delhi. The IAS officer today
takes with him to his district collector's post a rather definite set of priori-

[7] *Indian Administrative Service (Fixation of Cadre Strength) Regulations*, 1955, (as
amended), in Government of India, Ministry of Home Affairs, *Handbook of Rules and
Regulations for the All India Services*, 2nd ed., Vol. 2 (1960), pp. 1-17.

[8] David C. Potter, "Bureaucratic Change in India", Chapter 4 in Ralph Braibanti
and Associates, *Asian Bureaucratic Systems Emergent from the British Imperial Tradition*
(Duke University Press, 1966), Table 1.

[9] *Ibid.*, Tables 2 and 4.

ties as guide to conduct inherited from his ICS predecessor. The behaviour of an experienced IAS district collector in deciding between the alternatives of (1) moving quickly to pacify an imminent riot in his district town, or (2) keeping an appointment with his Chief Minister who has just arrived at the railway station, or (3) attending a scheduled meeting with important district politicians, or (4) signing papers, essential to the success of the district development programme, which must be sent with the jeep leaving now for the state capital, is predictable; he will move to the scene of the imminent riot and attempt to pacify it, or, if need be, to quell it. The maintenance of order in a district enjoyed absolute priority attention during ICS days; it is so today. The training of direct recruits to the IAS at the National Academy of Administration and the in-service training of all young recruits in the states, as well as the influence of more seasoned officers [including those remaining ICS officers in the IAS] under whom the young recruits work, stresses this priority although at the same time broadening the orientation to include the importance of development work as well.[10]

The national orientation as distinct from a particular regional orientation results from various structural features of the IAS. Fairly frequent rotation between district and state capital, with occasional assignments to important posts in New Delhi and then back again to the states, develops in an IAS officer a clear sense of the political unity in India—a sense of unity not shared by most Indians whose orientation is parochial or regional. Members of the IAS are recruited from every state in India and at least half of most states' IAS cadres consist of officers who were recruited from other states. Furthermore, the select and elite features draw to the IAS many of India's brightest college graduates and intellectuals, most of whom have a fairly clear sense of India as a distinct political entity. These and other factors condition the way an IAS officer behaves. This orientation results, for example, in IAS officers attempting to temper excessive particularistic demands of local politicians by relating such demands to broader national issues.

FEDERALISM AND THE IAS

What is the relationship of these structural and functional features of the IAS to India's federalism? I suggest that the IAS straddles and supports that federalism without violating it.

First, the IAS straddles it structurally with its all-India and elite features. There is a bias towards centralization in its occupancy, as a single organi-

---

[10] S. S. Khera, *District Administration in India* (London, 1964), underlines the general point in this paragraph. Khera, ICS, was for several years Secretary to the Cabinet of the Government of India.

zation, of key generalist posts in central, state and local governments. There is also a bias towards decentralization and some assurance of state autonomy in that it is composed of sixteen state cadres, not a single central cadre, and in the fact that formally an IAS officer in a state government acts on behalf of the state government, not the central government. The word "straddle" seems a helpful shorthand or describing this ingenious structural arangement.

The IAS supports India's federalism functionally by making a positive contribution to the continued existence of the Indian Union. The proposition "support the Indian Union" is stated in the broadest possible way, following David Easton, to include under "support" both overt support, or acting on behalf of, and covert support, or an orientation or predisposition to act on behalf of; and to include under "Indian Union" (1) the central government authorities, (2) the regime, or the basic procedures and norms by which political activity is conducted, and (3) the political community, or those persons who accept at least a minimal political division of labour.[11] I have not explored in any depth these six relationships although I suspect that such an analysis would be a profitable exercise in terms of any predictions about the continued existence of the Indian political system. By the way of suggestion, however, one can speculate that the law-and-order orientation of IAS officers in the districts supports covertly the central government authorities in that such officers are especially predisposed to maintain peace in India, thereby helping to sustain the present authorities in power. One can speculate that IAS officers in the district, state and central governments support overtly the regime on the asumption that most IAS officers share in general Congress Party ideology. One can speculate that the national as distinct from regional orientation of IAS officers in the districts supports overtly the political community by articulating constantly national ideology and regime norms in their exposed position before the people of India. And so forth.

It seems clear that the more one explores the notion of IAS support of the Indian union, the more clearly the IAS emerges as an effective centralizing and controlling force in the country as a whole. However, we are forced in this analysis to raise the question: Is the IAS so powerful a centralizing and controlling force that India's federalism is violated? We turn now to the contention that the IAS does not violate India's federalism.

Assuming the federal relationship between state and central governments, a point made at the outset of this essay, it is possible to argue that the IAS does not violate India's federalism if the following statement can be verified: IAS officers in the states are controlled by state governments and

---

[11] This formulation follows David Easton, *A System Analysis of Political Life* (New York, 1965), esp. Part III,

IAS officers on deputation to the Government of India are controlled by the national government. The formal position, unconvincing by itself, is that such a pattern exists. One could also cite instances where IAS officers in the states and at the centre have stated that they are responsible to their minister; but although such statements are much more convincing and important, they lack objectivity. A more objective approach is to examine the influence of Congress Party ministers on an individual IAS officer's postings and salary, matters of utmost importance to him. I have ploughed through the IAS Civil Lists for the year 1956-1968, which give information on each of the members of the IAS, and have come up with some rather startling, although still only suggestive, information. The most striking point which emerges from an analysis of the IAS Lists is the dominance in central government posts of officers in north-India cadres. The simplest way to handle these complex data is to compare the number of IAS officers in central government posts from major north Indian cadres to the number of IAS officers in such posts from major cadres outside north-India. Table 1 does this for the year 1968.

TABLE 1

PROPORTION OF IAS OFFICERS IN CENTRAL GOVERNMENT POSTS, 1968

State Cadre	Total IAS Strength	No. of IAS officers on deputation to Central Government or elsewhere	% of column (3) to column (2)
(1)	(2)	(3)	(4)
Bihar/Uttar Pradesh	478	171	36%
Andhra Pradesh/Madras/ Gujarat/Maharashtra/ West Bengal	872	205	23%

SOURCE: Compiled by the author from Government of India, Ministry of Home Affairs, *The Civil List of the Indian Administrative Service* (as on 1 January, 1968).

The States of Bihar and Uttar Pradesh are the two major north-India states. The states of Andhra Pradesh, Madras, Gujarat, Maharashtra, and West Bengal are the major states which are located outside north India. The data in Table 1 show quite simply that in 1968 roughly 36 per cent of the IAS officers from Bihar and Uttar Pradesh were holding central government posts or other deputation posts outside their state cadre, while roughly 23 per cent of the IAS officers in the other states were holding such posts. The officially authorized proportion of officers who should be holding such posts in all cases is roughly 21 per cent.[12] An identical analysisis of each of the IAS civil lists for the past ten years reveals similar north India dominance.[13]

This north-India dominance is shown more precisely by examining the state cadre identification of ICS officers (the most senior IAS officers) who hold central government posts paying 4,000 rupees per month (the highest bureaucratic salaries in India). Table 2 summarizes the position.

TABLE 2

ICS OFFICERS IN CENTRAL GOVERNMENT POSTS
PAYING RS. 4,000 PER MONTH, 1968

Year of entry into ICS	Bihar/Uttar Pradesh		Andhra Pradesh/Madras/Gujarat/ Maharashtra/West Bengal	
	Total officers	No. paid Rs. 4000	Total officers	No. paid Rs. 4000
(1)	(2)	(3)	(4)	(5)
1931	1	1	0	0
1933	3	2	2	2
1934	3	2	4	1
1935	3	0	4	1
1936	5	4	4	2
1937	6	3	7	3
1938	4	0	4	1
1939	5	4	4	1
1940	3	2	4	1
1941-1942/-1943/1944	13	0	13	0
TOTALS	46	18	46	12

SOURCE: Compiled by the author from Government of India, Ministry of Home Affairs, *The Civil List of the Indian Administrative Service* (as on 1 January 1968).

The data in Table 2 show that there were, in 1968, precisely the same number of ICS officers in the two north-India IAS cadres as there were in the five non-north-India cadres, and that the relative seniority of these two sets of ICS officers was roughly equivalent. Yet, the data also show that, despite this equivalence, 18 north-India ICS officers occupied these top bureaucratic

[12] Figure arrived at by the author from data appearing in Ministry of Home Affairs, *The Civil List of the Indian Administrative Service* (as on 1 January, 1968), Appendix I.

[13] e.g. Potter, "Bureaucratic Change in India", *op. cit.* pp. 166-69.

posts (Rs 4000 per month) while only 12 of the officers from outside north-India occupied such positions. The dominant position of north-India ICS officers in the most powerful and financially attractive posts in the central government is emphatically supported by these data.

There are several possible explanations for this north-India dominance. One plausible one employed in this analysis is that a causal connection exists between north-India bias in cadre postings in central government, on the one hand, and north-India bias in Congress Party national leadership, on the other. One unconfirmed assumption here is that national leaders from Uttar Pradesh and Bihar are predisposed to favor IAS officers from their home state. If confirmed (and motives aside), then one could suggest that the IAS officers in New Delhi believe themselves to be, and are, amenable to control by national Congress Party leaders in very important career matters involving postings and salary. Furthermore, if the regional bases of power in the Congress national leadership begin to shift away from north-India to other states, then we can look for corresponding changes in the regional identification of IAS and ICS occupants of senior posts in central government. One could then much more convincingly advance the proposition that IAS officers are controlled by Congress Party national leaders, rather than relying only on statements to that effect by IAS secretaries and Congress Party ministers. And if it is true that the Congress Party is able to control the behaviour of individual IAS officers, as is suggested here, then the Congress Party, with its federal features, is able to prevent the IAS from violating India's federalism.

By way of conclusion, although the preceding analysis is sketchy and based only slightly on scattered empirical observations, I am prepared now to state as a working hypothesis that the IAS straddles and supports India's federalism without violating it. If one believes that India's federalism and national political structure are capable of generating sustained development toward desirable social objectives, then it follows that the IAS can be judged as functional for the development process. If, however, one believes that the existing structures are incapable of achieving development objectives, then the hypothesis advanced above leads one to condemn the IAS as an anachronism and thus new and creative research must be undertaken which will result in concrete proposals for new bureaucratic and other structures appropriate to Indian society which can achieve those objectives.

4

ELITE IMAGES AND POLITICAL MODERNIZATION IN INDIA

MICHAEL BRECHER

THE FOURTH GENERAL ELECTION constitutes a watershed in the politics of independent India. From 1947 to 1967 the Congress exercised a monopoly of political authority at the centre and in all the states, except in Kerala for a few years. India's was truly a one-plus party system, comprising a massive majority party and a number of small opposition groups in the wilderness, that is groups that could not reasonably expect to assume authority in the foreseeable future. All this changed with the elections of 1967—from a rather static distribution of political power at the state and all-India levels to a new dynamic equilibrium, from a hegemonial Congress in Parliament to that of a bare majority, from a near-monopoly of Congress authority in the states to a fragmentation of control, dispersed among eight non-Congress governments. In short, India moved from a one-plus party system to an embryonic multi-party system. Moreover, the first "natural" succession contest occurred in the aftermath of the 1967 elections, as the incumbent Head of Government competed with an older and more senior Congress leader for the post of Prime Minister. The two preceding succession contests (1964, 1966) had been created by the death of the national leader and had been profoundly influenced by that setting. Thus the 1967 contest also marks a divide in India's political development, a challenge to stability during a period of a dramatic change in the system.

85

The Fourth General Election provided a valuable laboratory for behavioural research. Many aspects are being explored by political scientists,
Indian and Western. There is a great emphasis on electoral attitudes,
opinions, and choices, particularly at the constituency level, but at state
and all-India levels as well.[1] Other studies concern the selection process
for Congress candidates in parliamentary and assembly seats,[2] and the
consequences of the election results for India's political system.[3] An analysis of the 1967 succession contest, along with a comparison of the three
succession struggles for the Prime Ministership, was undertaken by this
writer.[4] In the plethora of research projects, however, there are no inquiries
into perceptions and attitudes of members of India's élite groups during
this critical transition phase.

This paper sets out the major findings of a study designed to fill that gap [5]
and examines their implications for political modernization in India. The
focus of attention is *élite images and opinions* about various facets of India's
political system. There were three main areas of investigation, through the
technique of a structured questionnaire.

Causes and Results of the Congress Setback in the Fourth General Election

This included élite perceptions of the general and specific causes of
Congress reverses at the polls, at the centre and in the states; of the
continuity of any charismatic role in voter behaviour; of Mrs. Indira
Gandhi's electoral appeal; of probable results; and of the consequences
of the election outcome on the balance of influence within the Congress
—between the party hierarchy and parliamentary wing, among geographic groups in the Party, between the Working Committee and the
Chief Ministers, between the Congress President and other loci of power,
personal and institutional. This section also examined élite images of
the impact of the election results on the candidates for Prime Minister.

---

[1] The most comprehensive project of this type was carried out in Kerala—before
and after the elections—by the Centre for the Study of Developing Societies in
New Delhi.

[2] By Professor W. H. Morris-Jones, Director of the Institute of Commonwealth
Studies, University of London.

[3] By various American and Indian scholars.

[4] See "Succession in India 1967: The Routinization of Political Change", *Asian
Survey*, Vol. VII, No 7 (July 1967), pp. 423-43.

[5] M. Brecher, *Political Leadership in India: An Analysis of Elite Attitudes*, Frederick, A. Praeger (McGill Studies in Development, 2), New York, 1968.

Qualities of Leadership and the Ranking of Congress Leaders

This explored opinions of the élite respondents about the requisite qualities for a good Prime Minister of India in the circumstances of 1967 and
of ranking, along a scale of 1 to 4, of the four best-known Congress
leaders—Mrs. Gandhi, Morarji Desai, Y. B. Chavan, and K. Kamaraj;
fifteen criteria or qualities of leadership were used to secure the assessment of strengths and weaknesses of the Congress leaders—national
image, international image, holding Congress together, maintaining
North-South unity, acceptance by the minorities, effective leadership,
strong leadership, flexible leadership, ability to deal with the Opposition
in Parliament, ability to deal with the states, maintaining harmony with
Congress leaders, the likely implementation of a socialist programme,
providing a better climate for business, the ability to solve economic
problems, and the pursuit of a successful foreign policy.

The Succession Contest of 1967

This included views of the altered date of election of the Congress
Parliamentary Party (CPP) Leader—causes of the change, decision-
makers of the change, effects on candidates' prospects, and the effect
on group influence within the Congress. It also examined opinions on
Mrs. Gandhi's selection as Prime Minister in 1966; on the appropriate
method of selecting a Prime Minister; on the actual method employed
in 1964, and 1967; on the consistency of choice; on the expectations of
the outcome if there had been a secret ballot; on the extent and character
of communication and consultation by participants in the 1967 process; on the initiative taken by participants. Finally, this section probed
opinions on the new Cabinet and the prospect for a full term of office
and for centre-state relations.

There are various intellectually valid conceptions of élite. In this study the
designation, "formal and informal decision-makers", was the common and
basic criterion; but not all groups within that designation were included
in the sample. Only three specialized élites were represented—political,
academic and journalist (or opinion leaders). The political group was
stressed because of the explicit foci of inquiry—the Fourth General Election
and the political process of selection of India's Prime Minister. The inclusion of other élite groups—military, civil service and business—would
have been desirable but of lesser importance..

The research value of élite interviews is substantial, especially in exploring
an élite-dominated political process. For one thing, they provide insight

into the conscious behaviour of those who make decisions, and in this instance the choice of CPP Leader rested with Congress members of Parliament (MPs) and with those who could exert influence on the parliamentarians, notably the organizational leaders of the Congress Working Committee and state chief ministers. Secondly, élite interviews illuminate images and attitudes that enter into élite decisions, and in 1967, the respondents' perception of the causes of the Congress setback at the polls sheds light on the acts (of omission and commission) by Congress leaders which contributed to the debacle. Thirdly, the candid ranking of Congress leaders by élite respondents offers the most accurate prediction of *probable outcome* had there been a secret ballot in the choice of CPP Leader. And in the elaborative comments, freely offered, the interviewees furnished guides to rooted convictions and preferences about many features of the political system. The value of such interviews is greatly enhanced by their paucity in studies of Indian politics. Pre-occupation with mass electoral behaviour, undoubtedly of great value, has led to indifference to élite behaviour and the associated images and attitudes that give rise to such behaviour. Yet there are certain processes and decisions in Indian politics, as in all politics, which are totally or overwhelmingly dependent on perceptions and choices of small numbers of persons within the system.

One cannot be certain about the truthfulness of articulated images and attitudes. Yet the interviews which form the basis of this paper seem to be of a high order of honesty. This judgment is based partly on fifteen years of direct interviewing contact with members of diverse Indian élite groups and the attentive public. It is also based upon the mannerisms of the respondents, the ample character of replies among those who did reply, the candour of many comments, the ease with which some declared that they would answer some questions but not others, the apparent trust in the interviewer's assurance that their names would not be divulged and, most of all, the immediate and co-operative reply to the request for interviews.

None was arranged in advance: there was no time to secure interviews by mail; nor is that the Indian way. The technique employed was a telephone inquiry, at the end of each day in New Delhi, from 11 to 28 March 1967. For each succeeding day an average of five appointments were made. The interviews were held either in the Central Hall or elsewhere in Parliament, or at the residence of the respondent. Only 2 persons with whom an interview was sought declined—because of lack of time; both were cabinet ministers. Some respondents declined to answer certain questions; for example, 9 out of the 80 did not engage in the ranking of the Congress leaders' qualities of leadership—but 71 did so. In short, of 82 interviews sought, 80 were actually held; and these persons answered the overwhelming majority of questions. Each interview averaged slightly more than 1 hour; many lasted $1\frac{1}{2}$ hours; none was less than 40 minutes.

On the whole, the respondents were very knowledgeable and articulate, though there were exceptions. All spoke English, the language in which the interviews were conducted. Some were surprised by the directness of the questions but most persons adjusted quickly. Many offered elaborative comments. The pervasive tone was a willingness—in some cases, an undisguised desire—to share attitudes and knowledge about the General Election and the third succession contest.

It should be re-emphasized that the survey questions were consciously phrased from an all-India perspective. The writer does not deny the importance of regional variations and the necessity for a regional framework in explaining both the defeat of several Congress state governments and the drastically reduced Congress representation in Parliament. The aim of this study, however, was to illuminate the images of *all-India élites* and thereby to fill a gap in the literature of Indian politics.

The sample is not of the random type. It grew out of the initial research focus on the contest for the Prime Ministership in the spring of 1967. Thus it was decided to include both governmental and organizational leaders of the Congress, i.e., cabinet ministers and members of the Working Committee. Because of their role as electors of the CPP Leader, Congress MPs were also included, and because of their influence, state chief ministers. It was also considered appropriate to include a few defeated and ex-Congress leaders or MPs because of the widespread schisms that occurred just before the General Election. To round off political élite representation, one leader from each of the seven Opposition parties in the Lok Sabha was included. Among the opinion leaders, nine prominent commentators and journalists in Delhi were selected, and with them two foreign correspondents with long residence in India. Finally, six professors at Delhi University and the Indian School of International Studies were added. The distribution by group will be found in Table 1.

TABLE 1

CLASSIFICATION OF RESPONDENTS

Politicians		63
Congress MPs	36	
Congress Cabinet Ministers	6	
Congress Working Committee	8	
Congress State Chief Ministers	2	
Defeated, Denied or ex-Congress MPs	4	
Opposition Party Leaders	7	
Academics		6
Opinion Leaders		11
Indian Journalists	9	
Foreign Journalists	2	
TOTAL		80

The 36 Congress MPs constituted one-eighth of the total number of Congress parliamentarians in March 1967; they include 2 from every state of the union, except Kerala and Madras (1 each, because of their decimated contingent in Parliament) and Uttar Pradesh, i.e. UP (4), and Madhya Pradesh, Maharashtra, Bihar, and Jammu and Kashmir (3 each, all but the last because of their size). They are not a random sample but they include all geographic groups; moreover, 11 of the 36 sit in the *Rajya Sabha* (Council of States), the Upper House of Parliament. As for the Congress leaders, the combined number of *Cabinet Ministers and Working Committee members* (14) constitute almost 40 per cent of those two bodies. The state leaders are, however, grossly under-represented. So too are the *Academics;* and no attempt is made to regard the attitudes of these two latter groups as representative. The Indian *Journalists,* by contrast include the best-known and the most influential in Delhi. Thus, whatever trends or conclusions are derived from the data do not represent *the élite;* they constitute the attitudes and images of *Indian élite respondents.*

The principal findings of the inquiry into the Indian élite images of the causes of the Congress setback at the polls may be summarized as follows:

Causes of Setback: Initiated Factors

1. A plurality of factors was ranked by the respondents, revealing sophisticated perceptions.

2. The opposition placed greater emphasis on economic discontent than did those in power. Congress leaders were more aware of the role of economic problems than were the Congress rank-and-file.

3. One fourth of the political respondents mentioned Desire for Change, and almost one half of the non-political respondents did so. Academics and journalists displayed acute perception of this intangible cause of Indian electoral behaviour in 1967. Congress MPs showed considerable awareness of this mood in the electorate; and political leaders of all persuasions were hardly conscious of this factor.

4. Only academics and the opposition interviewees gave United Opposition a high ranking.

5. Only Congress respondents were conscious of the impact of their party's schisms on electoral behaviour.

6. Congress MPs were less aware than others of the link between quality of leadership and voters' choice. All segments of the élite perceived this factor as marginal.

Causes of Setback : Suggested Factors

7. Only 4 of 80 respondents did not regard food or prices as relevant to the election outcome.

8. Four fifths of the persons interviewed cited or acknowledged Internal Quarrels.

9. The élite as a whole attached marginal inffuence to special issues.

10. In only 2 of the 6 factors—Internal Quarrels and United Opposition—is there a relatively equal frequency of initiation and responsiveness. Among the other 4 factors there is gross imbalance, heavily in favour of initiation in Economic Problems, and heavily in favour of responsiveness in special issues, Lack of Effective Leadership and Absence of Charismatic Leadership.

11. The élite as a whole perceived only 3 factors to be important in the General Election of 1967—Economic Problems, Internal Quarrels, and United Opposition.

12. A large proportion of respondents did not perceive any link between specific acts of the Government or Party and the election results; the governing élite was most emphatic in its denial of any connection. The only articulated exceptions was devaluation of the rupee in 1966—and only the journalists stressed its influence.

13. Government acts and Congress Party acts were perceived as synonymous by a majority of the respondents.

14. Almost half the respondents perceived charisma as a positive influence on the votes in the 1967 elections.

15. Morarji Desai was the clear alternative in the élite perception of appeal to Indian voters.

16. The incumbent political élites, academics and opinion leaders shared a sense of surprise about the results. Opposition leaders and defeated or ex-Congressmen did not.

Several analytic themes can be derived from these findings, but they are of necessity tentative. India is almost unique among the new states of Asia and Africa in its experiment in mass democracy : Indian élite images must be analysed within the context of a new and developing political system. Moreover, the analysis of élite images is a recent innovation. There is no body of literature which deals systematically with élite images of one's political system. Thus no hypotheses exist to link types of élite images with the functioning of political systems. Thirdly, this study of élite images dealt with one aspect of a political system, electoral behaviour, not with the system as a whole. For these reasons, the implications to be drawn from the data must be understood as preliminary work in an unexplored field.

It was noted (No. 2 above) that the two most frequently cited causes of the Congress setback were Economic Problems and the Desire for Change, that awareness of the impact of economic dislocation was greater among opposition members, and that Congress leaders were more conscious of that factor than were Congress MPs. This relatively low level of awareness by the governing party's rank-and-file is surprising and merits comment. Most of the literature on voting behaviour indicates the pre-eminence of "bread and butter" issues at the expense of "national" issues. Yet at a time of grave economic crisis in India, Congress MPs perceived Economic Problems as only one of three significant reasons for electoral revolt against Congress Raj.

Several explanations can be suggested for this attitude. Congress MPs are pre-occupied with preserving the cohesion and power of the Congress Party; as such, they place a greater emphasis on failures of organization than on failures of economic policy. Secondly, Congressmen may be aware of the enormity of the economic difficulties faced by India; but they may see no viable alternative to Congress rule nor viable alternative economic policies. In short, Congressmen perceive economic problems as long-range in character, with little direct connection between economic dislocation and defeat at the polls.

This hypothesis is supported by the Congress MPs' acute awareness of the impact of their party's internal schisms on electoral behaviour, a factor underplayed by all non-Congress respondents (No. 5 above). Deficiencies in the Congress party machine, dissidence and factionalism appeared to Congress interviewees as a major factor in the election outcome. This image of the causes of the Congress setback is focussed on *political institutions* rather than on *public policy*; it is essentially manipulative.

The opposition image also offers some insights. Only 1 to 7 opposition leaders mentioned Desire for Change as a siginificant cause of Congress defeat. As a group they placed much greater emphasis on Economic Problems and United Opposition than did the Congress, and they ignored internal Congress party schisms (Nos. 2-5 above). Opposition leaders, then, stressed both a manipulative factor—a United Opposition—and a grave issue of public policy—economic dislocation. As a group they are less concerned with the institutional aspects of election strategy, a logical attitude for a "permanent" opposition.

It was also noted that the Indian élite did not perceive the impact of specific policy acts on the election results (No. 12 above) in contrast to what the literature suggests. This, too, seems to underline the essentially manipulative image held by a substantial portion of the élite. Public policy in general, and specific acts of policy which may be subject to great controversy within the élite itself, are seen as irrelevant or marginal to electoral choice. Implicit is the élite view that voters respond at election-time to pre-established and long-held loyalties which have little or no connection with the content of governmental decisions.

Certain implications flow logically from this set of images. Policy-making becomes the exclusive concern of the élite. Moreover, the effect of both successful and unsuccessful policy is marginal within the political system as a whole. The gap in India is not between Congress and Opposition nor between the political and other élites; it is rather beween those who engage in the policy-making process—and are aware of its results—and the masses. In short, Indian élite respondents view the vast majority of Indian voters as "subjects"—unaware of both inputs and outputs of the policy process. The emphasis placed by both Congress and opposition respondents on institutional factors—Internal Quarrels and United Opposition—becomes meaningful within the context of a "subject"-oriented rather than a "citizen"-oriented population.[6] Yet there is some evidence that this all-India élite image does not wholly correspond to reality. Voting studies conducted at the village and city levels in India suggest a voter awareness of policy outputs that is, a "citizen" orientation. This awareness, however, is one that focusses on the relevance of policy decisions to local conditions.[7] Before any further implications can be drawn for the Indian political system, it is necessary to explore these images more deeply. If the Indian élite image is congruent with that of the voters, the making of policy and the winning of elections may be two entirely separate and unrelated tasks which the political élite of India must perform.

One futher point worth noting is the rather marginal influence attributed to charisma (No. 14 above). This is somewhat surprising, for the politics of development have often been described as "the politics of charisma". In the early years of the post-independence period, the giant shadow cast by the new leaders of India shaped and formed the political process. Mrs. Gandhi, as the daughter of Nehru, is the logical heir to the mantle of charisma. Yet less than one-fourth of the élite respondents considered Mrs. Gandhi's charisma a helpful factor at the polls.

This is one of the many indices of the transition in Indian politics. The élite no longer sees its leadership in charismatic terms; nor does it posit charisma as a prime requisite of leadership. The evidence uncovered here seems to support an earlier conclusion that India has managed to routinize

    [6] G. A. Almond and S. Verba, *The Civic Culture*, Princeton, New Jersey: Princeton University Press, 1963. Almond and Verba postulate three types: the "subject", who is unaware of inputs as well as outputs; the "citizen", who is unaware of outputs; and the "participant", who is aware of both inputs and outputs. They would characterize India as 'subject-participant'.

    [7] See, for example, F. G. Bailey, *Politics and Social Change: Orissa in 1959*, Oxford, England: Oxford University Press, 1963, and V. M. Sirsikar, *Political Behaviour in India*, Bombay: Manaktalas, 1965.

political change at the national level: the political élite no longer requires a charismatic leader as a necessary condition for a relatively stable political process.

Among the 15 base qualities later employed for leadership ranking, only 6 were cited more than once as Priority 1 in the initiating replies of the 80 persons interviewed. An even larger number of other, unstructured qualities (8) were introduced by the respondents, each at least twice. The order of frequency in the aggregate as Priority 1 quality was as follows:

Effective Leadership*	6
Strong Leadership*	6
Holding Congress Together	6
Maintaining North-South Unity	6
National Outlook†	6
Boldness, Courage, Dynamism†	5
Intellectual Distinction†	5
Ability to Deal with States	4
Mass Contact (or Support)†	4
Integrity†	3
Inspiration to people†	3

  * These 2 are essentially the same and may be combined to indicate a frequency of 12 for the quality of Effectiveness.
  † These qualities are not among the 15 base qualities of ranking.

Qualities mentioned as Priority 1 by 2 persons were Ability to Solve Economic Problems, Modern Liberal Outlook, and Patriotism. There was also a host of qualities mentioned as Priority 1 by one person, among them Honesty, Firmness, Restoration of Swadeshi Spirit, Empathy for Indian Spirit, Pragmatism, Adherence to Congress Ideals, Acumen, Adherence to Nehru's policies, and Building a Team. Thus Priority 1 in leadership was given by 73 actual replies to no less than 30 qualities—13 of the 15 base qualities and 17 others. In short, there was a remarkable diversity in the élite choice of the most important quality required for India's Prime Minister in 1967. This pluralist character of élite attitudes to leadership qualities is one index of political modernization.

Noteworthy is the absence of a single reference to Pursuing a Successful Foreign Policy. In 1967, not one member of a composite élite of 80 Indians considered foreign policy of sufficient importance to indicate skill in this sphere of public policy as necessary to a Prime Minister of India in the context of current affairs—in any of the 8 priorities of leadership qualities.

The other quality mentioned by none was Providing a Better Climate for Business, indicating a consensus in the élite as a whole that private enterprise occupies, at most, a marginal role in India's economic growth.

Elite attitudes to national leadership qualities were as follows:

  1.   The four most important qualities *initiated* by the élite as a whole were Effective Leadership, Strong Leadership, Holding Congress Together and Maintaining North-South Unity.
  2.   Congress MPs stressed Strong Leadership, Effective Leadership, Maintaining North-South Unity, Intellectual Distinction, Ability to Deal with the States and Holding Congress Together, in that order of importance. They paid scant attention to skill in handling economic problems.
  3.   Congress leaders displayed a wide range of emphasis, with special attention on Strong Leadership, Effective Leadership and Holding Congress Together.
  4.   Defeated, disillusioned and ex-Congressmen shared with opposition leaders the primary concern with Ability to Solve Economic Problems: two thirds of non-Congress respondents stressed this quality, while only 7 out of 45 Congress interviewees did so.
  5.   Academics and journalists revealed a pronounced pluralism in their selection of leadership qualities.
  6.   Stated in comparative group terms:

  (*a*)   Both sections of Congress respondents placed the greatest stress on Effective and Strong Leadership.
  (*b*)   Both sections of the Congress élite shared with two non-political groups this emphasis on Effective and Strong Leadership.
  (*c*)   The two segments of the élite diverged in their emphasis—non-Congress respondents emphasized Ability to Solve Economic Problems, while Congress respondents stressed Effective and Strong Leadership.
  (*d*)   The incumbent political élite did not appear to place a high value on economic prosperity and growth; the competing élites did.
  (*e*)   One non-political élite group, Indian journalists, shared with the non-Congress political groups an emphasis on Ability to Solve Economic Problems.

The ranking of the four Congress leaders was revealing:

  7.   There was a clear preference for Mrs. Gandhi among the élite respondents as a whole. Desai was the second over-all choice; and Chavan and Kamaraj were bunched together.

8. *Mrs. Gandhi* had the most positive image within India and in the world at large. She would contribute most to the Maintenance of North-South Unity, it was believed, and is most trusted by India's minorities. She was also regarded as the most flexible Congress leader and the ablest in dealing with the states, as well as the most highly skilled in the realm of foreign policy.

Mrs. Gandhi was ranked low in qualities of Strong Leadership and Ability to Solve Economic Problems. Most respondents thought her least likely to provide Strong Leadership. Yet this quality was given over-riding importance.

9. *Morarji Desai* was ranked highest in four qualities—Effective Leadership, Strong Leadership, Providing a Better Climate for Business and Ability to Solve Economic Problems. He was the clear but not deci-sive choice for most effective leadership. There was also a very broad consensus that he was the strongest personality among the four candidates.

Desai's shortcomings, in the élite view, extend to three areas: flexi-bility, relations with Congress leaders and implementation of a socialist programme.

10. *Kamaraj* ranked well in Holding Congress Together, but the data reflected a widely-shared and widely-expressed view that no single Congress leader could keep the party together; the same image applied to harmony among the Party Leaders. Kamaraj was regarded as the most likely to implement the Congress commitment to socialism, if he were in power; but only a minority of respondents thought that even he would do so.

He was regarded as the least effective of the four Congress leaders, the least qualified to deal with the Opposition in Parliament and with the states, the least capable of Providing a Better Climate for Business, and the least competent in Foreign Policy.

11. *Chavan* was not ranked the highest in any sphere, and he was rated the least qualified in four; thus his over-all standing in the élite assessment is lowest among the four Congress leaders. He was regarded as having the weakest National Image and International Image. Chavan was also ranked the least effective of the four in terms of the goal of Congress unity, but all four are individually weak in this respect. Finally, Chavan was perceived as the least-trusted by India's minorities, a spill-over from his image as a "Maharashtrian parochialist".

Congress MPs showed a high degree of consistency in ranking the requi-site qualities of an Indian Prime Minister in 1967: the most important qualities were perceived to be Effective Leadership, Strong Leadership,

Holding Congress Together and Maintaining North-South Unity (No. 2 above). As such, they articulated an over-riding concern with two problems—national integration and the unity of Congress: all other issues were secondary. This evidence supports an earlier hypothesis that the Congress rank-and-file have an essentially manipulative image: the task of leadership is to preserve the unity of the policy and of the party. It is striking that Congress MPs perceived no connection between political viability and the capacity to solve economic problems. Rather, their image of national integration was linked to North-South unity and to containment of state pressures on the federal government.

This emphasis on Holding Congress Together is entirely consistent with the awareness of the impact of party factionalism on the election results. Indeed the logical product of that image is the demand that the leadership improve the organizational performance of Congress. This reflects again a basic theme of Congress respondents—an image that is focussed on political institutions rather than on public policy.

The image of Congress leaders displayed almost the same pattern (No. 3 above). It was less diffused than that of the rank-and-file, with the greatest emphasis on Congress unity. The composite image of non-Congress respondents was strikingly different: two-thirds termed the ability to cope with India's grave economic crisis a prime requisite for the Prime Ministership; only 15 per cent of Congress respondents shared this perspective! In short, the incumbent élite, unlike competitive élites, does not appear to place a high value on economic prosperity and growth.

It was noted that not one person considered managerial skill in foreign policy necessary for the Prime Minister of India. This is both expected and surprising. It is expected because of the generally low level of Congress concern with all aspects of public policy and because foreign policy is a low-priority issue area in most democratic polities. It is surprising, however, in the light of the prominence of India's foreign policy in the past. The policy of "non-alignment" was defined as an extension of India's independence and gave India disproportionate influence and prestige for fifteen years. It is surprising, then, that in 1967 not one respondent considered skill in foreign policy an important quality for Prime Minister. Indeed, given India's developmental needs and its dependence on aid and trade, one would have expected this to be a significant element in the élite calculus of leadership. Viewed in a different perspective, however, the scant attention given by the Congress respondents to economic problems is consistent with the general indifference to foreign policy.

It was also noted that the élite as a whole stressed Strong and Effective Leadership; but the component groups gave this different operational content (No. 6 above). Non-Congress respondents perceived economic problems as the most important area of public policy. The Congress rank-

and-file emphasized problems of national integration and party unity. And the principal concern of Congress leaders was the continuing viability of Congress as a political party. This diversity reflects differing sets of priorities and differing images of the Indian political system as a whole.

The consistency of élite images merits notice, as they match candidates to qualities of leadership. A clear preference for Mrs. Gandhi was revealed (No. 8 above). Only in one case, that of Strong Leadership, was she given a low ranking. In the crucial area of national integration she emerged as best qualified. Not surprisingly, Mrs. Gandhi was rated weak in Ability to Solve Economic Problems; but given the relative indifference to economic problems within the Congress élite image, this deficiency was not a stumbling block to Mrs. Gandhi's re-election as Prime Minister.

Morarji Desai emerged as the clear alternative to Mrs. Gandhi, strong in areas where she is weak, and weak in areas where she exhibited her greatest strength (No. 9 above). Paradoxically, then, Desai emerged as the closest approximation to the ideal-type candidate of the opposition. Mrs. Gandhi emerged as the closest approximation to the ideal-type candidate desired by Congress MPs and leaders.

CONCLUSIONS

This inquiry into Indian élite images concentrated on two aspects of the political process—electoral behaviour and leadership at the all-India level. Any general conclusions to be drawn from the analysis must be regarded as tentative; they await similar explorations of related processes. Nevertheless, it is possible and desirable to place our findings in a theoretical framework for the analysis of political development.

Professor David Apter has suggested two ideal-types of developing political systems—mobilization and reconciliation.[8] Mobilization systems attempt to mobilize political energies and resources to attack the problems of poverty, ignorance and economic backwardness. They seek to reconstruct society, both attitudes and institutions, in order to achieve material advance. Indeed, the underlying premise can be stated as a simple proposition: economic progress is the basis for modern society. Mobilization systems are therefore characterized by hierarchical authority, total allegiance to the political system, tactical flexibility and ideological specialization. The political party or governmental apparatus serves as the central instrument of economic and social change.

The reconciliation system, by contrast, is a union of autonomous parts.

[8] David Apter, "System, Process and the Politics of Economic Development", in J. L. Finkle and R. W. Gamble, eds., *Political Development and Social Change*, New-York: John Wiley & Sons, 1966, 441-57. The following delineation of the structure and processes of the two types of political systems is based upon Apter's work.

It seeks a common denominator in order to satisfy all important constituents of the political system. High priority is thus given to compromise among competing political and interest groups. Reconciliation systems are usually characterized by pyramidal authority structures, multiple loyalties, the acceptance of compromise, pluralism and ideological diffuseness.

In both system-types, economic development is a significant issue and a constant policy problem. Each uses a quite different strategy to cope with this demand. Economic development receives the highest priority in mobilization systems. Institutions are created to remove social obstacles to economic growth, and governmental enterprise becomes the main engineering path to development. In reconciliation systems, however, economic objectives are more diffuse. The process of decision-making is less centralized, with the result that both the goal of economic development and progress toward its achievement are much more moderate. In mobilization systems, immediate satisfaction must be sacrificed for the sake of future benefits. In reconciliation systems, by contrast, possibilities for current savings are limited by the necessity for compromise between the demands of competing groups; there is a greater balance between developmental and system-maintenance decisions. In short, decision-making élites in reconciliation systems have a much more limited scope of action; a wider variety of constraints operates on development policies. In Apter's succinct formula, "mobilization systems fight society; reconciliation systems are prisoners of society".

Apter's mode can be readily applied to a study of Indian élite images of the political system. The perceptions of Congress respondents are typical of an élite operating within a reconciliation system. The attitudes of opposition leaders and of non-political respondents are more characteristic of an élite in a mobilization system.

Congressmen, that is, the incumbent Indian political élite, demonstrated a paramount concern with system-maintenance, not with development. They perceived deficiencies in the Congress party machine, dissidence and factionalism, as major factors in the outcome of the Fourth General Election. The rank-and-file gave high priority to problems of national integration and party unity, and they were principally concerned with the continuing viability of the Congress as a political instrument. Finally, in their ranking of the requisite qualities for an Indian Prime Minister in the conditions of 1967, Congress respondents stressed Holding the Congress Together and Maintaining North-South Unity.

All this reveals a high priority of goals related to reconciliation and integration. Moreover, Congress MPs were pre-occupied with the techniques of reconciliation: they focussed on the integrative role, not on the transforming role of the Congress party in the Indian political system. Their sensitivity to the scope and impact of regional variations in the election outcome, to shifts in the authority structure of the party, and to changes in the personal and institutional loci of decision-making—all these are consistent with the supreme value they placed on political reconciliation and their image of the Congress as its indispensable instrument. Further, in the light of this emphasis on system-maintenance, the choice of Mrs. Gandhi was perfectly consistent. Nor is it surprising that the Congress setback at the polls led to decline in the desire for change in Prime Minister.

Opposition and non-political élite images were more typical of an élite functioning within a mobilization system. Their emphasis on the ability to cope with India's economic problems as a prime requisite for leadership reflects the priority given to economic development; indeed non-Congress respondents perceived economic problems as the most important area of public policy. Morarji Desai was rated very highly in his ability to deal with economic crises and to provide a better climate for business. He was therefore the logical candidate of those persons whose goals are of the mobilzation type.

Two sets of data provide interesting evidence in support of these hypotheses. The first explores the consistency of élite attitudes to the choice of Prime Minister. Preliminary analysis appears to indicate a striking inconsistency in choice: fifty-five respondents ranked Economic Problems most important or second most important among the causes of the Congress setback in the 1967 General Election; a clear plurality of these persons ranked Morarji Desai as "best qualified" among the four Congress leaders to deal with Economic Problems; yet only 11 respondents (20 per cent) supported Desai for the Prime Ministership. The same zig-zag pattern emerges from the data on Mrs. Gandhi: only 9 of the 55 ranked her "best qualified" to cope with Economic Problems, 1 more than the lowest-rated in this sphere, Chavan; more than 40 per cent of the respondents rated her "least qualified"; yet 28 of the 55 persons, or slightly more than 50 per cent, supported her for the Prime Ministership. In group terms, the most pertinent comparison is the ranking and choice by Congress MPs who attached importance to Economic Problems in analyzing the election outcome: five ranked Mrs. Gandhi first in her Ability to Solve Economic Problems, and 7 ranked her fourth; yet 16 of the 25 MPs supported her for the Prime Ministership. There were 9 MPs who ranked Desai first in this skill, and 5 who ranked him fourth; but only 5 supported him for the Prime Ministership. More pointedly, 8 MPs ranked Kamaraj most capable in the economic sphere, but ony one MP favoured him as Prime Minister.

These respondents, it is evident, did not transpose their analysis of the election results to their analysis and choice of the best-qualified person for the position of Prime Minister. Several explanations may be suggested for this "gap". One is a discontinuity between the élite image of the kind of leadership required for an election campaign and the kind of leadership required for the country as the Head of Government. Another is a discontinuity between élite recognition of the political significance of unsolved economic problems and the importance of econmic skill in over-all leadership ability. A third theme is the widespread belief expressed by many respondents, that India's economic problems are too massive in scope and are too deep-rooted for any leader to be able to solve them alone. Thus other leadership qualities were regarded as more important in the choice of Prime Minister in 1967.

Another plausible hypothesis is that economic problems may be regarded by most foreigners and some Indians as the paramount task for India's leadership in the coming decades, but the ability in this sphere of policy is not pre-eminent among the élite's criteria for choice of a Prime Minister. In other words, skill in economic matters does not outweigh *all* other skills in the composite image of élite respondents.

These explanations are compatible. They also reflect the underlying realities of the political process in reconciliation systems. Economic skills can never outweigh skills of political bargaining and consensus-shaping. The apparent inconsistencies of élite attitudes to the choice of the Prime Minister disappear when economic development is treated as one of two or three priority goals rather than the over-riding objective of the system. It is not surprising that the Congress rank-and-file, who are regional in background, education and interest, have the clearest and most sharply attuned image of the reconciliation political process. The success of Mrs. Gandhi's candidacy can best be interpreted, then, in terms of her superior skill in bargaining and compromise.

The near-universal expectation about future centre-state relations was of greater tension or continuation of the status quo; not a single respondent anticipated a reduction of tension in the relations between Delhi and the states. Within this nearly uniform consensus there were variations of group emphasis: only Cabinet Ministers expected a continuation of the status quo; all others predicted greater tension.

There is evidence here of acute awareness of the nature of reconciliation problems within the Indian political system. The concensus in anticipating an increase in federal-state tensions demonstrates the interplay and conflict between priority objectives. The comment of one journalist, "secession, no, but real friction and tension within a year, yes; a real crisis of leadership now faces India", underlines the breadth of disintegrative potentialities within the Indian polity. The necessity for allocation of scarce resources to system-maintenance (rather than development) increases proportionately with the scope and intensity of disintegrative demands.

The Indian élite is composed largely of persons who are aware of the nature of the reconciliation process and of the intricate and complex techniques of bargaining and compromise which constitute its main features. A segment of élite—opposition leaders and communications specialists—have

M-8.

ordered their priorities differently, giving greater weight to the goal of rapid economic development. It is in this respect that they resemble their counterparts in mobilization systems. This is a healthy sign for the Indian body-politic because it reinforces incumbent élite awareness of the importance of economic growth.

Opposition and communications respondents probably attached greater weight to economic tasks because of their lack of practical and direct experience in the Indian policy-making process—until 1967. For this reason, it is likely that the images of Congress respondents are more congruent with the realities—both demands and constraints—of the decision-making process in all-India politics. Yet even the opposition and the non-political élites displayed extreme sensitivity to India's integrative problems.

During the first twenty years of independence a relatively stable reconciliation system was sustained in India. The interaction between the two sets of élite images, different only in their order of priorities, produced a viable mix of development and system-maintenance decisions; the emphasis was clearly on stability.

5

PREJUDICE AND POLITICS IN THE AMERICAN PAST AND PRESENT

SEYMOUR MARTIN LIPSET

THE SOCIAL tensions inherent in rapid economic growth, urbanization, immigration, migration, and shifts in the position of different ethnic groups, have repeatedly in American history stimulated the phenomenon of the political "backlash". Various groups have experienced such changes as challenges to their status, values, or interests, and have reacted by seeking to eliminate the source of these threats which they have often located in the supposed control over the government, or the institutions which dominate communications and culture, by an immoral, corrupt and un-American minority whose covert power has made the formal democratic process meaningless. Extremist movements such as the Anti-Masonic Party of the late 1820's the various nativist and Know-Nothing anti-Catholic parties and orders of the pre-Civil War era, the American Protective Association of the 1890's, the Ku Klux Klan of the 1920's, the Coughlinite movement of the 1930's, the McCarthyite syndrome of the 1950's and most recently the George Wallace movement in the 1960's, have each in different ways given expression to the sense of frustration of millions of Americans to a threat to their power and status, or economic position.

The use of prejudicial ethnic, racial and religious appeals against the supposed threat of minority groups is clearly almost as old as the American political system itself. The efforts of nearly every minority group in the

103

US to improve its situation have been viewed as a threat by some who possessed dominant status-charateristics, and some political leaders at almost every period have appealed to such resentments to get votes.

How do such extremist appeals become crystallized in a political movement or a political party? Working on the model proposed by Neil Smelser, we can postulate the following: There must be first a social strain or decline in status which is somewhat ambiguous and creates widespread anxiety. The adherents of extremist movements have typically felt deprived— either they have never gained their due share or they are losing their share of power and status. We might call these groups the "never-hads" and the "once-hads". These deprived groups are not necessarily extremist, but extremism usually draws its strength from them. The first type (never-hads) tends to experience primarily economic deprivation and consequently to seek redress by state action to achieve economic reforms; this typically has supported left-wing extremism, although it has occasionally fostered right-wing ones as well. The second type (once-hads) experiences or fears loss of status and influence; this group cannot be assuaged by government action. It requires a different course of action—usually the projection of grievances on to a minority group and attempts to discredit or destroy that group to relieve its own sense of anxiety; this typically takes the form of right-wing extremism, and it is with such extremism that we will be concerned, with our focus on prejudice.

Such reactions are not simply a response to political changes and demands. The fluidity of the American social struture, the fact that no dominant group has ever enjoyed a socially recognized claim to long-term status in the style of some of the more status-bound class-ridden societies of the old world, has meant that the problem of status insecurity has been an enduring characteristic of American life. New regions, new industries, new migrant groups, new ethnic and religious groups, have continually encroached upon the old. These changes have often been accompanied by adjustments in the prevailing norms concerning proper relations between parents and children, the drinking of alchoholic beverages, the use of drugs, the relations between the sexes, styles of dress, conceptions of religious morality, etc. Such changes in morality lead those adhering to the old norms to feel disinherited, dispossessed, displaced in their own land.

Groups who have a claim to status and cultural influence as a result of past or present achievements turn against existing political institutions when they feel that their claim is insecure, is under attack, or is actually declining. Such groups may include under present conditions some among the quite privileged such as doctors or heads of family-owned corporations who feel the weight of growing government controls—or on a less affluent level, working-class whites who after gaining economic security feel the pressure of Negro demands on their schools, neighbourhoods, and unions

—or on an ideological axis, those whose self-identity is closely linked to traditional religious and secular values which appear to be in the process of being supplanted by concepts and behaviour which they view as immoral. These are the prototypical situations which have fed the well-springs of right-wing movements. and, indeed, of right-wing extremism.

How do these groups whose status and values are threatened react to such insecurity? As Smelser suggests, they deal with it by designating a specific cause for that strain—not necessarily or typically the real cause, but a plausible cause. In many cases, ethnically or religiously indentifiable population groups have served that purpose well. They heavy immigration by ethnic groups who have allegedly introduced "unprotestant" and "un-American" values and modes of behaviour into this society has often been identified by "displaced" strata as the main threat to their values or position. So, for example, economic unrest has engendered mass anti-immigrant and anti-Catholic movements among the less privileged classes based on the charges that "alien" competition for jobs was the cause of unemployment. And loss of elections, the growth of urban machine politics, and changes in the general state of social morality have commonly been interpreted by groups losing their economic, social, political, or religious dominance as the fault of foreign and non-Protestant groups who have undermined the traditional structure of status and authority. Because nativism has so openly traded on religious and ethnic group appeals, it has been of primary importance in determining the correlations between party choice and membership in specific religious and ethnic groups. In most instances in this country the values that the declining majority has tried to preserve against the rising minorities have been the values of nativism, fundamentalism, and simplistic moralism.

Such moralism—operating as it does largely among the less educated, more fundamentalist, and more provincial—requires that the minority target group is held to be conspiring to destroy the very values that the deprived group is seeking to preserve. Conspiracy theories uniformly describe a high-powered core of intellectuals involved in devious manipulation of the national mind. As we shall see, conspiracy theories have provided the central drive for bigoted American political movements, because they suggest the course of direct action the deprived group must take: the remedy against the alleged conspiratorial plotting of a secret band of intellectuals at the helm of a distrusted minority group is exposure, repression, and even annihilation. And this course of action is presumably justified by the tenets of morality. The moralism of bigotry tends to be absolutist—the "enemy" is identified with the circulation of corrupt literature and with general debauchery. This black-and-white view insists that the enemy is debarred by its moral corruption and conspiratorial tactics from having any legitimate place in the normative political market-place. This entire process can be called backlash politics, and has characterized segments of American conservatism for much of our country's history.

The first such example involved New England Federalists, Congregationalists, and merchants who reacted to their decline by discovering foreign-based conspiracies, and by emphasizing religion and moralism. In the last years of the eighteenth century they placed the blame for the changing moral order, and their concomitant loss of political power, religious influence, and status on the conspiratorial activities of the Illuminati, an Enlightenment Society of intellectuals affiliated to the Masons, which existed for a brief period in Bavaria. Some European writers credited the group with responsibility for the French Revolution and other upheavals in various countries. The anti-Illuminati agitation involved an effort to defeat the rapidly growing Jeffersonian and Deist challenges to the position and values of the Congregationalist and Federalist elites by identifying these opponents as agents of a revolutionary conspiracy.

A quarter of a century later, a new wave of exposés of Masonic, and to some extent Illuminati, conspiracies arose during a comparable period in which conservative political and traditional religious forces felt themselves under attack from the rising Jacksonian democracy and irreligious elements. The politically potent Anti-Masonic movement drew much of its extensive support from lowly educated poor segments of the rural population which lived away from urban settlements, but ultimately joined forces with the conservative National Republicans to form the Whig Party. Both waves of agitation against Illuminati-Masonic conspiracies also involved links to ethnic and religious bigotry. The Illuminati of 1798 were identified with the revolutionary activities of the Irish in Ireland and America, while the Anti-Masonic party at times espoused nativist, anti-Catholic, and even anti-Semitic sentiments.

Such efforts to identify threats to the religious order and status system with hidden conspiracies as well as the repeated espousal of anti-Catholic nativism, first by the Federalists and later by the Whigs and related groups, in two decades before the Civil War illustrate, as we shall see, the willingness of segments of American elite to encourage extremism in their attempts to hold power. Among the masses, the rise of such movements has frequently represented the responses of evangelical Prostestants to changes that they feared were eroding their moral values or social status.

From the early days of the Republic down to the Great Depression, the most important source of prejudice in American politics was anti-Catholicism. Such sentiments have deep religious roots in this country: the Puritans and the Protestant sects, the Methodists and Baptists who came to dominate in terms of numbers, all hated the Papists. And this deep streak of anti-Catholic feeling was seized on at different times in American history to sustain movements which sought to preserve existing institutions against the threat of change—a threat that was attributed to the increased number of Catholics in the country and even to conspiracies directed by Rome.

Perhaps the earliest sustained anti-Catholic political effort occurred in New York in the first decade of the nineteenth century. The recently defeated Federalist Party, in an effort to regain strength by appealing to voters' religious prejudice, re-formed as the anti-Catholic American Party,[1] thus initiating the oft-repeated pattern of conservatives resorting to appeals to racial or religious bigotry when they find their power declining.

Anti-Catholicism made its first independent political impact during the 1830's, coinciding with the increase of immigration and with the rise of Jacksonian democracy. During this time a growing anti-Catholic literature reported the alleged sins and evil designs of the Church, including revelations of secret sexual activities which presumably went on in convents and monasteries (*Six Months in a Convent, The nun, etc.*). The Catholics were described as seeking to conquer and corrupt America through sheer numbers—the inpouring of masses of Irish and other immigrants. Scattered anti-Catholic parties appeared in eastern cities in the 1830's and grew in numbers and influence in the 1840's.

To a considered degree the success of this wave of anti-Catholic hysteria seems to be linked to the weakness in the cities in the 1830's and 1840's of the principal conservative party, the Whigs. With the mass base given to the Democrats by the Jacksonian populist image, the Whigs found it increasingly difficult to win elections. They began to blame their defeats at the polls on the fact that foreigners and Catholics were voting overwhelmingly for the Democrats. As more foreigners, particularly Catholics, came into the country, many Whigs feared they would be unable to compete effectively with their political rivals. This fear forced them on a number of occasions from the early 1840's on to compromise with their presumed dislike of appealing to prejudice by allying themselves with the more aggressively anti-Papist forces organized in the various small parties extolling an America-for-Americans nativism.

The use of anti-Catholicism by the Whigs played on a number of basic Protestant fears and values in an attempt to wean Protestants away from the Democrats: Orthodox Protestants saw in the growing number of Catholics and their increased political influence in the cities a threat to Protestant cultural dominance. The growing number of immigrants, Catholics and others, was regarded as a competitive economic and status threat by many Protestant workers. Futhermore, during this period of rapid population growth and geographic mobility, many Protestants moved from rural to

---

[1] This group was the first to introduce the name "American Party". Some version of the term "American Party" has been used by racists and bigots for well over a century and a half.

urban areas and, in doing so, severed their close social ties with the people and the institutions among which they were reared; they naturally feared the new ways of the city. The Protestants also feared the outcome of Catholic attempts to oppose Protestant teaching and the reading of the Protestant Bible in the public schools (the Catholics were supported in this demand by religious liberals, deists, and atheists, mainly united in the Democratic Party).

Exploiting all these fears of economic, cultural and moral displacement, the elaborately ritualistic anti-Catholic secret orders were able to recruit large numbers of Protestants, especially the poor and uneducated, to defend the old values and traditions. The literature that emerged in this period was not only anti-Catholic in general, but actually articulated a specific theory of Catholic conspiracy stemming from Rome, supposedly launched to undermine the American system. Belief in this theory presumably justified violent and democratic means to eradicate the conspiracy. From the 1840's to the mid-1850's violent anti-Catholic riots occurred. Churches and convents were burned and Catholics were beaten. Meanwhile, the Catholics were blamed for urban crime and the growth in immorality.

Given the rationale of moral absolutism, many of the same invidious things that are written openly or said privately about Negroes today were stated about other visible minority groups (primarily Catholic immigrants) at various periods before the Civil War. The themes of crime in the streets, immorality and unfitness, and conspiracy have been staples in the American diet of intolerance.

This rising tide of anti-Catholicism culminated in the emergence of the American, or Know-Nothing, Party in 1854. The latter became for a brief period the second-largest party in the United States, since the Whigs generally ceased to run candidates. It captured the government in many eastern cities as well as Baltimore and New Orleans. Its representatives constituted two-thirds of the Massachusetts Legislature and a majority in the Connecticut Legislature. In fact, the Know-Nothing Party had political hegmony in most of New England and in many of the Middle Atlantic states.

The political conditions which fostered the rapid growth of the Know-Nothing Party closely resembled those linked to the spread of the anti-Illuminati agitation in the late 1790's and of the Anti-Masonic Party at the end of the 1820's. The rise to prominence of these anti-conspiratorial movements seem to have been a reaction to the breakdown of the principal conservative political forces of each period. The anti-Illuminati frenzy coincided with the decline of Federalism under John Adams, the Anti-Masons arose with the defeat of his equally conservative son John Quincy Adams and the rise of Jacksonian democracy, and the emergence of the Know-Nothings as a mass movement occurred after the break-up of the Whig

Party following its defeat in the election of 1852.

Athough most American Party votes clearly came from former Whig supporters, the new party was able to win in traditional Democratic areas, particularly in cities, by capturing the backing of many Protestant workers who had previously voted Democratic. In some communities it even took on a left or populist aura on various social issues.

But the Know-Nothings had a relatively short political career. The party broke up by 1857, before it could do much about Catholics or immigrants. It was torn asunder by the slavery issue which was far more crucial for many devout Protestants than was the anti-Catholic cause. The northern supporters of the Know-Nothings were devoutly anti-slavery and its southern supporters were equally committed to slavery. A party so divided on so crucial an issue could not easily maintain itself.

In the North the Know-Nothings were absorbed in the new party which expressed the feeling of the middle-class, Protestant, formerly Whig community—the Republicans. The Republican Party after the Civil War was to take over the role of the Know-Nothings as the anti-Catholic party. Ulysses S. Grant had been a Know-Nothing for a brief period. As commander of the Union Army during the Civil War, Grant had tried to bar Jews from areas he controlled. As a Republican President, he made overtly anti-Catholic public statements. Addressing a reunion of Union veterans, he spoke out about the threat of a new civil war between the supporters of superstition (that is, the Catholics) and the true believers. He intimated that the Union Army might have to be recalled to defend the country against the conspiracies of the forces of superstition. Both of Grant's Vice-Presidents had been Know-Nothing leaders before the Civil War. Other Republican presidents and candidates like Rutherford Hayes and James G. Blaine were also active in the anti-Catholic fight. On the local level in the cities the role of the Republicans as an anti-Catholic party was even more obvious. The statement which supposedly defeated Blaine in the presidential election of 1884 was the Reverend Blanchard's accusation that the Democrats were "the party of rum, Romanism, and rebellion". Many historians have been so unaware of the role of religion as a perennial source of post-Civil-War partisan controversy that this one slogan was mentioned for a long time as having had a decisive effect on the election's outcome. Yet this single allegation could hardly have defeated Blaine, for thousands of Republicans had said the same or worse. Blanchard could legitimately be regarded as having merely epitomized what many Republicans were saying all along.

Two efforts to recreate a party called the American Party during this period failed. The first, which ran presidential candidates in 1876 and 1880, represented a minor effort by provincial Protestant fundamentalists to revive an Anti-Masonic movement, with tinges of anti-Catholicism. Some of the literature of this movement linked radical activities of the day, such as the Paris Commune of 1871 and the American strike wave of the '70s, with the continued activities of the Illuminati, previously credited with having organized the French Revolutions of 1789 and 1830. The second American Party of the post-Civil-War era was formed in the late 1880's and was primarily anti-Catholic and nativist. Although it tried to mount a national campaign, it, too, found little support for a third party.

Although efforts to form a new party based on Protestant fears of conspiracy failed, conditions had changed sufficiently by the end of the '80s to facilitate the growth of a militantly anti-Catholic movement, the American Protective Association (APA), which was founded in 1887.

At its high point in 1893, the APA and its allied organizations were credited with a membership of about two million people. In approach, the APA echoed the Know-Nothings. It repeated many of the Know-Nothing tales of Catholic conspiracy, warned Americans that the Catholics were aiming to seize power and kill off Protestants, and accused the Catholics of having assassinated Presidents Lincoln and Garfield. So intense was the anti-Catholic feeling and so widely held was the conspiracy theory that a responsible public official, the Governor of Ohio, in 1893 issued arms to Protestants to defend themselves against the alleged Catholic plan to kill them. The APA at the time was buying rifles and drilling troops because of its belief that on a specific day the Catholics were going to shoot the Protestants in a manner reminiscent of the St. Bartholomew's Day Massacre in sixteenth century France. Hundreds of thousands—perhaps millions—of Protestants took this allegation so seriously that they felt they must bear arms to defend themselves against the threat from the Catholic minority. The proportion of Catholics was then not more than that of Negroes now —about 15 per cent; the phenomenon of the 85 per cent of the population fearing it was going to be shot down in its beds and wiped out by the 15 per cent offers eerie parallels with the contemporary situation.

This dramatic rise of the APA in the early 1890's, like that of the Know-Nothings in the 1850's, seems to have been related to a visible threat to the political domination of the major source of evangelical Protestant control—in this case, the Republican Party. In the Congressional elections of 1890, the Republicans suffered their greatest defeat since their formation, shifting from a House majority to a minority of 88 members as compared to 235 Democrats and nine Populists. In 1892, the Democrats won the Presidency with their first decisive plurality since 1856. They also held political control of many cities in which Irish Catholics were beginning to take over as mayors and political leaders. Issues concerning teaching in the public schools continued to divide Protestants and Catholics. Many descendants of the first group of Catholic and Jewish immigrants who had come in before the Civil War were now prosperous second-and-third-generation Americans, demanding the right of access to high-status institutions. Other pressures during the 1890's came from increasing immigration from Europe and rapid industrialization and urbanization. In addition, the Depression of 1893, leading to increased competition for scarce jobs, further stimulated the growth of the APA among the fearful Protestant working class who constituted a large part of its membership at its height. The APA for the most part worked in and through the Republican Party (although in some areas it also received support from Populist leaders) much as some previous anti-Catholic, nativist movements had worked in and through the Whig Party.

The APA, like the Know-Nothings, flourished for only three or four years, declining in large part because the Republican leadership, many of whom had encouraged it while the Democrats were in power turned against it after their overwhelming victories in the Depression-influenced 1894 Congressional elections. This success, for which the APA tried to claim credit, suggested to party leaders like Mark Hanna that they had an opportunity to win over the urban Catholic and immigrant vote if they disassociated themselves from bigoted groups like the APA.

The repudiation of the APA by leading Republicans, some of whom likely McKinley had earlier encouraged it, illustrates an oft-recurring pattern in the political life of the United States. The moderate conservatives (Whigs or Repubicans) when at a low political ebb occasionally encouraged racism or political extremism—overtly—as a way of winning over some of the less privileged among their Democratic opponents. Such alliances were usually short-lived, since the moderates typically turned on the extremists following either electoral success or the growing revulsion against the increasingly overt bigotry of the extremists.

While anti-Catholicism was the main source of religious bigotry in the nineteenth century, anti-Semitism, which was to become so important in the twentieth century, was also beginning to send up visible shoots. Growing out of the soil of rural America, particularly in the West, anti-Semitism first appeared in political literature in the United States in the 1870's as part of the agrarian response to the Depression of 1873. Agrarian protest organizations blamed the decline of farm prices and the other economic difficulties of farmers on the banks which manipulated the value of money, held farm mortgages and charged high interest in New York and international exchanges.   In the late nineteenth century the international bankers who controlled these banks were often personified as Jews and financiers like the Rothschilds were treated as symbols of evil. The literature of the agrarian-based Populist Party of the 1890's sometimes talked darkly of international financial conspiracies designed to destroy America; some of the Populist leaders were overt anti-Semites as well as active APA members.

The APA, like the Know-Nothings, had considerable strength in the urban areas among workers, including trade unionists, particularly in Western states. Eugene Victor Debs, then a railroad union leader, found it necessary to wage a campaign against the divisive influence of the APA within union ranks. Populism, which had considerable support among provincial evangelical Protestants in the rural areas of mid-Western and Southern America, though in some communities linked to the APA, in general constituted an alternative rural form of protest against the urban cosmopolitan Eastern élites. And though strands of anti-Catholicism and anti-Semitism were present within it, on the whole the Populists defined the source of conspiracy which threatened their livelihood and social system in economic class terms, i.e. in the activities of bankers and businessmen. In a sense, both the APA and the Populists gave expression to a tendency of provincial Americans located away from the economically and culturally dominant cities of the East to regard these centres as dens of iniquity and economic exploitation. The process of pitting the provincial Americans, heavily small-town rural Protestant, against the secularized wealthy urban élites has been a continuous one in the political life of this country. As part of this process, after the turn of the century, some former Populists shifted their target from urban élites generally to the city-dwelling Catholics and Jews specifically.

The most prominent exponent of this new theme of bigotry was Tom Watson who had been the major Populist Party leader in the South. Watson had opposed the merger of the Populists with the Democrats in 1896. In various newspapers he continued the Populist diatribes against bankers, capitalists and railroad magnates, but also increasingly expounded a violent form of racial and religious bigotry directed at Catholics, Jews and Negroes. Watson's paper, *The Jeffersonian*, published in a small town in Georgia and circulated widely throughout the country, broadcast his contention that Jews and Catholics were united in a conspiracy to take over America. Watson became known before the United States entered World War I for his leadership in the effort to convict and later lynch an Atlanta Jew, Leo Franks, for the murder of a young girl. Watson seized on this case, and particularly on the efforts of Jews and liberals to defend Franks, as proof of the conspiracy of wealthy Jews to use and mistreat poor Christians.

Following World War I and during the prosperous decade of the 1920's, the United States experienced its most drastic period of repression, typified by the rise of the anti-Catholic, anti-Negro, anti-Semitic and anti-intellectual Ku Klux Klan. The Klan was founded in 1915 by the members of an organization originally set up by Watson to help convict Leo Franks. With an estimated membership in the 1920's of three to six million, the Klan drew its members not only from the South but from many northern states, and elected governors, mayors, and legislators all over the country.

It received considerable support in the burgeoning cities both in and out of the South—cities growing by virtue of the large number of recent small-town migrants. These migrants sought to preserve the rural values of their upbringing, and saw in the Klan a means to assure "law and order" in their new urban environment.

The Klan charged that Catholics and Jews had allied to dominate the cultural and economic life of the country and that in conjunction with the Communists they were seeking to take over the government by force.[2] The Klan also revived the charges that Catholics had been involved in the killings of Presidents Lincoln, Garfield and McKinley. It even argued that President Harding was mudered in 1923 by a secret undetectable Catholic weapon—presumably evidenced by the fact that his death certificate read "cause unknown" and autopsy was performed (it was generally agreed that Harding actually died of a coronary embolism). Anti-Semitism was also a leading Klan *leitmotif*. One Klan leader held that Jewish international bankers were responsible for starting World War I; others charged that the Jews had organized the Bolshevik Revolution and were behind Communism everywhere. Some Klan leaders combined the Catholic and Jewish conspiratorial themes, suggesting that Jews and Catholics were united in a plan to control the nation's press, economy, and political life. They pointed to New York as an example of a depraved city controlled by Jews and Catholics.

Given the concern with changing values, new "freer" ideas, and the loss of religious values, it is not surprising that the Klan leaders also attacked intellectuals, whom they identified with the growth of "liberalism". They were described by a Klan leader as "one of the chief menaces of the country, instead of the sane intellectual leaders they should be. They give an almost joyous welcome to alien criticism of everything American."

Although the Klan attacked immigrants and Negroes, who were economically deprived, it did not see itself as a conservative defender of white Protestant priveleges. Rather, according to Emerson Loucks, the most successful Klan spokesmen found that the best way to appeal to prospective followers was by creating "the native white Protestant not as belonging to the predominant and controlling group . . . but as the oppressed poor, oppressed sufferer, plundered by foreigners, tricked by 'Jesuits' and robbed of his birthright by scheming descendants of Abraham." Ironically, they too appealed to "the sympathy generally shown by the mass of Americans to the underdog, the fellow they feel hasn't had a fair chance." Thus the Klan, like its predecessors from

[2] At this period Negroes were not felt to be as much of a threat as Catholics or or Jews; although the Klan was strongly against Negro equality, its attacks of the early 20's did not fall on Negroes as heavily as on Catholics or Jews.

the Anti-Masons on, linked itself to the anti-élitist and equalitarian tradition of the country, while spreading bigotry.

The '20s also saw the emergence of Henry Ford as a respected spokesmen for right-wing extremism and religious prejudice. Through his violently anti-Semitic newspaper, the *Dearborn Independent*, Ford reached more than seven hundred thousand readers. For years the *Dearborn Independent* hammered away at the theme of an international Jewish conspiracy. A series of 80 articles in the paper were reprinted in book form as *The International Jew: The World's Foremost Problem.* More than half a million copies of this extremely anti-Semitic book were distributed throughout the US. The articles in it bore such titles as "Jewish Gamblers Corrupt American Baseball", "How the Jewish Song Trust Makes You Sing", "Jew Wires Direct Tammany's Gentile Puppets", "The Scope of Jewish Dictatorship in America", "The Jewish Associates of Benedict Arnold". In short, Ford blamed the Jews for everything from Communism to jazz, immorality, and short skirts.

Ford would not be of much interest to the story of political prejudice had he not been boomed as a possible presidential candidate in 1923. Then at the height of his well-publicized campaign of anti-Semitism, he was widely supported across the country. In fact, one of the early opinion polls reported that 35 per cent of its respondents preferred Ford for President.

Henry Ford's activities dramatized the entry into the American political arena of full-scale anti-Semitism. The Jews were eminently vulnerable to the new turn in conspiracy theory: they were visible in both radical and capitalist circles, although their numbers were wildly exaggerated. They were also castigated in the contemporary conspiracy theories that had been spawned for political purposes in Germany and in Tsarist Russia.

It is interesting to note the continuity in the conspiracy literature of the Right. The Ku Klux Klan reprinted and circulated many books and stories about Catholic activities which had originated with the Know-Nothings or their predecessors. Ford and the Klan repeated reports about the efforts of Jewish international bankers to control and undermine the American financial system which had first emerged among the agrarian and Populist movements of the 1870's and 1890's. Most interesting of all were the renewed references to the conspiracy of the Illuminati. The staid *Christian Science Monitor* published an editorial in 1920, "A Jewish Peril?", which seriously discussed for a column and a half whether the Elders of Zion or the Illuminati were behind various revolutionary events and political turmoil from Russia to America. The *Dearborn Independent* reminded its readers that, on two occasions in early American history, men had become aware that the country was threatened by hidden conspiratorial forces, *i.e.* in 1798, when the Illuminati had first been attacked, and in the late 1820's, during the campaign against the Masons. Ford's paper, however, argued that these earlier campaigns had failed because they had not realized that the true conspirators were the Jews, that the Illuminati were only a front for the Elders of Zion.

The 1920's not only had its extremist movements, such as the Klan, and its extremist political figures, such as Henry Ford; it also wrote its racial, ethnic, and religious bigotry and its moral absolutism into law. Thus the period between the end of World War I and the mid-1920's saw the enactment of the following: restrictive immigration legislation—legislation that not only limited the total number of immigrants very drastically but also set national quotas which clearly discriminated against people of non-Northern European, non-Protestant background, i.e. Catholics and Jews; the Prohibition Amendment outlawing alcoholic beverages; state laws barring people from wearing religious garb in schools that received tax exemptions; and laws prohibiting the teaching of evolution, particularly in the South.

All this legislation represented a significant victory for the forces of fundamentalism, nativism, xenophobia and moralism. Efforts to bring about such nativist and moralist restrictions have a long history going back almost to the beginning of the republic, but until the 1920's they achieved no widespread legislative success. Why should these crusades have won out in the 1920's? Why did the United States succumb at that time to a wave of repressive nationalist, moralistic, puritanical hysteria? There is no way, of course, to answer these questions with absolute certainty, but the analyses of this period by historians and social scientists suggest that these rightist actions represented the fear of many groups that persistent social change was finally destroying the kind of America they believed in, the Protestant America in which they had been reared.

Perhaps the most palpable sign of such social change was the growth of the cities. The rural-urban rivalry cited earlier was made much more pointed by the rapidly increasing urbanization of the country. The 1920 census reported that for the first time the rural population had become a minority in the United States. The big cities were the centres of communications and of visible cultural influence. They were also the centres of settlement of the tremendous waves of immigrants who had come from the non-Protestant areas of Europe. Most of the immigration from the 1890's to World War I was Catholic, Orthodox Christian or Jewish. Relatively little, proportionate to the total group, came from Northern European Protestant countries. By World War I and after, this influx was reflected in the visibly growing political power of Catholics through the urban Democratic machines and in the power of the rising Jewish middle class. The cities which were dominating the economy and political life of the country seemed to be controlled by the large numbers of non-Protestant immigrants. The rapidly growing cities, of course, contained large numbers of Protestants, many of them workers who had migrated from rural areas. This group provided the Klan with a considerable low-status urban base which resented and resisted the political power of the urban Democratic machines and the cultural liberalism of the urban cosmopolitan élites. And outside the urban areas the Klan drew strength from evangelical Protestants living in the small towns and rural areas who began to feel that they were isolated provincials, far from the mainstream, while the cities were controlled by élites with different values, attitudes and customs. As one Ku Klux Klan leader put it poignantly, "We have become strangers in the land of our fathers."

The earlier pre-twentieth century expressions of mass bigotry and belief in conspiracy theories had each arisen during periods marked by the sharp decline of the party supported by evangelical Protestants, Federalists, Whigs and Republicans. 1920 was also a year of drastic shift in party fortunes, but this time it was the Republican Party which gained. The conservative restorative politics of Warren Harding were endorsed by over 60 per cent of the electorate, the largest percentage ever received by a Republican, while the incumbent Democrats fell to little more than a third of the vote. Although the Klan in the North largely worked in and with the Republican Party in many states, clearly partisan weakness was not a source of Klan strength. Rather it would appear that the rise of the Klan, the appeal of Henry Ford, and the massive increase in the Republican support, each reflected, in different ways, the desire of many Americans to restore an America changed by war, urbanization and heavy waves of non-Nordic immigration, to once more reflect the values of rural moralistic Protestant society.

The Republican Party itself adapted to this shift in mood of its supporters. Campaigning for the presidency in 1920, Warren Harding spoke of the dangers to America inherent in "racial differences" and recommended that the United States should only admit immigrants whose background indicated that they could develop "a full consecration to American practices and ideas". His Vice-President and successor as President, Calvin Coolidge, wrote shortly before the new administration took office in 1921 that "biological laws show that Nordics deteriorate when mixed with other races". James J. Davis, Harding's and Coolidge's Secretary of Labour, went even further to argue for immigration restrictions on the ground that the older Nordic "immigrants to America were the beaver type who built up America, whereas the newer immigrants were rat-men trying to tear it down; and obviously rat-men could never become beavers." The third of the trio of Repubican Presidents of the twenties, Herbert Hoover, also joined the chorus at the beginning of the decade when, speaking as Secretary of Commerce, he declared that "immigrants now lived in the

United States on sufferance . . . and would be tolerated only if they behaved."

In reaction to a growing sense of displacement, the Protestant non-metropolitan Republicans of the North joined with the Protestant Democrats in the South against the big city Democrats in the 1920's. This first Dixiecrat-Republican coalition led to the passage of prohibition, restrictions in immigration, and other repressive legislation already mentioned. Although their successes could be taken as indices of the strength of these provincial and evangelical Protestant groups, it is probably more accurate to regard them as reflecting a backlash occurring at the very time when these interest groups were losing out. During the nineteenth century most Americans could have been described as white, Protestant, rural, small-town residents. Yet, all during the time that they constituted an overwhelming majority, their more extreme beliefs—nativist, fundamentalist, prohibitionist—were not massively incorporated into legislation. It was only as the group was declining, as it began to see other groups and other values taking over, that the necessary impetus—in this case, fear—was provided to enact these values into law.

The rights of dissenters got shrift during this period. On federal, state and local levels, officials' actions limited the rights of political opposition through explicit legislation, legislative investigations, and administrative fiat. In the hunt for radicals, the Department of Justice was guilty of illegal search and seizure, of intimidating interrogation, of levying excessive bail and of denial of counsel. Official action was matched by repressive private action, which included tarring and feathering and, in some instances, lynching political offenders. These offenders were typically regarded as being of the "wrong" colour, the "wrong" religion, the "wrong" ethnic stock.

The hysteria of the '20s gradually died away. It died partly because, as in the case of the Klan, the causes which it espoused were relatively successful. It declined also because its excesses, its use of violence, led the more respectable elements who had either supported or tolerated it in its early period to drop away and help turn the fire of community social pressure on it. The Klan lost much of its middle-class support by 1924 and increasingly remained as a declining organisation of less-educated workers and farmers. It failed finally because these movements, like the APA, and the Know-Nothings before it, were composed of extremists who tended to turn on each other in a bitter, aggressive and paranoid way and thus to split up. The last gasp of the bigotry of the 1920's was the highly prejudicial anti-Catholic campaign against the presidential candidacy of Al Smith in 1928.

As in the case of the previous mass expressions of bigotry, the hysteria

M-9

proved hard to maintain beyond a few years, but the legislation enacted during the '20s had long-lasting effects. Prohibition continued until 1933 with disastrous consequences for attitudes toward law and order. Biased immigration quotas lasted until just a few years ago. Although much of the politically restrictive legislation has been voided by the Supreme Court, some of it still remains on the books.

The decade of the '30s—with its massive economic depression, unemployment, and political pressures linked to revolutionary events in Europe—witnessed its share of extremist movements. Both left-wing groups gained adherents in this difficult period. The list of rightist proto-Fascist movements is almost endless: the Silver Shirts of William Pelley, the Black Legion of the Midwest, the Christian Defenders of Gerald Winrod, the Union for Social Justice of Father Coughlin, the Commitee of One Million of Gerald L. K. Smith, and so on. No one knows how many active members these groups had or how many others agreed with them.

Studies of the support of these groups indicate that they appealed heavily to the more religious, less educated and more provincial elements among both Protestants and Catholics. Their conspiratorial charges were directed mainly against Jews and Communists but occassionally also against Catholics. Gerald Winrod, a principal Protestant fundamentalist figure, was pro-Nazi and virulently anti-Catholic and anti-Semitic, and was given to ominous warnings about the plots of the Elders of Zion.

The most important of these right-wing extremists was the Catholic priest, Charles Coughlin. The Coughlinite movement demonstrated that many Catholics could hate just as well as Protestants could. Openly anti-Semitic and increasingly pro-Fascist, Father Coughlin had an audience of millions for his weekly radio programme. Reliable opinion polling, which began in the mid-'30s, showed that Coughlin's views were endorsed by more than 25 per cent of the adult population. His ideology sounded leftist to many since he strongly opposed private ownership of the banks and placed the responsibility for the Depression on the desire for profit of international bankers, most of whom were identified as Jews.

It is interesting that both Winrod and Coughlin believed in the continued existence of the conspiracy of the Illuminati, that the same society which had supposedly organized the French Revolution had fostered the emergence of subsequent revolutionary movements, including the Russian Revolution and now influenced the New Deal. Winrod, however, identified the Illuminati as the source of a Jesuit-Jewish alliance to dominate the world. Coughlin naturally did not speak of Catholic involvement but did link the Illuminati, and occasionally the Masons, with the efforts of the Elders of Zion and other Jewish groups to advance Communism.

The high point of Coughlin's support was attained early in 1936. His organization, the National Union for Social Justice, probably had close to a million members, reached out with organized groups through most of the country, and had a much larger population listening sympathetically to his weekly broadcasts. Most Congressional candidates endorsed by Coughlin in the 1936 primaries won their nomination fights. He disrupted the base of his support, however, by trying to turn his movement into a third party, the Union Party, behind the presidential candidacy of William Lemke. By so doing, Coughlin ran into the perennial difficulty of such efforts, their inability to prevent sympathetic voters from backing the "lesser evil" between the two major party choices. In this case, many underprivileged Coughlinites who were benefiting from the extensive programme of the New Deal chose to vote for Franklin Roosevelt. Lemke, who had the backing of eight per cent of the electorate in July according to the Gallup Poll, wound up with less than two per cent of the vote. Coughlin, thereupon, dissolved his National Union organization and temporarily withdrew from politics. Although he returned soon after, forming a new but much smaller organization of supporters and voicing much more explicit and virulent racist appeals, he never recovered from the failure of the Union Party campaign.

In the latter years of the '30s, the Coughlinites and the myriad of other bigoted movements strongly opposed American intervention in World War II, since they tended to support the Nazis. Indeed, various opinion surveys indicate that close to half the population had strong anti-Semitic atittudes at a time when the Nazis were riding high in Europe. But the impact of Pearl Harbour and, in some cases, direct government action killed these movements during World War II.

Following the war, racial tensions and concern with communism supplanted anti-Catholicism and anti-Semitism as the most salient sources of conspiratorial belief. The major racist efforts in this postwar period date from the Supreme Court's desegregation decision in 1954. That decision prompted the formation of White Citizens' Councils and other groups aimed at throttling the struggle for Negro equality. The most prominent right-wing movement of the early '50s, however was *not* racist. It was the anti-communist movement spearheaded by Senator Joseph McCarthy which emerged in 1950. McCarthy tended to concentrate his attention on the conspiratorial sources of the failures of American foreign policy; these failures, he claimed, represented the work of undetected communist agents who had infiltrated both the government and the key opinion-forming and policy-controlling institutions of the society. McCarthy alleged that these agents were particularly strong among the social elite, the graduates of Groton and Harvard, those who ran the newspapers, professors in the universities, the heads of the foundations, the personnel of the State Department and so on. He thus appealed to the status strains of many socially and economically inferior segments of the society and transposed into a new key the conspiracy theme that has characterized so much of American extremist politics. Analysis of opinion poll data bearing on support for McCarthy's activities indicated that it came disproportionately from the less-privileged strata, especially those among his Catholic co-religionists, and in ethnic groups, German and Irish, and sections of the country, the Mid-west particularly, which had been opposed to American entry into World War II.

Again typifying the conservative party's repeated reaction to extremist groups, many moderate leaders in the Republican Party generally encouraged McCarthy before 1953, seeing in his activities an opportunity to win over the support of many underprivileged Democrats, particularly Catholics, who reacted strongly against the rise of communism abroad and the seeming decline of American world power. Richard Rovere has suggested that this behaviour was a consequence of Republican reaction to Truman's unanticipated victory over Dewey in the 1948 elections. Republican congressional triumphs in 1946, plus optimistic reports from the opinion polls, had led party leaders to anticipate that, after sixteen years in opposition, they were about to take office. Defeat following on this sharp increase in their level of expectation undermined their commitment to the conventional rules of the political game and led them, like the Federalists and Whigs earlier, to tolearte or encourage the use of extremist tactics. Victory in the 1952 elections ended their need to rely on such measures. McCarthy's insistence on continuing his attack against the governmental élite, now in the hands of Republicans, ultimately resulted in his censure in 1954 by the Senate. Thereafter, he almost totally disappeared from sight; the mass media which had given extensive publicity to his attacks simply stopped covering him. His mass support, which also declined, may have been responding to these changes at the élite level as well as to the end of the Korean War which occurred about the same time.

After the McCarthy movement collapsed a host of smaller right-wing groups emerged. Some of them have focused on the Jews and Communists and have charged that the civil rights movements and efforts to improve the situation of Negroes are part of a Jewish-Communist conspiracy. The most publicized movement of the '60s, the John Birch Society, has not been anti-Semitic but it strongly opposes the civil rights movements. It has subscribed to the conspiracy theory, identifying many of the economic and social trends which it opposes as a consequence of the efforts of a "hidden conspiracy of Insiders", i.e., our old friends, the Illuminati. The Birch Society attributes both the rise of the welfare state and the growth of the civil rights movement to an alleged Illuminati-controlled communist conspiracy.

In his pamphlet, *The Truth in Time,* Robert Welch, the head of the Society, credits the Illuminati with being responsible for both World Wars, the Russian Revolution, the break-up of the colonial empires, the formation of the United Nations, centralized banking, the personal income tax, the direct election of Senators in the United States, and "everything in the way of 'security' legislation, from the first Workmen's Compensation Acts under Bismarck to the latest Medicare monstrosity under Lyndon Johnson". Like Henry Ford, Welch sees continuity both in the conspiracy and in the opposition to it. Thus he identifies with the Anti-Masonic movement of the early nineteeth century, stating that just as the Illuminati killed William Morgan, an opponent of Freemasonry whose kidnapping and disappearance in 1826 led to the formation of the Anti-Masonic movement, they had also eliminated Senator Joseph McCarthy when he became aware of their activities.

In an unsigned Introduction to a 1967 Birch Society edition of Robison's book, *Proofs of a Conspiracy,* first published in 1798, the Society makes clear who it thinks the Illuminati were and are:

> This was a conspiracy conceived, organized and activated by professionals and intellectuals, many of them brilliant, but cunning and clever, who decided to put their minds in the service of total evil . . . One tends to think of professors, philosophers and writers as sitting in their ivory towers, perfectly harmless to the world. Robison and history proved otherwise. . . From Woodrow Wilson—himself a professor—to Lyndon Johnson, we have had nothing but Presidents surrounded by professors and scholars. . . All of which brings to mind Weishaupt's plan to surround the ruling authorities with members of his Order.

And in discussing the current activities of the Illuminati, the Birch Society Introduction states that they no longer use Freemasonry. "Their main habitat these days seems to be the great subsidized universities, tax-free foundations, mass media communication systems, and a myriad of private organisations, such as the Council on Foreign Relations."

The Society, on the whole, eschews appeals to religious and racial bigotry, placing the brunt of its attack on the Illuminati and their Communist agents. It has expelled various members and some prominent leaders for anti-Semitic activities and statements. Although strongly against any efforts to foster civil rights or improve the socio-economic conditions of the black population through governmental action, it seeks to find conservative Negroes whose activities it can identify with and support. The tenor of its attacks on the civil rights movement, however, frequently leads Birchers to write and speak about Negroes in terms which can only be described as racist. It also strongly supports the rights of white minorities to rule in South Africa and Rhodesia on the grounds that they constitute the only real alternative to communism or anarchy.

Given its strong ideological attack on all forms of the welfare state and trade unionism, the Society has little or no appeal to the underprivileged. Analyses of the social composition of its membership, as well as of the six per cent or so of populations interviewed by opinion pollsters who are favourable to the Birch Society, indicate that it derives its support from a relatively affluent, well-educated stratum. Seemingly, according to studies of the Society's membership by Fred Grupp, Murray Havens, and Burton Levy, they come from the less prestigious segment of the affluent, those who did not finish college or went to inferior ones. Their top leaders tend to be heads of family-owned corporations located in relatively small provincial cities. Like the APA and the Klan, Birch Society chapters are more likely to be found in rapidly expanding communities, particularly in the South and West.

The combination of deep conspiratorial and ultra-conservative dogma has meant that the organization has remained relatively small (possibly 60,000 members at its height in 1965) and unpopular. Recognizing the difficulty of gaining wide support for its full programme, Robert Welch, the founder and head of the society, has defined its role as that of a vanguard organization modelling its tactics on that of the Communists, i.e., using "front organizations" in which Birch members can play controlling roles.

The largest and most important contemporary movement linked to racial concerns has been the American Independent Party headed by Governor George Wallace who ran for President in 1968. Almost every extreme right-wing group, almost every virulent racist in the country, backed Wallace. He produced a coalition of the Right such as probably never existed before, at least in the twentieth century. Birch Society members, in particular, played a leading role in the Wallace party and campaign organization in many states. In both his 1964 campaign in the Democratic presidential primaries and in his recent third party effort, Wallace made strong pro-Birch Society statements. His campaign speeches were clear, simple and insistent. Although he rarely mentioned Negroes as such, he campaigned strongly against government legislation which in any way involves enforcing integration or civil rights with respect to open housing, schools, unions, etc. He also spoke frequently about the need for force to deal with the breakdown in law and order, crime in the streets, and riots. Other frequent themes in his speeches dealt with fear of central government power generally and a concern for American weakness abroad, particularly as reflected in inability to win in Vietnam.

Unlike the Birch Society, however, which is explicitly élitist, Wallace directed an appeal to the common man of America who, he has argued, is brighter and more moral than the élite. His heroes are the taxi driver, the steel worker, the auto mechanic and the little man generally. He sees the "pseudo-intellectuals", in the form of college professors, the heads of the "tax-free" foundations, editors of leading newspapers and magazines, members of the Council on Foreign Relations, and high-ranking bureaucrats in Washington, as the source of evil and propagators of false doctrine. (The pseudo-intellectuals bear close resemblance to descriptions of the Illuminati in Birch Society literature.) Coming out of a Southern Populist tradition, he suggests the existence of an élitist conspiracy based on the Eastern Establishment. Thus, during the campaign he argued that the public opinion polls were being deliberately manipulated against him by the "Eastern money interest". Taking a leaf out of Senator Joseph McCarthy's book, he has identified Communism with the well-to-do rather than with the down-and-out, stating: "I don't believe all this talk about poor folks turning Communist. It's the damn rich who turn Communist. You ever seen a poor Communist?" Strongly antagonistic to the federal judiciary for their rulings on integration, the rights of Communists, and of defendants in criminal cases, Wallace proposed the plan first suggested by the Populists of the 1890's, the direct election of federal judges, a solution in line with his repeated emphasis on the moral and intellectual superiority of the common man.

Wallace's movement is not to be taken lightly. In the 1968 election Wallace received the support of 13.53 per cent of the electorate. His party was on the ballot in every state. This is no mean accomplishment. It is certainly the first time in half a century that a third party has been on the ballot in every state, which shows the degree of organization and competency of this movement. The strength of Wallace's appeal was even greater than the vote he received indicates. Both the Gallup and Harris Polls reported at the end of September that 21 per cent of the electorate preferred him to Humphrey or Nixon. As Election Day approached the Wallace supporters, recognizing that he could not win, began to feel the pressure to vote for the "lesser evil". Yet Wallace was able to retain more of his backing against such pressure than any other third party candidate in almost half a century. And it should be noted that, when the Gallup Poll inquired on a number of occasions in 1968, not how people intended to vote, but whether they approved or disapproved generally of George Wallace, more than 40 per cent indicated approval. But even granted the election showing represents his full support—votes for Wallace are more than a minor following.

Wallace finds his support in the same sorts of people sociologically as those who backed the earlier movements. They are disproportionately rural or small-town dwellers and Protestants (although he has considerable Catholic strength). They are likely to be less educated and poorer than the population at large. Outside of white Southern racist support, the largest segment of his backing in the 1968 election came from manual workers, many of them trade unionists. A special national poll of union members conducted by Gallup organization for the *New York Times* early in October reported that 25 per cent of them supported Wallace. A referendum conducted within the United Automobile Workers among elected local and regional *officers* found over 10 per cent choosing the American Independent Party nominee. A number of trade union locals in the North actually endorsed his candidacy. Journalists reported deep concern on the part of union leaders concerning their membership's enthusiasm for Wallace.

Many of these workers, who are steadily employed, are purchasing their own homes in neighbourhoods which are relatively close to expanding black areas and, bothered by higher taxes, are opposed to the welfare programme as a system which taxes the hardworking to help the lazy and unfit. To a considerable extent they identify these groups with the Negroes. Since white union members are much more likely to live inside the central cities than the more affluent middle class, they are also more directly and personally concerned with the problem of increased urban crime and with efforts at integrating urban school systems through modifying the concept of the neighbourhood school. Many workers see the pressures for school desegregation as coming from the well-educated middle-class which lives in the suburbs or sends its children to private schools. The issue for them has become one of the well-to-do forcing the white working-class to send its children to school with black children.

This disproportionate support given to George Wallace by American workers, a phenomenon akin to the backing received by the Know-Nothings, the APA, the Ku Klux Klan, the Coughlinite Christian Front, and Senator Joseph McCarthy, contradicts the assumption of many who identify the working-class and trade unionism with support for progressive social objectives. This phenomeoon of working-class endorsement for bigotry *and* for trade unionism and the welfare state coincides with the results of various sociological surveys which have found that the less-educated (and, therefore, also poorer) people are, the more likely they are to be prejudiced against minority groups and to be intolerant of deviance generally. Conversely, however, the less well-to-do a group, the more disposed it is to favour liberal-left policies with regard to issues such as the position of trade unions, social security, economic planning and the like. Workers and the less affluent generally vote for liberal-left parties because they see these parties as defenders of their economic and class interests against the conservatives who are identified in their minds with the well-to-do and big business. A candidate who seeks to appeal to their racial sentiments, but is also visibly opposed to their economic interests, such as Barry Goldwater in 1964, cannot gain their votes.

George Wallace, however, shied away from such positions and sought to identify the pressures for Negro equality and integration with the

Eastern Establishment and the intellectual élite. Not being a Republican also probably helped his image with many workers. They can more easily vote for a candidate and party which appeals to the common man than for a candidate and party which they identify with the wealthy. And Wallace did make a direct appeal for such support on economic lines by calling for a sharp increase in Social Security payments and for doubling the personal exemption on the income tax, a change which would particularly benefit the less affluent. His party platform also proposed liberalizing payments under the Medicare programme. It may be significant to note that the Harris Poll reported that many more Wallace supporters in the North chose the term "radical" to describe his political outlook than identified him as a "conservative".

Not surprisingly, the opinion polls indicated that Wallace supporters in the North tended to come from Democratic ranks (and those who abandoned Wallace before Election Day seemed to have voted for Hubert Humphrey). The opinion analyst, Samuel Lubell, reported in late October 1968 that "Pro-Wallace supporters in the northern cities ... voice strong working-class views which prevent them from voting Republican. . . Most of these Wallace followers maintain, 'Wallace is for the workingman. He couldn't be for anyone else.' Some even talk of the Wallace movement as 'the start of a new labour party'."

One relatively low-status occupation group which has been reported as heavily involved in the ranks of Wallace supporters is policemen. In this respect also the American Independent Party resembles its predecessors on the extreme right. Data bearing on the membership of the American Protective Association in the 1890's, of the Ku Klux Klan of the '20s and '50s, of the Black Legion and the Coughlinite Christian Front of the '30s, and of the Birch Society in the '60s, have indicated the disproportionate presence of policemen in their ranks.

A number of elements in their social background and work experience predisposes them to racial bigotry. As Gunnar Mydral noted almost three decades ago, they tend to be recruited from the lower-status and less-educated segments of the population. A recent study of the New York police describes the typical police recruit as being of "working-class background, high school education or less, average intelligence, cautious personality". Prejudice against Negroes is greater among persons with such backgrounds. Police work tends to reinforce and intensify such feelings since it brings policemen into contact with the worst elements in the Negro community.

The policemen's role is also particularly subject to creating feelings of resentment against society flowing from status discrepancies. On one hand, he is given considerable authority by society to enforce its law and is expected to risk his life if necessary; on the other, he receives little prestige and relatively low salary. A number of studies of the police report a common complaint that they are not respected by the public. And overt hostility and even contempt for the police are often voiced by spokesmen for liberal and left groups, and intellectuals. Insofar as the police find any segment of the body politic showing appreciation for their contribution to society, and for the risks they take, it is from conservatives, and particuarly from the far right. Thus, the slogan "Support your local police" was enunciated by the Ku Klux Klan in the early '20s, revived by the Birch Society in the '60s, and placed on the auto license plates of the state of Alabâma by George Wallace when he was Governor. The Birch Society has established awards for heroic policemen and has set up a fund for the support of the families of police killed in the line of duty. George Wallace went out of his way in campaign speeches to praise the police and to denounce their liberal intellectual critics.

Within the strata which disproportionately backed George Wallace, young people have been prevalent. Gallup and Harris surveys reported in October 1968 that 25 per cent, one out of every four, between 21 and 29 years old, were for Wallace, as contrasted with 20 per cent among the older groups. This phenomenon of disproportionate youth support for an extremist racist candidate has largely been ignored by those who have identified young America with left-wing campus demonstrators and student volunteers for Kennedy and McCarthy. In a real sense, the New Right of George Wallace, like the New Left, are both a direct outgrowth of a process of political polarization which emerged around the efforts to secure desegregation from the late '50s on. Many of the liberal white university students who joined the civil rights movement began to despair of American democracy when they witnessed authority in the South violating the law in order to preserve segregation. The tactics of civil disobedience and sitings first emerged among the student Left as a response to the civil disobedience initiated by such white segregationist leaders as Ross Barnett of Mississipi, Lester Maddox of Georgia and George Wallace of Alabama. At the same time, however, many white youth in the South and in the urban working-class areas of the North grew up during a period in which the issue of integration within their schools and communities has been salient. They were reared in an atmosphere in which the voicing of anti-Negro sentiments in their homes and neighbourhoods was common, in which members of the older generation discussed their fears concerning the adverse consequences of school or residential integration. Hence, while the upper-middle class scions of liberal parents were being radicalized to the left, southern and northern working-class youth were being radicalized to the right. The consequences of such polarization can be seen in the behaviour of the two groups in the 1968 election campaign.

The indications that the Wallace movement draws heavily among youth are congruent with the evidence from various studies of youth and student politics that young people are disposed to support the more extreme or idealistic version of the politics dominant within their social group. In Europe, radical movements, both of the left and the right, have been much more likely to secure the backing of the young than the democratic parties of the cenrtre. Being less committed to existing institutions and parties than older people, being less inured to the need to compromise to achieve objectives, youth are attracted to movements and leaders who promise to resolve basic problems quickly in an absolute fashion. Unfortunately as yet little data exist bearing on the extent to which the earlier American rightist movements also drew from youth.

The conclusion that concern over race and the related issues of "law and order" was the dominant sentiment among Wallace voters was borne out by the national opinion surveys. The pollster Louis Harris reported:

> The common bond that sews together this unusual assortment of political allies in this election is dominantly race. A heavy 73 per cent of all Wallace supporters want progress for Negroes to be halted. Almost as many, 67 per cent, say that they "feel uneasy personally due to the prospect of race riots in their own community".

Feeling about racial issues is, of course, not the only factor which has fostered the emergence of a New Right. The Wallace movement has disproportionate support among farmers and residents of small towns who are rarely in contact with the Negroes. Many in these groups appear to be responding to a concern over the changes in American religious and cultural beliefs. They are often religious or secular fundamentalists. They oppose changes in that old-time religion and/or in the traditional American individualist Way of Life. The religious fundamentalists, concentrated in rural areas and small towns or among migrants from such places to big cities, feel deprived by the fact that American society has become cosmopolitan and metropolitan. Fundamentalist values are treated as provincial and anachronistic by those who control the mass media and the cultural life of the nation. These cultural trends have, of course, intensified with the passage of time and to a considerable extent now dominate the major theological tendencies within both Protestantism and Catholicism. This now definitely minority group of traditionalist Christians has become a principal source of support for a politics of alienation and nostalgia. And to the resentments of the religious fundamentalists are joined those of many not particularly religious people who are deeply disturbed by changes in secular values.

It should be noted, however, that except among the minority of committed extremists, the Wallace movement as such failed to make headway with the bulk of affluent and better educated upper- and middle-class conservatives. A national opinion survey by *The New York Times* in mid-October 1968 of the presidents of *all* the companies whose shares are listed in the New York Stock Exchange, conducted by the anonymous questionnaire technique, reported that less than half of one per cent (three men) were for Wallace while 85 per cent endorsed Nixon, and 13 per cent backed Humphrey. While Wallace had more support in lower levels of the business and professional community, particularly in the South, it is clear from the polls that this stratum was also disproportionately opposed to him. Most of these people, though economic conservatives, are not afraid that the country is being taken over by Negroes or other minority groups and are not alienated from the body politic. Insofar as they are politically motivated, they are active in the Republican Party. In California they united in 1966 behind Ronald Reagan who embodies these conservative virtues. On a local and Congressional level they could find many candidates with kindred opinions within the GOP in 1968. Richard Nixon, who supported Goldwater in 1964 and who in turn was strongly supported by him before the Republican Convention in 1968, though not as conservative as some of them would like, still was sufficiently close to such views to retain their support.

The Wallace movement clearly is not a conservative tendency. Rather, it is a movement of the alienated adherents of religious and secular fundamentalism. It appeals to those who really feel threatened by the rise of the Negro in the cities, by the changes in the moral order which they can witness nightly on television, by the changing content of Protestantism and Catholicism, by mini-skirts, and by the decline of the United States on the world scene. There are many such frustrated individuals in America today. George Wallace has found a way of reaching many of them. In a real sense, he is trying to build a Poujadist movement out of those who reject "modernism".

The reactionary movements of the 1960's—the Wallace movement, the Birch Society, the Christian Crusade of Billy James Hargis and others— resemble the backlash politics that swept the country in the 1920's, many continue to be out of step with the dominant cultural trends of the society and to feel bitter about the decline of traditional Christian morality. It remains to be seen how powerful they will be this time. On the one hand their base in fundamentalists living in small towns and rural areas no longer constitutes the near-majority it did in the 1920's; now it represents only a small minority. But this group has been joined by the scions of the immigrants in the large cities, many of them Catholics, threatened by the inroads made by Negroes. Many of them react today to the growth in urban Negro population much as white Protestant workers reacted to the Catholic immigration in the nineteenth century.

The racial resentments of the provincial fundamentalist Protestants, including many who have moved to large cities, and of the children of immigrants, are playing a major role in the realignment of American politics
occurring in the 1960's. Once again their resentments are contributing
to the ranks of the more conservative of the two major parties as well as
making possible the rise of explicitly racially-oriented parties and movements. The fears of these people have been expressed in recent years by
many mayoral candidates, such as Louise Day Hicks in Boston, as well
as by a number of prominent right-wing Republicans who have appealed
to racism indirectly by discussing the dangers of crime in the streets, riots
or open housing legislation. Clearly, though many of them have not openly
talked about Negroes and race, they can say, as Mrs. Hicks did, "You know
where I stand."

Once again it must be said that a leader of the Republicans, Richard
Nixon, has sought to refurbish the strength of his party among traditional
Democratic supporters by appealing to those who have shown a readiness
to abandon their party allegiance in favour of a racist candidate. As *The
New York Times* (12 October, 1968, p. 10E) reported, using "the Wallace
slogan, 'Stand up for America,' he lauds Senator Strom Thurmond [the
presidential candidate of an earlier effort to create a third pro-segrega-
tionist party in 1948] as a man 'who has stood up for his state and will
stand up for America and I'm glad to stand with him today.'" Many
analysts of the 1968 election have described the campaign tactics of the
Republican Vice-Presidential candidate, Spiro Agnew, as an effort to "out-
Wallace Wallace". He spoke out repeatedly in strong terms about the
need to crack down on threats to law and order, explained the fact that
he did not campaign in Negro areas by saying "if you've seen one ghetto
area, you've seen them all", described Hubert Humphrey as "soft on Communism", and attacked "phony intellectuals [Wallace's favourite target] who
don't understand what we mean by hard work and patriotism". Since
Agnew maintained his Wallace-like posture throughout the campaign, there
can be little doubt that he was fulfilling a role assigned to him by party
strategists, i.e. to show Wallace-supporters that they could get what they
wanted from the Republican Party. Thus the major consequence of the
Wallace movement may be that it, like the Anti-Masonic and the Know-
Nothing American Parties, will serve as a transmission belt to bring the
more bigoted Democrats to the opposition conservative party which adapts
its policies to accommodate their concerns.

There is a real danger, however, that George Wallace will try to mobilize
his supporters in a new mass movement which, like some of the earlier
ones, will engage in extra-parliamentary confrontationist tactics including
taking to the streets to intimidate opponents. During the campaign he
openly discussed the possibility of a "white revolution" should be fail

to win, directed toward forcing the state governments "to physically take over the schools" to end integration. As he described the process, there would first be mass rallies and protest demonstrations throught the country. The vigour of such protests would press the states to bring about a halt in federal interference in local school policies. Wallace has argued that the common people are ready for drastic action and boasts of the fact that many in his campaign audiences became hysterical when he discussed law and order and school integration. Clearly, Wallace has been toying with the idea of turning his electoral party into a mass movement which will take to the streets to counter the activities of the "anarchists", the demonstrations and riots in the ghettoes and on the campuses. The implications of such an endeavour for the future of democratic politics in the United States are obvious.

As a final evaluative point, it is imporant to recognize that all of the earlier movements discussed here have been short-lived, even though most of them involved millions of people in their activities. Various analysts have explained their rise as a result of basic endemic tension-creating processes, explanations which imply that some of them should have continued to exist for much longer than they did, since the conditions which supposedly gave rise to them continued while the movements declined or died. Thus, the hey-day of the Anti-Masons was from 1828 to 1832. The Know-Nothing American Party was able to win elections in many states in the years 1854-1857, but quickly dwindled away thereafter. The American Protective Association became a multi-million member alliance in 1892-94 but disintegrated by 1896. The Ku Klux Klan presumably recruited close to four milllion members between 1921 and 1924 and helped elect many governors and other officials. It was an important force at both major party national conventions in 1924. By 1925 it had lost much of its membership and by the late '20s it was a small group. The two largest movements of the 1930's, which had considerable support according to the opinion polls, were Huey Long's Share-Our-Wealth movement and the Coughlinite organizations. Long's movement, which was formed in 1934, totally vanished with his assassination in 1935: his second-in-command, Gerald L. K. Smith, could not find a handful to follow him. Coughlin's high point with respect to membership and popular support occurred in 1936. Thereafter, he led a declining movement which disappeared into limbo after Pearl Harbor. The phenomenon known as McCarthyism lasted four years, from 1950 to 1954.

Looking over this record suggests the need not only to determine the conditions under which different groups of Americans become disposed to form and join movements which are far outside of the American "consensus", but also why they decline so quickly. Some of them, e.g., the Anti-Masons and possibly the Ku Klux Klan, lost out after seemingly achieving their most prominent objectives. Others, like the APA, the Klan and McCarthy, lost support after segments of the more established elements which supported them in their early period turned against them, either because they had achieved some of "their" objectives, i.e., the political defeat of their opponents, or because the extremist tactics of the movements make it difficult for respectable individuals to remain identified with them. Some, like the Know-Nothings and the APA, splinter because they include many who differ widely on issues other than the main one which brought them into existence. A few, particularly the Klan, have declined after revelations that their leaders were involved in fraudulent activities or had begun to fight among themselves.

Although no one has presented an adequate general explanation for the the short-lived character of American protest movements, a few statements can be made. *First*, those which have tried the "third party" route have been unable to break through the constraints placed on such efforts by the American constitutional structure, which makes of the entire country one constituency for the one important election, that of the presidency. Like the Know-Nothings in 1856 and the Coughlinites in 1936, they wind up in presidential elections with much less support than they had previously. One of the major parties usually makes some efforts to appeal to their supporters, and many of them vote for the "lesser evil" on Election Day. The movements, as distinct from the parties, often attract leaders and activists whose values and personalities make it difficult for them to compromise on new issues facing the group. The intense factional struggles which often arise result in such acrimonious bickering as to discourage many of their members and supporters. Those movements which become more extreme in their tactics often find the more moderate groups withdrawing. The Establishment, in the form of the media, community, church and political leaders, ultimately unites to place extremist movements which show a capacity to survive outside the pale of socially tolerated activity. But whatever the cause of decline, the fact remains that all such extremist efforts have quickly subsided. And although the social strains which led millions to join or follow these movements presumably continued to exist, efforts to continue or revive them, once the process of decline has started, have invariably failed. There is no secular tendency connected with any of them.

This concludes a brief analysis of the appeals that have been made to racial and religious prejudice in efforts to preserve the status or values of groups with a prior claim to the American tradition. The story has been discouraging, but this does not mean that no changes occur. On the positive side one may point to the fact that overt support for bigotry has become much more shamefaced than in the past. No prominent American politician speaks directly about the negative traits of minority groups in the way that leading Whigs and Republicans did in the nine-

teenth and early twentieth centuries. Lest we forget, it should be noted
that the three Republican presidents of the 1920's—Harding, Coolidge and
Hoover—all openly spoke or wrote about the threat to American values posed by Americans of non-Anglo-Saxon backgrounds. Except in the South, no
politician dares any longer to attack Negroes by name. Racist appeals
of course continue, but they now take the form of discussion of the
"problems" created by unspecified groups. To the inhabitants of the ghetto
such changes may seem trivial, when men can still get elected by appealing to the fears and bigotry of whole sections of the population. Yet the
fact that the major party politicians who speak of the problems of law
and order also feel obliged to advance a programme which is ostensibly
designed to improve economic and educational conditions in the ghetto,
does attest to an improvement in the attitudes of white America. All the
opinion polls agree that there has been a decline in expressed anti-minority
attitudes whether these be towards Negroes, Catholics or Jews. It is striking to note, for example, that the religious affiliation of Robert Kennedy
and Eugene McCarthy was never mentioned during the 1968 campaign.

Given the existence of institutionalized sources of discrimination, such
a change in attitudes implies no more than unrealized potential. American
institutions are still fundamentally biassed in favour of whites, but Americans as a people are closer to expressing a belief in the American creed
of equality than they have ever been. Whether they believe in it deeply
enough to live by it is another question. The struggle for a genuinely
equalitarian society is obviously far from having been won. There will be
many reversals, but the long-term direction of the change remains consistent. Unfortunately, the pace of change is slow relative to needs. Thus
one can still safely predict that if we all come together a decade or two
hence to discuss patterns of prejudice there will be plenty of new evidence
of the propensity of Americans to organize to suppress others because of
their racial, religious or ethnic traits.

There is, of course, the additional problem posed by race. The fact that
race is such a visible chracteristic, the fact that Negroes cannot become
physically indistinguishable from other Americans simply by virtue of
changes in their educational and occupational status—this undoubtedly
means that racial prejudice is going to be much more difficult to eradicate
than religious or ethnic prejudices. But one observation about institutions
can give us some encouragement: the political system not only functions as
an arena within which religious or racial tensions can be expressed; it
also serves as the avenue through which minority groups have gained
first symbolic and later real power and status. Parties have nominated
and elected members of minority groups which have been disliked by the
great majority in order to gain the votes of the minority. As Gunnar Myrdal

pointed out a quarter of a century ago, many politicians who are personally prejudiced have often supported measures fostering equality. Electing
blacks to high office is an excellent way to improve the status of a group
traditionally stereotyped as lowly. Hence, in addition to measures directly
concerned with improving the educational and economic situations of
the black population, it is important that both major parties be pressed
to nominate and help elect black leaders. In this way a new and much
more hopeful chapter can be written in the doleful history of politics and
prejudice.

As a final note on the politics of prejudice, it is important to recognize
that right-wing political protest in America has almost invariably taken
on an anti-élitist and often specifically anti-intellectual cast. In spite of
the fact that such movements are seeking to preserve existing privileges
and traditional values, they reflect the deep commitment to egalitarianism
with the concomitant anti-élitism inherent in the American value system.
When bigoted movements attacked Catholics and Jews in the past, they
did so in part by identifying these groups with positions of political,
economic and cultural power. The Catholic danger to America was supposedly a result of deliberate conspiracy by the Catholic hierarchy and the
Pope, in league with Catholic politicians, to take over America and subject
it to their European élitist structure and values. The Jewish threat was
identified with the dire activities of international bankers. Even Communism must be presented as a threat flowing from within the élite, not
from the poor. And when ethnic élites have not been available as a target,
the focus of hostility has been directed against the Illuminati as the surro-
gate for the intellectuals.

The current upsurge of anti-intellectualism expressed by the Wallace
movement has repeated the oldest populist American conspiracy theme,
that which identifies changes in values and institutions with the deliberate
subversive efforts of the intellectual élite. The Negroes, on the other hand,
cannot be and are not identified as part of the élite. They, therefore, are
not the real villains; rather they are perceived as pawns manipulated by
the Illuminati, the Communists or the intellectuals, to achieve their subversive ends. Those involved in anti-civil rights movements can, therefore,
honestly feel that they are not racists, that they are not anti-Negro. The
poor Negro who seeks to move out of the ghetto, who desires to put his
child in an integrated school, who presses on white unions for membership,
is only a weak tool, more to be pitied than hated. That the Birch Society,
the Christian Crusade, or the American Independent Party, focus their
resentments on intellectuals rather than Negroes does not make the situation of the Negroes any better. It does point up, however, how the stress
on racial and religious bigotry in America may decline at the same time

that extremist movements designed to protect white supremacy and fundamentalist values are fostered. The enemy in America must always be associated with the élite, never with the common man, whether he be black
or white.

BIBLIOGRAPHICAL NOTE

THIS ARTICLE is based on research in process for a comprehensive book on the American
radical right in historical perspective by Earl Raab and myself, which hopefully
should appear in print published by Harper and Row during 1970. The detailed
sources, both published and unpublished, for many of the statements presented here
will be found in the above volume. Both this article and the larger book lean heavily
on the theoretical approach for the study of mass movements presented
in Neil Smelser, *A Theory of Collective Behavior* (New York: Free Press of Glencoe,
1963). Various of my previous writings deal with ideas and substantive work presented
here. These include: Chapters 4 "Working-Class Authoritarianism", and 5 " 'Fascism'
—Left, Right, and Centre", in *Political Man* (Garden City: Doubleday, 1960), pp.
97-178; two articles, "The Sources of the Radical Right" and "Three Decades of
the Radical Right: Coughlinites, McCarthyites, and Birchers", in Daniel Bell, Ed.,
The Radical Right (Garden City: Doubleday, 1963), pp. 259-377; chapter 9 "Party
Systems and the Representation of Social Groups", in *The First New Nation* (Garden
City: Doubleday-Anchor, 1967), pp. 327-65; chapters 2, 5, 8 and 9, "Revolution
and Counterrevolution: The United States and Canada", "Class, Politics, and Religion in Modern Society: The Dilemma of the Conservatives", "Religion and Politics
in the American Past and Present", and "The Right-Wing Revival and the 'Backlash'
in the United States", in *Revolution and Counterrevolution* (New York: Basic Books,
1968), pp. 31-63, 159-76, 246-332; "On Politics of Conscience and Extreme Commitment", *Encounter*, 31 (August 1968), 66-71; and George Wallace and the US New
Right", *New Society* 12 (3 October 1968), pp. 477-83.

Some of the literature which pertains to the movements discussed here may be
found in a variety of published works as well as in Masters' essays and Doctoral
dissertations. These include:

General Historical Works

Ray Allen Billington, *The Protestant Crusade, 1800-1860* (New York: Rinehart and
Company, 1938); John Higham, *Strangers in the Land; Pattern of American Nativism,
1860-1925* (New York: Atheneum, 1963); Gustavus Myers, *History of Bigotry in the
United States.* New York: Capricon Books, 1960); Edward J. Richter and Berton Dulce,
Religion and the Presidency (New York: Macmillan, 1962); Richard Hofstadter,
Anti-Intellectualism in American Life (New York: Alfred A. Knopf, 1963).

The Anti-Illumaniti Agitation and the Anti-Masonic Party

Richard Hofstadter, *The Paranoid Style in American Politics* (New York: Alfred A.
Knopf, 1965), esp. pp. 3-40; Vernon Stauffer, *New England and the Bavarian Illuminati*

(New York: Columbia University Press, 1918); John Robison, *Proofs of a Conspiracy* (Boston, Western Islands, 1967, first published in 1798); David Brion Davis, "Some Themes of Counter-Subversion: An Analysis of Anti-Masonic, Anti-Catholic and Anti-Mormon Literature", *Mississippi Valley Historical Review*, 47 (September 1960), pp. 205-24; Charles McCarthy, "The Anti-Masonic Party: A Study of Anti-Masonry in the United States, 1827-1840", *Annual Report of the American Historical Association for the Year 1902*, Vol. I (Washington, D.C.: Government Printing Office, 1903); Leland M. Griffin, *The Anti-Masonic Movement, 1826-1838* (Ph. D. Thesis: Department of Speech, Cornell University, 1950); Lorman A. Ratner, *Anti-Masonry in New York State* (M.A. Thesis: Department of Government, Cornell University, 1958); George H. Blakeslee, *The History of the Anti-Masonic Party* (Ph.D. Thesis: Department of History, Harvard University, 1903).

Nativist and Anti-Catholic Movements Before the Civil War

Ray Allen Billington, *op. cit.*; L. D. Scisco, *Political Nativism in New York State* (New York: Columbia University Press, 1901); Lee Benson, *The Concept of Jacksonian Democracy* (Princeton: Princeton University Press, 1961); Lawrence F. Schmeckebier, *History of the Know-Nothing Party in Maryland* (Baltimore: Johns Hopkins Press, 1899); John R. Mulkern, *The Know-Nothing Party in Massachusetts* (Ph.D. Thesis: Department of History, Boston University, 1963); Robert D. Parmet, *The Know-Nothings in Connecticut* (Ph.D. Thesis: Department of History, Columbia University, 1966); William G. Bean, *Party Transformation in Massachusetts with Special Reference to the Antecedents of Republicanism* (Ph.D. Thesis: Department of History, Harvard University, 1922); Leon D. Soule, *The Know-Nothing Party in New Orleans: A Reappraisal* (Ph.D. Thesis: Department of History, Tulane University, 1960).

Nativist and Anti-Catholic Movements in the Latter Part of the Nineteenth Century

John Higham, *op. cit.*; Charles L. Sewrey, *The Alleged "Un-Americanism" of the Church as a Factor in Anti-Catholicism in the United States, 1860-1914* (Ph.D. Thesis: University of Minnesota, 1955); Alvin P. Stauffer, *Anti-Catholicism in American Politics, 1865-1900* (Ph.D. Thesis: Department of History, Harvard University, 1933); Donald L. Kinzer, *An Episode in Anti-Catholicism: The American Protective Association* (Seattle: University of Washington Press, 1964); Irwin Unger, *The Greenback Era* (Princeton: Princeton University Press, 1964); Humphrey J. Desmond, *The APA Movement* (Washington: New Century Press, 1912); Priscilla F. Knuth, *Nativism in California, 1886-1897* (M.A. Thesis: Department of History, University of California, Berkeley, 1947).

Bigotry in the First Three Decades of the Twentieth Century

John Higham, *op. cit.*; Oscar Handlin, "American Views of the Jew at the Opening of the Twentieth Century", *American Jewish Historical Society*, 40 (1951), pp. 323-44; C. Vann Woodward, *Tom Watson: Agrarian Rebel* (New York: Oxford University Press, 1963); Leonard Dinnerstein, *The Leo Frank Case* (New York: Columbia University Press, 1968); David M. Chalmers, *Hooded Americanism: First Century of the Ku Klux Klan 1865 to the Present* (Garden City: Doubleday, 1965); Arnold Rice, *The Ku Klux Klan in American Politics* (Washington, D.C.: Public Affairs Press, 1962); Jonathan N. Leonard, *The Tragedy of Henry Ford* (New York: G. P. Putnam's Sons, 1922); William Preston, Jr., *Aliens and Dissenters: Federal Suppression of Radicals,*

1903-1933 (Cambridge: Harvard University Press, 1963); John Mecklin, *The Ku Klux Klan* (New York: Harcourt Brace, 1924); Emerson Loucks, *The Ku Klux Klan in Pennsylvania* (Harrisburg: Telegraph Press, 1936); Charles C. Alexander, *The Ku Klux Klan in the Southwest* (Lexington: University of Kentucky Press, 1965); Gordon W. Davidson, *Henry Ford: The Formation and Course of a Public Figure* (Ph.D. Thesis: Department of History, Columbia University, 1966); David L. Lewis, *Henry Ford: A Study in public Relations* (Ph.D. Thesis: Department of History, University of Michigan, 1959); Carey McWilliams, *A Mask for Privilege: Anti Semitism in America* (Boston: Little, Brown and Co., 1948); Kenneth T. Jackson, *The Ku Klux Klan in the City* (New York: Oxford University Press, 1967; Benjamin H. Avin, *The Ku Klux Klan, 1915-1925 Ph.D.* Thesis: Georgetown University, 1952); Kenneth E. Harrell, *The Ku Klux Klan in Louisiana* (Ph.D. Thesis: Louisiana State University, 1966); John A. Davis, *The Ku Klux Klan in Indiana, 1920-1930* (Ph.D. Thesis: Department of History, Northwestern University, 1966); Norman F. Weaver, *The Knights of the Ku Klux Klan in Wisconsin, Indiana, Ohio and Michigan* (Ph.D. Thesis: Department of History, University of Wisconsin, 1954); William P. Randel, *The Ku Klux Klan* (Philadelphia: Chilton Books, 1965).

The Extremisms of the Thirties

Morris Janowitz, "Black Legions on the March", in Daniel Aaron, ed., *America in Crisis* (New York: Alfred Knopf, 1951), pp. 305-25; Morris Schonbach, *Native Fascism During the 1930's and 1940's* (Ph.D. Thesis: U.C.L.A., 1958); Marie Ann Buitrage, *A Study of the Political Ideas and Activities of Gerald B. Winrod* (M.A. Thesis: Department of Political Science, University of Kansas, 1955), Ralph Roy, *Apostles of Discord* (Boston: Beacon Press, 1953); Donald S. Strong, *Organized Anti-Semitism in America* (Washington, D.C. American Council on Public Affairs, 1941); Victor C. Ferkiss, *The Political and Economic Philosophy of American Fascism* (Ph.D. Thesis: Department of Political Science, University of Chicago, 1954); David H. Bennett, *The Demagogues' Appeal in the Depression, The Origins and Activities of the Union Party: 1932-1936* (Ph.D. Thesis: Department of History, University of Chicago, 1963); Charles J. Tull, *Father Coughlin and the New Deal* (Syracuse: Syracuse University Press, 1965); Nick A. Masters, *Father Coughlin and Social Justice* (Ph.D. Thesis: Department of Political Science, University of Michigan, 1955).

The Radical Right in the Post-War Era

Edward Shils, *The Torment of Secrecy* (Glencoe: The Free Press, 1956); Daniel Bell, Ed., *The Radical Right* (Garden City: Doubleday, 1963); Michael P. Rogin, *The Intellectuals and McCarthy: The Radical Specter* (Cambridge: MIT Press, 1967); Jack Anderson and Ronald W. May, *McCarthy the Man, the Senator the Ism* (Boston: Beacon Press, 1952); Reinhard H. Luthin, *American Demagogues* (Boston: Beacon Press, 1954); James Rorty and Mosche Dechter, *McCarthy and the Communists* (Boston: The Beacon Press, 1954); Richard Rovere, *Senator Joseph McCarthy* (New York: Meridian Books, 1960); Nelson W. Polsby, "Towards an Explanation of McCarthyism", *Political Studies,* 8 (October 1960), pp. 250-71; Martin Trow, "Small Businessmen, Political Intolerance and Support for McCarthy", *American Journal of Sociology,* 64 (November 1958), pp. 270-81; William R. McPherson, *Parallels in Extremist Ideology* (Ph.D. Thesis: Department of Social Relations, Harvard University, 1967); Burton Levy, *Profile of the American Right: A Case Study of Michigan* (Ph.D. Thesis: Department of Political Science, University of Massachusetts, 1966); Fred Grupp, *A Study of the Membership of the John Birch Society and the Americans for Democratic Action*

(Ph.D. Thesis: Department of Political Science, University of Pennsylvania, 1968);
J. Allen Broyles, *The John Birch Society* (Boston: Beacon Press, 1966); Benjamin
Epstein and Arnold Forster, *The Radical Right, Report on the John Birch Society
and its Allies* (New York: Vintage Books, 1967); Ira Rohter, *Radical Rightists: An
Empirical Test* (Ph.D. Thesis: Department of Political Science, Michigan State Uni-
versity, 1967); Brooks H. Walker, *The Christian Fright Peddlers* (Garden City:
Doubleday, 1964).

6

THE PROBLEM OF INDIVIDUAL IDENTIFICATION WITH THE NATIONAL GOVERNMENT IN INDIA

EVERETT E. HAGEN

IN THIS essay I discuss the question of the individual's identification with (or loyalty to) a national government as opposed to a smaller or narrower political or social group, and apply the analysis to India. I combine with more purely sociological analysis of the factors that determine the unit to which the individual gives primary loyalty, newer theory concerning qualities of personality that may affect his attachment to a local or a national entity. In a previous work, *On The Theory of Social Change*,[1] I have elaborated a theory of these personality factors and their determinants. I refer to various sections of this volume in occasional footnotes below.

In 1946 and 1947, as negotiations with the British Labour government for independence proceeded, the India-Pakistan schism occurred, but the Indian part of the sub-continent presented the aspect of a single nation, united in its demand for independence. Admiration by many intellectuals and officials for the British did not alloy the pride in separate national identity. But within the past few years the expressions of state and communal separatism in India have raised doubts about the strength of Indian national identity. Are national attachments weakening? Is the social unity of India disintegrating? Was there always latent disunity which is now

[1] Homewood, Illinois: Dorsey Press, 1962.

138

coming to the surface? Or are the recent manifestations of localism a superficial and temporary phenomenon?

These questions are floating in the Indian air. Their presence perhaps makes it appropriate to discuss in this essay the forces which cause individuals to feel a national identity or on the contrary to cling to local attachments, feel hostility to other groups or regions within the nation, and threaten or even destroy national unity. The discussion is in general terms, but the relevance to India of various points in the argument will be suggested.

An individual's identification with his nation, relative to that with both smaller and larger groups, is of course a matter of degree, even though the individual often draws an especially sharp line between individuals within the nation, who are fellow citizens, and those outside. He identifies himself politically with smaller groups but more strongly, in some sense, with the nation—or the reverse. While in this essay I shall be especially concerned with identification with the nation, the problem of degree of identification with groups of varying size—shades of identification within concentric social circles, so to speak—will also arise.

All identification is a matter of differentiation. Nothing can be defined except by contrast with something else. If there were only a single colour in the universe, the concept of differences in colour would not exist. If all sounds were of one pitch, there would be no concept of differences in pitch. In these cases, men would not know that they possessed organs capable of perceiving differences in colour or pitch. If all animate beings were men, the human brain would not conceive of the differences between men and other animals.

Similarly, a group can conceive of itself as a group only in contradistinction to other groups. "An Indian" is a person who is not something else. He is a Hindu, which defines him only if there are also non-Hindus. He believes in a certain form of government, which means that he does not believe in other forms of government. He has a certain history, which has meaning only if other persons have other histories. The question of an individual Indian's emotional identification with the nation is a question whether he regards the qualities he has in common with all or almost all other Indians, in contradistinction to non-Indians, as more or less important than the qualities he has in common with members of a smaller group, in contradistinction to Indians who are members of other smaller groups. These statements, which relate to "identification" in the sense of "definition", also relate to "identification in the sense of "emotional association with". Emotional identification with something is heightened by antipathy to some contrasting thing. Political and social identification are questions of hostilities and antipathies as much as of positive loyalties.

Before the last several centuries, the largest groups with whom non-élites identified themselves were much smaller than is true in the large nation-states today. The affiliation was with a tribal or ethnic group, not with a geographic area. Members of each group looked upon all other groups as alien and often as enemies. Examples in Europe, Asia, Africa, and the Americas are numerous; they need not be recounted. To superficial observation, present India historically was more fragmented (though some of the "fragments" were rather large) than present China, and the peoples of Western Asia (the "Middle East") more than the people along the Nile. The superficial observations may be correct. At any rate, India was fragmented; it is well known that small groups of Europeans were able to conquer coastal areas not merely because of their superior arms but also because the local groups were so alien to each other that they did not unite in resistance. It is usually stated that the local princes or leaders were hostile to each other, but I suggest that it is put in this way mainly because history pays most attention to political leaders. In fact the lowly members of the local groups felt alien to each other also. If they had thought of each other as "we Asians" or "we Indians" being attacked by "those Europeans", movements for united resistance would probably have arisen.

Empires were of course formed, but they were held together for a time, not by any sense of identification of the masses with the imperial unit, but by the submission of disparate social groups to force. Only a few élites felt primary political loyalty to the empire. The question, Why do individuals identify themselves with local units rather than with the nation? would have had little meaning in ancient or medieval Europe or in pre-British India because the concept of identification with larger nation-states hardly existed.

Perhaps, then, the question to be analyzed is: Why have the people of some areas come to identify themselves with nations? rather than, Why do the peoples of some areas identify themselves predominantly with local groups? I think that the problem is illuminated most if it is approached from both viewpoints. I shall try to answer both questions. Even if local groups may be said to be the "natural" political units, "natural" does not mean "without causes" or "not needing explanation".

The largest of the modern nation-states, in terms of population, are the Soviet Union, the United States, China and India. (In terms of area, Canada and Brazil belong in the group. However, the four provide adequate illustration of questions to be discussed here.) One of these was formed by the extension of power from Moscow, that is, by conquest. Perhaps the nation of China may be said to have been formed in the same way, though China also has a history unique among these four of unity, repeated breakup into virtually independent smaller states, and renewed reunification. The United States was formed by the occupation of "empty lands". India was unified by a colonial power. Does improvement in communication in modern times provide a sufficient basis for believing that these entities of unprecedented size will continue to be national units? Or should we anticipate their possible disintegration, just as ancient empires disintegrated?

EDUCATION AND COMMUNICATION

It is somtimes assumed that national unity, that is, primary political loyalty to the nation-states, can be achieved by deliberate policy. Specifically, it is assumed that information, education, and verbal exhortation (the sort of communication which when done by our enemies we term propaganda) can arouse identification with the nation in persons whose attachments previously were ony local. Certainly, on occasion, when an eloquent leader has spoken, a rush of support for the nation has arisen from groups that seemed previously to have only local attachments. However, in each such case there seems to have been an underlying bed of emotion which the words of the leader merely touched off. Without minimizing the importance of the words or of the leader's model, given the situation, it is reasonable to suggest that leadership by an individual is at best a joint cause of identification with the nation. It sometimes seems to be merely the overt symbol of an event that was "waiting to happen" and was inevitable. This may be the case far more often than we realize. It is apparently true that Gandhi merely mobilized, and did not create, a sense of the rightness of passive resistance.

Some persons have faith that such exhortation or eloquence can arouse national unity among individuals who are passive or indifferent. This faith is related to the concept that formal education can have an important effect on the attitudes of a passive or indifferent audience. There is no firm evidence for this hypothesis. At least some of the persons who have this faith think of the minds of the "lower classes" as blank slates on which a leader can write what he will. This was the attitude, for example, of American policy-makers toward the Vietnamese. It may be the attitude of some Indian élites toward Indian peasants. However, the further social psychology progresses, the more evidence it accumulates that the class "people without strong unverbalized attitudes toward other groups" is an "empty set". It is becoming increasingly clear that the infancy, childhood, and adolescence of all individuals, including peasants and urban menials, in any country, whether educated or not, and whether limited to local knowledge or not, give them predispositions toward the world that are likely to affect their attitudes more powerfully than deliberate propaganda or education.

That education can impart knowledge and skills is clear; but the belief that it has important effects on attitudes may result more from the fact that men do not understand how the attitudes of humbler men arise, and would feel lost, and anxious, if they did not believe that education can influence them, than from any objective evidence that the belief is valid.

Where differences in the attitudes of two individuals or groups are associated with differences in their education, we tend to *assume* that the education determined or strongly affected the attitudes. It does not occur to us to consider that persons who seek more education than others demonstrate by that fact that they already have different attitudes. Surveys show an association between educational differences toward modernization, nationhood, etc., but these surveys may record not cause and effect but merely the co-existence of two concomitant effects of a prior difference in personalities.

The evidence that the degree of national unity is importantly affected by verbal communications is therefore weak. A somewhat different case can be made for the thesis that good transport and communication among groups (as distinguished from propaganda directed at them) may tend to bind local groups together. But, when one looks hard at the evidence, one must admit that sometimes good communication unites but sometimes not. If local groups prove to be congenial when they are brought into contact, then the contact will unify them. If the initial attitudes are aggressive or hostile, contact may bring conflict. A few examples are the Romans and the "barbarians", the Germans and their neighbours during much of modern history, the component units of the Austro-Hungarian empire, and the Ibos and the Yorubas in Nigeria. If the reader objects that in these cases there were underlying causes of conflict, the answer is that this is precisely the point. It is the underlying forces, rather than the communication, that seem to have the dominating effect.

The same point is made by considering cases in which communication has failed to alleviate previous hostilities. Consider the continuing frictions in the United States between the North and the Old South; the continuing bitter hostility of the Walloons and the Flemish in Belgium; the movements for autonomy from the English, even today, in Wales and Scotland; and the violence which erupts periodically in the confrontation between Ulster and Eire, or within Ulster. The spectacular case in South Asia of contact that did not preserve unity is of course that of contact between Muslims and Hindus.

There is some evidence that, for individuals, acquaintance with alien groups moderates both favourable and hostile preconceptions about them toward the middle. A survey of the attitudes of a number of American businessmen before and after they had a number of contacts with businessmen abroad showed this result.[2] However, it would be hazardous to draw many general conclusions from this study. These were individuals, not groups; they were individuals making casual contacts with foreigners and expecting to return to their own undisturbed society; and they were businessmen whose mission in life requires maintaining effective working contacts with customers and suppliers.

Let it be granted that where groups brought together by improved communication feel some communality, the contact will bind them together. The question then arises, What qualities or forces cause them to feel some communality? I attempt to answer this question below. Meanwhile, the general point being made here is that the "historical" forces which determine the degree to which the individual identifies himself with social groups or political units, and the degree of his antipathy to units outside his group, are far less subject to deliberate control, and far more determined by forces outside that control, than we would like to believe.

THE "HISTORICAL" FORCES

Even a cursory examination of the world's history suggests some causes of the size of nations. Common ethnic origin is obviously of some relevance; ethnic differences have often been associated with bitter divisions. But one may ask the simple-minded question, Why?, rather than take these differences as a cause that needs no explanation. Moreover, common ethnic origin is a matter of degree, and the degree necessary for or favourable to national unity is often known only *ex post*. The Germans may be regarded as one ethnic group, but if Austria and Germany were a single nation, the collective would, with some justice, be regarded as a single ethnic group, whereas, if there were a strong separatist movement in southern Germany, the ethnic differences between Prussians and South Germans would no doubt be adduced as a cause. In some vague sense, all or most of the Russians can be said to have an ethnic relationship, but if the Soviet Union were six nations, ethnic differences would be said to account for the divisions.

Conquest has accounted for the union of ethnically diverse groups, and identification with the large national unit has sometimes followed. But conquest and enforced contact for some time thereafter is not enough. All of the peoples of greater Russia now feel identity with the large entity, the USSR. But when Charlemagne died, the state he had built up disinte-

[2] I. Pool, S. Keller, and R. Bauer, "The Influence of Foreign Travel on Political Attitudes of American Businessmen", *Public Opinion Quarterly*, XX, No. 1 (Spring, 1956).

grated quickly. The examples of conflict after contact, cited above, are also pertinent.

Certainly a more loosely defined historical factor, the sharing of common experiences of emotional importance, is relevant. Persons of Hungarian origin, persons who fought a war together, persons who shared a great and hazardous migration—these and their descendants for some generations may feel some sense of unity. The pride of "all the Russians" in the technical achievements of the Soviet Union surely is an important factor in the present unity of the nation. The pride of United States citizens in their "conquest of the West" and the technical achievements and power of their country surely is an element in the geographic unity of the United States. (In writing this, I recognize lingering regional differences, for example between the North and the Old South, and the racial differences that divide the country, but the latter are not geographical and the former create no serious desire for separation.)

Physical features of course are also factors of importance. They are a practical explanation of the fact that the South European conquerors of Latin America formed a dozen and a half small countries, while the North European occupiers of northern America formed two. But they are not a complete explanation; no one looking at the mountain ranges of of Latin America would have drawn all of the national boundaries where they now exist, and certainly the fragmentation of "Grancolombia" in north-western South America, and the emergence of four Central American states, require further explanation.

Lastly, "historical accidents" must also be allowed for.

Explanations of this "historical" sort clearly have great force. Yet the total result of such analysis is not entirely satisfying. One is left with the judgment that these forces may be adduced in one combination or another, to explain anything that has happened, but would also have been adduced, with a different weight given to each, to explain alternative or opposite events. To conclude for this reason that these are not pertinent and sufficient causes would not be justified. It may be that we have merely not been able to quantify them, to assign the appropriate weight to each, and to deduce the resulting effect the combination at work in any given case would have had. However, it seems more probable that the so-called historical explanations do not probe deeply enough. The few additional suggestions I offer somewhat speculatively will not make prediction concerning the formation or break-up of nations more reliable than it is at present, but they may possibly add a link or two in the chain of understanding, so that some future advance may be made.

PERSONALITY FACTORS

I start by introducing some considerations of personality theory. Some of these are commonplaces to laymen; others are not. Certain qualities of personality offer a likely explanation of some differences in the size of the social groups with whom individuals identify in differing degrees. The relevant qualities are ones shared by all men, but the degree of each quality and the mix of the qualities vary among individuals within a group and among groups. With some hesitation I shall introduce some technical terms. Their use creates the risk of permitting formula explanations, by which reference to the technical term takes the place of thought, but their use also permits a shorthand reference which is convenient and economical.

(1) One of these qualities is the need of virtually every individual to live within a group. Loosely, this is what is meant by the term "need for affiliation" or, for brevity, "need affiliation". Quite apart from practical problems, the sense of being isolated from all other individuals is depressing, and the individual would have to find some group with which to identify himself mentally or physically, if the structure of his society did not provide groups for him.

The nature and size of the group or groups needed to be satisfying depends in part on the psychological make-up of the individual. (Some conceptual analysis of how each individual's needs for affiliation are formed is possible, but will be omitted here.) It depends also on the external pressures. The greater the sense of threat from some external source, the larger or more sturdy or reassuring in nature the group within which the individual will seek reassurance. Moreover, it is probably easier for an individual to identify himself with large groups when communication facilities give him wider contact than when they do not.

(2) A second of the relevant qualities of personality is "need for dependency" or "need dependency", the anxiety-motivated desire to turn to someone else for decisions in matters with which one does not feel able to cope.

(3) A third is "need aggression", or a tendency to be aggressive.

One feels need dependency initially because some of one's explorations of the world in infancy and early childhood were frustrated—frustrated by one's incapability or by restrictions and control (rather than support) by parents or other powerful individuals around one. Hundreds of times, a mother or father, nurse, older brother or sister, or other powerful person checks the explorations of a baby or a child for reasons which to the child are sheer unexplained interference with his use of his developing capabilities. Or the powerful person orders him to behave in one way or another for no understandable reason. Everything he desires to do seems wrong.

The result, insofar as these impressions of frustration or abandonment dominate over the sense that one is supported and can have confidence in oneself, is to create repeated anxiety and cause the child to fear taking any action without waiting for direction from someone around him. The result, that is, is to create need dependency.

The frustrations and abandonments also create anger. Typically the child quickly learns to repress it for if one expresses anger at, say, one's mother, who has restricted one or left one frightened without relieving one's fear, the resulting sense of having driven her away and being isolated and without support is more than one can bear. But the repressed anger remains inside one and, especially for individuals in whom it is great, may provide the energy for any number of acts of aggression and violence throughout life.

The degree to which one's need dependence is satisfied in adult life and the degree to which one's need aggression may burst out in aggressive behaviour are closely related. For insofar as one's anxiety is relieved by the considerate response of a superior to one's call for help, one need not feel much anger. But if one's need for relief of anxiety is denied, one's anger and sense of frustration rise. The greater one's need dependence, the more readily and repeatedly one will become convinced that superiors and, if one dares, will demand it as today's rebellious students do, and the more readily and repeatedly one will become convinced that superiors are not responding considerately to one's needs. In the more extreme cases, the individual became so convinced in his early life that no one will support him or has any regard for him that he acts violently as an adult, if he dares, without testing the environment.

(4) Individuals in whom this set of personality traits is strong carry within them a sense that some force outside them threatens them.[3] Like Pirandello's six characters in search of an author, such individuals search for some threat in the environment to explain their unease, and find one somewhere, which then becomes the scapegoat of their sense of danger. This tendency probably explains a large part of the fear of something vaguely called "Communism" by many Americans, and a large part of the Russian fear of the United States; a large part of the fear of each other by India and Pakistan; communal conflicts within India; the fear felt by Germans of Hitler's generation that the Jews in Germany would dominate them; the "white backlash" toward blacks in the United States; and so

---

[3] This sense is a displacement of the early life sense that parents or other persons important in the home were restrictive and arbitary. This perception is too dangerous to be borne, so the individual represses it, then later in life "explains" his sense of a threatening force by finding such a force elsewhere—either his superiors in adult life, or, more often, by a more far-reaching displacement, some "alien" force.

on. Where each of two countries is hostile toward the other for this psychological reason, the hostility of each is an objective fact to the other, and confirms the psychological impression. Alien ethnic or cultural qualities provide an easy rationalization for the judgment that those "different" people are to be suspected. The combination of need aggression, the need to find a source of danger outside oneself, and the presence of differences in behaviour patterns is probably a much more important cause of conflicts and tensions among ethnic groups, in every part of the world and throughout history, than are the objective circumstances that are the rationalizations of such conflicts.

(5) Contrasting with need dependence, but not a fifth separate characteristic, is "need autonomy", or satisfaction in arriving at decisions through one's own judgment rather than depending on the verdict of someone else. The two needs are in a sense at the opposite ends of a continuum. The higher one's need dependence, the lower one's need autonomy, and vice versa. There may be a wide circle of problems with respect to which one feels satisfaction in exercising one's own judgment, and only a few with respect to which anxiety leads one to accept someone else's decision blindly, or the reverse. There is reason to believe that the number of persons whose need autonomy is fairly high and fairly wide in scope varies within a society at different eras, and hence varies also among societies. Perhaps the peasants and menials of traditional societies were (or are) especially high in need dependence. However, a fact that is relevant at this point is that a large majority of individuals in all societies feel rather high need dependence, especially concerning problems of interpersonal relationships, and rather high need aggression; and visualize some group or force outside themselves as threatening (even though dispassionate observers judge the threat to be greatly exaggerated or mythical). At times, for large minorities or even majorities, the fear is almost hysterical. This has been true at times in the United States.

(6) Closely related to need autonomy is need achievement. The latter term may be misleading; it refers, not to the need to attain great position, but to satisfaction in facing and solving problems. This, too, in a sense, is at the other end of a continuum from need dependency. Need achievement and need autonomy are undoubtedly inculcated, beginning in infancy, by the individual's experience that his explorations *are* successful; that his initiative yields satisfying results, not harm or alarm; that the world (i.e., important persons) around him supports him, guides him understandably, and feels pleasure, which gives him pleasure, at his development. The more satisfying the individual's development in this this way, the less need dependence, the less need aggression, and the lesser perception that there is evil and danger outside him, he will build into himself. It is important to note, however, that his behaviour in each

respect will depend also on the objective circumstances that do face him not merely on his inner attitudes and reactions.

A world in which everyone's need autonomy and need achievement were high and his sense of external threat was low would be an ideal world, in which mutual understanding among groups would be high and international agreements easy to reach. Unfortunately, however, persons who are high in these qualities are few; most of us are characterized by fairly high need dependency, need aggression, and sense of external threat.

PERSONALITY AND SOCIAL STRUCTURE

It is an interesting fact that the structure of traditional authoritarian and hierarchical societies satisfied these psychological needs at least as well as more democratic societies do. The small social groups within which historically there has been a sense of unity have with very few exceptions been ones with hierarchical and authoritarian social and political structure. Such a structure provides an effective arrangement for the satisfaction of this set of needs so long as the people at the base of the little pyramid feel that those above them have some regard for their needs. And in such small groups or tribes they do have reason to feel this. In this case, there is a local élite individual to whom the peasant or menial can turn for decisions concerning matters that give him anxiety; in their own somewhat wider problems those local élites can turn to more élite persons above them; and they in turn can depend on the chieftain or priest. Thus need dependency is satisfied.

At the same time, *everyone* in a traditional group comes to occupy a position of authority as he grows older. The lowliest peasant boy becomes an elder brother, a husband, and later a village elder. In each position, he experiences the aggression-satisfying role of dominating someone below him. Anticipation of these successive roles relieves his need aggression even before he actually reaches the position, just as, in the days when second-year students in colleges traditionally hazed first-year students, each first-year student assuaged his humiliation in two ways: by the knowledge that this was a proper part of the system, and by the anticipation: "Just wait until next year."

(7) There is an additional aspect of the attitudes of individuals who are high in need dependency and need aggression that has made such hierarchical relationships satisfying. Such individuals often fear their own aggressive tendencies. I refer, not to their fear of retaliation from without, but to their fear of what their own aggressiveness, if released, will do to them. One's reaction to one's own early expressions of aggressiveness did give one a sense of desolation, as noted above. Throughout life, this anxiety may persist. (In extreme cases, an individual with high need aggression may

be the most passive, bland, and non-aggressive of men. He tightly curbs his own need aggression, denying to himself that it exists.)

Fear of his own need aggression and fear of dangers outside him combine to make an individual uneasy at any conflict of judgment or purpose with other individuals, or at any uncertainty about his position relative to others. In hierarchical traditional groups, these fears were avoided by the fact that relative positions were so clearly and rigidly structured that everyone know in almost all situations to whom he had to defer, and who would defer to him. As an anthropologist in an Asian country said, "In my society, if any man looks at the man on either side of him, he knows one thing immediately: they are not his equals. Each is either above him or below him." For "my society", read "any traditional society".

In situations in which no simple rule of relative status guided interpersonal relationships, they had to be worked out painstakingly to avoid the threat posed by inter-individual tensions. Historically, in apparently every traditional society there was a group of elders—village elders, clan elders, or the like—who talked out dissensions within the group, painstakingly avoiding the imposition of majority rule on a minority, until consensus was finally reached about what had to be done, so that the decision seemed inevitable rather than imposed. Then the headman voiced the consensus as his decision, and to the maximum extent interpersonal grievance was avoided.

The sanctioned subdued aggressiveness of exercising one's authority on the persons socially below one might not be sufficient to relieve one's need aggression. For, if the society was to continue to work well, one could not be ruthlessly domineering; there had to be some consideration for the welfare of the individual beneath. (The lessening and sometimes almost complete absense of this considerations in recent times, under the stresses to which traditional élites have themselves been placed, is probably a major cause of mass unrest.) However, there was another outlet for need aggression. I have explained above why any group may tend to see alien groups as hostile or at least dangerous. Where unsatisfied need aggression is high, this view of aliens also rises in intensity, and a group or nation may satisfy its perception of external danger and its need aggression by attacking an alien group. It does so "in self-defense", which sanctions the violence.

Within such a group, then, one's need dependence may be satisfied by the availability of men above one to give directions and thus relieve anxiety. One's need aggression may be satisfied in the main, at each moment in life, by one's present and prospective authority statuses. Any residual need aggression may be satisfied by conceiving of outside groups as hostile and living in antagonism to them.

M-11

PERSONALITY, SOCIAL STRUCTURE, AND POLITICAL IDENTIFICATION

All of this may now be related to the question of the individual identification with the nation. Throughont history up to modern times, not only have nations been hierarchical and authoritarian; they have also been small. Obviously, non-personality factors such as communication difficulties and geographical barriers were factors in the small size. Ethnic differences were certainly a factor. But in a number of cases, these were surely not the deciding factors, and in some cases where, say, wide rivers or mountains divided nations, they were barriers only because human attitudes were what they were. The core personality barrier was simply that the need aggression bred into human personalities was sufficiently disruptive to militate against the formation of large nations. In Latin America, the emergence of Ecuador, Peru, Colombia, Venezuela, and four Central American states, rather than a single north-western state of Gran-colombia, seems to me to be largely due to this influence. The persistence over a long period of relatively small states in the sub-continent of South Asia also seems to reflect this influence. Conquests and reconquests created temporary boundaries of princely states; perhaps only the need aggression that caused petty differences to flare into lasting barriers permitted these boundaries to remain.

Merger into larger nations may occur where need aggression is not so high. Neighbouring groups may then be seen as not so hostile, it may be easier to perceive the advantages of political merger, and a larger nation may arise. (Of course this requires a *mutual* lesser degree of need aggression.) Less likely, a larger nation may arise becaue there is present in individuals a high fear of their own need aggression. The result may be an uneasy sense that aggressive hostility toward neighbouring groups is not right, and the size of the society over which a single ordered hierarchy holds sway may grow.

The history of England from the fifth to the tenth centuries is a history of progressive unification after the invasions of the Angles, Saxons, Jutes and Vikings. Reading that history, one gets the impression that unification occurred not merely because of the victories of able leaders but also because anxiety at the continuing strife outweighed the satisfaction yielded by fighting. The people found relief in unity.[4] Where this force is at work, the society will continue to be hierarchical and authoritarian, as was true of England during this era.

The ideal version of European feudalism envisioned a single Europe-wide hierarchy of *statutes* extending upward through successively higher levels of nobles through a king up to God. The aggressiveness of no-

---

[4] For a discussion of this thesis, see *On the Theory of Social Change*, pp. 265-69.

bles and kings (élites typically have less fear of their aggressiveness than do lower social classes) kept this ideal from being realized, but even its conceptual existence must have given some psychic satisfaction to individuals uneasy about their need aggression.

Differences among societies with respect to such personality factors may account in part for the differential success of attempts at unification.

Explanation of this sort is subject to abuse. It is not helpful to replace careful historical study by a facile assertion that personality factors are important. The brief historical references in this essay are subject to this criticism, and I would emphasize again at this point that these are merely suggestions of possible hypotheses, not firm assertions. Moreover, it is not helpful to treat personality differences as a residual, to which all developments not readily explainable otherwise are attributed.

However, with due wariness concerning these dangers, it should be recognized that there is good foundation in personality theory for believing that the needs and other personality attributes described above are identifiable qualities bred into personality (in varying degree) by the (varying) circumstances of early life. There is reason, quite independent of group conflicts and quite independent of the existence of aggressive acts, for believing in the reality of need aggression, and for believing that it may exist in different societies, and in different eras, in differing degrees. Since this is true, historical interpretation may be aided in moving beyond mere one-thing-follows-another analysis by recognition of these factors.

This consideration may be put in another way. The analysis of societies and of history has in the main proceeded on the assumption that "human nature" is pretty much the same throughout the world. It follows that differences in behaviour must be the direct result of differences in the events impinging on men. True, historians occasionally have recognized personality differences by such statements as: "In its original habitat, Islam was a very aggressive religion" or "The desire for self-government gradually deepened and broadened in western Europe." In the main, however, either such statements have been *ad hoc* observations limited to extreme situations or the changes in human attitudes have been assumed to be "rational" results of such events as gradually broadening knowledge. The knowledge of experts in the field, personality psychologists, concerning the influences that shape human attitudes has not been applied. In the main, the assumption of invariant "human nature" has implicitly been maintained. What is suggested here is merely that the possible presence of one added sort of variable, variation in human needs and values caused in the micro-world of the individual's early life, should be recognized. No direct historical evidence of differences in the early life environments of individuals is possible, but in this as in many other matters circumstantial evidence is not without value.

There are sociologists who would reject such an hypothesis as "psychological reductionism". This term may have two meanings. Adducing personality factors as any part of the causation of events may be rejected as "psychological reductionism". This viewpoint has no sensible foundation. Certainly the personality that has been bred into an individual by his heredity and his life experiences up to a given moment is one determinant of his behaviour at the moment. The other use of the term is to refer to adducing personality factors as the sole explanation of behaviour. With the condemnation of "psychological reductionism" in this sense of the term I agree wholeheartedly. Of course social structural factors are always *also* important, as the discussion that follows illustrates.

THE EMERGENCE OF NATION-STATES

I turn now to a more general discussion of the emergence of nation-states. More specifically, I turn to the question of how individuals have come to feel emotional identification with a nation-state rather than merely with much smaller local groups; for until such identification occurred, nation-states had no solid foundation. In this context, identification with the nation-state—or loyalty to it—may mean either of two things: satisfaction with the geographical scope of the nation, as opposed to a desire to have part of it split off to form a separate state; and contentment with the political structure of the nation. In discussing the forces that brought about the formation of nation-states, it is not necessary to distinguish between these two meanings, for the formative forces brought loyalty simultaneously to a new, larger political entity and to its political structure.

Two forces may have contributed to the persistence of petty states. One is pre-modern limitations on communications facilities. A nation-state can emerge only over an area in which people are in effective communication with each other. In the early days of the United States, some observers in the Atlantic seaboard states doubted that the new nation could stretch as far west as the Mississippi, because of the difficulty of maintaining communication over such a large area. However, this factor should not be stressed too much. The ancient empires maintained communication channels that were sufficiently fast for the centre to be kept reasonably well-informed of events on the periphery. While a nation-state undoubtedly requires better communication than an empire whose stress is primarily on ruling, groups with a will to unite would probably not have found problems of communication a major barrier.

The other barrier is a force analogous to inertia. If a petty princedom or tribal state (or any other political entity) is once in stable existence, each successive generation of men, as it gains political knowledge, will become acquainted with the fact of this state in operation, and will tend to accept the *status quo* unless there is some positive incentive for change. A nation-state has emerged, replacing smaller units, where persons constituting the predominant majority of its population have gained a sense of being engaged in a common enterprise valuable to them. More specifically, a nation-state has emerged when each individual in that predominant majority gained a sense that the entire group was engaged in an enterprise that indicated respect for his worth, an enterprise that provided him emotional security. When such a perception is gained, each individual feels that the social group as a whole accepts him, values him, and can be trusted. Men who feel this about each other are drawn together.

The type of enterprise that has most commonly aroused this perception is one that combined skilful, effective, united achievement with relief of anxiety. The archetype, of course, is military defence against a foreign enemy. Presumably, military defence that was unsuccessful would achieve the result, if it seemed capable and heroic to the defenders; but since in case of defeat there was often no nation left to feel united, the cases of historical importance are cases of *successsful* defence of the nation. Both the sense of common threat and that of united achievement are cohesive forces, for reasons which the discussion above of personality attributes probably makes clear. The execution of a united achievement requires that transportation and communication facilities make such a common enterprise technically possible; this is probably an important reason why the super-large nation-states—China, India, the Soviet Union, the United States—emerged only in modern times.

Even when no external threat is involved, a common national enterprise of emotional importance will minimize the psychological need for aggression, since the individual's need dependency or need affiliation or both are being satisfied, and his sense of the existence of some threatening force outside him is dulled. However, defence against an external threat is especially likely to be of emotional importance precisely because it offers protection against a threat. Moreover, need aggression can focus on that threat.

A few examples will illustrate the process.

Consider first the smaller of the large nations. Before the Tokugawa era, Japan oscillated between national unity (which included less than the present area of Japan) and division into virtually separate states. The dates fifth century, 710, 1185, and 1600 may be taken as marking the beginning of successive periods of union, though the apparent precision of the dating is spurious. To a person with the predilections of the writer, it seems likely that this osciliation was due to the fact that during the periods of local conflict fear of own need aggression resulted in growing support for a single national hierarchy, and then, after some generations, chafing at the lack of outlet for need aggression produced disintegration, whereupon after an interval the cycle occurred again. At any rate, explanation merely in terms of periodic military ascedancy by an unusually able general seems rather superficial.[5]

By 1600 some Japanese leaders felt the threat of European encroachment moving around Asia and into the Pacific. It is likely that the mass of the population and even many of the élites did not. Except for two new facts the revolt of the "outer clans" in the middle of the nineteenth century against domination by the Tokugawa might have led to the break-up of the nation into regional units, as revolt against national hegemony had done at previous times. One of these two facts was that the Tokugawa had pursued policies of imposing national burdens on individual outer clans, and of holding families of clan leaders hostage at Tokyo and thus requiring annual ceremonial pilgrimages from the western end of Honshu to Tokyo. These policies brought an unprecedented degree of nationwide communication between 1600 and 1850.

Perhaps the more important new fact was the arrival of Commodore Perry in 1853. The fact that Japan was threatened by the West was made vividly apparent to every Japanese during the ensuing fifteen years. The reality and immediacy of the threat must have been a powerful force for national unity. The threat continued after the Meiji Restoration of 1868. The drive for national strength was a result of it. Pride in that national effort further cemented national unity.

The formation of the German nation also seems explained by outside pressures on the group of predecessor states. The group of little states had no natural boundaries. Pressures from the East and from the West were conspicuous. Reaction to a common external threat, rather than merely the military and other talents of Prussia's leaders, seems to me to explain the unification of Germany.

During much of the period from the eleventh century onward, the territorial struggles between English and French rulers reflected shifting feudal claims. However, as time passed, the claims became polarized as those from across the channel and those from this side. Joan of Arc symbolized and clarified a conception of a single nation whose existence was threatened, but she certainly did not create it. The threats drew the small French counties, dukedoms, and royal lands together. Their psychological effect helped to create identification with the larger entity.

[5] For a more extended discussion of Japan, see *On the Theory of Social Change*, Chapter 14.

Later, if anything beyond Napoleon's exploits was needed to reinforce national unity, the threat of Prussia must have served the purpose.

Consider now the four super-nations. One may doubt that there was a great deal of national unity or even much national control over outlying constituent states in Russia before the nineteenth century. The earlier wars of Moscow with Denmark and Sweden probably caused little reverberation in Tashkent or around Lake Baikal (though closer historical investigation may show that this is incorrect). The fact that the outlying states did not revolt is not necessarily evidence of identification with greater Russia; they were largely autonomous even within the Russian orbit. Even in the first World War the evidence is mixed. However, the great scientific and technical advance that followed the accession to power of the Communist regime must have aroused a proud sense of community, and the second World War must have created an acute sense of a common external threat. These events, it may be presumed, were important unifying factors.

Throughout her history, China has undergone an oscillation between unity and break-up somewhat like that in Japan. Many Chinese felt humiliation at Western incursion from the sixteenth century on and felt a resulting need for national unity. The impact on the people in the interior may or may not have been great. It certainly became significant in the nineteenth century, if it had not been so before, and even more in the twentieth. It may be argued that national unification would have come in any event, as it had come at intervals previously. The speculation was advanced concerning Japan that the oscillation between regional autonomy and national unity represented overfulfilment of one need at the expense of an opposite one, then a pendulum swing to the opposite extreme. Conceivably this was true in China also, that the pressure from without merely augmented such a swing. It follows that one must consider the possibility of a reverse swing of the pendulum. This possibility is discussed below.

The unifying force in India was surely colonial rule. The important impact, I suggest, was not the creation of national administrative machinery, a national bureaucracy, and a national legislature by the colonial rulers, but the humiliation of rule by aliens contemptuous of the indigenous culture.

The area that is now Pakistan experienced the same rule. Why did not the reaction to that rule draw Muslims and Hindus together? If unity had survived, no doubt I would attribute its survival to the binding effect of common humiliation. After the fact of separation, one may speculate as follows: the Muslims were a geographically distinct minority, even though in the border zone there was much overlapping. The difference in religion is associated with other cultural differences; the religious contrast is not merely a surface accident. Intense need aggression had been held in check by colonial controls (and also, by a complex process that cannot be discussed here, perhaps also generated by them over a period of generations). Now its need to find a target overcame the unifying effect of joint success in a common struggle, found a scapegoat in the cultural differences, and burst out. It was of course the Muslim minority that demanded separation. Though the association between Islam and high need aggression was mentioned above, it does not necessarily follow that separation was due to higer need aggression among Indian Hindus. If Hindu groups had been in a minority in a Muslim state, they too might have demanded a separate state.

Lastly, the American nation was formed by migrants who moved in tiny bands from settled civilizations across a great distance (far greater than the same number of miles today) and setted a wilderness They must have been anxious groups ill at ease in their home cultures. The trauma of the migration must have created a bond; this was strengthened by the sequence of events that led to the revolt against colonial rule. That bond was sufficient to draw the thirteen colonies into union in spite of the great need for freedom from controls that had led the northern colonists into the wilderness. Later, their descendants plus other migrants progressed across successive areas of wilderness to the Pacific. That achievement, the great and continuing technical surge of the nation, and the common cultural background of many of the people created and maintained strong bonds.

Yet no external pressures held the new nation together, the Rocky Mountains constituted a difficult barrier between East and West, and the question may be asked why the puny movement for independence in California did not flare into a greater flame. Perhaps there were three reasons. The men who settled California were not a separate cultural group; they were individuals from the East. Secondly, a larger than usual sprinkling of the settlers, all the way across the continent, may have been men whose needs were satisfied by achievement rather than by aggression.[6] And, more important than either of these factors, their need aggression was satisfied by many other outlets: the colonial revolt, the War of 1812, the Civil War (which of course prevented secession by another group), the destruction of Indian tribes, and continuing individual violence in the none too tightly organized new land. The enslavement of blacks in the South, their treatment since the Civil War, the "white backlash" at their recent attempts to gain equity, the somewhat hysterical nature of American fear of Communism, and various recent American

---

[6] For a discussion of the influences that may cause the emergence in a society of a larger than usual number of such individuals, see *On The Theory of Social Change*, Chapters 8-12.

adventures occasioned by reaction to that fear, are both indications of persisting need aggression and of the outlets found for it.

THE FUTURE OF THE SUPER-STATES

Within this framework of analysis, what can be said about the prospects for continued national unity in the nation-states? To prevent this essay from growing to undue length, I shall omit discussion of Japan, France, and Germany, except for one comment. In nations of this size the day-to-day meshing of economic, political, and social activity throughout the country provides a "common enterprise" in a pedestrian sense of that term. The resulting contacts must be a great force for the preservation of the nation, especially when added to the factor discussed above under the label of "inertia". These factors also militate toward the continuance of the four super-states, though in somewhat lesser degree, especially in the case of China. All of the other considerations relevant to analysis of the future unity of the smaller nation-states become apparent in the discussion of the four super-states.

In this discussion, it is necessary to distinguish between loyalty to the geographical unit and loyalty to the political structure. All four nations are undergoing tensions among classes or groups that indicate something less than completely satisfying identification with the political structure and may in time change that structure materially. However, geographical fission is a quite separate matter. It seems to me that the threat to national geographic unity is greater in India than in any of the other three, and greater in China than in the Soviet Union or the United States, though even in India the odds are surey against fission of the nation in the foreseeable future.

The positive national achievements which have constituted a source of national unity in the United States probably have lost some of their old appeal. The conquest of a nation and the forging of a great industrial system probably symbolized for almost every American his own dreams, even though he did not put this fact into words in his own mind. However, great industrial power is no longer unique; mere continuing expansion of productive capacity does not have the same appeal; and there are new divisive forces that much outweigh, for large segments of the population, any sense of participation in the nation's material achievements, and any sense of pride in the technical progress manifested in the space probes. The most powerful internal forces holding the United States together are probably inertia and the common bonds of daily life, plus sheer pride in size.

However, among the four nations— so it seems to an outsider— India seems most conspicuously to lack a national programme that would convey to the members of the population in general a perception that the society regards each of them as having worth and is acting in his behalf. Reference to a "national programme" here is not necessarily to a governmental programme; In India neither a governmental programme nor a general private endeavour of wide appeal seems present. Provision to peasants of the new "miracle seeds" and of sufficient water and fertilizer to make their use possible is the one prominent exception; this programme may have given a new sense of effective membership in the society to those peasants whom it has reached. However, beyond this, the successive development plans have left many millions of Indians unemployed or greatly underemployed. National leaders give the problem too low priority to execute the bold and imaginative and difficult programme that would be necessarily to meet it. Land reform remains on paper in many regions; the party in power gives the impression to many Indians of still being a "party of landlords". In Calcutta, a usually well-informed Indian told me, only one new school had been built since 1948, and little expansion or renewal has taken place in the old schools, because concern about education of the children has given way to disputes concerning the location of schools and the allocation of credit and benefit. And so on.

Some of these statements may be inaccurate. The important point is that they seem to reflect a general perception of the nature and quality of national programmes. That perception is not one conducive to identification by the individual with the nation.

Futhermore, the cohesive force of perception of an external threat is less present in India than in the other three nations, and, especially, is more pale now in India than it was a generation ago. On the contrary, in China the perception of an external threat to all the people, against which the nation offers protection, is probably more vivid now than in previous periods. It can be argued that the objective basis for a Chinese image of a foreign threat is not as sturdy as it once was. However, it is difficult to see why the Chinese should perceive this. The past reality was European encroachment in Chinese ports and Western imposition of unequal treaties. The present objective basis is the presence of American military power in Vietnam, Taiwan, and South Korea, and in the ocean along the entire Pacific perimeter of China, combined with knowledge of the towering total military strength of the United States. Probably much less important, but not inconsequential, are the claims of Chiang Kai-shek. That this combination of facts conveys to the Chinese a perception of a threat hanging over all of them and that this perception increases national unity is hardly to be doubted.

A similar perception must be common in both the United States and the Soviet Union. The missile strength of the United States must seem a threat to virtually every man in the Soviet Union except a few intellectuals. The missile strength of the Soviet Union has the same effect in the United States. Altogether, China, the Soviet Union, and the United States form a triangle in which the perception by the great mass of the population of each of threat from the other two must constitute cohesive forces of some importance. That importance should not be exaggerated. In the United States, after Khrushchev's visit revealed to Americans that the dictator of the Soviet Union was only a human being, and even a rather earthy and erratic human being, rather than a vague sinister figure, fear of the Soviet Union subsided considerably. Nevertheless, the threat certainly exercises some unifying effect.

There is surely no comparably strong perception of external pressure in India. The great external pressure was colonial. The colonial power is gone; it would be difficult to argue that in the present world atmosphere many Indians have a foreboding that it will return. While some Indian intellectuals talk and write of the menace of economic imperialism, it seems equally doubtful that this menace weighs heavily on any appreciable percentage of the Indian public. It is difficult to weigh the effects of the confrontations with China and Pakistan, but the fact that a call for national unity against these dangers did not seem to arouse much response in recent elections suggests that no great danger is in fact perceived from these nations by the Indian population in general.

Hence, the forces for national cohesion seem weaker in India than in the United States, the Soviet Union, or China. On the other hand, the channels in which need aggression can express itself in India threaten national unity more than do the channels open in the Soviet Union or the United States, and probably also more than those open in China. Need aggression within the Soviet military can find an outlet in measures against "reactionaries" and "counter-revolutionaries" in the satellite countries and also within the Soviet Union itself, and in a missile programme to strengthen the USSR relative to the United States. There is no evidence of frustrated need aggression in the population at large; one must conclude, *ex post*, that the positive programme of the government—technological, military, and social—satisfy the dependency and affiliative needs of the Russian people well enough so that need aggression is subdued. The discontent of intellectuals in the USSR, even if it were politically significant, is directed at the bureaucracy and has no significant divisive effect. Class tensions that might spill over into ethnic divisions seem hardly to exist.

In the United States, need aggression, and the need to create fantasies of threats pressing upon the individual, is obviously high in individuals making up a large proportion of the population. There is no need to discuss here the releasing of American need aggression in Latin America and in Vietnam (followed by an increasing sense of guilt among·

many—not all—Americans, as reality replaced fantasy). For the point that is pertinent here is the nature of release of need aggression within the nation. That has taken the form of rejection of blacks, and when the nation adopted measures toward racial equity, a "white backlash" of fear and hatred. For many individuals the expression of need aggression has also taken the form of regarding the poor as incapable, un-worthy, and even threatening.[7]

While these, the major forms of release of need aggression within the nation, undoubtedly have resulted in grave dissatisfaction with the poli-tical structure among the blacks and many of the poor, the structure is sufficiently satisfying to the great majority to make its stability certain.

These class and group tensions find no geographical lines of possible fission. Neither the blacks nor the poor are so concentrated geographically that they can demand political separation, nor can the hatreds of the white middle-land working-class majority find geographical focus. Many individuals of the Midwest distrust the "intellectual East"; the self-styled individualists of the mountain states shudder at the "collectivism" of the North and East; and above all the whites of the Old South detest the "Negro-favouring" policies of the national government; but these tensions are weak compared to the bonds which tie the nation together.

The picture presented by China is less clear. It is clear that tensions within the country are great. It is incorrect, I think, to assume that they reflect merely a struggle among individuals for power or a struggle bet-ween conservative and radical Communist ideologies. Underlying that struggle seem to be a-rational motives. The tension seems to be between a Maoist sense of unease unless the country is being swept along on a tumultuous wave, and an opposing desire for ordered hierarchy. Mao's success earlier in life was by means of leading a surge from below. One may guess that such action is psychologically important to him. However, it would not have succeeded if it were important to him alone. It is also important to a very large number of the youth of China. The disorders of the "cultural revolution" were probably sparked by a distrust of and hostility to authority as such, not merely to the policies of the cur-rent authorities. The unconscious emotional motivations were as impor-tant, in any judgment, as the conscious ideological ones. This surge of youth against authority seems similar in its unconscious motivations to the New Left and the college rebels in the United States, but that in China was much more important because much more widespread and because sanctioned by Mao.

The need for ordered hierarchy is felt strongly by the military in

---

[7] Compare this with the neglect of mass unemployment and underemploy-ment in India.

China, as it is by the military everywhere. Many Chinese generals are powerful, each in his own region. In earlier eras of history, when a period of national disorder occurred, each general seized the opportunity to establish his own autonomous orderly structure in his region. That the Chinese military is powerful at present is evidenced by the fact that it was able to force election of military officers in 1969 as approximately one half of the 174 members of the Central Committee of the Communist Party. At present, however, Chinese generals no doubt share the perception felt by other Chinese of a need for national unity, and the sense felt by other Chinese of potential great national achivements. These perceptions hold them together.

The tendency for mass surges of the young against the authorities over them will almost certainly persist in China, for it must have roots in the early lives of individuals, and early life environment is not likely to change greatly. If encouraged or sanctioned, the tendency may break forth in disorder or unrest now and again in the future. The unity of China will then depend on the reaction of the generals. For the reasons just stated, the generals will probably maintain unity, especially if there is national progress during the next decade or so that confirms their sense of national destiny.

In India, where there is neither any great pressure from without nor any strong sense of national acheivement to give cohesion to the country, the most obvious targets for each groups frustrated need aggression is the national government and the other ethic groups of the country.

If there were full-scale war with Pakistan, or if China were to invade India, the regional divisions would no doubt disappear. If there were a sense of vital national enterprise aimed at enchancing the dignity of individuals, the divisiveness would no doubt disappear. In the absence of either, the danger exists that regional and ethnic alienation will increasingly become the outlet for individual frustrations. Nevertheless, because of inertia and the bonds of daily communication, it seems unlikely to this writer that in the foreseeable future there will actually be a division of present India into a plurality of separate nations. Conceivably this unlikelihood results from the reluctance of an observer to look with sufficient boldness into the future. Assuming that the forecast of a continuing single nation is correct, for the reasons indicated India seems more likely than China, and much more likely than the Soviet Union or the United States, to experience a degree of localism that will be a serious political problem.

7

REFLECTIONS ON NINETEENTH CENTURY MODELS OF ECONOMIC MODERNIZATION IN INDIA

WILLIAM J. BARBER

THE MAJOR concern of this essay is with debates over the economic problems and prospects of India in which British economists of the first half of the nineteenth century engaged. Attention to this material, however, is prompted by a mid-twentieth century question: namely, what types of economic models are called for in the analysis of less developed countries or—more specifically—are economic models devised in the rich countries readily transferable to poor ones?

A moment's reflection on current controversies in the theory of economic development will illustrate the point at issue. In the past two decades, theoretical discussions of development problems have tended to diverge into one of two camps, each operating from distinctly different methodological bases. Advocates of what might be described as the "standard" position (which, for purposes of this essay, will be referred to as Position I) hold that the techniques of economic analysis and the types of questions relevant for investigation are much the same in all societies. In short, the economist's tools are universally applicable; empirical research should be directed to filling economic boxes cut to much the same specifications in whatever environment it is undertaken. Important differences between the more and the less developed economies are, to be sure, recognized.

162

Such differences, however, are held to be ones of degree, rather than of kind. No fundamental modifications in conventional analytical procedures are thus called for. Examples of Position I perspectives on the under-developed world abound. Perhaps the bulk of the output on the economics of development to be found in the more prestigious journals proceeds from presuppositions similar to those sketched above.[1]

A second— and diametrically opposed—view of theorizing on economic development might be described as the "Conceptual Luddite"[2] position (or, for convenience in this context, as Position II). Like the machiner-smashers of the early days of the Industrial Revolution, spokesmen for Position II tend to regard standard tools with suspicion. Their view is built on the premise that standard economics as developed in advanced economies is remote from the realities of the underdeveloped world. Its proponents do not, however, rest their case on a judgment that economic behaviour in poorer countries is either more or less "rational" than is the case in any other economic environment. Instead the basic argument of Conceptual Luddites is that the economic structure of most underdeveloped countries calls the standard categories of analysis into question. In the re-cent literature, this charge has been pressed against a number of conven-tional concepts: among them, aggregate income, aggregate capital-output ratios, the labour force, etc. None of these notions, it is alleged, is ideally suited to societies which are heavily agrarian. In these economies, a sub-stantial part of real product is produced and consumed within the house-hold and a major contribution to labour input is made by non-wage family workers.[3]

[1] Two examples, among many possible ones, may serve to illustrate types of ana-lysis proceeding from Position I premises:

"It is the relative size of sectors and their increase in time, and the relative importance of the instruments of policy, which vary and thereby change the prac-tical appearance of the problems, but the core of programming, the attempt to arrive at a consistent picture of potentialities and desirabilities, does not change; neither do the fundamental relations between the main economic phenomena." (Jan Tinbergen, *The Design of Development,* published for the Economic Development Institute of the International Bank for Reconstruction and Development, Johns Hopkins Press, Baltimore, 1958, p. 28.)

Emphasis on "uniformities" in the development process in all countries—regulari-ties which are alleged to transcend contrasting institutional structures—is also characteristic of "Stage" theories of economic growth:

"We shall be concerned here . . . with certain 'particular factors of reality' which apepar to run through the story of the modern world since about 1700." (W. W. Rostow, *The Stages of Economic Growth,* Cambridge University Press, London, 1960, p.1.)

[2] I owe this phrase to Professor Paul Streeten.

[3] Critiques of this type have been developed, for example, by Gunnar Myrdal, *Asian Drama; an Inquiry into the Poverty of Nations,* 3 vols., Twentieth Century Fund, New York, 1968; and Dudley Seers, "The Economics of the Special Case", *Bulletin of the Oxford Institute of Economics and Statistics,* 1963.

Those of a Position II persuasion would not maintain that it is impossible to produce numbers to fill many of the standard boxes. Indeed, considerable energies in many countries are engaged in precisely such exercises. Given the institutional structure, however, the task of generating data to fit the standard format requires heavy dosages of arbitrary imputation. The realism of the results can thus be legitimately challenged. To Conceptual Luddites, such procedures are subject to a more important criticism: that of misallocating research energies. In this view, it would be more productive—both intellectually and practically—to focus attention on the economic implications of the special characteristics of underdeveloped economies. The differences—rather than the similarities—between the institutional and structural circumstances of the richer and poorer economies deserve to be at the centre of the stage.

The methodological positions juxtaposed above clearly call for different types of analytical approaches. Each implies different research priorities and each is likely to offer a different reading of the options available to policy-makers. It does not appear, moreover, that these positions are readily reconcilable. There is little to suggest that a consensus among development economists on basic methodological procedures is emerging. More often than not, spokesmen for these two positions talk past each other.

II

The remarks above are some distance removed from the nineteenth century. Nevertheless, an inspection of the central themes to be found in earlier controversies may speak to our present condition. It is at least conceivable that a review of the controversies on the Indian economy during the heyday of classical economic theorizing will shed light on some of the unsettled questions of our own day.

Economists in the British classical tradition were deeply committed to the study of long-period economic growth. Indeed this theme supplied the organizing principle of their thought. Their sights, in the first instance, were on the possibilities for economic growth in their own country. But they also sought to understand the phenomenon of growth (or of stagnation) on a global scale. It was no accident that "nations" appeared in the plural in the title of Adam Smith's major work.

To economists in this tradition, India held a special fascination. For many of them, the attraction of Indian affairs was more than a matter of intellectual curiosity. Most members of the first team of British economic thinkers of this period had more than a casual involvement with Indian problems. Two of them were in important policy positions: James Mill— the friend and disciple of Ricardo—and his son, John Stuart, served in the London headquarters of the East India Company. Though less directly involved, David Ricardo was reasonably well informed about Indian problems as a shareholder, and sometime commentator at Court of Proprietors' meetings, on the East India Company's activities. Another important contributor to economic literature in the classical period, T. R. Malthus, served as the first professor of political economy in the College at Haileybury founded by the East India Company to train cadets for the Indian administration. Official connection with the East India Company and its administration was not, however, a necessary condition for informed comment on India's economic problems. The reader of the *Westminister Review, Edinburgh Review,* or *Quarterly Review,* or the citizen who followed Parliamentary proceedings with care had regular access to materials on Indian affairs.

Economists writing on India addressed themselves to two fundamental questions: what could explain the apparent stagnation of the Indian economy? and what policies would best contribute to the promotion of economic improvement? Those strongly influenced by utilitarian thinking saw opportunities in India to increase enormously the sum of human happiness.[4] Others sought prosperity for India, both for its own sake and for its potential contribution to the longer run growth in demand for British exports. None defended the commercial monopoly privileges of the British East India Company. On the contrary, most of them—including those in the employ of the company—were sharply critical of many of the company's practices. It should also be noted that none of the economists consciously sought to organize the Indian economy to yield a tribute to Britain. By their own lights, British classicists involved in Indian affairs sought economic uplift, not exploitation, for India.

Though classical economists analyzing Indian affairs asked much the same questions, they did not speak with one voice in the answers they supplied. The factors which accounted for different readings of events are themselves worthy of inspection. When allowances are made for changes in analytical style between their day and ours, some persisting patterns in debates about the economics of development can be identified.

III

By the 1820's, Ricardian economics had become a major intellectual influence and its impact on the discussion of India's development problems was nearly as marked as it was on British domestic issues. In the formulation of strategy for India, economists of a Ricardian persuasion divided into two streams: one attached primary weight to the insights afforded

---

[4] For an excellent discussion of this point, see Eric Stokes, *The English Utilitarians and India,* Oxford Universty Press, 1959.

by the doctrine of differential rent; the other emphasized the importance of international trade as a stimulus to growth and urged steps to perfect the market to allow full scope for the operation of comparative advantage.

James Mill was the central figure in the school which saw a grand design for India's progress in Ricardian rent doctrine. In his view, the fundamental task of the East India Company's administration was to organize the tax system to trap the net product of the soil. As the differential rent was a windfall gain to the owner of land and did not enter the costs of production, revenue could thus be raised without distorting factor costs. Moreover, as the rental share of income could be expected to rise with future growth in population, the state could enjoy an elastic revenue base. As James Mill put the matter in 1831:

I conceive . . . that the peculiarity of India, in deriving a large proportion of its revenue from the land, is a very great advantage. Nine-tenths probably of the revenue of the government in India is derived from the rent of land, never appropriated to individuals, and always considered to be the property of government; and to me that appears to be one of the most fortunate circumstances that can occur in any country; because in consequence of this the wants of the state are supplied really and truly without taxation. As far as this source goes, the people of the country remain untaxed. The wants of the government are supplied without any drain either upon the produce of any man's labour, or on the produce of any man's capital.[5]

If the rent doctrine provided guidelines for policy, it also offered an explanation for the persistence of misery in pre-British India. This question was not a trivial one to late eighteenth and early nineteenth century men. How, they had asked, could one account for the decline of India from an apparent situation of wealth and power to such weakness that sovereignty over large areas of the sub-continent could be assumed by a handful of merchant adventurers? Adam Smith had attempted to deal with part of the problem by arguing (incorrectly) that the principles of the "Gentoo religion" prohibited the lighting of fires at sea and that the development of long distance sea-borne commerce by Indians had thereby been precluded.[6] Much of the international trade in which Indians participated had thus been organized by foreigners who had appropriated the bulk of the gains from trade for themselves. A much more satisfactory solution to the problem could be found in rent theory. Now it could be

[5] James Mill, "Minutes of Evidence before the Select Committee on the Affairs of the East India Company", *Parliamentary Papers, 1831*, Vol. 5, p. 252.
[6] Adam Smith, *The Wealth of Nations,* Edwin Cannan. Ed., 6th edn. London, 1950, Vol. II, p. 180.

demonstrated that traditional rulers had been misguided by claiming a share of the gross—rather than the net—product of the soil. The peasantry had been over-assessed because taxation had encroached upon the non-rent shares of income. In consequence, both the ability and the will of the average cultivator to save and invest productively had been stifled. Malthus, one of the co-discoverers of differential rent, was the first to draw this inference.[7] The explanation he offered for the decay and stagnation of pre-British India was soon widely accepted.

Diagnosis and remedy could thus be brought together in one stroke. Moreover, the remedy—if faithfully applied—offered the prospect of a bright economic future. A tax confined with the net product of the soil would be neutral with respect to factor costs and would help to perfect the operation of market forces. Moreover, as the rent formula for taxation seemed to promise rising revenues through time, the government would be well placed to finance measures to foster economic improvement. In Mill's judgment, top priority on the expenditure side should be assigned to the provision of impartial and incorruptible administration. If security for persons and property could be assured, the climate for accumulation and growth would be favourable. Traditional Indian rulers, in his judgment, had failed to provide this pre-condition for progress.[8] He was confident that good government, combined with self-imposed limits on its taxing authority, would unleash private initiative.

In this model of economic development for India, the crucial ingredient was the theory of taxation derived from Ricardian distribution analysis. Mill, in his capacity as a policy-maker in the East India Company's headquarters, could translate theory into practice. In some parts of British India, however, his freedom of maneuver was restricted. This was the case in Bengal where Cornwallis's permanent settlement of 1793 had created a group of large landowners who were to pay a land revenue which would be fixed in perpetuity. In Madras, on the other hand, an approach guided by Ricardian principles was possible. Mill instructed revenue officers there to adjust the land tax to the "net product" of the soil. With this purpose in mind, assessments of the natural fertility of individual peasant plots were undertaken. In addition, Mill sought at least partial correction for the mistakes which had been made in Bengal. When the holdings of Zemindars came on the market, he urged that they be purchased by the government.[9] The state would thus become a landowner in its own right and collect the rent at source.

[7] T.R. Malthus, *Principles of Political Economy*, London, 1820, pp. 155-56.

[8] For a fuller discussion of this point, see William J. Barber, "James Mill and Theory of Econome Policy in India" *History of Political Economy*, 1969.

[9] James Mill, "Minutes of Evidence Before the Select Committee on the Affairs of the East India Company", *Parliamentary Papers, 1831*, Vol. 5, p. 310.

To men of these convictions, the attractions of recasting the Indian
land system in a form suited to the requirements of Ricardian theory
were compelling. They could claim that India—by virtue of its association
with Britain—was beneficiary of the latest and highest developments in
economic thinking. The scientific tax could be applied there, free of the
political constraints which would frustrate its implementation in the
United Kingdom. Growth and progress could thus be reasonably well
assured.

IV

Within the framework of orthodox Ricardianism, another strategy for the
economic development of India could be devised. A representative spokes-
man for an alternative position was J. R. McCulloch, a political economist
whose credentials as a disciple of Ricardo were nearly as well validated
as were those of James Mill. McCulloch regarded himself as a missionary
for the propagation of Ricardian doctrine and played a role not unlike
the one performed by Alvin Hansen more than a century later when
he widened the audience for Keynesian teaching in the United States.

Indian affairs were not a central concern for McCulloch. Yet on these
matters—as well as on most public issues of his day—he felt obliged
to comment from what he understood to be the Ricarian point of view.
His interpretation of the message assigned primary weight to the widening of space for the free play of market forces. Mill, to be sure, was not
unsympathetic to this goal. He had argued, however, that it could be
successfully reached only if preceded by fundamental reform in the Indian
land revenue system.

In McCulloch's brand of Ricardianism, such massive governmental
intervention in the economy was dangerous. As early as 1827, he voiced
his suspicion of the grand planner:

It seems . . . as if there were some strange fatality attending the
government of India; and that the greatest talents and best intentions,
when applied to legislate for that country, produce only the most
pernicious projects.[10]

McCulloch did not challenge the analytic soundness of the rent doctrine.
His quarrel was with the practical effect of claiming the net product of
the soil (or at least a substantial part of it) as public revenue. Such a
demand on the part of the state, he maintained, left too little discretionary

---

[10] J. R. McCulloch, "Revenue and Commerce of India", *Endinburgh Review*,
March 1827, p. 354.

purchasing power in the hands of the cultivator. As he saw matters:

> We must either make the ryots the proprietors of the soil, under payment of a moderate quit-rent to Government, or we must let the land to them for a period of years certain, *at such reduced rent as they may be able to pay without difficulty.* Under either of these systems industry would revive and the peasantry would become attached to government. But so long as we compel them to raise crops, not for their own advantage, but for the exclusive advantage of Government and the host of harpies it is obliged to employ, so long will the scourge of universal poverty continue to afflict the country...[11]

In McCulloch's view, tax reduction for the peasantry would stimulare the economy in a variety of ways. In the first instance, the capacity of the cultivating population to accumulate productively would be enlarged. In addition, the growth of effective demand for consumer goods would revitalize the domestic non-agricultural economy. Nor was he insensitive to the possibility that the demand for British exports would also be increased. But this result, in turn, could be expected to generate healthy longer-run growth effects for the Indian economy. Consumption horizons would thereby be widened and, correspondingly, new incentives for efficiency in production would be generated. There was no elasticity pessimism in this position. As McCulloch wrote in attempting to refute a widely-held view:

> Notwithstanding all that has been said as to the immutability of Hindoo habits, the fact is not to be denied, that a taste for European products and customs is rapidly spreading itself over India. And the fair presumption is, that it will continue to gain ground according as education is more diffused, and as the natives come to be better acquainted with our language, arts, and habits.[12]

McCulloch's vision was one of uplift led by the stimuli of a free market. Nevertheless, he was doubtful that the Indian economy—in the absence of resources supplied from abroad—could quickly lift itself by its own bootstraps. Indian poverty was too massive. For this reason, inflows of foreign capital and skill occupied an important place in the growth strategy for India. Not only would the limited supply of local savings thereby be augmented; but—perhaps more importantly—skills from abroad could be imparted to the local population. In his view:

[11] *Ibid.*, p. 358. (Italics in the original.)
[12] McCulloch, *Dictionary of Commerce*, 1842, p. 502.

. . . the increase and diffusion of the English population, and their
permanent settlement in the country, are at once the most likely means
of spreading a knowledge of our arts and sciences, and of widening
and strengthening the foundations of our ascendancy. ... Nor will it, I
conceive, be doubted that the diffusion of useful knowledge, and its
application to the arts and business of life, must be comparatively
tardy, unless we add to precept the example of Europeans, mingling
familiarly with the natives in the course of their profession, and
practically demonstrating, by daily recurring evidence, the nature and
value of principles we desire to inculcate, and of plans we seek
to have adopted.[13]

McCulloch's programme, however, called for one important institutional
reform: the creation of a modern monetary and banking system.[14] India,
he held, was inadequately served with reliable savings institutions. A
soundly structured banking system would foster productive accumulation
activating savings which would otherwise be dissipated in idle hoards.
Both commerce and industry would be stimulated by such an innovation. This institutional recommendation was thoroughly consistent with
McCulloch's *laissez-faire* approach to India's economic uplift.

This type of development model—though different from James Mill's
—was still clearly in the Ricardian lineage. Whereas Mill saw reform
in the tax structure (and indirectly in the land tenure system) as the
key to improvement, McCulloch's strand of Ricardianism sought the creation of modern monetary institutions. Whereas Mill attached high importance to the role of government in creating a climate conducive to
an economic "take-off", the market-led growth school preferred lower
taxes and greater reliance on private initiative. These streams of
Ricardian thought divided on an issue of political preference, rather
than on any fundamental point of economic analysis. Mill, at heart,
was a planner who favoured a high degree of direct governmental intervention to achieve the structural reforms necessary for the implementation of the scientific tax. Continuity of sound administration could
then be assured and the social infrastructure needed for sustained economic progress could be put in place. At the same time, Mill was reluctant
to offer an enthusiastic welcome to foreign investors in India.[15] He anticipated that foreign investment on a substantial scale would be linked

[13] McCulloch, *Dictionary of Commerce*, 1859, p. 563.
[14] McCulloch, *Reasons for the Establishment of a New Bank in India With Answers
To The Objections To It*, London, 1836.
[15] Mill's scepticism on this point is apparent in his testimony before Parliamentary
Committees of Inquiry on the Issue of a dual court system in India. It was argued
in the 1830's that the prospects for foreign investment and European settlement in

with European settlement. It would then be likely that European settlers would soon demand participation in government. This state of affairs would not be readily compatible with his image of a far-sighted Indian administration run by a group of Platonic guardians. McCulloch shared none of these reservations. He championed full-blooded *laissez-faire* in India's international economic relations as well as in the domestic Indian economy.

Despite differences in their approaches to India's modernization, these variations on Ricardian themes shared a significant characteristic: both attempted to extend to India the blessings of the latest economic conditions in Britain. Spokesmen for both schools recognized that economic conditions in India and Britain were far from identical. Yet both adopted a Position I attitude: solutions to India's problems were to be sought by drawing on modes of analysis and types of policies which had been formulated against the background of British conditions.

V

It requires only a modest stretch of the imagination to find mid-twentieth counterparts to these nineteenth century debates. James Mill's general posture is not far removed from that of planners who have more recently sought to transform the Indian economy. Post-Keynesian growth models have now displaced Ricardian distribution analysis as the supplier of the organizing categories of thought. This substitution has, in turn, meant that another set of strategic variables has been brought to the forefront of discussion. Thus, a modern plan frame is developed around saving-income ratios and capital-output ratios, rather than around the concept of rent. Yet past and present meet in a commitment to the use of the latest theoretical developments in the advanced economies to guide strategies for economic modernization and to a large dose of state intervention to fulfil the objectives of planning.

Nor does one need to scratch far beneath the surface to find a classical analogue to another latter-day approach to planning. It is frequently argued nowadays that actual factor prices in many underdeveloped countries do not accurately reflect the real scarcities of factors. It is then recommended that "shadow prices"—set to approximate the equilibrium prices—should guide choices on the combinations of labour and capital. James Mill did not approach the problem in the same manner. He was, however, on the scent of the same issue when he insisted that taxes should be directed to and confined within the net rent.

India were dim unless Englishmen could be assured of access to courts manned by English judges administering English law. Mill opposed any concessions on this matter.

Within a framework of classical reasoning, taxation would then be neutral and would not impinge on the natural prices of labour and capital.

Similar analogies in modes of reasoning of the past and of the present can be found among those who recommend a *laissez-faire* route to economic modernization. Indeed, one scarcely needs to change the vocabulary. McCulloch in his day had confidence in the capacity of widening markets to stimulate economic advance and to act as educators and promoters of uplift. Overtones of this faith come through in the following paragraph written in 1966:

Why should the presence of rich countries damage the development prospects of the rest? The former serve, and have for a long time served, in varying degrees, as markets and sources of supplies of skills, know-how and capital for poor countries. External contacts introduced new ideas, attitudes, crops and methods of production in poor countries. They often induced a new outlook to material progress and helped to undermine attitudes and customs most harmful to it. These processes are commonplaces of social and economic history. Over the last century, external contacts have enormously widened the economic horizons of a large part of the underdeveloped world.[16]

McCulloch, with his proposals on the banking system, added another ingredient to his package of recommendations for uplift to the Indian economy. Again there is a striking parallel between his views and those of recent contributors to the discussions of this issue. The case developed by Gurley and Shaw, for example, on the contribution of financial intermediaries to development has much in common with arguments McCulloch advanced.[17]

In short, a common methodological thread runs through both variants —past and present—of Position I approaches. Whether the writers in question are more disposed to interventionist solutions or to market solutions, both streams of thinking proceed from the premise that salvation for the underdeveloped world is to be sought by applying wisdom accumulated elsewhere.

VI

Ricardian orthodoxy—in one or another of its forms—dominated thought

---

[16] P.T. Bauer, "The Debate on Development: including an exchange of letters based on an article entitled the 'Poverty of Economics'", *The Spectator*, London, November 4, 1966.

[17] John G. Gurley and E.S. Shaw, "Financial Structure and Economic Development", *Economic and Cultural Change*, 1967.

about India at the policy level during the most of the first half of the nineteenth century. But voices of dissent were also to be heard during this era.

Prominent among the critics was Richard Jones, the successor to Malthus in the chair of political economy at the East India Company's College at Haileybury. Jones took aim on the claim that the insights afforded by Ricardian rent theory had universal applicability. Those who made such assertions were, in his judgment, responsible for "circulating error" because they had "confined the observations on which they formed their reasonings to the small portion of the earth's surface by which they were immediately surrounded; and have then proceeded at once to erect a superstructure of doctrines and opinions, either wholly false, or if partially true, as limited in their application as was the field from which the materials for them were collected."[18]

Jones was prepared to allow that Ricardian rent doctrine provided a reasonably satisfactory analysis of circumstances in England. The residual income share, attributable to the net product of the soil and appropriated by owners of land, could there be accounted for with Ricardian principles. That this was possible in English conditions, however, depended on two supporting conditions: in the first place, labour and capital were priced in competitive markets; secondly, the bulk of the outputs of land were sold in organized markets. The rent share could thus be derived by deducting the claims of labour and capital from the gross revenues of the agricultural enterprise.

Similar conditions, to be sure, did not prevail in India—or, for that matter, in most of the rest of the world. As Jones put it:

Mr. Ricardo, overlooking altogether the peasant tenantry, which occupy ninety-nine hundredths of the globe, had persuaded himself that the existence of a gradation of soils of different fertility was the only cause why rents ever existed at all.[19]

One is tempted to follow the lead of Professor Stigler—who has described Ricardo as holding a "93 per cent labor theory of value"[20]— by characterizing Jones' position as an accusation that Ricardo held a "one per cent theory of rent".

Major difficulties clearly emerged if one attempted to establish the magnitude of the net rent in a traditional agrarian system in which

[18] Richard Jones, *An Essay on the Distribution of Wealth and the Sources of Taxation*, 1831, p. xxiii.

[19] *Ibid.*, pp. 205-06.

[20] G.J. Stigler, "Ricardo and the 93 Per Cent Labor Theory of Value", *American Economic Review*, 1958.

little of the total output was marketed and in which most of the inputs were supplied by family labour. Equilibrium values for the various income shares could not then be readily identified. Only a total agricultural product was visible. No market criteria were available to distribute that product into shares for suppliers of land, labour, and capital. James Mill recognized this difficulty as a practical matter, but he did not regard it as an insurmountable obstacle to the implementation of his programme. The net rent could be approximated, he maintained, by direct assessment of the differential fertility of individual plots of land. Accordingly, revenue officers in the field were instructed to make cadastral surveys for the purpose of adjusting the tax demand to the fertility of the soil. Jones regarded this undertaking as "a gigantic task, that never could be efficiently done!" [21]

But the main issue was a conceptual, not an administrative, one. Jones maintained that the procedure adopted in India—particularly in Madras —in the attempt to apply Ricardian rent theory had, in fact, turned the doctrine upside down. Rent, as approximated by the tax demand, had a prior claim on the peasant's product. The shares of labour and capital—not the rent—now became the residual. Indeed, in face of the contrasting economic structures of India and England, it was difficult to imagine how the outcome could have been different.

This line of critique struck directly at the analytic foundations of Mill's strategy for the economic uplift of India. Jones asserted that the framework of Ricardian concepts, when extended to that part of the world, was misleading and mischievous. This challenge to orthodoxy was largely ignored in his lifetime. That it did not have more impact is not to be explained entirely, however, by the fact that his conclusions ran counter to official doctrine. Perhaps more important was Jones' failure to develop his argument tightly enough to pass Ricardian standards of analytical rigour.

Conceptual Luddite arguments, however, were not directed exclusively to the presuppositions underlying the interventionists' use of the Ricardian model in India. Another line of critique was addressed to the *laissez-faire* model of growth. One of the issues in this discussion turned on the question: does an apparent expansion in market transactions provide an unambiguous indicator of economic improvement in predominantly agrarian societies?

The form which this debate took can be seen in the sharply divergent interpretations of the behaviour of agricultural prices in South India following the land revenue settlements there. The available evidence

[21] Jones, *Literary Remains, Consisting of Lectures and Tracts on Political Economy,* William Whewell, Ed., 1859.

seemed to point to the conclusion that prices of basic agricultural products had tended systematically to fall after land revenue settlements had been made. John Stuart Mill had interpreted this outcome as a result of the favourable effects on production of orderly government and a predictable tax structure.[22]

But could inferences about the level of agricultural production legitimately be drawn from evidence on market prices? Richard Jones cautioned against a preoccupation of economists with exchange transactions. He maintained that it required "little reflection to perceive that there are many articles of wealth which are consumed by producers, and never become the subjects of exchange; and, therefore, that a portion of the wealth of nations is excluded from the view of those who confine Political Economy to the study of exchanges."[23] In India, it was conceivable that the volume of marketed agricultural produce bore no clear relationship to total agricultural output. This was certainly a possibility after the government had fixed the tax demand at a stipulated level for a period of years and further insisted that tax payments be discharged in cash. Markets might thus grow, but on a forced basis. Indeed, the effects of the tax system might generate the appearance of progress while the volume of output retained in peasant households diminished. Jones failed to develop this point systematically, though it is latent in his argument.[24]

A related issue surfaced in the attempts of Position I economists to interpret the fluctuations of silver imports into India. When a considerable drain of silver to the East began in the 1850's—after having been arrested for several decades,—orthodox writers found the phenomenon difficult to explain. There appeared to be neither the price effects that might have been expected if output had been stagnant, nor did there appear to be increases in production sufficient to insure price stability as the money supply increased substantially. Those who investigated this matter—as McCulloch did—were inclined to fall back on the view that the adjustments had taken place in the velocity of circulation.[25] Much of the inflow of precious metals had, they alleged, found its way into idle hoards. In addition, it was argued that the still inefficient state of the monetary and financial system had meant that an inordinate per-

[22] John Stuart Mill, *Memorandum on Recent Improvements in the Administration of British India,* 1858, p. 9.

[23] Jones, *Literary Remains,* p. 196.

[24] It should be noted that economists in the British classical tradition did not seriously consider the possibility of "backwash effects" on the traditional economy which might accompany the growth of monetized exchange. It was Marx who attached considerable weight to this matter.

[25] McCulloch, *Dictionary of Commerce,* 1859, p. 560.

centage of India's silver inevitably was wasted through wear, tear and loss. These considerations seemed to salvage the essential tenets of orthodox doctrine.

A critic of classical quantity theory—such as Sir James Steuart nearly a century earlier—could argue that the whole problem had been misconstructed by this conceptualization. Steuart's scepticism of the orthodox view was addressed particularly to its application in agrarian societies. On this point, he observed:

> In all countries where there is little industry; where the inhabitants are mostly fed directly from the earth, without any alienation of her fruits taking place; where agriculture is exercised purely as a method of subsisting; where rents are low, and where, consequently, the free hands who live upon them for the price of their industry, must be few; the demand for grain in the public markets must be very small, consequently, the price will be very low whether there be little or whether there be much money in the country. The reason is plain. The demand is proportioned here, not to the number of those who consume, but of those who buy: now those who consume are all the inhabitants, but those who buy, are the few industrious only who are free, and who gain an independent livelihood by their own labour and ingenuity.[26]

These words, written in 1759, were intended as a critique of Hume's version of the links between the quantity of money and the general price level. With only minor modifications, Hume's formulation of the quantity theory was incorporated into the classical orthodoxy of the nineteenth century.

Steuart carried his heterodox views into the discussion of Indian monetary affairs in 1772 when, at the invitation of the East India Company, he prepared an analysis of the Bengal currency system. His report was prompted by the alleged scarcity of silver which had developed after Clive's assumption of the Diwani. The acquisition of taxing power by the East India Company had led to the termination of the regular silver inflows which had formerly provided the working capital needed for the company's trading activities. The change in the Company's role now made it possible to use revenue collections for this purpose. In the 1760's, the Company's agents in the field complained that this change in the mode of operations had deranged the monetary circulation, had

---

[26] Sir James Steuart, *Principles of Political Economy* (as reprinted in *The Works of Sir James Steuart*, 1805, Vol. II p. 91).

produced a fall in prices, and—in some cases—had made it impossible to collect taxes in cash.

Steuart's recommendations on the steps which should be taken to deal with the scarcity of silver would hardly have been acceptable to an orthodox classical monetarist. He described his objective as one of endeavouring "to find out a method for conducting those resources which proceed from herself namely, the money which she at present possesses) into a channel which may set new engines to work in order to augment circulation and encourage her manufactures; instead of serving as a bare equivalent for those at present produced".[27] To achieve this, he urged that a note-issuing bank be created and that some extraordinary powers be afforded to it. The bank should be equipped to extend credits to stimulate the growth of production and to facilitate the collection of taxes. But it should also be flexible enough to adjust its operations to the reality of an agrarian and largely non-monetized economy. Hence, the bank should be prepared to provide facilities for payment of tax obligations in kind. In this vein, he noted:

In the proximity of great cities, and in very populous districts, granaries might be established, and part of the rents might be received in grain for the supply of markets, at a price proportionate to the plenty of the year. Even these granaries might be converted into banks for grain, according to a plan which might be contrived for the circulation of subsistence, and even of paper credit within a small district.[28]

Not only would claims on the money supply be diminished when such transactions could be settled in kind; provision could also be made for accumulation of the basic stock—food—required for sustained growth in the non-agricultural sectors of the economy.

This expansionist view of the role that monetary management might play in stimulating production was largely alien to the thinking of Position I economists. After all, classical quantity theory taught that monetary changes had a neutral effect on real output, though they might have important consequences for the general price level. Moreover, imprudent expansion in the money supply could be expected to produce serious complications for a country's balance of payments. This did not mean that the performance of the economy could not be improved by

[27] Sir James Steuart, *The Principles of Money Applied to the Present State of the Coin of Bengal: Being an Inquiry into the Methods to be used for Correcting the Defects of the Present Currency; for stopping the Drains which carry off the Coin; and for Extending Circulation by Means of Paper Credit*, 1772, p. 80.

[28] *Ibid.*, p. 74.

equipping India with more sophisticated institutions for channelling savings into productive uses; McCulloch (and others) had called for the creation of a more effective system of financial intermediation. Deliberate monetary expansion, however, was a different matter and should be carefully circumscribed lest India's foreign trading position be jeopardized.

Steuart shared few of these concerns. In his view, monetary stimuli might be injected without necessarily compromising a developing economy's position in export markets. What mattered to a country's trade were the prices established by the state of "demand and competition" in particular markets. The influence of the total money supply and of the general price level on these specific prics was, at best, remote. Indeed, Steuart was prepared to argue that—in an economy with the type of structure to be found in India—quite remarkable price effects might be associated with changes in the money supply. He saw no reason to rule out the possibility that prices of goods exchanged against money might not rise following a reduction in the money supply, rather than fall (as an orthodox monetarist would expect). This might happen, for example, if former sellers of goods responded to a shortage in the monetary medium by shrinking their offerings to the monetized portion of the market and withdrawing into barter transactions or into purely subsistence production. These considerations received little hearing in the nineteenth century.

One further matter attracted the attention of an occasional Conceptual Luddite in the nineteenth century: the organization of India's foreign trade and its impact on the growth prospects of both India and England. In this connection, one figure—the Earl of Lauderdale—deserves particular mention. Lauderdale, whose ambitions to become Governor-General of Bengal had once been frustrated, became one of the most outspoken critics of the East India Company and of the Board of Control which Parliament had created in 1784 to supervise its activities.

Lauderdale mounted his most systematic attack on the consequences of this arrangement in a pamphlet published in 1809. Why, he asked, should a territory with such vast resources as India was then alleged to possess, be such an unpromising market for British exports? As he stated the apparent paradox:

That such prosperity, and so great an increase of wealth as was loudly boasted of, should take place, without producing any extension of commercial transactions, appeared to our merchants and manufacturers repugnant to what experience had taught them to regard as the certain consequence of growing opulence; and, as they did not feel the effects of that increase of demand, of which they could not doubt the existence, they were led to suspect, that it had found some other channel. . .[29]

Commentators on this phenomenon who spoke within the orthodox classical tradition (including James Mill and McCulloch) explained it as the result of the stultifying influence of commercial monopoly.

Though no less critical than they of the East India Company's trading monopoly, Lauderdale maintained that the problem went much deeper. It was to be found in "the formidable bar, which the system itself had placed to the possibility of extending the sales of our exports, even if the monopoly had been done away".[30] The root of difficulty lay in the use of the territorial revenues of India for the acquisition of goods to be exported to Europe. The company's position as a sovereign "at once furnished means of supplying the British market with Indian produce, independent of all export from Europe, far beyond what the stock of the Company, acting as merchants, could antecedently command".[31] This turn of events had transformed the terms on which international trade was conducted:

There was no exchange of commodities; nothing was given by this country in return for what it annually took away. The extent of demand which regulates all commercial transactions, no longer form a rule for the conduct of those concerned; for it was the amount of the tribute that could be collected, and of the fortunes the Company's servants wished to remit, and no consideration of the state of our European markets, that decided the quantity of exports from India, whilst, on the other hand, there could exist, comparatively speaking, no such thing as imports; for a country from which all was taken, and to which nothing was returned, could not partake of those desires originating from the possession of surplus wealth, which gave birth to a demand for foreign commodities.[32]

In Lauderdale's judgment, this system was ruinous to both countries. India's resources were drained to generate the sizeable export surpluses required to manage this "trade of pure remittance".[33] At the same time, some sectors of the British economy were threatened by the dum-

[29] Lauderdale, An Inquiry into the Practical Merits of the System for the Government of India under the Superintendence of tht Board of Control, Edinburgh, 1809, p. 125.
[30] Ibid., p. 132.
[31] Ibid., p. 135.
[32] Ibid., p. 138.
[33] Ibid., p. 163.

ping of competing Indian goods. With an argument similar to that employed by Keynes in his denunciation of German reparations set by the Versailles conference of 1918-1919,[34] Lauderdale maintained that the prosperity of home manufacturers (particularly textile producers) was likely to be incompatible with a heavy volume of transfers from India. The interest of British producers could not be protected in this system "unless the industry of India is diverted into some new channel, in which it may be instrumental in producing such raw materials as our climate cannot furnish, and thus aid and assist the prosperity of our manufacturers, which must otherwise suffer from the rivalship of a remittance trade; always ruinous to those, the produce of whose industry enters into competition with it, because its extent is neither bounded by the demand for goods its conveys, nor by the loss it occasions to the adventurers on whose account it is conducted".[35]

These arguments, like most others in the Conceptual Luddite stream, were almost totally ignored at the time. Lauderdale's pamphlet appears not to have received even the courtesy of a rebuttal—an omission which is in itself noteworthy. Most critics of the East India Company in that day and age at least had the satisfaction of seeing their views attacked by an officially inspired—though usually anonymous—pamphleteer. Lauderdale, on the other hand, seems not to have been taken seriously at all. Members of the orthodox classical school recognized that sizeable transfers from India to England regularly occurred, but they addressed themselves to another aspect of this matter. James Mill and McCulloch, for example, were at pains to dispose of the idea that England extracted a tribute from India. As Mill saw the issue:

Never did an opinion exist, more completely without evidence, contrary to evidence, evidence notorious, and well-known to the persons themselves, by whom the belief is entertained. India, instead of yielding a tribute to England, has never yielded enough for the expense of its own government.[36]

(It should be noted that Mill held this view before he had any official association with the East India Company.) India, as Mill was well aware, needed to generate a surplus in its merchandise trading account in order to cover the costs incurred in England (known as the "home charges") in support of the East India Company's administration. It was main-

---

[34] J.M. Keynes, *The Economic Consequences of the Peace*, Macmillan, London, 1920.

[35] Lauderdale, *op. cit.*, pp. 173-174

[36] James Mill, the article "Colony" in the Supplement to the *Ecyclopedia Britannica*, 1826, p. 17.

tained, however, that these transfers—far from being a tribute—represented payments for essential administrative services which India herself could not supply. Though this argument was sufficient to satisfy most members of the orthodox school that India was being benefitted by the British connection, it nevertheless failed to address a central analytical issue: the consequences of the transfer mechanism itself on the trading prospects of India.

VII

Discussions of economic issues have increased enormously in their levels of sophistication in the last century and a half. Even so, significant traces of intellectual kinship can be found among the Conceptual Luddites of earlier periods of history and the economists who now maintain that the categories of analysis developed in rich countries should be transferred only with great caution to the poorer countries of the world.

The echoes of Richard Jones' appeal for a recognition of the special properties of peasant systems can be heard, for example, in the works of the Russian agrarian economist, Chayanov (whose major contribution has recently been translated into English)[37] and in A.K. Sen's revisionist theorizing about peasant economies.[38] Jones' broader crique of the Position I claim that its analytical categories are universally applicable has been taken up by a number of modern economists—perhaps most notably by Gunnar Myrdal.[39] In Jones' day, the attack was directed at the extension of Ricardian distribution analysis to the less developed countries. Latter-day commentators have instead focussed their attention on the inappropriateness of many of the aggregative concepts upon which post-Keynesian theory is built to economies which are structurally segmented and in which markets are far from ubiquitous. It is thus argued that the contrasts in the institutional structures of the richer and the poorer societies seriously call into question the use of concepts such as aggregate income, aggregate capital-output ratios, or full employment in planning for development.

Similarly, many of the overtones of Steuart's criticisms of the classical monetary orthodoxy recur in the rejoinder of the "structuralists" to the orthodox monetarist analysis of inflationary pressures in developing

[37] A. V. Chayanov, *The Theory of Peasant Economy* (Eds. Daniel Thorner, Basile Kerblay, and R.E.F. Smith), English translation published for the American Economic Association by Richard D. Irwin, Inc., Homewood, Ill., 1966.

[38] A.K. Sen, "Peasants and Dualism with or without Surplus Labour", *Journal of Political Economy*, 1966.

[39] Myrdal, *Asian Drama.*

M-13

182   MODERNIZATION OF UNDERDEVELOPED SOCIETIES

countries.[40] These debates have been mounted more vigorously in Latin America than in South Asia. Nevertheless, a continuity with the main themes of earlier discourse is striking.

Though it calls for a bit more elasticity in the imagination, a common element can be found in questions Lauderdale raised about the economic consequences of the transfer process from India to England and in those re-opened by such critics of orthodox international trade theory as Raul Prebisch.[41] A difference of a century and a half in time has obviously meant that the specific details of argument are not identical. Yet, at the analytic level, the target is the same. In both cases, Position I thinking on the distribution of the gains from the trade is attacked on the grounds that the structure of international commerce generates a systematic bias in the terms of trade to the disadvantage of the weaker trading partners.

On balance, it would thus appear that much of the scepticism of orthodoxy voiced in contemporary discussions of development problems is by no means unique to the past two decades. Again, past and present meet in a commitment to a common methodological theme: that the special circumstances of the underdeveloped world restrict the transferability of models which presuppose institutional conditions found in the more advanced economies

VIII

A review of streams of argument on the economic modernization of India is a matter of interest for its own sake. But it also reveals a remarkable persistence in patterns of controversy over the analysis of economic development. Indeed, what we witness nowadays is very much a case of "old wine in new bottles". The analytic fluids are much the same, though twentieth century fashions (rather than nineteenth century ones) now influence the packaging and labeling. In short, much of the ground of current controversey has been traversed before.

Two further conclusions also emerge from a reconsideration of nineteenth century discussions of India's modernization. In the first place, there would appear to be good reason to counsel caution to those who would readily use the latest models from advanced countries to guide analysis and policy in the less developed ones. After all, such economics by extension has been practiced before. Few are likely to maintain that the standard models applied in India in the nineteenth century led to

[40] See, for example, Dudley Seers, "A Theory of Inflation and Growth in Underdeveloped Countries Based on the Experience of Latin America", *Oxford Economic Papers*, 1963.

[41] Raul Prebisch, "Economic Development or Monetary Stability: The False Dilemma", *Economic Bulletin for Latin America*, March 1961.

altogether satisfactory results—at least if conspicuous improvement in real income is taken to be the measure of satisfactory performance. Disappointing outcomes in the real world do not, of course, invalidate an analytic model. Nevertheless, there is some *prima facie* evidence to support the view that the highest analytic techniques may be inappropriate in the poor countries. Moderation in the claims to universality for models derived from Position I premises may thus be in order.

The failure of the Conceptual Luddites to win a wider and more influential audience suggests another conclusion. On specific issues, the points made by Position II commentators have often been telling. Yet the critical stance of a Conceptual Luddite does not easily lend itself to the construction of an alternative theoretical system. Therein lies a major explanation for the failure of the critics to exert more intellectual influence. If study of the history of economic theory yields any single moral, it must surely be that inappropriate conceptual systems are never shaken by confrontation with awkward facts. They are only successfully challenged by superior theoretical models.

8

MODERNIZATION OF ECONOMIC LIFE IN UNDERDEVELOPED COUNTRIES

PARESH CHATTOPADHYAY

I

By MODERNIZATION of economic life we mean the act of modernizing the economy of a country; in other words, the act of effecting the economic development of a country that is, for the moment, economically backward compared to some other countries that are more advanced economically. From this point of view our position seems to tally broadly with that expressed by Daniel Lerner in his definition of modernization: "Modernization is the process of social change in which development is the economic component." [1] In other words, for the purpose of this paper, we take modernization to be broadly equivalent to what is currently known as economic development of an underdeveloped country. But what is an underdeveloped country and what is economic development?

By an underdeveloped country the bourgeois economists generally mean a country which is economically "backward" compared with the advanced capitalist countries of the West, this "backwardness" showing itself through lower per capita income in the former compared with the latter. By implication this would mean that such a country is roughly speaking at a stage in which the present-day capitalist countries themselves were

[1] *International Encyclopaedia of Social Sciences* (1968), Vol. 10, p. 387.

one hundred and fifty or two hundred years ago. Even though, from the point of view of real income per head, there may be some truth in this statement, such a statement passes in complete silence the very substantial qualitative differences in the two situations.[2]

The structure of the economies of the present-day advanced capitalist countries in the "pre-industrialization" period did not show excessive growth of some sectors, those linked with foreign capital and foreign markets, at the expense of the rest of the economy. Their economies did not develop or stagnate following fluctuations in world market conditions of primary products nor were their new-born industries compelled to compete with already established ones dominated by world monopolies. Finally, these advanced countries were not, at the stage of their "backwardness", economically dependent upon others for sheer survival in the sense in which the present-day underdeveloped countries are.[3] Thus the bourgeois treatment of an underdeveloped country, at least by implication, hides the most essential characteristic of underdevelopment—the domination and exploitation of such a country by world monopoly capital.

By economic development the bourgeois economists generally mean raising the per capita real income of a country.[4] As to the factors that determine this rate of growth their point of view is well represented by the President of the International Economic Association, Professor E. A. G. Robinson of Cambridge, when he points out, with reference to the "advanced" countries, that such factors include, besides the supply capital, everything that we regard as contributing to industrial efficiency: better education, better research, better choice and planning of industrial processes, better transport and economies of scale, quicker transfer of knowledge from firm to firm and from country to country; and above all a dynamic and progressive outlook and a determination and freedom to achieve progress. As to the "underdeveloped" countries, Professor Robinson adds, they need not increase the world's stock of scientific knowledge and skills for their progress. They need only "to increase the rate of its transfer".[5]

Thus economic development is, for all practical purposes, reduced to, first of all, production activity artificially separated from other economic

[2] See C. Bettelheim: *Planification et Croissance Accélérée* (1964), Third Essay.

[3] For a not so satisfactory comparison see S. Kuznets, "Present Underdeveloped Countries and Past Growth Patterns" in his *Economic Growth and Structure* (1965).

[4] See W.A. Lewis: *Theory of Economic Growth* (1955), p. 9. The non-English-speaking economists offer a rather broader definition involving mental and social changes among a people leading to higher income. See. F. Perrou: *L'Economie du XX Siècle* (1961), Ch. III.

[5] Opening Address at the International Congress on Economic Development, Vienna, September 1962, in *Problems in Economic Development*, Ed. E. A. G. Robinson (1965), pp. XVI-XVIII.

activities. Secondly, even the production activity itself is reduced to the technique of production which concerns itself, as purely *the* "economic phenomenon", only with the relation of man to nature, only with what Marx called the "forces of production". Of course reducing the problem of economic development basically to technology [6]—though admitting the relevance of social factors described as "non-economic" factors and hence relegating them to a place outside the pale of the economists—is a particular manifestation of the more general attitude towards the process of production in economics shown by what Marx called "vulgar political economy" after the decline and fall of the classical political economy.[7] The classical political economy, during the heroic period of the bourgeoisie's fight against feudalism, was not satisfied simply with studying the so-called "technical" aspect of production but was also occupied with its "social" aspect. That is, in Marx's terminology, their analysis comprised both the "forces of production" and the "relations of production" —both the relation of man to nature and the relation of man to man through classes. The classical economists did not fight shy of discussing the production relations along with the productive forces because they wrote on behalf of the class that represented the new, capitalist mode of production in its fight against the old, feudal mode of production. It was, rather, precisely in their interest to show the defects of the old mode of production and the merits of the new. One may refer, in this connection, to Adam Smith's discussion of the division of labour and of "productive" and "unproductive" labour as well as to Ricardo's definition of political economy.[8] After the bourgeois mode of production was firmly established it became, however, increasingly uncomfortable for the apologists of the system to raise any basic question concerning the relations of production in economics and the post-Menger post-Jevonian academic economics unceremoniously dropped any serious discussion on the subject. Thus the contemporary bourgeois economists have reduced the study of the

[6] Among the modern economists J. A. Schumpeter seems to be a notable exception in this respect. See his *Theory of Economic Development* (1934), Ch. II.

[7] The classical political economy, according to Marx, began with Petty in England and Boisguillebert in France and ended with Ricardo in England and Sismondi in France-Switzerland. See his *Zur Kritik der Poilitischen Okonomie* (1859) in Marx-Engels: *Werke* (1964) B. 13. S. 37. By classical political economy, he wrote, "I understand all the political economy since Petty which inquires into the real interrelations of bourgeois production [Zusammenhang der bürgerlichen Produktionsverhältnisse] in opposition to the vulgar economy which deals with the *appearance* of such interrelations."—*Das Kapital*, I, 1867, in ME: *Werke* (1962) B. 23 S. 95. Our italics.

[8] See A. Smith: *Wealth of Nations* (1776), B. I, Ch. I; B. II, Ch. III; and D. Ricardo: *Principles of Political Economy and Taxation* (1817), Preface.

process of production and consequently of economic development mostly to an analysis of productive forces, shunting off the so-called "non-economic" factors, that is the relations of production, to the sociologists. Thus by abstaining from all class analysis these economists have, for all practical purposes, reduced the problem of economic development to a "technical" problem, thereby hiding its vital, essential element—the role of domination and exploitation in underdevelopment.

As a matter of fact the phenomenon of economic development/under-development of a society cannot be meaningfully analysed save in the context of what Marx called "social economic formation" Ökonomische Gesellschaftsformation) that manifests itself through the prevalent mode of production of the society in question[9]. The state of the economy of a society at a particular moment of time corresponds to a definite stage in the social-economic formation of that society whose structure and development is principally explained through production relations.[10] Though the concept of "social-economic formation" is a perfectly *general* concept one must at the same time emphasize its *specificity* which is no less important. In other words, though it is true that the relations of production form the structure of a society and that these relations correspond to a definite stage of the development of productive forces that does not itself explain the specific character of a particular mode of production. As Marx pointed out in a passage of a relatively neglected text, "if there is no production in *general,* there is also no *general* production ... whenever we speak of production we always think of production at a *definite* stage of social development".[11] Thus, even if we leave aside the pre-capitalist modes of production, the capitalist mode of production itself undergoes changes at its different phases over time, besides showing different forms in different countries at the same period of time. As is well known, Lenin's contribution to scientific political economy related to both these aspects. On the one hand he analysed the changes that capitalism as a world system had undergone since the days of Marx and Engels and, on the other, he showed how in the particular case of Russia, though capitalism was developing

[9] See *Zur Kritik* - Vorwort in *MEW* (13) S. 9. Also *Das Kapital* I, Vorwort zur ersten Auflage in *MEW* (23) S. 16.

[10] See Lenin: "What the 'Friends of the people' are and How They Fight the Social Democrats" (1894) in *Collected Works* (Moscow), Vol. I, p. 141. To Lenin "economic formation of society" is "the sum total of given production relations". (*Ibid.,* p. 142)

[11] Einleitung zur Kritik der politischen Okonomie (1857) in *MEW* (13), S. 616, 617. Our italics. The text forms a part of *Grundrisse der Kritik der Politischen Okonomie (Rohentwurf)* [1857-58]. S. 5-31 of the 1953 edition. The text was posthumously published by Kautsky in *Neuezeit* (1903).

in all its general features, yet it did not develop exactly in the way that Marx had envisaged in the context of Western Europe in his principal theoretical work.

In the abstract model—an abstraction that is both necessary and scientific—set up by Marx in his principal theoretical work capitalism has two basic features: it is essentially competitive and it has, in the main, vanquished all pre-capitalist modes of production. For, as we know, contemporary England was the model of capitalism for him.[12] Lenin enriched Marxism on both these counts. First he showed that capitalism was no longer competitive; it had entered the monopoly stage.[13] Secondly he demonstrated that in an economically backward country like Russia, in the epoch of world monopoly-capitalism, it was no longer possible for the capitalist mode of production to suppress entirely the pre-capitalist modes. They had to co-exist.[14]   Both these strands of Lenin's thought found their unity in his famous formulation of the law of uneven development of capitalism.[15]

Capitalism is of course an integral world system. But the whole consists of parts that are extremely uneven. At the same moment there are countries where capitalism is far advanced and others in which it is being born, where the pre-capitalist modes of production still predominate— though both forming parts of the single world capitalist market. Similar differences show themselves also in the interior of each country or even in the same sector of production. Now the development of capitalism to an advanced stage in some countries—belonging essentially to Western Europe and North America—depended precisely, as Sweezy has recently emphasized in an excellent paper, on the underdevelopment of the rest of the world.[16] This dialectical interdependence of development and underdevelopment—to borrow Sweezy's expression—had two facets. On the one hand the wealth plundered from the underdeveloped countries became the basis of advancement of the developed countries. This was in

[12] See *Das Kapital* I, Vorwort zur ersten Auflage in *MEW* (23) S. 12

[13] Mainly in his classic *Imperialism, The Highest Stage of Capitalism* (1916).

[14] Referrng to Russia Lenin wrote about the "tremendous relics of corvée economy and all kinds of survivals of serfdom" along with the development of capitalism, in the preface to the second edition (1907) of his *Development of Capitalism in Russia* (First edition, 1899). See also Ch. VIII, Section VI of the same book. Some years later he characterized Russia as "bourgeois-feudal". See his article "Two Utopias" (1912).

[15] Indications of this law are not completely absent in Marx. For example, he wrote, "The country more developed industrially shows to the less developed only the image of its own future . . . Not only the development of Capitalism but also the incompleteness of its development inflict suffering on us [the Germans]. Alongside of modern evils a whole series of inherited evils oppress us arising from the passive survivals of the old mode of production." *op. cit.*, S. 12-15)

[16] "The Future of Capitalism" in D. Cooper (Ed.): *The Dialectics of Liberation* (1967).

fact the external source of primitive accumulation of capital in these
countries—the internal source being the forcible expropriation of the
masses of agricultural producers from the soil within these countries.[17]
To facilitate this primitive accumulation the capitalist countries tried, on
the other hand, to destroy the pre-capitalist modes of production that
were prevailing in the rest of the world. The term "modernization" used
by bourgeois scholars in the context of an underdeveloped economy is
only a euphemism for the phenomenon of the pre-capitalist modes of
production being invaded by the capitalist mode, the latter being introduced by the so-called developed countries. But by the very nature
of things the capitalist countries have no interest in seeing capitalism develop fully in the colonial countries. The former are interested
in destroying the old modes of production only in so far as they put
obstacles in their path to rapid accumulation of capital. In the event, the
process of colonial exploitation resulted in small areas of capitalism arising
and maintaining themselves like islands in a vast sea of pre-capitalist
modes of production in these countries. Marx had already an idea of the
confrontation between the two systems—"the contradiction between the
two diametrically opposed economic systems" as he calls it in the last
chapter of the first volume of his principal theoretical work.[18] This contradiction has only recently gained admission to the main corpus of bourgeois political economy under the name "dual economy"—one part of the
economy being "modern" the other, the major part, remaining traditional,
the task of economic development being to modernize the traditional
part.[19]

There are certain important aspects of this "dualism" that we must
take account of. *Firstly*, in a fundamental sense dualism in economy is
a universal phenomenon in capitalism—true for its advanced as well as
its underdeveloped parts. In every country under the sway of capitalism
there is a developed and there is an underdeveloped sector.[20] *Secondly*,

[17] For the importance of merchant capital in primitive accumulation see Marx:
Grundrisse, S. 375 ff and *Das Kapital* III, in *MEW* (25) S. 335 ff.

[18] *Das Kapital* I, *op. cit.*, S. 792.

[19] The two important references are (1) J. H. Boeke: *Economics and Economic Policy
of Dual Societies as Exemplified by Indonesia* (1953) and (2) B. Higgins: "The
'Dualistic Theory' of Underdeveloped Areas" in *Economic Development and Cultural
Change* (1956). There have been quite a few exercises in model building on this
theme in bourgeois economic literature beginning with W. A. Lewis's paper, "Economic
Development with Unlimited Supplies of Labour" in *Manchester School* (1954).

[20] The advanced and underdeveloped countries may *appear* to present basic differences in this regard, inasmuch as the former are fully capitalist whereas the latter are
predominantly under pre-capitalist modes of production. But the differences are more
apparent than real because the pre-capitalist modes of production are, in the final
analysis, dominated by the world capitalist market.

even in the underdeveloped countries there is no Chinese Wall between
the so-called "modern" and the "traditional" sectors—between the developed and the underdeveloped sectors, contrary to what the dualist
theoreticians usually imply. Though the developed sector is broadly
speaking capitalist and the underdeveloped sector pre-capitalist, the
latter is being constantly, though slowly, undermined by the former under the auspices of world monopoly capital. *Thirdly*, this dualism in an
underdeveloped country has itself a dual character as far as exploitation is concerned. The country as a whole is exploited by an external
imperialist bourgeoisie, concretely through the so-called "modern" sector;
and inside the country itself the indigenous bourgeoisie, in alliance with
the feudal or semi-feudal elements, and very often in subordination to the
foreign imperialist bourgeoisie, exploit the rest of the people. *Fourthly*,
and this follows from what precedes, modernization or economic development cannot be viewed as a class-neutral phenomenon, or merely
as a "technical" phenomenon in abstraction, apart from the production
relations underlying the phenomenon. In order to make a meaningful study
of modernization in an underdeveloped country one must be prepared
to analyse which path this modernization is following—capitalist or
socialist.

In order to eliminate dualism in the sense in which it appears in underdeveloped countries—the co-existence of capitalism and pre-capitalism
—the capitalist sector should be in a position to dominate and finally to
absorb the entire pre-capitalist sector within its fold. This was indeed
the classic way in which capitalism achieved complete victory in Western
Europe. But this is no longer possible in present-day underdeveloped
countries. Imperialism, indeed, broke up the old modes of production but
only to the extent that such destruction was necessary for extracting
raw materials and foodstuffs from these countries. The development of
full-fledged capitalism in the colonies or semi-colonies would however
go against its own monopoly interests. Even when these countries became
formally politically independent and had a sizeable bourgeoisie—India is
obviously a case in point—it was no longer possible for the class to
effect the necessary transformation. In the context of the victory of
socialism over a considerable portion of the globe and particularly after
the triumph and consolidation of the Chinese, Vietnamese and Cuban revolutions and the forward march of the national liberation movements,
the consolidation between this class on the one hand and feudalism
and imperialism on the other is no longer antagonistic, even if it ever
was; whereas the contradiction between this holy trinity and the people
has become antagonistic. Hence it is no longer in the interest of the indigenous bourgeoisie—mainly the big bourgeoisie—to carry the fight against
the pre-capitalist modes of production to its logical conclusion as this

would alienate the other propertied classes connected with them. The real solution of the problem of dualism in underdeveloped countries—in the sense of the co-presence of the different modes of production side by side—lies in following the socialist path of "modernization", after the working class in alliance with the immense majority of the people seizes political power in these countries.

II

SECTION I

The process of "modernization" in the sense defined above, i.e. the dissolution of the old mode of production and the introduction of the new, started in India fom the moment she was conquered and colonized by England. For what the British did in India was, as Marx pointed out in his well-known articles on India in the fifties of the nineteenth century, nothing short of a social revolution unlike any that India had experienced in the past.

First, the conquest of India by England was no ordinary foreign conquest. It placed India directly under the domination of a class of commercial bourgeoisie that was in the vanguard of developing capitalism. Marx pointed out that this domination at once played a destructive and a regenerating role for India. The destructive aspect showed itself, in the early years of the British rule, through extortion, plunder and such other naked forms of exploitation of the Indian people and, in the later years, through measures of contracting the sale of Indian manufactures in England and expanding the sale of English manufactures in India. Thus "India," to quote Marx, "the great workshop of cotton manufacture for the world since immemorial times, became now inundated with English twists and cotton stuffs." [21] The immediate effect was the depopulation of manufacturing towns and the consequent pressure of population on land. Accompanying this was a measure of far-reaching consequence. This was the establishment of a land revenue system in India on a completely new basis—broadly under the names of *zemindari* and *ryotwari*. Under *zamindari* the intermediary of old, who had administrative and fiscal duties but no rights in land, was made the landed proprietor who would serve as the intermediary revenue collector between the tenant-cultivators and the government. This system was ordinarily known as the Permanent Settlement though there was also Temporary Settlement under the *zamindari* system. Under the *ryotwari* system, there was

---

[21] "The East India Company; its History and Results", *New York Daily Tribune*, 11 July, 1853.

no intermediary; the individual peasant, who had only customary rights,. was now vested with full ownership of his holding and paid land taxes direct to the government. What is important here is to note that in either case the principle of private property in land was directly introduced; for the purpose of revenue individual assessment replaced the old system of collective assessment of the whole village and land became a commodity to be bought and sold. This was accompanied by collection of tax in cash instead of kind, as had formerly been the case. The introduction of this land system together with the invasion of low-priced English manufactures on a massive scale—ruining the weavers and spinners in the villages—contributed significantly to the break-up of the traditional. village system in India.

The regenerating aspect of the British rule in India showed itself through the establishment of unprecedented political unity, the formation of an educated Indian class "imbued with European Science" and, what was perhaps the most important of all, the introduction of railways. The railways, besides breaking down the isolation and self-sufficiency of the village, represented the import of British manufactures. to India and the export of India's raw materials and foodstuffs to England. The introduction of railways also involved the investment of British capital in plantations, mines and factories in addition to railways. and led to the growing application of machinery even to those branches of industry not immediately connected with railways. Thus the railways. not only made India an integral part of the world capitalist system but also and at the same time became, in Marx's words, "the forerunner of modern industry".[22]

Again, the process of turning India into an agricultural colony for the exclusive purposes of supply of raw materials and food to England in exchange for her manufactured goods gave rise to a considerable amount of trading and commercial activities inside India. This development of trade and commerce, even as it undermined the foundations of the traditional Indian society, at the same time considerably strengthened the mercantile bourgeoisie—the forerunners of the industrial bourgeoisie—and greatly widened the class of wage labourers consequent upon the process of "de-industrialization".

Thus the very process of colonization of India contained within itself the elements of its own negation. The effect of the introduction of the new land system—whether *zamindari* or *ryotwari*—was far-reaching for the countryside. In the *zamindari* area the introduction of the English landlord system, "a caricature of English landed estates",[23] accompanied

---

[22] "Future Results of British Rule in India", *Ibid.*, 8 August, 1953.
[23] Marx, *Das Kapital* III, S. 346 (Berlin, 1964).

by English bourgeois legal conceptions, resulted in the large-scale evic-
tion of peasants—now turned tenants—from land, besides creating a horde
of intermediaries between the nominal proprietor and the cultivator. A
basically similar development took place in the *ryotwari* areas through the
process of subletting and through the dispossession of the original cultivators by moneylenders. As a consequence, the countryside witnessed,
in course of time, a sharp differentiation of classes accompanied by an
enormous growth of the number of landless labourers—the agricultural
proletariat. Thus, according to the Census Reports, within a decade between 1921 and 1931, the number of landless labourers among those engaged in agriculture rose from one-fifth to one-third. At the same time, the
process of commercialization of agriculture, already begun with the introduction of money economy in the form of cash assessments, was hastened
by the improved means of transport and communication and by the
cultivator's urgent need of cash to pay the interest on his debt to the
moneylender.

By the middle of the last century the indigenous industries were by
and large destroyed. At about the same time the railways experienced
remarkable progress—from a little over 400 miles in 1859 they extended
to more than 5,000 miles in the next decade. This was also the epoch
when British capitalism was entering a new stage—the stage of
monopoly capitalism associated with the growing importance of the export of capital, in contrast to the export of commodities that had marked
the stage of the earlier industrial capitalism. As a matter of fact, the
growth of railways, as mentioned earlier, led to the investment of British
capital not only in the railways but also in plantations, mines and factories. This was the beginning of industrialization on a fully capitalist
basis. However, this "industrialization" was based almost exclusively on
British capital invested in enterprises directly related to the production
and export of raw materials. The only modern industry in the organization of which Indian capital took the initiative was cotton spinning and
weaving. On the whole, there was a steady growth of *existing* industries.
Thus, between 1890 and 1914, cotton spindles more than doubled, cotton
powerlooms quadrupled, jute looms increased four and a half times and
coal raising six times, while the extension of railways continued at the
rate of about 800 miles per annum.[24] Meanwhile, the iron and steel
industry, owned and managed by the Indian bourgeoisie, had come into
existence. In the same period the average daily number of employees
in the factories increased more than threefold.[25] The progress of indus-
dustries continued on the whole during the later years. The counterpart

[24] D. H. Buchanan: *Development of Capitalist Enterprise in India* (1934), p. 159.
[25] *Ibid.*

of this progress was of course the growth of British investments in India over the years. Thus according to the estimate of George Paish the share of British investments in India in her total foreign investments was 11 per cent in 1910.[26] The corresponding figures rose to about 20 per cent on the eve of the Second World Dar.[27] According to the Reserve Bank's estimate, the share of British investments in the total foreign investments in India was 72 per cent in 1948.[28]

However, there were forces developing inside the country that were already undermining the British position in India. The very forces unleashed by imperialism were responsible for the birth and development of capitalism and the bourgeoisie in India. From a small beginning, Indian capitalism began to develop along with the overall growth of modern industries. Most of the industries that grew in the inter-war period and during the Second World War—namely, cotton textiles, sugar, cement, iron and steel, paper, chemicals, ferro alloys, diesel engines, non-ferrous metals, machine tools, etc.—were Indian-dominated industries. Then the share of manufactured goods in India's total exports rose from 30 per cent in 1938-39 to 55.5 in 1948-49.[29] Similarly the share of India's traders in India's external trade rose from about 15 per cent in 1930-31 to about 60 per cent in imports and 75 per cent in exports in 1951.[30] At the same time there was a steady growth in the size of the working class in the organized industrial sector. There seems to have been a fourfold expansion of factory employment between 1900 and 1939 followed by an increase of 20 per cent between 1939 and 1945.[31]

However, we must avoid giving an exaggerated idea of the development of capitalism in India at the end of British rule. Thus, although there was a definite *absolute* growth of manufacturing industry prior to 1951, very little change in the *relative* position of modern industry had occurred. Thus in 1951 the proportion of the total labour force employed in factories with 20 or more workers and employing power was only 2.1 per cent, contributing 6.5 per cent of the national income, there being practically no change since 1931.[32] This signifies that capitalism, besides being backward on the whole, manifested itself mostly in small-scale production. However, there can be no doubt that capitalist relations were

[26] *Journal of the Royal Statistical Society*, 1911.
[27] Wadia and Merchant, *Our Economic Problem* (1956), p. 561.
[28] Reserve Bank of India: *Census of India's Foreign Liabilities and Assets* (1950), p. 84.
[29] Cited by R. L. Varshneya, *India's Foreign Trade* (1954), p. 95.
[30] *Report of the Central Banking Enquiry Committee*, 1931, and *R.B.I. Bulletin*, February 1954.
[31] W. Malenbaum: *Prospects for Indian Development* (1962), p. 152.
[32] Planning Commission (GOI): *Papers relating to the Formulation of the Second Five-Year Plan* (1955), p. 203.

growing in India at a steady rate and were giving rise to a class of bourgeoisie that was more and more thinking in terms of independent capitalist development in India. The secret of its strength did not however lie so much in the economic resources it commanded as in its ability to ally itself with and lead a political movement that more and more threatened the foundations of imperialism.

SECTION II

When we arrive at the contemporary scene, that is at the epoch following the transfer of power in 1947, we find that the process of the dissolution of the old mode of production, which started under the British, has continued at a greater pace. We shall be almost exclusively concerned with the two basic spheres of production—agriculture and industry.

First we discuss agriculture where we start with agricultural production. With 1949-50 = 100, the index of production rose from 95.6 in 1950-51 to 161.8 in 1967-68.[33] This shows that the growth rate of agricultural production has been rather slow exceeding only slightly the rate of growth of population which is about 2.5 per cent per year. But, then, this modest rate of growth seems to be quite high compared with the rate of growth during the previous regime. Thus between 1900 to 1924 foodgrain production in India seems to have increased at an annual rate of 0.3 per cent and between 1924 and 1948 it declined at the rate of 0.2 per cent per annum,[34] whereas the compound annual rate of growth of foodgrains production in India during 1949-50 to 1964-65 has been 2.98 per cent.[35] A part of this growth is explained by the extension of the area of cultivation. But from the middle fifties the last factor seems to have played a comparatively minor role in the increase of production. In fact, since the middle fifties, the dominant trend is that of higher yield from the acreage cultivated. Increasing application of better inputs in agriculture seems to have been an important factor in this growth though favourable weather conditions undoubtedly also had a non-negligible share. Thus the area under irrigation has increased from 51.5 million acres in 1950-51 to 96.9 million acres at the end of the Third Plan.[36] With regard to agricultural machinery, the increases are given in Table 1. As regards fertilizers, the consumption of nitrogenous and phosphatic fertilizers has gone up, between 1956-1957 and 1965-1966, from 130,636

[33] *Indian Agriculture in Brief*, Government of India (1968), pp. 118-21.
[34] Cited by S. R. Sen in *Commerce*, Annual Number, 1967, p. 43.
[35] *Growth Rates in Agriculture*, Government of India (1966).
[36] *Third Five-Year Plan* (Govt. of India). p. 382, and *Fourth Five-Year Plan: A Draft Outline* (Govt. of India), p. 9.

tonnes to 540,803 tonnes and from 21,967 tonnes to 156,489 tonnes respectively.[37]

It follows that this development of production and the forces of production, by all evidence much faster than that in the pre-1947 period, though far from satisfactory considering our requirements, could not have been achieved on the basis of a totally stagnant agrarian structure. Let us now see what modifications this structure has undergone and in which direction.

TABLE 1

INPUTS IN AGRICULTURE

	1951	1956	1961	1966
Tractors (000)	8.6	21	31	53.97
Oil engines (000)	82	123	230	441
Sugarcane crushers (000)	526	568	624	587
Electric pumps (000)	8.5	47	160	366

SOURCE: *Indian Livestock Census, 1956*, Vol. I, p. 4, and *Indian Agriculture in Brief* (*op. cit.*), p. 53.

The Indian bourgeoisie who, by and large, had led the national movement against imperialism was bent upon carrying India along an independent capitalist path. But this was out of the question as long as the countryside remained semi-feudal, to which state it was reduced by imperialism. The Congress Party, the political party of the Indian bourgeoisie, was aware of this at the hour of transfer of power. In fact the report of its Agrarian Reforms Committee published in 1949 was a very radical document from the bourgeois point of view. It recommended the abolition of intermediaries, the giving of land to the actual tiller, protection of the tenant from rack renting, commutation of rent in kind into cash. The Committee envisaged small and medium-sized farms following the allotment of land to the tenants. Thus the whole programme seems to have envisaged full-fledged capitalism in agriculture based on peasant proprietorship, resembling, in important respects, what Lenin called the "American path of land distribution" in contrast to the "Prussian Path" leading to landlord-type capitalist farming.[38] By the time the Congress governments in different states were enacting and later "implementing"

[37] *Indian Agriculture in Brief* (op. cit.), p. 189.
[38] Two important references are his *Agrarian Programme of Russian Social Democracy in the Democratic Revolution* (1907) and Preface to the Second Edition (1907) of *Development of Capitalism in Russia* (1899).

the land legislation the original programme of the bourgeoisie was how-ever greatly diluted in favour of the rural vested interests—both as regards heavy compensation and as regards the definition of personal cultivation, resulting in the intermediaries taking on huge amounts of land by evicting millions of tenant-cultivators.[39]

There were several factors behind this step backward. The local and state leaderships of the ruling party were much more seriously compro-mised with the landed interests than the national leadership. Secondly, the widespread mass struggle in the country at the hour of transfer of power, specially the armed struggle of the Telengana peasants that pre-ceded the legislations, had a dual effect on the bourgeoisie—on the one hand it felt the necessity of undertaking land reforms to a certain extent to eliminate the stark exploitation in the countryside and, on the other hand, it did not want to go too far in this for fear of antagonizing the powerful vested interests in the rural area who could be its allies when faced with a popular upsurge. Thirdly, the triumph of the Chinese Revolution, followed by the popular victory in the first phase of the national liberation war in Vietnam also had almost an identical dual effect on the Indian bourgeoisie. Consequently the land reform measures did not come to much; however, to a certain extent, they resulted in some modifications of the old mode of production, though unevenly as between different States. For example, in the State of Saurashtra, a sample study among 124 girasdars—i.e. the landlords—showed that whereas before the land reforms they had 4,455 acres of self-cultivated land, after the reforms they had 5,764 acres, 26 girasdars securing additional lands under khudkasht[40] allotments—all of which could be effected through the evic-tion of the previous tenants. On the other hand in Rajasthan the khudkasht area held after the reforms was 26.4 per cent less than the operational holdings of the intermediaries before the reforms.[41]

The success of land legislation regarding prohibition of sub-letting or leasing of land was also mixed. In Andhra, for example, leasing increased from 8.8 per cent of owned lands before the reforms to 10.7 per cent after the reforms, while in UP the extent of sub-tenancy, including share cropping, was estimated to have declined from 13.98 per cent to 10.50

[39] Thus a keen American observer of the Indian agrarian scene, Daniel Thorner, pointed out that in the State of Bihar the landlords, taking advantage of the defini-tion of personal cultivation as given in the legislation, could retain 500, 700 and 1000 acres of land in the post-reform" era. See Daniel Thorner, *The Agrarian Pros-pect of India* (1956) p. 34.

[40] *Khudkasht* signifies land under the personal cultivation of the landlord.

[41] See the consolidated study by P. T. George in the *Indian Journal of Agricultural Economics,* July-September 1968,

per cent of the total cultivated area of the sample villages.[42] On the whole, as a competent student has observed, "There is no evidence to show that the tenancy practices changed for the better as a result of the abolition of the intermediaries' though the former tenants became owners *under the law*."[43]

The ceiling on land holdings offers us more or less the same story. The law in various States fixed the ceiling on existing holdings in such a way that it would preserve the middle holders and rich peasants; for with more than 60 per cent of landholdings in India under five acres, the ceiling fixed by the different States ranged from 14 to 300 acres.[44] At the same time, the intermediaries were able to retain huge amounts of land by underhand means. Thus in West Bengal between a quarter and a third of land that could be available under the legally fixed 25 acres ceiling went to the landlords through *mala fide* transfers.[45]

We shall say a few words here about usurious capital. It is well known that, historically, usurious capital, which is often connected with merchant capital, manifested through private money-lending, has preceded the capitalist mode of production.[46] But *ipso facto* neither usurious nor merchant capital leads to the capitalist mode of production. Everything depends on the particular stage of historical development.[47] However, it is perhaps not too much to say that usury, even if it does not, *per se*, strengthen the feudal or semi-feudal mode of production, at least does retard its dissolution and the corresponding transition to commodity production and capitalism.[48] In our country about 54 per cent of the rural households are indebted and the share of private moneylenders in the total farm credit is 62 per cent.[49] However there has been some, though modest, progress here over a decade. Table 2 shows that the grip of private moneylenders has to some extent diminished and the share of government and cooperatives in total farm credit has to some extent increased over a decade.

One of the first things that strikes a student of India's agrarian situation is the extreme differentiation among the peasantry as regards both the size of landholdings and the value of different assets possessed. Table 3 shows the distribution of operational holdings in Indian agriculture as it

[42] P. T. George: *op. cit.*, and Singh and Misra: *Land Reforms in Uttar Pradesh* (1964), p. 160.

[43] P.T. George: *op. cit* (Our emphasis).

[44] *Third Five-Year Plan* (Govt. of India), pp. 236-38.

[45] Basu & Bhattacharya: *Land Reforms in West Bengal* (1963). p. 82.

[46] Marx: *Das Kapital* III, S. 607 (ed. cit.).

[47] *Ibid.*, p. 608.

[48] Lenin: *Development of Capitalism in Russia* (1899), Ch. XIII.

[49] *National Sample Survey Report No. 95* (July 1960-June 1961), and *All-India Rural Debt and Investment Survey* (Reserve Bank of India) 1961-62.

prevailed in 1961-1962. On the basis of the table we find that a little less than two thirds of all the operational holdings having less than 5 acres— which is well below the average of 6.5 acres—hold about a fifth of the total area operated; whereas, at the very top, 3 per cent of the households with more than 30 acres have under them about a quarter of the total area operated. As regards the assets at the disposal of the peasantry their distribution also shows great differentiation as indicated in Table 4.

TABLE 2

SHARE OF VARIOUS CREDIT AGENCIES IN THE WHOLE FARM CREDIT

Credit Agency	Percentage share	
	1950-51	1961-62
Government and Co-operatives	6	15.4
Traders	6	7.2
Agriculture & Professional Money-lenders	70	62.0
Relatives	14	6.4
Landlords	2	0.9
Commercial Banks	<1	<1
Others	The rest	The rest
TOTAL	100	100

SOURCE: *All-India Rural Credit Survey* (1950-51) and *All-India Rural Debt and Investment Survey* (1961-62).

TABLE 3

HOUSEHOLD OPERATIONAL HOLDINGS AND AREA OPERATED BY SIZE (ALL INDIA)

Size groups (acres)	Percent of holdings	Percent of total area
1. up to 0.49	8.55	0.32
2. 0.50— 0.99	8.58	0.95
3. 1.00— 2.49	21.94	5.59
4. 2.50— 4.99	22.62	12.32
5. 5.00— 7.49	12.84	11.73
6. 7.50— 9.99	6.96	8.97
7. 10.00—12.49	5.05	8.25
8. 12.50—14.99	2.90	5.95
9. 15.00—19.99	3.75	9.58
10. 20.00—24.99	2.29	7.39
11. 25.00—29.99	1.31	5.38
12. 30.00—49.99	2.18	12.05
13. 50.00 and above	1.03	11.60
Average size: 6.49 acres		

SOURCE: *National Sample Survey*, 17th Round, Setember 1961—July 1962.

The same story is told by fixed capital formation in farm business. Table 5 sets out the global data.

The cause as well as the consequence of the differentiation among the peasantry is reflected in the data concerning profit and loss per acre as the size of the holding increases. The farm management data from different States, studied by the Ministry of Food and Agriculture, show that the loss decreases and profit increases per acre as the size of the holding increases. Figures for the Punjab are given in Table 6.

TABLE 4

DISTRIBUTION OF CULTIVATOR HOUSEHOLDS ACCORDING TO THE VALUE OF ASSETS (ALL-INDIA)

Asset group	Percent of households	Aggregate value of assets (crores of rupees)
Less than Rs. 500	6.5	99.4 (0.3)
Rs. 500— 1,000	9.7	366.3 (1.1)
1000— 2,500	24.8	2,124.1 (6.3)
2500— 5,000	23.3	4,215.9(12.5)
5000—10,000	18.6	6,587.8(19.5)
10000—20,000	10.7	7,498.6(22.2)
20000 and above	6.4	12,885.6(38.1)
All Asset Groups	100.0	33,777.6(100.0)

Figures in brackets are percentages to total for all asset groups.

SOURCE: *All-India Rural Debt and Investment Survey,* 1961-62, Table 1 in *Reserve Bank of India Bulletin,* June, 1965.

TABLE 5

FIXED CAPITAL FORMATION IN FARM BUSINESS (ALL-INDIA)

Asset Group (Rs.)	Proportion of cultivator households reporting (%)	Average per household Rs.	Aggregate (crores of Rs.)
Less than 500	10.1	3.4	1.1 (0.7)
500— 1,000	13.1	4.2	2.0 (1.2)
1000— 2,500	16.9	6.7	8.4 (5.1)
2500— 5,000	22.2	12.9	15.1 (9.2)
5000—10,000	27.5	30.9	28.9 (17.6)
10000—20,000	35.3	65.4	35.3 (21.4)
Rs. 20,000 and above	49.3	229.5	73.9 (44.9)
All asset groups	23.3	32.7	164.7 (100.0)

Figures in brackets show the percentage contribution of each asset group to the total for all asset groups.

SOURCE: *All-India Rural Debt and Investment Survey,* 1961-62, Table XVII in *Reserve Bank of India Bulletin,* June, 1965.

With minor definitional differences and some minor internal variations this picture is basically confirmed by the more recent data on larger farms in the same state presented in Table 7. This implies that small farmers find it increasingly difficult to stay on in farming and first try to supplement their land income through non-farming occupations and ultimately swell the ranks of landless agricultural labourers. An official re-

TABLE 6

PROFIT AND LOSS PER ACRE ON CROP PRODUCTION
(Average of 1954-1955—1956-1957)

Holding size group (acres)	Profit or loss per acre (in Rs.)
0 — ∠ 5	− 39.33
5 — ∠ 10	− 16.99
10 — ∠ 20	− 7.33
20 — ∠ 50	− 0.02
⩾50	+ 16.3

Profit or loss has been derived by deducting the value of input from the value of output. A minus sign precedes loss and a plus sign precedes profit.

SOURCE: *Studies in the Economics of Farm Management in the Punjab*, Combined Report (1963), Table 4.10.

TABLE 7

PER GROSS ACRE SALE RECEIPTS, 1967-1968

Size groups (acres)	Net cash receipts (in Rs.)
20— 25	179.92
25— 30	162.15
30— 40	174.10
40— 50	194.71
50— 75	164.22
75—100	182.98
100—150	255.78
<—150	591.52

Net cash receipts are arrived at by deducting total cash expenditure from total sale receipts.

SOURCE: Ashok Rudra, "Big Farmers of Punjab", Table 17, in *Economic and Political Weekly*, (Bombay) 27 December 1969.

port in the early fifties already spoke of the first phenomenon.[50] Normally we should expect that the process will first lead to an increase in the agricultural labour as a percentage of active agricultural population and ultimately to an increase in the landless agricultural labour as a percentage of total agricultural labour. The reality, however, does not present us with such a straightforward answer. On the basis of available data it seems that forces are moving in two opposite directions. Thus, according to the Census Reports, of the total agricultural active population, cultivators excluding agricultural labourers increased from 70 millions in 1951 to 99.5 millions in 1961, thus registering an increase of 43 per cent, whereas agricultural labourers increased from 28 millions to 31.5 millions only during the same time, thus registering a rise of only 14 per cent.[51] There may be several reasons for this apparently paradoxical phenomenon. To start with, the definition of the particular categories of the agricultural population differed as between the two censuses.[52] But a more important reason seems to be a gradual lessening of the inequality in the size distribution of operational holdings among agricultural households. Thus, if we compare the national sample survey data for two years, 1953-1954 and 1961-1962—that is, roughly speaking, those taken before the implementation of land reform legislation and those taken after—we see that, whereas according to the earlier data about 71 per cent of the households at the bottom having less than 5 acres operated 15.6 per cent of the area, according to the later data about 61.7 per cent of the households having less than 5 acres operated about 19 per cent of the area.[53]

We shall later give some indication of crop sharing in the different states of India.

It is also necessary to examine to what extent small and impoverished cultivators are migrating to other occupations in the rural or urban areas —a phenomenon into which, unfortunately, we cannot enter here for the lack of comprehensive data. However we do not doubt that the accentuation of the process of the formation of agricultural labour, like other manifestations of transition to commodity production and capitalism, has been seriously hampered by the old mode of production which is still very strong in the countryside. On the other hand we get a clear picture of the increase in landless labour as percentage of agricultural labour, as the figures in Table 8 show.

There is an important consequence of this disintegration of the peasantry. If we refer to the data on the size distribution of operational

[50] See *All-India Rural Credit Survey* (1954), Vol. II, Chapter 30.
[51] *Census of India*, 1961, Paper No. I of 1962, Appendix III.
[52] See the Reference already cited.
[53] *National Sample Survey*, 8th Round, 1953-54 and 17th Round, 1961-62.

holdings we find that on the supposition of 7.50 acres constituting an economic holding (striking a balance between 5 acres suggested by Nanavati and Anjaria and 10 acres suggested by Professor Dantwala), about 70 per cent of the area cultivated is already organized into units above the size of economic holdings operated by a quarter of the households. It should be obvious that the bulk of the produce from this area is meant for the market. In other words, it seems commodity production prevails in about two-thirds of the area cultivated in India. That the extent of commodity production has in fact been growing is also seen from the data on comparative growth-rates of foodgrains crops and non-foodgrains crops as well as the respective areas under them. Thus the compound growth rates per annum of production of foodgrains crops and area under them between 1949-50 and 1964-65 have been, respectively, 1.34 per cent and 2.98 per cent. The corresponding figures for non-foodgrains crops are higher, they being 2.52 and 3.61 per cent respectively.[54] Our position is further strengthened by the figures of inter-state movement of cereals by rail and river. Thus quantities of cereals moved were 3.20 million tons in 1955-56 and grew to 9.25 million tons in 1966-67.[55]

TABLE 8

PERCENTAGE OF AGRICULTURAL LABOUR HOUSEHOLDS (ALL-INDIA)

	1950-51	1956-57	1963-64
With land	49.93	42.87	38.83
Without land	50.7	57.13	61.17
TOTAL	100.00	100.00	100.00

SOURCE: *Agricultural Labour in India* (Labour Bureau, Department of Labour and Employment, Govt. of India), 1968, Table 2.12.

From our discussion above it appears that there is a definite, though slow, trend towards the disintegration of the old mode of production in agriculture. But can we speak of capitalist mode of production already prevailing in agriculture? The most definite evidence of the degree of capitalist penetration should be the extent of wage labour in agriculture.[56] According to the census figures roughly a quarter of the active agricultural population in India consists of agricultural labourers, which com-

[54] *Growth Rates in Indian Agriculture*, Government of India (1966).
[55] *Indian Agriculture in Brief* (1968), Table 6.2.
[56] Cf. Lenin, *New Data on Laws of Development of Capitalism in Agriculture* (1914-1915), Part I, Sec. 16.

pares favourably with the US and the German figures at the turn of the century.[57] *Secondly,* as we have already noted, there has been an increase in the share of landless labourers among the agricultural labourers. *Thirdly,* the share of wages in the income of agricultural labour households rose from 76 per cent in 1950-51 to 81 per cent in 1956-57.[58] However, as against these "advances"—in the objective, historical sense —there were some retreats. The ratio attached to casual labour increased between 1950-51 and 1956-57 from 10.90 to 27.73.[59] Secondly, the share of cash in wage-payment declined from 56 per cent to 49 per cent in the same period.[60] Finally, we can only mention that according to the calculations of the Soviet author, G. Kotovsky, the area cultivated wholly or mainly by hired labour in the middle fifties was 25 to 30 per cent, which perhaps enables one to say that a quarter of the area cultivated was then under the capitalist mode of production.[61]

One must however guard against getting an exaggerated idea about the dissolution of the old mode of production—basically semi-feudal[62] and the development of the capitalist mode in Indian agriculture. It is here, more than anywhere else in India, that "dead holds the living in its grip". First, in spite of some undoubted progress—qualitative and quantitative—in the instruments of production in the post-1947 era compared to what prevailed before, it does not come to much if we take the absolute picture. Thus, after a decade of economic development, the total value of the equipment used in farm business—excluding transport equipment—was of the order of Rupees 486 crores, constituting a paltry 0.3 per cent of the total value of tangible assets of the cultivator households of India which was of the order of Rupees 33,275 crores.[63] Secondly, even after the "implementation" of the land reform legislation, survivals of the old system are still very strong. Unfortunately exact data on tenancy, share cropping, and lease of land are very difficult to come by. Still some ideas can be had from the accounts given in this

[57] Cited by Lenin, *op. cit.,* Sec. 5.

[58] *Report of the Second Agricultural Labour Enquiry* (1960)), Appendix IV.

[59] *Ibid.*

[60] *Ibid.*

[61] See G. Kotovsky, *Agrarian Reforms in India* (1958-59), Eng. Translation, 1964, p. 158.

[62] Here we follow Bettelheim's characterization of India's agrarian structure which is not fully feudal but shows the features of a declining feudalism such as absence of a labour market over a large part of the rural sector, personal subservience of the immediate producer to the landowner, excessive importance of land rent, use of produce mostly to satisfy immediate needs, underdeveloped social division of Labour (Bettelheim, *India Independent,* 1968, p. 23).

[63] *All-India Rural Debt and Investment Survey,* 1961-62, Table II in *Reserve Bank of India Bulletin,* June 1965. (one crore = 10,000,000)

regard by a report of the Planning Commission concerning different States. Thus "in Andhra where substantive areas were cultivated through tenants and share croppers ... they were not recorded. The Andhra Tenancy Act has been ineffective". In Assam "large areas are cultivated through tenants-at-will and share-croppers. According to 1961 Census 37 per cent cultivators were either tenant-cultivators or part owner—part tenant cultivators". In Bihar "crop-sharing is widely prevalent. According to Census of 1961 about 25 per cent cultivators were part tenant and part-owner cultivators and another 7.5 per cent were pure tenants. The tenants usually pay half the gross produce". In Madhya Pradesh "Tenancy Law which was soundly conceived had become ineffective due to lack of adequate steps for implementation—the Law prohibits leasing (except by disabled persons). In practice, much leasing goes on in the form of crop-sharing and the share croppers are generally not recorded". In Madras "in several districts large areas are cultivated through tenancies, mostly oral leases. There was thus much concealed tenancy". In Mysore "in several parts of the state large areas are cultivated through share croppers and other tenancy arrangement but land records do not contain information about them". In Orissa "there is fairly common practice of cultivating land through share cropping. The share-croppers have no security of tenure in practice. They were being evicted at the will of the landlord. The rents paid by them amounted in many cases to half of the gross produce". In Uttar Pradesh "the law prohibits leasing but permits partnership in cultivation. In practice, leasing or crop-sharing is increasing. The share croppers usually pay half the produce as rent. They are not allowed to remain on land for any length of time lest they claim tenancy rights. Such arrangements are not generally recorded, and the sharp-croppers are unable to claim any rights under the Law". In West Bengal "according to 1961 Census about 34 per cent cultivators were pure *bargadars* that is, share croppers (13.4 per cent) or part owners and part *bargadars* (21%). Between 25 to 46 per cent area in different districts is cultivated through share-croppers. The rent payable is 50 per cent of the produce if the landlord provides plough, cattle etc., and 40 per cent in other cases". And so on.[64]

Thirdly we have seen earlier that though there has been some progress as regards rural indebtedness, still more than 60 per cent of the total farm credit in India comes under usurious practices of private moneylenders. Worse still; interest paid by the agriculturists—excluding agricutulral labourers—more than doubled from 4.7 per cent to 10.3 per cent of the total income from agriculture over the period 1951-52 to 1961-61.[65]

[64] Planning Commission (Govt. of India), *Implementation of Land Reforms* (1966), pp. 2-13

[65] S. A. Shah and M. Rajagopal, *Economic Weekly* (Bombay) 12, Oct. 1963.

From the foregoing it follows that there were no real agrarian reforms in the countryside—some of the reasons for which we have already referred to earlier. The result was that the over-all growth of the economy began to be seriously hampered by the lagging agricultural sector. The planners were practically convinced by the static agricultural level during 1960-61 to 1963-64 that the state of agriculture was seriously undermining the industrial development of the country. In 1964 the planners announced "a fresh consideration of the assumptions, methods and techniques as well as the machinery of planning and plan implementation in the field of agriculture".[66] Two points were emphasized. First, development efforts would be concentrated in the areas having assured supplies of water—constituting about a quarter of the total cultivated area; and second, within these areas there would be a systematic effort to extend the application of science and technology. In October 1965, the new policy was put into practice under the so-called Intensive Agricultural Areas Programme (IAAP). A model for this existed in 15 districts under the so-called Intensive Agricultural Development Programme (IADP), beginning in 1961. This new approach—which under the so-called High Yielding Varieties Programme (HYVP) was later called the New Agricultural Strategy—in essence emphasized the necessity of providing the cultivator with a complete "package of practices"—including credit, modern inputs, price incentives, marketing facilities and technical advice—in order to increase yields. Shorn of all verbiage, this "new strategy", boils down to the strategy of accelerating the growth of capitalism in agriculture without basic agrarian reforms—a modified version of what Lenin called "the Prussian Path", that was being followed, though in a different context, in pre-revolutionary Russia by Stolypin. Though the full effects will take time to mature there is no doubt, on the basis of available evidence, that there has been an accentuation of class differences in the districts operating under the "new strategy". Some valuable work in this regard has recently been done by an American author.[67] As is to be expected, the large and to some extent the middle farmers have increasingly taken advantage of the official assistance in relation to credit and new inputs, in modern investments of production and in relation to high prices for agricultural products and low taxes. After a careful survey of the "green revolution" in four districts in widely separated parts of India, Francine Frankel comes to the following conclusion:

The gains of the new technology have been very unevenly distributed.

[66] Planning Commission, *Memorandum on the Fourth Five-Year Plan* (1964), p 26.

[67] Francine Frankel, *Agricultural Modernization and Social Change: Case Studies of Five Districts* (mimeographed), September 1969.

In Ludhiana (in Punjab) where the majority of cultivators have economic holdings of 15 to 20 acres or more ... the benefits of the new technology have been most widely, albeit still unevenly, shared. Probably only the bottom twenty per cent of farmers holding ten acres or less, have experienced a serious relative deterioration in their economic position for profitable adoption of the new techniques. Yet, Ludhiana is atypical even for Punjab and much more so for large parts of wheat growing belt. For example, in Bihar and Uttar Pradesh both major wheat growing areas, over 80 per cent of all cultivating households operate farms of less than eight acres. It is therefore not unreasonable to assume that the relative percentage of cultivators who have received significant benefits from the new technology compared to those who have been left out are almost exactly the reverse in these areas than in Ludhiana. Certainly, this has so far been the case in the rice growing region where the overwhelming majority of the cultivators have uneconomic holdings of two and three acres ... (There) it appears that only the small minority of cultivators with holdings of ten acres or more have been in a position to mobilize surplus capital for investment in land development as an essential precondition for the efficient utilization of modern inputs. Farmers with twenty acres or more have made the greatest absolute and relative gains, partly by mechanization but also by diversifying their cropping pattern to include more profitable commercial crops. The majority of farmers—probably as many as 75 per cent or 80 per cent in the rice belt—have experienced a relative decline in their economic position; and some proportion representing unprotected tenants under oral lease have suffered an absolute deterioration in their living standard .... Given the much higher cultivation costs of the new varieties—under the so-called HYVP—and an even greater premium on timely agricultural operations—including a rigid schedule for the application of fixed amounts of water to achieve maximum potential yields—the economic disparities between the minority of cultivators who can finance the improvements and the majority who cannot, is bound to widen further. In fact, in areas where the high yielding varieties of rice have been successfully introduced, this tendency towards economic polarization between large farmers on the one hand, and the majority of small owners, owner-cum-tenant cultivators and share croppers on the other, has already begun. . . . The IADP and now the HYVP have not only intensified the process of economic polarization in the rural areas, but they have also contributed to an increasing social estrangement between the landlords and tenants and landowners and labourers.[68]

[68] *Agricultural Modernization and Social Change*, op. cit., pp. 78-83.

INDUSTRY

Next we turn to industry. The pattern of industrial development in the post-independence era shows interesting features from the point of view of the development of capitalism in India. First we note that industrial production has grown at a fairly rapid rate and much more rapidly than agricultural production—thereby widening the differences between town and countryside almost at all levels. Thus the index of industrial production went up from a level of 74 in 1951 (with 1956 = 100) to 182 in 1965— an increase of 146 per cent in 14 years.[69] At the same time the number of workers employed in large-scale factories (that is factories employing 50 or more workers with the aid of power and 100 or more workers without the aid of power) rose from about 1.5 million in 1949 to about 3.5 million in 1965, that is more than doubled in less than two decades.[70] Also the total productive capital—that is fixed plus working capital— in large-scale industries increased from about Rs. 509 crores in 1949 to Rs. 6,446 crores in 1965, that is by about twelve times.[71]

This picture does not give any idea of the structural changes that the industrial sector has undergone. First, not all industries grew at the same rate. Thus during the period under consideration the large scale (i.e. factory) sector grew faster than the small-scale (i.e. non-factory) sector. In 1948-49, the ratio of large-scale to small-scale was 40:60. In 1966-67 is rose to 70:30.[72] Secondly, we have two important indices of increasing capital intensity in Indian industries. In the first place the ratio of total productive capital to wages, salaries and benefits increased from about 3 in 1949 to about 6.6 in 1965.[73] In the second place, according to one estimate the index of electricity consumption per industrial worker rose from 100 in 1951 to 334 in 1967.[74] Thus it seems that the organic composition of capital in the industrial sector is rising. Next, within the large-scale sector itself, in general, consumption-goods industries have shown a lower rate of growth than capital-goods industries. Thus whereas, for example, food manufacturing, beverage, textiles and leather products show, respectively, 3.2, 6.1, 2.0 and 3.0 per cent rates of growth, electrical machinery, non-electrical machinery, chemicals and petroleum products show, respectively, 14.9, 17.7, 9.1 and 20.8 per cent rates of

[69] Fourth Five-Year Plan: A Draft Outline (Planning Commission, Govt. of India), p. 10.

[70] Statistical Abstract, India, 1962 and 1968 (Central Statistical Organization, Govt. of India).

[71] Ibid.

[72] Commerce, Annual Number, (1968).

[73] Our calculation on the basis of data given in the Annual Survey of Industries (Govt. of India).

[74] Commerce, Annual Number, (1968).

growth during the period under consideration.[75] The same idea is obtained another way. The share of consumer goods in total industrial production declined from 67.9 per cent in 1950-51 to 34.0 per cent in 1965-66 and the share of non-consumer goods rose, correspondingy, from 32.1 per cent to 66.0 per cent during the same period.[76]

The figures on the rate of growth of industries cited above should not give rise to an exaggerated notion about the extent of industrialization of India. The share of industries, including mining, in Net National Product of India, at 1948-49 prices, actually *fell* from 17.1 per cent in 1948-49 to 16.6 per cent in 1960-61, while it rose only slightly, at 1960-61 prices, from 20.2 per cent in 1960-61 to 22.4 per cent in 1967-68.[77]

There is conclusive evidence that the progress of industry has strengthened the bourgeoisie. First, there has been a steady rate of increase in the industrial profits of the joint stock companies over the third plan period. Thus, according to the Reserve Bank of India, between 1950 and 1956 (1950=100) gross profits of joint stock companies rose by 65 per cent while the gross profits of public limited companies rose by 42 per cent between 1955 and 1959 (1955=100) and by about 51 per cent between 1960-61 and 1965-66 (1960-61=100). The comparable figures for the private limited companies during the same two periods were respectively 65 per cent and 67 per cent.[78] On the other hand as regards the real earnings of factory workers earning less than Rs. 200 per month the index rose from 100 in 1951 to 123.7 in 1955 and then gradually declined to 104.6 in 1964.[79] In fact an official report has admitted that "during 1951-64, real wages have shown little improvement, while in 1964 there has been a substantial decline". [80] It adds that "the provisional data for 1965 and 1966, now available, don't indicate any change in the trend".[81] Then again, the paid-up capital of joint stock companies increased by about five times between 1947-48 and 1965-66.[82] The particularly rapid expansion of large companies confirms that the big bourgeoisie has reaped the greatest advantage from this development. Thus as Professor Hazari has shown, the four largest groups of capitalists—Tata, Birla, Martin Burn, and Dalmia Sahujain—had increased their share of capital on non-government public companies from 18 per cent in 1951 to 22 per cent

[75] Calculated from *Economy Survey*, 1968-69 (Govt. of India).
[76] Calculated from *Fourth Five-Year Plan : A Draft Outline* (Govt. of India), p. 10.
[77] *Economic Survey*, 1968-69. In the latter so-called "revised" estimate as between 1960-61 and 1967-68, construction and electricity were added to industries and mining.
[78] *Statistical Abstract, India.*, 1958-59, 1962 and 1968.
[79] *Indian Labour Statistics*, 1968.
[80] *Report of the National Commission on Labour* (Govt. of India) (1969), p. 189.
[81] *Ibid*.
[82] *Statistical Abstract, India*, (1958-59 and 1968).

in 1958.[83] An official report listed, as of 1963-65, the top 75 groups of monopolies who, owning less than 6 per cent of non-government non-banking companies, held about 47 per cent of their total assets.[84] In 1967-68 the share of these groups in the total assets of the non-government non-banking companies, of which they owned about 8 per cent, rose to about 54 per cent.[85]

Who are the agents behind the development of capitalism in India? We have seen above that the Indian bourgeoisie wanted to take India along an independent capitalist path. This most mature bourgeoisie in Asia outside of Japan was conscious of the difficulties faced by a backward capitalism and was aware that private enterprise alone could not deliver the goods. It had two non-exclusive alternatives—intervention by the State—*their* State—in the economy at an accelerated pace and collaboration with foreign capital.

That the Indian bourgeoisie opted for a large public sector is clear from Nehru's account of the big business component of the Congress National Planning Commission [86] as well as from the fact that the so called *Bombay Plan*, formulated towards the end of the Second World War by Tata, Birla, and six other big capitalists, provided for a considerable extension of State ownership and management of the economy. An examination of the Govt. of India's Industrial Policy Resolutions of 1948 and 1956 shows that the State has agreed to step in only where the private enterprise for various reasons cannot do the job alone. The intervention by the State in the Indian economy was meant *primarily* to create conditions for the rapid development of capitalism and *secondarily* to prevent excessive concentration and monopoly of economic power—this last being promoted by the exigencies of parliamentary democracy and the necessity of not alienating the small and the middle bourgeoisie from the big bourgeoisie; in other words, in order to serve interests of the capitalist class as a *whole* even at the cost of the interest of *particular* capitalists. As to the secondary purpose of the State intervention we have seen above that it had very little negative effect on the growth of concentration and monopoly.

As to the primary purpose, it is proved by the essentially capitalist character of the State intervention itself and by the growth of the private sector during the planning period. For the first point it is enough to go through the measures of nationalization effected so far including the much

[83] *The Structure of the Corporate Private Sector* (1966), p. 305.

[84] *Monopolies Enquiry Commission Report* (1965), pp. 121-22.

[85] B. Datta, "Growth of Industrial Houses" in *Company News and Notes*, (May 1 & 16, 1970), Dept. of Company Affairs, Ministry of Industrial Development (Govt. of India).

[86] *Discovery of India* (4th ed.), p. 404.

vaunted bank nationalization. If we consider the nationalization of air transport in 1953, the Imperial Bank in 1955 and life insurance in 1956 we see that each of them was undertaken with some specific objectives in view and none formed part of any concerted anti-private enterprize strategy. The same holds good for bank nationalization in 1969. In the first case the resources at the disposal of air transport were insufficient; in the second case there was the necessity of having an extensive credit structure well beyond the scope of private moneylenders; in the third case, there was the uncertainty of being able to mop up savings for large industrial investments as well as the need for cleaning up of an industry that was inefficient and corrupt; in the fourth case, an important reason was the need to extend credit and banking facilities to agriculture in order to widen the basis of capitalism in the countryside. Obviously the basic question is who holds the State power. As this power is essentially held by the big bourgeoisie, in alliance with the landlords, the character of state intervention cannot but be capitalist. Even the share of the State in the economy need not make one enthusiastic. Thus, towards the end of the Third Plan period, about nine-tenths of the domestic product was still at the disposal of the private sector and the share of the government rose by about 4 per cent over a period of fifteen years.[87]

Also to be noted is the rapid growth of the private sector over the planning period—a growth that has been facilitated by the activities of the public sector. We have already cited some data in support of this contention. As an ex-Cabinet-Minister of India has observed, "the private sector could not have achieved the expansion that it has but for the public sector investment in economic overheads and heavy industries".[88] We also know that the State has helped the private sector by extending long-term credit to big industries through its financial institutions.

Can this capitalist development be called *independent*? Certainly not. This is seen from a look at the intervention of foreign capital in the Indian economy. Till the mid-fifties the Indian bourgeoisie was not very enthusiastic about foreign capital lest it might jeopardize the very purpose for which it had fought the British rule, namely, independent capitalist development. That justifies the remark of an American observer, "until the late 'fifties the total inflow of foreign private capital into India was sluggish. The inflow of American private capital amounted to little more than a trickle".[89] Later on, however, the deepening crisis of following the capitalist path led to a marked shift in the whole trend of foreign capital inflow, so much so that of the total number of foreign collaboration

[87] *India : A reference Annual*, 1966 (Govt. of India), p. 150.
[88] Manubhai Shah in *Eastern Economist*, 21 July 1967.
[89] J.P. Lewis, *Quiet Crisis in India* (1962), p. 211.

agreements amounting to 2200 between 1948 and 1964, 1900 were effected between 1956 and 1964.[90] Secondly, over 70 per cent of the 827 private sector companies, covered by a recent survey of the Reserve Bank, had technical collaboration agreements.[91] Thirdly, the aggregate book value of foreign investments in the private sector—that is, the sector involving commercial and industrial undertakings including State-owned enterprises —rose from Rs. 679.8 crores (1961) to Rs. 935.8 crores (1965).[92] Industrywise, about two-thirds of the fresh inflow in each of the years 1963-64 and 1964-65 was absorbed by manufacturing industries of which chemicals, transport equipment, minerals, metals and metal products and machinery and machine tools accounted for about 40 per cent.[93] Similarly, machines and machine tools, electrical goods and chemicals accounted for 55 per cent of the total foreign collaboration agreements.[94] This shows the control of the vital sectors of our economy by foreign capital. Then again there is the dwindling share of the national resources in the investments made by the State capitalist sector as is seen from the fact that the share of foreign assistance in total public sector outlays has grown from 9.6 per cent in 1951-56 (First Plan period) to 44.99 per cent in 1967-68.[95] The lion's share in the total foreign assistance to India—it goes without saying—is provided by the United States. This has amounted to more than 9 thousand million dollars between 1951 to 1969—an amount that is higher than all the rest of the foreign assistance over the same period put together.[96] All this proves that we are following a *dependent capitalist path*.

From our extremely rapid survey of the principal spheres of production of the Indian economy we see that the process of modernization well started during the British period received momentum after power was transferred to the bourgeoisie and their allies. This modernization, however, proceeded along the line of commodity production and capitalism. In agriculture, though commodity production has spread to a wide area, capitalism itself is proceeding slowly. On the whole, semi-feudal production relations still predominate in Indian agriculture. This explains, to a great extent, the crisis in agriculture that we all know. On the other hand, industry's progress has been much faster but the rate of progress is far from satisfactory both from the point of view of

[90] Reserve Bank of India, *Foreign Colloboration in Indian Industry* (1968), p. 4.
[91] *Ibid*, p. 99.
[92] *Reserve Bank of India Bulletin*, January, 1967.
[93] *Ibid*.
[94] Reserve Bank of India, *Foreign Collaboration in Indian Industry, op. cit.*
[95] Planning Commission (GOI) as given in *Records and Statistics, Quarterly Bulletin of the Eastern Economist*, November, 1968.
[96] *Fact Sheet: US Economic Assistance to India*, No. 20 USIS, 1969).

our requirements and from the point of view of performances of some of the countries in the underdeveloped world. This is again because our agriculture remains semi-feudal and hence backward. This co-existence of a vast semi-feudal sector with a small, though growing, capitalist sector pulls down our entire economy and is the basic cause of the crisis we are passing through. As we pointed out earlier, it cannot be otherwise under the present set up, that is as long as the State power essentially remains in the hands of the exploiting classes—that is, the bourgeoisie, turning increasingly comprador, and its national and international allies. Not before India's semi-feudal production relations are destroyed will her state of economic underdevelopment cease. The completion of anti-feudal tasks is of course vitally linked with the successful struggle against India's subservience to imperialism.

9

PERCEPTIONS, LEARNING, AND INITIATIVE IN COMMUNITY DEVELOPMENT

WALTER C. NEALE

THE THEME of this essay is that differences in folkview—differences in how people perceive the world around them—create a gulf in understanding between the originators and leaders in Indian community development and the lower level, operating extension officers who carry out the programme. In consequence of this gulf officials at the operating level learn different lessons from their experiences to those which the leaders learn; the lessons operating officials learn do not increase their ability to adapt or initiate; and leaders and social scientists may misunderstand some aspects of the behaviour of operating officials. I shall illustrate the theme with the contrast between the views of effective extension work held by the world community of originators and leaders of community development and the view of Indian operating extension officers that *morality is causative*.

An event, an order, a programme is understood differently because "folkviews"[1] vary. It is widely understood that different experiences, different aims, and viewing life and specific problems from differing situations leads people to understand any specific event or the core of any

---

[1] I use the term *folkview* broadly to encompass all the ideas—of cause and effect, of justification and condemnation, of realism and foolishness, of rightness and wrongness, of decency and disgustingness—all the ideas by which we order the world around us in our minds and by which we reach conclusions and judgments.

problem differently. What is perhaps less widely recognized is that concurrently with the process of "learning from experience" there is also a "simultaneous translator" at work fitting the lessons of an experience, a sentence, a programme into a consistent picture of the world which is already largely formed and with which the new experience must be made consistent—"must be" in the sense that the event remains upsetting or meaningless until it is made consistent with the existing picture.

The process of integrating events with an existing, stuctured folkview by reinterpreting the events can be illustrated by an incident involving perceptions of health and medical practice. On a tour in Punjab I once totally lost my voice. A local practitioner of the health arts offered to brew me a glass of *banufsha*.[2] I was most hesitant to accept the offer because my immediately previous acquaintance with local medical practice was witnessing a practitioner tying ribbons to thumbs and toes of a man clearly in great pain, and then rolling a green bottle on his stomach "in order to relocate his displaced centre of gravity". But then, reasoning that to "brew" a medicine involved "boiling", I decided that it would be "safe" and drank a glass of "boiled grass". Thirty minutes later, to my surprise—but to my surprise alone—my voice returned in full force. When I recounted this tale to medical friends at the Ludhiana Hospital their consternation relaxed into smiles when they realized (or decided?) that *banufsha* contained a drug known to British pharmacology. In other words, "It was all right".

Three differing folkviews are revealed by this experience of mine: (1) the local medical health practitioner's view that it was a "health brew"; (2) my view that it was "boiled"; and (3) the doctors' view that it was a "proper drug". Whatever the correct version of the local medical practioner's folkview may be, it is clear that the event took place only because I reinterpreted "brewed" as "boiled", and that the doctors could accept the propriety of the incident only when they could reinterpret *banufsha* as "suitable drug".[3]

For analysis in the social sciences it is unimportant whether a folkview is, by whatever standard one wishes to judge truth, a true view: it is only important that the people holding the folkview believe it to be true—or, if not true, then proper or moral or decent. The *folk* who hold the view are any group of people with a common understanding of cause, relevance, and morality in respect to a kind of situation, or any number of kinds of situation.

[2] The transliteration is mine, from memory, and my ear is bad.

[3] I have since recognized a further peculiarity in my own folkview: I was willing to drink the brew because it was "boiled", but had it been boiled arsenic or strychnine of silvers of glass I would now have been dead long ere this, Pasteur or no Pasteur.

Folkviews are not the views of "simple folk" alone. We all have folkviews, and we all (i.e., all us humans) have folkviews about everything
with which we deal. Thus the scientific community has a folkview which
it calls science or scientific method or scientific process. This folkview
asserts that understanding and meaning come from prediction-and-testing,
that arguments must follow the rules of logic, that only observations may
be introduced into argument as data. I, and probably most readers of this
volume of essays, regard these as proper rules to follow, and science as
"true"—but this is itself an assertion of a folkview about how the universe works and how one knows man's place in it. But for me or those
who agree with me to argue that the scientific method is "better" than
other folkviews—even "truer"—hardly establishes the scientific as not a
folkview or as a better one, for the *very criteria by which* we argue the
superiority or difference of our folkview are part of our folkview. Reject
the criteria inherent in our folkview and our arguments have no force—
no more force than arguments in defense of myths of origin have for us
when we reject the criteria by which those who believe them judge truth
and falsity, relevance and foolishness.

So folkview as used here refers to the *rules* of reasoning, the criteria
of relevance, the *nature* or causation, as well as to the *propriety* of action
of any group. The academic community has a folkview—and we understand each other pretty much around the world because academics in
New York, Ibadan, London, Bombay, Manila, and Tokyo have pretty
much the same folkview about the way in which the world is put together. Similarly, the higher levels of the Indian administration have one
folkview (which happens to be much the same as the folkview of the
academic community); lower level officials in community development
have another; and the farmers with whom they deal a third. But whereas
communication is "pretty easy" between academics and IAS (Indian Administrative Service) officers, communication is not so easy between people from these groups (i.e., "us") and others who are involved in community development because the academic or IAS view of relevance and
causation and criteria for evaluating propriety is different from the views
on these matters of VLW's (Village Level Workers) and cultivators.

The folkviews of the leaders of community development are essentially
operational. In their discussions and evaluations, the aims and attitudes
of development officials are never divorced from the specific techniques
which extension workers use, or ought to use. The adaptation of techniques to achieve developmental objectives is seen as a response to a
feedback mechanism which constantly readjusts the operational procedures
in a trial-and-error process of sucessive approximations until the techni-
ques-in-operation come close to achieving the results as originally conceived. Or, as may happen in the light of experience and of the needs, de-

mands, hopes, and fears of the rural people, the specific ends and criteria of success are modified in response to the "messages" generated in the feedback process.

The key words in their folkview are ones such as "demonstration", "supply-line", workability", or "persuasiveness". Whether demonstrations have been conducted, whether the supplies desired or promised have been delivered to the right place at the right time, or whether the results of the demonstration have approximated the anticipated results ("workability" in the specific circumstances)—these questions are answerable operationally, often with numbers.

The semantic order of these terms contrasts with the semantic order of such words as "cooperativeness", "goodwill", or "nation-building". Whereas the originators and leaders of community development share with almost all officials and volunteers in a community development process a high regard for attitudes which fit such semantic rubrics as "cooperativeness", the essence of their approach lies in an emphasis upon specific extension techniques such as keeping accounts for cooperative societies or supplying farmers with calendars on which to keep track of the laying rates of hens.

"Being right", and therefore "persuasive" and "workability" are the operational tests of effectiveness in community development, and effectiveness is the test which justifies. Good intentions which pave the way to hell are not operational techniques (which this international community regards as the core of successful extension work) nor are they ever considered a justification for failure to achieve objectives. No matter what the foundation in intention, no matter what the foundation in previously-belived-to-be-true "knowledge", if in any particular case the demonstration does not show what it was designed to show, then the demonstrator has failed.[4]

Furthermore, although it is true that all people involved in furthering the processes of community development personally admire the characteristics of cooperativeness and goodwill, they do *not* base their proposals and techniques upon the hope that people will behave cooperatively or in a spirit of joint action for the benefit of their community. Rather, they are strongly aware that the motives of most people are (in significant part at any rate) selfish, and that people learn from experience as it

---

[4] Which does not, of course, mean that the demonstrator must be reprimanded or "punished". Circumstances would dictate how the administration should act to prevent recurrences of the failure. The point here is that in the originators' folkview a mistake was made, the demonstration was done wrongly, and no antecedent or surrounding circumstances can correct the mistake, turn "wrongly" into "rightly", or remove the failure from the historical sequence of causes and consequences to be considered in deciding what to do next.

affects themselves far more readily and thoroughly than they do from reports of how experience has affected others. Thus their test of workability requires that the clientele with whom community extension officials work be satisfied—and if this clientele is not satisfied it remains unpersuaded and the extension work has therefore failed the test. For instance, an argument that people will benefit financially must be validated in the conduct of each particular project by clear financial benefits to the clientele, and—no matter how unjustified this further criterion may seem to an extension worker who has tried hard and done his duty—it must be validated by the recognition of the clientele that they have benefited financially. The same *double criteria* of achievement of the specific result and recognition by the clientele that the specific result had been acheived applies equally to all branches of extension work: from establishing the effectiveness of fertilizers in increasing crop yields through increasing longevity and reducing infant mortality to helping children to achieve a different life by attending the educational institutions provided in the rural areas.

These beliefs, attitudes, and approaches contrast with the views of a great many people involved in the actual carrying out of community development programmes in India.[5] The contrasting semantic order of thought among Indian extension workers is that development and extension work is a moral matter. Moral criteria run through instance after instance in reports on projects, in formulations of projects, and in discussions of problems in community development. The characteristics of a "good" extension officer are moral ones: dedication, humility, selflessness, honesty, faith, respect for law and authority. Success is attributed to these characteristics; failure to their absence or the presence of their opposites. Differences of opinion or of effort between the extension official and the villager are not phrased as conflicts of interest but as failures to arouse the

---

[5] My sources for statements about the folkviews of extension officers and their superiors in Indian community development are mimeographed reports of block development and extension officers on their experiences (reports which they wrote for syndicates at orientation centres); reports of these syndicates; reports of syndicates at the National Institute of Community Development in Hyderabad; two reports of and a number of interviews with people involved in a long-term private extension project in India; and interviews at village, block, and district levels during 1964-65. Because my treatment of cases may appear to be derogatory (although I certainly do not intend them to be), and because much of my information was given me informally in trust, I refrain from citing specific written sources or citing particular people and interviews. The points which I wish to make are about underlying folkviews and perceptions and not about particular cases which might be attributed to errors in the judgment of particular people.

proper moral values in the villagers and, less frequently, as improper moral attitudes among villagers.[6]

The moral criteria applied to themselves by the extension officers are also applied by them to village leaders, and in consequence the extension officer believes that a major part of his job is to instill the correct values in the villagers with whom he works. It is for this reason, I think, that Block Development Officers, Extension Officers, and Village Level Workers have earned a reputation for exhortation rather than for action. If my hypothesis is correct, it is wrong—it is unfair—to charge the officers with substituting sermons for explanations, talk for demonstrations; for *in their view "sermons" are action*. The officers have not, as it is often said they have, tried to disguise their incompetence or laziness. Rather, they are working hard to "upgrade" the attitudes of their "parishioners". Whatever judgment one may pass on their technical competence as evangelicals of social change, it reflects well upon their courage that they assault the problems of rural India on such difficult ground as moral conversion.

A story told by a BDO (Block Development Officer) illustrates the force of the folkview that, somehow, effectiveness and efficiency ought to flow from "properly motivated" action and inefficiency from "improperly motivated" action. In this case the BDO organized a dairy marketing cooperative covering a number of villages. He argued—to himself in jus- tifying his efforts and to the villagers in persuading them to join the cooperative—that the elimination of the middlemen in milk-marketing would increase the returns to the farmers. Now, in the folkview of an economist there are simple tests for the appropriateness of that dairy marketing cooperative at that place at that time: (*a*) Did the farmers enrich themselves by joining in the cooperative marketing arrangements? and (*b*) Did the farmers feel that they were better off? As the BDO tell his story, the criteria of appropriateness which he employed were of a different order.

The middlemen had been going around to the farmers in the villages, buying milk from each of them, bulking it, bringing it into town, and selling it there. They paid the farmers on the spot when they took the milk from them. The cooperative proposed to pick up the milk at several collection points, bulk it, bring it into town, and sell it. As is the normal

---

[6] I suspect that the much greater frequency of citations of "failure to create right attitudes" and of "failure to educate" compared to the infrequency of statements about village selfishness is a result—to what degree is a question—of the quasi-public character of the orientation centre discussions: in fact, it is probably an exhibition of that "humility" and of that "faith" which is elsewhere so strongly urged upon the "good" extension officer. But whatever the reporters' motives, the fact is that the issues are phrased as moral ones.

procedure of cooperative societies, the farmers were to receive payment for the milk after all transactions had been completed and the balance in the cooperative society's books struck. Originally, when the society was being organized, the farmers did complain about having to take the milk to the collection points, a procedure which they regarded as inconvenient compared to the procedure in dealing with the private milk marketers. However, an appreciable number of farmers did enroll in the cooperative. For exactly what reasons they enrolled we do not know; but the BDO and his extension officer used the arguments that the cooperative would not cheat the farmers, that the farmers would have a larger cash income in consequence, and that the milk handled by the cooperative would be unadulterated and honestly marketed.

When the time came to pay the proceeds of the cooperative's operations the member farmers received less than they had been paid by the middlemen under the earlier arrangements. It was not the case that the middlemen had raised the prices which they offered to the farmers in order to fight the cooperative society, but rather that the cooperative society simply did not earn as much net as the middlemen had normally paid in spot cash.

The farmers felt that they were paying three penalties for joining the cooperative society: (1) the inconvenience of bringing milk to the collection point; (2) the inconvenience (and implicit cost?) of waiting for their money until the marketing period was over, and (3) the reduced cash income which they received. In consequence, the farmers began deserting the cooperative and dealing again with the milk-bulking middlemen.

The BDO and his extension officers then went around to the farmers again in order to persuade them to stick with the cooperative. They argued that the cooperative had the best interest of the farmers at heart, whereas the middlemen were indifferent to the farmers' welfare; that the farmers would be better off if they sold their milk through the cooperative rather than to middlemen; and that middlemen "would stop at nothing" to fool the farmer, to mislead him, and to make him suffer.[7]

This was the story as the BDO told it.

Running through his story is the theme that middlemen are bad and cooperatives are good; that middlemen cheat and cooperatives are honest; that middlemen hurt farmers while cooperatives benefit them. These appear to be core beliefs in the folkview of lower level officials. They ought to have been, as the BDO told the story, sufficient arguments to persuade the farmers to stick with the cooperative society. In reading the BDO's

---

[7] In the event, the cooperative did stay in business, albeit on a much reduced scale of operations.

story, it is impossible to tell whether he used accounting arguments or arguments about long-run costs and gains; but what is significant is that he did not consider this kind of argument important enough to mention in his tale of how he handled the situation. The BDO presented no evidence about the financial or costing operations of the cooperative or about those of the middlemen; nevertheless it was apparent to him that the society was good for farmers and good for development, the middlemen bad for famers and bad for development. While the position is not consistent with the economistic biases drilled into such as me by parents, childhood friends, and graduate school, it is consistent with the view that good results are founded upon right attitudes and ill effects upon selfish motives. Cooperative money is good money, but middlemen's money is bad—and hence cannot have beneficial effects.[8]

Contrast this study and its implicit values with the view of an economist. In the economist's view the outstanding element in the history of the milk marketing cooperative society was the inability of the marketing society to compete in the market with the middlemen. The economist reads this as a statement that the marketing cooperative was economically inefficient in comparision with the middlemen; that the arguments originally used to establish the marketing cooperative were invalidated by the history of the cooperative; that the cooperative society had in fact failed; and that the farmers had *already learned* (and that further learning would probably only increase their desire to work through the middlemen rather than through the society). To the economist the society had failed the operational tests of fulfilling its promises and becoming what it was hoped that it would be.

A curiosity in the BDO's tale—a curiosity at any rate to one holding a different folkview of the world—is the BDO's emphasis upon the argument that the cooperative society would deal honestly and sell unadulterated milk. From the point of view of the consumer and from some points of view of the "public good" the sale of milk in pure form is desirable. However, as a commercial operation the matter is not so clear. If middlemen gain by watering the milk, one can understand (even if one does not approve) their actions. Furthermore, if the middlemen were adulterating the milk, this may well have been the reason why they could afford to pay the farmers more for whole milk than could the cooperative society. One consequence would have been that the farmers

[8] The BDO's ultimate solution was that the farmers would learn and come to understand how important cooperative societies were. The comments of the co-members of the syndicate and the orientation centre instructor indicated that they agreed that the BDO had done his best and that it was just one of those sad, frustrating cases.

themselves were in effect party to profiting from the adulteration of the milk.[9]

A second case has in common with the first the establishment of a cooperative society under the impression and with the argument that there would be benefits to farmers who did business with the cooperative rather than with private merchants and processors. In this case the cooperative society was to process groundnuts into oils and sell the oil in the town market or to bulk buyers, but to keep back some oil to sell to the members of the society. As in the other case, the sponsors of the cooperative used the argument—and there is no reason to doubt the sincerity of belief in the argument—that the net financial return to the farmer would be greater if he joined a cooperative society rather than sold on the market. In addition, it was argued, the cooperative society's retention of some of the oil for sale to members would relieve the members of the inconvenience of going to a market town to buy oil and would guarantee the quality of the oil sold for domestic consumption.

The cooperative established, the area under groundnuts was extended by the farmers. In the first year of operation the processing society was unable to pay as much at the end of the season to the supplying members as the market was willing to pay at the time of delivery by the farmers. The consequence in this case, as in the milk marketing case, was that the farmers deserted the cooperative and sold their groundnuts to merchants. The "loss of loyalty" was attributed by one sponsor of the cooperative to the *legal* incapacity of the society to pay the full value of the groundnuts in cash at the time they were delivered. Part of the failure of the processing society to make sufficient profits to pay as much net as the private dealers did was attributed to the interest payments to the district cooperative bank. Another reason given was that the cooperative society had to pay octroi and market dues on the groundnut oil, charges which were proportionally higher for oil than they were for groundnuts in the unprocessed state. The financial difficulties of the processing society were thus attributed, among other things, to unfairness inherent in the law which required the cooperative society to pay octroi and market charges which were evaded by middlemen and to the dishonesty of the private dealers who made false declarations about what

[9] Whether or not the farmers knew that they were benefiting from the adulteration is a point not covered in the source. Whether one takes a rather jaundiced view of mankind and assumes that the farmers did have an idea that they benefited in this way, or whether one takes the view that the farmers—no doubt like the BDO and the authors and readers of this volume—were dead set against adulteration is in the event unimportant because in fact the farmers did benefit. One might note, however, that the farmers, when faced with the choice between turning to the middlemen again or sticking with the cooperative—whose agents had made a point of its honesty—did return to dealing with the middlemen.

their sales were and who paid petty bribes to octroi and market officers in order to evade taxes and fees legally due.

Economists or political scientists or the original sponsors of community development would hardly absolve the private merchants of moral culpability, and many would oppose giving processing cooperatives "special privileges" in marketing as a "conspensatory" device. Some would and many would not suggest that the cooperative too should engage in false invoicing and in bribery. *But* all would take the view that the cooperative must operate in a world where private traders did these things; that the cooperative society would have to succeed by satisfying its members in this particular world; and none would pin hope of success upon the inherent virtuousness of the cooperative ideal and of the aims of the sponsors of the cooperative. Their folkview would lead them to a kind of cautiousness in launching a cooperative venture, and perhaps to kinds of adaptations once the cooperative was started, which would be different: perhaps political activity, or perhaps efforts through the administration to change the ways in which market and octroi officials behaved. The results might be no better and perhaps the hopes and moral faith of extension workers would achieve more in the end. But the point is that the leaders in community development would not be talking about the same adaptations as are the sponsors of processing societies because their folkviews—assumptions about what will happen, what will work—are different.

The view that economic development follows from "right action" and that "right action" follows from "right attitudes" also accounts for officials' aversion to village politics. It leads to disapprobation of campaigning for village office on the part of political parties or party members. It leaves officials equally unhappy when the political parties are absent and they find "factions" instead. A party or a faction is by definition "immoral" because (1) it is seeking gain of some sort (office, jobs, a share in the resources being made available by government); and (2) it is attempting to deprive others. Since these *objectives* of political activity *are immoral* —for instance, striving for office evidences lack of humility—the *consequences* of political action *must be undesirable.*

Not only do "right attitudes" lead to "right action" and hence to development. The proposition has a symmetrical corollary and "wrong attitudes" lead to "wrong action" and stagnation. The "improper" attitudes of village leaders thus become more than an inconvenience when faction struggles delay decisions: they are perceived as absolute barriers to progress because development cannot occur when wrong attitudes exist. It therefore becomes an extension officer's duty to raise the level of village morality by eliminating "wrong", factional attitudes.

The moral aversion to politics is illustrated by an account-and-comp-

laint about formalities of the authorization of a loan by a district cooperative bank. What was legally required in this case was the submission of
a proposal which fulfilled the criteria set forth by the state government,
the deposit of the equity (share capital) contribution of members of the
cooperative in the bank, and the submission of various ancillary guarantees
and agreements. The board of the bank could grant a loan or reject the
application, and if the loan were granted the manager was then to autho-
rize the handing over of the money or the crediting of the cooperative
society's account. All formal requirements of filing and delivery could be
met by a single person representing the society (or by a few people if it
was felt necessary to keep the representative honest).

What happened was that a large portion of the society's membership
was asked to come to district headquaters to witness the granting of
the loan. This, in the view of the extension worker who had sponsored
the society, was a gross imposition upon the time, convenience, and
budgets of the attending members. They were asked to attend "only to
satisfy politicians" on the board of the bank. Clearly, argued the extension worker, these mass trips to the bank should cease since they were,
on the one side, legally and financially irrelevant and, on the other,
inconvenient.

Now, in the United States it is legally necessary only that the incoming
President, Vice-President, and Chief Justice attend the Presidential In-
auguration. In India, as in the United States, it is legally necessary only
that the bride, groom, a couple of witnesses, and a priest or official attend
a wedding. Yet thousands attend the Inaguration and dozens attend many
weddings—at some inconvenience and at a good deal more cost than
taking a bus twenty miles to the district town.

Where lies the difference between the case of the cooperative bank
loan and the wedding? In the folkview of the extension officer. Wherein
lies his ability to change the system (so that he himself raised a crowd of
villagers to attend the granting of a loan to the processing society)? In his
own folkview and the folkview of the villagers.

From the point of view of local politicans it is important that their
followers *see* that they are effective and important in the process of
authorizing loans. It is also important to them that their political allies
and opponents *see* that they are able to marshall active support, evidenced by a group of followers appearing at the bank. But to people
engaged in community development work the careers of politicians appear
irrelevant. Since the effect of this political activity is inconvenience to
villagers and perhaps delay in the granting of loans, the development
worker perceives these activities of the politician as harmful. So far, his
view may not differ from the views of scholars and national leaders. But
these latter are apt also to perceive the politician as having other useful,

even vital functions; and therefore to perceive his activities in cooperative banking as a reasonable or even necessary part (and cost) of the democratic process. Conversely, the development worker attaches little if any functional value to the politician's actions because he attaches no moral value to them. The question asked is, "Why should villagers have to come to the bank? The obvious answer—obvious, that is, to the political scientist—is "To help their political leader in the democratic competition for support, office, and the power to carry out the policies for which they stand." [10] That the extension worker asks the question is evidence that the answer is either not "obvious" to him or, more likely, that he considers it an irrelevant answer. Thus does folkview or perception colour judgment, and thus does folkview put an extension officer in conflict with a (potentially allied) politician.

A secondary theme which reinforces the phrasing of issues in terms of morality and is itself reinforced by moral phrasings is the view that authority is a good thing and that the good person is obedient. But the view of authority goes beyond admiring obedience. Authority itself is right: a programme is effective because authority says it is; a statement is true because authority makes it. Here again we find alternative interpretations of the actions of extension officers. It is often said that appeals to higher echelons in the administrative hierarchy is "passing the buck"; that they are evidence of the unwillingness of lower level officials to accept responsibility. But appeal to higher echelons is perceived as appeal to greater authority and hence the decision from above is more right, the suggested programme is better than the decision or programme at which an officer could arrive by himself.

A story which I enjoyed as much as did the BDO who told it illustrates how reliance on the rightness of authority affects judgment. The BDO told the tale in order to illustrate how the national programme for population limitation could run into trouble and how such trouble could be overcome; but, as I shall argue below, his tale only illustrates his lesson if one accepts his assumptions about the nature and consequences of appeal to higher authority.

The story is that a husband underwent a vasectomy only to find some time later that his wife was pregnant. The man had complete faith in his wife's chastity but was made miserable by neighbours who lacked his devotion to the Mrs and enjoyed speculating about the possibilities. The BDO sent the poor chap to a hospital where the operation was performed again. The hospital surgeon reported that in the first operation

---

[10] The politicians' personal motives for standing for or for carrying out such policies are not, in the political scientists' view, relevant to his functional relationship with his followers.

some vasicles had not been severed. The BDO found this happy ending to the story.

The point for social science is not, of course, whether or not the wife was in fact chaste, but that the BDO's folkview permitted, even encouraged him to find that the story had a happy ending. Although the BDO learned two lessons from the experience—(1) that vasectomies should not be done badly, and (2) that when such a job is done badly it is good to repair the damage—he also managed to conclude that the wife's chastity was proved and that the husband would no longer be plagued by his neighbours. In order to reach this conclusion the BDO had to assume not only that the surgeon—*authority*—was right (telling the truth), but also that the man's neighbours would believe authority's explanation of the pregnancy. If the man's neighbours did not have the same faith in authority—if, say, they had a view somewhat closer to mine—the whole affair, whatever the truth of the matter, cannot be regarded as a success. In another folkview than the BDO's, the BDO would have done better not to send the man back to the hospital, for at best that implied that vasectomies can be ineffective, whereas leaving the poor wife in disrepute would also have left surgeons' reputations for effectiveness unsullied.

Contrast the views of operating extension workers with those of social scientists and leaders in community development. The former see co-operatives as inherently developmental because they are inherently right; that is, properly motivated to good ends. This is the case in spite of setbacks which, to social scientists, are clearly a consequence of mismanagement or of the inappropriateness of the cooperative institutions in those particular contexts. That extension officers regard the problem as moral, as calling for increased will-power and more sincere effort rather than for different managerial or commercial techniques is shown by their reaction to failure: they attempt to do "more of the same" rather than to change either arguments or techniques. Superior officers may feel that such subordinates are not trying hard enough or that they are totally lacking in initiative. But this, I submit, may be a mistaken view. A capacity in the extension worker to adapt, to use what we would call "initiative", is perhaps not so much lacking as it is misdirected because the extension worker's folkview of cause and effect, of what constitutes persuasiveness, differs from that of the more operationally oriented social scientist or leader in community development.

For the historically oriented reader, the argument in this essay may help to explain some of the frustrations which have occurred during the history of Indian community development; for the policy-oriented reader, the lesson of this essay is not so clear. If it is clear that further orders and exhortations are inappropriate since they will be translated by the recipient of the messages to accord with the recipient's own folkview, it does not follow that one should try to change the folkviews of extension workers. Such advice of good intention might turn out to be the advice of despair.

Whether social scientists and leaders in community development can phrase directives and communications which, when translated by extension workers into their own folkviews, will produce a "coincidence of differing perceptions" which leads to the results desired is indeed an open question; but achieving successful community development is likely to be an even more burdensome task in the absence of an effort to do so.

10

EDUCATION AND MODERNIZATION

M. S. GORE

EDUCATION AS AN INSTRUMENT OF SOCIAL CHANGE

WHATEVER MAY be the substantive content of the concept of modernization it is clear in the context of underdeveloped economies and traditional societies modernization involves a process of change—social, economic and political. Actually, the change goes even deeper and encompasses cultural values and personality orientations as well.

In so far as modernization is considered a desirable process and a goal to achieve, the relevant question to ask about education vis-a-vis moder· nization is: what kind of education and under what conditions will generate and strengthen the process of modernization in a society? This is a different kind of question from the one usually formulated, viz. Will education lead to social change?

From a sociological point of view education is one of the major agencies of socialization—an agency which by its very nature is intended to ensure continuity rather than discontinuity or change. If therefore, we conceive of education as a likely instrument of change we are guilty of at least an apparent contradiction. Why then do we think of education in the context of change?

One possible answer is that, since in all large societies—including peasant societies, there is always a multiplicity of value-systems which are in a state of relative co-existence and/or mutual competition, education can never completely serve as a mediator for all the different value-systems. In a society which allows freedom in the organization of education different educational institutions would reflect or serve as socializing agents for different sub-cultures. Where the control of educational institutions is differentially distributed between different sub-cultures either as a result of direct regulation by law or as a result of differences in access to economic, political and social centres of decision-making in a given society, the system of education may tend to reflect the values of those groups which are in charge of education and those which support and control education. Teachers belong to the former category and to the latter belong the policy-makers and administrators in government and the trustees of educational institutions. But both of these groups may belong to the sub-culture which is distinguishable from the sub-cultures of other groups in society.

In this situation one can conceive of education as an instrument of social change—a situation in which the élite, i.e. those who control or impart education, seek to impart their values, aspirations and attitudes to the children not only of their own groups, but also children of other groups who may be apathetic, if not hostile, to the value-system of the élite.

In a discussion of education as an instrument of social change we must identify three components of the situation: the agents of change, the content or message of change, and the attitude and social backgrounds of those who are sought to be changed. There is also an important fourth component which can be separately identified, viz. the socio-economic context within which the change is expected to take place or in terms of which the proposed change is to be measured. But it is likely that this fourth component can well be regarded as present in a discussion of each of the first three components.

INDUCED CHANGE THROUGH EDUCATION—A NINETEENTH CENTURY EXPERIMENT

When in the middle of the nineteenth century, the question of devising an appropriate system of education was being considered there were two schools of thought—one made up of those who wished to continue the Vedic, Arabic or Persian patterns of scholarship and education, and the other of those who wished to adopt the western model. This was not so much a division between the British and the Indian sections of opinion as a division within each of these groups. After much debate those who argued for a system of education approximating the English education model won their case. But even here the expectations of the British from the new system of education were not the same as those of the different

M-16

sections of the Indian population, and among the Indians again there were differences between groups regarding what the new education would and should contribute to Indian social life. Some among the British officers expected that the new system of education would provide them with a group of English-speaking, English-thinking subordinates to man government services in India. They expected that the ideas that would be communicated through this system would make the educated Indian more appreciative of and loyal to British rule. Among Indians some looked upon the new system of education as the channel to secure governmental jobs and such other positions of bureaucratic authority as were open to Indians. But there were others who primarily saw the new system of education as a way of introducing young Indians to the new knowledge of science and there were still others who hoped that the new education at the college level with its emphasis on the study of nineteenth century liberal philosophers would open a new vista of thought and philosophy and help promote social reform in the country.

It would be interesting to speculate whether these differences in expectations of what "English" education would contribute were only differences between different segments of the population.

AGENT OF CHANGE

It appears that the group of social reformers were conscious of the potentiality of the new system of education as an instrument of social change. Generally they expected that "English" education, particularly at the higher levels, would lead to a change of social values. Their movements for the amelioration of the condition of women in Indian society and their plea for the removal of caste disabilities were based on the concepts of human dignity and equality; their "petitions" to the British rulers seeking a greater voice and participation for Indians in the governance of the country were based on the premise of the desirability of democratic institutions. The Indian social reformers looked to the liberal philosophy of nineteenth century Britain for inspiration and they evpected that the spread of education in India would ensure the spread of new values which would support the demand for many of the social and political reforms they were seeking. Typically, the social reformers strove for the spread of education as good in itself: education was commonly represented as the flame or light of knowledge which dispelled the darkness of ignorance.

It seems doubtful whether the teachers in the primary and secondary schools who were the agents for the spread of education were aware of the hopes and aspirations of the liberal reformers and it is reasonably certain that, with a few exceptions, they were not in sympathy with the goals of the social reformers. Even those who taught at the college level did not act "liberally" in their personal lives whether with reference to women or to persons of the lower castes.

THE MESSAGE OF CHANGE

The second component in the exercise of induced change consists of the content or the message of change. Ideally it should consist of a statement of what aspects of life are sought to be changed and in what manner. Since the different agents of change have different expectations from the same common programme of action it is natural that they are unable to provide a single or agreed statement of the objectives of change. This was true of those who devised and promoted the new system of education in India. A reference has been made above to the differences between the social reformers and teachers who manned the new schools and colleges. But apart from this difference the social reformers themselves were selective in their perception and propagation of the message of liberalism. A belief in social equality, in popular democracy or representative government and in rationality are the three major aspects of liberal thought. Of these the social reformers emphasized social equality and political democracy. Rationality was perceived somewhat less clearly as a value and then primarily in its relationship to modern science. The acceptance of the liberal message by the rest of the population was probably even more selective. Generally one may say that, of all the values of liberal philosophy, the value of popular democracy received the greatest measure of acceptance and emphasis.

THE SOCIAL CONTEXT

This raises the question why certain aspects of a system of thought are more easily perceived, accepted and communicated than certain others in a given society at a given time. It is here that the role of the social, economic and political context becomes important. With reference to a system of education this factor may simultaneously influence the policy-makers, the teacher-agent of change as well as the pupil-recipient of the message of change.

In a recent study, *Western India in the Nineteenth Century*, occurs the following interesting observation on the role of the brahmans of Maharashtra as the refracting medium for the spread of liberalism:

Since the concepts of social equality and popular democracy which they [the liberal brahmans] promoted were designed to undermine the institution of caste, and to destroy the supremacy of the brahmans, brahman community looked upon their programme of social action with considerable hostility. The brahmans of Mahrashtra, given the choice, would have preferred to follow the orthodox shastris, who were committed to values which ensured brahmanical supremacy and which rejected progress and social mobility. But the inability of the shastris to perform their secular role adequately under the British Government compelled the brahman community to turn to a group of new brahmans who reconciled progress with brahmanical supremacy, and who saw no contradiction between popular democracy and the institution of caste. The "orthodox" new brahmans shared the political objectives of the "liberal" new brahmans. But unlike the latter, they refused to countenance social action which was designed to weaken the traditional structure of Hindu society. Since the orthodox new brahmans did not attack brahmanical supremacy, and because they believed that political emancipation could be achieved independently of social reform, they enjoyed a popularity in the brahman community which was denied to liberal antagonists like Ranade.

     —Rabinder Kumar, *Western India in the Nineteenth Century,* London, Routledge (1968), pp. 331-32

In the minds of most, the relationship beween education and white collar employment was well established and it served to define the aspirations of successive younger generations for the better part of a century between 1860 and 1960. But the message of liberalism grew thinner and the renaissance sought for by the "liberal brahmans" never came. The concept of popular democracy was accepted, passed on and took roots; the concept of social equality was revived later through the influence of Gandhi's humanism and Nehru's socialism and found a place in the Constitution though we are still far from being on our way to equality. But the value of rationality in social action has not yet found an echo in the Indian mind—despite protestations on behalf of a secular polity and the overly articulate demand for the spread of science.

The discussion of the experiment in ushering in liberal values through the mediacy of the educational system was undertaken to highlight the problems of bringing about social change with the help of education but more particularly with the hope that it would sensitize us to the problems we may anticipate in an effort to use education for the spread of the values of modernization.

MODERNIZATION THROUGH EDUCATION

The concept of modernization has been discussed widely by scholars. The concept is obviously a complex one and there are notable differences between societies which may all be referred to as "modern". Of the attributes which are said to characterize modern societies there is one on which there is unanimity, viz. the characteristic that the economies of modern societies are highly productive and that they are based on the adoption of a scientific technology whether in industry, agriculture, fishery, dairy-farming or sheep—and cattle-rearing. When the word modernization is used, it is primarily the modernization of the country's economy that is being thought of. This is particularly likely to be the case when one speaks of the modernization of the erstwhile colonial, newly independent, underdeveloped countries of the world. One suspects, at any rate, that despite some indication to the contrary, the term modernization is used in India as synonymous with industrialization and economic development. This raises the possibility that, just as in the preoccupation with the political goal of freedom one aspect of the liberal philosophy— viz. representative democracy—received greater emphasis and acceptance in the nineteenth and early twentieth centuries, the preoccupation with the economic goal of increased productivity may lead to an emphasis being laid on the creation of appropriate economic institutions to the exclusion, again, of the social aspects of modernization.

This is all the more likely to happen because, unlike liberalism, modernization is not a philosophy and a movement with a clearly articulated value-system. It is a process that first characterized the societies which changed from being primarily agricultural to primarily industrial economies. As this happened these societies simultaneously underwent other changes in their social practices and value premises which have been recorded, discussed and analysed by social scientists and by literary men. These changes have been identified as constituting the process of modernization. In this sense it may be said that modernization is a descriptive and analytical concept rather than a normative one.

Some social scientists have moved beyond the assertion of a correlation between the economic and social aspects of the modernization process to a statement that the social aspects of modernization are a necessary condition for the facilitation of the process of economic modernization. It is this that has added urgency to an understanding of the nature of modernization and to the potential usefulness of education as an instrument for achieving modernization.

LACK OF VALUE CONSENSUS AMONG THE ELITE

There are two more or less clearly differentiated social-political frameworks within which the process of economic development has taken place in the countries of the world. One of these is characterized by a representative form of government and by an assertion of individual freedom. The other is characterized by a totalitarian form of government and by a limitation of the individual's freedom of expression and association. Modernization of the economy can and has been achieved by countries in both these contexts. Of these two socio-political systems India has chosen the democratic system based on a concept of civil liberties and individual freedom. It is no secret, however, that there are organized political parties which are not committed to this system and some of whose leaders talk of using constitutional means for wrecking the constitution.

The same doubts arise with reference to the other concomitants of the process of modernization. Sociologists have, for instance, argued that the development of a sense of national community is a facilitator if not a pre-requisite for the process of industrialization. It can be argued that India as a national community already exists and to that extent the condition for the emergence of a modern society is fulfilled. In support of this one can point to the spontaneous national upsurge when India was attacked by China and later, again, by Pakistan. But we also know that regional loyalties and sub-regional loyalties are no less in evidence and they can even threaten at times the normal functioning of civic life. The development of a national community implies the emergence of a relatively homogeneous system of values and pattern of living in at least the dominant sections of the community—the educational, the business and the political élite. It is these particular groups in our society that are most articulate about their separate regional identities and are involved in organizing strong interest groups based upon regional—as different from national—affiliations.

The same can be said about our secular aspirations and professions. Apart from the sporadic communal and inter-religious riots that take place in different parts of the country, we witness in our society the phenomenon of avowedly communal organizations functioning as recognized political parties.

A third component of modernization is the spread of rationality—at least with reference to social and political life. As mentioned earlier, the liberal social reformers failed in gaining acceptance for this value and there is no evidence that the system of education over the last hundred years has succeeded in making a serious dent in a way of life largely governed by tradition and ritual. Our leaders are known to consult astrologers, we depend on the *muhurat* for celebration of marriages and are continually inhibited by considerations of what is auspicious or inauspicious.

When education is sought to be utilized as a channel for the spread of modernity the need for consensus is all the greater. As stated earlier, the use of education as an instrument of social change raises minimally three questions—one relating to the agent of change, another relating to the message of change, and a third relating to those who are to be exposed to the message of change.

EDUCATION: AN UNCOMMITTED ADVOCATE

About the first component, viz., the agent of change, several questions can be raised. What is the extent of the agent's commitment to the goals of change? How far has his own thinking and behaviour been influenced by the specific ideas that are germinal to the changes that are proposed? An effort to answer this question immediately draws one's attention to the fact that the *agent* of change is not a homogeneous entity. The agents of change are a plurality of individuals and agencies. They differ in their social positions, their perspectives and, maybe, even in their interest-groupings. These differences are important in so far as they are likely to lead to differences in articulation and emphasis on the different aspects of the goal of change. A society which is characterized by a plurality of groups with rival interest orientations would find it difficult to develop a system of education which moves in a linear fashion to one agreed set of change objectives.

There is, besides, a structured source of heterogeneity among the agents of change. It was mentioned above that the agents of change in respect of the system of education are to be found in several groups—the policy-makers, the trustees and the teachers. Assuming that the policy-makers and the trustees are a relatively homogeneous group—an assumption which is by no means universally true— there is still an identifiable and patterned difference between the policy-makers on the one hand and the teachers who execute the policy on the other. In most societies the two belong to two different strata of society. In a traditional society and in a society in its early stages of transition these differences are likely to be particularly marked where the teachers may be drawn from a set of castes or ethnic groups different from those from which the power or business élite, who function as policy-makers, are drawn.

If there is lack of consensus—and in fact open disagreement—even among the élite in society about the social-political framework and the values of modernization the first question that arises is, "Who will educate?" Obviously if the agents of change are themselves unpersuaded about the message they are supposed to transmit and at any rate are unable to incorporate it in their own lives, how can they carry it to others? It is possible that among educators at the school and college levels there is probably acceptance of the value of democracy and of the need to adopt scientific technology, but it would be difficult to say that they are equally sanguine about the values of secularism and rationality. It would be even less justifiable to assert that in their life the teachers practise the values that they avow. Neither democratic attitudes nor scientific objectivity have reached the classroom in all our schools and colleges. Secularism and rationality have, of course, yet to gain a firm acceptance even at the verbal level.

The report of the Education Commission spells out with unusual direct-ness the values and the characteristics of a modern society. The problem, however, is that the report seems to assume a measure of consensus on political values which is not fully justified by recent political events and an acceptance of social values which, while often professed, are rarely practised. Even if India were to see a return to the type of political consensus and stability characteristic of the mid-fifties, the path of modernization through education is not likely to be an easy one— the reason being that even today there is not a sufficiently large body of educators committed to the values of modernization. The task of educating the potential educators has yet to be performed. One wonders whether this can be acheived in the classrooms of teachers' colleges!

THE AMBIGUOUS MESSAGE

The second question that needs discussion in the use of education as an instrument of modernization is the one relating to the clarity of the concept of modernization and its implications for education. It has been suggested above that, apart from lack of consensus on the validity of the particular values of modernization, there is also a lack of clarity about the meaning and implications of some of these values. It is not unusual for political leaders and sometimes even academicians to give a call for a rapid modernization of our society and simultaneously ex-press the opinion that this should not be done at the sacrifice of our traditional values. Since neither the values of modernity nor the values of traditional society are clearly spelt out those who listen to a leader's call can agree or disagree with him depending upon their own mood and temper and upon whether, otherwise, they like or dislike the leader. In this atmosphere pleas for combining the values of science and spirituality do not help in clarifying issues.

It may be argued that new values do not emerge through a process of reasoned clarification and that their acceptance by individuals is at least as much an emotional as a rational process. This may well be so, but the point remains that, unless there is an understanding on what the new values are, there is bound to be a problem in propagating them. This is specially the case in respect of the values of secularism and individualism. In our public life the word "secularism" has come to mean religious tolerance. Actually secularism should mean a rejection of any religious element in the formation of a social or political policy.

A secular policy may not be anti-religious or irreligious, but it is certainly a policy which is non-religious. Secularism is based on a firm acceptance of rationality as the guide to action. The problems arising out of the ambiguity of the concept of secularism are seen best in the effort to develop the teaching of moral science in primary and secondary schools. At some point or the other the authors of the textbooks on moral science have to fall back upon the sanctions of a supernatural power. It may well be that as a people we do not find "rationalism" an acceptable basis for organizing individual and social life. Even so, this would call for a clearer redefinition of the concept of secularism in its Indian usage.

The same ambiguity characterizes our use of the term individualism. Individualism means the right of the individual to think for himself, to differ from others, to not conform to traditional or customary expectations, to make his own decisions. Individualism, of course, requires the individual to develop his own criteria of judgment or, at any rate, to accept socially defined criteria not out of a need to conform but of his own choice. It is not certain that individualism in this sense is accepted by the proponents of modernity in India, for individualism in this sense is likely to threaten the integrity of the familistic and the caste-based loyalties of Indian society.

The need for a clarity in the message of change is important not only for the reason that it can then be incorporated didactically or otherwise in the textbooks and through other means of direct verbal communication but also because it can then become the basis for working out a pedagogic philosophy and practice based upon the values which make up the message. In the absence of such clarity or in the event of the non-acceptance of these values by the teachers as a basis for their own individual life and action all the prescriptions of "progressive education" become another set of rites observed in form but often violated in spirit. It is similar to the situation that would arise by recruitment of family planning workers who do not practise family planning and of village health extension workers who peddle latrines for sale to the village community but themselves prefer the use of open spaces. Teachers who wish to promote independent thinking cannot hope to do so if they give no evidence of independence in their own thinking, nor can they hope to do it so long as they "help" students to perform better in examinations by dictating to them notes and model answers.

At present our pedagogic philosophy is in the nature of a verbal borrowing from the western, particulary the American, context. The American philosophy of education is based, like their philosophy of life, on individualism and on the acceptance of competition and rivalry in social and economic life. If India is to have a socialist society it may be necessary to examine whether this does not call for a modification of educational philosophy and practice. The Education Commission has referred to the need for reconciling the goal of "individual fulfilment with social purpose"; but the changes in approach that such a reconcilation would call for have yet to be indicated.

THE STUDENT AND HIS BACKGROUND

The social and economic background of the students is varied. Except for those who come from urban, professional families, there is often little in the background of the others that can help them to make a meaning out of the message of "modernizm". The "modern" to him, as to many others, means the western and a good deal of his knowledge of this subject is obtained from the film and from fiction. The Indian films reflect the same confusion and ambiguity. There is a simultaneous copying of western fashions in clothing, music and the love-before-marriage theme and verbal glorification of "Indian" culture and Indian values.

The themes of secularism, national consciousness and individualism are not sustained by the life-experience of students. The parental family gives him security but also holds him much too closely to itself to enable him to understand personal freedom or experimentation. The lack of economic opportunity reinforces the student's dependence on the parental family. It also provides the basis for pettiness and for fostering a type of rivalry which is founded not on individual merit and achievement but on claims of language, region and caste. The values of liberalism and modernizm developed in the west during an era of expanding opportunity. Rugged individualism and self-confidence were consistent with the existence of a yet-to-be-conquered world which lay beyond the seas or in the "wild west". Indian youth have yet to experience this sense of economic opportunity and challenge. From this point of view the "green revolution", if it can be consolidated and sustained, may do at least as much for the spread of modernizm as the uncommitted advocates in the schools and colleges can.

This paper on Modernization and Education has discussed the subject from one specific point of view, viz. the use of education as an instrument for the spread of modern influences. It would have been possible to discuss the subject from a different standpoint in an effort to bring out the consequences of modernization for education. But the author chose the former as, in his judgment, the more important of the two foci for discussion.

There is an assumption in much of the discussions of social change that education offers the best and the only instrument of change. There is no intention to deny the usefulness of education as an instrument of change, but education can achieve the desired goals only under certain minimal conditions. These conditions are: a commitment on the part of the agent of change to goals of change, a relative clarity about the message of change, and the existence of an objective situation in which the new values seem to provide guidance and legitimacy to an increasingly larger section of the population that is influenced by education. It appears that these conditions are not fulfilled in India today.

11

PROBLEMS OF MODERNIZATION OF
EDUCATION IN INDIA

B. V. SHAH

1. WHAT IS MODERNIZATION?

MODERNIZATION IS a multi-dimensional process. It is not merely an economic process concerned with maximization of physical power and
improving of tools to increase the productive potential and thereby increase the levels of living of a given society. It is a political, social and
cultural process as well. It is a complex process which touches the entire life of the members of a given society. It is a process which
frees the potential in them in various spheres of their lives and maximi-
zes their ability to share in defining the goals of their society, to interna-
lize them and to participate creatively and effectively in their realization
in the wider society.

In the economic sphere it results in industrialization which brings in
large-scale production and large-scale organization of men, money and
materials, mechanization, monetization and urbanization. It emphasizes
distictions between private and corporate property and separates place
of work from place of residence. It provides individuals freedom of
choice of occupation and requires them to be rational and mobile. It
expects them to develop new attitudes to earning, purchasing, saving
and investing in consonance with the goals of society. *In the political*

sphere it develops a secular and welfare state with enlarged functions to include concerns such as education, health, housing, employment etc. It establishes the rule of law and provides to all equality before the law. It gives freedom to people in choice of rulers and form of government as well as freedom to change them and requires their conscious participation in the political processes. *In the social sphere* it necessitates an open system of stratification and emphasizes achieved status rather than an ascriptive one. It emphasizes equality of opportunity for all and lays stress on individual freedom in matters of family, marriage, occupation, religion etc. *In the individual sphere* it emphasizes change as a value and encourages individuals to have faith in the efficacy of human effort for bringing about desirable social changes. It expects them to be secular, cosmopolitan, rational, scientific and universalistic in their outlook and approach to life and its problems, equalitarian and democratic in their relationships with others, and innovative and creative in their contribution to societal problems and development.

2. GOALS OF THE MODERN INDIAN SOCIAL SYSTEM

In spite of may diversities in Indian society, a general consensus was arrived at in the Constituent Assembly as regards the goals of Indian society. This general consensus has been incorporated in the Constitution. The Preamble of the Constitution with the Fundamental Rights and Directive Principles of State Policy lay the foundations on which a new democractic India is to be built. Their basic objective is to establish a democratic, secular republic with a view to securing justice, liberty, equality and fraternity to all its citizens. They aim at securing a blend of political democracy with economic and social democracy that may ultimately lead to the establishment of a welfare state. In short, they seek to modernize the political, economic and social institutions of Indian society with a view to securing a better standard of life for all citizens. Thus India has decided to become modernized in a big way. From being a society with ascribed, authoritarian and stable values and ways of life, denying its members the right to decide and choose in various spheres of their life according to their inclinations, abilities and achievements and compelling them to conform to group goals of joint family and caste, it aspires to become a society with achieved, democratic and modernistic values and ways of life, giving its members the right to decide and choose themselves according to their own individual inclinations, abilities and achievements. Instead of fixed social interaction, immobility and authoritarian and hereditary, hierarchical social relationships, it aspires to provide to its members free social interaction, mobility, and voluntary, democratic and equalitarian social relationships, be they in the family or in the educational, economic, political or other spheres.

This decision has been taken by a responsible élite for the good of the people. Besides, the élite has decided to induce planned change in consonance with these goals. As the change is to be induced, it is bound to be faster than change that comes naturally through historical development of social forces. However, the change is not to be violently forced; it is to be brought about voluntarily, in accordance with the rule of law, through persuasion and provision of opportunities and facilities to be able to change. Many are expected to participate in this development wherein the already modern are expected to help the transitionals and both are expected to help the traditionals to become modern.

The institutionalization and internalization of the new goals and the consequent social changes cannot take place very smoothly and efficiently unless the large mass of people themselves desire to change and do change in consonance with these goals. They must be prepared to give up ascriptive norms and adopt achievement ones; they must be prepared to adopt specificity rather than diffuseness in a large proportion of their social relationships; they must be ready to give up the long-cherished religious beliefs and be secular and rational in their behaviour; they must cease to be fatalist and resigned to the will of God and be optimistic about fashioning the social future of individuals and groups by human effort. Instead of being interested only in their personal affairs and affairs of their kin, caste and village members, they must take an interest in public affairs and cultivate personal opinions on public issues— local, regional and national. Instead of restricting their loyalty to a small caste or village community, they must enlarge it to the complex and large-scale nation community and participate in the political process as responsible citizens. They must develop new attitudes towards government, legislatures and law as well as towards the individual's role as a citizen. They must have, as Lerner puts it, "a mobile sensibility" and "empathy skills" and readiness to play new roles and participate in new relationships at all levels without losing efficiency.

All this necessitates a big change in the values, interests, attitudes and behaviour of the large mass of people in their social relationships, in their knowledge and abilities and in the technical and social skills they possess in all spheres of their social life.

3. Goals of the Indian Educational System

(i) Agencies of Socialization

A large-scale modernizing society has not only to socialize its younger generation but it has also to resocialize its members into acceptance and internalization of new values and skills. These tasks are shared by several agencies such as the family, school and other educational agencies like adult and social education services, extension education agencies, local, regional and national level voluntary associations in the economic, political and cultural spheres and their leadership, and mass media such as the press, films, radio, etc. In India also the task of socialization is being shared by these agencies. The state, as the community watchdog, is assisting, encouraging as well as controlling these agencies to enable them to perform the task well and in the desired direction. Some of them are directly run or controlled by the state and some are only partially controlled by it in the interests of the community.

These various agencies of socialization and their leadership may work harmoniously and in the same direction or may work in opposite directions: some of them may be more effective than others; some may be more effective with respect to only certain groups. There is no empirical evidence to enable us to get a comparative picture of the content of the socializing effect of these different agencies and the degree of their effectiveness. Research in this direction would be useful.

(ii) Formal Education as a Socializing Agency

Though the task of socialization of the young is shared by several agencies in a modern large-scale society, formal education is considered more important than others. In developing societies which attempt to introduce rapid social changes through democratic and peaceful ways, education is considered the chief activity that can initiate and speed up the mobilization and transformation of human resources that are needed for modernization. It can impart different levels of technical and social skills that are needed for the performance of variegated new roles. It can create and sustain a modernizing élite by preparing it for leadership in various fields by providing high level training in technical and social skills. It can make the masses literate enough to be able to support the modernized political, economic and other institutions actively and efficiently and help to accelerate the process of modernization. As Lerner says, "Literacy, once acquired, becomes a prime mover in the modernization of every aspect of life ... gives people access to the world of vicarious experience ... and becomes the sociological pivot in the activation of psychic mobility, shared skill which binds a modern man's varied daily round into consistent life-style." (Lerner, Daniel, 1963, p. 341).

(iii) Goals of the Indian Educational System

As Indian society has decided to modernize its social, political and economic institutions very rapidly and without force, it wishes its educational system to play a modernizing role. It believes that the educational system can play a major role in bringing about necessary changes. This is reflected in the constitutional directives of state policy, in the governmental efforts to reconstruct the educational system, and also in declarations of governmental educational policy.

In the post-independence period, a major concern of the Government of India and the State Governments has been to give increasing attention to education as a factor vital to national progress and security. The Government of India in its recent resolution on national policy in education concurs with the Report of the Education Commission (1964-66) which sub-titles its Report "Education and National Development", and states in its very first sentence that "the destiny of India is now being shaped in its classrooms" and, after discussing some of the changes that are required for national development, concludes that "if this change on a grand scale is to be achieved without violent revolution, 'there is one instrument, and one instrument only, that can be used: EDUCATION." (Government of India: Ministry of Education, 1966, pp. 1 and 4) The resolution clearly states that

the Government of India is convinced that a radical reconstruction of education on the broad lines recommended by the Education Commission is essential for economic and cultural development of the country for national integration and for realizing the ideal of a socialist pattern of society. This will involve a transformation of the system to relate it more closely to the life of the people, a continuous effort to expand educational opportunity, a sustained and intensive effort to raise the quality of education at all stages, an emphasis on the development of science and technology and the cultivation of moral and social values. (Government of India: Ministry of Education, 1968).

Government also laid down in its resolution that "investment in education should be gradually increased so as to reach a level of expenditure of 6 per cent of the national income as early as possible". Thus the goal of the present-day educational system in India is to develop in the younger generation new technical and social skills, and new values, attitudes and behaviour in consonance with a rational, democratic, equalitarian, secular achievement-and-change-oriented and participant society. It remains to be seen how far the educational system has been able to perform this role and reflect the desired changes.

4. MODERNIZATION OF EDUCATION IN INDIA—A SPECIAL PROBLEM

The modernization of education in India poses a -special probem in several ways.

India has adopted the path of economic development within the framework of a free society and therefore cannot adopt authoritarian means to modernize education. The centre has to get the willing consent of the states and each state has to get the willing consent of its elected representatives in their legislative assemblies before introducing any major change in the allocation of resources to education or in the educational system itself.

Secondly, India has no colonies to depend on for resources to meet the expenditure on modernizing its educational sytem. It has to depend on and find its own resources which are bound to be very limited at this stage of development. On the other hand, there is an advantage also. Advanced countries and international agencies, like UNESCO, have developed programmes to assist educational development in developing countries. India can get assistance for them.

Thirdly the process of modernization is not completely new to India. It started with the impact of the Britishers and is now about a hundred years old. This has added to the diversities in India. Its economy has become mixed, including modern factories along with traditional agriculture; its tribal, rural and urban groups show very wide contrasts in their physical and social conditions of living. It has some highly educated and sophisticated groups of people with achievement-orientation and a firm belief in their own ability to mould their life and society according to their goals as well as illiterate primitive groups of people who resign themselves to God and believe that not even a blade of grass moves without His will. On the one hand "there exists a number of linguistic regional societies largely following the traditional ethic or value pattern which is constituted of the twin loyalties to caste and joint family and on the other hand there is, located in each of these linguistic regional societies, a new urban society spread all over India, which largely follows the ethic of liberalism, democracy and secularism." (Panchanadikar, K. C., 1961, p. 14-35) These different levels of development at which the various sections of society stand differentiates their educational needs and complicates the problem of educational development. The aims, methods and organization of education which may be functional for one group may be dysfunctional for the other. There may be differences among the people in matters of allocation of scarce resources. Some may give priority to a quantitative expansion of primary education to the masses and some others may lay emphasis on a qualitative improvement of all levels of education before expanding them.

In western societies economic modernization preceded political and social modernization. Consequently, in their educational thinking they could lay more emphasis on the needs of the individual than on the economic needs of the country. In India all aspects of modernization are brought into motion more or less simultaneously. Being largely agricultural and poor, India has to think of the economic needs of the country before it thinks of individuals. It cannot initially afford to "waste" its resources on educational programmes that are not productive in economic terms. The problems of outputs proportional to inputs in terms of economic needs are likely to loom large and to be attended to more than the problems of quality of education in the earlier period of its development.

5. THE PROBLEM OF ORIENTATION OF EDUCATION

In a modernizing society the orientation always has to be towards the future; towards the new goals and values cherished by the new society, though in doing so it does not discard the social heritage completely. It draws from it wherever it helps to realize the new goals but rejects it wherever it hinders this process. Most Indian traditions inhibit modernity. India's ethical values are other-worldly and secular values like *artha* and *kama* are subordinate to them. Its social institutions are authoritarian and group-oriented and individuality and free enquiry are not encouraged. The narrower loyalties to kin and caste groups do not allow wider civic responsibilites and national loyalties to develop. Tolerance of differences arises out of shutting one's self in one's kin and caste group and not out of a recognition of the right of others to be different. India has very little in her traditions that can support modernity. How can education assist the supplanting of traditional orientations by modernistic ones? What elements of traditions can be reinterpreted and transformed to assist modernity?

6. PROBLEMS OF QUANTITATIVE EXPANSION

A modernizing society needs a large base of functionally literate people, a fairly adequate supply of technicans, and a considerable number of trained people who can lead the masses in the desired direction. It needs, therefore, a leadership commited to extending education to masses, a rising demand for it among the people, and sufficient resources to meet the demand The first two are present in India. As for the third, India has to proceed by stages, as the resources become available from public or private sources.

The questions that can be raised here are as follows: How can we estimate realistically the manpower needs that will guide sound educational expansion at different levels of development: How much of educational expansion can be made in primary, secondary and higher education? What allocation of resources would be sufficient to ensure this? Which agency—government, local body, public corporation, private trust or any other—will best be able to organize educational institutions at different levels in terms of national goals as well in terms of the needs of different sections of society? Where private inititative is permitted to organize educational institutions, what government or university controls and directions will be necessary to ensure that no commercial and non-academic considerations enter into their organization and conduct and that regional or rural-urban imbalances in the provision and type of educational facilities are not generated? Even if only academic considerations weigh with public or private organizers of education, is education sufficiently diversified at different levels in content, and both in methods of teaching as well as in organization to suit the differential needs of different sections of Indian society which stand at different levels of traditionality and development? In what ways should educational institutions adapt themselves to serve the needs of low-ability students coming from non-intellectual backgrounds without lowering the level of their services to satisfy the needs of high-ability students? Though education may be open to all, the backward and poor sections of society may not be able to take to it. It is necessary to examine, therefore, to what extent the nature of existing facilities unequalize the chances of admission of certain sections to certain courses of instruction, as well as of continuance and success? Is there sufficient provision of economic and other assistance to enable them to overcome this handicap? The problem here is: Can the student body at different levels be made more socially representative of different classes in society without losing quality?

Wastage and Stagnation
In a developing society, unless education is diversified enough at different levels to suit the differing needs of groups at different levels of development, it is likely to create the problem of wastage and stagnation.

Educated Unemployment
In a developing society, the traditional notion that education bestows status persists for a long time. Though this has decreased in India to some extent, a large number of people still take up education to achieve status and not to fit them for any active work. The upper castes refuse to be satisfied with secondary or vocational education and go in for whatever university education they can get. The masses also demand the same kind of education as the élite take, even though it has no relevance to their immediate needs. The educational system does not discourage the excessive production of trained persons in unneeded skills and encourage increased production of trained persons in needed skills. There is over-production of persons with skills needed for white-collar, high-level jobs and a shortage of skilled middle-level technicians, laboratory assistants, medical asssistants and supervisory-level workers,

This creates a continuously growing class of educated unemployed and a class of educands who are unsure about getting employment at the completion of their education. The more able are likely to be lured by opportunities of further studies and employment in more advanced countries. This is evidenced in the increasing brain-drain to the more developed countries. The less able swell the number of frustrated youths.

Rise of Private Educational Entrepreneurs
The quantitative growth of education with limited public resources leads the government to rely on private initiative and resources. This gives rise to a class of private educational entrepreneurs who organize education at different levels. In dealing with the Indian situation Srinivas (1968, p. 36) says that "education becomes a status symbol for the community and a source of economic and social influence for the entrepreneur". The more they organize schools and colleges, the more extensive becomes their power and influence. Some of them may be academically oriented and may maintain standards; but a large proportion of them are commercially and politically oriented and are quite content to run substandard institutions as long as they serve their main purpose.

Rural Students
The quantitative educational expansion brings in a large number of rural students into schools and colleges. A large number of them come from illiterate families. This double exposure to education and urban environment, coming as it does for the first time, makes severe demands on their intellectual and moral resources. This creates problems of adjustment in schools and colleges as well as in the urban environment in which they have to live.

Educational Institutions in Rural Areas
Quantitative expansion leads to schools and colleges being located in rural areas also where traditional loyalties to kin, caste and village community are still very powerful. It is very likely that the pressure of these primary group loyalties will circumvent or undermine adherence to achievement criteria in admission and promotion of students as well as in recruitment of teachers and adherence to rules and regulations in maintenance of standards. This is more likely to happen in educational institutions which are run by private entrepreneurs.

Adult Education
Education for change must be education at all levels of society and especially among adults. An educational programme that concentrates on the

new generations only cannot effect major changes because the influence of the adult world is too strong. Though the younger generation may rebel against the standards of the adults, in the long run they are more likely to give up the values newly acquired in childhood and accomodate themselves to the world of accepted adulthood. It is necessary that the values of childhood get reinforced in adulthood. This is possible only if adults are also educated in the acceptance of new values along with the younger ones.

7. PROBLEMS OF QUALITY

In our educational planning more attention is paid to devising procedures for effectively expanding the quantity of education and less to improving its quality, though the latter is much more important. Here we can think of three different levels of quality as Beeby (1966, pp. 10-12) has defined them:

(1) *Classroom Conception of Quality* as seen by the inspector of schools. This may include measurable skills in the three R's, acquisition of a given range of facts about certain subjects and measurable aspects such as habits of industry, tidyness, accuracy, attitude of respect towards authority, love for country, manipulation of facts, independent thinking, initiative and creativity.

(2) *Economic Conception of Quality* measured by its productivity of suitably trained persons in suitable proportions for different economic activities to be performed at a particular stage of development.

(3) *Social Conception of Quality* which includes social goals and values cherished and the degree of their internalization by the educands through the educational process.

Economic and Educational Approaches

With regard to the question of education we have two approaches, that of the economist and that of the educator. As Beeby puts it:

the educator still continues secretly to believe that, if the economist really sets his mind to it, he could find some hidden source of funds for a purpose so obviously essential as education. ... The economist, on the other hand, while maintaining that his primary interest is not in cutting expenditure on education, but in that, if educators could only drop their conservatism and come into the 20th century, they could "develop a new "education technology" that would raise the productivity of the school and produce better results with little or no rise in costs. (Beeby, C. E., 1966, pp. 21-22)

Economists regard the conservatism of educators and of the educational system as one of the important barriers to both education and economic progress. The question is whether they are needlessly conservative. How far is resistance to change due to conservatism for its own sake and how far is it in the very nature of the teaching and learning within the school system in a developing country? A new educational technology may fail not merely because the teacher does not want to take to it or is conservative or suspicious about it; it may fail because it calls for knowledge and understanding, abilities and qualities which the teacher does not possess; it may fail because the pupils do not respond as they may not possess skills and qualities that the new technology requires of them; it may fail because the necessary materials and equipment it requires are not available or its costs are too high to meet. The question we can therefore raise here is: Is it better to improve the quality of education by raising the educational and training level of teachers or by providing the existing teachers with improved educational technology and training them in their use? Is it better to use new technology only as a supplement or as an alternative to the giving of more general education and training to the teacher?

The quality of educational institutions may vary and the measures that may be suited for improvement of those that are at a higher-quality level may not be suited to those that are at a lower-quality level. It is necessary, therefore, to devise a classification of educational institutions according to their quality level in terms of all the three conceptions of quality before selecting measures to improve them.

Recruitment of Educational Decision-makers
The controllers and supervisors of the educational system at different levels play a very crucial role in facilitating or obstructing changes in the educational system in the desired direction. In order to ensure that the right type of persons are recruited to positions of educational planners, education ministers, directors and inspectors of education, vice-chancellors, chairmen and members of various educational boards and communities, etc., the recruitment procedures must be sufficiently impersonal and objective and the basis of recruitment must be merit and achievement that are relevant to the position involved. Do relevant achievement criteria receive prime consideration? To what extent do ascriptive and other non-academic criteria enter into such recruitment?

Orientation of Supervisory and Inspectional Personnel
Do the educational supervisors and inspectors consider themselves to be mere controllers, censors and fault-finders or do they regard themselves as constructive guides of the teachers?

Principals, Teachers and Management Boards

How are principals and teachers recruited at different levels? Are the recruitment, promotion and dismissal procedures sufficiently impersonal and objective? Do relevant merit or demerit and achievement or non-achievement receive prime importance or are ascriptive and other non-academic considerations involved?

Does the structure and composition of the management boards provide effective weightage and power to the principal in all academic matters? Are teachers represented on the management boards? To what extent are administrator-teacher relationships democratic? Do principals regard teachers as equal partners and involve them in academic policy-framing?

Teacher-student Relationship

How is the teacher's role conceived? Is he to be an all-knowing person whose authority cannot be questioned and whose only role is to pass on what he knows to the students? Or is he expected to encourage students to think independently and raise doubts and questions? Is he expected to lead them to accept the prevailing social norms or develop ability in them to rationally question them, to reject them wherever they find it necessary, and to adapt themselves efficiently to the new developing norms?

Student Recruitment and Role

Are students of only high and medium ability recruited or are low-ability students encouraged to join for mere economic benefit? In India, private educational institutions often admit low-ability students in large numbers. These students, under a belief that high academic requirements will un-equalize their chances of success, resist their enforcement and resort to anti-intellectualism and movements to lower the academic standardss in order to increase their chances of success (Shah, B. V., 1968, p. 62).

Laboratory work is regarded as equivalent to manual labour, require-ment for purchase of textbooks is considered a hardship on impove-rished students and failing examinations indicate that the passing mark was set at too high a level. Under this pressure there is a tendency for standards to drop to a point where the payment of fees and registra-tion are the only requirements. In some countries government Univer-sities have allowed their standards to drop to the level where they meet the level of student preparation. In others government schools (and colleges) have sought to hold their standards, but private schools (and colleges), which are in reality little more than diploma mills, make a handsome profit by passing out diplomas in return for tuition. Hunt, Chester L. 1966, p. 121)

How is the role of the student conceived? Is he expected to study only and be an expert in his field? Should he care merely for the development of his personality or should he work for the enlargement of his social consciousness by a proper understanding of public issues that involve locality, region, state and nation and prepare himself for assuming civic responsibility? Has he any role to play in the welfare of the wider society?

Content of Education

In a modernizing society the content of education must be liberal and must reflect the new values—democracy, equality, rationality, scientific attitude, secularism, achievement orientation, readiness to change and faith in the ability of effort to effect social change. To what extent does the emphasis given to different subjects and their content reflect these values?

Examinations

Do examinations encourage only memorization of information unrelated to life or do they encourage analysis, interpretation and independent, innovative and creative thinking and inculcate a scientific approach and insight into the problems of society?

Language Problem

The confusion created by unsettled language policy and vested interests in language teaching has affected the quality of education, specially at higher levels. Lack of resources for production of literature in regional languages and apathy and unwillingness of senior and experienced teachers to write books in regional languages has further aggravated the situation.

Unsupportive Role Played by Family

Due to the wide gulf between the goals and needs of the school and those of the illiterate parents of children coming from rural areas, the family is not able to play a supportive role to the role of the teacher and the quality of learning acquired suffers.

8. THE PROBLEM OF FIXING PRIORITIES

The limited resources of the community create the problem of fixing priorities. Would it be better to give priority to economic development over educational development? Would it be better to attend to problems of quantity first or to those of quality? Should we start with improving primary education or begin with higher education? Should improvement of physical facilities, technology of education, structure of organization of education, recruitment procedures, examination patterns, etc. be given priority or should improvement of quality and attitudes of human material involved in the process be our prime concern? We can also raise the question of the very efficacy of education as a major agent of social change.

9. Is Education a Major Agency of Social Change?

Education is not the only agency of social change. Other agencies such as voluntary associations, motion-picture, press, radio, etc., also operate. Besides,

> the interdependence of education and the total cultural framework means that it is folly to rely on education as the sole or even a major agent of social change. This statement does not invalidate the premise that an educational programme working in conjunction with changing agriculture, business, political and industrial patterns may do much to accelerate the rate of change. (Hunt, C. L., 1966, p. 132).

By expecting more of education than it can deliver at any given stage, education is made to appear dysfunctional in developing societies. It is necessary, therefore, that developing societies regard education as only one of the agents of social change that can bring only limited results and look to other agents also and gear them in the desired direction to make the effect more cumulative and lasting.

These are some of the questions that can be raised with respect to modernization of education in India. They may not be all. Nor have I attempted to answer them fully but have left them open for discussion.

REFERENCES

Beeby, C. E. : *The Quality of Education in Developing Countries*, Harvard University Press (1966)

Government of India, Ministry of Education: *Report of Education Commission 1964-66 (1966); Resolution on National Policy on Education*, (24 July 1968)

Hunt, Chester L. : *Social Aspects of Economic Development*, McGraw Hill Book Company (1966)

Lerner, Daniel : "Towards a Communication Theory of Modernization" *in Communications and Political Development* by Lucian W. Pie (1963)

Panchanadikar, K. C. : "Determinants of Social Structure and Social Change in India", *Sociological Bulletin*, Vol. XI, pp. 14-35, (October 1961)

Shah B. V. : "Students' Unrest—A Sociological Hypothesis", *Sociological Bulletin*, Vol. XVII-1, pp. 55-64 (March 1968)

Srinivas M. N. : "Education, Social Change and Social Mobility in India" in T. A. Mathias (ed.) *Education and Social Concern*, Jesuit Educational Association of India, Delhi pp. 18-43 (1968)

12

SOME THEMES IN THE CULTURE OF INDIA

DAVID C. MCCLELLAND

To ATTEMPT to make any generalization about India is immensely difficult and for a foreigner, somewhat presumptuous. It is not only a huge
country with a long and complex history, but a tremendously varied one.
Is it proper to speak of a "culture" embracing all of India? As Narain
in his book *Hindu Character* observes: "The Hindus are an old and
complex people. It is by no means an easy task to understand and explain
them." (1957, p. 34)

Yet many have tried, perhaps because, despite the obvious variety,
certain Hindu characteristics such as the stress on non-violence or the
caste system have appeared so striking, even to the casual observer.
Furthermore, one suspects that the core values of Hinduism must have
represented a strong unifying force since they have managed to resist
and transform several major attempts to take over the country politically
by foreign invaders such as the Greeks under Alexander the Great, the
Moghul emperors, or more recently the British empire-builders. Even though
such attempts were buttressed by other major religious traditions, like
Christianity and Islam, one gains the impression that in some sense Hindu
character overwhelmed and transformed them all. So there must be some
hard core unity in all this diversity and many have sought to discover
what it is—including Indian scholars like President Radhakrishan (1948)
or Nirad Chaudhuri (1965) and Westerners like W. S. Taylor (1948) or
Morris Carstairs (1957). Such contributions have been ably reviewed by

Narain (1957) who has also added much himself to our knowledge of Hindu character.

What gives me the right to try to join such a distinguished company of observers? If Narain feels handicapped by his inability to read Sanskrit or any South Indian languages, how much more handicapped am I—I who cannot read *any* Indian language? I have not even lived in India for any extended period of time. In fact I have made only three short visits there touching base in such key spots as a North Indian village, Delhi, Bombay, Hyderabad and two smaller cities in South-central India—Kakinada and Vellore, yet missing such major centres as Calcutta. Perhaps my one claim to some first-hand knowledge in depth is based on our intensive work over a period of years with some businessmen in Kakinada and Vellore who joined us in an effort based on modern psychological knowledge to develop the spirit of enterprise in their cities. This project has been fully written up elsewhere (McClelland & Winter, 1969), though paradoxically my experience with it left me with the predominant feeling that Indian businessmen are pretty much like businessmen I have worked with everywhere else—in the United States, in Spain, in Tunisia, and in Mexico. Perhaps there is some advantage in studying a culture at a distance. The closer you get to it, the more you become aware of our common humanity.

Narain has also pointed to this possibility: "to study the culture in which one is born is a double-edged affair—he can see things from within, but he cannot look at them from without" (1957, p. 186). To look at them from without, and from a distance, may give one more perspective but it is also extremely dangerous. For if one cannot see very well or very clearly, he tends to imagine what is there. As modern psychology has demonstrated again and again, people tend to project into an ambiguous stimulus what they themselves wish and believe. And Westerners have for a long time tended to create an image of the "mysterious East" which fulfils their own desires to escape from the hectic demands of an achievement-oriented civilization. From Thomas Mann and Hermann Hesse to Timothy Leary extolling the virtues of the LSD experience, the Westerner has all too often created an image of a peace-loving other-wordly East in which people live out a kind of trance-like existence unaffected by the materialistic demands that confound the western world. So while the Indian may feel too close to his culture to see it clearly, the Westerner has his special problem of coping with his need to see things that aren't necessarily there.

As if these problems were not enough, the dominant view among behavioural scientists today is that national character studies should not be attempted without national sample surveys. Inkles and Levinson (1954) argue that the only scientific meaning that national character can have is in reference to modal personality traits—that is, beliefs, attitudes or acts factually shown to characterize the mode for a random sample of the human beings living in a given nation state. Clearly no data of this kind exist for the Indian sub-continent nor are they likely to exist in the near future. So from what factual base are we to infer the themes which characterize Indian culture? Why attempt something that can have no scientific basis in national sample statistics? The answer lies in my some· what different conception of the nature of the task involved in delineating national character or finding themes in a given culture. Certainly national sample statistics are helpful in such an effort, but they are not essential. To me culture is a shared cognitive system. Members of the culture learn to operate in terms of this system often quite unconsciously in much the same way as they learn to speak a language. They learn to speak the language correctly—that is, according to the implicit rules of the linguistic system—but they may be quite unable to formulate those rules and describe them to an outsider. It is the job of the behavioural science observer—the anthropologist, sociologist or psychologist—to try to discover those rules and formulate them as simply and parsimoniously as possible. For this purpose, it may be much more efficient to go directly to the rule books rather than to try to infer what the rules are from the actions of modal classes of people in a culture. By "rule books" I mean those documents which lay out more or less explicitly in words the cognitive systems which the members of a culture are supposed to share. In the case of India they would certainly include such popular epics as the *Bhagavad Gita* and the *Ramayana* as well as such other forms of popular culture as the films and proverbs analysed by Narain (1957). I personally have found children's stories particularly useful for this purpose because they often express the general rules of conduct quite simply and directly. In fact if they are explained simply enough for children to learn, perhaps even the behavioural scientists can understand them! The genesis of this paper lies in an analysis I made of 21 such stories sampled at random from third-grade readers used all over India (see McClelland, 1961). I had undertaken the task because I thought the results might be helpful to the Indian businessmen when they were considering the virtues of a greater achievement-orientation in the light of certain traditional Indian values. We had planned to discuss the themes I had observed in the stories, reading them more or less as a clinical psychologist would, in terms of whether they promoted or inhibited the changes in their activities that these men were considering. But the discussions never took place partly because I could not be present personally to conduct them and partly because the Indian staff responsible for the courses wondered how these "psychological insights by an American" would be received. It proved better to deal more indirectly with possible value conflicts between tradition and new ways of behaving under discussion in our achievement motivation courses for businessmen.

So while I found the culture of India fascinating and its children's stories even more so, I have hesitated to publish these notes for fear of being presumptuous. In fact I would not have had the nerve to do so even now had it not been for the urging of A. R. Desai and D. Narain of the University of Bombay. Even with their kind invitation I hesitate to expose these ideas to the public. They are certainly less authoritative than I would like them to be, based as they are on an inadequate knowledge of Indian languages, history, religion and culture. Perhaps the only excuse for publishing them is that they represent an approach which in more knowledgeable hands may be pushed to a more authoritative conclusion. The reader should realize that what follows is, at best, only a very rough sketch of a few of the main features of the cognitive map in terms of which Indians appear to operate.

THE ANALYTIC APPROACH

Let me begin by stating more precisely the nature of the task as I understand it. The goal is to explain, understand or account for the characteristics of Indian culture—its customs, beliefs, institutions, or the typical actions of members of the culture. To accomplish this purpose two steps are necessary. First we must make a list of the facts that are to be accounted for. And second, we must discover the fewest possible themes or propositions that seem to account for them. Hopefully the themes themselves can be organized into a coherent whole on the assumption that the culture "makes sense" psychologically in much the same way that a language does. That is, the different rules dicsovered should "hang together" or "make sense" in some way or at least not contradict each other totally. This is not to say that there will be no conflicts among the various themes, but if there are, there at least should be culturally defined ways of coping with them.

What facts need to be accounted for? Obviously the universe is very large. Table 1 on page 258 presents a sampling of such facts, some of which have often figured in previous interpretations of Hindu character, and some of which have not. The list illustrates a number of points about an analysis of this kind.

To begin with we must deal with a sample of facts. We could not possibly list them all or account for them all. Furthermore, we are sampling facts, not people, as in a national sample survey, but in deciding how to sample facts we may follow the same principles used in sampling people. That is, just as we want a sample of people to be representative

TABLE 1

SOME MISCELLANEOUS OBSERVATIONS OF HINDU
CULTURAL CHARACTERISTICS

1. Crowded occupancy of space
2. Wide variations in personal life style (in everything from dress to religion)
3. Non-violent ideal (vegetarianism)
4. High rate of litigation and disputation
5. High dominance and succorance (asking for help) rates in children, compared, to other cultures
6. Sacredness of the cow
7. Why are gods and goddesses represented as having four arms and hands?
8. Caste system, *dharma* (duty in "calling")
9. The law of *Karma* (action and reaction, permanent record of merit)
10. *Moksha*—the goal of enlightenment, withdrawal from the world
11. Stress on ritual purity, non-contamination (touch taboos)
12. Feeding and food offerings as signs of devotion and respect
13. Not eating (fasts) as means of constraining the behaviour of others, showing anger, curing disease
14. Two types of leaders—wealthy men, men of no wealth (*sadhus*)
15. Yoga as self-purification
16. Traditional restriction of freedom of movement of women
17. Women mythologically considered dangerous, active
18. Women have higher positions of political power in modern India than any other nation
19. Excessive concern over privileges in bureaucracy (size of office, rug, desk, number of peons, etc.)
20. Insistence that even important men must be always available to callers in their offices, even though they are already in conference
21. Fights between mothers-in-law and daughters-in-law
22. Dangers of open praise for another's performance (or beauty and good health of a child)—Emphasis on criticism
23. Side-wise head shaking
24. Love of discussion of abstract moral issues
25. Importance of sexual imagery in worship (the *lingam* in the *yoni,* etc.)

of all the different classes of people in India, we want a sample of facts to be representative of all the different classes of facts. If it is truly representative, the sample need not be large. Unfortunately we do not as yet have an agreed upon system for classifying facts, though a few simple categorizations readily suggest themselves. For instance, we ought to sample facts from different areas of cultural life—from child-rearing, from political behaviour, from religion, from art and so on—in fact from all the major categories in an anthropological handbook like *Notes and Queries.* Secondly, we should sample not only from the ideal but the real. For instance, we readily note that Indians stress the ideal of non-violence, yet we must also account for the fact that in reality they are among the most disputatious people in the world (see below). We must account not only for their highly abstract philosophy of religion but also for the fact the the common people worship tree spirits. Thus Table 1 includes facts of apparently very different levels of importance. Thus we have included the doctrine of *Karma*, which everyone would doubtless agree is of central importance, along with such apparently trivial facts as the tendency of gods and goddesses to have four hands or of people to shake their heads in a sidewise motion in conversation. According to the theory being presented here, any analysis of Indian character must account for the trivial as well as the sublime, for folk culture as well as for consciously idealized culture. So to test the generality of interpretations or their inclusiveness, it is desirable to include a random sampling of facts, both trivial and sublime, from all areas of cultural life.

The careful behavioural scientist may want to know when a fact is a fact. While he must agree that many Indians are vegetarians, if he is at all knowledgeable, he will be quick to point out that many millions of Indians eat meat and have always eaten meat. In what sense then can we say that it is a fact that vegetarianism is a characteristic of the culture of India? Why shouldn't we say that non-vegetarianism is a characteristic of the culture of India? Is the matter to be decided by majority vote? Obviously not, according to the mode of analysis adopted here. Vegetarianism is a fact characteristic of the culture of India in the sense that practically every Indian knows that vegetarianism is an ideal practised by many Indians. It is part of his culture in exactly the same sense as a word might be part of his vocabulary which he could understand if it was spoken, even though he might never use it himself.

But vegetarianism is more important even than that to our understanding of Hindu character. Even though it were practised only by a minority and although the majority did not know about it, it could be particularly helpful in our analysis because it is relatively unique cross-culturally. Unique, uncommon, or strange facts are particularly useful in making inferences about national character because of the logic of inverse probability. In making an analysis of this kind we are trying to infer an explanation A, from a manifestation of it B. But unfortunately under normal conditions we cannot infer A from the existence of B. There are many other antecedent conditions, X, Y and Z, which may have been responsible for B. There is only one condition under which we can safely infer the antecedent A from the consequence B. That is when A and *only* A can produce B. If B is a common event like eating meat, we would be lost trying to make any inferences as to the reasons why people eat meat since most peoples eat meat and there presumably are all sorts of reasons for doing so. However, if B is a rare or unique event, such as not eating meat, we have a much more restricted universe of antecedent events A from which to pick an explanation. We are much more likely to be in a position to say that A and *only* A could produce B. The reader with a more technical interest in this problem should refer to discussions of the laws of inverse probability (cf. Bakan, 1967).

But our skeptical methodologist may still not be wholly satisfied. He might be willing to accept the fact that the cow is considered sacred in India even without a national sample survey, but he is certain to question our assertion that there is "excessive concern" over privileges among bureaucrats in India. What do we mean by excessive? Is it truly greater than in any other bureaucracy? What proportion of Indian bureaucrats are "excessively" concerned about privileges? To be sure it would be better if we had some statistics to answer these questions because the way the "fact" is stated implies a comparison of some kind. Thus we feel much more comfortable about fact 5 in Table 1 because we know that careful comparative studies made by Whiting and associates (in preparation) [1] have demonstrated that dominance and succorance are the highest among Khalapur Rajput children in comparison with samples of children from five other cultures where the observations were made under identical conditions. Still, in the absence of such comparative data, we are not quite willing to abandon the statement about "concern over privileges" altogether because Indians themselves so often talk about how prevalent concern over privileges is. Whether on an international comparative basis Indian bureaucrats are more concerned with privileges or not, it is a fact that Indian commentators find the concern that exists objectionable and in this sense, at a minimum, the privileges issue is one that needs to be accounted for in any complete picture of Indian national character.

One other characteristic of the "facts" listed in Table 1 deserves mention. So far as possible they represent "observables" rather than interpretations. Note that I have tried not to list traits such as "femininity" or "other-worldliness" which are sometimes attributed to Indians. The reason is that femininity seems more like an intepretation than a fact. As such it belongs in the second part of the analysis. In the first part we may place something like the stress on non-violence, but if we wanted to intepret that as meaning femininity, we would have a great deal of work ahead of us yet. That is, we would have to show that women are less violent than men cross-culturally, that Indian men are in fact non-violent, and so forth. We would also have to define other behaviour

---

[1] Throughout this paper, I have relied heavily on information gathered in a field study of a North Indian village sponsored by the anthropologists, Drs. John and Beatrice Whiting as part of a systematic comparative study of six cultures. Publications include Minturn and Hitchcock, 1963, and Whiting, Whiting Lombert and Longabaugh, in preparation. The Whitings carefully stress that their findings are based on studies of 38 households in Khalapur, Uttar Pradesh, India, and can be generalized to other groups in India or India as a whole only with extreme caution.

characteristics of women and see if Indian men display them more than men in other cultures do.

In making an analysis of the sort proposed here, it is methodologically essential to list the facts in advance of their interpretation. Otherwise we fall into an unsystematic, anecdotal method of making a few informal interpretations and then looking around for illustrations that bear them out. Science is devoted to the notion of being more careful than that, of setting the facts up in such a way that they could seriously jeopardize interpretations offered. The listing in Table 1 is by no means definitive. In fact it is something of a random jumble, but at least it has the merit of having been made in advance of the interpretation so that we cannot readily be accused of selecting the facts to fit the theories. And furthermore if any one does not like the interpretations about to be offered, he has an opportunity of developing his own alternative hypotheses to explain such facts as those listed. Or he can insist that certain key facts must be included in the list that have been overlooked. And when we have finished we can look back and see whether we have accounted for all of these facts reasonably well and whether any of them are left over. Only by systematically checking our interpretations in such ways can we lay any claim at all to being engaged in a scientific enterprise.

Given the facts, how do we go about finding interpretations for them? It is certainly dangerous to attempt to give psychological explanations based on Western experience. For example, suicide threats are commonly associated in the West with low self-esteem, often coming from desertion by a loved one. Yet it would be a mistake to interpret suicide threats in India in these terms, as we shall see in a moment. Instead we must turn to the explanation Indians themselves give for what they do. There are three main sources of information on such matters. First in importance are the formal rule books—the sacred texts containing religious and philosophical explanations understood by every knowledgeable adult. Thus it is not hard to find out why cows are considered sacred in India. "The Vedic writers held cows in high regard, used them as their standard of exchange, and identified them with earth, nourishment, and motherhood" (Minturn & Hitchcock, 1963, p. 268). In India great popular epics like the *Ramayana* and the *Mahabharata* which includes the *Bhagavad Gita* are examples of such important religio-philosophical texts. Narain quotes President Radhakrishnan as saying that the *Gita* "is the most popular religious poem of Sanskrit literature. . . It is a book conveying lessons of philosophy, religion and ethics." Narain continues.

the Hindu turns to it when he is serene as well as when he is ruffled. It may be a daily ritual with him or it may be his only hope when crisis threatens. The occasions on which the Gita is read and its teachings

M-18

are taken to heart are as numerous as they are varied. From a minor emotional disturbance to the most intense spiritual distress, the *Gita* is looked up to as the last word and the unfailing source of help. It has exerted on the Hindu mind an immeasurable influence. Its teaching percolated in some form or other to the common people. (1957, p. 78).

Narain then devotes an entire chapter to analysing the psychology and philosophy of the *Gita*. The *Ramayana* is scarcely less important as it has been told and retold down through the ages. Nowadays it forms the basis for a series of films which are immensely popular in India. The student of national character is fortunate in the case of India because it has such a well-defined set of popular religious texts which provide explanations for the kinds of facts listed in Table 1.

Yet obviously the formal explanations have some limitations. They deal more with the ideal than with the real. So it is often necessary to interview ordinary people to find out just how they understand formal religious and psychological doctrines. For example, Minturn and Hitchcock (1963) report that Rajput adult men understand very well the principle of non-violence which they accepted as a traditional Hindu ideal. Thus, when asked by anthropologists about quarrels and stick fights, they at first denied any knowledge of them. However, on further questioning by an Indian adult male like themselves, they admitted that fights occurred frequently and that in fact they encouraged their boys to learn how to defend themselves in stick fights. Here the formal rule about not fighting was obviously being supplemented by an informal norm that encouraged fighting in self-defence. Or to take another example, many abstract philo-sophical explanations can be found for the law of *Karma*, but the way it is understood by an ordinary man should also be taken into account. Minturn and Hitchcock report, for instance, that

a Rajput man explained this concept by saying that God keeps something which resembles a court file. During the course of man's life meritorious deeds are entered on this file, together with his sins. The file is first consulted when the man dies. At this time the balance between his good deeds and his bad deeds determine the length of his soul's stay in a "small heaven". . . . The file is consulted a second time when the soul is to be reborn. This time the balance between good deeds and bad determines the status into which the soul is to be reborn. (1963, p. 276)

Whatever the merit of this explanation in abstract philosophical terms, it is important for trying to define the themes that characterize Indian culture.

Finally there is popular literature—such as the films and proverbs that Narain has analyzed or more specifically the children's stories which will form the basis of our analysis. Popular literature will often provide clues for psychological interpretations that cannot be obtained from explanations in formal texts. Suppose we wanted to know why Hindu gods and goddesses sometimes have four hands. The *Ramayana* makes it clear that demons have a hundred hands as a symbol of their power. But why are hands a symbol of power and why are extra hands also attributed to gods? One of the children's stories suggests the psychological meaning of an extra pair of hands. A tailor is given one wish by a tree spirit which he has disturbed. He dreams of becoming a king but his wife insists that he ask for two more hands. "With four hands you could make more cloth, sell it and make more profit." In other words hands are for making and getting things, for increasing the exchange one has with the world. Giving and receiving are a central attribute of existence and the goods symbolize that fact by having extra hands as we shall see later. One might have guessed this in advance but finding it in a text tends to diminish the likelihood that the interpreter is putting his own thoughts and desires into the explanation.

To take another example, we also find in the stories an instance of a suicide threat. A crocodile has befriended a monkey but unfortunately the crocodile's wife conceives a desire to eat the monkey's heart, and insists that her husband get it for her.

Immediately the he-crocodile told his wife, "How can you make such a request! How can I ever kill my friend? If you want, I will get you some more fruits." The she-crocodile threatened her husband and said, "If you don't get me the monkey's heart, I will go to the land and commit suicide." Now what could the he-crocodile do? With tears in his eyes he went near the monkey.

It is clear that the suicide threat has nothing to do with grief or mourning over a lost love object, as one might be inclined to interpret such an act in the West. Instead the explanation given is that the suicide threat is a power play explicitly designed to force somebody to do something that you want done. One might obtain such an explanation from an Indian informant for such threats seem to be fairly common (see Chaudhuri, 1965, and Minturn & Hitchcock, 1963), but the stories provide a quick and convenient way of finding interpretations for acts that might otherwise be quite puzzling. Futhermore, the fact that the explanation occurs in a popular text of this sort gives it somewhat greater credibility than if it were given by one or two informants. For the stories are produced for and read by millions of children. One can assume that they therefore represent quite directly the shared cognitive system of members of the culture. Here, for example, is what the translator had to say about the Hindi stories included in our sample:

> This Reader has been compiled and published in the state of Uttar Pradesh [Northern India] in Hindi—the language which is officially becoming the national language of the country. It is prescribed as a textbook for children aged 9 and 10 in the public schools throughout the state which has a total population of 60 million. . . . The stories in this Reader are steeped in the culture of the country, are drawn from Hindi mythology, from the great epics, from Indian history and from social customs and scenes. . . . Three of the stories are from the ancient Hindu epics—the *Ramayana* and the *Mahabharata*. Every Indian, young and old, is familiar with these and can aptly quote from them. Sentries on duty and children on playgrounds shout happily from them and scenes from them are performed annually by communities throughout the country.

But Indians read and speak in many different languages. Which stories were chosen for analysis? Obviously it was desirable to make some attempt to obtain a sample which would be representative of the whole of Indian culture by selecting stories from different cultural-linguistic areas. So 20 stories were chosen completely at random, six from Hindi readers, seven from Telugu readers, and eight from Tamil readers. The sample is short on stories from North India and the Hindi-related languages, but perhaps this will compensate somewhat for the North Indian bias that appears in our other sources of information, in particular the detailed anthropological account of the Rajputs of Khalapur. Furthermore, a comparison of the themes found in the three sub-sets of stories does not suggest that they differ in major ways. Rather they strongly support the impression that despite linguistic-cultural differences, there are certain common themes that run through the popular culture of India.

THE MAJOR THEMES

The themes were actually arrived at inductively beginning with an analysis of the children's stories. That is, the various ideas presented in the stories were gradually sorted out and classified under major headings which were then used to attempt to explain such facts as those listed in Table 1. But it would be tedious to take the reader through this laborious process. Instead we will reverse the procedure and present the themes which were arrived at as the end result of the analysis.

If I were to try to sum up the core theme in Indian culture in one word, I would choose the word *giving*. Of course no one word is really adequate for so awesome a responsibility, but *giving* does the job fairly well if it is understood in its fullest sense. Giving implies a giver, a gift, and a receiver. It also implies an *exchange,* an event that takes place in time with a beginning, a middle and an end which can occur over and over again and is not going anywhere in time as for example in a means-ends progression like building a road across a country. Let us try somehow to put all this into a sentence.

1. *Giving as a kind of repeated exchange is at the centre of the natural and moral universe.*

This basic idea is formulated at many different levels of abstraction in Hindu culture. In the *Upanishads,* theological texts written in the sixth century B.C., "the Absolute is described as a Being not only transcendent but also immanent. All created beings are only His partial manifestations" (Sarma, 1961, p. 23). Each man's soul, the *Atman,* represents a portion made manifest of the world soul, the Ultimate Reality, *Brahman.* "The souls of animals, plants, and even inanimate objects are merely separate manifestations of this world soul" (Minturn & Hitchcock, 1963, p. 269). But of course these material manifestations keep changing. Men, as well as plants and animals, are born, live for a while and die. Thus a gift, so to speak, of the world soul is being made manifest for a time in a man's life but when he dies he is reabsorbed into the infinite. In fact man's ultimate goal is to return to and become one with the world soul so that *Atman* and *Brahman* become one. The idea of an exchange between the spiritual and the material world, of a going back and forth between the divine and its manifestations, is explicit in this doctrine.

At a somewhat more concrete level the Hindu conception of *Trimurti* or the three-fold form of God also expresses the same idea. God is to be worshipped in his creative aspect (Brahman), his protecting or preserving aspect (Vishnu), or his dissolving or destroying aspect (Shiva). Once again this image seems to symbolize the "gift of life" or a concrete manifestation which comes into being, lasts for a while and then dissolves into the original source of creation. If the idea of exchange, or to-ing and fro-ing, is so central, it is not so puzzling to observe that the gods are often pictured as having four hands—not only those concerned with wealth like Ganesh and Lakshmi, but the three main aspects of God himself— Brahman, Vishnu and Shiva. The extra hands symbolize, as we have already noted, exchange, giving and getting, which is of the very nature of God. The world is made up of an endless series of exchanges between the spiritual and the material world and it is the nature of the gods as personifications of this process to be involved in, or to facilitate, those exchanges.

The idea of exchange was worked into a moral code for man in the law of *Karma*. A man is supposed to build up merit in one manifestation as a living person so that he can be reborn at a higher level in his next incarnation until finally he is able to escape material manifestations altogether and become one with the divine world soul. The notion of giving and geting now becomes considerably more concrete and has strong moralistic overtones. One of the children's stories explains in down-to-earth ethical terms what is involved in the birth, death, rebirth cycles that all men are involved in. It begins:

The world is an illusion. Wife, children, horses and cows are all just ties of fate. They are ephemeral. Each after fulfilling his part in life disappears. . . . As long as we live it is wise not to have any attachments and just think of God. . . . Don't get entangled in the meshes of family life. Just to learn that wife and children are ties of fate, listen to this story.

It then goes on tell tell about a man who took his child as soon as it was born out to the graveyard and asked, "Who are you? Why are you born to me?" The child replied that in his previous life he had sold the man a load of wood but was not paid for it. "I am born to you so that I can get it." So the man gives him what he owes him and the child dies. After this happens a few more times the wife begins to suspect that her husband is burying live children. Finally, however, a child is born to him who actually owes him money from a previous existence. So the child will stay alive so long as the parents never collect this debt by taking anything from him. Unfortunately one day after he has grown up, his mother accidentally picks up some money that belongs to him and immediately he dies because he has paid his debt to them.

What are we to make of this strange story? The idea of exchange has now been given a distinctly moral tone. It involves concrete obligations of one individual to another. A child is born to collect a debt or to pay a debt. Life represents so to speak an incomplete exchange. As soon as the exchange is correctly completed, the person dies. Ideally it is better to escape the whole business, which is a theme to which we will return below. For now it is enough to note that giving and getting are central, and that they are part of a prescribed code governing interpersonal obligations.

The central idea of giving or exchange can be broken down into several subsidiary themes which may be more explicitly stated. Implicit in what has already been said is the notion that the world soul, the source of life, of everything given, is clearly superior to any of its material manifestations and deserves to be worshipped either in its personifications as various gods or as an abstract principle. The reverence for the creative life-force is often coupled with an explicit or implicit rejection of its opposite, the world of matter, but since the rejection of the material world has other motivational roots, we will postpone a discussion of it until later.

The second theme may be summarized then as follows:

2. *Worship every living thing as a gift or manifestation of the divine.*

The respect Indians show for living things—even including plants and animals—is too well known to need elaborate description here. Some of its more obvious forms include: representations of animals as major gods and heroes (Ganesh, Hanuman) vegetarianism (arising from dislike for killing animals), non-violence because aggression is likely to cause injury to life, and respect for the cow which has become particularly symbolic of the nurturant, life-giving force in the universe since it yields so many valuable products—calves, milk, curd, butter, urine and dung—all of which are sacred even among farmers today (Minturn & Hitchcock, 1963, p. 269). The prominence of sexual imagery in various aspects of Hindu religion can also be derived from this theme. For the sexual act symbolizes particularly well the workings of the creative principle in the universe. It involves exchange which is symbolized by the *lingam* or phallic-shaped stone (male principle) resting in the *yoni* or saucer-shaped stone (female principle) in thousands of temples throughout India. Certain priests to Vishnu use a similar sign painted on their foreheads, a straight line penetrating a semi-circle, representing coitus. The sexual act creates life and a child is particularly valued as a representation of the divine life-force. Thus, fertility in women is highly prized. Pregnancy is celebrated by a special ceremony and a prominent abdomen is an object of pride and display among traditional Indian women, not something to be hidden so long as possible as in some Western cultures.

Importance of worship for life is brought home in one of the children's stories called the "Child Monster." It gives an "ant's eye" view of what a "monster-child" is like whose height is "like a small hillock" and who "killed hundreds of people [ants] with his hands and feet and for the sake of play". The moral is clearly drawn: "We should not give trouble to insects like ants and flies. ... Those who do not sympathize with living beings are like monsters." However, worship for life does not automatically imply sympathy and care of the individual living being. Indians can be quite cruel to animals, leaving them diseased and starving, twisting bullocks' tails until they are broken, etc. But such acts are not seen as inconsistent with respect for the divine spark so long as they do not put it out. Pain and suffering belong to another less real world anyway.

If one worships a kind of life-giving force, it is a logical moral step to infer that if one wants to be a good person, he should imitate that divine principle by giving also.

3. Attain merit by giving.

In its simplest and earliest forms giving took the form of sacrifice or *Yajna*.

> *Rita* was originally the order of natural events such as the succession of seasons or the harvest of crops. But soon it came to mean not only the cosmic order but also the moral order. . . .The order of the universe was supposed to be maintained by sacrifices. In fact, according to the famous *Purusha-Sukta*, the universe itself is the result of a sacrifice performed by the gods. Thus *Yajna* or sacrifice became the means, and *Rita* the end. (Sarma, 1962, p. 5)

These gifts or sacrifices were a way of imitating the divine creative force and a way of initiating an exchange with the gods. Animal sacrifices were early given up since they violated respect for life. They were replaced by gifts of food specially prepared for nearly all Hindu ceremonies to this day. These gifts of food among the village people are interpreted as exchanges with the gods— either in the form of *do ut des*—"I give in order that you give"—or *do ut abeas*—"I give in order that you stay away" (with particular reference to the disease goddesses). This kind of ceremonious giving of food to divinities and upper castes is very common in Indian vilage life (Minturn & Hitchcock, 1963, p. 275). For example, Brahmans representing the most spiritual class are fed by the lower classes and provide spiritual guidance in return.

Self-sacrifice is the most meritorious form of giving. One of the children's stories is about a king who agreed to give protection to a dove that was being pursued by a hawk. The hawk was indignant arguing: "I am dying of hunger. How can you take away my food? This dove is my food. If I die of hunger you will commit the sin of killing an animal." Note that the hawk is well aware of theme 2 above (worship of life, e.g., his own). So the king in order not to harm the hawk or the dove finally cuts off his own flesh and says: "Eat me." The story ends that the gods were pleased and sent him to heaven. The moral of the story is that the most meritorious form of giving is literally of one's own resources—of one's own flesh if other food is unavailable. The Rajput mothers have difficulty controlling their children because they cannot conceive of punishing them by withholding rewards. "What we have, we give," they say over and over again (Minturn & Hitchcock, 1963, p. 29). At a practical level, self-sacrifice often takes the form of not eating or fasting, as when wives go without food to help their husbands get over an illness. The reason self-denial is so meritorious apparently lies in the fact that it represents an attempt to reject the material world and to become one with the divine spirit of the universe (Themes 1 and 2 above). Self-sacrifice is an attempt to become pure and holy.

One can also find here another reason why aggression is considered so bad. It not only can result in the sin of wiping out a life; it is also the direct opposite of the most meritorious act which is to sacrifice oneself in the act of giving and becoming one with God.

It also is clear that one must: 3 (a) *accumulate in order to give*. We now begin to run into some of the conflicts within the Indian value formulas. At first sight it seems paradoxical to ask a person to get (which is the opposite of giving) in order to give. Yet how can a person give if he has nothing? The paradox is reflected in the respect that Indians give not only to poor wandering *sadhus* with no worldly possessions but also to men of wealth and power. In the Rajput village the leaders are clearly those with the most possessions in land and worldly goods. The Indian businessmen repeatedly wrote stories about men who were successful and became wealthy *so that they could be of service* to the people.

The contradiction is more apparent than real, though it can at times lead to some interpersonal difficulties as we shall see in a moment. The norm is clearly explained in a children's story which tells of some birds that deserted a banyan tree after they had eaten up all its fruit. The tree complains: "Till now the birds were living happily with me. Now I have neither leaves nor fruit. Therefore ... they leave me. Only if we possess something will people go after us." The moral seems to be that respect comes from having material things like fruit to give to others. But the author of the story draws a somewhat different moral. "Boys! The words of the tree are true. Therefore you must read well. Only if you read well you can live well. Then all people will be searching after you." Apparently knowledge, like the knowledge obtained from reading, is like material possessions. It too can be accumulated and given. It is for this reason that the *sadhus* and wandering holy men should also be respected. They have no material possessions, but they have accumulated much wisdom and spiritual strength which they can share with others.

There is also the notion implicit here that: 3(b) *giving exhausts the giver* (the tree has no more fruit). In a sense then all giving is self-sacrifice because it involves giving away some of one's resources and one must constantly accumulate and store up resources if one is to go on giving. As a rather curious example of this point, Carstairs has noted that loss of male semen is considered debilitating, so much so that one drop of semen is equivalent to the loss of forty drops of blood.[2] Summed up in this idea are several of the themes already mentioned: Semen as representing the life-force is valuable; it is given in an exchange which starts life; but the gift weakens the giver; it is in a sense a sacrifice of the self which is the most meritorious form of giving.

But trying to attain merit by giving has some decided drawbacks psychologically speaking. They are certainly not well formulated in the formal ethical codes so characteristic of Indian thought, but that is not to say that they do not figure frequently in everyday discussions, folktales, and children's stories. So we cannot find the following theme in more or less formal statements as we have the previous ones, but must infer it from descriptions of what life is like in India.

4. Giving leads to interpersonal power struggles.

Why? There are all sorts of reasons. The most obvious is that giving is what is now popularly called a zero sum game: I can only give what others will receive. And if I give and you receive, I am by definition more meritorious and more powerful than you are. It was this implication of the act of giving that the philosophers and sages did not understand very well. Giving implies a receiver and what merit does the receiver acquire by accepting the gift? The answer is never worked out in a completely satisfactory way in the value system, although as we shall see there are many ways in which the system attempts to lessen the seriousness of the problem. At the simplest, most overt level, there is supposed to be reciprocity in giving. A mother gives endlessly to her son and he is supposed to reciprocate by giving her love and respect in return. In fact the more a parent gives, the more the child must give back in respect if he is not to be "put down" in a merit system in which giving is primary. Thus in one very well known story, Ganesh (the elephant child) wins a competition to see which God will be worshipped first, by showing the greatest respect for his parents. The Creator has decreed that the God who is first able to circumnavigate the universe will be worshipped first. While bigger and stronger gods hasten off on their quest, Ganesh rides a mouse around and around his parents and wins because he has defined them as the "universe". Note that *giving* the most respect again wins most merit and makes one worthy of being given the most respect (wor-

---

[2] He does not note that this idea is common also in other cultures. As recently as the 1930's the official handbook of the Boy Scouts of America also warned that loss of semen led to loss of manliness—as a way of warning boys against masturbation.

shipped first). Note also that Ganesh, the elephant God, is one god of material resources.

But giving respect in return for gifts permits the development of some extraordinarily hierarchical systems in which men gain control over resources so that they can obtain merit by giving them to those beneath them. It is in these terms that one can understand most easily the extent to which Indian bureaucrats can get emotionally involved over the privileges they are entitled to. Why should they care so much whether they are assigned a larger office, a larger number of peons, or a car with a driver? In many cases these items are not demonstrably related to doing a more efficient job of work. But they are tremendously important if one is seeking to be in a position to be of service to other people. One must accumulate resources in order to give, and privileges represent resources.

I know of an instance in which the head of a Government of India Institute was upset because it seemed to him his car was being driven too rapidly through a crowded section of the city. Yet he could not bring himself to speak directly to the driver to ask him to slow down. Instead he had to ask someone who was in the car with him to ask the driver to please slow down. Why could he not speak directly to his driver? It is certainly only a half-truth to claim that he was mimicking his former colonial masters, the British. No, the explanation lies centrally in the Indian value system. One must accumulate resources in order to be useful. Privileges represent accumulated resources and the meritorious leader is one who can help others precisely *because* he has privileges which symbolize control over resources and put him in a position to help others and be worthy of respect. So not speaking to someone does not signify disrespect as it would in many cultures, but ideally it means: "I am maintaining a position in which I can be of service. Maintaining my distance from people is one of the ways in which I can show that I have power and only if I have power can I be useful." Needless to say the person not spoken to does not always see it this way, unless he is clearly of lower status. So endless squabbles and fierce fights break out if two people of undetermined or nearly equal status are each trying to get into the position of having more resources, power and privileges than the other. And yet it is obvious to Indians that these unseemly struggles for power are directly opposed to the part of their value system which stressed humility and self-sacrifice. Thus the Indian who told me the story about the Institute head and his driver was very critical of him for behaving in this over-bearing manner. Newspapers in India are more critical of men in power than perhaps any newspapers in the world. Chaudhuri in *The Continent of Circe* excoriates practically every person or group in Hindu society that might have any pretence to power. In fact he seems to like only the aboriginals or tribal peoples, presumably because they have no claims to any power or resources whatsoever. But in doing so he is operating solidly within the value system we are attempting to describe: the irony of it all is that no one seems to realize that the system has a built-in inconsistency. It demands that people accumulate resources in order to be able to give but then punishes them severely for attempting to do so because it violates the ideal of being humble.

Competition over resources is a key theme in the children's stories. For example, one deals with a beauty contest. The teacher decided that "the child who appears most beautiful is to be awarded a prize of a book and play materials". The girls in the class are very excited and put on "their best dress and ornaments and beautify themselves". Note that the competition is over a resource—an asset like beauty—not over an achievement like who can spell the best or solve the most math problems. Sakuntula was the prettiest and her parents thought she would win the prize. Rupavathi wore the costliest ornaments with great pride. So Sakuntula became jealous of her and refused to speak to her. But of course the poorest girl, Valliyammal, won the prize although her face was black and she gave away her only ornament. She won because she was not proud, but was cheerful, and self-sacrificing. The nature of the goal of the contest—to see who has the most merit in terms of assets—is clearly stated and also the means of winning it—by being humble, self-sacrificing and by not trying to win.

The insistence that one must not *seek* resources is so strong that it seems practically counter-phobic, as if everyone recognized that the pressure to do so is very great in a system which requires people to accumulate resources to attain merit. For instance, Indian mothers report that they almost never use praise or reward as a technique of teaching children to learn because "praising children 'to their faces' will spoil them and make them disobedient" (Minturn & Hitchcock, 1963, p. 325). In hundreds of behaviour observations they found only one or two instances of a parent praising a child (p. 326, p. 359). Instead the children were constantly criticized and scolded; the work they did around the house was belittled to others, etc. Why? It is almost as if praise would bring to the surface in an unbearable way the power struggles that are actually going on all the time. If a child were praised, that might encourage him to be proud and to seek merit directly by aggressive action rather than by renunciation and humility as practised by the girl who won the beauty contest. Of course the Indian children are being encouraged to accumulate resources as we have seen—to become more knowledgeable, for example, so that they can give wise advice to others—but the system requires that they deny that they have any resources, belittle themselves, etc. In fact in the comparative study of six cultures by Whiting and associates (in preparation), Indian children, both boys and girls, turn out to *dominate others* more often than children from any of the other cultures. In other words, Indian boys and girls, whether they are older or younger, spend more of their time telling each other what to do than children in any of the other five cultures. This seems paradoxical in the light of the advice they are constantly getting to the effect that they should be humble and non-dominating. Yet it can be understood if it is remembered that they are also being told that they should accumulate, let us say knowledge, in order to give good advice to others. The reason the behaviour seems paradoxical lies in the natural tendency for pro-social dominance to short-circuit into what the Whitings call ego-dominance. For a child to say to another, "Stop eating that, it will make you sick", is perfectly all right in the value system: it is pro-social dominance or giving good advice to another. However, it very often shortens simply to "Stop eating that," with no reason being given for the command other than the implicit one that "I, an important person, commanding much knowledge, having much prestige, etc. tell you to do it; I am simply demonstrating my moral superiority." Thus what in the formal value system is a good (pro-social dominance) readily turns into something which the same system rejects as bad (ego-dominance). It is small wonder that often Indians see themselves as two-faced because in the effort to become holier than the next person they end up being extraordinarily unholy to each other at times.

Consider the conflicts between mothers-in-law and daughters-in-law which are proverbial in Indian culture. Narain (1957) is a little puzzled by the intensity of this particular conflict. Why, he asks, shouldn't there be similar conflicts between father-in-law and son-in-law or between mother-in-law and son-in-law, if it is just a matter of being forced to live together? But in terms of the themes we have been discussing, the intensity of this particular conflict is easily understandable. It is a *competition in giving* of the sort most conflict-producing for Indian culture. The mother has attained merit by giving all her life to her son. Now a daughter-in-law enters the picture who threatens her position of superior merit established by years of prior service. Of course the mother-in-law usually wins out at first because of prior stronger claims to merit, but the daughter-in-law cannot help but try to emulate her because she too is under a compulsion to attain merit by giving to her husband. The only trouble is that the husband has some limit on what he can receive. If he accepts attentions from his wife, he cannot then accept them from his mother and she is jealous of her daughter-in-law. On the other hand, if he accepts them from his mother, he makes his wife jealous because she is being put down in the system of merit by her mother-in-law who is managing to do more for her son. The situation is made worse by the fact that the fierce inter-personal competition is completely disguised and moralized in terms of who can be more self-sacrificing or giving. The husband/son understands well enough that there is some kind of struggle going on, but there is little he can do to mitigate its intensity. So for the most part he tries to withdraw and in time the young wife learns to turn her attentions to her son rather than her husband.

Some rather unpleasant psychological consequences flow from the fact that there isn't supposed to be a power struggle going on, or if there is, the person is supposed to win by not trying or being humble. For the fact of the matter is that ordinary mortals learn that there *is* a power struggle and that in fact they don't always win by being humble. So what happens is what Chaudhuri (1965) describes as a kind of "double consciousness". He illustrates his point with the case of the wife who exhibits

> the split personality most typically. In one of her personalities she does not seem to remember any grievance, and goes about quietly doing her work, and even shows affection to the husband. But once a quarrel has begun, it does not remain limited to the occasion; every quarrel since the day of the wedding is recalled; all the grievances become connected; in retrospect the sorrows gain accumulative fury, and the anger is poured out in red hot streams of lava. Listening to the words, one would naturally imagine that a resumption of married life could not take place, and as long as the fit lasts both the husband and wife think so. But in actual fact no such calamity comes about. ... So one might say that for most Hindu husbands the wife is a beautiful bath of gleaming porcelain with both cold and hot water taps, with this difference, however, that the taps are not under control but flow as they list, and by turns the husband is bathed in the cool spray of love or scalded in the geyser of anger. (1965, p. 277).

He has described with wit and vividness how the moral code of being a self-sacrificing wife can build up a tremendous reserve of hostility if her husband doesn't notice and appreciate sufficiently what she is doing. And as the story of the crocodile's wife mentioned above makes clear, suicide threats on the part of a wife are quite baldly power plays aimed at forcing the husband to do something she wants. In other words self-sacrifice may seem highly moral but it is also an ill-disguised power play. The explosive character of Indian aggression has often been noted: since aggressive impulses are denied and projected, when they do explode, they often show a kind of uncontrolled quality not characteristic of cultures in which aggression is used openly and regularly in a "socalized" way to gain one's ends.

Interpersonal competition of course arises most directly when two or more people are trying to gain control of the same resource. The children's stories are full of instances in which children get jealous of each other, because both want to sit in the father's lap (King Uttanpad and Dhruva) or because only one can be made king (Ramayana). In the story of Ganesh cited earlier, the gods themselves had a quarrel over such a matter. "In council the question came up as to which god should be worshipped first during an auspicious occasion. Each god wanted to be worshipped first. Therefore nothing could be settled between them." In another story when a bird was away, a rabbit moved into his nest in the bank of a river. When the bird returned he said: "This is my house. Get out." The rabbit replied, "How can you say it was yours? When I came here it was empty. So I occupied it." In similar fashion land disputes and arguments over prestige and preference are endemic in Indian villages (see Minturn & Hitchcock, 1963). They found in interviewing 38 men between the ages of 25 and 65 in Khalapur that they had been involved in a total of 59 separate court cases, eliminating duplications and not counting all the disputes that never got to court. Nearly all of the disputes involved control of resources—disputes over land ownership, allocation of income from land, water rights, alleged thefts, etc. In many cases what was actually involved materially speaking was quite trivial, but material gain was not the point of the dispute: the real struggle is for the respect and merit which derives from control of resources. In fact in India, as in many cultures, it is common to think that resources are by their very nature limited so that what one person gains inevitably means that another person loses. So by definition people are trying to accumulate the same resources. Sinha (1967) has been very critical of our attempts to develop achievement motivation in Indian businessmen precisely on this ground. He believes that since India is a country of limited resources, motivating businessmen will only make them compete with each other more for scarce resources and the net effect on the community as a whole will be bad because they will get in each other's way. Part of this belief in limited resources derives from the conviction that India is a poor country. It is a commonplace to pick up almost any Government of India publication and find sentences like "the Indian farmer is poor and backward". He may in fact be neither of those things. It would be just as possible to write "the Indian farmer has rich soil which is amply watered, and given the conditions under which he works he does a remarkable job of farming the land". But as we have already noticed, it is against Indian values to praise or point with pride. One must always be critical and humble if one is to be morally superior. So the idea of the "limited good" derives in part from the Indian's tendency to belittle everything. He is convinced "there isn't enough to go around" and what there is, everyone is trying to accumulate so that he can attain merit by giving it.

4(a) *Competition in giving leads to psychic withdrawal.*

We are now in a position to understand the reasons why Lord Krishna advised Arjuna in the *Gita* to give up his attachments to the world in perhaps the most famous passage in Hindu epic literature. Arjuna is pictured as unnerved and in doubt as to whether to go into battle because it may involve killing his relatives. Krishna advises him that he must fight because it is his duty, but he should fight without any concern for the outcome. "To action alone hast thou a right and never at all to its fruits; let not the fruits of action be thy motive; neither let there be in thee any attachment to inaction." He develops the doctrine of detachment from the world even further by arguing that sensory attachments, pleasure and pain, love and hate, all these are temporary and the wise man fit for immortality is he who remains steadfast ignoring all of these earthly feelings and attachments. This doctrine has been extremely influential in Hindu thought but it is also puzzling. As Narain points out "Krishna's psychotic concept of mind can only lead to wholesale banning of emotions" (1957, p. 95). As he further explains, "Krishna has outlined a chain of reactions which originates in attachments to sense objects and ends in the destruction of the individual" (p. 97). This chain may be summed up as follows :

Sensations→attachment to material objects→desire→ anger→bewilderment→loss of memory→destruction of intelligence→ death.

The only way to escape this chain of disaster is to give up attachment to sense objects and desires altogether. But Narain asks quite sensibly, why should desire automatically lead to anger? In fact if desires are fulfilled, they lead to pleasure and satisfaction. It seems as if Krishna has left out an important part of the chain of connected events; desire leads to anger only if it is disapointed. Narain points out that in terms of modern psychology this doctrine is quite self-defeating because it never permits a person to learn to cope with his disappointments, and use anger in socialized ways. After all frustrations, sorrow and pain can be quite *constructive* forces in the development of character if properly handled.

While I agree with this analysis, it is still an interesting psychological question to ask why the author of the *Gita* overlooked this obvious psychological fact. Why did he think that desire would automatically lead to anger? Surely it is not reasonable to think that the author of the *Gita* did not understand that desire does not always lead to anger. Rather I would credit him with a profound intuitive understanding of the central conflict in the Indian value system. In fact desire for material objects *will*

lead to anger in a system in which giving is the virtue of highest importance, precisely because giving is a power game which *inevitably* and
by definition involves people in intense interpersonal competition. In other
words, giving *automatically* produces the disappointments and feelings
of inferiority that evoke aggression. It involves people in an "if I win, you
lose" game. There is simply no way to play the giving game that does
not involve one in this kind of situation, as all the above comments have
hopefully made clear. So from this point of view, Krishna's advice was
really quite reasonable; he said that one should play the prescribed giving
game (doing one's duty), but without having any of those dangerous feelings of love, hate, attachment, pleasure and pain that would inevitably
lead to hostility in such a game. It would be very good advice if ordinary people could follow it with any regular hope of success. And it is
just one among several of the devices developed by Hindu culture to cope
with the psychological conflict induced by making giving the central
value in the culture.

It should of course be stressed that giving is a value in most cultures.
After all one of the favourite sayings of Christianity is that "he who
loses his life shall find it".[3] But the whole tenor of our argument is that
giving is more deeply imbedded in the whole structure of Hindu culture.
It is not simply *a* virtue as it is in many cultures, but *the central* virtue.
Perhaps a simple example will make the point clearer. Suppose we imagine a culture which is primarily achievement-oriented and secondarily
giving- or service-oriented. Let us further suppose that there is a farmer
in such a culture who wants to improve the yield of wheat grown in the
area. His primary concern is a better quality of wheat; secondarily he may
recognize that if there is a better quality of wheat people may make
more money and eat better in the area and that therefore his contribution
to improved wheat production would be of service to others. He should
spend his time reading up on different strains of wheat, trying them out
if he already owns some land, or trying to persuade others to try out the
new varieties if he doesn't. In a certain sense he doesn't care what people
think of him; he doesn't care whether he is respected or considered influential in the community. He only cares whether he can improve wheat
production. He may have disappointments in the process: there may be
droughts or floods, or pests which destroy the crops. These disappointments should lead him only to search for new varieties or methods of
controlling floods or somehow solving his problem of improving wheat
production. His central value centres around his relationship to the environment (the wheat crop) rather than to his fellowman.

---

[3] But even here the statement is not "he who loses his life shall be worshipped
first".

M-19

Now contrast him with a farmer living in a system in which the central value is that merit comes from being in a position where one can be of service to other people. If he is interested in better wheat production, his first and foremost goal is to get himself in a position where he can provide such a service to other people. It becomes centrally important to him to own a piece of land where the wheat could be produced or at least to get into a government institute where he can provide this service through the resources he controls. But in either case he will be involved in competition with other people who may also want to control (give) those resources. He is told that he must not compete, that he who is most humble is certain to win, (note however, that winning is important). He is almost certain to become angry at those who try to prevent him from being meritorious, at himself for seeming to be pushy, at others for not noticing how humble and worthy he is. He is locked into power struggles within himself and with others which are extremely painful and self-defeating. Small wonder that Krishna counsels withdrawal from such a world!

But withdrawal is not the only means available for mitigating such conflicts. Let us consider some of the culture's main "defense mechanisms".

5. Inter- and intra-personal power struggles can be eased by renunciation, rules, requests, and reasoning.

5(a). Renunciation

As we have just seen, the simplest way to handle power struggles is just to deny they exist, at least so far as the individual's personal involvement is concerned. That is, he cannot avoid acting and participating in a power struggle as in Arjuna's war with his family, but he can give up all feeling or caring about the outcome of his actions. He must go through life impervious to the "slings and arrows of outrageous fortune", concentrating wholly upon God, unattached to the world of the senses and material objects. As President Radakrishnan puts it, Hindus regard themselves naturally "as strangers and pilgrims on earth, fit for heaven but of no earthly use" in the sense that they seek for union with the supreme, universal spirit and regard earthly attachments as standing in the way of that goal. As Narain points out (1957), Krishna's advice to Arjuna sounds like a Western psychiatric textbook description of how to be schizophrenic. For in the West a schizophrenic is defined as someone who acts without appropriate feelings and emotions and who has become detached from the world of "reality" as it is defined by others. In fact there may even be a hint here as to one of the root causes of schizophrenia. For the giving, nurturing function is cross-culturally more characteristic of the

the female role (see McClelland, 1965) and McClelland and Watt (1968) report that sex role alienation commonly occurs among schizophrenics. That is, male schizophrenics reject the normal male assertive role in favour of the giving, yielding role more universally characteristic of females. Furthermore, May (1968) has shown that male schizophrenics are much more comfortable than normal males with scenes depicting a man in a nurturing role, as when he feeds a woman. Thus the double bind resuting from power struggles over giving which forces withdrawal as an Indian cultural trait may more universally force a similar kind of withdrawal in individuals whose extreme cases are labelled schizophrenic. It is curious that at the present time in the West certain psychiatrists like Szasz (1961) and psychologists who have been experimenting with psychedelic drugs like Leary (1967) have been arguing that Krishna's advice is essentially correct, that it is precisely the nonattached "schizophrenics" who are normal and the normals who are crazy because they are so involved with the world, because they care too much about the outcome of actions. One of my ablest former students, Dr. Richard Alpert, is putting this belief into practice, after having been generally influenced by this point of view. He has undergone rigorous training to become a Hindu guru and goes by the name of Baba Ram Dass. Yet even for these men, the goal is still power, *spiritual* power to be sure, but power nevertheless, in the traditional Hindu sense of gaining merit by renunciation. Thus they do not escape the power struggles, though they may be able to escape thinking about them.

The average Indian of course does not carry matters so far. He may manage to avoid involvement or commitment to a degree that some Westerners find extraordinary. For instance, the side-wise headshaking so characteristic of Indian encounters is at first baffling to the Westerner. Is the man saying yes or no? The answer is that he is doing neither. He is avoiding commitment for the moment, but is attempting to facilitate the interpersonal exchange by saying in effect: "Go ahead; I read you loud and clear." My wife is an artist who has drawn people in public places all over the world—Ethiopia, Tunisia, Italy, Mexico, Hong Kong, Bangkok. The problem everywhere is that the people she draws get curious to see what she is doing. They become self-conscious and compulsively interact with her by asking her questions and interrupting what she is doing. But not in India. She found it easier to draw ordinary people in India than in all other countries. They seemed unbothered by her attention, quite remote from her, as if they were indeed strangers and pilgrims on earth.

Practically speaking, this means that very young infants and old people who are about to leave the world are considered holier because they are less involved. The death of an infant was not traditionally considered a major tragedy in a village family since a child is a recent spark from the divine returning home unsullied by the world, but ideally in old age "a man and his wife should retire to a forest and live there as celibate hermits, devoting themselves to a life of religious contemplation" (Minturn & Hitchcock, 1963, p. 274). Few practise the ideal, but it shapes their view of the materialistic world as unworthy. The hierarchy of the caste system is essentially built on this same notion: the most revered castes are the most spiritual and have the least contact with material things which can pollute them; the untouchables as the lowest caste must handle the most "materialistic", sense-arousing objects—like slop and faeces. Rajput women cannot handle blood or fluid-stained clothes after childbirth and must wait for a lower caste midwife to come and clean up. Anything material that arouses the senses and the passions is potentially polluting by making a person less holy or spiritual.

5(b). *Renunciation often masks hostility*

Yet folk wisdom shows that the people understand what often lies behind the facade of renunciation and withdrawal. In the children's story described earlier involving a dispute between a bird and a rabbit over property rights, the two finally went out to search for someone to settle the dispute. They finally "found a cat sitting by the side of a small pond. He had a string of beads on his head. He had had his birth in the pond, applied sacred ashes to his forehead and started contemplating. The bird and the rabbit thought he was a saint." So they decide to ask him for help in settling the dispute, but the cat claimed he was hard of hearing and insisted that they come closer. They were a little afraid, but he reassured them as follows: "Don't you see what I am now? I have committed many sins in my life. I am waiting for my death. What more hatred have I got? I am just thinking of God and spending my life. So don't be afraid." So they came closer, got lost in their argument until "the cruel cat caught them within his paws all of a sudden and killed them." Or in another story a tiger got so old that it could no longer search for its food. So it sat "with a golden bangle by the side of a lake with eyes partly closed like one who performs penance". A traveller sees him and starts to run but the tiger calls out: "Brother, why are you running? I don't kill anybody. My teeth have fallen out. Moreover it is a sin to kill lives. If you come to me, I shall give you the golden bangle." Again the hapless traveller draws near to get the bangle, gets stuck in the lake and is killed by the tiger. The message of such stories seems clear. *Renunciation often disguises hostility.* That is, the people understand that renunciation is often just a ploy in the power struggle, a means of gaining one's ends, as in the case of the crocodile's wife who threatened to commit suicide to make her husband do what she wanted. So renunciation doesn't always solve power struggles. It may make them worse.

5(c). Rules for avoiding power struggles

Another technique for handling conflicts is to work out a set of *rules* for who does what for whom under what conditions and gets what in return. The Hindu view of the life cycle helps soften the full force of Krishna's advice to Arjuna by putting off withdrawal to the end of life. The pupose of life is four-fold,

> namely, *dharma* (duty), *artha* (wealth), *kama* (desire) and *moksha* (liberation). The first three of these constitute the path of *pravritti* (active life) and have to be gained in domestic life. That is, a man has to be a member of society and discharge his duties as a householder and citizen. He has to acquire wealth, gratify his legitimate desires and at the same time practise virtue. The final stage of life for which his whole career has been a preparation is one of *nivritti* or complete surrender and hence *moksha* or liberation (Sarma, 1961, p. 21).

The caste system of course consists of the most elaborate set of rules for determining who has more claim to merit. It is particularly useful in avoiding conflict to base a claim to merit on things that have happened in previous incarnations since the merit therefor is not open to dispute at this time. If a man can prove by his genealogy that he is a Brahman or Ksatriya (of the warrior-ruler caste), he is by definition superior to an untouchable who must show him respect. Great emphasis is therefore placed on defending and maintaining clan or family status by elaborate rules governing who can marry, touch, or eat with whom or by developing genealogies which lay claim to high status through connection with a famous ancestor (Minturn & Hitchcock, 1963, p. 216). Again it has always seemed paradoxical to observers that Indians who stress so much the virtue of humility spend in fact so much of their time demonstrating that they are members of a superior caste. Yet their activity is quite functional in the sense that it certainly serves to ease power conflicts that would arise if all people had equal claims to merit and had to fight it out with everybody else.

The position of women in Indian life is particularly interesting because they would seem to have a superior natural claim to power in a giving-oriented culture. Like the cow they give birth to children and provide milk to nurse them, in ways biologically denied to men. Here a "rule of nature" should help establish the merit hierarchy. As we have noted, the mother-son nurturing relationship is particularly important. In folk-tales and mythology, women are in fact seen as having lots of power. The female consorts of the gods Shiva and Vishnu are more active than the rather passive males. In the children's stories, the crocodile's wife forces her compliant husband to go after his monkey friend's heart, and the tailor's wife forces him to ask for another pair of hands even though he wants something else. In modern films wives often play very forceful roles, even to shooting lovers (see Narain, 1957). But usually they are seen as bad—powerful but dangerous. Thus, it is almost as if the men realized that women have a superior natural claim to merit and power in the Indian value system and that therefore they have to be checked and confined. In fact, in traditional households they could not even leave the courtyard after marriage. As these "old-fashioned" checks on women's power are eased in the modern sector, one would predict that Indian women should rise to positions of leadership and importance more often than in other cultures because both they and the men know that in a value system which stresses power from accumulation of resources, they have a special claim to strength. In fact this is what is taking place in India which today has more women heads of states than any other country in modern or probably ancient times. Women may also be chosen because none of the men has a natural claim to higher merit according to any traditional rules or roles, and it is difficult to seek leadership in a culture which stresses renunciation as a path to power. Thus, a woman becomes a natural choice both because she avoids intense competition among men for leadership positions and because she does have a natural claim to superior strength in this value system.

5(d). *Requesting help as a way of establishing a merit hierarchy*

A rather simple way to avoid competition for power in a giving-oriented society is to *request help*. The person who asks for help is automatically assuming an inferior position and admitting from the outset: "You are stronger and more powerful than I am. Therefore give to me." To ask for help is in itself a sign of respect since the asker tacitly acknowledges the superiority of the person asked. By the same token a person would not ask help of someone he clearly perceived as his inferior, unless it were a service expected in a clearly subordinate role. In this system self-reliance training for children obviously has no particular merit; instead children learn to ask or demand from their parents since the parents have clearly superior status. In fact Indian children show far more demanding behaviour than the children from any of the five other cultures studied under comparable conditions (Whiting & others, in preparation).

The extent to which the children were capable of insistently demanding was brought home to us almost daily. ... Throughout our stay we were rarely out of earshot of the whining cry "Give me my photo"....

Nor did the mothers reprimand their children for this persistent begging. Many mothers were, in fact, only slightly less demanding in this regard than their offspring (Minturn & Hitchcock, 1963, p. 336).

This has sometimes been called the "Bapu" or dependency syndrome in which Indians seem to be endlessly asking for protection, advice, and assistance of all kinds from superiors. In fact, Arjuna shows it in the *Gita* when he gives up in effect and says to Krishna, "With my mind bewildered about my duty. I ask thee, Tell me, for certain, which is better, I am thy pupil; teach me, who am seeking refuge in thee."

Westerners or even Indians who are bothered by this insistent demanding might be somewhat more tolerant of it if they understood better that the suppliant is in effect doing the man he asks a favour by acknowledging openly that he is superior and has a greater control over resources. Competition for power can be avoided simply by one person acknowledging at the outset that the other has more to give. The person asked is supposed to be grateful for the acknowledgment of his superiority and give if he can, but to do so privately. If he were to give publicly, he would make the suppliant seem even more inferior and could enrage him. Anyone interested in the niceties of these moral points need only read Chaudhuri's description (1965) of how angry he got when someone announced publicly that he had given him a typewriter.

5(e). *Reasoning as a means of establishing a merit hierarchy*

Another technique for coping with power struggles is to try to rationalize them in a way that will prove someone's moral superiority. So *reasoning* and discussion are highly valued in Indian culture. One of the most striking characteristics of Hindu religious thought is its extraordinary variety and subtlety. Its philosophers have been famous for millenia. New sects or religious movements have constantly appeared based on rather subtle theological differences. The Rajput villagers spend hours on the men's platform talking and arguing. They must be able to reason cleverly in the many lawsuits they are involved in. Indians appear to enjoy discussion the way some other peoples enjoy action. By contrast one need only point out that New England farmers can spend hours together sitting around a stove in winter scarcely exchanging a word.

Reasoning not only helps work through power struggles. It has many virtues in the Indian value system. It involves exchange among people, the giving and receiving which is so basic a part of the Indian worldview. It avoids the dangers of commitment to action (which entangles one in its consequences). It is part of the whole push toward dematerializing or intellectualizing the universe, for it attempts to replace the world of the senses and emotions with talk. But above all it is necessary for the manoeuvering that goes on, in court and out, to gain control of resources since direct instrumental activity is in theory forbidden.

Some of the quality of this type of reasoning is captured by one of the children's stories about four businessmen who bought a cat to keep the rats from getting into the bales of cotton they kept in a warehouse. Each man owned a leg of the cat. One day the cat injured a leg; the owner of that leg tied an oily rag to it which caught on fire when the cat went near the fireplace and so the whole warehouse was burned to the ground. There had been a serious loss of resources. So something had to be done. The three businessmen brought suit against the man who tied the oily rag to the cat's leg on the ground that he was responsible for their misfortune and should pay damages. The magistrate after considerable argument delivered the following judgment: "The leg on which the defendant tied the oily rag was an injured one. Therefore it was unfit for walking. It was only because of the other three legs owned by you three that the cat ran. The great loss occurred only because the cat ran. Therefore you three have to pay for the loss of the defendant." Thus, the humble man who renders a service wins, as he always should in an Indian morality tale, but the reasoning by which this outcome is reached is typically Indian in its subtlety and the cleverness with which the tables are turned on he who thought he had a superior moral position at the outset.

The Meaning of Work

So far the discussion has centred almost entirely around how the Indian copes with the problem of trying to gain moral superiority by giving. Little of what has been discussed seems to bear directly on such this-worldly problems as getting a job of work done and managing other people so as to achieve some collective goal. How does the average Indian look at work? To judge by the critical comments of a number of observers, he isn't very focused on the problem of getting a job of work done. The following episode reported by an American Peace Corps volunteer is apparently fairly typical of what often happens:

Storm ripped an opening in the Block's poultry house. "We've got to get this fixed," I told the Block Development Officer. "Yes, yes," he agreed. Nothing happened, however. When I asked him about this several weeks later, he said the engineer was preparing a detailed estimate of cost involved.

Six weeks passed. In the meantime, a mongoose got into the poultry house through the hole made by the storm. Half of the birds were slaughtered by the mongoose or crushed in their frenzied efforts to escape.

The day after this happened I asked the engineer if the cost estimates had been prepared. The engineer turned to the Block Development Officer and said something in Hindi. They didn't think my Hindi was good enough to understand—but I understood. The BDO hadn't told the engineer to prepare the estimate.

(Bradford, 1968)

Observations like these of course are not limited to Westerners. Khush-want Singh, one of India's most distinguished men of letters, has provided us with a witty and perceptive account of how little Government of India clerks manage to accomplish in a day in his story, "Man, How the Government of India Run!", published in *A Bride for the Sahib and Other Stories.*

Can it be that the BDO didn't care about the chickens, that he and the clerks of the Government of India are just plain lazy and disinclined to work? There is another possibility:

6. *Work is viewed as a form of giving, as providing service to others.*

Lord Krishna, supported by many Hindu sages, has advised all Indians as follows: "Work alone art thou entitled to, and not to its fruit. So never work for rewards nor yet desist from work. Work with an even mind, oh Arjuna, having given up all attachment." So one must not focus on the outcome of work, on getting something accomplished that will give satisfaction. Of what value then is work? It can rather easily be fitted into the major theme of giving or providing services to others. A Block Development Officer, a clerk or a Joint Secretary is in a sense doing a favour to people by working; that is, he is providing services, out of his resources, for others. But of course he must *have* some resources—e.g., privileges, prestige, respect. So his major focus of interest is not the outcome of a job of work but whether or not he has the resources to do the work. Viewed from this perspective the Peace Corps volunteer who advised the BDO that he should fix the poultry house effectively *prevented* him from doing anything. The person who gives advice, in the Indian value system, as we have seen, has more power. By receiving and acting on it the BDO would have been admitting his inferiority and to admit inferiority is to say that you do not have the resources to do your job properly. A person wise in the ways of getting things done in India knows that suggestions for action of this sort must be made very indirectly and if possible in such a way that the superior feels that it was his idea. Only then will he feel that he has not been undercut in his capacity to do his job. Similarly the clerks may feel it is far more important to show how fatiguing their jobs are (after all, giving exhausts the giver), than actually to do the job. From this point of view, it is not totally unreasonable to spend a lot of time in tea breaks since they emphasize how tiring the work is and how important it is for the workers to build up their resources to cope with it. Thus, the clerk is more involved in the question of his *capacity* to do the work than in actually doing it.

It also follows that high value would be placed on working *for others* rather than working for oneself. Thus, one can avoid the dangers of taking initiative and admit humbly, as Arjuna did, that he doesn't know what to do but needs to be told by a superior. Working for another person can obviously be perceived also as a form of giving. The ideal situation is one in which the person is working for a superior master (e.g., the Government of India) who tells him what to do, yet at the same time establishes his great importance as a public servant, working for others rather than himself. Once again the key issue is not the work he accomplishes, but his moral position, as an important person who, from his accumulated resources, can provide services for the people.

In all of this there also seems to be some actual fear of too much involvement with work. In the children's story, the tailor who received four hands as a gift from the tree spirit was stoned to death as a freak by the other villagers when they saw him. Apparently, giving and getting too much, or working too hard on one's own, is presumptuous, perhaps because it imitates the gods too closely who make and unmake the world. As we have already noted, people are afraid to praise others for their work. Instead they use almost entirely criticism as a means of attempting to control the behaviour of others, but psychology has shown that punishment is a much less effective way of encouraging learning than reward. In fact it tends above all to instill a fear of failure in work, a fear that what one does will be criticized. The fear seems to be so intense in Indian schoolboys that in studies of achievement motivation made by Mehta (1967), he found that certain story characteristics like mentions of personal failings or difficulties in the world were not mentioned at all in India, in contrast to stories written by similar children in other countries in the world. That is, they were so counterphobic about difficulties that they failed ever to mention them even as possibilities. Again this may come from several sources, but at least in part it seems to derive from the conception that work is an interpersonal service so that failure is perceived as some kind of *moral* failure to do one's duty rather than more simply as a task failure or inability to do something for lack of knowledge or skill.

As for public order, there is very little in the value system of India to back up maintaining it. Rather the theme seems to be something like:

7. *No one should be prevented from representing God in his own way.*

A major characteristic of Hinduism is its tolerance of other religions. At the village level, the Rajput farmers adopted a Moslem saint. In modern Hindu temples leaders of all great religions are represented and worshipped—Christ, Mohammed, Buddha, etc. "No true Hindu ever tries to uproot another man's faith nor revile his God nor boast of the superiority of his own religion. For you may accept any creed, follow any prophet and belong to any organization, provided you are able by these means to reach your goal of realization of God." (Sarma, 1961, p. 234) The extent to which the ideal of toleration is practised in everyday life in India is at first startling to the Western observer, for it appears as if there are no norms of dress or behaviour or more particularly as if no one ever interferes with another in the name of public order. The range of permitted behaviour is greater than in almost any culture. Men can wear dhotis, "pajammas" or Western clothes, refuse to cut a hair on their heads like the Sikhs or wear no clothes at all for fear of crushing tiny insects like a few very religious Jains. No one objects or tries to foist his convictions on another.

Streets, even in major cities, are often in indescribable confusion. Every living being, including especially cows, has a right to go anywhere, in any direction. No one really likes to make streets one way, to prohibit them to animals, or even to push cows out of shops. Chickens, cows or goats are seldom fenced in, not because farmers are too poor—in many places all they would have to do is pile stones into a wall—but because it is not really right to interfere with other living beings. Above all one must not sacrifice one life for the welfare of another. It is inconceivable for the average Indian that he might drown three kittens in a litter of five so that the remaining two would have enough to eat to live well. Everyone has a right to life no matter how miserable. It has proven extremely difficult even in major cities to get ordinances enforced for killng off packs of diseased, starving dogs.

The result of such tolerance has been a great deal of public disorder. Few have been willing to put the common good above the welfare of individuals. Hinduism is interested primarily in *individual* not group salvation. Thus conservation is difficult to teach because it often means weeding out the unfit for the sake of the rest. Public health measures do not arouse interest because they often require a family to stop doing something (like fouling a water supply) which is bad for the general public.

Public cleanliness suffers the same fate. Indians are intensely interested in being personally clean (uncontaminated by the material world), but they see nothing especially valuable in clean *public areas*—sidewalks, streets, bathrooms—since maintaining public cleanliness may interfere with the personal habit of keeping clean by throwing refuse into the public domain.

In politics factions develop as people manoeuvre to accumulate their resource base from which to exercise power, but they are tolerated, even respected. Husbands and wives or brothers and sisters may head different political parties which struggle fiercely against each other, but no one would think of invoking family solidarity to try and silence his opponent (see Erikson on Gandhi, 1969). One may manoeuvre to form a stronger faction, but one should not invoke party discipline to keep a splinter group in line. Even the fairly mild party discipline of Western democracies is alien to the traditional Indian spirit. The severe discipline of the Communist Party is even more so.

Tolerance inevitably promotes disorder, though Indians have not always seen the two phenomena as intimately connected. If one carries respect for individual differences to the extreme, it inevitably encourages disorder. There must always be some system for promoting the public interest, for at least on some occasions sacrificing the freedom of the individual for the welfare of the group. All societies maintain some kind of a balance between individual freedom and public order. India for centuries achieved a semblance of public order by an hereditary caste system which constructed a fixed model of social organization within which all individuals and groups had a place. At times she also achieved order by rule imposed from without as during the Moghul or British periods. It has often been noted how much more successful Indians seem to be outside their own country in communities scattered from East Africa to Southeast Asia. One reason may well be that they can function better in a society where *someone else* imposes the public order which they are reluctant to impose on themselves.

Let these seven themes complete the analysis. Obviously many more could be added, but one of the goals of this type of effort is to keep the analytic structure as simple and parsimonious as possible, lest it grow and become in the end as complicated as the facts it is trying to interpret. What I have tried to do is show that many apparently paradoxical facts about Indian culture can be interpreted in terms of a few relatively simple variations on the central theme of giving or exchange. In the process of course I feel that I have not managed yet to state the themes exactly right. My hope is that these ideas may be helpful to some Indian scholar who with a better background than I have can work them into something closer to the truth.

But what about our methodological test? Many facts not listed in Table 1 have been introduced in the discussion to support various points of the analysis, but have all the facts we listed in advance been accounted for? Table 2 provides an answer. It shows that practically all of the 25 observations listed in advance can rather easily be understood in terms of one or more themes. There is one partial exception—the first fact listed in the Table as the "crowding of public spaces". As noted, this may be explained in part from Theme 7, the unwillingness to interfere with people for the sake of public order, but this is only part of the story. E. T. Hall has observed that beaches in India and America fill up very differently as people arrive (1966). In America individuals typically arrange themselves as far as possible from any other individuals or family groups on the beach, so that if one flies over a beach in a helicopter he observes a series of evenly spaced dots. In India, on the contrary, if there is one man on the beach and another arrives he goes over to join him, until as more and more later arrivals are added, a knot of humanity can be observed from a plane. Why? None of the seven themes really explains this behaviour very well, although one could argue of course that if people are interested in exchange, in dominating and demanding, they have to do it with other people so that they go where there is an opportunity to behave in the way that makes them feel most comfortable. Yet one feels that the point deserves further study, perhaps by experimental psychological methods before a final conclusion is drawn. And that could be said about many other interpretations made in this essay.

TABLE 2

CLASSIFICATION OF OBSERVATIONS BY THEMES IN INDIAN CULTURE

1. Giving and exchange are central in the universe
   7, 9, 23, 25
2. Worship the divine source of every material gift (spirit over matter)
   3, 6, 11
3. Attain merit by giving
   12, 13, 14, 15
4. Giving leads to interpersonal power struggles to attain superior moral worth
   4, 5, 19, 21
5. Interpersonal power struggles can be eased by renunciation, rules, requests, and reasoning
   5, 8, 10, 16, 17, 18, 20, 22, 24
6. Work is a form of giving or service to others
   19, 20
7. No one should be prevented from representing God (the Divine source) in his own way
   2

Not fully covered by any of the themes
   1

One final point about the analysis: it should be obvious, but perhaps it ought to be stressed, that I have attempted to avoid evaluative remarks throughout. Nothing that I have said should be interpreted as meaning that I believe this aspect of Indian culture is good or that aspect bad. In fact my overwhelming conviction after doing several national character studies like this (1963) is that the so-called "defects" of a culture, often as seen quite clearly by its members, arise nearly always from an excess of its "virtues". Thus, self-sacrifice and tolerance would doubtless be acknowledged in nearly every culture as important virtues. They become handicaps for certain purposes in India only because they are practised to an extreme seldom reached in other societies.

THE PROBLEM OF MODERNIZATION

One way in which cultures tend to be judged in the 1960's is in terms of whether their value systems promote or impede economic and social progress as defined in these days. So without attempting to make any ultimate value judgments, one can still legitimately ask to what extent the themes just described will interfere with rapid economic progress. Many have argued of course that Indian values are obstacles to development: the stress on otherworldliness, the lack of a concern for concrete achievements, the social discriminations built into the caste system that prevent upward mobility, etc. do not seem very compatible with a rapidly growing industrial society. Yet on this point I would urge caution to judge from my own experience. To begin with, it needs to be stressed again that what we have been describing is a traditional culture pattern in a kind of abstract, ideal, or extreme form. There must be millions of Indians—certainly I know personally of them—whose thinking and acting are influenced by this traditional ideal-typical pattern only slightly if at all, and then only in marginal ways. Even if one assumes these values antithetical to rapid modernization, there are very probably enough Indians who do not share them to any significant degree to bring about changes in the country.

My specific reason for being doubtful about the braking influence of traditionalism lies in some research results we obtained in our efforts to promote achievement orientation among businessmen in Kakinada and Vellore. We studied intensively the traditionalism of the participants in our training courses. That is, in interviews and questionnaires we attempted to find out what their attitudes and practices were on a whole range of issues in the areas of religion, family, caste, eating habits, work attitudes, etc. We then classified the men as to whether they were very traditional or very modern in their attitudes and practices. The traditional men, for instance, said that they went more often on religious pilgrimages, refused to eat meat or kill diseased cows, consulted *gurus* or astrologers regularly, would not eat food prepared by a member of a lower caste, would arrange a marriage for their daughter, did believe that there was little use in human effort because fate determined the outcome of all human activities, etc. We then followed the men up for two years after the training and discovered which ones became unusually active and which ones did not. To our surprise, in view of all the previous writing on this subject, there was no relationship between traditionalism and becoming more active in business after training in achievement motivation—supposedly a very Western, "modern" concept (McClelland & Winter, 1969). For every modern man who changed, there was an orthodox Hindu who also changed. Both men were actively contributing to the economic development of their city and India, but traditionalism in the one case did not seem to be any particular handicap. How can we understand this result?

To begin with, it is well to remember, as Kluckhohn and Strodtbeck (1961) make clear, that every culture has dominant and substitute or variant value orientations. While countries in the West may at the present time be achievement-oriented, at a secondary level of importance they are also service-oriented. Even though India has stressed non-violence the Ksatriyas have traditionally been supposed to be brave, strong and fearless in battle. Thus in training these businessmen, we were dealing probably with the group in all of India which was most achievement-oriented to start with, at least in the sense that they were in business, an achievement-oriented occupation. This is not to say that they individually had high needs to achieve, but at least they were in the kind of occupation where results of efforts could readily be measured and checked for an improvement. Thus it was probably easier to talk to them in terms of the concepts of the course than it would have been to other groups—say, government clerks where it is by no means so obvious that individual effort and improved performance leads to better functioning of an office. So one might argue that economic development depends in the end on the extraordinary activities of a rather small fraction of the population—the entrepreneurial fraction—and that there are enough men in India now with an orientation toward achievement to promote rapid economic development, if their latent energies are mobilized. That is, while the dominant orientation may be to see work as described in Theme 6, there are enough people who see it in a different way to bring about rapid economic development.

But more than this, even the traditionalism among some members of this group did not prevent them from becoming active in a way which they *might* have regarded as self-seeking and immoral. What we learned was that value patterns of the sort described are not rigid and inflexible but they can be reinterpreted in ways that are consistent with change. For instance, in this case the courses stressed over and over again the fact that achievement motivation training would benefit not only them individually in their businesses, but also their communities, India as a whole, and even the entire world as they showed the way for others to follow. That is, it was argued that by improving their business, they were *making a contribution* to employment, income demand, and ultimately economic growth. In apparently doing something for themselves, they were doing a great deal for others. It can reasonably be argued that it was only because we were able to link an achievement orientation with an altruistic conception of providing services to others that we succeeded in enlisting the wholehearted cooperation of these businessmen. They would not have been excited by a course which stressed selfish gain nor would they have been likely to be moved by appeals solely to altruistic giving. It was the combination of these two motive systems that seemed to be effective. Certainly attempts to make Indian businessmen more achievement-oriented did not run into any insuperable obstacles from traditional value themes in Indian culture.

More difficulty may arise in the area of using power to control the behaviour of some for the benefit of the whole. This is a problem which every modern state must solve, but as we have seen, it is particularly difficult for Indians. The prescribed way of doing it—public self-sacrifice as in Gandhian fast—has proved remarkably effective on occasion, but it seems hardly likely to lead to an orderly and regular exercise of authority. Indians will have to find some way of reconciling the use of authority for the public good with their traditional values. The problem is a difficult one, and I hope this essay has made it clear why it is. My own conviction is that once the problem is seen more clearly, perhaps as it has been explained above, Indians will find a way of reinterpreting the problem in traditional moral terms. It may be that some kind of a calculus of greater and lesser damage to the life-force may work: in terms of modern knowledge a diseased cow or diseased dog may be responsible for the death of hundreds or even millions of other animals (manifestations of the life-force). Or it may be that an argument can be made that it is wrong to permit any casual, material manifestation of the divine to go its own way, completely unhindered. Such an attitude in a sense represents a fixation on a particular materialistic form that is in fact antithetical to the fundamental belief that spirit is more important than matter. Thus, it is actually to worship the divine spirit better if one prunes its material manifestations to let the light shine through more clearly or even in some cases to destroy a particular manifestation, e.g., a diseased cow, so that the divine may manifest itself again in a purer material form. As Krishna reminded Arjuna, in a certain ultimate sense there is no such thing as killing. The *Atman* is the only reality.

But it is beyond my capacity to solve this problem. It is enough to point out that it is there, that it is deeply imbedded in the Indian value system, that it will have to be solved probably to produce an effectively governed modern nation, and that the solution will have to be a moral one. Beyond that I cannot go. I have been presumptuous enough already in terms of the Indian value system. But perhaps its tolerance of me as a foreigner will excuse my lack of humility in trying to explain to Indians what they already know much better than I do.

REFERENCES

Bakan, D. "Clinical Psychology and Logic". In *David Bakan on Method*. San Francisco, Calif.: Jossey-Boss, 1967.

Bradford, A. *The Volunteer and the Bureaucrat*: *Case Studies from India*. Washington, D. C.: Peace Corps, 1968.

Carstairs, M. *The Twice Born*. London: Hogarth Press, 1957.

Chaudhuri, N. *The Continent of Circe*. Bombay: Jaico Publishing House, 1965.

Erikson, E. *Gandhi's Truth*. 1969.

Hall, E. T. *The Hidden Dimension*, New York: Doubleday, 1966.

Inkles, A. & Levinson, D. J., "National Character: The Study of Model Personality and Sociocultural Systems", Chapter 26 in *Handbook of Social Psychology*, Volume II: "Special Fields and Applications", Cambridge, Mass.: Addison Wesley, 1954.

Kluckhohn, F. R. & Stodtbeck, F. L. *Variations in Value Orientations*. Evanston, Ill.: Row Peterson, 1961.

Leary, T. *High Priest*. New York: World Publishing Co., 1967.

McClelland, D. C. *The Roots of Consciousness*. New York: Van Nostrand, 1963.

McClelland, D. C. "Wanted: A New Self-image for Women". In R. J. Lifton (Ed.) *The Woman in America*. Cambridge, Mass.: Houghton Mifflin, 1965.

McClelland, D. C. & Watt, N. F. "Sex-role Alienation in Schizophrenia". *Journal of Abnormal Psychology*, 1968, 73, 3, 226-39.

McClelland, D. C. & Winter, D. G. *Motivating Economic Achievement*. New York: The Free Press, 1969.

Mehta, P. Level of *n* Achievement in High School Boys. New Delhi, India: National Institute of Education, 1967.

Minturn, L. & Hitchcock, J. T. "The Rajputs of Khalapur, India". In B. B. Whiting (Ed.), *Six Cultures*. New York: Wiley, 1963, pp. 203-361.

Narain, D. *Hindu Character*. Bombay: University of Bombay Press, 1957.

Radhakrishnan, S. *The Hindu View of Life*. London: G. Allen and Unwin, 1927.

Radhakrishnan, S. *Indian Philosophy*. London: G. Allen and Unwin, 1948.

Sarma, D. S. *Hinduism through the Ages*. Bombay: Bharatiya Vidya Bhavan, 1961.

Sinha, J. B. P. "Effects of *n* Ach/*n* Cooperation on Group Output and Interpersonal Relations under Limited/Unlimited Resources Conditions" Patna, India: A.N. S. Institute of Social Studies, 1967.

Szasz, T. *The Myth of Mental Illness*: *Foundations of a Theory of Personal Conduct*. New York: Hoeber-Harper, 1961.

Taylor, W. S. "Basic Personality in Orthodox Hindu Culture Patterns". *Journal of Abnormal and Social Psychology*, 1948, 43

Whiting, J. W. M., Whiting, Beatrice, Lambert, W. & Longabaugh, R. *Children's Behaviour in Six Cultures* (in preparation).

13

SOCIAL ORGANIZATION AND SOCIAL CHANGE

CHARLES P. LOOMIS

INTRODUCTION

An effort to focus discussion. In my consideration of social change I wish
to limit my efforts to those alterations which reduce the human effort
and suffering required to attain a level and/or standard of living desired
by members of a given society. I assume that adoption of improved
practices in agriculture which increases income or health practices which
reduce sickness and disease are examples of this kind of change. In
famine-ridden over-populated areas, adoption of birth control procedures
may also involve this kind of change. I wish to include in my discussion
of alterations which reduce suffering the increasing of liking and affec-
tion of actors for one another and the decrease in dislike and hostility of
actors for one another. I assume that social organization is not neutral
but may either increase or decrease the efficiency of the use of human
energy or increase or decrease human suffering.

It seems unnecessary before a group of social scientists to elaborate a
definition of social organization. For our purposes in this paper I shall
assume that the Indian village *panchayat*, with its role and power structure,
like the schools, the governmental ministries which supply electrical power,

* Presented at the Second World Congress of Rural Sociology, Enschede, Netherlands, 5 August 1968.

roads, law and order, agricultural and health services, etc. are social organizations.

The basic assumption of the paper is that, by and large, gains in human efficiency and decreases in human suffering are the products of science and invention. In other words I assume that increasing scientific knowledge and inventions if effectively used in the interests of mankind may increase the efficiency of human activity and reduce suffering. These are, of course, only assumptions. I shall not attempt to prove them. I assume that human knowledge is increasingly produced in knowledge centres and that the effective linkage of these centres with the people who attend schools, use electric power, mass media, agricultural and health extension services, etc. may increase human efficiency and reduce suffering.

The source of data used in analysis. Data will be drawn primarily from studies in which I have been directly or indirectly involved. These studies will be referred to below in the text by the italicized portion of the title after the numbers which follow: 1. *The Study of Awareness of Change in India.* In this all-Indian study, based upon a modified probability sample, 364 villages were studied in which 1,414 influentials, 3,375 randomly chosen males and 2,435 randomly chosen females all 21 years of age or over were interviewed.[1] 2. *Agricultural Innovations in Indian Villages.* A study of 108 villages in the three Indian States of Andhra Pradesh, Maharashtra and West Bengal included interviews with 856 leaders. Parenthetically it may be noted that this study followed and profited from the benchmark study phase in a UNESCO-financed communication experiment involving "treatments" such as radio, farm forums, and functional literacy classes. The following two studies benefited from both of these studies.[2] 3. *Patterns of Agricultural Diffusion in Rural India.* A study of the 680 heads of farm households in the three states just mentioned who were all 50 years of age or younger and cultivating at least 2.5 acres of land in 8 of the 108 villages mentioned above. The publication with the above title specifically treats adoption of improved agricultural practices. Another based on the same data treats family planning.[3] 4. *Study of Urban Mexico.* A probability sample of Mexican city dwellers 21 years or older including 1,126 respondents.[4] 5. Study of *Rural Michigan.* A probabiity sample of rural Michigan (places 2, 500 or under) including 306 respondents 21 years of age or under.[5] 6. Study of the *United States General Public.* A probability sample of the mainland including 1,528 respondents all 21 years of age or older.[6]

Hypotheses, queries, and sources of data. In the paper which follows no formalistic procedure is followed by which general theory and accompanying assumptions are specified after which hypotheses are generated. There

---

[1] Notes at the end of the paper.

are other unorthodox features of the paper in part explained by the uncompleted state of analysis and gaps in the data at hand. Thus if the subject under discussion is variation in change orientation and behaviour of influentials as compared with non-influentials and data in one hemisphere where data are available provides clues, we do not hesitate to present them even if we do not have the data to make comparisons from the other samples and places. This does not mean we think it is permissible to extrapolate from Indian to Mexican data or vice versa. We have merely used the data available to raise and in some instances answer queries.

OVER-ALL VIEW OF ORGANIZATION AND SOCIAL CHANGE IN RURAL INDIA

The awareness of change study. When we began the study of India's villages we were more aware of Marx's denunciation of them than we were of the changes that are now taking place there. We asked ourselves, "Do the village leaders want to turn back the clock in some of the ways in which the sainted leader, Gandhi, recommended?" And ringing in our ears was Karl Marx's famous statement:

". . . we must not forget that these idyllic village communities (which the English trade is destroying), inoffensive though they may appear, had always been the solid foundation of Oriental despotism, that they restrained the human mind within the smallest possible compass, making it the unresisting tool of superstition, enslaving it beneath traditional rules.... We must not forget that these little communities ... brought about a brutalizing worship of nature, exhibiting its degradation in the fact that man, the sovereign of nature, fell down on his knees in adoration of Hunuman, the monkey, and Sabbala, the cow".[7]

Tables I—IV compare the village leaders with other randomly selected villagers in the 364 villages. I draw your attention to the way in which the leaders were selected for interview. By the procedure used in choosing the leaders we hoped to ascertain the evaluation villagers make of advocated changes in agriculture, health and family planning and to relate the social organization of the village to this evaluation. The elected president of the village *panchayat* was always included. From sociometric choices made by the randomly selected informants, three influentials other than the president of the village *panchayat* were selected for study, namely, the best farmer, the most important person, and an implementor of group action. Table I describes the social characteristics of the sample.

As hypothesized, these influentials had adopted and were adopting many more of the practices under study than the informants in the randomly chosen sample. This is indicated by Table II. They were much more

TABLE I

SOCIAL CHARACTERISTICS OF INFLUENTIALS AND OF THE RANDOM SAMPLES OF

MALES AND OF FEMALES

(ALL-INDIA DISTRIBUTION)

Characteristics	Influentials (Per cent)	Random Samples	
		Males (Per cent)	Females (Per cent)
Brahmins or high-caste non-Brahmins	55.4	34.2	35.6
Finished middle school or more	33.6	10.5	3.3
Finished primary school	28.9	18.0	8.1
Illiterates	23.7	60.5	84.5
Cultivators	87.2	74.3	57.2
Agricultural labourers	0.9	10.0	15.1
Have seen a movie	75.2	54.0	37.8
Read newspapers	53.5	20.0	5.7
Listen to radio	75.6	57.5	46.0
Number of respondents	1,414	3,375	2,435

TABLE II

MODERNIZATION OF RURAL INDIA: PERCENTAGES[*] OF RESPONDENTS WHO ADOPTED

AGRICULTURAL, HEALTH AND BIRTH CONTROL PRACTICES

(ALL-INDIA DISTRIBUTION)

Improved Practices	Influentials (Per cent)	Random Samples	
		Males (Per cent)	Females (Per cent)
Chemical fertilizer	76.4	43.2	36.0
Improved seed	67.5	31.5	25.4
Insecticides	52.8	25.4	23.8
Improved plough	41.1	15.2	11.3
Smallpox vaccination	85.5	78.7	73.6
TABC[†]	66.3	51.1	44.4
Family planning[‡]	10.1	4.5	3.2
Number of respondents	1,414	3,375	2,435

* Percentages which fall in the following categories for each of the practices are available: (1) Have heard, was interested, have tried and used (or adopted). (These are the figures above.) (2) Heard, interested and tried only. (3) Heard and interested only. (4) Heard only. (5) Not heard. (6) No answer. See Charles P. Loomis, "Change in Rural India," op. cit.

† Typhoid and cholera inoculation.

‡ For those who gave answers to the following question: "If you knew of a simple harmless method of not having more children than you want, would you approve or disapprove of its use?", the percentages of those answering in the affirmative for influentials, males and females, respectively, were 66.0, 50.4 and 44.9. Negative answers were 21.1, 26.1 and 21.7. The remaining informants were classified as "Don't know" or "No answer". For this question, the coding 0=disapprove and 1=approve constitutes the index for approval of birth control. (See Table IV.)

actively linked with official change agents, they were much more cosmopolitan and more *Gesellschaft*-like or rational. By all measures, they were modernizing more rapidly. Table III compares linkages of the influentials with those of the randomly chosen sample. We note from Table II that, whereas three-fourths of the influentials had adopted chemical fertilizer on their farms, less than one-half of the randomly chosen males had done so. For other practices, the same pattern prevailed, with influentials reporting themselves as the most frequent adopters, randomly chosen females as the least frequent, and randomly chosen males in between. Take inoculation against typhoid and cholera, for example. Sixty-six per cent of the influentials, forty-four per cent of the randomly chosen females and fifty-one per cent of the randomly chosen males reported having adopted it. For birth control, the percentages of those who adopted were lower—ten, three and four, respectively.

TABLE III

LINKAGES OF INDIAN VILLAGERS TO MODERNIZING STATUS-ROLES: PERCENTAGES OF RESPONDENTS WHO SPOKE MORE THAN 10 TIMES WITH OFFICERS AND AGENTS (ALL-INDIA DISTRIBUTION)

		Random Samples	
Officers and Agents	*Influentials* (Per cent)	*Males* (Per cent)	*Females* (Per cent)
Block development officer	30.0	5.6	2.0
Agricultural extension officer	25.7	4.3	0.7
Co-operative extension officer	20.1	2.9	0.6
Village level worker*	61.2	25.7	10.9
Block doctor†	20.2	6.5	6.5
Number of respondents	1,414	3,375	2,435

* The percentages respectively of influentials, males and females who report "knowing" the Village Level Worker are 92.5, 63.2 and 38.1. The percentages who report "liking" the VLW are as follows: 84.2, 54.5 and 30.0.

† Percentages who respectively report as in the footnote above for the Block doctor are as follows: 56.9, 35.6 and 24.3 for "knowing" and 47.3, 29.1 and 19.2 for "liking".

The paradox of the traditional thriving right alongside the modern was common. For example, while over half of the randomly chosen informants believe that evil spirits cause disease, and an even larger fraction would go to a religious leader or to a temple for treatment if they got smallpox, three-fourths had either themselves been vaccinated or reported that members of their families had been vaccinated. A comparison of the influentials with the randomly selected villagers in Tables I and II,

TABLE IV

MATRIX OF PRODUCT MOMENT CORRELATION COEFFICIENTS § BETWEEN SCORES ON INDEXES OF ADOPTION OF MODERN PRACTICES IN AGRICULTURE, HEALTH AND FAMILY PLANNING AND INDEXES ON OTHER SOCIAL, CULTURAL AND ECONOMIC VARIABLES IN 364 VILLAGES (ALL-INDIA DISTRIBUTION)

Indexes for Adoption of Modern Practices in A=Agriculture; B=Health; C=Birth Control; D=Approval of Birth Control

Indexes	Influentials (N=1414×1/5)				Males (N=3375×1/10)				Females (N=2435×1/10)			
	A	B	C	D†	A	B	C	D†	A	B	C	D†
SOCIO-CULTURAL												
Educational aspiration	.26**	.27**	.28**	.10	.31***	.16**	.28***	.13*	.28***	.14*	.31**	.14*
Extension contacts	.49***	.33***	.38***	.31***	.44***	.12**	.31***	.21**	.26**	.19***	.29***	.10
Knowledge	.56***	.38***	.51***	.34***	.42***	.19***	.47***	.26***	.24***	.06	.30***	.20***
Social participation	.39***	.07	.24***	.26***	.35***	.17***	.33***	.17***	.23***	.11	.20***	.03
Sacred-secular	−.23***	−.20***	−.15*	−.12*	−.08	−.16**	−.16**	−.04	−.10	−.008	.07	−.01
Empathy	.24***	.10	.26***	.20***	.27***	.02	.29***	.09	.11	−.04	.26***	.12
Film exposure	.19***	.19***	.32***	.19***	.25**	.14*	.27***	.22***	.27***	.17**	.30***	.04
Radio contact	.36***	.32***	.31***	.27***	.33***	.22***	.38***	.23***	.09	.04	.28***	.16*
Urban contact (cosmopolite)	−.02	.05	.12*	.05	.16**	.07	.16**	.10	.05	.12*	.20***	.13*
Age	−.06	−.14*	−.09	−.02	−.01	.01	−.05	−.11	−.11	.02	.09	−.09
Educational attainment‡	.28***	.12*	.04	.13	.09	.18***	.13**	.16**	.07	.10	−.03	.04
ECONOMIC												
Land cultivated	.39***	.21**	.13*	.12*	.42***	.01	.11	.19**	.37***	.03	.11	.22**
Tenure status	.26***	.01	.08	.06	.36***	−.11	.09	.13	.32***	−.04	.06	.21**
Productivity index	.40***	.16**	.19**	.09	.50***	−.01	.13*	.07	.29***	.09	.10	.15*
Agricultural income	.42***	.30***	.29***	.15*	.40***	.07	.21**	.13*	.44***	.10	.20**	.00

§ Calculated for this paper and for further collaborative usage by Lalit K. Sen, with Prodipto Roy, Satish Arora and the present author: all now or at one time members of the National Institute of Community Development, Hyderabad, India, are conducting the study on national awareness of community development.
* Statistically significant at the P < .05.
** Statistically significant at the P < .01.
† The coefficients under D measure biseral correlations because approval of family planning was measured on a dichotomous scale.
‡ Note the amount of illiteracy and other data on educational attainment in Table 1.

and the correlation co-efficients in Table IV, presage findings which are presented in the study of *Agricultural Innovations in Indian Villages* and *Patterns of Agricultural Diffusion in Rural India.* Influentials have higher caste status, have more contact with professionals whose responsibility it is to get innovations to the people, are more frequently literate and educated, utilize mass media more, and scored higher on the scales measuring secularization, rationality or *Vergesellschaftung;* and urban or cosmopolite contact.

Indian village and patterns of diffusion studies. As noted above, the Awareness of Change Study was followed by studies which permitted the use

TABLE V

ZERO-ORDER AND TWELFTH-ORDER PARTIAL CORRELATIONS OF ALL VARIABLES REMAINING
FROM THE PREVIOUS ANALYSIS WITH AGRICULTURAL ADOPTION

	Zero-order Correlations*	12th-order partial correlations*	Least square fourth-order partial correlations†
Index of agent contact with village [9] ...	.50	.11	.36
Index of leaders' contact with agents [10] ...	.52	.19	
Extension performance index [11] ...	.39	—.05	
Secular orientation (leaders)‡	.45	.35	.45
Urban contact through males migrating (per capita) [12] ...	.16	.12	
Index of access to mass media (distance from post-office, library, cinema) [13] ...	.31	—.04	
How often leaders attended cinema [14] ...	.43	.03	
VLW headquarters in village [15] ...	.38	.15	
Agent's choice of media (personal versus impersonal contact) [16] ...	.17	.29	.21
Proportion literate, males ...	.39	.11	.21
Electricity in the village [17] ...	.47	.32	.37
Number of political parties [18] ...	.43	.13	
Number of voluntary organizations [19] ...	.42	.10	

* For the zero-order coefficients the relevant degrees of freedom are 100, with a coefficient of .164 or larger needed for significance. For partials, 90 degree of freedom and a coefficient of .173 are more appropriate.

† A least square deletion computation deleting insignificant variables singly was conducted and these five variables remained. Together they explain 53 per cent of the variance, and the highest order partials are presented for the five-variable solution. The results are similar to the 12th order partials except that agent contact is substituted for leader contact and male literacy becomes more important.

‡ For the construction of this scale see the text of this paper.

SOURCE: Frederick C. Fliegel, Prodipto Roy, Lalit K. Sen and Joseph E. Kivlin, *Agricultural Innovations In Indian Villages,* (Hyderbad: National Institute for Community Development, 1968).

of multivariant analysis and a more definitive statement concerning the power various factors manifest in explaining the adoption of innovation.[8] Table V presents data which could lead to basic changes in policy of agricultural development. Obviously providing villages with electric power may possibly not guarantee more rapid adoption of improved practices and the high coefficient of relationship between this factor and scores made on agricultural adoption by villages may be due to some intervening factors such as the social power of the leaders. Nevertheless, electricity does drive pumps and mills and extend the demand for various items purchasable on the market for those who have the money to buy them.[25] That the extension contacts whether on demand of the leader or on the supply of the agent are important should lead to more quantity and quality inputs into this service. In terms of the subject under discussion in this paper, such social organizations as the agricultural extension ser· vice, ministries responsible for the information and broadcasting services, the village schools which may not only increase literacy but provide knowledge, and the suppliers of electricity to villagers which are related to village innovations and modernization should plan coordinated action to get the greatest return for the investment. Not unimportant in providing extension, school, electrical and other services is the planning of market-town growth centres which are now emerging in India. The studies prove that inputs of these services will pay off in greater modernization. Experience in more developed societies which have made the transition from the village-centred to the trade-town-centre society demonstrate that high schools, extension service headquarters, electrical distribution centres, various marketing and sales services, can most economically be located at growth centres. Great wastage may result from spreading or scattering these services among small places not likely to grow in wealth and power.[26]

Table VI presents the results of the study of 680 farmers in 8 villages in the 3 states mentioned above. As will be noted, the level of living index manifests the highest relationship with the agricultural adoption index. The index was constructed on the basis of owning specific household and personal items such as a clock, flashlight, wooden or metal furniture, mosquito nets, bicycle, shoes, wrist watch, etc. as well as size and type of house.[27] The index may mask many influences and since it is presented in the form of an index, it does not permit an item analysis of its several components in terms of their motivating force in creating desire for money to buy consumer goods. It seems to be particularly effective in masking the influence of such factors as caste and educational attainment of informants in their relation to scores on the adoption or innovation index.

Credit orientation was measured by responses to the question: "Did you use any credit for farm purposes last year?" and would you have used (some/some more) had it been available at reasonable interest?"[28]

Of course, Table VI argues in favour of extension of credit to farmers. With official sanctions prohibiting the enlargement of farms, the following summary statement concerning this factor bears notice: "[The] size

TABLE VI

ZERO-ORDER AND HIGHEST-ORDER PARTIAL CORRELATION COEFFICIENTS OF AGRICULTURAL INNOVATION WITH 15 SELECTED VARIABLES (N=680)

Variable	Zero-order Correlation	Highest order Partial Correlation
1. Level of Living†	.59*	.32*
2. Mass media contact†	.50*	.08*
3. Extention contact [20]	.49*	.22*
4. Value of agricultural products raised [21]	.43*	.21*
5. Political knowledge†	.37*	.09*
6. Education of respondent	.36*	−.07
7. Urban contact	.30*	−.01
8. Caste rank [22]	.29*	.06
9. Secular orientation†	.27*	.19*
10. Social participation [23] (holding office)	.24*	.04
11. Educational aspiration	.19*	−.08*
12. Urban pull†	.18*	.11*
13. Empathy†	.14*	−.07
14. Credit orientation†	.13*	.21*
15. Deferred gratification [24]	−.02	−.06

* Significant at the .01 level.

† For the construction of these indexes or scales see the text of this paper.

SOURCE: Prodipto Roy, Frederick C. Fliegel, Joseph E. Kivlin and Lalit K. Sen, *Patterns of Agricultural Diffusion in Rural India,* (Hyderabad: National Institute for Community Development, 1968).

of farm operation seems to be a necessary precondition to modernization. We feel that the ox is now before the cart and the pace of modernization will inexorably force the size of farm units upwards, resulting in a greater polarization of modern, large-size farm operators and traditional, marginal, small farm operators. This latter group may be viewed as a welfare problem. . . ." [29] We thus face another organizational concern common in all developing countries, at least temporarily increasing poverty. For India it may be for the many, once "larger farms which are modernizing [and] are intensifying labour inputs"[30] turn to more economical means of increasing their production. Care for the needy must be planned for. Should they not help build the electric power lines and roads which may lead out to the villages from the growth centres mentioned above?

SECULARIZATION, VERGESELLSCHAFTUNG AND DISENCHANTMENT
OF TRADITION

The reader if he has studied Tables IV, V and VI closely must be impressed with the fact that, no matter what factors have their influence partialled out, secularization retains its significant relation to the adoption of innovation. In Table IV the fact that sacredization, *Gemeinschaft* and traditional thinking as incorporated in the sacred-secular or *Gemeinschaft-Gesellschaft* scale inhibits the adoption of improved agricultural, health and family planning practices is indicated. This scale as used in Table IV was built from the following questions: "1. Can evil spirits cause disease? 2. Have you ever made a sacrifice to prevent sickness? 3. What do you do when some gets smallpox? 4. Should Harijans [formerly called untouchables] be allowed to draw water from all wells in the village? 5. Should Harijan children and other children take meals together in schools? 6. Who do you think is superior, a village Brahmin who is illiterate or a Harijan who has a college degree?" In the scale as employed in Tables V and VI the following items were added: "7. Do you think Harijans should be allowed to enter and worship in all temples of the village? 8. What do you do with bullocks who are too old to work?"; for "2" above the following substitution was made: "Should non-Hindus be allowed to eat beef?"; and for "3" the following was substituted: "If your son wanted to marry a lower caste girl would you allow it?"

In Tables V and VI the scale is reversed to measure secularization, *Vergesellschaftung* and disenchantment. Therefore, the signs on the correlation coefficients measuring relations between this factor and the score on the adoption index are positive. Even after the influence of such factors as caste rank, the masking variable-level of living, value of agricultural products, social participation, educational attainment and literacy, among others, are partialled out the score on the sacred-secular or *Gemeinschaft-Gesellschaft* scale as related to the score on the adoption of agricultural practices remains significant at the P .01 level. From these tables and Table IV, almost anyone interested in speeding up the adoption of innovations, although he would certainly advocate electrification of villages on some rational plan as mentioned above, increasing and improving extension and impoving credit and education, would want to launch a campaign against enchantment which the process of secularization or *Vergesellschaftung* attacks. This variable of secularization is related to radio exposure ($r = .11$), literacy ($r = .10$), educational attainment ($r = .16$) and level of living ($r = .23$). In the *Study of Awareness of Social Change in India* the scores on the sacred-secular scale were all significantly related to the empathy scores and to the knowledge score at the P .01 level for influen-

tials and randomly chosen informants. For the latter it was significantly related at the P .01 level with educational attainment for randomly chosen
informants. This latter correlation coefficient is not yet available for influentials. For the *Study of Patterns of Agricultural Diffusion* it is also related to urban pull ($r = .11$) as determined by the question, "If you are
offered a job in a city with double your present income, will you go?";
self-reliance ($r = .27$) as determined by the question. "How much of
your future depends on yourself? Out of a rupee, would you say 16
annas, 8 annas, 4 annas or none?"; income aspiration ($r = .13$) as determined by the question: "How much money does your family need per
month to live comfortably in this village?"; political knowledge ($r = .12$)
as determined by questions concerning, who the Prime Minister of India
is, who the Chief Minister of the State is, and who the elected representative
to the State Legislature of the area was, and empathy ($r = .13$) as determined by a set of questions in the form: "If you were.................[a
role] then what would you do to..............................[solve a relevant
problem]?" The roles suggested were those of district administrative
officer, the block development officer, village *Panchayat* and a day labourer.

The secular orientation measured by the sacred-secular or *Gemeinschaft-Gesellschaft* score has been described as revolving around the two
major themes that still dominate the rural ethos in India—the caste system and the sacredness of cattle. Secular orientation was measured by the
degree of deviation, expressed in terms of attitude, from the norms regarding the two themes. "... The significant relationships between urban pull,
political knowledge, education, radio exposure and literacy on the one
hand and secular orientation on the other, are indicative of the fact that
a person's psychic linkage with systems external to the village encourages
him to deviate from traditional norms."[31]

EDUCATION AND SECULARIZATION OR VERGESELLSCHAFTUNG

As noted above, in rural India secularization or *Vergesellschaftung* is
significantly related to both educational attainment as measured by the
school grades the informant claims to have completed and literacy as
measured by whether the informant claims he can read a newspaper or
not. As yet we have not completed analyses of the impact of education
on the attitudes incorporated in the secularization scale as students in
India proceed to a different levels of educational attainment. In terms
of the themes of this paper, namely, what the schools may be contributing to secularization, the data from the studies of urban Mexico, rural
Michigan and the general public of the United States may be of interest.[32]

Figure 1 illustrates how the proportion of urban Mexicans and
Americans who answer the question: "When you have a decision to

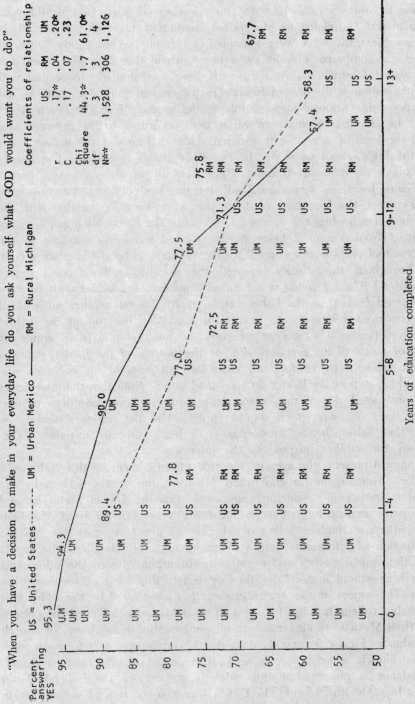

FIGURE 1

EDUCATION & SECULARIZATION—Percentage of informants answering, Yes, to the question:

"When you have a decision to make in your everyday life do you ask yourself what GOD would want you to do?"

US = United States------   UM = Urban Mexico   ———   RM = Rural Michigan

* Statistically significant at the P<.05 level.
** Unless otherwise specified the number of informants for subsequent figures are with minor variations the same as these.

make in your everyday life do you ask yourself what God would want you to do?" is related to educational attainment. Over 95 per cent of the urban Mexicans who were classified as having no education answered "Yes" as compared with 58 per cent of urban Mexicans with more than 13 years of education. American schooling was similarly associated with secularization with some difference in pattern in rural Michigan. As will be noted in various figures to follow, the impact of secularization which may be charged to education varies both according to the measure used and the level of schooling considered. Thus in Figure 1 the impact made in the high school years in Mexico (9-12) grades is evident. The impact of college or university training is great for all three groups. As Figure 2 indicates for those who "ask God" for the kind of guidance considered in Figure 1, the frequency of doing this is negatively correlated with the amount of schooling the informant reported. The Rural Michigan data are omitted from Figure 2 because the reduced numbers reporting in the high school years were too small for the averages to be stable in some cells.

Throughout the studies reported the so-called self-anchoring device was used.[33] The informant was handed a picture of a ladder with 10 steps numbered from 0 at the bottom through 10. To get another measure of self-conceived religiosity he was then hold "At the *top* of the ladder stands a person who is *very religious*. To him, religion is an important part of much of his everyday life. At the *bottom* of the ladder stands a person whose religion *does not enter into all parts of his everyday life*. On which step of the ladder do you stand now?" Note that the interviewer was instructed that if the "respondent inquires about definitions of religion, it is his own which should apply". Also the reader should know that the "self-anchoring" procedure had been carefully introduced previously for another purpose in the interview.

Figure 3 presents the average reported for placement on this "religiosity ladder". Here again for the urban Mexicans the grades 9-12 make the greatest impact in "reducing" religiosity. For the United States general public the impact is greatest in the lower years but for rural Michigan the pattern is similar to that of Mexico. Figure 4 presents data on the production of informants with varying amounts of schooling who report that they are agnostics and/or atheists. In urban Mexico the informants with high school and college training report this form of secularization most. The impact on the American samples as measured by this index was slight but college training for those in rural Michigan followed the pattern of urban Mexico. Another measure of secularization is frequency of church attendance. Figure 5 presents data on the proportion of informants who attend church at least once a week. The impact of education on church attendance as measured in this index is greatest for the respondents in the urban Mexican sample. In fact a larger proportion of informants in

FIGURE 2

EDUCATION & SECULARIZATION—Frequency of asking yourself what GOD would want you to do? (See Figure 1)

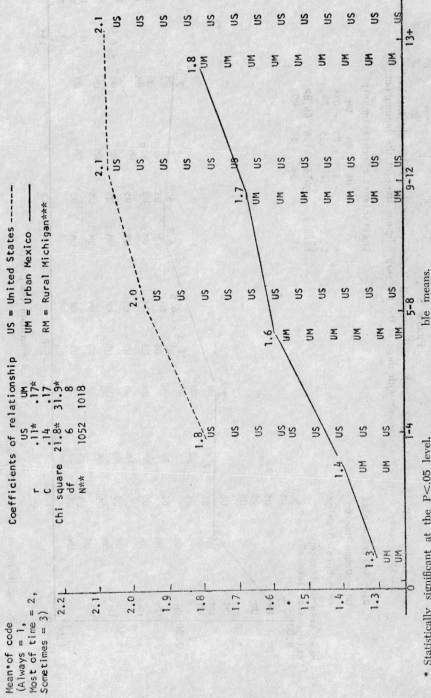

* Statistically significant at the P<.05 level.
** Those answering "No" to the question omitted.
*** Omitted because numbers in small cells were too small for sta

Figure 3

EDUCATION & SECULARIZATION: Self-perceived Religiosity on the "Religiosity Ladder." Mean scores from self placement with those at the top very religious those at the bottom not.

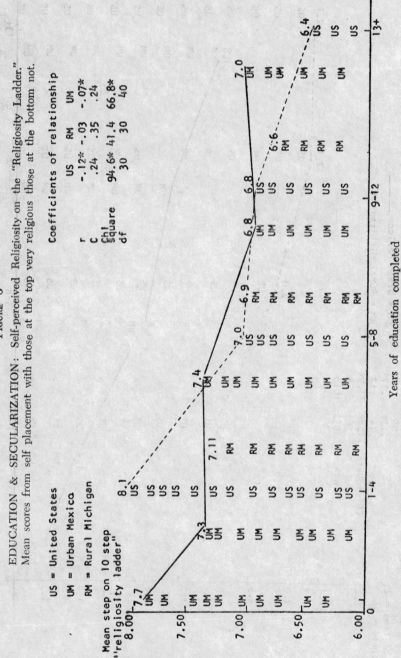

US = United States
UM = Urban Mexica
RM = Rural Michigan

Coefficients of relationship

	US	RM	UM
r	-.12*	-.03	-.07*
C	.24	.35	.24
Chi square	94.6*	41.4	66.8*
df	30	30	40

Mean step on 10 step "religiosity ladder"

Years of education completed

* Statistically significant at the P<.05 level.

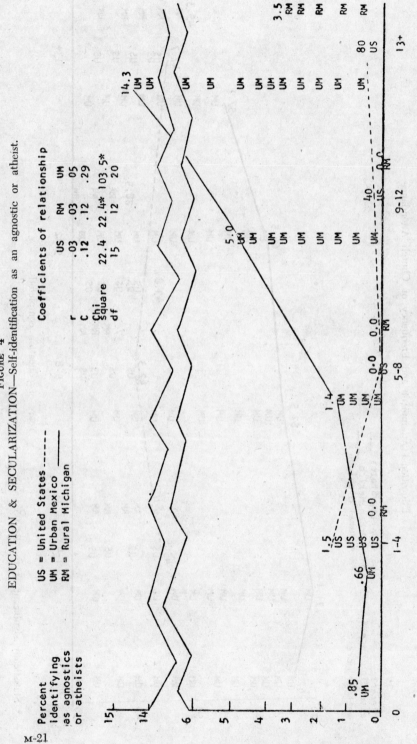

FIGURE 4

EDUCATION & SECULARIZATION—Self-identification as an agnostic or atheist.

US = United States ------
UM = Urban Mexico ———
RM = Rural Michigan

Percent
identifying
as agnostics
or atheists

Coefficients of relationship

	US	RM	UM
r	.03	.03	.05
C	.12	.12	.29
Chi Square	22.4	22.4*	103.5*
df	15	12	20

Years of education completed

* Statistically significant at the P<.05 level.

M-21

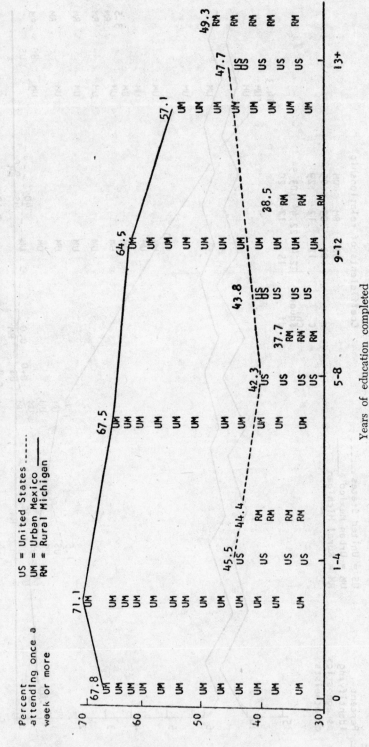

FIGURE 5

Educational Attainment and Frequency of Church Attendance

* Statistically significant at the P<.05 level.

rural Michigan and the general public of the United States with college education report attending church once a week than do others. The greater religiosity of Mexico when compared with the American samples as reflected by this index is apparent. Neverthelss, educational attainment in Mexico is generally more highly related to these indicators of secularization than in the United States.

AUTHORITARIANISM, STRATIFICATION, SOCIAL CHANGE AND EDUCATION

In most American sociological literature which treats the promotion of modernzation, a case is made for reducing stratification and authoritarianism based upon ascription. Equalitarianism is advocated. The "democratic way"[34] is advocated if for no other reason than for increasing the ability to emphasize or play the role of others.[35] In the studies reported on above, something like half of the variation in adoption of agricultural practices was explained through all the variables used in the analyses (See Tables V and VI). Of this, caste rank explains about 8 per cent.[36] For leaders of the 108 villages studied, caste rank explained about 13 per cent of the variation in agricultural adaption.[37]

Through multivariant analysis [38] it was determined for the study of innovations in the 108 Indian villages that "the effect of caste was most telling on leaders' empathy and their opinion of extension programs . . the effect of empathy and favourable opinion of extension programs on adoption are mainly functions of caste status. The association between caste, which refers to a traditional ranking system, and these modern variables show that tradition is not always contradictory to modernity".[39] In the study of patterns of diffusion in 8 villages in rural India "caste status was found to be significantly related to adoption levels. . . . The correlation at $r = .29$ explains eight per cent of the variance. . . .".[40]

Against the background of the importance of caste rank in the modernization of India the leap-frog modernization of various totalitarian regimes under the secular religion of Marxism may be noted. Elsewhere I have attempted to make a case for the use of force to speed up the rationalization of human effort and life.[41] Let us now ascertain whether education may erode stratification and authoritarianism in the manner that it appears to be associated with the disenchantment of the religious world as discussed above. Since we have not yet analyzed the Indian data available on this subject I must turn to the three samples from the western hemisphere. Informants in the urban Mexican, rural Michigan and general US public samples were asked whether they (1) strongly agree (2) slightly agree, (3) don't know or have no opinion, (4) slightly disagree, or (5) strongly disagree, with the following statement: "Everyone should think the same about what is right and wrong ." Figure 6 presents the rela-

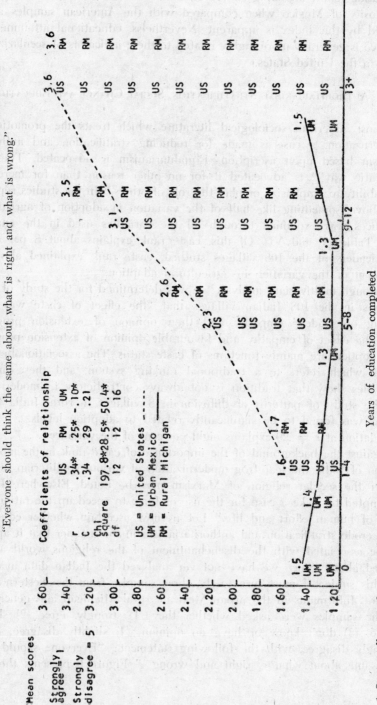

Figure 6

EDUCATION & AUTONOMY vs AUTHORITARIAN CONFORMITY—Extent of agreement with the statement: "Everyone should think the same about what is right and what is wrong."

* Statistically significant at the P<.05 level.

tionship between level of educational attainment and response to this statement. The differences in the urban Mexican and the American samples as reflected in Figure 6 are startling. If one makes an assumption which, of course, is contrary to fact that instead of cross-section data the population shown in Figure 6 in the three samples are cohorts passing through the various levels of education in the various stages of the life cycle, the erosion of authoritarian conformity and the increase in autonomy in America as represented by this statement begins immediately upon entering school and continues regularly throughout the schooling career. For urban Mexicans schooling is not related to this measure of authoritarianism. Figure 7 treats the statement "Whatever we do, it is necessary that our leaders outline carefully what is to be done and exactly how to go about it", as the previous statement was handled. Here again basic differences in the American and Mexican data show up with schooling appearing to erode authority in the case of the former and not in case of the latter. Figure 8 treats the following item on authoritarianism and autonomy as was done in Figures 6 and 7: "I find it easier to follow rules than to do things on my own." As before, the US general public sample indicates a freeing of the individual with the beginning of schooling. The rural Michigan and urban Mexican samples follow a similar pattern with the "freeing" process beginning with high school and extending through college. In general it appears that schooling in the United States has different consequences for informants reacting to these statements than does schooling in Mexico. Of course we can only talk of relationships here and schooling may merely reflect other more important intervening variables. However, with authority playing such an important role in social change in authoritarian societies under the influence of the secular religion of Marxism and with caste rank playing such an important role in social change in India, the American dogma of anti-authoritarianism and equalitarianism may be called into question.

LITERACY AND/OR EDUCATIONAL ATTAINMENT AS POSSIBLE INTERVENING VARIABLES

Among the variables in Table IV which subsequent analysis proved to be closely related to educational attainment are the following:[41]* 1. Educational aspiration for children and/or grandchildren ($r = .51$); 2. General Knowledge ($r = .50$); 3. Contacts with extension agents ($r = .50$); 4. Social participation index score ($r = .52$); 5. Empathy ($r = .42$); film exposure ($r = .37$) and urban contacts ($r = .42$). The economic indexes showed less close relationships with the productivity index being highest ($r = .36$). The question then arises, is education a causal factor in producing social change or are there various intervening variables, perhaps some not included in the study, which are responsible? In the study of

FIGURE 7

EDUCATION & AUTHORITARIANISM: Extent of agreement with the statement: "Whatever we do, it is necessary that our leaders outline carefully what is to be done and exactly how to go about it."

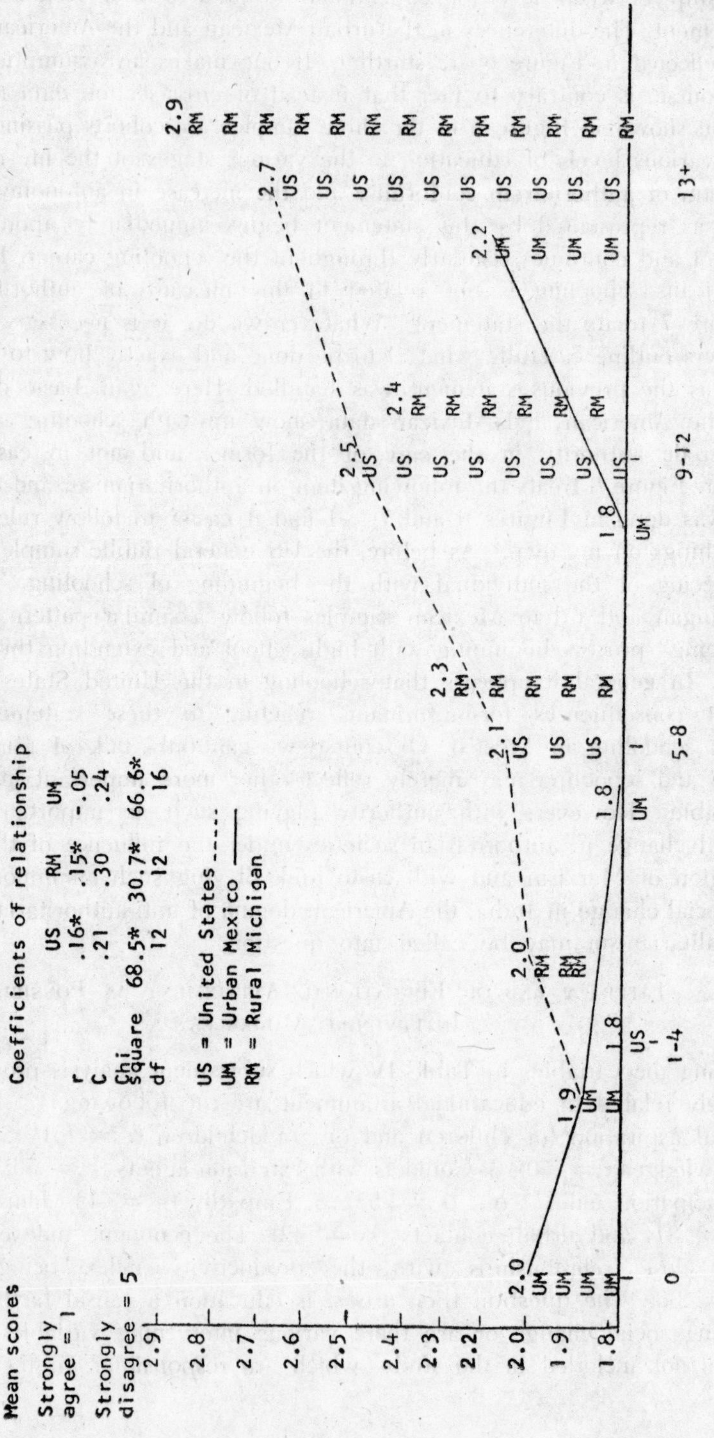
Mean scores
Strongly agree = 1
Strongly disagree = 5
Coefficients of relationship
US RM UM
r .16* .15* -.05
C .21 .30 .24
Chi square 68.5* 30.7* 66.6*
df 12 12 16
US = United States
UM = Urban Mexico
RM = Rural Michigan
2.9
2.8
2.7
2.6
2.5
2.4
2.3
2.2
2.0
1.9
1.8
2.0
1.9
1.8
2.0
1.8
2.1
2.3
1.8
2.5
2.4
2.2
2.7
2.9
0
1-4
5-8
9-12
13+
Years of education completed

* Statistically significant at the P<.05 level.

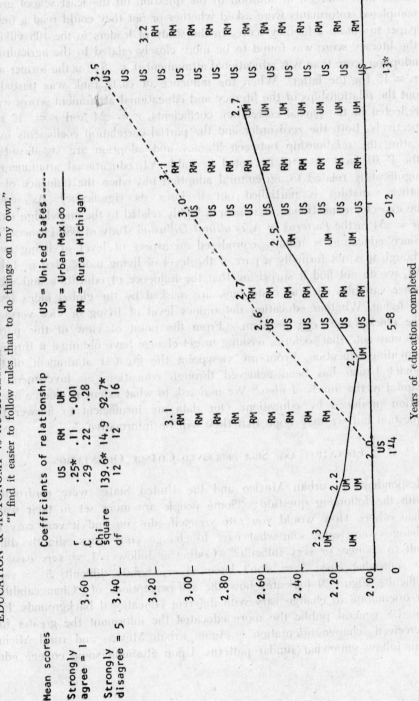

FIGURE 8

EDUCATION & AUTONOMY vs AUTHORITARIANISM: Exten of agreement with the statement: "I find it easier to follow rules than to do things on my own,"

US = United States ------
UM = Urban Mexico ———
RM = Rural Michigan ------

Coefficients of relationship

	US	RM	UM
r	.25*	.11	-.001
c	.29	.22	.28
Chi Square	139.6*	14.9	92.7*
df	12	12	16

Mean scores

Strongly agree = 1

Strongly disagree = 5

* Statistically significant at the P<.05 level.

agricultural innovations in 108 villages and the study of patterns of diffusion in 8 villages, in addition to the question on the least school grade completed, informants were asked whether or not they could read a newspaper to obtain a literacy score. In the study of leaders in the 108 villages the literacy score was found to be more closely related to the agricultural adoption score than was educational attainment ($r = .34$ for the former and $r = .15$ for the latter). When the influence of caste rank was partialled out the relationships of the literacy and educational attainment scores were reflected in the partial correlation coefficients, $r = .24$ and $r = .12$ respectively. Both the zero order and the partial correlation coefficients indicating the relationship between literacy and adoption are significant at the P .01 level. As will be noted in Table VI, educational attainment is significantly related to agricultural adoption but when the influence of 14 other variables is partialled out it loses its significance. As would be expected educational attainment is highly related to the knowledge index ($r = .54$ in the *Patterns of Agricultural Diffusion* study of 680 farmers).[41]** Since education is usually considered an aspect of level of living even though it is not formally a part of the level of living index used in Table VI, we do not find it surprising that the influence of education and some other variables such as caste rank are masked by the global index level of living. Whether education determines level of living or vice versa is the chicken and egg problem. From the point of view of this paper we may note that societies wishing to get change have obtained it through providing education. From my viewpoint the greatest attainment of the Soviet Union has been achieved through education, an investment of capital in the minds of men.[42] We may ask to what extent is change orientation produced by education? Our data are insufficient to answer the question but we may hope that they will be informative.

EDUCATION AND SELF-PERCEIVED CHANGE ORIENTATION

Respondents in urban Mexico and the United States were confronted with the following question: "Some people are more set in their ways than others. How would you rate yourself—do you find it very easy to change your ways, somewhat easy to change your ways, slightly difficult to change, or very difficult?" (Coding as follows: 1 = very easy; 2 = somewhat easy; 3 = don't know; 4 = slightly difficult; 5 = very difficult). Figure 9 indicates how the self-perceptions of "Changeability" or orientation to change vary with different educational backgrounds. For the US general public the more educated the informant the greater his perceived "change orientation". Again urban Mexico and rural Michigan follow somewhat similar patterns. Upon attaining some college edu-

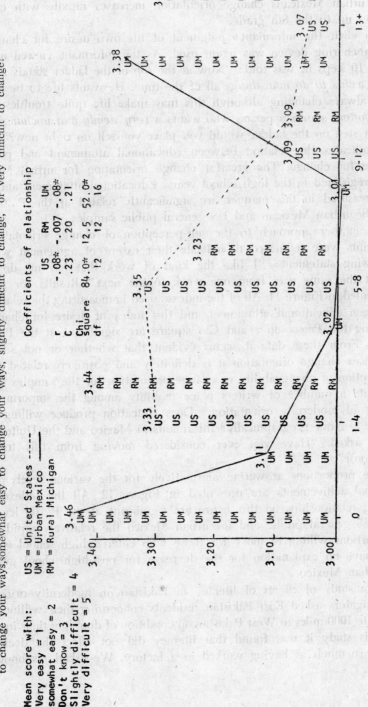

FIGURE 9

EDUCATION & SELF-PERCEIVED CHANGE ORIENTATION: Responses to the question:

"Some people are more set in their ways than others. How would you rate yourself—do you find it very easy to change your ways, somewhat easy to change your ways, slightly difficult to change, or very difficult to change?"

Mean score with:
Very easy = 1
somewhat easy = 2
Don't know = 3
Slightly difficult = 4
Very difficult = 5

US = United States ----
UM = Urban Mexico ——
RM = Rural Michigan

Coefficients of relationship

	US	RM	UM
r	-.08*	-.007	-.08*
C	.23	.20	.21
Chi square	84.0*	12.5	52.0*
df	12	16	16

Years of education completed

* Statistically significant at the P<.05 level.

cation the self-perceived difficulty in changing for some reason increases. For urban Mexicans change orientation increases rapidly with entry in school up to the 8th grade.

To elicit the informant's judgment of his own desire for change the self-anchoring device was again used. As the informant viewed a ladder with 10 steps he was told: "Now at the *top* of the ladder stands a person who *wants to do new things* all of the time. He wants life to be exciting and always changing although this may make life quite troublesome. At the *bottom* stands a person who wants a *very steady and unchanging life*. What step on the ladder would you place yourself on right now?" Figure 10 indicates the relation between educational attainment and perceived desire for change. The greatest change orientation for urban Mexicans was registered in the high school years. Educational attainment and desire as measured in this manner are significantly related at the P .01 level for the urban Mexican and US general public samples.

In another approach to the self-perception of change orientation, informants were requested to indicate their extent of agreement with the following statement: "I like the kind of work that lets me do things about the same way from one week to the next." Results for this are presented in Figure 11. All of the indexes used in measuring the relationship between educational attainment and this index of desire for change including the Personian r and Chi square are significant at the P = .05 level. From these data it seems evident that whether or not schooling produces change orientation it is definitely and positively related to self-perception of changeability or change orientation for the samples studied.

Quite a number of writers place mobility among the important indicators of modernity orientation.[43] Does education produce willingness or desire to move geographically? Informants in Mexico and the United States were asked. "Have you ever considered moving from this town (or location)?"

The proportions answering affirmatively for the various levels of educational achivements are presented in Figure 12. All the indexes measuring relationships on this figure are significant at the P. .05 level. For the US general public and for urban Mexico the relatively rapid rise in proportions willing to move for those who entered high school is noted. We have no explanation for the decrease for post-high-school graduates in urban Mexico.

In a study of effects of literacy in Pakistan on modernity orientation, investigators asked East Pakistan residents concerning their willingness to migrate 1000 miles to West Pakistan on condition of doubling their incomes.[44] In this study it was found that literacy did not affect the decision to move so much as having worked in a factory. We asked respondents in

FIGURE 10

EDUCATION & SELF-PERCEIVED CHANGE ORIENTATION—Mean scores from placement through the "self-anchoring technique" on a ladder with the 10th step or top representing "a person who wants to do new things all of the time . . . wants life to be exciting and always changing . . ." (and) the bottom . . . " a person who wants a very steady and unchanging life."

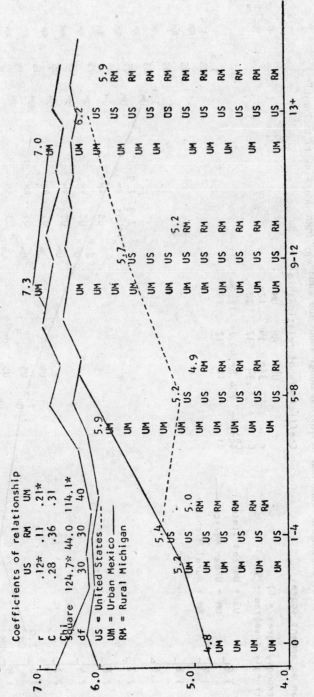

* Statistically significant at the P<.05 level.

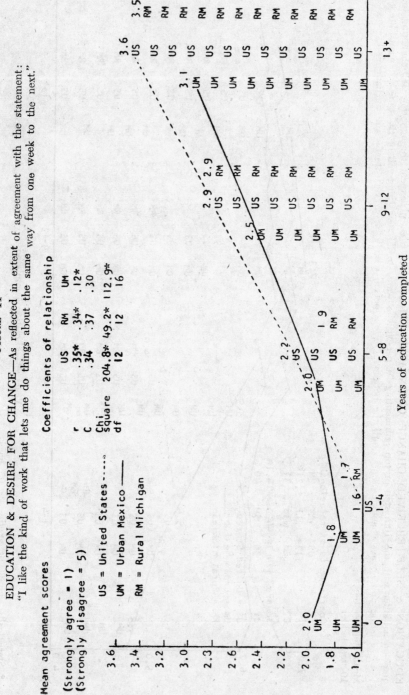

FIGURE 11

EDUCATION & DESIRE FOR CHANGE—As reflected in extent of agreement with the statement: "I like the kind of work that lets me do things about the same way from one week to the next."

* Statistically significant at the P<.05 level.

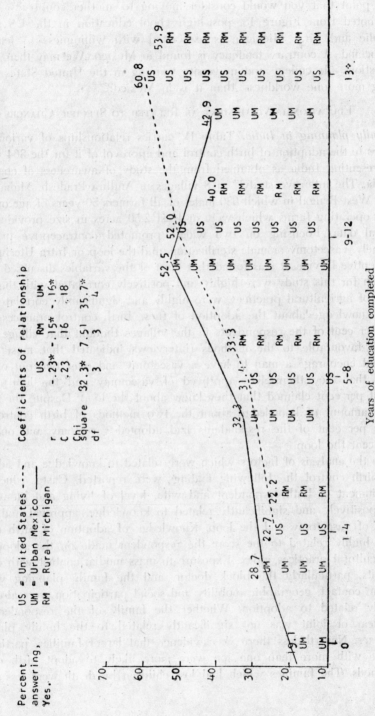

FIGURE 12

EDUCATION & CHANGE ORIENTATION via MENTAL MOBILITY OR READINESS TO MOVE—as indicated by answers to the following question: "Have you ever considered moving from this town (place)?"

Percent answering, Yes.

US = United States - - - -
UM = Urban Mexico ———
RM = Rural Michigan ———

Coefficients of relationship

	US	RM	UM
r	-.23*	-.15*	-.16*
C	.23	.16	.18
Chi Square	32.3*	7.51	35.7*
df	3	3	4

Years of education completed

* Statistically significant at the P<.05 level.

Mexico and the United States: "Can you imagine things would get to the point that you would consider moving to another country?" As may be noted from Figure 13, post-high-school education in the US general public and rural Michigan is associated with willingness to leave the homeland. A contrary tendency is found in Mexico. We may then ask the question: "Is college and university training in the United States producing more 'one worldness' than it is in Mexico?"

Educational Attainment as Related to Specific Changes

Family planning in India. Table IV carries relationships of various variables to the adoption of birth control and approvol of it for the 364 villages representing India as obtained from the study of awareness of change in India. The intensive study [45] of 8 villages in Andhra Pradesh, Maharashtra and West Bengal in which 680 males of all farmers 50 years of age or under and operating farms which were at least 2.50 acres in size provides additional data. Focusing on two widely promoted contraceptive practices, namely, vasectomy or male sterilization, and the loop or Intra Uterine Contraceptive Device, it was found that most of the variables discussed above, which for this study were highly and positively correlated with the adoption of agricultural practices, were highly and significantly correlated with the knowledge about the adoption of these birth control practices. Some 53 per cent of the respondents in the villages thought that village norms were favourable to the methods (interviews indicated that most people would encourage a man to have a vasectomy and over two out of three said that they themselves approved of vasectomy and the loop). Fifty-eight per cent claimed that they knew about the loop. Despite the surprising amount of knowledge about the two methods of birth control only nine per cent of the respondents had adopted vasectomy and only two per cent the loop.

In the analysis of factors which were related to knowledge and adoption of birth control the following findings were reported. Caste, educational attainment of both respondent and wife, level of living and literacy are all positively and significantly related to knowledge, approval and adoption of vasectomy and the loop. Knowledge of adoption of birth control was highly related to the score the respondent made on the adoption of agricultural practices index. Exposure to mass media, contact with change agents, particularly the block doctor, and the family planning worker, urban contact, geographic mobility and social participation were also positively related to adoption. Whether the family of the respondent was nuclear or joint was not significantly related to the family planning indexes. Nevertheless there was evidence that larger families, particularly those with more than one son were more likely to adopt birth control methods. The families which had lost children by death were less apt to

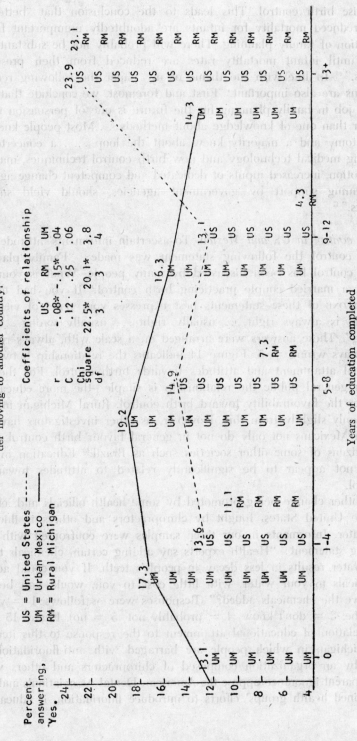

FIGURE 13

EDUCATION & CHANGE ORIENTATION via MENTAL MOBILITY OR WILLINGNESS TO LEAVE THE HOME COUNTRY—as indicated by answers to the following question: "Can you imagine conditions could get to the point that you would consider moving to another country?"

practise birth control. This leads to the conclusion that "better health and reduced mortality for infants are adoubtedly unimportant factors in adoption of family planning. There will probably not be substantial adoption until infant mortality rates are reduced from their present high levels." [46] In line with the theme of my paper the following recommendations are also important. "First and foremost, we conclude that the primary job in family planning for the future is one of persuasion to adopt, rather than one of knowledge about methods. . . Most people knew about vasectomy and a majority knew about the loop . . . a concerted effort uniting medical technology and new birth control techniques, mass media promotion, increased inputs of dedicated and competent change agents and continuing support by government agencies, should yield substantial results." [47]

Birth control in US and Mexico. To ascertain informants' attitudes toward birth control the following statement was made: "Family planning or birth control has been discussed by many people. What is your feeling about a married couple practicing birth control? If you had to decide, which ONE of these statements best expresses your point of view? Birth control is always right, . . . usually right, . . . usually wrong, . . . always wrong". These answers were arranged on a scale with, always right = 1 to always wrong = 5. Figure 14 indicates the relationship between educational attainment and attitudes towards birth control. For the United States general public the relationship is simple—the more education the greater the favourability toward birth control. Rural Michigan informants vary only slightly from this. However, as other investigators have noted, urban Mexicans not only do not in general favour birth control as much as citizens of some other societies such as Brazil. [48] Education in Mexico does not appear to be significantly related to attitudes toward birth control.

Another change being promoted by some health officials and, especially in the United States, fought by chiropractors and others is fluoridation of water. Informants in our three samples were confronted with the following statement: "Health experts say adding certain chemicals to drinking water results in less decay in people's teeth. If you could add these chemicals to your water, with little cost to you, would you be willing to have the chemicals added?" (Responses were as follows: 1 = yes; 2 = may be; 3 = don't know; 4 = probably not; 5 = no). Figure 15 presents the relation of educational attainment to the response to this item. Only in Michigan in which people are barraged with anti-fluoridation literature by an organization composed of chiropractors and others who out of apparent ignorance oppose the American Dental Association's and various combined health groups' efforts to introduce fluoridation, is education not

FIGURE 14

EDUCATION & WILLINGNESS TO CHANGE via PRACTISING BIRTH CONTROL—Mean scores of respondents' answers to the following questions plotted against educational attainment: "Family Planning or birth control has been discussed by many people. What is your feeling about a married couple practising birth control? If you had to decide, which ONE of these statements best expresses your point of view?" Always right (scored as 1); Usually right (scored as 2); Don't know (scored as 3); Usually wrong (scored as 4) and Always wrong (scored as 5).

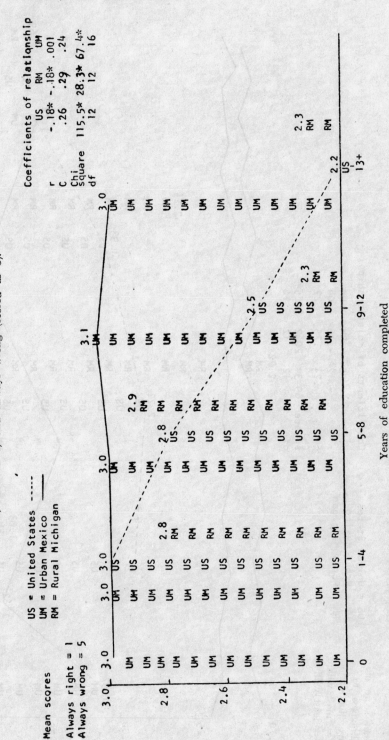

M-22

* Statistically significant at the P<.05 level.

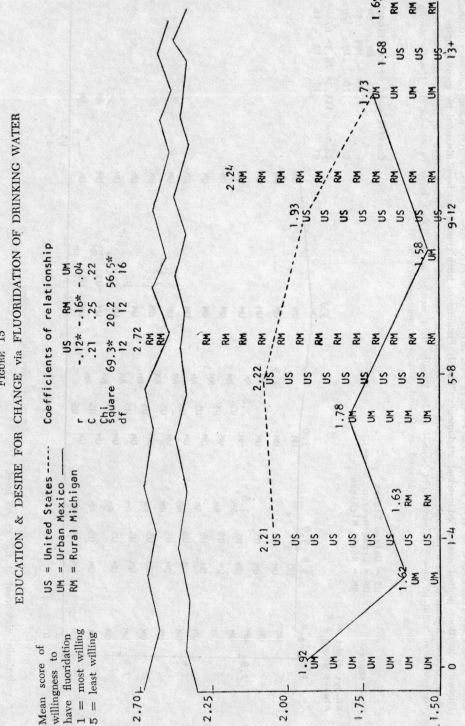

FIGURE 15

EDUCATION & DESIRE FOR CHANGE via FLUORIDATION OF DRINKING WATER

US = United States -----
UM = Urban Mexico ———
RM = Rural Michigan

Mean score of
willingness to
have fluoridation
1 = most willing
5 = least willing

Coefficients of relationship

	US	RM	UM
r	-.12*	-.16*	-.04
C	.21	.25	.22
Chi square	69.3*	20.2	56.5*
df	12	12	16

Years of education completed

* Statistically significant at the P<.05 level.

significantly related to desire for fluoridation. In Michigan the 69 informants in the category of having completed 5-8 grades of education stand out as a sore thumb for those who want fluoridaton. Evidently people with this level of education respond to anti-fluoridation propaganda. In Mexico there seems no great opposition to fluoridation at any level of educational attainment.

EDUCATION AND SOCIAL DISTANCE

All informants in Mexico and the United States were read and/or shown a list of categories of persons and asked the question: "Are there any of these groups you would *prefer not to have* as citizens? ... neighbours? ... family members by marriage? ... co-workers on the job?" In the United States the categories of persons involved in this social distance evaluation were the following: Protestants, Catholics, Jews, Negroes, Japanese. Mexicans, Whites, Other (specify)——. In Mexico the list contained the following additional categories with North Americans substituted for Mexicans: Indians who speak Spanish and Indians who do not speak Spanish. At the end of each list of categories for each of the status roles, namely, citizen, neighbour, family member and co-worker, a response "all are acceptable" was provided. Figure 16 reports for the 3 samples the relationship between the proportions of respondents who specified that all are acceptable as citizens tabulated in relation to educational attainment of the respondent. In Mexico educational status is very closely related to acceptance of the categories mentioned as citizens. In fact, in Mexico the relationship between educational attainment and tolerance, as measured by the various social distance scales, is very high for all the status-roles involved. These data have been reported in detail elsewhere but the relation to education has not been specified as in Figure 16.[49] In the United States, although overall tolerance may be greater, the relation of education to the tolerance or social distance scores is not so great as in Mexico. It appears that if scarce resources are to be spent on education to reduce tensions among minority groups and between the two nations they could be best spent in Mexico.

In Figure 17 the proportions of informants who do not have cross-the-border friends [49*] and who answer the question, "Would you like some (cross-the-border) Mexican (North American) friends?" in the affirmative is plotted against educational attainment. If again we would assume that these cross-sectional data are not that but represent 3 cohorts of students proceeding through school it would appear that from indifferent beginnings all three "cohorts" on arriving at college or university opt to have "cross-the-border" friends in large proportions. Thus only 11 per cent of rural Michigan informants in the lowest grades of school want Mexican

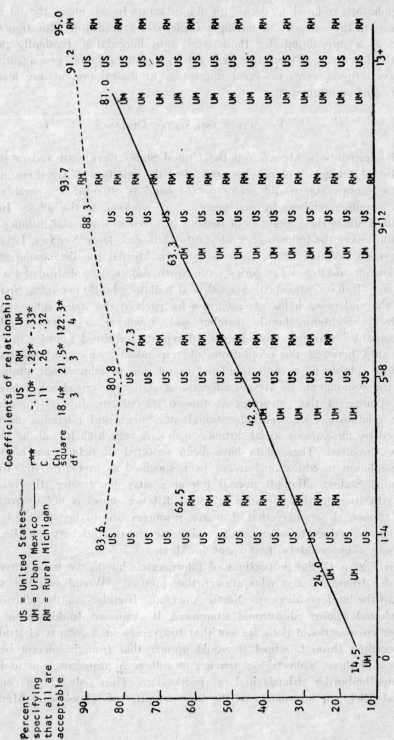

FIGURE 16

EDUCATION & SOCIAL DISTANCE—Percentage of respondents who said that "all are acceptable" when asked, "Are there any . . . you would PREFER not to have as citizens of our country?" Plotted against educational attainment.

* Statistically significant at the P<.05 level.
** Social distance score was coded as follows: 1 = all are acceptable. Hence the negative coefficients.

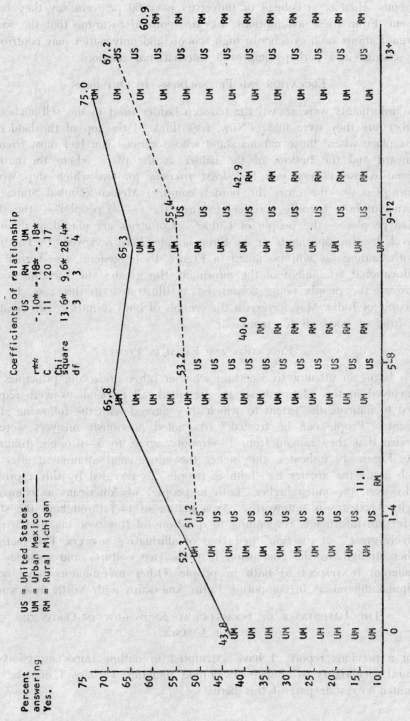

FIGURE 17

EDUCATION & POTENTIAL FOR LINKAGE—Percentage of Mexicans and North Americans not having cross-the-border friends but wanting some as indicated by responses to the question: "Would you like to have some Mexican (North American) friends?"

US = United States
UM = Urban Mexico
RM = Rural Michigan

Coefficients of relationship

	US	RM	UM
r**	-.10*	-.98*	-.18*
C	.11	.20	.17
Chi Square	13.6*	9.6*	28.4*
df	3	3	4

Percent answering Yes.

Years of education completed

* Statistically significant at the P<.05 level.
** The biserial distribution lead to negative coefficients because the answer, yes, was coded 1 and the answer, no, 2.

friends whereas in college or university over 60 per cent say they want them. From these assumptions, we are tempted to argue that the social organizations such as schools, high schools and universities may contribute to change and perhaps improved international relations.

EDUCATION AND FRIENDLINESS TO OUTSIDERS

As informants were shown the ten-step ladder used in the self-anchoring procedure they were told: "Now, let's think of the top of the ladder as the place where those nations stand whose PEOPLE you feel most *friendly* toward and the bottom of the ladder as the place where the nations stand whose PEOPLE you feel *least friendly* to. On which step would you place——(the cross the border country) Mexico (United States) in terms of how friendly you feel towards the (——) people?——the Russian people,——the people of Cuba?" Countries are placed at different levels by the informants in the three samples here reviewed.[49]** This notwithstanding, as will be noted in Figure 18 in general, the higher the educational attainment of the informant, the greater the friendliness felt toward the people being considered as illustrated, in this case, by the people of India. May we credit the schools of both countries with creating a fund of goodwill for mankind?

EDUCATION AND FAITH IN PEOPLE

To begin an attempt to ascertain whether other underlying principles are involved in the relationships just presented, all respondents were reques-ted to indicate the extent to which they agreed with the following statement: "People can be trusted." (As noted previously answers were so coded that they ranged from 1—strongly agree, to 5—strongly disagree.) As Figure 19 indicates, the higher the educational attainment after the 8th grade the greater the 'faith in people" as revealed by this approach. However, the much higher "faith in people" of Americans as compared with Mexicans is noteworthy. As a matter of fact throughout the study Mexican informants responding to questions of this type manifest a relatively great "set reaction" in favour of affirmative answers. This fact further strengthens the conclusion that the two cultures and societies are different in respect to faith in people. Other investigators have noted similar differences in comparing Latin Americans with North Americans.[50]

THE IMPORTANCE OF SOCIOLOGICAL KNOW-HOW IN ORGANIZING FOR CHANGE

In a previous report[51] I have attempted to outline important efforts of rural sociologists to change developing societies. Perhaps I may be permitted to restate part of this here:

FIGURE 18

EDUCATION & DESIRE FOR LINKAGE WITH OTHER PEOPLES—Illustrated by placement of India by the "Self anchorage" technique on a "friendship ladder" at the top of which "those nations stand whose people you feel most friendly toward" and the bottom "(those) people you feel least friendly to."

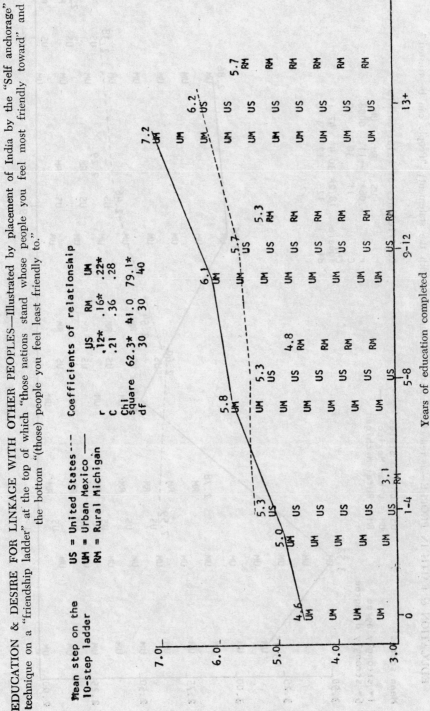

* Statistically significant at the P<.05 level.

FIGURE 19

EDUCATION & FAITH IN PEOPLE—as reflected in extent of agreement with the statement: "People can be trusted."

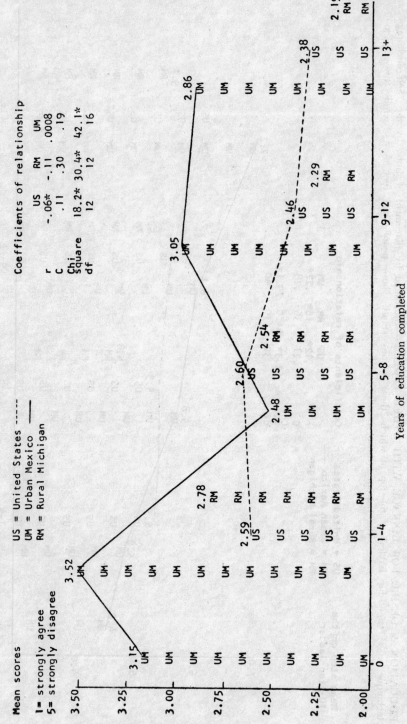

Mean scores   US = United States ------
                     UM = Urban Mexico ———
1= strongly agree   RM = Rural Michigan
5= strongly disagree

Coefficients of relationship

	US	RM	UM
r	-.06*	-.11	.0008
C	.11	.30	.19
Chi Square	18.2*	30.4*	42.1*
df	12	12	16

Years of education completed

* Statistically significant at the P<.05 level.

An imaginative application of the social sciences together with the use of appropriate techniques for the development of agriculture, management, health, education, and other facets of social organization may be found in some of the programs in developing countries. The 'basic democracies' which are being cultivated in Pakistan and the credit organizations in Korea[52] might be cited as programs which have made differences in the lives of considerable numbers of people. But for boldness of range and magnitude of undertaking, we must turn to the Indian story. To be sure the attempt to remold that huge nation by means consistent with its democratic tradition far exceeds the application of rural sociological principles. For present purposes, only a small part of the whole story whose end, of course, is nowhere in sight, will be recounted: the social change generated by the virtual partnership between the government of India and the Ford Foundation's Indian program, the latter under the administration of an American rural sociologist.[53]

The method chosen to move the country forward was that of government-led development programs intended to raise per-capita income and set growth in motion through a series of five-year plans applied under free democratic conditions.[54] A realistic catalogue of agricultural needs characterized the first two five-year plans, but their implementation proved to be somewhat too fragmented to achieve the desired results. Some of the projects undertaken during the first two planning periods were Training centers for village workers, aid to extension departments for agricultural colleges, training centers in village crafts, training women for village extension work in home economics, organization and leadership of village youth activities, in-service training for village development personnel, strengthening the role of village teachers in rural development personnel, rural health service, research and training centers for village planning and rural housing, and scholarships to superior Gram Sevaks (Village Level Workers).[55]

These measures had varying degrees of lasting success but evaluations of the total program attributed the increased aggricultural yield in considerable measure to expanded crop acreage. Since there was little more land which could come into production, and since the combined projects left the food problem far from solved, alternatives were sought in the Third Plan. The Intensive Agricultural District Program, or what is more commonly called the "package program", was then undertaken.

Unlike the earlier programs, which although mutually reinforcing, were undertaken separately, the package program stressed improved practices which were to be used in combination—such practices as selection of improved seed; treatment of seed to prevent plant disease;

improved tillage and equipment, fertilizer and plant protection; improved harvesting, storage and marketing. Also, unlike the earlier programs, the package programs were pilot programs, strategically located in respect to visibility and success probability and constituted so that whatever progress they might accomplish would virtually be a showcase demonstration of improved agricultural practices.

The objectives for the Stage I part of the long-term project are considered to have been accomplished in view of the following: yields have increased by 20 to 25 per cent among the million or more farmers in the pilot projects who have recovered two or three times as much money as they have invested in such inputs as fertilizer and insecticides; supporting organizations have been developed, such as represented by the ten thousand agricultural officers at various governmental levels; warehouse organizations are now capable of making accessible to the farmer fertilizer and other supplies; effectiveness of co-operative societies is claimed to have increased. Diffusion practices and standard-of-living studies are discernible in the workings of the pakage program presently nearing completion of a phase as the five-year plan draws to a close. This phase has been characterized by an approach new to India, by which the staff, through a district extension operation, is learning to understand, educate, and work with rank-and-file farmers in large numbers both in groups and as individuals. Stage II is presently emerging, the social targets of which are joint program planning between extension workers and village leaders, full program participation by all farmers, more complete farm planning, the simultaneous development of all farming enterprises using simple practices, better use of village resources in production and joint efforts to make the co-operatives and other institutions more effective.

The concerted attack on underproduction of sufficient food for the nation is coupled with a similar emphasis on control of the stupendous swelling of the Indian population. . . . Practically all that is known about social organization, social rank, the use of power, effective communication systems, the diffusion process, ecological methods, the end for which men strive, and the norms they employ in their striving has been applied and modified in this ongoing story of a great nation's first steps toward agricultural self-sufficiency.[56]

A footnote to this effort may now be added. As I returned to India this summer I was told by experts that for the first time in history India will have sizeable surpluses of food. Of course, the new varieties of grains developed, taken together with improved cultural procedures, and many other factors, have brought about this condition. Although serious drought conditions could change the situation, what was reported above about the effectiveness of the professional and other agents, increasing availability of improved fetilizer and seed, and economic incentives taken with the foresight of the government and the Ford Foundation in developing the "package progam" for strategic pace-setting sectors of the country must be given credit for this near miracle claimed by many to be impossible, and still doubted by some.[57]

The Indian segment of UNESCO's experiment with radio forums and literacy projects.[58] Where illiteracy is high and desire for learning great, if the chief objective is diffusion of improved agricultural, health and family planning practices, will the procedure of radio forums or carefully planned functional literacy for adults produce greater knowledge about and adoption of these items? Between 1964 and 1966 communication experiments were begun in Costa Rica and India with the objectives of: 1. determining the impact of different means of communication on the spread of these practices; 2. determining the factors affecting the acceptance of innovations; and 3. describing the total process of diffusion of innovations. In 1964 benchmark data on caste, age, family size, education, farm size and operations and level of living were gathered. In 1966 and 1967 surveys for measuring the impact of the experiments were made.[59] During 1965 "communication treatments" of literacy classes and radio farm forums were applied to each of two pairs of villages. To a third pair on which benchmark data were also obtained the treatments were not applied. All these villages are located south of Lucknow.

Through the All-India Radio network farm forums were introduced to enhance the informational and motivational value of radio listening.

A forum consists of 10 to 20 villagers who gather together to listen to programs about farm programs. They elect a secretary who keeps minutes of the discussion meetings which follow the broadcast. A rotating chairman who leads the discussions is elected for each broadcast. Requests for additional information or about adaptations of recommendations to local conditions may be sent to the radio station. Hired action leaders are also used. These guide discussion if necessary and give advice on putting the information to use. For example, if a farmer had losses from rats he would be encouraged to obtain poison and told how to use it in his own storage shed. There was a radio farm forum in each of the two radio treatment villages. Each forum was provided with a transisterized radio set and members listened to about 100 talks, which focused on improved agricultural and health practices.... For example, talks on the modern plow and on fertilizer usage were given before both the *Rabi* (winter) and *Kharif* (rainy) planting seasons .... Attendance varied considerably, from 30 to 90 per cent . . . many who were not members . . . attended . . . .[60]

We may use the advocacy of rat poisons as an example of how the forums worked. Although cultivators knew about rat poison few would use it openly because this meant killing a living thing. Caste and religion were believed to proscribe this Some who used rat poison secretly might discourage others from using it for the reasons here involved. In one of the villages the problem was particularly acute. A large number of *chamars* (a caste near the bottom of the Hindu social ladder) were trying to raise their caste status through carefully obeying the Hindu norms. In this village the first radio programme and discussion of rat poison was understandably not very successful. A second discussion vividly called attention to the losses caused by the rats. This increased interest. In subsequent discussions the case was made for the poisoning of rats as a perfectly moral act. Thereafter, "knowledge and adoption of rat poison reached such high levels by 1966 that the practice no longer discriminated" *chamars* from others and in 1966 the comparison was dropped.[61]

Literacy classes like the radio farm forums were used as vehicles for spreading information about improved practices and for promoting their adoption. In addition, literacy classes had a major separate goal. This was the teaching of reading and writing. Only male literacy classes were started in the experiment and rarely did women attend. Literacy House, an adult literacy training centre in the city of Lucknow, organized the experiment. Both literate and illiterate men were included in the experiment. Toward the end of the classes, after reading proficiency had been obtained, groups were converted into reading forums. The objectives were not alone to teach reading and writing bct to "make participants functionally literate so that they would be stimulated to use reading and writing in their daily life".[62]

In each of the literacy treatment villages 25 to 30 participants met for two and a half hours daily six days a week from 8:00 to 10:30 p.m. Hindi Devanagari script was used. Participants ranged from 15 to 45 and were from widely different castes. Attendance ranged from 30 to 100 per cent. Pamphlets were developed locally to promote improved practices. Thus two titles were "Increase Wheat Yields with Improved Seed" and "Rat— An Enemy of Crops". In the reading forum discussions of the material used in the literacy classes were held. Rotating group leaders guided discussion. An action worker was on hand at times to guide discussions and promote adoption of innovations.

Although the six villages differed some, the two receiving treatments of radio forums, the two receiving treatments of literacy training, and the two receiving none of these treatments were in general similar in their important aspects for such an experiment.

In 1967 the radio farm forum treatment villages showed significantly more progress than the literacy and control villages. This was true whether measured by adoption of practices or by other variables. There was some tendency for the literacy villages to score higher than the control villages but usually these differences were not statistically significant . . .

Knowledge of family planning increased markedly form 1964 to 1967. About 80 per cent of the respondents could mention at least one birth control technique which he knew about. Differences in knowledge about family planning *per se* among the three sets of villages in 1967 were not significant but radio villages knew about significantly more methods of family planning than either the literacy or control villages. . . .[63]

The various factors usually found to be significanty and positively correlated with the adoption of improved agricultural practices were in general found to increase more in the radio forum villages than in the others. Although the "literacy villages scored highest on a seven word test of functional literacy. . . [they did not score] significantly higher than radio villages."[64] "An index attempting to measure secular orientation [as discussed above] also disclosed radio villages to have the highest scores but differences were not significant and there were only slight increases in all three sets of villages from 1964 to 1967."[65]

We may close our discussion of this study with the following observations and recommendations by the investigators: "We would advise increased use of radio farm forums where they can be organized to elicit villager participation. Forums should take up only highly relevant and technologically sound practices."[66] We concluded that literacy classes not only do not make a very good vehicle for promoting acceptance of innovations, but that they require a great deal of input for a payoff in increased literacy . . . We do not, of course, condemn or slight literacy training programmes . . . . the villagers themselves indicated [that] literacy programs have high social value . . . . Literacy programs [however] as our experience has shown, are expensive . . . they should be considered either as a long-term investment in development or as social welfare."[67]

SUMMARY AND CONCLUSIONS

1. *Change and awareness of change in village India.* In one of the earliest and largest studies of social change conducted by India's Institute of Community Development, four village influentials in each of 364 villages in India were compared with randomly chosen males and females in the same villages. Because the 1414 influentials were, either as in the case of the president of the village governing body, the village *Pancha-*

yat, elected by popular vote, or determined by sociometric procedures calculated to reflect the values of the people (the most important person, the best farmer and the villager who could help most in getting school or other facility), the comparison of influentials with the randomly selected informants was considered especially important (see Tables I - IV). Whereas three-fourths of the influentials had adopted chemical fertilizer on their farms, less than one-half of the randomly chosen males (N = 3,375) had done so. For the adoption of improved agricultural, health and family planning practices and for the variables related to motivation toward change, the pattern of influentials having the highest score, randomly selected females (N = 2,435) the lowest and randomly selected males in between, held. For instance, 66 per cent of the influentials had adopted typhoid and cholera inoculation, whereas 44 per cent of the randomly chosen females and 51 per cent of the randomly chosen males had adopted it (Table II). Only scales such as the secular-sacred or *Gesellschaft-Gemeinschaft* index influentials fell further toward the secular or *Gesellschaft* pole than did the randomly chosen informants. They had higher caste status, were better educated, had higher empathy scores, were more cosmopolite, had higher incomes, operated more land, etc.

2. *What organizations and instrumentalities produce change?* Following the awareness study in India an effort was made through further intensive investigation to pinpoint leverage points by which change can be introduced. Multlivariant analysis revealed that for all the studies the secular orientation, rationality or what Weber would have called *Vergesellschaftung* was always significantly related to adoption even when the influence of other important factors were partialled out (Tables V and VI). Examples of such important factors, which were closely related to innovation and adoption scores as shown by both zero order and partial correlation coefficients, were such factors as caste rank, credit orientation, educational attainment, extension contact, level of living, mass media contact, size of operation and other influences which, when partialled out, did not negate the importance of secularization. We are left with the impression that those organizations and influences which increase secularization likewise increase change. The apparent importance of this variable led us, in the absence of comparable India data, to explore the relation between education and secularization in Mexico and the United States (See Figures 1-5). This will be discussed briefly below.

If factors are sought by which to predict which villages will stand high on measures of adoption of improved agricultural practices several others emerge from the studies. As may noted from Table V the contact which professionals whose responsibility it is to extend practices to the villagers have with the villages is very important and highly related to adoption of agricultural practices. These agents' choice of procedures for reaching the villagers was important; those using such techniques as demonstration being the most successful. In addition, as may be noted from Table V, secularization of leaders, literacy of males and availability of electricity in the village were important. If one were to use only a half dozen or so predictors in selecting villages which are adopting improved agricultural practices, these mentioned here and as indicated in Table V would be most effective. Other possible factors which could be used in predicting which villages are adopting agricultural practices would be the caste rank of leaders, the proportion of agriculturalists paying at least a 10 rupee tax (the larger the proportion the higher the adoption), the number of labourers per cultivator, the leaders' contact with mass media, the number of electric pumps and oil engines per capita, the number of religious structures, the accessibility of roads, the number of voluntary and marketing organizations, the number of political parties, and a certain amount of reported conflict due perhaps to change. These, of course are not unrelated to those discussed above, For the theme of this paper it is important to note that when influences of village size and affluence (measured by the per cent of families taxed 10 rupees) are partialled out, the proportions of males and females who are literate is significantly related to the agricultural adoption scores of the villages.[68]

From the study of 680 farmers with land operations of $2\frac{1}{2}$ or more acres and under 50 years of age in the 8 villages as noted in Table VI,the multivariant analysis singles out value of agricultural products raised, level of living, secularization, educational aspirations, credit orientation, political knowledge, mass media and extension contact and urban pull as most significant for predicting which farmers will adopt agricultural innovations. As noted in the text of the paper, I believe that the level of living index as constructed for this study masks several factors in change such as caste rank and literacy or educational attainment and these would stand out as important if the influence of this index were not removed.

For the future of rural India, few of the relationships mentioned previously in the paper and revealed in Table V are more important than the influence of size of operation as revealed by "value of agricultural products raised". The high relationship between this variable and scores of informants on agricultural innovations indicates that those who wish for rapid increase in agricultural production may effectively attain this objective by facilitating and strengthening the larger operators. Forces seem to be in motion which will increase the size of alert operators.

3. *The case for organizing future rural trade centre communities about growth centres.* One of the most distressing problems for extension orga-

nizations and political entities in rural India, and a problem which promises to become more acute, arises from the condition that the village is losing many of its important original functions but very generally there are now no effective centres between the village and the huge urban district centres about which community life is organized. If forces are put in motion which further increase agricultural production, the economically strong farmer will become stronger and the weak, weaker. The need for social services may become greater but these cannot be administered without a centre in a place larger than the village and closer than the district centre. Trade, credit, marketing, general servicing, recreation, relief work on roads and electric lines, and other activities should shift to emerging "growing centres", but this shift may not lead to the optimum development unless planned.

In the pages above, the importance of rural electrification as related to the adoption of improvel practices is stressed. Despite the great importance of village electrification it should be noted that "only a little over 11 per cent of India's villages are within 'easy reach' of present transmission lines ...".[69] This and the fact that rural electrificaltion is generally not the most profitable procedure by which 'to sell electric power requires that the allocation of electricity for centres be planned for optimum growth and change. I suggest that every effort be made to put rural electrification fiirst in village and/or town growth and market centres from which it may be fed out to villages in the service area. If, in future, high schools, small hospitals, rural banks, credit and cooperative facilities, centres for agricultural, health and family planning, services and supply stores of all kinds could be focused together in growth centres which would serve from 20,000 to 50,000 people in accordance with planned development, much capital and human wastage common to some past modernization experience might be eliminated. The above review points to the need for more and better credit, marketing, mass media and other services. Perhaps the planned growth-centred-community which should supply these and many other services will be the answer to Karl Marx's condemnation of the Indian village as a "brutalizing worship of nature".

4. *Radio farm forums vs. literacy classes.* Experimentation with radio farm forums and functional literacy classes for adults casts doubt on the practicality of the latter as means of introducing agricultural, health and family planning innovations to villages at least from the short run point of view. As determined by the UNESCO experiment directed by India's National Institute for Community Development, radio forums seem not only to be an appropriate means of speeding up the process of adopting improved practices, but when effectively organized and presented

they appear to be a means whereby factors known to be related to and useful in predicting the extent and nature of adoption of innovations may be changed. Thus, they may increase general knowledge, secularization, empathy etc.

5. *Education as a crucial capital input in the minds of men.* As indicated by Figures 1-5 educational attainment is positively correlated with various indicators of secularization as these were studied in Mexico and the United States. Educational attainment was much more closely related to the depreciation of authoritarianism in the United States than in Mexico. The importance of authority and stratification in promoting change is illustrated by the function of caste rank in India in promoting innovation. Not all traditional features of society oppose change and modernity. The heavy emphasis upon anti-authoritarianism in American schools is evident from Figures 6-8.

The direct approach to an analysis of change and the perception of factors concerning their own orientation is made in Figures 9-13. Education seems important in supporting the desirability of change as a self-perception. Figures 14 and 15 indicate the relationship between educational attainment and attitudes concerning birth control and fluoridation in Mexico and the United Sstates. Figures 16-17 indicate that education in both the United States and Mexico creates a fund of goodwill toward others at home and abroad and a desire to become involved with them. These findings must, of course, be subjected to further analysis to ascertain whether variables other than education are more important in producing these results. Actually, of two variables positively related to scores for both the desire for and the actual linkage of citizens of Mexico and the United States across the mutual border, educational attainment was found to be more closely and positively related than income.

Thus in summary we found from the studies in which we participated and from the available literature that India is modernizing. Influentials chosen for interview because they represent the value system of the villagers are adopting agricultural, health and family planning improvements more rapidly than others. Key organizational problems for India as revealed by the study centre on getting more and better facilities, including fertilizer, electricity and roads, and other practices and stocks, including seeds, to the people, more and better extension services to assist in their use, and more and better educational services of all kinds. In general, the thesis has been that neither India nor any other developing country can delay establishing the educational and other systems required to make men rational, knowledgeable, and committed to the well-being of mankind.

M-23

NOTES

[1] Charles P. Loomis, "Change in Rural India as Related to Social Power and Sex", *Behavioural Sciences and Community Development*, Vol. I, No. 1, March 1961, and *Kurukshetra*, Vol. 15, No. 9, June 1967. These are publications of a paper read before the Rural Sociological Society, 1 September 1966, Miami Beach, Florida. See also a summary statement in the author's presidential address before the American Sociological Association as printed in the *American Sociological Review*, Vol. 32, No. 6, December 1967. For specification of sampling procedures and additional data see Lalit K. Sen and Prodipto Roy, *Awareness of Community Development in Village India*, Hyderabad: National Institute of Community Development, 25 October 1966.

[2] Frederick C. Fliegel, Prodipto Roy, Lalit K. Sen and Joseph E. Kivlin, *Agricultural Innovations in Indian Villages*, Hyderabad: National Institute of Community Development, 1968. The acknowledgements specify that "The research reported here is part of a larger study entitled 'Diffusion of Innovations in Rural Societies', directed by Everett M. Rogers of the Department of Communication, Michigan State University, under contract with the United States Agency for International Development, and has included three countries: Brazil, Nigeria and India." No one reading the interview schedules used in this study and the related one reported in the next footnote will fail to observe the contribution of the previous "Awareness Study", reported in Note 1 above to these later studies.

[3] Prodipto Roy, Frederick C. Fliegel, Joseph E. Kivlin and Lalit K. Sen, *Patterns of Agricultural Diffusion in Rural India*, Hyderabad: National Institute of Community Development, 1968. For an analysis based upon the same field data see Joseph E. Kivlin, *Correlates of Family Planning in Eight Indian Villages*, by the same publisher. The same acknowledgements are appropriate for these two publications as for the publication under Note 2 above.

[4] Charles P. Loomis, Zona K. Loomis and Jeanne E. Gullahorn, *Linkages of Mexico and the United States*, East Lansing, Michigan: Agricultural Experiment Station, Michigan State University, Research Bulletin 14, 1966. (For acknowledgment for financial support and other contributions see footnote page 4.)

[5] *Ibid.*   [6] *Ibid.*

[7] Karl Marx, "The British Rule in India", in Karl Marx and Frederick Engels, *Selected Works*, Moscow: Foreign Languages Publishing House, 1962, pp. 350-51.

[8] See Fliegel, *et al.*, Ch. 2, for the development of the village agricultural adoption index. It included 17 items such as number of improved cattle supplied, or in the village; percentage of cultivators buying improved seed for the cash crop; number of leaders using fertilizer; pesticides; etc.

[9] This index was constructed from the following data: 1. Agricultural extension officers' visits to the village in the last six months, 2. Village level worker's visits to the village in the last six months, 3. Per cent of the VLW's time in the village, 4. Number of demonstrtions in two years.

[10] See Fliegel, *et al.*, p. 38. This index is based upon such items as 1. Leader's visits to block headquarters, 2. Average number of times the leader talked with VLW, BDO and AEO, etc.

[11] The performance index was based upon leaders' answers to questions concerning the work of the VLW, BDO and AEO. *Ibid.*, p. 42.

[12] The number of males who had migrated to the city as a ratio of the size of the village is the basis for this index.

[13] For the construction of this simple index see *ibid.,* p. 49.

[14] *Ibid.*   [15] *Ibid.*

[16] This index relates to the choice the agent made of media. *Ibid.,* p. 48. It is noted that the index "relates positively [to the adoption index] with use of radio, newspapers, demonstrations and meetings as compared to the use of group discussions and farm visits."

[17] *Ibid.,* p. 59. The authors note "the presence or absence of electricity in the village is the most highly related of any variable . . . [considered among the village resources] and its effects is not much altered by control of population size." p. 59.

[18] *Ibid.,* p. 67. This variable along with the number of voluntary organizations (other than political parties) remained signficantly correlated with the agricultural adoption index after influence of population size was partialled out. "Forty-two villages had no formal political party represented, 28 villages (of the 108) had one party only, 30 had two, and eight had three parties represented.

[19] This is a count of groups other than religious and political organizations. "Youth clubs and theatrical groups" are mentioned.

[20] See Roy, *et al., op. cit.,* ch. 2. This index is, of course, differently constructed than that used in the village study. It is based upon the interviews with the 680 farmers in the villages. The basic factor is whether or not the informant had tried such agricultural facilities or practices as the following: inoculation of cattle, insecticides, rat poison, super phosphate, green manure, improved cattle, an improved cultivator, etc. The study was focused on 10 specific practices.

[21] This was obtained by multiplying the quantity of earth product reported by published, actual market price appropriate for each product. *Ibid.,* p. 43.

[22] See Roy, *et al., op. cit.,* p. 67. "Caste ranking were obtained for the analysis by asking knowledgeable respondents in each village to rank photographs of people at work in caste occupations in terms of ritual status for that village." For some Muslims no meaningful caste rankings could be obtained. "Ritual status was defined on the basis of interdining and sharing water. Later, the separate rankings for the eight sample villages were standardized and combined into a single rank order". p. 67.

[23] *Ibid.,* p. 70. Only 25 per cent of the informants were members of any formal organization. Holding office in an organization was found to be significantly correlated with adoption behaviour but membership was not. Therefore, holding office was used as an index.

[24] Deferred gratification was measured by the open-ended question, "Suppose that your cash returns from the farm last year had been twice your actual income, what would you do with the extra money?" The response categories used for scoring from low to high were: 0—family expenses or consumption on food, clothes, furniture, jewelry, repairs or additions to home: 1—social obligations, wedding, birth rite, feast, pilgrimage; 2—pay off debts; 3—save without qualification; 4—purchase or save to purchase land; 5—purchase or save money to purchase agricultural inputs; 6—invest or save money to invest in non-agricultural business; 7—education.

[25] High correlation coefficients signify the relationship between the scores on agricultural adoption and such items as electric pumps per capita ($r = 40$) This correlation and that of presence of oil engines per capita ($r = 23$) retain their statistical significance as does the fact of having electricity in the village even after such other influences as size of the village are partialled out. See Fliegel, *et al., op. cit.,* p. 54.

344   MODERNIZATION OF UNDERDEVELOPED SOCIETIES

[26] *Market Towns and Spatial Development in India,* New Delhi: National Council of Applied Economic Research, 1965.

[27] Roy, *et al., op. cit.,* p. 122. The level of living index was based upon the following items: (1) ownership of good dress, shoes, good jewelry, wrist watch or clock, torchlight, wooden or metal furniture, mosquito nets, and bicycle; (2) houses with brick or stone wall, shuttered windows, bathroom, well, and number of stories; (3) number of rooms in the house. A much longer list was presented. Only items which showed fair distributions were retained. For the presence of each item in (1) and (2) above a score of 1 was given. For (3), a score of 1 was given for each room. The index was a summation of these scores.

[28] *Ibid.,* pp. 105-6, 29.   [29] *Ibid.,* pp. 138-9.

[30] *Ibid.,* p. 139.   [31] *Ibid.,* pp. 115-6.

[32] The distribution for education in the three samples was as follows:

| Level of education | United States | | Mexico |
	General public	Rural Michigan	Urban
None	—	—	19.0
1-4 years	5.0	4.4	40.0
5-8 years	30.1	36.2	30.0
9-12 years	42.5	42.0	8.0
13 years and over	22.3	17.4	2.0
Don't know, no response	.1	—	1.0
TOTAL PERCENT	100.0	100.0	100.0

[33] E.P. Kilpatrick and Hadley Cantril, "Self-anchoring; Scaling; A Measure of Individual's Unique Reality Worlds", *Journal of Individual Psychology,* Vol. 16, No. 2, November 1960.

[34] David Horton Smith and Alex Inkeles, "The OM Scale: A Comparative Socio-Psychological Measure of Individual Modernity", *Sociometry,* Vol. 29, No. 4, December 1966, and Alex Inkeles, "What Makes a Man Modern?" transcription of paper given at Interdepartmental Symposium on "Problems of Cross-Cultural Research in Developing Areas", at Michigan State University, 25-26 May 1967. Also see Melvin M. Tumin, *Social Class and Social Change in Puerto Rico,* Princeton, New Jersey: Princeton University Press, 1961, p. 248.

[35] Daniel Lerner, *The Passing of Traditional Society,* New York: The Free Press of Glencoe 1958.

[36] Roy, *et al., op. cit.,* p. 135.

[37] Fliegel, *et al.,* p. 77. The secular orientation score is highly related to caste rank for the leader of the 108 villages studied (r = 49). *Ibid.,* p. 78. Nevertheless when the influence of caste rank in partialled out in a study of the relation between secular orientation of leaders and the village adoption score the latter relationship remained statistically significant (r = .33) *Ibid.,* p. 77.

[38] *Ibid.*

[39] Fliegel, *et al., Ibid.,* p. 78.

[40] Roy, *et al.,* p. 67.

[41] Charles P. Loomis, *op. cit., American Sociological Review.* See also "Systemic Linkage of El Cerrito", *Rural Sociology,* Vol. 24, No. 1, 1959, and "Tentative Types

Directed Social Change Involving Systemic Linkage", *Rural Sociology*, Vol. 24, No. 2, 1959.

41* Unpublished data by Lalit K. Sen.

41** Roy, *et al., op. cit.*, p. 13.

42 T. W. Schultz, "Investment in Education", in A. H. Halsey, Jean Floud, and C. Arnold Anderson, eds., *Education, Economy and Society,* New York: The Free Press of Glencoe, Inc., 1961, pp. 55ff; and T. W. Schultz, *The Economic Value of Education,* New York: Colombia University Press, 1963.

43 Arnold S. Feldman and Wilbert E. Moore summarized the matter as follows: "The *economic* function of mobility in a labor market is the facilitation of 'correct' or 'optimum' occupational placement relative to given states of capital, technology, and organization." See their book, *Labor Commitment and Social Change in Developing Areas,* New York: Social Science Research Council, 1960, p. 46.

44 Howard Schuman, Alex Inkeles and David H. Smith, "Some Social Psychological Effects and Non-effects of Literacy in a New Nation", *Economic Development and Cultural Change,* Vol. 16, No. 1, 1967.

45 Joseph E. Kivlin, *op. cit.*

46 *Ibid.*   47 *Ibid.*

48 Joseph A. Kahl, "Modern Values and Fertility Ideals in Brazil and Mexico", *The Journal of Social Issues,* Vol. 23, No. 4, October 1967.

49 Loomis, Loomis and Gullahorn, *op cit.*

49* The proportions in the US, RM and UM samples reporting cross-the-border friends were respectively as follows: 18.7, 19.5 and 15.8. Educational attainment was significantly related statistically to reporting such friends for the US and UM samples. The more education the more friends were reported for these two samples.

49** Charles P. Loomis and Prodipto Roy, "the Place of India in the Minds of the Peoples of Mexico and the United States of America", *Monthly Commentary on Indian Economic Conditions,* Vol. 6, No. 6, January 1965. See also, Loomis, Loomis and Gullahorn, *op. cit.*, p. 35.

50 William F. Whyte, "The Cultural Environment and Industrial Relations: The case of Peru". Paper prepared for the New York State School of Industrial and Labor Relations Symposium, 1962.

51 Charles P. Loomis and Zona K. Loomis, "Rural Sociology", Ch. 24 in Paul F. Lazarsfeld, William H. Sewell and Harold L. Wilensky eds., *Uses of Sociology,* New York: Basic Books, Inc., 1967.

52 Harald A. Pederson and Linwood L. Hodgdon, personal correspondence. Edgar A. Schuler was also influential in the development in Pakistan. See his early contributions to the *Journal of Pakistan Academy of Village Development.*

53 Douglas Ensminger has been the Ford Foundation's Representative in India since the inception of its programme there in the early 1950's. The short presentation of its current agricultural programme is based on *The Ford Foundation and Agricultural Development in India,* New Delhi: The Ford Foundation, March, 1965. See also Carl Taylor, Douglas Ensminger, Helen Wheeler Johnson, and Jean Joyce, *India's Roots of Democracy* (Bombay: Orient Longmans, 1965).

54 *Ibid.*, p.9.   55 *Ibid.*, p. 12.

56 Loomis and Loomis, *op. cit.*

57 Gunnar Myrdal, *Asian Drama,* New York: Twentieth Century Fund, 1968.

[58] Joseph E. Kivlin, Prodipto Roy, Fredrick C. Fliegel and Lalit K. Sen, *Communication in India: Experiments in Introduction Change*, Hyderabad, National Institute of Community Development.

[59] Prodipto Roy, *The Impact of Communications on Rural Development in India*, Hyderabad: National Institute of Community Development, 1968. Note also: Joseph E. Kivlin, *et al., Ibid.*

[60] *Ibid.*, MS p. 4.   [61] *Ibid.*, pp. 5-6   [62] *Ibid.*, p. 7

[63] *Ibid.*, p. 42.   [64] *Ibid.*   [65] *Ibid.*   [66] *Ibid.*   [67] *Ibid.*

[68] Fliegel, *et al., op. cit.*, pp. 54ff.

[69] National Council of Applied Economic Research, New Delhi, *Market Towns and Spatial Development in India*, p. 126.

14

DEVELOPMENT OF SOCIOLOGY IN "DEVELOPING SOCIETIES": SOME OBSERVATIONS (WITH SPECIAL REFERENCE TO INDIA)

RAMKRISHNA MUKHERJEE

I

OUR UNDERSTANDING *of social change* is usually based on the following premises:

(1) An "alteration" observed in a society refers to a societal arrangement which may be economic, technological, demographic, political, cultural, psychological, and so on in character.

(2) An alteration in a societal arrangement will alter a corresponding behaviour pattern of the people, and this will take the form of emergence, revision, or disappearance of the social category identified in the given context.

(3) The altered behaviour pattern will have repercussions on other behaviour patterns, and will ultimately lead to the emergence of those social groups which would represent symbiotically the altered economic, ideological, political, cultural, and other patterns.

(4) The emergence of social groups, representing the new and altered behaviour patterns, will replace the previously existing groupings and, thus, social transformation will take place.

347

As I have discussed elsewhere (Mukherjee 1968: 31-55), these premises are relevant to the evaluation of social change but they are not precise enough to permit us to appreciate the phenomenon unequivocally and comprehensively. Fallacies occur with reference to each of these premises. With reference to premise 1, fallacies are seen to occur in two ways mainly: (1) the imputation of any alteration from the given fact may be wrong, and (2) the observed alteration may not refer to the societal arrangement it is imputed to refer to. The first is concerned with social research *per se,* viz. the evolution of appropriate techniques and methods to study any societal phenomenon.[1] This sort of fallacy, therefore, we need not discuss in exclusive reference to the "developing societies". The second kind of fallacy, however, has a distinct relevance to our discussion.

For example, the number of radios per 1,000 population in a nation-state has been used as one of the "political and social indicators" in an authoritative publication (Russet *et al* 1964: 120-25). The obvious assumption is that an increase in the number of radio listeners in a society indicates alteration in its "value arrangement" relating to the social, political, and economic orientation of the people. It is known, on the one hand, that an alteration has taken place in the number of radio listeners and, on the other, that the transmitting authorities have the communication of a particular set of values as one of their major objectives, and that for this purpose they transmit (in between the music and drama programmes) various kinds of "talks" and other special programmes designed for factory workers, peasants, students, women, etc. The validity of this assumption, however, is seriously questioned for the "developing societies" since the listeners in many of these nation-states usually avoid the special radio programmes, as it has been found for India (Mukherjee 1968: 44-45).

In a "developed" society, on the other hand, the above assumption may be valid, as in the USA (NORC 1948: 123-24). For the members of a "developed" society make use of their radio sets more frequently for newscast or special programmes than for the regular music and drama sessions, since they have access to more effective aids for the latter (e.g., TV, tape-recorder, etc.) and a large number of them can also afford to

---

[1] For example, what should be comparable points of reference to ascertain inter-generational occupational mobility? Why is a correlation analysis between family types and fertility rates often proved to be fallacious? How can we appraise a course of nuclearization of joint family structures since the increasing incidence, over time, of nuclear to joint family structures in a society may be due to a fission of joint structures or change in the demographic profile of the people with reference to their age of effective marriage, fertility pattern, expectation of life, etc.? (See, for details, Mukherjee 1968: 45-46, 48-50; 1969b: 49-73)

visit movies, theatres, concerts, etc., regularly (see, for example, NORC 1948: 126; BBC 1959: 6ff; NHK 1969: 10-14).

The example suggests that the indicators of social change, formulated in one particular social context, cannot automatically attain a universal validity: a point which has also been illustrated by Professor Alatas from instances in the life and living in Southern Asia (Alatas 1969). Obviously, the indicators will have to be formulated with specific reference to the place, the time, and the object of change: the three dimensions of variation which must be taken into account to appreciate a phenomenon, as expressed in Indian logic under the phrase *sthāna-kāla-pātra*. Afterwards, the indicators obtained from various nation-states may be systematized in a global perspective, which cannot be equated beforehand to the situation in one or a few "developed" nation-states.

Later, we shall have the occasion to discuss further the pernicious effect of the wilful or unconscious *imposition* of any meaning to social change and development in the "developing societies". To continue presently with the aforesaid four premises of social change, the following major fallacy is associated with premise 2: the observed alteration may have a bearing upon a societal arrangement but it does not necessarily alter the corresponding behaviour pattern of people, and this for one of two reasons: (1) the alteration observed is casual or transitory, and (2) although the alteration in the given societal arrangement is lasting, it either does not alter peoples' behaviour pattern or the results are inconsequential.

The relevance of this fallacy is now fairly obvious with reference to changes in the material culture of a people. Changes to this effect, therefore, are not generally assumed to indicate social change *per se* (as distinct from societal change of any kind) but as having a contingent role to play in the process. The point has to be discussed, however, with regard to the emergence of "value differentials" in the society, which are often considered to reflect alterations in the value system of a people as they are registered in the structure, function, and process of the people's behaviour patterns. The assumption is fallacious; also to consider "value differentials" as representing the incubative phase in the course of social change is conjectural.

Obviously, there are four possibilities in reference to (a) the emergence of "value differential" in a society, and (b) the corresponding change in the behaviour pattern of the people. These are: (1) the score on both counts is negative, (2) the score on (a) is positive but on (b) negative, (3) the score on (a) is negative but on (b) positive, and (4) the score on both counts is positive.[2] The first possibility is irrelevant to the present

----

[2] There is also the point that the imputation of "value differentials" from the given fact may be wrong because: (1) the informants may not have crystalized

discussion. The fourth possibility assigns an explanatory, and not a diagnostic, role to the emergence of "value differentials" in a society vis-a-vis changes in the behaviour patterns, since the changes are no longer anticipated but have already taken place. As we shall discuss latter, this possibility, therefore, is relevant to a historically accomplished phenomenon; viz. when a course of social change, as laid down by the four premises stated at the beginning of this discussion, has taken place. In terms of an ongoing process of social change, on the other hand, only the second and the third possibility are relevant, but they denote an indeterminate situation. India abounds in examples to substantiate this point and draw the following conclusions (Mukherjee 1968: 34-36, 46):

(1) The inference regarding the emergence of "value differentials" in society may be valid, but the alterations are of only casual relevance to changes in the corresponding behaviour patterns of the people. For example, although the informants may state a preference for an alteration at one moment (e.g., to break caste taboos), the stated preference is no longer indicated at the time for the translation of the "value arrangement" into practice (see, in reference to the caste taboo on commensality, Karve and Ranadive 1965: 224-25, 228-29, 278-79).

(2) "Value differentials" may be durably established in regard to some aspects of the society, but they may not alter the corresponding behaviour patterns of the people. For example, the emergence of certain "value differentials" is seen to have led to the legal sanctioning of a behaviour which was previously prohibited (such as, the passing of the Widow Remarriage Act of 1856), but even a century later this lasting alteration in the societal arrangement did not lead to a frequent practice of the hitherto prohibited behaviour pattern (Gopalaswami 1953: 76).

(3) "Value differentials" may not have been forceful enough to make a lasting alteration in the relevant societal arrangement by means of a legal sanction (such as, the failure to pass a law in British India against the practice of polygamy), but the corresponding behaviour pattern may have undergone extreme alteration (as in the case of polygamy, possibly because of the continually growing economic difficulty of maintaining more than one wife).

Findings of this sort are *sui generis* to a "developing society" since

opinions or attitudes on the subject under reference but are obliged to furnish *some* information, or (2) they may be able to guess and supply the "desirable" answers without actually subscribing to their professed views on the way of life, family, marriage, caste, religion, etc. (see, for some details, Mukherjee 1968: 34-35; 46). Either way, this is a problem for social research *per se*, as noted for a corresponding situation with reference to premise 1. We need not, therefore, discuss it in exclusive reference to the "developing societies".

(a) the opinion, attitude, idea, and the belief of the people are in a state of flux, and (b) causality in social change works in more ways than can be comprehensively assumed or anticipated in the current state of our knowledge. With reference to many aspects in their life and living, the people learn in one way at home and in another way through formal education; and, then, realities may compel them to think in a third way when they grow up, and act in a fourth way. In the contemporary perspective, therefore, we are not in a position to draw an invariant relation between the emergence of "value differentials" in a society and the *anticipated* change in the behaviour pattern of the people. Consequently, the "value differentials" will denote their usefulness as contingent facts in the evaluation of social change, and they should be taken note of on that merit alone. The implication is untenable that they represent *ipso facto* a causal or a concomitant role in the ongoing process. Yet this is how social change is not infrequently anticipated for the "developing societies", which places sociology in the realm of conjecture and speculation.

The speculative character of the study of social change in the "developing societies" is brought out more forcefully with reference to two major fallacies associated with the last two of the four premises mentioned at the beginning of this discussion. They refer to the following contingencies (for details, see Mukherjee 1968: 36-41,46-50):

(1) Even though alteration in one behaviour pattern will begin a chain reaction, it is not justifiable to assume that alterations in certain other *specified* behaviour patterns will inevitably follow; or, even if alterations take place in some or all the specified behaviour patterns, they may not register change in the expected manner.

(2) An altered behaviour pattern, or a set of altered behaviour patterns, is not necessarily a replacement of the previous behaviour patterns in the society. So that, *social accumulation,* instead of *successive replacement,* may be the essential character of the changes taking place in a society.

Both the fallacies are operative in India. The current course of industrial and rural development, and urbanization and spread of education, has certainly initiated a chain reaction in the society with reference to the newly emerged behaviour patterns. The chain, however, does not invariably follow the expected course or culminate in the anticipated target of social change. For example, it has not destroyed the joint family or the caste system, which industrialization and urbanization, in particular, were supposed to do. There is also no evidence to indicate that social change in these respects will take place in the near future. Even so, the disappearance of the joint family and the caste system has been repeatedly anticipated with certain drastic alterations in the societal arrangements such as: (1) the introduction of railways and machinery by the British since the middle of the nineteenth century; (2) the enforcement of the Caste Disabilities Removal Act XXI of 1850, and additional rules and regulations to this effect later; (3) the proclamation of Queen Victoria in 1858 that Indians "of whatever race or creed, be freely and impartially admitted to offices in our services, the duties of which they may be qualified, by their education, ability, and integrity, duly to discharge"; (4) the rapid spread of English education and Western liberal and scientific ideas since the middle of the nineteenth century; (5) the noticeable formation of a class of English-educated Indians, from about the end of the last century, with progressive and, in some cases, revolutionary ideas; (6) the disintegration of the subsistence economy in rural areas since about the beginning of the present century; (7) the growth of the Indian working class since the First World War; (8) the development of mass political movements since the 1920's (9) the measures taken to develop India since 1947; and so on.

If we look into the social history of India we find that it is characterized by an assortment of different behaviour patterns, by their accumulation, adjustments and compromise, and not always by their successive replacement (Kapp 1963: 30-40; Mukherjee 1957: 59ff; 1958: 140ff; 1961: 157-67; 1965: 15-58, 185-213; 1969b). Changes are, no doubt, taking place in the society, but they do not necessarily destroy the existing social systems; at any rate, the governing ones. For exmple, what has happened, and is happening, with regard to the joint family and the caste system is that change takes place within the systems and this results in the emergence of various forms of joint family structures, many new *jātis* (caste-units); and wtihin and between all these variants of family and caste structure, the newly emerged behaviour patterns are adjusted with those existing from earlier times.

This characteristic of "unity in diversity" is possibly strongly underlined for India, since it bears a continued history over two thousand years. Similarities in this respect, however, are not unlikely in some other "developing societies"; as for example, in Indonesia (Wertheim 1956: 1ff). Also, possibly because of their course of conditional changes in a colonial or semi-colonial atmosphere in the recent past the above four fallacies referring to sequential alteration and replacement of specified behaviour patterns are found applicable to virtually all "developing societies". A simple *sequential model of social change*, therefore, is inadequate for these societies when the phenomenon is studied in the contemporary perspective.

II

The model may be found ineffective for the contemporary analysis of social change in the "developed" societies also; while, for all kinds of society, it may be appropriate for the study of social change in a historical perspective. In that case, change is a *matter of deduction* after it has taken place and new social formations have replaced the corresponding previous formations.[3] Within such a frame of reference, a set of indicators of social change may be formulated deductively; "value differentials" in a society may be treated as causal or concomitant facts to explain change in the value system of the people and, subsequently, in their behaviour pattern; and a sequential relation may be drawn up among the new and old behaviour patterns according to the schema of eventual replacement of the latter patterns by the former.

If, however, social change is invariably regarded as a matter of deduction and any alteration in any behaviour pattern (as a consequence of any alteration in any societal arrangement) is considered as evidence of "social change", then the concept loses its analytical relevance for diagnostic investigations in the contemporary perspective. It will merely substantiate the obvious fact that any society, at a given point of time, is in a state of *dynamic equilibrium* and alterations are inevitably effected in a social organism. It is necessary, therefore, to distinguish between studies of social change from the *historical or the contemporary* perspective and as an *explanatory or a diagnostic* proposition. In the latter event, the fallacies we have discussed attain a crucial importance while, for the former, the four premises of social change may be considered in a straightforward sequence.

This distinction is particulaly relevant to the investigation of social change in the "developing societies" because the perspective is contemporary and the attempt is diagnostic. For our purpose, therefore, a deductive approach to the investigation of social change is inappropriate; and, correspondingly, the theories of social change, evolved out of this approach, would be inadequate. It would also be fallacious to employ any other theory deductively. Possibly because we do not pay serious

[3] For example: (a) the former social structure of India, which was based on the four *varnas,* was replaced, at one stage of her history, by a matrix of an inceasingly large number of *jatis;* (b) the emergence of the Bahima aristocracy and Bahera serfs replaced the previous social relations of the Bahimas and the Baheras when the kingdom of Ankole came. into being in Africa in the pre-British days; (c) the majority of the peoples in Uganda had passed beyond the tribal stage and were in the feudal stage of historical development (with tendencies among the Baganda and some other people towards further change) when the British occupied their territory; and so on. (See, for details, Oldenberg 1897: 267-90; Oberg 1950: 121-62; Mukherjee 1956: 46-101).

attention to these two points, we are not consistently aware of the fall-acies involved in a simple sequential analysis of social change.

The theories of social change have mostly been evolved out of the historical experience in the "developed" societies, in an attempt to explain how the West European societies have undergone change since the European renaissance and how the spill over of the social forces in the New World led to the development of the North American societies. A few painstaking theoreticians endeavoured to prove the general validity of their theories by applying their respective models of social change to other societies. The most rigorous of them have also pursued an inductive course of validation of their theories. However, with reference to the contemporary situation in the "developing societies", we are still in the position exemplified by the Indian fable of seven blind men and the elephant. Under the circumstances, the deductive application of any change (which may be attempted covertly or overtly) will not be useful.

To be sure, the "developing societies" are not respectively unique. Social science has progressed far enough to preclude a discussion like that which Lenin and Plekhnov had to undertake with reference to Mikhailovsky's and Danielson's unique characterization of the Russian society (Lenin 1894, 1899; Plekhanov 1895). Each of the "developing societies", however, will exhibit some specific characteristics of its own, while the categorization of these societies as different from the "developed" societies may denote certain characteristics of particularity. Universality in the development of sociology, therefore, will not be attained by a-contextual and imitative application of any theory to these societies. Instead, empirical research on the mechanics of these societies (viz. the *what, how*, and *why* of their statics and dynamics) will lead us to this goal.

In this venture, social research in the "developing societies" can make profitable use of the current theories of social change provided they are not upheld *ipso facto* but are employed to formulate hypotheses for testing in the fields of variation duly specified by their place, time, and object dimensions. For example, to maximize the contended difference among the theories prevailing today, hypotheses may be formulated in the light of the Marxian and the Weberian concepts of social dynamics, and these hypotheses may be tested in the same field of variation. Pursuantly, the pocedure for testing the hypotheses will follow from an inductive-inferential course of research based on the logic of probability. This is a long-drawn process, but there is no short-cut to success, however brilliant the short-cuts may appear for a short while.

In order to draw objective and unambiguous generalizations from this approach, we require a commonly agreed frame of reference which locates a set of hierarchically structured units of observation, analysis and inference. The constitution of the frame will improve along with the course of research, as we learn successively from the limitations of the earlier undertakings. To begin with, however, the smallest of the relevant units of observation and analysis may be given by Max Weber's concept of *social action*: "Action is social in so far as, by virtue of the subjective meaning attached to it by the acting individual (or individuals), *it takes account of the behaviour of others and is thereby oriented in its course*" (Weber 1947: 80. Emphasis added).

To the anti-Weberians this ultimate point of reference may appear to be subjectivistic and equivocal. However, Marx also stated: "Social activity and social mind by no means exist *only* in the form of activity or mind which is *manifestly social*" (Bottomore and Rubel 1963: 91). Moreover, we are not concerned with actions at random. As Homans said very aptly: "It is hard to believe that social scientists could have worked out many generalizations about the behaviour of men in groups, if there had been no persistences in this behaviour" (Homans 1950: 311). For our purpose, therefore, individual actions must be affiliated to one or another set of mutually distinct but analogous social actions, and this set will characterize a specific *behaviour pattern*. On this premise also we may muster a general agreement; for, as Marx said: "What is society, whatever its form may be? The product of men's reciprocal action" (Marx 1846).

Proceeding on this basis, we may consider a set of mutually distinct but analogous behaviour patterns to denote a specific *social relationship*. Here, again, we may muster agreement among different ideologies and orientations towards social research. For example, Weber wrote:

The term "social relationship" will be used to denote the behaviour of a plurality of actors in so far as, in its meaingful content, the action of each takes account of that of the others and is oriented in these terms. The social relationship thus *consists* entirely and exclusively in the existence of a probability that there will be, in some meaningfully understandable sense, a course of social action. (Weber 1947: 107)

Marx had stated, correspondingly:

The production of life, both of one's own in labour and of fresh life in procreation, now appears as a double relationship: on the one hand as a natural, on the other as a social relationship. By social we understand the co-operation of several individuals, no matter under what conditions, in what manner and to what end. (Marx 1942: 18)

Following therefrom, a set of mutually distinct but analogous social relationships will denote in *institution* which comprises specifically patterned actions and relationships in reference to what Malinowski characterized as an "organized, powerful system of human effort and achievement" (Malinowski 1944: 51). Defined in this manner the concept of institution will conform to an agreed characterization of this phenomenon among social scientists and, thus, register a relevant landmark in the hierarchically structured configuration of units to constitute the required frame of reference; as employed, for instance, by Marx and Weber (see, for some relevant comments, Gerth and Mills 1958: 65-66).

Next, the particular characteristics of a set of mutually distinct but analogous institutions will refer to a specific *social group;* and a set of these mutually distinct but analogous social groups will define a society bounded by its three dimensions of identification in place, time, and object.

The tiers of social actions, behaviour patterns, social relationships, institutions, and social groups will, thus, express the mechanics of any society. The content of these hierarchically structured units, and their interrelationships may be differently emphasized by the persons concerned according to their ideological orientation, terms of reference to social research, and methodology. It has been argued, for instance, that Weber was "polemical against ... the Marxist use of objective meanings of social action irrespective of awareness of the actor" (Gerth and Mills 1958: 58). It is true that Marx was primarily interested in the social relations of production (Marx 1859). The institutions may be examined in the sociological sense or, restrictedly, in the juridical sense by different pesons or by the same person in different contexts of research (see, for Weber's comment on this point, Rheinstein 1954: 157-58). The social groups, as identified in the present context, may be regarded as one of the many empirical possibilities to identify groupings in a society. These variations, however, are either subsequent or external to the proposed unit-characterization of the sociological phenomena of social action, behaviour pattern, social relationship, institution, and social group. Also the hierarchical structuring of these units of observation, analysis and inference is not affected by any differential emphasis put on their contents. These tiers, therefore, may represent the frame of reference required to specify a field of variation in an objective and accountable manner, and irrespective of any intrinsic evaluation of the current theories of social change.

The field may compromise one or more than one society, provided they are identified in terms of their place, time and object dimensions; so that the constitution of the field will remain flexible in theory and unconstrained in practice, while the appraisal of social change will be based upon the relations drawn unrestrictedly from among the ascertained characteristics of social actions, behaviour patterns, social relationships, institutions, and social groups, depending on which one of them deserves priority of attention; what their respective roles in social dynamics are; which one of them is therefore, *relevant, necessary,* or *sufficient* to evaluate social change in the given society.

For this course of research the field will be conceived as comprising, theoretically, infinite but enumerable varieties of social actions, and the *null hypothesis* will be that no change takes place in their respect. The inductive-inferential approach can, then, be pursued the most effectively. For, in practice, all the social actions in the given field cannot be brought under examination. *Alternate hypotheses,* proposed in the light of current theories and our *a priori* knowledge of the society under reference, will, therefore, focus our attention on particular sets of social action. So that, over a time-series projected from, say, t_n to t_k, we may examine the cause and the characteristics of variation in the social actions from their individual operation—and through their impact on behaviour patterns, social relationships, institutions, and operation of social groups—to the configuration of the total field = the society or the societies under reference.

The test of the hypotheses will require a research design which is based on the concept of statistical probability and which is conducive to multivariate analysis of the quantitative and/or qualitative data, as found appropriate and available (cf. Mukherjee and Bandyopadhyay 1964: 259-82). Thus the course of objective and unambiguous testing of the hypotheses will indicate the usefulness of taking particular sets of social action into account and suggest, further, the necessity of considering others from the total field of variation. The content of the field, therefore, will not suffer from subjective constraints and will yield ever more precise and comprehensive information on social change, as the course of research is successively improved and enlarged.

In this context, the distinction drawn between change by replacement and casual fluctuations around a central tendency becomes relevant to any research undertaking, for: (a) the casual fluctuations lead to what has been described as social accumulaion, and (b) when a course of accumulation reaches a critical point, without sequential transformation, the result is frustration, chaos, imbalance, and disorganization, as exemplified in some ways or other in virtually all "developing societies" today.

In order to be comprehensive in this respect, we should take into account three modes of social change, which with reference to two mutually distinct but analogous social actions, behaviour patterns, etc., may be posed as follows: (1) x is removed from the social scene by force, with or without x' being deliberately introduced in its place; (2) x disappears without replacement or is replaced by x' in a situation which is not deliberately induced and achieved; and (3) x survives with x' by accumulation in a situation which may or may not have been delibe-

M-24

rately induced. The first and the second possibility refer to a historically accomplished phenomenon; the only difference between them is that for the former we merely *state* the resultant change, and for the latter we *deduce* it from empirical investigation. The third possibility, on the other hand, is the one in which we are primarily concerned with; and, in this case, change becomes a *matter of inference* to be drawn on a probability basis. For, that which could be considered as "change" over the time period $(t_1...t_i)$ could also be considered causal fluctuations around the behaviour pattern over the time period $(t_1 ... t_i ... t_n)$. Correspondingly, the inference of change over the time period $(t_{(n+1)} ... t_r)$ may be superseed by the inference of casual fluctuations over the time period $(t_1... t_i... t_{(n+1)})$, in which the nature and degree of fluctuations may have varied among themselves over the total time period.

A suitable example to this effect is the previously mentioned recurrent inference drawn on the disintegration and disappearance of the caste system in India under a broad categorization of the temporal points as, say: $t_1 =$ the onset of the Bhakti movement in about the twelfth century; $t_i =$ the final phase of development of the movement in about the seventeenth century; $t_i =$ the eighteenth and the first phase of the nine-teenth century; $t_{(n+1)} =$ the second half of the nineteenth century; and $t_r =$ 1947 to the present (see, for details, Mukherjee 1958: 182-91, 313-28, 423-29). Such a situation calls for empirical investigations on the basis of "no change" as the null hypotheses formulated in light of our *a priori* knowledge on the phenomenon and the prevailing theories on the origin, development, and persistence of the caste system in the society.

The formulation of alternate hypotheses in reference to the prevailing theories on a societal phenomenon may not be a simple task since there may be a general agreement among the contending viewpoints on the constituents of the phenomenon. In that case, difference may be noticed in the allocation of relative importance to the various factors producing and sustaining the phenomenon in the society or in the assumption of varying intensity of their regression upon one another. It is necessary to underline this point because, more often than not, social research on the "developing societies" is pursued on the basis of sweeping generalizations on one or another theory or a deductive selection of a particular course of argument in any of them. What is required, instead, is a content analysis of the writings, which record the development of respective theories, as a prelude to the formulation of the alternate hypotheses. This is a painstaking and time-consuming task, but it should be an obligatory part of social research if the development of sociology is not to be distorted by dogmatic adherence to any particular theory, dissipated by the so-called "open minded" and "hit and run" method of empirical research, or rendered futile by imaginary or sterile polemics.

For example, both Marx and Weber were of the opinion that the caste system of India formed a syndrome of economic, social and ideological factors (cf. Marx 1853a; 1949: I, 350-52; Weber 1958: 101-33). The difference between Marx and Weber in this context, therefore, may be obtained in their attribution of decisive importance to one or the other factor in the origin, development, and persistence of the societal phenomenon. Thus, to quote a few of their significant statements in this respect:

Marx: The primitive forms of property necessarily dissolve into the relation of property to the different objective elements conditioning production; they are the economic basis of different forms of community, and in turn presuppose specific forms of community. These forms are significantly modified once labour itself is placed among the *objective conditions of production* (as in slavery and serfdom), ... [Where] the particular kind of labour—i.e. its craft mastery and consequently property in the instrument of labour—equals property in the conditions of production, this admittedly excludes slavery and serfdom. However, it may lead to an analogous negative development in the form of a caste system. (Marx 1964: 101-02)

Weber: All factors important for the development of the caste system operated singly elsewhere in the world. Only in India, however, did they operate conjointly under special Indian conditions: the conditions of a conquered territory within ineffable, sharp, "racial" antagonisms made socially visible by skin color. ... [This] well integrated, unique social system could not have originated or at least could not have conquered and lasted without the pervasive and all-powerful influence of the Brahmans. It must have existed as a finished idea long before it conquered even the greater part of North India. The combination of caste legitimacy with *karma* doctrine, thus with the specific Brahmanical theodicy—in its way a stroke of genius—plainly is the construction of rational ethical thought and not the production of any economic "condition". (Weber 1958: 131)

Marx: When the crude form in which the division of labour appears with the Indians and Egyptians calls forth the caste-system in their State and religion, the historian believes that the caste-system is the power which has produced this crude social form. While the French and the English at least hold by the political illusion, which is moderately close to reality, the Germans move in realm of the "pure spirit", and make religious illusion the driving force of history. (Marx 1942:30)

Weber: ... what was decisive for the Hindu caste system in particular was its connection with a belief in transmigration, and especially its connection with the tenet that any possible improvement in one's chances in subsequent incarnations depended on the faithful execution in the present lifetime of the vocation assigned him by virtue of his caste status, ... Among the Hindus, the Biblical emphasis echoed in Luther's injuction, "Remain steadfast in your vocation", was elated into a cardinal religious obligation and was fortified by powerful religious sanctions. (Weber 1965: 42-43)

Marx: We know that the municipal organisation and the economical basis of the village communities has been broken up, but their worst feature, the dissolution of society into stereotyped and disconnected atoms, has suvived their vitality. ... Modern industry, resulting from the railway system will dissolve the hereditary divisions of labour, upon which rest the Indian castes, those decisive impediments to Indian progress and Indian power. (Marx 1853b)

Weber: Modern industrial capitalism, in particular the factory, made its entry into India under the British administration and with direct and strong incentives. But, comparatively speaking, how small is the scale and how great the difficulties. ... So long as the *karma* doctrine was unshaken, revolutionary ideas or progressivism were inconceivable. ... It was impossible to shatter traditionalism, based on caste ritualism anchored in *karma* doctrine, by rationalizing the economy. (Weber 1958: 113-14, 123)

It follows from the issues we have discussed so far that the content and the manner of examination of social change in the contemporary perspective and as a diagnostic proposition are reduced, ultimately, to interpretation and prediction. It need not, however, be conjectural. Hence, to be precise and objective in drawing appropriate inferences, we cannot depend on the four sequential premises enumerated at the beginning of this discussion. We cannot, on the other hand, consider any societal change as social change. In between these two extreme situations, therefore, the following set of questions should provide us with the guidelines to pursue our researches unambiguously and fruitfully:

(1) What is the rationale behind the selection of a set of social actions for observation and analysis; that is, what are the alternate hypotheses put forward against the null hypothesis of "no change", and why?

(2) How have the relations among the selected social actions been drawn to represent particular behaviour patterns, social relationships, ins-

titutions, social groups, and, ultimately, the total field = the society or the societies under reference?

(3) How precise are the parameters to define the *place* and the *project* under reference; and what is the rationale behind the time-series taken into account (e.g., $t_n \ldots t_k \ldots t_j \ldots t_a$), and why?

(4) What is the nature of alterations, over the time-series, in the societal arrangements which have altered one or a set of the specified social actions, behaviour patterns, etc.?

(5) What are the specific characteristics of the altered social actions, behaviour patterns, etc., over the time-series; and how and why have they altered?

(6) What is the chain of alteration effected by the altered social actions, behaviour patterns, etc., over the time-series?

(7) Has that chain been ascertained precisely, unambiguously, and comprehensively at the existing state of our knowledge; and is the design of research amenable to a better appraisal of the chain of alteration in the future along with our ever-accumulating knowledge in this respect?

(8) How and why has the chain of alteration taken a particular configuration over the time-series, and not any other?

(9) What is the likely configuration of this chain of alteration in the immediate future, as can be predicted objectively?

(10) How can we make our predictions increasingly efficient in the light of our continually increasing knowledge on the subject?

III

Let us now examine the concept of social development. While the concept of social change has been in vogue for some years, the concept of social development has been introduced fairly recently to appraise the dynamics of the "developing societies". This is an improvement in research methodology, for the latter was previously submerged in the former and the term "social change" implicitly connoted "social development". Social change was, thus, a value-loaded concept, which hampered its objective evaluation even more than has already been discussed. Social development, however, remains a value-charged concept, having the implication of particular kinds of social change from a particular base and towards an ultimate goal.

Attempts are now being made—significantly by the economists and statisticians—to enumerate the content of social development under subject-categories, like nutrition, shelter, health, education, leisure and recreation, security, and opulence level (Drewnowski 1967: 131-34); or under categories like output and incomes, conditions of production, levels of living, attitudes towards life and work, institutions and policies (Myrdal 1968: III, 1860). These attempts help us to ascertain social development on the basis of precise and objective information (e.g., McGranahan 1969: 1-22) in place of its superficial and esoteric evaluation. They will not, however, make the concept of social development value-free.

The values are imposed by the respective social philosophies of development. This is obvious when the world is dichotomized into the "free" sector and its counterpart, or when a three-fold distinction is drawn among the Western World, the Socialist World, and the Third World. It is also implied when human society is dichotomized as capitalist and communist; trichotomized as monopoly-capitalistic, bourgeois-democratic, may be further indicated by the distinctions drawn within any one of communist; trichotomized as monopoly-considerations" in social development these sectors; for example, by the Russian and the Chinese outlook within the gamut of socialist development. Also, another social philosophy may totally upset the accepted constellation of development indicators for an "affluent" society. For example, the growth of GNP, rise in per capita incomes, increasing levels of investment, industrialization and urbanization, etc., will be of no relevance to the Gandhian outlook of social development.

The concept of a "welfare society" or faith in the overall "humanitarian values" also will not impose an equal "value-load" on all possible courses of social development and, thus, make the concept of social development operationally value-free. Consensus on such a concept or understanding will be obtained only at the level of such generalized truth as "all men are mortal". In effect, on the other hand, differential emphasis on the developmental measures will depend on "value considerations" of politicians, planners, reformers, etc., in a local, regional, or the global perspective, even when they subscribe to a specified kind, and a particular brand, of social philosophy. The "developing societies" furnish, currently, many examples of this kind.

Conceptually as well as operationally, therefore, we cannot consider that social development is value-free. Bendix has attempted to override this problem by distinguishing between a "nominal" and the "real" definition of "development". To quote Bendix:

There is nothing inherently wrong about using the history of Western societies as the basis of what we propose to mean by *development*— as long as the purely nominal character of this definition is understood. The history of industrial societies must certainly be one basis for our definition in this field. Trouble arises only when it is assumed that these are "real" definitions, that development can mean only what it has come to mean in some Western societies. (Bendix 1964: 5-6)

Such an attempt, however, only further substantiates the fact that social development is a value-loaded concept. Therefore, in place of ignoring or by-passing the inherent characteristic of this phenomenon, we should consider the point: how efficiently can we employ the concept of social development to appraise the dynamics of the "developing societies" under the proviso that it is value-loaded.

"Tradition to modernity" is the schema frequently employed nowadays to evaluate social development. This is a useful schema so long as we adhere to its basic connotation that tradition denotes the base of particular kinds of social change and modernity denotes the goal of these changes. Usually, however, we do not specify the contents of "tradition" and "modernity", and consider them to be axiomatic. For example, Deutsch defined "social mobilization" as "an overall process of change, which happens to substantial parts of the population in countries which are moving from traditional to modern ways of life" (Deutsch 1961: 493). We need not discuss the overall fallacy of this approach since it has already been pointed out (Mshvenieradze 1964: III, 33-37). It would, however, be useful to note additionally that the schema stimulates the image in the mind of many social scientists that the "developing societies" of Asia, Africa, Occeania, and South America are "traditional" and the "developed" societies of West Europe and North America are "modern". This dichotomy is implicit, and occasionally explicit, in the writings of several reputable social scientists (e.g., Black 1966: 1-55; Shils 1968: 7-11). Even to countries like the USSR and Japan they may accord a "developed" status only in parenthesis, while China is hardly ever mentioned in this context. The upshot is that the schema loses its objectivity, ignores the inherent dynamism of any society at any time-period, and conforms to a particular course of ideology and action.

Insofar as the concept of modernity is concerned, doubts about the usefulness of equating it to the "social, political, and economic characteristics of Western democracies" have already been expressed (Nettl and Robertson 1968: 42). Equally it is necessary to examine the utility of a blanket characterization of the "developing societies" as traditional, and to specify how the schema of "tradition to modernity" can be employed fruitfully. For, if we treat "tradition" as a value-free concept and as merely referring to that body of social actions, behaviour patterns, social relationships, and institutions of a social group (or of the society *en bloc*), which has been transmitted from the past to the present, then the schema loses its analytical relevance. There is not a single society, at any point of time and space, which has not a tradition behind it. If, on the other hand, "tradition" is regarded *on its own merit* as a value-charged concept, then the hitherto applied dichotomy of tradition and modernity cannot but resurrect the concept of "primitive" and "civilized" which is anathema to "modern" man and is also unreal as representing discrete entities. For the schema, therefore, tradition acquires a meaning only as *subjunctive* to modernity, and as denoted by that body of transmitted facts which is antithetical to the purposively conceived characteristics of modernity.

Viewed in this manner, the tradition (or, more appropriately, the traditionalism) of a society cannot be specified by some innate characteristics like, the lack of achievement orientation, the joint family system, the caste system of India or any ascriptive system in other "developing societies", and so on. Correspondingly, modernity cannot be denoted by certain generalized concepts or attributes like, rationality, nuclear family organization, etc. The procedure may give a wrong characterization of what is transmitted or provide those indicators of modernization which are irrelevant or even harmful to the desired course of social development.

For example, according to the Brahmanical tradition, which has permeated into virtually all sectors of Indian society, all social actions fall under one of the four categories of *dharma* (relating to religious practices), *artha* (relating to wealth and material well-being), *kāma* (relating to the fulfilment of desire), and *mokśa* (relating to ultimate salvation). The evaluation of any social action, however, refers to whether it is a *dharma* action (i.e., righteous) or an *adharma* (i.e., not-*dharma*) action. The category *mokśa*, in this context, consumes all actions. Therefore, the "traditional" social actions categorized as *artha and kāma* but evaluated as *dharma* can be achievement-oriented at any time period, and this possibility is reinforced by the fact that the gamuts of *dharma* actions are immutable. Otherwise we fail to explain instances like that of a Brahmin working even at the production-bench of a shoe factory who does not consider himself to be commiting an *adharma* action, which he would reckon he was doing if he was earning his livelihood as a cobbler.

Thus, the lack of achievement-orientation *per se* is not a characteristic of the so-called Indian tradition, as we are sometimes told in the course of an imitative and a-contextual application of a model of modernization. What we should consider, instead, is whether the "traditional" achievement-orientation in the society is conducive or not to the desired course of social development. Similar situations should be searched in other "developing societies" instead of trying to establish an "achieving society" on a utopain basis.

If we pursue the example of "traditional" social actions in India, we find that the consequence of *dharma* and *adharma* actions is assessable in the future perspective according to the doctrine of *karma* and the theory of reincarnation of souls. Accordingly, contemporary actions are cumulative and the net effect on the presumed next birth is derived by subtracting the total consequence of *adharma* actions from that of *dharma* actions. Causality or concomitance of all these actions is not specific to the place (*sthāna*), time (*kāla*), and *object* (*pātra*). So that, within the "traditional" set-up, certain *adharma* actions can be performed with impunity since they will be expiated by the corresponding performance of suitable *dharma* actions. Rationality, in the contemporary situation, can thus be purposively applied to optimize the relation between ends and means, without moving out of the sphere of "traditional" ideology and action. Possibly, it is only in this or in a similar manner that many apparent incongruities in the "developing societies" can be duly explained: for example, the "anti-social" activities of many "achieving" persons; the contradictory role of the entrepreneurs in their economic versus their ideological life, of the elites in their social versus their political life; and so on. Rationality *per se*, therefore, is not a suitable indicator of any course of modernization.

The assumption that it is the role of the caste system to obstruct the modernization of India, and similar assumptions concerning ascriptive systems in other "developing societies", should also be examined in terms of their actual effect on the programme laid down to attain the particular goal of modernity. Facts like people identifying themselves by caste, rank, or religion, or the political parties making use of the caste, rank, or the religious affiliation of people to gain votes in elections, are inconsequential until we learn how and why that action or behaviour-pattern obstructs a particular course of social development. There is ample evidence to substantiate the fact that the "traditional" modes of identification in many "developing societies" serve as a cloak to cover specific class or economic interest in the contemporary situation (see Mukherjee 1957 for the situation in West Bengal). We also notice, contextually, that political parties with religious or similar appellations are not uncommon in may "developed" societies.

On the other hand the supposition that the joint family system hinders social development and others like it may be irrelevant or have a harmful effect on that very course of development in the given conditions. For example, the frequently found joint family in India is of a 2- or 3-generation lineal structure with the principal or the only provider for the family located at: (1) the topmost generation-level, or (2) at the intermediate level, if the top is represented by the widowed "mother" or aged "parent(s)" (Mukherjee 1969b: 75-97). In both cases, therefore, the maintenance of the joint structure may hinder a course of modernization if (*a*) it is in a position to provide economic and the corresponding opportunities to all able-bodied persons, (b) more than one such person is found in the respective families, and (c) these persons are found to relinquish or undermine the opportunities offered to them in favour of a partial or a fully parasitic existence upon their parent(s)' earnings. These three condition are really met with simultaneously in India or other "developing societies", while the second form of joint family structure denotes that: (a) its maintenance may be an inevitable burden on the nuclear sub-unit since the old people cannot be provided for in any other way, or (b) it is a boon to the working couple since their children can be looked after by the "grandparent(s)" when they are out to earn for the family. Thus the formation of a nuclear family organization is not necessarily an indicator for even the commonly implied goal of modernization. Goode also noted (1963: 2): "Just *how* industrialization or urbanization affects the family system, or how the family system facilitates or hinders these processes, is not clear."

Many more examples can be cited to substantiate the obvious fact that, at the present state of our knowledge of the "developing societies", traditionalism and modernization cannot be indicated by a set of attributes evolved out of an a-contextual theoretical construct. Just as modernity cannot be comprehended in one and the only way, and the traditionalism of a society is predicated by a specific characterization of social development, so the attributes of traditionalism and modernization will have to be formulated for each society from empirical investigations. And, if we accept this aspect of reality, we find that the enforced dichotomy of "developing" and "developed" societies loses its meaning for social research. No society is finally developed, whatever may be the chosen goal of social development. Also, the so-called "developed" societies may choose a different goal of development. Either way, an objectively formulated schema of "tradition to modernity" is applicable to any and all world societies.

A discussion on the relative merits of different goals of social development is beyond our present terms of reference. We may note, however, that appraisal of any course of social development in a society will primarily require answering the following questions:

(1) What is the goal of social development, and why has that goal been chosen?

(2) What is the immediate target of social development; what are the successive targets; and how are they sequentially related?

(3) What are the social actions, behaviour patterns, social relationships, institutions, and social groups necessary for the realization of the successive targets and, eventually, the ultimate goal of social development?

(4) What are the characteristics and intensity of the social actions, etc.,

which are found currently in the society and which are inimical to those formulated for (3) above?

(5) How and why have the social actions, etc., under (4) been transmitted from the past? What are their traditional roots and current viability? And, how can they be replaced by those under (3)?

(6) What is, therefore, the programme of the desired course of development? How can it be communicated to the people, and how can they be motivated to strive for it?

Answers to these questions will provide the basis for an examination of social change in the given society in an induced situation. The questions posed earlier to appreciate social change *per se* will, therefore, follow in order to evaluate the dynamics of the society precisely, unambiguously, and comprehensively.

IV

Pursued in this manner, the development of sociology in each society will have a specificity of its own. It will require an intrinsic knowledge of each society with reference to what it was, what it is, and what it should be: a point which, with reference to India, has been discussed elsewhere in some detail (Mukherjee 1969a). In terms of the prevailing dichotomy, the available experience from the "developed" societies will help us in this pursuit of knowledge in the "developing societies"; but that experience, crystalized in currently available theories, cannot be imposed upon the latter in the search for certain selected traits of change and development, of tradition and modernity. On the contrary, a true grasp of the reality in the latter group of societies will enrich the currently available theories and practice and, thus, lead to the development of world sociology.

Universality of science has not been attained in any discipline without an objective comprehension of its particular manifestations. History tells us that apparently irreconcilable theories and practices have reached synthesis at higher levels of effectiveness and our ever-accumulating knowledge on the analogous systems of variation. The process has been particularly manifest in the last few decades in economic science and technology. A proper development of sociology in the "developing societies", therefore, will be useful not only to the respective societies but also to the world society at large.

REFERENCES

Alatas, Syed Hussein (1969): "The Captive Mind in Development Planning", paper submitted to the 11th World Conference of the Society for International Development, New Delhi, 14-17 November, 1969.

BBC [British Broadcasting Corporation] (1959): *The Public and the Programmes.* London, BBC.

Becker, Howard; Barnes, Harry Elmer (1952): *Social Thought from Lore to Science.* Washington D.C., Harren Press.

Bendix, Reinhard (1964): *Nation-building and Citizenship.* New York, Jom Wiley & Sons Inc.

Black, C. E. (1966): *The Dynamics of Modernization.* New York, Harper and Row.

Bottomore, T. B.; Rubel, Maximilien (1963): *Karl Marx: Selected Writings in Sociology and Social Philosophy.* London, Pelican.

Deutsch, K. W. (1961): "Social Mobilization and Political Development", *American Political Science Review.* 55(3): 493-514.

Drewnowski, Jan (1967): "Some Suggestions for Measuring Social Variables", in: *Social Change and Economic Growth.* Paris, Development Centre of the Organization for Economic Co-operation and Development.

Gerth, H. H.; Mills, C. Wright (Eds.) (1958): *From Max Weber: Essays in Sociology.* New York, Oxford University Press.

Goode, William J. (1963): *World Revolution and Family Patterns.* London, Collier-Macmillan Limited.

Gopalaswamy, R. A. (1953): *Census of India, 1951* I (IA). New Delhi, Government of India Press.

Homans, George C. (1950) *The Human Group.* New York, Harcourt, Brace and Co.

Kapp, K. William (1963): *Hindu Culture, Economic Development and Economic Planning in India.* Bombay, Asia Publishing House.

Karve, I.; Ranadive; J. S. (1965): *The Social Dynamics of a Growing Town and Its Surrounding Area,* Poona, Deccan College.

Lenin, V. I.;
1894: *What "Friends of the People" Are and How They Fight the Social-Democrats.* (English translation). Moscow, Foreign, Languages Publishing House.
1899: *The Development of Capitalism in Russia.* (English translation). Moscow, Foreign Languages Publishing House.

Malinowsky, B. (1944): *A Scientific Theory of Culture and Other Essays.* North Carolina University Press.

Marx, Karl
1846: "Letter to P. V. Annenkov", in: Karl Marx, *The Poverty of Philosophy.* (English translation). Moscow, Foreign Languages Publishing House.
1853a: "British Rule in India", *New York Daily Tribune.* 25 June 1853.
1853b: "The Future Results of British Rule in India", *New York Daily Tribune,* 8 August 1853.
1859: "Preface", *A Contribution to the Critique of Political Economy.* (English translation). Moscow, Foreign Languages Publishing House.
1942: *The German Ideology.* London, Lawrence and Wishart.
1949: *Capital: A Critical Analysis of Capitalist Production.* Vol. I. London, George Allen and Unwin.
1964: *Pre-capitalist Economic Formations.* London, Lawrence and Wishart.

McGranahan, Donald V. (Director) (1969): *Research Notes.* Geneva, United Nations Research Institute for Social Development.

Mshvenieradze, V. V. (1964): "Objective Foundations of the Development of Society:

Critical Study of Some Sociological Theories", *Transactions of the Fifth World Congress of Sociology*. Louvain (Belgium), International Sociological Association, Vol. III. 33-37

Mukherjee, Ramakrishna
1956: *The Problem of Uganda*: A Study in Acculturation. Berlin, Akademie-Verlag.
1957: *The Dynamics of a Rural Society*. Berlin, Akademie-Verlag.
1958: *The Rise and Fall of the East India Company*. Berlin, Verlag der Wissenschaften.
1961: "Caste and Economic Structure in West Bengal in Present Times", in: Saksena, R. N. (ed.). *Sociology, Social Research and Social Problems in India*. Bombay, Asia Publishing House. 157-167.
1965: *The Sociologist and Social Change in India Today*. New Delhi, Prentice-Hall.
1968: "Some Observations on the Diachronic and Synchronic Aspects of Social Change", *Social Science Information*. Paris, 7 (1): 31-55.
1969a: "Empirical Social Research on Contemporary India", *Social Science Information*. Paris, 8 (6);
1969b: *Family in India: A Perspective* (mimeoed). Calcutta, Sociological Research Unit, Indian Statistical Institute.

Mukherjee, Ramkrishna; Bandyopadhyay, Suraj (1964): "Social Research and Mahalanobish's D^2", in: Rao, C. R. (ed.). *Contributions to Statistics*. Calcutta, Statistical Publishing Society; Oxford, Pergamon Press.

Myrdal, Gunnar (1968): *Asian Drama*. London, Allen Lane, The Penguin Press.

NHK [NHK Public Opinion Research Institute] (1969): *Public Opinion Research of NHK*. Tokyo, NHK.

NORC [National Opinion Research Centre] (1948): *Radio Listening in America*. New York, Prentice-Hall.

Nettl, J. P.; Robertson, Roland (1968): *International Systems and the Modernization of Societies*. London, Faber and Faber.

Oberg, K. (1950): "The Kingdom of Ankole in Uganda", in: Fortes, M.; Evans-Pritchard, E. E.; (eds.). *African Political Systems*. London, Oxford University Press.

Odaka, K. (1964): "Traditionalism and Democracy in Japanese Industry", *Transactions of the Fifth World Congress of Sociology*. Louvain (Belgium), International Sociological Association, Vol. III, 39-49.

Oldenberg, H. (1897): "Zur Geschichte des indischen Kastenwesens", *Zeitschrift der Deutschen Morgenländischen Gesollschaft*. 51: 267-90.

Plenkhanov, G. (Beltov, N.) (1895): *The Development of the Monist View of History*. (English translation). Moscow, Foreign Laguages Publishing House.

Rheinstein, Max (ed.) (1954): *Max Weber on Law in Economy and Society*. Cambridge (Massachusetts), Harvard University Press.

Russet, Bruce M.; Alker Jr., Hayward R.; Deutsch, Karl W.; Lasswell, Harold D. (1964): *World Handbook of Political and Social Indicators*. New Haven and London, Yale University Press.

Shils, Edward (1962): *Political Development in the New States*. Mouton and Co. Netherlands.

Weber, Max
1947: *The Theory of Social and Economic Organization*. London, William Hodge & Co.
1958: *The Religion of India*. Glencoe, (Illinois) The Free Press.
1965: *The Sociology of Religion*. London, Methuen and Co.

Wertheim, W. F. (1956): *Indonesian Society in Transition*. The Hague, Bandung, W. van Hoeve Ltd.

15

THE NEW SOUTH: EXEMPLAR
OF HOPE FULFILLED

JOSEPH J. SPENGLER

The South is on the way to a Promised Land.

—RUPERT B. VANCE

THERE ARE many approaches to the study of a nation's economic development, ranging from the historical to the model-based theoretical. Within this set of approaches fall the regional, itself divisible into several sub-types.

Economies progress unevenly much as do nations, though not entirely for the same reasons. Sometimes forces making for convergence are ascendant, and sometimes forces making for divergence. Within the international econmic arena the forces making for divergence have been ascendant ever since the industrial revolution got under way effectively and began to spread selectively. Indirectly, evident of this increasing international differentiation is increase in income disparity. For example, L. J. Zimmerman estimates that the top quartile of the world's population received 57.8 per cent of the world's income in 1860 and 72.1 per cent in 1960.[1] Presumably the circumstance generating the "Matthew Effect"—unto every one that hath shall be given—worked strongly

---

[1] *Poor Lands, Rich Lands: The Widening Gap*, New York, 1965, p. 38.

against those in less favoured situations. The beneficiaries of these circumstances have been the industrial countries where, in 1961, Gross
National Product and national income per capita were 10-11 times as
high as in the non-industrialized countries.[2]

Within countries regional disparity is less persistent. Of this we have
evidence in the United States in 1967 in that average income in New
York, the state with the highest income, was not quite double that in
Mississippi, the state with the lowest average income. Forces making
for convergence, though outweighed at times by forces making for divergence, tend to be more powerful in the longer-run, though not powerful enough to remove all differentials. Interregional migration and interregional flows of physical and human capital, together with enterprise
and management, exercise powerful and equalizing effects. For these
flows are not slowed or interrupted by international boundaries, under-
girded by the apparatus of state and often reinforced by linguistic
differences.

It is my purpose in this paper to review briefly the experience of the
American South, a region usually defined to include those states in
which the institution of slavery persisted until destroyed by the Civil
War of 1861-65. It includes Virginia, the two Carolinas, Georgia, Florida,
Kentucky, Tennessee, Alabama, Mississippi, Louisiana, Arkansas and Texas;
sometimes Oklahoma and/or West Virginia are also included.

HISTORICAL OVERVIEW

The South was originally the product of two complementary forces, the
introduction of Negro slavery from Africa and the emergence of cotton
as a widely demanded staple. When that prescient 26-year-old French
political philosopher, Alexis de Tocqueville, came to the United States
in 1831 and carried on the inquiries that resulted four years later in
his *Democracy in America*, he divined the significance of the then South
for America's future, only to die two years before his forecast was
partly borne out. He pointed out that the "Southern States are almost
exclusively agricultural" whereas the "Northern States are more peculiarly commercial and manufacturing". The South was as interested as the
West and the North in preserving the union of the three regions in one
state, since the South profited from the union even as did others. In
particular the South, containing as it did "an enormous slave population", one "already alarming, and still more formidable for the future",
was "induced to support the Union" not only because of commercial and
related advantages but also in "order to avail" its people of the "protec-

[2] United Nations, *The Growth of World Industry*, New York, 1965, p. 194.

tion" which the Union might afford "against the Blacks". Slavery had
not, therefore, "created interests in the South contrary to those of the
North".

Slavery could, however, threaten the Union. "Society can only exist
when a great number of men consider a great number of things in the
same point of view." This condition slavery might undermine. "The equality of fortunes, and the absence of slavery in the North, plunge the
inhabitants in those same cares of daily life which are disdained by
the white population of the South." In the North "the imagination is
extinguished by the trivial details of life"; prosperity is the sole aim of
exertion", and "little value" is set "upon the pleasures of knowledge".
"The citizen of the South is more given to act upon impulse; he is more
clever, more frank, more generous, more intellectual, and more brillant."
He has "the tastes, the prejudices, the weaknesses, and the magnani-
mity of all aristocracies" whereas the citizen of the North has "the
characteristic good and evil qualities of the middle classes".[3] The adverse effect of difference in manners tended to be accentuated by the
superiority of the North to the South in commerce, manufacture, and
growth of population and wealth, since it resulted in a growing sense
of weakness on the part of the South in relation to the North and thus
weakened their sense of a commonality of interest. America's rapid
growth ought therefore to be viewed "with sorrow and alarm" instead of
"with exultation since it threatened the continuance of the American
Union through withdrawal of the Confederate States if not through a
veakening of the Federal Government.[4]

While the South's future did not unfold precisely as De Tocqueville
anticipated, its unfoldment did not really belie his projection. In particular, it bore out his emphasis upon the role of manners. For nearly
130 years later commentators on the course of economic development
in the South stressed the importance of subjective components of Southern culture. A leading economic theorist and historian writes: "Few
Southerners have yet faced up to the question of whether they want
industrialism badly enough to give up firmly held Southern traditions
which are inconsistent with it."[5] One finds somewhat similar views.
expressed by other students of the modern South.[6]

---

[3] *Democracy in America* (Henry Reeve, trans.), London, 1836, Vol. II, pp. 379-
82, 385-88.

[4] *Ibid.*, pp. 394-98, 401-03.

[5] W. H. Nicholls, *Southern Traditions and Regional Progress*, Chapel Hill, 1960,
p. 155.

[6] E.g., see Rupert B. Vance, "Beyond the Fleshpots", *Virginia Quarterly Review*,
XLI, Spring, 1965, pp. 219-30; papers in *The Graduate Journal of the University
of Texas*, Vol. 3, Supplement. 1960.

The South was not doing badly at the time De Tocqueville was writing. In 1840 per capita income was 60 per cent higher in the West South Central states than in the nation; it was 84 per cent as high in the South Atlantic states as in the nation, and 85 per cent as high in the East South Central states. After the Civil War, which ended in 1865, terminated slavery, and temporarily imposed military occupation upon the South, Southern incomes lagged markedly behind the national average. As late as 1880 per capita income in the West South Central, East South Central, and South Atlantic regions was only 60, 45, and 51 per cent as high as per capita income in the nation. Nor was there improvement in the rest of the century, since in 1900 the corresponding percentages approximated 61, 45, and 49. Thereafter conditions improved relatively, in part as a result of the impact of World War I, and average incomes in the three Southern regions rose to 72, 59, and 52 per cent of the national average, only to be pressed back to 62, 55, and 50 in the decade ending in the Great Depression apparent already in 1930. Recovery setting in during the late 1930's, the averages for the three regions rose to 81, 71, and 61 per cent, respectively, of the nation's average by 1950.[7]

The South's quite good relative position around 1840 was not an absolutely good position. Indeed, per capita income in the United States was barely one-fifth as high (if that) around 1840 as in 1929 when per capita income approximated 857 dollars of 1929 purchasing power.[8] The data suggest that the decline in the relative position of the South after the Civil War was a result of that war. This was not essentially the case, however.

The South was easily distinguishable as a region both on the eve of the Civil War and in the period that followed. Moreover, the culture of some of the states that bordered on the Old South—Maryland, Delaware, Missouri, and later Oklahoma—reflected cultural influences mainly originating in the South. It has long been evident that any historical-analytical account of the economic evolution of the South after the Civil War must focus on its overriding components, the Negro and agriculture, especially cotton culture. The *key* explanatory variable, Anderson points out, is neither the Negro nor cotton culture, but the

[7] See R. A. Easterlin, "Interregional Differences in Per Capita Income, Population and Total Income, 1840-1950", in W. N. Parker, ed., *Trends in the Nineteenth Century*, Princeton, 1960, pp. 85-89, 139-40.

[8] See U. S. Bureau of the Census, *Historical Statistics of the United States, Colonial Times to 1957*, Washington, D. C., 1960, p. F 1-21; Paul A. David, "The Growth of Real Product in the United States Before 1840: New Evidence, Controlled Conjectures", *Journal of Economic History*, XXVII, June, 1967, pp. 151-97.

association of these two.[9] Cotton production was concentrated in the lower and western South on the eve of the Civil War and thereafter spread outward somewhat while becoming more intense within parts of the area cultivated already in 1859.[10] This pattern and movement persisted until World War I. Indeed, the pattern was not much modified by the great exodus of Negroes from the South, which came in the wake of the boll weevil and the cutting off of foreign immigration, first by that war and then by post-war immigrant-restriction legislation. Of course, the Great Depression slowed down the momentum of the movement of the Negro out of the rural South. Even so, in 1930-60, 3,237,000 Negroes and 1,111,000 whites emigrated from the 13-state South; only Florida and Texas gained migrants. Nonetheless, until relatively recently, the rural Negro depended on cotton, and cotton depended on him. Moreover, most Negroes were rural. When one compares a map of cotton production in the South as of 1909 with a map of cotton acreage on farms operated by Negro tenants, the patterns of the two maps are identical. The post-Civil-War croppers and tenants were the descendants of the pre-Civil-War slaves, and their distribution in the rural South did not really begin to be modified greatly until the advent of World War II. As late as 1900 Negroes made up 34.3 per cent of the South's population and 2.4 per cent of the non-South's. In one-fourth of the counties in the eleven most southerly states, Negroes constituted the majority of the population. Yet, by 1950, only a seventh of the counties had a Negro majority, and by 1960, the Negro fraction of the population of the 13-state South had fallen to 21 per cent while that of the non-South had risen to 6.6 per cent. With this decline in the relative number of rural Negroes, the dependence of the Negro on cotton growing contracted, with cotton production becoming more confined within the "core area of pre-1860 dominance". Indeed, the area under cotton has shrunk over half, as a result of government controls, the development of ever-more versatile man-made fibres, the development of cotton production in western-state irrigated areas (California, New Mexico, Arizona), and increase in output per acre. Cotton's relative importance as an agricultural income producer in the South was only two-fifths as high in 1960 as in 1929.

It may be noted parenthetically that the redistribution of the Negro population may have reduced the intensity of racial discrimination. For

[9] C. Arnold Anderson, "Den Amerikanska Södern—En Region I Omvandling", *Svensk Geografisk Arsbok*, Lund, 1955, pp. 199-232. Eleven tables and twelve charts illustrate Anderson's argument.

[10] In his *Human Geography of the South*, Chapel Hill, 1932, C. Arnold Anderson explains why some Southern areas were not planted to cotton. See also S. Bruchey, Ed., *Cotton and the Growth of the American Economy: 1790-1860*, New York, 1967.

as the concentration of the Negro population declines, and the distribution of the Negro population approaches that of the white, the taste for discrimination probably tends to decline. Accomplishing such a distribution of population would have entailed an emigration of 6 million Negroes from the South as late as 1960. Not surprisingly, therefore, discrimination remained intense as late as 1950, in part because about two-thirds of the nation's Negro population still lived in the three Southern divisions. By 1960 this fraction had declined to about three-fifths, with the Negro population constituting about one-fifth of the South's population.

Returning now to the linkage of cotton growing with the distribution of the Negro population, we find that this linkage became a deterrent to economic progress in the period after the Civil War, when average income in the rest of the country began to pull away from that in the South. It was not the South's defeat in the Civil War that was responsible, though this view was held at one time, especially in the South. It was not tenancy, as such, since it is sometimes a rung on the ladder to ownership. It was the South's traditional form of agriculture, one carried out largely by Negroes with little education and skill, and not infrequently, by whites, many of whom were both poor and badly educated. The Negro was subject to subordination and segregation, especially in the rural areas where he lived in the main. There, as Booker T. Washington observed, he pulled many a white man into the ditch with him. Urbanization proceeded slowly, with the result that urban alternatives were limited. As late as 1900, the South remained 82 per cent rural, at nearly the level found in the whole of the U.S. in 1850; even as late as 1930, the South remained 66 per cent rural, or slightly above the national level as of 1890. By 1960, the South was only 42.3 per cent rural compared with 25.6 per cent in the Non-South; but the ratio of the South-Non-South percentages (42.3−25.6=1.65) remained at the 1900 level.

The South after the Civil War thus answered to the description of an underdeveloped country. It was saddled with an underdeveloped rural people, of quite limited education and, in the case of the Negro, with restricted access to occupations in the cities. Indeed, some occupations formerly open to him, such as barbering, became partly closed, around the turn of the century. Rural people could, of course, move to Southern cities, or outside the South, or remain on the farm. In fact, as early as 1880, they were moving outside the South, and from 1880 on continued to do so, especially after 1910. Negroes in particular were moving out of the South, in small numbers before World War I, but in large numbers while that war was in progress and thereafter when the country became largely closed to white immigration from abroad. Even in the depressed 1930's there was a considerable net movement from the South, and in the 1940's, 1950's and 1960's it became very high, largely because of the Negro exodus. So long as this reserve army of underemployed hung over the South's labour market, it was difficult for the wage levels to rise appreciably, since high rural fertility tended in some degree to counterbalance high emigration from the farms and from the South. As a result, low incomes persisted. Moreover, as we shall indicate, incomes still remain low despite the transformation of the Southern economy over the past 40 years, especially since 1940.

These changes have reduced the homogeneity of the South; one may argue that the South no longer is a region, but rather a collection of entities with elements in common. Don Bogue's description of the United States in regional terms brings out this heterogeneity.[11] Southern states do, however, have some things in common, relatively low incomes, relatively heavy Negro population, relatively less population concentration, relatively small-scale agriculture other than in Florida and Texas, and so on. We may, therefore, think of the South as a collection of contiguous states with similar rankings on indicators, probably because positions on these indicators are somewhat intercorrelated.

INCOME SITUATION

Average income has continued to be relatively low in the South, for reasons having their origin in the South's distinct history. Even so, the ratio of Southern to Non-Southern income has risen.[12] Per capita personal income in the South around 1900 was only about 51 per cent as high as that in the nation, but this fraction rose under the impact mainly of World War I to approximately 61 per cent by 1920, only to be depressed to 52.6 per cent by 1930, with the deepening of the Great Depression. Recovery in the later 1930's elevated this fraction to 60.1 per cent by 1940, virtually the 1920 level. Since then the relative condition of the South has continued to improve, with this fraction rising to 75.5 per cent by 1960 and several points since 1960. In sum, while the South's economy

---

[11] See my "Demographic and Economic Change in the South, 1940-1960", in Allan P. Sindler, Ed., *Change in the Contemporary South*, Durham, 1963, pp. 49-52.

[12] For information on the South see C. B. Hoover and B. U. Ratchford, *Economic Resources and Policies of the South*, New York, 1951; James Maddox et al., *The Advancing South*, New York, 1967; Nicholls, *op. cit.*, and his detailed studies there cited; Anthony Tong, *Economc Development in the Southern Piedmont 1800-1950*, Chapel Hill, 1958; Rupert Vance, *All These People*, Chapel Hill, 1945; Sindler, *Change in the Contemporary South*; J. C. McKinney and Edgar T. Thompson, *The South in Continuity and Change*, Durham, 1965; M. L. Greenhut and W. T. Whitman, eds., *Essays in Southern Economic Development*, Chapel Hill, 1964; also my "Population Problems in the South", *Southern Economic Journal*, April, July, October, 1937. State income data are published annually in the *Survey of Current Business*. The March, 1968, *Monthly Labor Review* is devoted to "Labor in the South",

has fluctuated and trended as has the national economy, average income
has risen faster since 1940.

This continuing improvement has not sufficed to carry many of the
Southern states out of the category of states with relatively low per
capita incomes. In 1963 as in 1929 all thirteen Southern states (including
Oklahoma) were included among the 17 lowest in per capita income,
with 9 at the bottom. In 1967, 11 of these states still remained among
the 17 lowest. Florida had been carried out at last by a heavy influx of
tourists, well-to-do retirees, and some modern employments, and Virginia,
by expanding government employment based on the national capital as
well as some industrial development. Texas retained its relatively high
position within the South, but did not experience a sufficiently rapid
growth to move out of the category made up of the nation's 17 states
ranking lowest in average income. Within each Southern state one
encounters pronounced income differentials, by county, by race, by profession, by rural-urban orientation, by industry, and by location of
employment.

Why was average income in the South so low 40 years ago, particularly
when contrasted with that of the Non-South—only 42.5 per cent as high
in 1930-31 and only about 65 per cent as high in 1947-48? The immediate
explanation is that the Southern economy was dominated by industries in
which output per worker was very low by national standards and that
even in these industries average output or income often was lower in
the South than elsewhere. Underlying these conditions was the preponderance—51 per cent in 1920—of agricultural employment in the South,
with much of it made up of individuals of little education, many of whom
were Negro and hence subject to adverse economic and social discrimination as well. In 1960-61 when per capita personal income in the South
was 76.5 per cent of the national income, post-tax Negro family income
in the South was 56.6 and 51.9 per cent, respectively, of Southern and
national post-tax white income.

Several of these conditions may be noted in greater detail. As late as
1930 Negroes made up 26 per cent of the South's population, but not
quite 3.5 per cent of that of the Non-South; nor was there much change
by 1940 when these percentages remained 25 and 3.8. As late as 1940
34.9 per cent of the South's labour force were engaged in primary industry, mainly agriculture, compared with 12.8 per cent in the Non-South.
Agricultural output per agriculturist was only about half as high in the
South as in the United States in the 1930's. Responsible, besides a widespread lack of education, was the relatively poor quality of the soil and
hence the considerable input of fertilizer required, together with the
relatively small amount of farm land per worker, an amount much lower
in the South than elsewhere. This ratio improved after 1940 as a result

of a decline of 4 million or 26 per cent in the South's farm population between 1940 and 1945 while elsewhere it declined only about one-tenth. Education, as already remarked, was deficient, with the rate of illiteracy twice as high in the South as elsewhere and with 42 per cent of all persons 25 or more years old possessed of less than 7 years of schooling as of 1940, compared with about 21 per cent in the Non-South. The deficient state of education in the South reflected high fertility and the lowness of Southern incomes, since the South spent as large a fraction of its income on education as did the Non-South. Natality was about one-seventh higher in the South than in the Non-South in the 1930's, thus contributing to the fact that about 43 per cent of the South's population was under 20 years of age in the 1930's, compared with about 34 per cent in the Non-South. Conditions in today's Negro ghettoes in large cities reflect the defective state of Southern education in the 1930's, especially among Negroes, since it was at that time that many were in school, in schools the federal government failed to help finance. Health conditions in the South were somewhat inferior to those in the Non-South and so was the usual diet.

World War II set in motion the forces which have been carrying the South forward ever since. Most important has been the movement of excess population out of agriculture and the redistribution of the Negro population. Between 1940 and 1960 the Negro population of the South-east increased only 9.4 per cent compared with 39.1 per cent for the white, while both the Negro and the white rural-farm populations decreased, the former by about 65 per cent and the latter by 61 per cent.[13] Whereas in 1940 half the nation's agricultural employment was in the South where it occupied 35 per cent of all employed persons, by 1960 the number of agricultural workers had declined by three-fifths, constituting only two-fifths of the nation's agricultural labour force and engaging only 10.4 per cent of all Southern workers. This movement out of Southern agriculture has been continuing since 1960 making possible a further reduction in the number of farms and increase in the average size of farms, now more than double what it was in 1940, together with adjustment of Southern agriculture to the requirements of modern farm technology. Associated with this movement out of agriculture has been emigration of the Negro from agriculture which employed only about 16 per cent of nonwhite workers in 1960 compared with 43 per cent in 1940. The number of nonwhites in Southern agriculture declined by 923,000 in 1940-60, or about 64 per cent, while those engaged in other occupations rose by only 773,000. Emigration of Negroes from the South,

---

[13] S. C. Mayo and C. H. Hamilton, "The Rural Negro Population of the South in Transition", *Phylon*, 1963, pp. 160-61.

about 3.2 million in 1940-60, accounts for the small decline in the non-white labour force between 1940 and 1960 as well as for the decline in the fraction nonwhites constituted of the population, 21.3 per cent in 1960 compared with 25.3 in 1940.

Non-agricultural employment increased in quality as well as in relative amount between 1940 and 1960. Non-agricultural employment rose from about 65 to about 90 per cent of all employment. Employment in industries with above average growth rose from about 38 per cent to about 65 per cent, mainly as a result of decline in agricultural employment and increase in diverse employments, especially in trade, professional services, and construction. The South's share of employment in fast growing industries remained about one eighth below that of the nation as a whole.[14] Even so, one may say that a considerable degree of convergence to the national standard has been attained. It was not complete, however, in part because Negroes had less access than whites to superior employment in the nation as a whole and particularly in the South. This lack of access was associated with poor quality of education, reflected in the fact that in the United States as late as 1960 the median number of years of education for persons 25 years and older was only 8.2 years for non-whites compared with 10.6 for whites. By 1966, however, these figures had risen to 9.1 and 12.1 years, respectively.

The condition of Negro education in the South has, of course, been inferior to that in the country as a whole. In 1940, of the nonwhite population 25 years old and over, 50 per cent had less than 5 years of elementary schooling while only 5 per cent had 4 or more years of high school; by 1960 the corresponding percentages were 34 and 14. Among whites the corresponding percentages were about 16 and 24 in 1940 and about 11 and 40 in 1960. In the United States as a whole the corresponding percentages in 1960 were about 7 and 43 for whites and 24 and 21 for nonwhites.

It is evident that a major reason for the relatively low level of average income in the South has been the predominance in the Southern economy of industries and employments in which the average level of income has been relatively low. This is not the only reason. Straight-time hourly earnings of production or non-supervisory workers in the South often are over 20 per cent below those received elsewhere.[15] When workers are mobile as are professional people and highly skilled craftsmen,

[14] Maddox *et al.*, *op. cit.*, chap. 4; V. R. Fuchs, "Determinants of the Redistribution of Manufacturing in the United States Since 1929", *Review of Economics and Statistics*, XLIV, May 1962, pp. 167-77; olro E. S. Dunn, Jr., *Recent Southern Economic Development*, Gainesville, 1962.

[15] *Monthly Labor Review*, March 1968, p. 77; but see *ibid.*, March 1969, pp. 44-45.

their levels of remuneration in the South do not differ notably from those received elsewhere in the country.

One often encounters complaint that in the past the South's leading industries have been industries characterized by low wage levels and often by low rates of growth inasmuch as their growth in the South was in part the result of inmigration from other sections of the United States. Illustrative is the textile industry. This type of complaint, and it is still common, overlooks the fact that the South was, and may still be in slight measure, a region with an unemployed or underemployed labour reserve, one situated mainly in agriculture and suited primarily to labor-oriented industries in which skill requirements are low or to those in which Southern raw materials predominate (tobacco). The development of these industries in the South was favoured by absence of strong trade unions as well as of minimum wage legislation designed, as Colberg wisely observes, "to reduce competition from Southern labour-surplus areas". Much unemployment in the South as elsewhere is traceable to successful trade-union and governmental efforts to jack the prices of types of Southern labour above what the market will bear, thereby eliminating the advantage industrialists need in order to overcome such defects in the Southern economy as shortage of capital, lack of education and industrial experience, etc.[16]

"Historically, the South, compared with the United States as a whole, has been a high-consumption, low-savings economy, a state characteristic of many regions in the process of economic development." So reported a Southern banking review in 1965. Back in the early 1930's savings per capita in the Sixth Federal Reserve District were only 30 per cent of the national average; but by 1964 this fraction had doubled. Meanwhile, of course, businesses generated their own savings, and increasingly as activity increased after 1940. Some capital flowed in from outside the South as well, together with managerial and scientific resources. Around 1950 Hoover and Ratchford estimated that the South was absorbing only 15-18 per cent of the nation's annual investment whereas it required over 25 per cent for 15-20 years to put its economy on a par with that of the rest of the nation.[17] Available information suggests that in the early 1960's only about 22 per cent of the nation's total net investment in plant and equipment took place in the South, compared with just

---

[16] M. R. Colberg, *Human Capital in Southern Development, 1939-1963*, Chapel Hill, 1965, pp. 122-24; George J. Stigler, "The Economics of Minimum Wage Legislation", *American Economic Review*, XXXVI, June, 1946, pp. 358-65; D. E. Kann, "Minimum Wages, Factor Substitution, and the Marginal Producer", *Quarterly Journal of Economics*, LXXIX, Aug., 1965, pp. 478-86, and "Wage Adjustments in the Appalachian States", *Southern Economic Journal*, XXXII, Oct., 1965, pp. 127-36.

[17] *Op. cit.*, p. 195.

over 18 per cent in the late 1940's.[18] The total amount of capital formed in the South is much higher, of course, including housing, public capital, various types of construction, etc.

Of great importance though still commonly neglected is "human capital". Colberg estimates the value of human capital in the South at about 30 per cent of that for the United States as a whole. He estimates also that between 1939 and 1959 human capital grew about 1½ times as fast in the South as in the United States.[19] The absolute amount in 1959 was about 13 times net investment in plant and equipment in the South that year. For the nation as a whole Colberg's method of estimating makes human capital as of 1959 approximate something like 35 per cent of the national wealth. A corresponding relation probably obtains for the South. It is apparent, therefore, that investment in human capital is a major source of the South's capital equipment.

THE FUTURE

While the South made great progress between 1940 and 1960, it will require at least 25 years, perhaps 50 years, to catch up economically with the rest of the nation. For, as noted earlier, average income in 1960 was only 75.5 per cent as high in the South as in the nation. In 1966 per capita income in the population living in Standard Metropolitan Statistical Areas was 84 per cent as high in the Southeast as in the nation; the corresponding percentages in 1929 and 1950 were 64 and 79.[20] The incidence of poverty, as arbitrarily defined, is higher in Southern rural areas than in other areas of the nation and among nonwhites than among whites. The latter condition reflects in part the fact that if Negro males classified by education and age, were paid at the some rates as white males correspondingly classified they would earn about 50 per cent more on an average.[21] In the South, median earnings of nowhite males are roughly 55-64 per cent as high as those of white males of comparable education and age. In the Non-South the corresponding percentage range is 70-83.[22]

The South's future will be conditioned by the composition of its population. Given continuation of the movement of the 1950's when net out-

[18] Maddox et al., *op. cit.*, pp. 48-51; J. T. Romans, *Capital Exports and Growth Among U.S. Regions*, Middletown, 1965; L. E. Galloway, "Regional Capital Estimates by Industry, 1954-57", *Southern Economic Journal*, XXIX, July, 1962, pp. 21-25.

[19] M. R. Colperg, *Human Capital in Southern Development 1939-1963*, chap. 8. Colberg's mode of estimation results in aggregates lower than those yielded by some other modes.

[20] *Survey of Current Business*, August 1968, pp. 34-36.

[21] Maddox, *op. cit.*, p. 146.

[22] *Ibid.*, pp. 136-37.

migration of Negroes approximated 1.5 million compared with a net immigration of 381,000 whites, one would expect only a small increase in the Negro population and a large increase in the white population. This is not what U.S. Census projections suggest. Modernization of the South's economy is slowing outmigration but not eliminating it. Only Florida is expected to experience a large amount of net inmigration—between 2 and 3 million—by 1985, with Virginia attracting less than 100,000 and Texas only a few, if any. Other Southern states will experience outmigration. Only Virginia, Georgia, Florida, Louisiana, and Texas are expected to experience as high a rate of population growth as the nation. Even so it is expected that in the South the ratio of the Negro to the entire population will not differ markedly from what it was in 1960, just over 21 per cent.[23] These data signify that the task of bringing the educational level of the population to parity with that of the nation will not be easy and inexpensive. This task will be complicated by the fact that, on the basis of experience, nonwhite fertility will be roughly 25 to 40 per cent above white fertility. As a result a considerable number of Negro families will include more children than parents can support adequately and thus will experience poverty.[24]

Turning again to the capacity of the South's economy to catch up with that of the rest of the United States, we find the South to be well endowed with space, water, and climate, better than most regions, and with an urban population distribution that still allows easy access to natural amenities.[25] In the past the presence of unskilled labour, together with natural resources, served to attract industry to the South.[26] Today, however, as result of the technological revolution, it is increasingly "brains" that attract industry, especially modern growth industry, and "brains" in turn are attracted by "pleasant physical surroundings", a forward-looking political climate, cultural and recreational amenities, and an educational system that is both excellent and abreast of scientific progress.[27]

[23] For migration projections by state, see U.S. Bureau of the Census, *Current Population Reports*, Series P-25, No. 375, Oct. 3, 1967, and on projected metropolitan growth, *Ibid.*, No. 415, Jan. 31, 1969.

[24] On family size and poverty see H. L. Sheppard, "Effects of Family Planning on Poverty in the United Stater", a Staff Paper, W. E. Upjohn Institute for Employment Research, Kalamazoo, Mich., Oct. 1967.

[25] See my "Southern Economic Trends and Prospects", in McKinney and Thompson, *op. cit.*, pp. 103-09; also J.W. McKie, "The Southern Industrial Fuel Economy", *Southern Economic Journal*, XXXIX, April 1963, pp. 269-78; C. T. Taylor, "What Kind of Economy Can the South Expect?", *Monthly Review*, Federal Reserve Bank of Atlanta, Sept. 1967.

[26] Fuchs, *op. cit.*

[27] B. W. Zumeta, "What Attracts Growth Industries?", *Business Review*, Federal Reserve Bank of Philadelphia, July 1964, pp. 8-13. See also Elizabeth B. Deuterman, "Brains in the Old Manufacturing Belt", *ibid.*, October 1966, pp. 3ff.

The South is well suited to meet the demand for some of the amenities associated with affluence, but not yet all. Moreover, the South is less well equipped as yet with skilled personnel than other regions. This is not so true of the distribution of scientific talent as such.[28] The South has, however, gained relative to the rest of the nation in respect of science connected with atomic energy,[29] and it will gain on a broader front through the establishment of such centres as "the Research Triangle";[30] and in some measure, too, by efforts to attract business firms by facilitating their settlement in suitable areas.[31]

The composition of the South's labour force remained inferior to that of the rest of the country in 1960. In the Southeast 35 per cent of all employees fell in the relatively unskilled category compared with about 10.3 per cent in the United States. Corresponding percentages for professional, technical, proprietory, and clerical personnel were 24.1 and 35.7. These distributions reflect the fact that nonwhites in 1960 constituted about 20 per cent of the working population in the South, but only about 10 per cent in the United States, together with the fact that the percentage of Negro workers classified as skilled and/or white collar workers constitutes a very small percentage, by industry, of the percentage of white workers so classified.[32] This distribution also reflected in some degree, as did the lowness of income, the effect of low educational attainment, especially among the Negroes.[33]

Projections of educational attainment in the United States suggest that the South can catch up. For the country as a whole median school years completed by persons aged 25-29 years were 12.3 in 1957-59 and 12.5 in 1964-66. Medians projected for 1975 and 1985, respectively, are 12.6 and 12.7. In 1960 the median years of school completed by whites 25 or more years old was close to the national average, 10.9 years, in all but three Southern states. Accordingly, with current almost universal continuation of education into secondary schools and considerable continuation into colleges, the median for whites in the South should correspond closely to that in the nation in the near future. It will take

[28] Ira Horowitz, "The Regional Distribution of Scientific Talent", *Southern Economic Journal*, XXXI, Jan. 1965, pp. 238-50.

[29] W. G. Pollard, *Atomic Energy and Southern Science*, Oak Ridge, 1966.

[30] W. B. Hamilton, "The Research Triangle of North Carolina: A Study in Leadership for the Common Weal", *South Atlantic Quarterly*, LXV,, 1966, pp. 254-78.

[31] E.g., see Evan B. Alderfer, "Angling for Industry", *Business Review*, Philadelphia Federal Reserve Bank, April 1968, pp. 100; E. Lichtenstein, "Higher and Higher Go the Bids for Industry", *Fortune*, April 1964, pp. 118ff.

[32] See tables in *Monthly Labor Review*, March, 1968, pp. 19-20, 83.

[33] For a study of experience outside the South, see Walter Fogel, "The Effect of Low Educational Attainment On Incomes: A Comparative Study of Selected Ethnic Groups", *Journal of Human Resources*, I, 1966, pp. 22-40.

longer to bring the nonwhite level in the South up with that outside the South as well as with that of the South's whites. In 1960 the median for nonwhites in the South was a year or two below the national level of 8.1 years. The real spread between nonwhite and white tends to be accentuated by disparity in the quality of education by level of education, a disparity it will take some years to eliminate.[34]

In the past the South far more than any other region of the United States has been saddled with a relatively large underemployed population, resident mainly in rural aras. This component of the South's population has been reduced, as noted earlier, by emigration (much as in Puerto Rico) and by the growth of non-agricultural employment, even in smaller towns and rural areas which are becoming more attractive to industry as a result of spatial and related advantages they offer in an age of widespread transport. Associated with the introduction of new industrial employment are the jobs generated by employment multipliers —by increase in service and industry-supply activities—the magnitude of which is positively associated with the level of productivity in the newly introduced industries. Even so, considerable underemployment and unemployment remains, mainly in agriculture and rural areas. Between 1960 and 1967 the white and nonwhite portions of the nation's farm population declined 4.5 and 10 per cent per year, respectively, with the rates higher in the South than outside. It will decrease further in the South however, since modern labour-saving agricultural technology remains less widely diffused in the South than elsewhere.

The upward pressure against wage-levels may be expected to increase faster in the South than elsewhere. On the one hand, the labour surplus is being absorbed, or will be too dispersed to hold down wage levels as in the past. Second, when workers in a labour-market area become concentrated in high-wage industries, the wages in what have been low-wage industries tend to be pulled up. As a result pressure to increase output per worker will increase, along with emphasis upon the importance of education and human capital as a whole.

At present, what may be called growth points are unevenly distributed over the South. Their distribution can be made less unequal, however, inasmuch as both labour and most of the imputs complementary to labour are quite mobile and hence susceptible of combination in a variety of places where transport, water, and amenities are actually or potentially available.[35] Moreover, with the integration of Southern industrial units into larger national networks, the economy of the South should

[34] Cf. Maddox, op. cit., pp. 138-42, 208-16, and chap. 5; also E. Waldman, "Educational Attainment of Workers", Monthly Labor Review, March 1969, pp. 14-22.
[35] See Sindler, op. cit., pp. 49-50; McKinney and Thompson, op. cit., pp. 122-31.

be as stable as that of the nation.[36]

IMPLICATIONS FOR INDIA

The implications of the South's experience for India are not unique. Net emigration from agriculture, essential to the South's catching up with other regions, was facilitated not only by the inflow of inputs complementary to the South's labour force, but also by the access which the South's labour surplus had to other regions. This opportunity is not open to India's population as a whole, though it is available to those living in India's less industrialized regions. Movement out of agricultural areas was made easier because natural increase, while higher than outside the South, was relatively low, and because Southern agriculture underwent both a grass revolution [37] and a technological revolution that greatly reduced the optimum man-land ratio. Indian agriculture is now experiencing a productivity-increasing breakthrough that should render it virtually self-sufficient in terms of food, but it can remain so and at the same time make possible a rapid decrease in India's agricultural population only if rural natural increase is greatly reduced. Indeed, should natural increase be reduced below one per cent, the capital required to absorb migrants from agriculture will presently become available. Movement out of agriculture was aided also by the fact that wages were not made artificially higher through the intervention of the state and trade unions, at least until recently.

India faces a problem somewhat distinct from that faced in the South. India has an absolutely large but relatively (to its population) small core of highly skilled scientific and industrial personnel. How this core is distributed can greatly affect the magnitude of India's Gross National Product over time. The South, by contrast, had a small and slowly growing core, but could eventually draw on external sources in a degree not open to India.

The South may have had another advantage. The drive for its development came from the private sector and was animated by the drive for profits. Augmentation of the incomes of the mass of the population was not the goal directly sought, though this was achieved almost in proportion as enterprise succeeded. India, by contrast, counts in much greater measure upon the state, without inquiring closely into the capacity of the state

[36] E.g., see L. R. McGee, *Income and Employment in the Southeast*, Lexington, 1967.

[37] Grasses were developed in the past 25 years that produce the equivalent of a high maize yield on what was inferior land and that are well suited for cattle feed. This grass revolution recalls the grass revolution that took place in Europe some time before the Industrial Revolution.

to perform the role performed in the west by private enterprise, or to hold down consumption and elevate savings in a consumption-oriented society.[38]

While the experience of the South points to the importance of education, especially in the region's development, it also indicates how much can be accomplished in some lines of industry by a labour force whose formal educational attainments were low. It is essential, in an age when something called "education" has become a fetish, that its capacity to increase output per capita not be exaggerated, particulary if savings are in short supply.[39] The South, like India, has at times been subject to "brain drain." Unlike India, however, the South has since become free of this leakage. Indeed, it now is attracting "brains" on balance and will do so in increasing degree as its economy progresses.

Contrast of India's economic situation and potential with those of the South suggests that in the main it is comparison at the quite general level that is both possible and fruitful. As one moves from the general to the quite detailed, however, marked differences increasingly mask implications at the general level and thus limit the inferences that mav be drawn.

---

[38] See Henry Wailich's analysis in "Some Notes Towards a Theory of Derived Development", in A. N. Agarwala and S. P Singh, Eds., *The Economics of Development*, New York, 1963.

[39] E.g., see A. Harbarger's essay in C. A. Anderson and M. J. Bowman, eds., *Edrcation and Economic Development*, Chicago, 1963, pp. 11-50; S. Kannapan, "The Brain Drain and Developing Countries", *International Labour Review*, July 1968, pp. 20-21 and notes. See also R. S. Eckau's paper in S. J. Muchkia, ed., *Economics of Higher Education*, Washington, 1962, pp. 102-28.

16

ADAPTING TO MODERN LIFE
IN A CANADIAN ARCTIC TOWN

JOHN J· HONIGMANN

UNDERDEVELOPED AREAS exist not only in Asia, Africa, and Latin America but are also found in North America, especially on the northern geographical margin of the continent in northern Alaska and the vast Canadian North. It is with the latter region where Canadian government agencies have recently launched considerable efforts at development, including the foundation of two new towns, that I will be concerned.[1]

The prospects and problems of development and modernization are sometimes discussed on macroscopic levels. We talk of development in an entire country which may consist of millions of people and even of the modernization of the whole "third world", the underdeveloped countries taken collectively. While consideration of the subject on such levels conforms to the level of generality found, for example, in theories of social evolution and has allowed new theoretical insights to be forged, it fails

[1] The National Science Foundation (grant number GS-939) financed my research on incipient urbanization in northern Canada of which the Inuvik study forms part. The Northern Research Group of the Canadian Government supported Irma Honigmann's work with native children in Inuvik. Analysis of data and conclusions deriving from analysis owe much to her assistance. A shorter version of this paper was presented at the 1968 annual meeting of the American Anthropological Association in Seattle, Washington. We worked in Inuvik from March to August, 1967.

to reveal that subgroups and individuals in a large population respond variably to modernization. Consequently planners and administrators may remain unaware of precisely where their efforts are proving most effective.[2] The viewpoint adopted in this paper confines itself to a more molecular level. It will examine how individuals belonging to three different cultural groups, each characterized by a different cultural tradition, are responding to certain challenges of modern life being presented to them in a single, newly created town.

Objectives

The principal object I set for myself upon undertaking research in the Arctic town of Inuvik, located in the Northwest Territories near the mouth of the Mackenzie River, was to compare the adaptation to modern life being made by three ethnic groups.[3] They are, first, Athapaskan-speaking Indians from the Lower Mackenzie Valley and other parts of northwestern Canada and Alaska; second, Eskimo from the Mackenzie Delta and the adjacent Arctic coast of Canada and Alaska, and a third group that I call Other Native. This third population consists chiefly of persons who are the offspring of Indian-white unions that sometimes occurred as far back as the third preceding generation. I hasten to say that my usage of ethnic labels like "Indian", "Eskimo", or "white" refers most importantly to different cultural traditions as well as different legal statuses. My theory allows me to attach no importance to the genetic makeup of the population. By adaptation in general I mean the effectiveness with which a group functions, judged by how it responds to opportunities, expectations, and problems presented to, or encountered by, its members. Later I will present explicit criteria by which I propose to judge the adaptation of the different ethnic groups in Inuvik.

The native people living in Inuvik are not complete strangers to currents of modern life.[4] Even the Eskimo coming from the Western Arctic coast have been exposed to traders, trade goods, Christian missionaries, and other features of western culture for at least one hundred years. Yet in that period the full ideological content of the dominant culture, its world view and values, have not been fully assimilated by any of the

---

[2] Community development for example may like international development most promote the economic development of those who are already advantaged to begin. See Honigmann 1960.

[3] For a related study of modernization in another part of this region see *Eskimo Townsmen* (Honigmann and Honigmann 1965).

[4] For a list of criteria of modernization generally applicable in northwestern Canada see Roberts and McBee 1968: 607.

three groups.[5] It is fair to say that each continues to resist becoming more completely converted to the values and other behavioural traits followed in dominant middle-class North American society.[6] Although acculturation has been of long duration in the region, and the aboriginal culture was long ago abandoned, culture change has not been accompanied by any marked psychological breakdown in the population such as change is sometimes thought to promote almost necessarily.[7]

I began this paper holding two opposed theoretical orientations that I deliberately avoided trying to reconcile. One of those positions emphasizes the importance of an external situation in controlling behaviour or in developing new behaviour, particularly of a modernizing kind; the second position stresses the dominant role of internal states or of the internalized culture pattern over how persons behave, including how they change and modernize. Debate between proponents of each view has been carried on using a variety of terms for two positions that I will label "situationalism" and "essentialism", respectively. Situationalism explains behaviour by alluding to the sufficiency of incentives, social structure, or the contemporary situation to induce behaviour;[8] it views opportunities as triggering change;[9] counts on role learning (including adult socialization) to modify behaviour,[10] and relies on making knowledge (like family planning information) readily accessible to ensure that people will adopt it.[11] Situationalism sees adaptations as on-going[12] and more a matter of becoming than of being. What one becomes is largely contingent on the current conditions under which one lives.[13]

Essentialists explain behaviour by reference to psychological dispositions ("essences") that motivate behaviour,[14] including values and needs (most notably the need of achievement)[15] which are laid down in childhood and persist as part of the stability of personality. Essentialists think in terms of a "mental virus"; when a certain "virus" is present, an individual behaves in a certain way.[16] The two positions may, of course, be

[5] For problems connected with "structural duality" see Eisenstadt 1965.
[6] Honigmann and Honigmann 1960. Cf. Stewart 1952.
[7] Spencer 1959: 2. For a somewhat different view emphasizing the fact that some people have been only poorly able to adjust see Clairmont 1963 and Chance 1965.
[8] LeVine 1966: 89.
[9] Weiner 1966: 9-10.
[10] Murphy 1947: 868.
[11] Jaffe and Polgar 1968.
[12] Durkin 1968.
[13] Liebow 1967: 208.
[14] Rubenfeld 1968: 25.
[15] LeVine 1966; Hagen 1962.
[16] McClelland 1966.

reconciled, as in fact they are in what has been called "field theory".[17] There is nothing basically illogical about either point of view, and both find facts to support their arguments. However each position has different consequences for planning social change or trying to promote modernization. An extreme essentialist orientation, holding psychologically motivating dispositions to be invariant or the internalized culture pattern as being well-nigh immutable, makes change difficult in terms of the time and energy it will require. A situational approach implies that change can come quickly provided men are willing to jettison unworkable institutions and wise enough to create attractive new ones that will promote a desired response.[18]

Thinking like a situationalist, I began research on the adaptation of the ethnic groups in Inuvik believing that the new town with its attractions and opportunities might be sufficiently strong to swamp any internalized cultural traditions or socially standardized psychological traits pertaining to motivation of the Indians, Eskimo, and Other Natives. Hence I expected that each group would closely resemble the other in its mode of adaptation. On the other hand, I could not deny that cultural differences existed which were accompanied by different social personalities from one people to the next. Such knowledge led me to think in essentialist terms. I expected that substantial differences in adaptation might appear between the three ethnic groups as a result of the fact that each was culturally endowed with different proclivities for modernization. The Eskimo, I thought, would be especially inclined and able to modernize. Evidence for that expectation goes back to observations made by the Arctic explorer, Sir John Franklin, who reached the Mackenzie Delta in 1826. He describes the Eskimo's desire to secure the white man's goods as being so sharp that they resorted to stealing.[19] Alexandre Taché in 1870 had several travellers' reports on hand allowing him to generalize that Eskimo "are more susceptible of being educated . . . than their neighbors", meaning the Indians.[20] Rasmussen, too, in 1924 was much impressed with the advantages and prosperity that the Mackenzie River Eskimo had secured for themselves compared to their Indian neighbours.[21] Those writers suggest that though Eskimo and Indians had the same external opportunities to modernize in the early days of contact with explorers and during later fur-trade time, internal

[17] Jessor et al. 1968.
[18] Honigmann 1966.
[19] Franklin 1828.
[20] Taché 1870.
[21] Ostermann 1942: 51, 53.

(i.e., cultural) factors enabled the Eskimo to demonstrate greater alacrity in doing so.

However, some observers report the northwestern Canadian Indians—Athapaskan-speakers like those living in Inuvik—to have also been adaptable (though the reports do not make an explicit comparison with the Eskimo). Several anthropologists,[22] including, Lowie, Boas, and Jenness, are among writers who have characterized the northern Athapaskan Indians as resourceful in meeting new economic conditions.

My personal experience as an anthropologist studying northern Canadian Indians and Eskimo has demonstrated the successful modernization of Eskimo in Frobisher Bay;[23] my students have revealed similar behaviour among the Eskimo of Churchill, Manitoba,[24] and other writers have described evidence of Eskimo modernization elsewhere in Canada.[25] I know of no reports documenting comparable transformations of Indian culture in the same region. The ethnic distribution of vocational trainees from the Northwest Territories who in 1966 received out-of-school vocational training supports the likelihood that Eskimo participate at a higher rate in modernization.[26] Of 444 trainees, 34 per cent were Eskimo, 17 per cent Indian, and 45 per cent of "other ethnic origin". Yet Eskimo in 1965 constituted 36.1 per cent of the territorial population, Indians 23.4 per cent, and "others" 40.5 per cent. The percentage of Eskimo trainees is proportionate to the strength of Eskimo in the total population, but Indians are under-represented.

The available information led me to entertain seriously the possibility that Indians in Inuvik compared to Eskimo would for some culturally related reason turn out to be relatively disinclined to modernize or for some socially patterned "internal" reason would be handicapped in doing so.

However, even if Eskimo turned out to be better adapted than the Indian, that would not necessarily mean support for an essentialist theory. The possibility of alternative explanations exists, including one in which situational factors operate more favourably for the Eskimo than the Indian. I refer to the fact that during the past fifteen years—the period of intense modernization in the Far North—administration of the two ethnic groups in the Northwest Territories was divided between two arms of the Federal Government. The relatively recent Northern Administration Branch looked after Eskimo affairs while the older Indian Affairs Branch

[22] Lowie 1909; Boas 1910; Jenness 1955: 35; Morice 1928: 77.
[23] Honigmann and Honigmann 1965.
[24] Egloff, Koolage, and Vranas 1968.
[25] Iglauer 1966; cf. Arbess 1966.
[26] Northwest Territories 1966: Vol. II, 77; 1967: Vol. III, 226.

handled Indian matters. Historians will probably be able to document what circumstances allowed the, Northern Administration Branch to be far more imaginative in, and concerned with, actively promoting Eskimo modernization than the Indian Affairs Branch. In addition to Eskimo and Indian administration coming under different bureaucratic arms of the government, white administrators and other workers in the North have often unabashedly preferred Eskimo to Indians and have found it more congenial to associate with the former.[27] Whether these conditions operated in Inuvik since the town was established around 1957 cannot be said with certainty, or even whether they existed in the Mackenzie Valley and along the Arctic coast where Eskimo and Indians lived and trapped. Nevertheless if Eskimo turn out to be better adapted than Indians, the possibility of discriminatory attitudes and treatment operating on the former must be borne in mind.

Another possible disadvantage facing the Indian in Inuvik must be borne in mind. One of the measures of adaptation to modern life that I will use is wage employment (which in turn opens up access to modern satisfiers for the employee and his family). However a relatively high percentage of Indian men are over 55 and hence may not be readily employable. (Six per cent of the Indians are over 55 compared to 4 per cent of the Eskimo and 3 per cent of the Other Natives.) Examining only the employment of family heads in each group will reduce the disproportion of older men in the Indian population, but it will not overcome another potential demographic handicap confronting the Indians: a high frequency of woman-headed families. We shall see, though, that women family heads among Indians appear not to face great difficulty in securing steady work.

Compared to my expectations concerning the adaptation of Eskimo and Indians, my ideas concerning Other Natives (mostly Indian Métis) remained much less crystalized. On the one hand, I knew from previous field work that Métis often rank high in prestige vis-a-vis Indians living in the same community.[28] On the other hand, I had also learned that Métis, being legally equivalent to whites, stand at a disadvantage compared to Eskimo and Indians because of Federal services available to the latter two groups.[29] Furthermore, being of mixed ancestry Métis might for that reason be subjected to personal discriminations and other

[27] Honigmann and Honigmann 1959: 7-8; see also Egloff, Koolage, and Vranas 1968: 23, 75-76. For the role of patrons see Honigmann and Honigmann 1965:225-228 and Arbess 1966.
[28] Honigmann 1946: 128, 131.
[29] Slobodin 1966: 143-44; Cohen 1962: 91.

handicaps.[30] I was also aware of several reports documenting difficulties that Métis in northern Manitoba, Alberta, and Saskatchewan were experiencing in becoming full-fledged members of modern society.[31] Perhaps similar difficulties would turn up further north in Inuvik.

THE TOWN

Inuvik, a planned town, has been fully occupied only since 1957. Most of the native and white inhabitants depend on wage work for their livelihood and only a few families continue to rely heavily on trapping, formerly the dominant occupation of the region. The 1200 white inhabitants are from southern Canada and in the main hold skilled, supervisory, and professional jobs. High wages, modern government housing with all amenities located in the East End of town, and the promise of a good school for their children attracted those not in military service to work above the Arctic Circle for a few years. The 1100 Indians, Eskimo, and Other Natives with whom I am concerned are less well prepared to compete for skilled jobs and so hold mostly low-skilled employment. Native men working for the government, the largest employer, earn from $500 to $900 gross pay monthly, or mostly about $550. The larger sums, of course, go to the few men in each of the three native groups who hold such skilled or prestigious jobs as airplane pilot, policeman, clerk and heavy equipment operator.

Native people typically live in lower-grade housing located in the town's West End. Their homes lack access to town services like running water or flow sewage. A few white families also reside in the West End, mostly those committed to a life in the North who are not employed as government servants. With few exceptions, the transient population living in the East End and the native population in the West each runs on its own track. Though children from both sides attend school together, and the two groups join as passive spectators of athletic events and entertainments, relatively little sustained interaction and few common interests unite the two populations. They don't even consciously compete for the same jobs. However, marriage to transient white men has enabled a few native women to move into the East End.

Among Indians, Eskimo, and Other Natives in the West End the style of life has a "frontier" quality. Outdoor-type clothing, slacks for women, heavy shoes, and other features give the native population a distinctive cultural character that contrasts sharply with the middle-class style of

[30] Kerckhoff and McCormick 1955.
[31] Card et al. 1963; Lagasse et al. 1959; Zentner 1967; see also Kerckhoff and McCormick 1955.

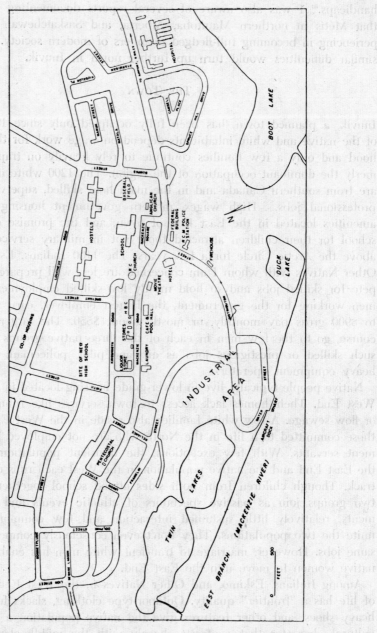

life that predominates in the eastern end of the community. Yet many of the same elements of culture and similar values occur in both styles of life. Economic enterprise is one such shared trait, demonstrated for example by both husband and wife holding steady or fairly steady jobs in order to augment family income. Other common traits result from the way both East and West End youngsters are eager to keep up with prevailing fads, including new music.

An assortment of business establishment, including a bank, food store, bakery, cinema, and restaurant, is situated in the central part of town along with government offices, a government-operated liquor store, and a hotel that serves alcoholic beverages during stated hours. The integrated school is likewise located in the centre of town. It serves not only pupils from the two neighbourhoods of Inuvik but also several hundred youngsters who come from remote settlements scattered along the Arctic coast and in the Mackenzie Valley. Two large hostels house the latter pupils during the school year and also accommodate a few children of Inuvik trapping families who spend much of the year out of town, living on the land. Through universal schooling as well as advanced training offered to persons who promise to benefit from it, the territorial and Federal governments are trying to implement the goal of staffing most jobs in the Far North with local (especially native) workers within the next ten years. But Indians, Eskimo, and Other Natives in Inuvik were familiar with schooling before they moved to the town. Many adults have had 4, 5, or more years of residential school in the region and practically everybody speaks and can read English.

Indians, Eskimo, and Other Natives are mostly Catholic or Anglican. There is also a Pentecostal Church in town whose members come chiefly from Eskimo families. The history of missionary activity in northwestern Canada best explains why some native people (for example, many Mackenzie Valley Indians) are nominally Roman Catholic and others (many Eskimo), Anglican. Attendance at church by natives is light; the lack of involvement with religion reflects a secular outlook that expects little about the world to be supernaturally explicable. In other words, people largely believe that man has it in his own power to plan and to succeed, whether it be through trapping or in jobs; hence theological world views cannot relieve most of the ambiguities and anxieties of life. Yet occasionally we hear that God alone could accomplish something, like curing a person from a compulsion for heavy drinking; and the appeal of the Christian Assembly (Pentecostal) church to a number of Eskimo has been partly due to its uncompromising opposition to alcohol.

TESTING ADAPTATION

A variety of administrative records furnished most of the objective information I have used to compare the way Indians, Eskimo, and Other Native are adapting in three systems of behaviour. For adaptation in female family heads' employment, the amount family heads recieved in social assistance and the number drawing welfare payments, and the number of heads who continue to make a living trapping furs. Steady employment constitutes evidence of good adaptation; occasional or rare-employment or no evidence of any employment record as well as relatively great dependence on social assistance indicate poor adaptation.[32] The significance of trapping will be explained later. Legal convictions of persons 15 years or older for offences committed under laws regulating the use of alcohol have provided information for judging adaptation in the Normative System. Not one or only one conviction means good adaptation. In the Educational System I have looked at how native children 15 to 20 years old adapt to expectations and problems presented to them through the integrated Federal school in Inuvik. For this purpose 378 children were grouped by the ethnic status of their family head, my assumption being that home conditions vary with ethnicity and influence children's adaptation in school. Criteria of adaptation are age-grade level, test results, and attendance. In addition I have information on youngsters 15 to 20 years old who without finishing their education dropped out of school, thereby revealing poor adaptation to the institution.

The three systems in which I test adaptation of course embody an ethnocentric bias. In effect they define successful adaptation as meeting opportunities and expectations presented to native people by the larger Canadian society or its employers, teachers, and administrators. One cannot conduct research without admitting some bias. Considering the situation in which town living had placed the native people of Inuvik, using the demands of the larger society as criteria for judging adaptation seems quite reasonable. I do not imply that Indians, Eskimo, and Other Natives who are not adapting well by employment, legal, and educational criteria are morally obliged to. Using convenient criteria in measurment also implies nothing about the existential-phenomenological value of those criteria for the people being studied. Nevertheless many people do seek jobs, value the income that jobs produce, want to stay out of trouble with the police, and wish to see their children successful in school. That most Indians, Eskimo, and Other Natives believe jobs, lawabidingness, and education to be important augments the significance of the criteria I have chosen and also indicates the extent to which both they and I belong to a common cultural tradition that recognizes value in the same things.

[32] Information about employment came from checking with all government and most private employers and noting the number of months during which persons had been employed between January 1966 and July 1967. Steadily employed means employed 90 to 100 per cent of the time for which information was available; fairly steadily employed, 70 to 90 per cent of the time; occasionally employed 34 to 69 per cent of the time; rarely employed, less than 34 per cent of the time.

TABLE I

ETHNIC GROUPS COMPARED FOR FAMILY HEADS' ADAPTATION IN
THE ECONOMIC SYSTEM

| Criteria | Number and Percent in Each Ethnic Group | | |
	Indian	Eskimo	Other Native
	%	%	%
Total Number (N=100%)	(34)	(86)	(45)
Employment			
Steady or Fairly Steady	32	47	58
Occasional, Rare, and No Record	68	53	42
Social Assistance			
Received Welfare	44	57	24
Trapping			
Professional Trappers	12	15	20

Economic System. I chose family heads as the group with which to test
adaptation in Economic System of behaviour because people holding
that status recognize a normative responsibility to support their households. This responsibility can be fulfilled through drawing social assistance (not easy to come by and not overly generous), working for wages
in town, or by career on the land such as professional trappers persist in
following.[33] Family heads are both male and female, and the total group
of 165 heads includes 38 women. The ethnic groups differ in the number
of women who head families; out of 34 Indian family heads, 14 are women;
out of 86 Eskimo, 15 are women, and out of 45 Other Natives, 7 are
women. The median age of Indian family heads is 41.4, Eskimo 42.3,
and Other Natives 36.8.

Job information on family heads in Table I shows a clear gradient in
the proportion of each ethnic group steadily or fairly steadily employed.
Other Natives lead, 58 percent having held jobs steadily or fairly steadily
in the period covered by my sample. Then follow Eskimo (47 per cent),
and Indians (32 per cent). These figures reveal that a large proportion
of family heads in each ethnic group only occasionally or rarely work
for wages, Indians being worst off in this regard, for nearly 70 per cent
of that group have been employed at best only occasionally.

Indians, it will be recalled, have the largest proportion of female-
headed families. Facts fail to bear out the possibility that women in this
position are less inclined than male family heads to seek, or less capable

[33] A professional trapper is a person considered by informants to be primarily
devoted to trapping as an occupation and committed to living in the bush during a
large part of the year. In summer some trappers take a job in town.

of maintaining, steady and fairly steady jobs. Almost the same proportions of Indian male and female family heads are steadily or fairly
steadily employed, 32 and 33 per cent respectively. Differences in the
median age of each ethnic group by themselves also seem irrelevant for
explaining the distribution of members in the various employment
categories.

Government social assistance is, of course, a means of buttressing
family security during unemployment and other crises, but I regard it as
a token of marginal adaptation. Welfare is not a major source of income
in Inuvik, and the amounts distributed are not high; about half of the
welfare recipients drew assistance for only 1 or 2 months and got less
than $ 100 total in a sample of 9 months (1966-67). One might expect
that Indian family heads with their relatively infrequent employment
would have received social assistance proportionately more often than
Eskimo or Other Natives, but the facts do not bear that out. Welfare
payments were drawn by 57 per cent of the Eskimo, 44 per cent of the
Indian, 24 per cent of Other Native family heads. These figures, which
make the Eskimo seem more poorly adapted than the Indians, must be
interpreted carefully. Fourteen of the 49 Eskimo family heads who
received social assistance also held steady or fairly steady jobs compared
to only 1 out of the 15 Indian recipients. Eskimo are for some reason
either more willing than Indians to apply for social assistance even
though they are working, or they are for some reason in a favourable position when it comes to having their welfare application acknowledged
favourably. Mean amounts paid over the sample period better reflect
relative need and adaptational status. The Indian family head recipient on
the average recieved $490 total in the 9-month sample period; the Eskimo,
$292, and Other Native, $195. By this measure and by my reasoning Indians,
who draw the largest average amount in social assistance, are most poorly
adapted.

Informants identified 26 of the 165 family heads as professional trappers. These men and one woman make Inuvik their headquarters for
selling fish and fur that they produce; here too they purchase their food
and other supplies. Proportionately more Other Natives are professional
trappers than Eskimo or Indians, the percentages being 20, 15, and 12
respectively. Indians relatively rarely found in the ranks of steadily or
fairly steadily employed, are also the group least devoted to exploiting
the land's natural resources. Professional trappers and their families may
live fairly comfortably away from Inuvik, but because they make
little attempt further to modernize their lives through adopting town-
based roles and because their earnings tend to be low compared to
steadily employed persons, I regard professional trapping as part of
a pattern of marginal adaptation. Yet, as I will show, trapping offers a

truly adaptive niche for people disinclined or ill-equipped to adopted fully social roles in the town.

Now to summarize adaptation in the Economic System. Other Native family heads occupy the most favourable economic position. The high proportion of them with steady or fairly steady employment leaves comparatively few whose economic position is marginal. Of those whose position is marginal, a surprisingly large proportion gain their income by living on the land. Consequently the town itself contains few Other Native families with only precarious means of support and therefore in need of social assistance.

At the opposite extreme stand the Indians. They occupy the least favourable economic position. Only a small proportion of the family heads in this group have worked steadily or fairly steadily, and a large proportion are therefore marginal. Of the marginals only a relatively small group live by professional trapping. This means that a large percentage of Indians living in town lack steady or fairly steady work and don't regularly secure country products; so they depend on welfare payments.

Eskimo economic adaptation is in-between that of the Other Natives and Indians.

Normative System. To gauge adaptation in the Normative System, I consulted information about the extent to which the three native groups got into trouble with police over alcohol on at least two occasions.[34] Police in Inuvik secure an overwhelming number of convictions for offences committed under the liquor laws, offences like public drunkenness, underage drinking, and giving an alcoholic beverage to a minor. The volume of such cases supports native informants who claim that alcohol constitutes one of the most problematic areas of town living. My information covers 108 persons convicted two or more times in 18 months out of a total population of 580 men and women 15 years or older. Conviction, however, furnishes only a partial indicator of difficulty connected with drinking; it says nothing about economic problems and physical injuries resulting from use of alcohol.

In Table II Other Natives contain the smallest proportion of persons 15 years or older who encountered trouble with the police; only 10 per cent had two or more convictions. Indian are at the other extreme, 24 per cent being in the group convicted at least twice, and Eskimo are in-between. But with a conviction rate of 20 per cent Eskimo are closer to

[34] Data on convictions covering 18 months from 20 January 1966 to 6 July 1967 derive mostly from a record maintained by one of the town's two regular justices of the peace. Most convicted persons pay fines but sometimes they are sentenced to a short term in jail or choose several days in jail rather than paying a fine.

TABLE II

TABLE II

ETHNIC GROUPS COMPARED FOR FAMILY HEADS' ADAPTATION IN
THE NORMATIVE SYSTEM

Age Groups and Criteria	Number and Percent in Each Ethnic Group		
	Indian	Eskimo	Other Native
	%	%	%
Persons 15 Yrs. or Older, Total Number (N=100%)	(129)	(327)	(114)
Two or More Convictions for a Liquor Offence	20	24	11
Persons 15-24 Yrs. Old, Total Number (N=100%)	(44)	(143)	(55)
Two or More Convictions for a Liquor Offence	32	30	13

the Indians than to the Other Natives.[35]

The ability of Other Natives to avoid running afoul of the liquor laws becomes even more noteworthy when we learn that Other Natives over 21 years old who bought alcoholic beverages at the government liquor store during a sample of 84 buying days covering the period from June 1966 to July 1967 did so more generously than any other native group. Out of 59 Other Native buyers, 34 per cent spent from $151.00 to $538.05, the largest amounts recorded. Out of 140 Eskimo buyers, only 26 per cent are in that category, and out of 73 Indian buyers, only 16 per cent.

Comparing youthful offenders between 15 and 24 years old to all convicted persons 15 years older (Table II) reveals that, in every native group, persons getting into recurrent legal difficulty on account of alcohol were usually young. Again the Other Native group shows the best adptation to alcohol, only 13 percent of those between 15 and 24 having been convicted 2 or more times. Indian youths especially get into trouble, 32 per cent having been convicted. The Eskimo keep their in-between position but with 30 per cent convicted are very close to the Indians.[36]

[35] Omer Stewart (1964) was one of the first anthropologists to have examined Indian adaptation to modern life using police data. He observes Indians in his sample have a high rate of arrests compared to whites and other races, and that they are especially vulnerable to arrest for drunkenness. He explains the preponderance of Indian arrests for drunkenness on two grounds, first, selective prohibition on Indian drinking for a hundred years and, second, close management of Indians' affairs by other people. See also Jessor et al. 1968: 184-87.

[36] Althorgh Indians and Eskimo have relatively high proportion of young people (15 to 24 years old) making up the population, the conviction rates of the 32 and 30 per cent of young Indians and Eskimo respectively exceed the percentage of

Educational System. How have native children adapted to expectations and problems presented to them through the Federal day school that operates in Inuvik? For the purpose of comparison 378 children have been grouped not by their own ethnic status but by the ethnic status of their family head (usually own or adoptive parents), resulting in three groups: family head Indian, family head Eskimo, and family head Other Native. A fourth group, composed of a small number of children with a white family head (over half of whom have a native mother), will be included to extend the comparison.[37] Three sets of criteria will be employed to judge adaptation in school: age-grade level, performance on achievement tests, and attendance.[38] Increasing age lowers both age-grade level and attendance but the proportion of children above and below age 15 does not vary in a statistically significant way from one ethnic group to another; hence no control for age has been applied. As a final measure of adaptation to school, I examine dropouts, children who have quit school without completing 12 grades or graduating, and their frequency from one group to another.

A child will show up low in age-grade level if he is older than the average age of his grade, high if he is younger than the average age, and average if he ranges from less than one year younger to one year older than the average age. In computing age-grade levels we used only children in our sample, excluding children going to school in Inuvik who live in remote settlements and white children living in the East End of town.

that age group in the population (22 per cent in each case). Other Native youths make up only 14 per cent of the Other Native population.

[37] The Other Native group includes 27 children whose own ethnic status is Other Native but the family head (usually the father) is white and 18 children whose own ethnic status is white. Although the paper covers a 100 per cent native sample of school-age children, it includes only those white children who live in the West End of town.

[38] Records provided the following information for each child: his age, school grade, results on three nationally used educational achievement tests, and number of days attended the previous year. Those data served in constructing 5 measures of school adaptation in the following manner. After calculating the average age only of sample (mostly native) pupils in each grade of the school, each child was ranked as either high, average, or low in his age-grade level. Achievement-test results allowed each child to be ranked high, average, or low depending on his score. Attendance figures furnished the basis for grouping each pupil in a quartile of days present, ranging from high to low. The pupils were then divided into two groups, those above the median days present and those below. In each group of pupils grouped by the family head's ethnic status an index number was calculated for each measure of school performance except attendance. The lowest rank on any measure received a weight of 100, and the next 300. The weight was multiplied by the number of pupils in the group who had earned that rank. Results were summed and the sum divided by the total number of pupils, yielding an index for each measure. The higher the number, the higher the group's standing on that measure.

Results in Table III show that sample children with a white family head are by far the best placed with regard to age-grade level. They are followed by Other Native, Indian, and Eskimo children in that order.

TABLE III

ETHNIC GROUPS COMPARED FOR ADAPTATION IN THE EDUCATIONAL SYSTEM: CHILDREN 6-20 YEARS

Criteria, Groups, and Number of Children (N=100%)	Percent and/or School Performance Index (Children Grouped by Ethnic status of Family Head)			
	High or Above Median Standing %	Average Standing %	Low or Below Median Standing %	Index
Age-Grade Level				
Indian (N=38)	18	63	18	200
Eskimo (N=147)	14	62	24	190
Other Native (N=70)	34	50	16	219
White (N=41)	56	34	10	246
Metropolitan Achievement Test for Reading				
Indian (N=15)	47	40	13	233
Eskimo (N=58)	17	76	7	210
Other Native (N=30)	40	50	10	230
White (N=17)	65	35	0	265
Metropolitan Achievement Test for Arithmetic				
Indian (N=15)	47	33	20	227
Eskimo (N=59)	36	63	2	234
Other Native (N=17)	63	37	0	263
White (N=17)	65	35	0	265
New Basic Reading Tests				
Indian (N=32)	13	31	56	156
Eskimo (N=116)	18	34	48	170
Other Native (N=50)	24	40	36	188
White (N=29)	31	34	34	197
Attendance†				
Indian (N=37)	35	—	65	
Eskimo (N=108)	43	—	57	
Other Native (N=52)	44	—	56	
White (N=34)	65	—	35	

† Children living at home only (town children living in hostel excluded); proportions are those with above and below median attendance.

Children were also compared on three educational achievement tests, two of which (the Metropolitan tests for reading and arithmetic) have been standardized in northern schools of the region containing Inuvik. Table III reveals that children with white family heads always take precedence over children with native family heads on such tests and that youngsters with Other Native home background are in second place. The Indian group has an index number lower than the Eskimo on two tests but ranks ahead of the latter on one. The lack of consistency, however, suggests caution in interpreting the results, especially since the Indian group regularly on the three tests has a larger proportion of testees with low standing than the Eskimo and a larger proportion of testees who achieve high standing on two.

What it means for native children's intellectual development to live in a town rather than a remote settlement is dramatically revealed by our data which indicate that the town children more often achieve high and average standing when their scores are compared to regional norms. Also fewer town children have low standing when compared to regional norms.[39]

On attendance children with a white family head again show the best record, meaning that they meet expectations of the school with the greatest dependability of any group. Pupils from Other Native and Eskimo homes follow next in order and they are so close that ranking seems unadvisable. Indians do most poorly on this measure of adaptation to school.

TABLE IV

ETHNIC GROUPS COMPARED FOR ADAPTATION IN THE
EDUCATIONAL SYSTEM: DROPOUTS 15-20 YEARS

| | Number and Percent in Each Ethnic Group (Children Grouped by Ethnic Status of Family Head) | | | |
| | Indian | Eskimo | Other Native | White |
	%	%	%	%
Total Number (N=100%)	(22)	(73)	(28)	(12)
Dropouts	45	44	29	8

Table IV reports on 51 dropouts who are between 15 and 20 years old. Young people with a white family head have most rarely quit school; they

[39] For details of how local norms were established for two tests see Northwest Territories Testing Program 1969.

are followed by Other Natives. The difference between Indians and Eskimo is too slight to warrant further ranking.

To sum up what the four criteria reveal: youngsters from homes with a white family head cope most successfully in school and are usually followed by those with an Other Native as head of family. Homes marked by an Indian and Eskimo family head appear to be relatively disadvantaged when it comes to helping a child adapt to the demands and expectations of the school system, with the Indian group showing no consistent tendency to be the worst off.

SUMMARY AND CONCLUSIONS

Eskimo, Indians, and Other Natives. When Other Native family heads are compared with Indian and Eskimo family heads they show up to be best adapted in the Economic and Normative Systems of town life. Children with an Other Native family head are also better able to cope with the expectations of the school system than those with an Indian or Eskimo family head. The advantage held by the Other Native group of youngsters is lost, however, when they are compared to children with a white family head. In general Other Natives turn out to be successfully adapted in Inuvik compared to the experience of Indian Métis further south in Canada, who are often handicapped economically and in other ways.

Indians and Eskimo. Comparing only Indian and Eskimo family heads shows that Eskimo tend consistently to be somewhat more successfully adapted in the Economic and Normative Systems of town life than the Indians. However the standing of the two groups is sometimes closely similar. No advantage similar to that enjoyed by Eskimo adults shows up for children with an Eskimo family head, and it is hard to claim firmly that either the Eskimo or Indian group copes more successfully with the expectations of the school. Note, however, that children from Indian homes fail to repeat the pattern of consistently poorest adaptation that we observed in the Indian adults.

The contrasting performance of Eskimo vis-à-vis Indian adults in the Economic and Normative Systems of town life conforms to my assumption concerning the greater adaptability of Eskimo and their greater ability or willingness to modernize compared to the Indian. On the other hand the similar performance of the Eskimo and Indian children's groups in the Educational System contradicts my expectation. Failure of results in the three systems consistently to correspond offers no support for an essentialist-type of theory, one that sees unique cultural traditions which have been internalized governing adaptation. The inconsistent results in the three systems also run contrary to a situationalist hypothesis holding that objective conditions in town life will act similarly on all ethnic groups regardless of cultural traditions they embody. The comparatively successful adaptation of Other Native adults and children and the outstanding success of children with white family heads further undermines any purely situationalist explanation.

Our tests have produced facts that beg for explanation. First, Eskimo family heads adapt better than Indian family heads in the Economic and Normative Systems. Another fact to be accounted for is why Other Native and white groups of children do better than the Eskimo and Indian groups in the Educational System.

Accounting for Eskimo and Indian family heads' modes of adaptation in Inuvik. Frankly my knowledge of Other Natives is still too inadequate to explain their ability to cope successfully with various aspects of town life. However, longer personal experience with Eskimo and Indians in northern Canada and a more voluminous literature about them that can be applied to those populations in Inuvik make me somewhat more confident about explaining the behaviour of those two groups.

The Indian adults' behaviour in Inuvik is illuminated by applying features of the Indian social personality which I discovered in my work with other Athapaskan-speaking Indians in northwestern Canada in 1944 and 1945.[40] These psychological elements, which distinguished the Indian from the Eskimo, while suitable for adaptation to bush life, complicate his adaptation to demands made on him by conditions he encounters in town life. The structure of Indian social personality may be briefly summed up by noting that the Indian's world and self views waver between an idea that experience is manageable and the contrary apprehension that life is overwhelmingly difficult and social relations are threatening. As long as his life remains routinized and calls for no major adjustment to crisis, the Indian feels resourceful and even optimistic, albeit cautious. In the face of excessive demands on him, his feelings of capability and resourcefulness quickly collapse, presumably to the accompaniment of anxiety and guilt.

In Inuvik we have collected data showing the Indian, when he is engaged in wage labour, to experience any rebuke or remonstrance from a white supervisor as critical and stressful. Apparently his self-image becomes threatened. At any rate, he tends to respond to such situations by overt anger and sometimes by quitting. Indians are strongly introverted. Hence they tend to overlook the importance of some external cues and standards that nevertheless bear on them because of the social situations

---

[40] Honigmann 1949; for Eskimo see Honigmann and Honigmann 1965, especially Chapter 6.

M-27

they have entered. Their own standards to which they are primarily attuned don't suffice to guide them, especially not in a new and complex social situation like life in a comparatively large town where they must live and work closely with others, including people psychologically differently equipped as they are. However when external standards fortunately coincide with inner needs, then the Indian can adapt successfully to his external situation.

Compared to the Indian, I believe that the Eskimo has generally been reared to possess a less complex, less vulnerable personality. As one of my Other Native informants said in comparing the two groups, the Eskimo is an easier-going person who is better able to bear frustration and slights to his ego. Indians are more sensitive, touchy, and proud, meaning stubborn. The defence structure of the Eskimo is simple, particularly in that he is less concerned with maintaining a facade. Also he is not as much inclined to blame others or external circumstances (like alcohol) when things go wrong for him. Under threat or adversity, the Eskimo is likely to take extra care in selecting his mode of response or to exert extra effort to meet responsibilities. In my opinion it is the social personality of the Eskimo that has favourably impressed administrators and other white residents of the Far North and has sometimes moved the latter to become dedicated patrons and sponsors of Eskimo endeavours. Psychologically the Eskimo is in a better position than the Indian to respond to an agency like the Northern Administration Branch containing persons dedicated to promoting the native people's modernization. I know of no evidence showing that the Eskimo is more strongly oriented to achievement than the Indian. In fact, I would predict that in an achievement test Indians would show up more strongly endowed with that need than Eskimo.[41]

What governs children's adaptations to school in Inuvik? Our results confront us with the fact that children with Eskimo and Indian family heads tend to conform to each other in their adaptation to school. Speaking bluntly, they often tend to find school troublesome and perform more poorly with respect to the system's expectations than youngsters with Other Native and white family heads. Contrary to differences separating the Eskimo and Indian family heads' adaptations in the Economic and Normative Systems, the behaviour of their children is being standardized in Inuvik. Apparently the attractions, opportunities, problems, and demands of town life—including the school—constitute incentives powerful enough to promote a common style of response. Other data which are not reported

[41] For supporting evidence see Parker 1962. If Indians to have high n-achievement, it may not be motivating them because of overt discriminatory and emotional factors See Staats 1968: 431.

in this paper also point to a bifurcation of cultural groups occurring in Inuvik. Behaviourally speaking, Indian and Eskimo adults and children are mostly (but not exclusively) in one group while Other Natives are in the other; the behaviour of the latter in certain respects emulates the middle-class Canadian style of life more than it approximates that of the other two native groups.[42]

Successful adaptation to school is closely governed by the degree to which middle-class North American norms, values, disciplines, and related cultural traits are present in the child's home. Such elements are in fact characteristic of homes marked by Other Native and white family heads but tend often to be lacking in homes with Indian and Eskimo family heads. Hence the success with which the former two groups adapt to school compared to the latter. Such success, however, is further dependent on the large degree to which nondeliberate cultural bias inheres in the Federal school in Inuvik. Although government is zealous in providing educational opportunities for all children regardless of ethnic background, and official policy has been to promote adaptation to town life through formal education of native children,[43] in effect the school discriminates against children with native cultural backgrounds and for children with a middle-class North American cultural background.

The principal object of this paper, to compare the adaptation of three ethnic groups to modern life in Inuvik, has been fulfilled. Results support neither an exclusively essentialist or wholly situational explanation of the results. The explanations offered for the way adults are adapting economically and to the liquor laws and children to the expectations of school in effect combine both viewpoints, indicating how they may be fruitfully used to complement each other. The process of becoming depends on how people of given age, status, and experience, who possess certain internalized culture patterns and motives, learn to respond to opportunities and challenges presented by their situation. The same objective situation may have quite diverse meanings for, and impacts on, persons with different cultural backgrounds and personality systems.

Assuming that the authorities want to change behaviour, where should the major effort be put—on changing the situation in Inuvik or on changing the cultural backgrounds and personality systems of the ethnic groups that are adapting poorly? The answer would seem to be clear. Changing the situation promises to be far more economical and feasible than trying to alter attitudes and other cultural features. If such cultural alteration

[42] Cecil French (1967) reports cultural bifurcation of a somewhat different sort occurring in northern Alberta where lower-class values are pulling Indians and Métis in a common direction.

[43] Phillips 1967: 240.

is done with an eye to native people's existing social norms and values, a situation will be created that can facilitate further adaptation without unrealistically demanding total conversion to a middle-class North American style of life.

REFERENCES

Arbess, Saul E. 1966. *Social Change and the Eskimo Co-operative at George River Quebec.* Ottawa: Northern Co-ordination and Research Centre, Department of Indian Affairs and Northern Development, publication 66-1.

Boas, Franz. 1910. "Ethnological Problems in Canada." *Journal of the Royal Anthropological Institute* 40: 529-39

Card, B. Y., G. K. Hirabayashi, and C. L. French. 1963. *The Metis in Alberta Society,* Edmonton: Committee for Social Research, University of Alberta.

Chance, Norman. 1965. "Acculturation, Self-Identification, and Personality Adjustment." *American Anthropologist* 67: 373-93.

Clairmont, Donald H. J. 1963. *Deviance Among Indians and Eskimos in Aklavik, N.W.T.* Ottawa: Northern Co-ordination and Research Centre, Department of Indian Affairs and Northern Development, publication 63-9.

Cohen, Ronald. 1962. *An Anthropological Survey of Communities in the Mackenzie Slave Lake Region of Canada.* Northern Co-ordination and Research Centre, Department of Indian Affairs and Northern Development, publication 62-3.

Durkin, Roderick. 1968. Some Social Psychological Aspects of the Ongoing Adaptation of Personalities to Social Systems. Unpublished paper presented at the 1968 meeting of the American Anthropological Association.

Eisenstadt, S. N. 1965. "Processes of Modernization and of Urban and Industrial Transformation Under Conditions of Structural Duality." *Information* 1965: 40-50.

Egloff, Margaret Stephens; William W. Koolage, Jr., and George Vranas. 1968. *Ethnographic Survey of Churchill.* Chapel Hill: Institute for Research in Social Science, University of North Carolina.

Franklin, John. 1828. *Narrative of a Second Expedition to the Shores of the Polar Sea in the Years 1825, 1826 and 1827.* London: John Murray.

French, Cecil. 1967. "Social Class and Motivation Among Metis, Indians, and Whites In Alberta.: Arthur K. Davis (ed.), *A Northern Dilemma.* Two volumes Bellingham. Wash.: Western Washington State College.

Hagen, Everett E. 1962. *On the Theory of Social Change.* Homewood, Ill.: The Dorsey Press.

Honigmann, John J. 1946. *Ethnography and Acculturation of the Fort Nelson Slave.* New Haven, Conn,: Yale University Publications in Anthropology, no. 33.

———. 1949. *Culture and Ethos of Kaska Society.* New Haven Conn.: Yale University Publications in Anthropology, no. 40.

———. 1960. "A Case Study of Community Development in Pakistan." *Economic Development and Cultural Change* 8: 288-303.

———. 1966. Education in the Modernization of Cultures: Pakistan and Indian Villages Compared to Eskimo in a Canadian Arctic Town. Paper prepared for the International Sociological Association's VI World Congress.

——— and Irma Honigmann. 1959. "Notes on Great Whale River Ethos." *Anthropologica* 1: 1-16.

————.1965. *Eskimo Townsmen*. Ottawa: Canadian Centre for Anthropological Research, University of St. Paul.

————.1969. Success in School: Native Youngsters in a New Canadian Arctic Town. Manuscript.

Iglauer, Edith. 1966. *The New People*. New York: Doubleday and Co., Inc.

Jaffe, Frederick S. and Steven Polgar. 1968. "Family Planning and Public Policy: Is the 'Culture of Poverty' the New Cop-out?" *Journal of Marriage and the Family* 30: 22-35.

Jenness, Diamond. 1955. The Indians of Canada. Third edition Ottawa: National Museum of Canada, Bulletin 65.

Jessor, Richard, *et al*. 1968. *Society, Personality, and Deviant Behaviour*. New York: Holt, Rinehart and Winston, Inc.

Kercphoff, A. C. and T. C. McCormick. 1955. "Marginal Status and Marginal Personality." *Social Forces* 34: 48-55.

Lagasse, Jean H., W. E. Boek, J. K. Boek, W. M. Heady, and B. R. Poston, 1959. A *Study of the Population of Indian Ancestry Living in Manitoba*. Three volumes. Winnipeg: Department of Agriculture and Immigration.

LeVine, Robert. 1966. *Dreams and Deeds*. Chicago: University of Chicago Press.

Liebow, Elliot. 1967. *Tally's Corner*. New York: Little, Brown and Co.

Lowie, Robert H. 1907. "An Ethnological Trip to Lake Athabasca." *American Museum Journal* 9: 10-15

McClelland, David C. 1966. "The Impulse to Modernization." In: Myron Weiner (ed.), *Modernization, the Dynamics of Growth*. New York; Basic Books.

Morice, A. G. 1928. "The Fur Trader in Anthropology and a Few Related Questions." *American Anthropologist* 30: 60-84.

Murphy, Gardner. 1947. *Personality*. New York: Harper and Row.

Northwest Territories. 1966. *Council of Northwest Territories Debates, thirty-third session, Resolute, N.W.T., Oct. 31-Nov. 18, 1966*. Two volumes. Ottawa: The Commissioner of the Northwest Territories.

————. 1967. *Council of the Northwest Territories Debates, thirty-fourth session, Ottawa, Ont., March 9-April 10, 1967*. Three volumes. Ottawa: The Commissioner of the Northwest Territories.

Northwest Territories Testing Program. 1966. *Tentative Norms for Metropolitan Achievement Test Batttery*. Ottawa, Curriculum Section, Education Division, Northern Administration Branch, Department of Northern Affairs and National Resources.

Ostermann, H. (Ed.). *The Mackenzie Eskimos*. Copenhagen: Report of the Fifth Thule Expedition, 1921-24, Vol. 10, Pt. II.

Parker, Seymour. 1962. "Motives in Eskimo and Ojibwa Mythology." *Ethnology*, 1: 516-523.

Phillips, R. A. J. 1967. *Canada's North*. New York: St. Martin's Press.

Roberts, Robert E., and George W. McBee. 1968. "Modernization and Economic Development in Mexico: A Factor Analytic Approach." *Economic Development and Cultural Change* 16: 603-12.

Rubenfeld, Seymour. 1965. *Family of Outcasts*. New York The Free Press.

Slobodin, Richard. 1965. *Metis of the Mackenzie District*. Ottawa: Canadian Research Centre for Anthropology, University of St. Paul.

Spencer, Robert F. 1959. *The North Alaskan Eskimo: A Study in Ecology and Society*. Washington: U. S. Government Printing Office.

Staats, Arthur W. 1968. *Learning, Language, and Cognition*. New York: Holt, Rinehart, and Winston.

Stewart, Omer C. 1952. "Southern Ute Adjustment to Modern Living." In: Tax (Ed.), *Acculturation in the Americas, Proceedings and Selected Papers of the XXIXth International Congress of Americanists.* Chicago: The University of Chicago Press.

Taché, Alexandre A. 1870. *Sketch of the North-West of America.* Translated by D. R. Cameron. Montreal: John Lovell.

Weiner, Myron (Ed.). 1966. *Modernization, the Dynamics of Growth.* New York: Basic Books.

Zentner, Henry. 1967. "Reservation Social Structure and Anomie; a Case Study." In: Arthur K. Davis (Ed.), *A Northern Dilemma: Reference Papers.* Two volumes. Bellingham, Wash: Western Washington State College.

17

IRRIGATION POLICY IN SPAIN AND SPANISH AMERICA*

KARL A. WITTFOGEL

THE ONLY major system of irrigation agriculture in Europe emerged in medieval Spain. Stimulated by African experiences, there developed on the Iberian peninsula a hydraulic ("Oriental") civilization that under the Caliphate of Cordoba became world famous. But the forces of a semi-pastoral feudal society competed with, and ultimately overwhelmed, the great hydraulic civilization created by the Moors.

Not long after this fateful event, the aggressive warriors of Navarre and Castille encountered in America societal conditions that agro-politically (but not culturally) were quite similar to those they had destroyed in their homeland. And they destroyed the hydraulic core of the high American civilizations with the self-same political and economic weapons they had used against the centres of Moorish irrigation—Cordoba, Seville, and Granada.

In the arid regions of Spain irrigation is vitally important for an effective intensive agriculture.[1] To a limited extent intensive agriculture was

*The data and arguments of this inquiry elaborate certain ideas suggested in my comparative study of total power, *Oriental Despotism* (New Haven 1957) concerning the socio-economic impact of conquest on various types of hydraulic societies, including India.

[1] P. Hirth, "Die künstliche Bewässerung". *Kolonial-Writschaftliches Komitee*, XXI, No 3. Berlin 1928, pp. 57 ff.

practiced in Spain during the pre-Moorish and Roman periods.[2] The Goths engaged in cattle-breeding and agriculture, but they favoured cattle-breeding.[3] And they succeeded in spreading their proto-feudal order over the entire country.[4] They deprived the peasant-owners of two-thirds of their holdings;[5] and they established large private estates,[6] that utilized serfs (*coloni*) and slaves (*mancipii*) as cultivators.[7] Irrigation continued to be practiced[8] and irrigation water remained common property,[9] not because the big landlords were greatly concerned with intensive agriculture,[10] but because they accepted it as a fact.[11]

II

Historians differ in their evaluations of the agricultural policy of the Goths, but they all agree that in Spain, the Arab conquerors developed patterns of hydraulic farming[12] comparable, and even superior, to those they had known in the hydraulic centres of North Africa and the Near East.

In consequence of this development, water administration[13] and water laws[14] assumed a new significance; and land tenure underwent important changes.[15] The latifundia were broken up, serfdom was eliminated, and

[2] W.H. Hall, *Irrigation Development. Report*: Part 1, Sacramento, 1886, p. 363.

[3] *Memoire sue le perfectionnement de l'agriculture et aur les lois agraires . . .* redige par . . . Gaspar Melcho de Jovellanos.
The Memoire which was written in 1795, is reproduced in A. de Laborie, *Itineraire descriptif de l'Espagne*. IV. Paris, 1808, pp. 103-294.
For the above statement see p. 107.

[4] J.M. de O. Martinus, *A History of Iberian Civilization*. London, 1930, p. 66.

[5] *Op. cit.*, p. 78.

[6] Martinus, *op. cit.*, p. 84; cf. also Memoire, *op. cit.*, p. 161.

[7] Martinus, *A History of Iberian Civilization*, pp. 82-83.

[8] E. Levi-Provencal, *L'Espagne Muselman a Xème siècle*. Institutions et vie sociale. Paris 1932, p. 166.

[9] Hall, *op. cit.*, p. 365.

[10] The *Memoire* claims complete lack of agricultural interest for the Gothic conquerors of Spain, (*op. cit.*, p. 107).

[11] As assumed by several writers, such as Laborde, *op. cit.*, p. 29.

[12] See L. Viardot, *Historie des Arabes et des Mores d'Espagne. Paris* 1851, II, p. 91; cf. also Levi-Provencal, *op. cit.*, p. 166; Laborde, *op. cit*, I, p. xxxvii: IV, p. 29; Hall, *op. cit.*, p. 363; A. G. Palencia, *Historia de la España Muselmana*, Barcelona-Buenos Aires, 1925, p. 112; L. M. Echeverria, *Geographia de España*. Barcelona-Buenos Aires, 1928, I, p. 162; R. Ballester, *Geographia de España*. Gerona 1918, p. 155. Even the patriotic author of the *Memoire* admits bashfully the spread of Arab agriculture wherever it could be applied profitably in Eastern and Southern Spain. (*op. cit.*, p. 107).

[13] Hall, *op. cit.*, pp. 395 ff.

[14] *Op. cit.*, pp. 367 ff.

[15] Laborde, *op. cit.*, p. 177.

the peasants became small cultivators, their zeal increasing as their gains increased.[16] Thus situated, the peasantry of Arab and Moorish Spain[17] was not only industrious,[18] but extremely numerous.[19] The Andalusian hinterland of the Guadalquivir which in 1800 had only slightly more than 200 villages had six times that many under the Caliph of Cordoba.[20]

Moorish Spain, whose population exhibited a "hydraulic" density, was also "hydraulic" in its form of government,[21] its mode of selecting officials,[22] its bureaucratically controlled fiscal[23] and military organization,[24] its theocratic leadership[25] and its great interest in astronmy.[26]

To be sure, the economy of Moorish Spain was not exclusively agricultural. Both Arabs and Berbers had a long tradition of pastoralism, and the highlands of Spain offered excellent opportunities for its continuance.[27] Moreover, its irrigation centres were not concentrated in a single river valley or plain, but were spread out over many disconnected regions. This constellation facilitated the dissolution of the Moslem state into a number of smaller units.[28] It also permitted the persistence in the north of those independent Christian territories that grew stronger as the Moslem world disintegrated and that, after a series of victories, destroyed it altogether. Institutionally speaking the conquest of Moorish Spain by the "Catholic Kings" was the triumph of a cattle-breeding feudal society over an agricultural civilization of the hydraulic type.

III

Cattle was not the sole property the Christian refugees took with them

---

[16] Levi-Provencal, op. cit., pp. 160 ff.

[17] The Arabs conquered Spain; later their African cousins, the Moors, superseded them as the rulers of the Islamic part of the country.

[18] Viardot, op. cit., 1, p. 392, (Voltaire called the Moors, "labourieux dans le pays de la paresse. . .").

[19] Op. cit., II, p. 33.

[20] Laborde, op. cit., p. 8. For a similar figure see Viardot, op. cit., II, p. 33.

[21] Levi-Provencal, op. cit., p. 62; see also H. Schurtz, "Die Pyrenaische Halbinsel", in Hans F. Helmolt, Weltgeschichte, IV, Leipzig and Wien, p. 491; and R. Dozy, Histoire des Muselmans d'Espagne. Leyden, 1932, II, pp. 153 ff.

[22] Op. cit., pp. 100, 118, 120. Cf. also Viardot, op. cit., II, pp. 11-12

[23] Levi-Provencal, op. cit., p. 73; Viardot, op. cit., II, p. 47.

[24] Levi-Provencal, op. cit., p. 135; Viardot, op. cit., II, p. 41.

[25] Levi-Provencal, op. cit., pp. 45 ff.; Viardot, op. cit., II, p. 6.

[26] Levi-Provencal, op. cit., p. 171; Viardot, op. cit., II, p. 100.

[27] Levi-Provencal, op. cit., p. 163; see also Laborde, op. cit., IV, pp. 56 ff.; according to Schurtz, the Arabs settled in regions such as fertile Andalusia, while the Berbers originally occupied the mountainous territories of the northern frontier of Central Spain, and the South. (Schurtz, op. cit., 489).

[28] Cf. R. Dozy, Histoire des Muselmans d'Espagne, III. passim.

when, in the 8th century, they retreated before the Arab invaders,[29] but herding was the core of their material existence. And the growth of their political power is closely linked to their expanding pastoral activities, which, in the later Middle Ages, received a new economy.[30] While making full allowance for other contributing factors, it does seem that the course of events on the peninsula was largely determined by the growing importance of wool production and wool trade in the militant kingdoms of Northern Spain.

The import of Spanish wool by England began "at least as early as the 12th century".[31] In 1172, Henry II tried to suppress it.[32] But whatever his success, from 1300 on, fine Castillian wool is mentioned more and more regularly in the trade reports of England and Flanders. In Bruges, Spanish wool merchants set up a trading-post, and after 1303, the arrival of Spanish wool in Southhampton, Sandwich, and Portsmouth is mentioned annually.[33]

The production and trade of wool was well under way before the Great Pestilence of 1348-1350. However, the decimation of the rural population encouraged the promotion of cattle-breeding. This is precisely the kind of development that occurred in Castille which had "by far the most active and productive pastoral industry of any country in Europe in that period".[34]

The further history of the wool trade in Spain need not be discussed here. Enough to say that under Ferdinand and Isabella the promotion of wool exports was "the key note of the commercial programme." [35] In the the first decades of the 16th century, Spain's wool trade reached an all-time high.[36]

The economic weight of sheep-breeding is clearly expressed in the revenues obtained by the central government from a tax on migratory sheep. The *servicio y montazgo* brought into the treasury [37]

4.7 million maravedis in 1513
8.5 „ „ in 1535
10.2 „ „ in 1543
19.6 „ „ in 1563

[29] This is Jovellanos' claim. See Laborde, *op. cit.*, p. 165.

[30] See Kulischer, *Allegemeine Wirtschaftsgeschichte*, I, pp. 218, 245, and 261; also Sombart, *Der Moderne Kapitalismus*, I, pp. 282 ff.

[31] J. Klein. *The Mesta. A Study of Spanish Economic History 1273-1836*. Cambridge 1920, p. 34.

[32] *Loc. cit.*

[33] *Loc. cit.*

[34] *Op. cit.*, p. 35.

[35] *Op. cit.*, p. 37.

[36] *Op. cit.*, p. 325.

[37] *Op. cit.*, p. 279.

These facts substantiate the statement made in 1567 that "the exploitation and conservation of the pastoral industry is the principal sustenance of these kingdoms".[38] Indeed, the country's "chief staple" was the wool[39] that "had long been Spain's principal and almost only export commodity".[40]

Northern Spain's expanding sheep-herding and wool trade found organized expression in "the Honorable Assembly of the Mesta of the Shepherds" created by Alfons of Castille in 1273.[41] Once established, the Assembly became a powerful agent in furthering the wool trade. By pushing pastoral interests at court it protected this increasingly remunerative economy from local administration and taxation.[42]

The Mesta, which strengthened the government fiscally and politically,[43] did much to strengthen the centralization of the state. Its leaders drew closer and closer to the hub of political power; in 1454, the hereditary chief of its judicial affairs became a member of the Royal Council.[44] One last step remained to complete the union of the Mesta and the state—and this step was taken in 1500 when Ferdinand and Isabella established the office of the Presidency of the Mesta, which was to be headed by "the eldest member of the Royal Council".[45]

When the Northern states expanded southward, this union attained a more than local significance. The Spaniards, encroaching upon the irrigated fields in the Moorish territories, developed their pastoral economy and its controlling centre, the Mesta. Which force would prevail? Would the small land holdings characteristic of intensive agriculture obstruct the formation of large estates needed for extensive pasturage? After the expulsion of the Moors, the agricultural resources which were impaired by the wars of liberation could have been restored. But "Ferdinand and Isabella lost no time in displaying that marked partiality toward the pastoral exploitation of their kingdoms which was to be so conspicuous throughout this period".[46] It soon became apparent that "the monarchs were determined to support the extravagant contentions of the sheep owners against all southern and western landowners."[47]

[38] *Nueva Recopilacion de las Leyes destos Reynos, hecha por . . . Felipe II*, (1567), quoted in Klein, *op. cit.*, p. 317.
[39] W. H. Prescott, *History of the Reign of Ferdinand and Isabella the Catholic*, III, Philadelphia 1864, p. 459.
[40] Klein, *The Mesta*, p. 317.
[41] *Op. cit.*, p. 12.
[42] *Op. cit.*, pp. 175-77.
[43] *Op. cit.*, pp. 188, 192, and 201 ff.
[44] *Op. cit.*, pp. 209, 83.
[45] *Op. cit.*, p. 52.
[46] *Op. cit.*, p. 317.
[47] *Op. cit.*, p. 324.

After the reconquest, Granada's irrigation agriculture was in "a chaotic state".[48] There, as in Murcia, "any local attempts to improve agriculture ... were openly forbidden";[49] and, in consequence, the water works of Granada were "small, poorly maintained and miserably managed";[50] On the other hand, "every effort" was made to extend pasturage, "not only in Castille, but in other parts of the peninsula".[51] Along the highways followed by the sheep, from the estates of military orders, royal domains and town commons, land was turned over to the insatiable sheep owners.[52] In case of conflict, the agriculturalists who could produce no legal "evidence" to validate their claims to the ownership of their fields lost them to the herdsmen.[53] To increase pasturage so that the sheep could be adequately fed in the winter, forests were burned over and small trees cut down.[54] The *hojo* system was encouraged which prescribed that fields should lie fallow every second year and thus provide more grazing ground.[55] These several measures were crowned in 1505 by the famous *Leyes de Toro* which, by giving legal recognition to the large entailed estates (*mayorazgos*), established the herding economy as "unquestionably supreme over all other forms of rural life throughout the realm".[56]

The effect of this policy was double-edged. Spain's sheep wealth grew by leaps and bounds as did the wool trade, and government revenues soared. But agriculture shrank; in some regions it virtually disappeared. Much less land was cultivated and what was cultivated was often less well tilled than under Moorish rule. Summarizing Spain's economic stagnation after several hundred years of a pro-pastoral and pro-Mesta policy, Laborde remarks: "The greater part of the kingdom's lands entailed on the families of the nobility or belonging to religious corporations remains untilled".[57] There were fields without people[58] and people without fields. Indeed, much valuable terrain was transformed into pastures and yielded nothing.[59]

Irrigation had been the backbone of Moslem agriculture. Attempts to preserve or restore the Moorish water works,[60] were largely futile, since

[48] Hall, *Irrigation Development*, p. 430.
[49] Klein, *op. cit.*, p. 317.
[50] Hall, *op. cit.*, p. 430.
[51] Klein, *op. cit.*, p. 317.
[52] *Op. cit.*, pp. 318 ff.
[53] *Op. cit.*, p. 319.
[54] *Op. cit.*, p. 320.
[55] *Loc. cit.*
[56] *Op. cit.*, p. 325.
[57] Laborde, *op. cit.*, I, p. lxxxix.
[58] *Op. cit.*, IV, p. 11.
[59] *Op. cit.*, p. 53.
[60] Cf. Hall, *op. cit.*, pp. 508-9.

the government consistently favoured sheep-herding and the establishment of big estates.

It is true that, in regions such as Valencia where the ancient water works remained intact, irrigation continued to be practiced and agriculture flourished.[61] But the masters of the new latifundia were not content to control the cultivated land; they also wanted to control the water. Ultimately water became private property; and the consequences of this change were far-reaching. In Alicante, some people "have much more water than they require, while others have not nearly enough".[62] In Elche, private ("capitalist") control of water brought a halt to all agricultural progress.[63] In Murcia, the separation of the water from the land caused "a great deal of trouble, dissension, and many failures of crops from short supply and bad management".[64] Devastating as were these legal strangleholds on land and water, the situation was greatly worsened by a policy that discouraged the restoration of an irrigation economy which had been seriously damaged by the wars of reconquest.

IV

As agriculture declined, the population shrank. A preponderantly pastoral economy requires fewer operators than does an intensive agriculture. Klein ascribes the depopulation of Spain at this time to an increase in sedentary sheepbreeding which he distinguishes from the migratory herding encouraged by the Mesta.[65] Dillon, on the other hand, is convinced that the depopulation of Spain resulted from the policy of the Mesta. He argues that "where there is no Mesta, every part is populous ... the Mesta not only depopulated Estramadura but also the kingdoms of Leon and Castille".[66]

It is possible that sedentary sheep-breeding played a more important role in the "dismal process of agrarian decay"[67] than Dillon realized, but Klein's conclusions are not always consistent with his data. Clearly, the extension of large landholdings and heavy taxation[68] were merely different aspects of the same policy—a policy that first promoted the rise of the Mesta and then the growth of sedentary pastoralism. It is not too much to say that most of the causes enumerated by Klein were rooted

[61] Op. cit., pp. 384 ff., 395 ff.
[62] Op. cit., p. 408.
[63] Op. cit., p. 413.
[64] Op. cit., p. 432.
[65] Klein, op. cit., pp. 342 ff.
[66] J. T. Dillon, Travels Through Spain, London, 1780, p. 62.
[67] Klein, op. cit., p. 337.
[68] Op. cit., p. 336.

in the pro-pastoral policy of the government. Their coordination led inevitably from agricultural distress to decay and ruin.[69]

The wide empty spaces over which Don Quixote drove his stumbling mare testify eloquently to the pastoralization and depopulation of the Spanish countryside. Some areas never recovered from the pestilence and reconquest.[70] Others were allowed to lie fallow during the 16th [71] and 17th centuries:[72] and in Castille formerly flourishing fields [73] were "smitten with the curse of barrenness",[74] because sheep-breeding had been allowed "to run riot throughout the land and to annihilate almost the last vestiges of agriculture that still remained".[75]

Laborde paints a sad picture of Spain's depopulation. He gives a detailed description of more than 1,141 ruins of former settlements in Catalonia, Aragon, Leon, Valencia, Mancha, Castille, etc. around the year 1800. Of the 1,200 villages in Guadalquivir under the Caliph of Cordoba, only 200 survived; of the 50 in Malaya, only 16; of the 748 in one section of the diocese of Salamanca only 333, of the 127 near *des partidos de Baño y peña del rey* only 13.[76]

Laborde supplements this depressing catalogue by figures on the population in general which, although they require some correction in detail, in essence confirm the contemporary statements. In some cases Spain's population decreased more rapidly after the 16th century than before; but often the sharpest decline occurred immediately after the Moors and Jews were expelled. At this time even those regions whose population decline was greatest in the subsequent centuries suffered serious losses. The table on the next page, assembled from several sources, strikingly underlines the general trend.

The masters of the reconquest reflected the new economic climate even in their moments of relaxation and play. The Moslem nobles had often been keenly interested in the cultivation of the fields; even the Caliph might use the pruning knife.[77] The Spanish nobles behaved differently. The new lords of the pasture entered the arena and fought the bull. In fact, "Charles V himself on one occasion charged the bull with his lance".[78] And it was in the reign of Charles V that Cortez conquered Mexico and Pizarro conquered Peru.

[69] *Op. cit.*, pp. 336-37.   [70] See above.
[71] Cf. Klein, *op. cit.*, p. 321.
[72] *Op. cit.*, pp. 342 ff.
[73] Prescott, *Ferdinand and Isabella*, III, p. 462, note 85.
[74] *Op. cit.*, p. 461
[75] Klein, *op. cit.*, p. 343.
[76] Laborde, *op. cit.*, IV, p. 9.
[77] Viardot, *Histoire des Arabes et des Mores d'Espagne*, II, p. 91
[78] Cf. M. Haverly, *Wanderings in Spain*, London 1847, II, p. 294.

Territory or city	Under the Moors	In the 16th century	ca. 1800[79]
Merida	40,000		5,000
Seville	300,000[80] (in 1247)	200,000	96,000
Cordoba	1,000,000[81] (under the Caliphs)	60,000	35,000
Toledo		200,000 (14th-16th century)	25,000
Baeza	150,000[82]		15,000
Granada			
the Kingdom	3,000,000		661,661
the city	250,000 (in 1492)	80,000 (in 1614)	50,000

V

This historical background is prophetically significant when the policies of the *conquistadores* are studied. In Spain herding had been the easy and noble road to riches in silver and gold. In the New World, it was believed this road could be travelled even more quickly. Here the treasure was untapped, the rewards great and the Spanish invaders were well prepared to fight for them. The recent Spanish experience proved an excellent model. Through the *repartimiento, the encomienda,*[83] and the

[79] Laborde's "population actuelle". His work was published in 1806. (Laborde, *op. cit.,* IV, p. 9).

[80] 1247 was the last year of Moslem rule. The city was reconquered in 1248. If really "400,000 of the inhabitants went into voluntary exile" (article "Seville", *Encyclopedia Britannica* eleventh ed., XXIV, p. 732), then the city must have been still more populous.

[81] Native Arab chroniclers ascribed to Cordoba not less than 200,000 houses, a figure that would indeed indicate a population of at least a million people, if the average household comprised 5 members. The author of the article "Cordoba" in the *Encyclopedia Britannica* (eleventh ed., VII, p. 143), though considering the figure 200,000 "probably exaggerated", accepts an accelerated decline of population after the reconquest.

[82] According to the article "Baeza" in the *Encyclopedia Britannica* (eleventh ed., III, p. 192) the "flourishing Moorish city" was credited with 50,000 inhabitants.

[83] L. B. Simpson, *Studies in the Administration of the Indians in New Spain,* III. The Repartimiento System of Native Labor in New Spain and Gautemala". Berkeley 1938, pp. 6 ff. Cf. also *Documents from Early Peru.* "The Pisarros and the Almagros, 1531-1578". The Earkness Collection in the Library of Congress, Washington, 1936, *passim,*

mita,[84] they forced the natives to toil for them in the silver mines and gold fields.[85] It is clear from the early documents that during the first half of the 16th century "a considerable percentage of the Indian population of New Spain was being used in the mines".[86]

In Mexico the use of commandeered labour in the mines continued until the 18th century [87] and in Peru until the beginning of the 19th.[88] For both countries the hardships and horrors of this type of exploitation have been reported in authentic sources. It hardly needs saying that it sharply reduced the manpower available for agriculture.[89] And the agricultural manpower was further reduced by the requisitioning of natives for other kinds of work.

But the negative effects of these measures were grimly aggravated by the devastation that followed the seizure of Indian lands and the establishment of great plantations and cattle-ranges for the benefit of the new rulers. Cortez and Pizarro bestowed upon deserving *consquis- tadores* control not only over the land, but also over the persons of the defeated non-believers. Humboldt says: "All the vices of the feudal government passed on from one hemisphere to the other, and in Mexico the abuses were the more dangerous in their effects, since it was more difficult for the supreme authority to cure the evil and to mobilize its energy at such an immense distance. The soil of New Spain like that of Old Spain finds itself in great part in the hands of several powerful families who had gradually absorbed the private property. *In America, as in Europe, great communities are condemned to cattle-herding and permanent sterility.*" [90]

This statement of American policy is highly illuminating, but Humboldt's notion that the supreme authority in Spain sought to check the excess is based on an erroneous conception of the primary economic interests of the contemporary Spanish government. In Spain as well as in the Americas, many conflicts occurred between the central government and cattle-owning nobles; but their dominant aims were not contradictory. The conquest of the new lands was not undertaken to preserve the tra-

---

[84] A. de Humboldt, *Examen critique de l'histoire de la geographie du nouveau siècles.* Paris 1837, III, pp. 290 ff.

[85] Hussey, *Economic Colonial Life,* p. 321.

[86] Simpson, *op. cit.,* p. 44.

[87] *Op. Cit.,* pp. 46-65. Report concerning ill treatment of the forced mine workers continued until the "dangerous riots in the eighteenth century" (Simpson, *op. cit.,* p. 45; see also pp. 53 ff., 55, 61 and 65).

[88] Humboldt, *op. cit.,* III, p. 290, note 2.

[89] See A. de Humboldt, *Essai politique sur le royaume de la Nouvelle Espagne,* Paris 1811, II, p. 424.

[90] *Op. cit.,* III, p. 289. Italics mine,

ditional economy of an alien and heathen population, but to increase the wealth and power of the crown and its loyal servants. In time the search for economic gain might induce the conquerors to modify their traditional economic concepts, yet it was only natural that these concepts would determine their first steps and reactions. Wherever the early *conquistadores* went, they searched eagerly for good pasturage as well as for precious metals. Landing in Tabasco, Cortez immediately observed that the fertile coastal plains offered facilities for grazing all kinds of animals.[91] In Cholula, he was impressed by its highly developed irrigation agriculture; but he found the area attractive for a very different reason: "It is the best adapted for Spaniards to live in of any I have seen since leaving the port, *as it has some uncultivated lands and water for the purpose of raising cattle, such as have no others we have seen so far.*"[92]

Cortez' statement is as direct as it is consistent. It perfectly expresses the "economic ethos" of self-conscious cattle-breeders who after a long struggle had demonstrated the superiority of their type of material production. Of course, it is conceivable that a different situation might have compelled the sons of Mesta radically to alter their traditional attitude. But no such revolution was required by new circumstances.

America's rich numeral resources stimulated more than altered the habits acquired in industrial Europe. Although many features of the American rural landscape were strange to the conquerors, the change from small Indian holdings to large sugar and cocoa plantations paralleled Spain's own change from a small peasant agriculture under the Moors to an economy built on large estates.

Of course, agriculture had to be preserved, for, whatever its size, the population had to be fed. Thus a limited cereal agriculture was preserved and at times even promoted.[93] But in large part arable land was given over in the lowlands to the production of such export crops as sugar and cocoa and, in the regions offering good pasturage, to cattle-breeding.

VI

The background of the *conquistadores* encouraged violence against, and contempt for, the subdued non-believers. But it would be a grave mistake to explain a policy of centuries as having been set by a short period

[91] *Letters of Cortez*, translated and edited by F. A. MacNutt. New York and London, 1928, I, pp. 160 ff.

[92] *Op. cit.*, p. 221. Italics mine.

[93] Cf. Humboldt, *Essai politique*, III, pp. 14 ff.; Simpson, *op. cit.*, p. 93; Hussey *op. cit.*, pp. 319 ff; A. S. Aiton, *Antonio de Mendoza. F. M. viceroy of New Spain.* Durham, 1927, p. 110.

of transition. The attitude of the Spaniards in America was not shaped by the long-range advantages they were able to attain. Ships were small and freight charges high. Not much would be gained by exporting grain to Europe. Until the end of the 18th century the commodities that were important in local trading were not exported to Europe.[94] Silver was the most highly valued article of export; but handsome profits could also be made in sugar and cocao, dyewoods and dye-stuffs,[95] and hides.[96] The "great gains" accruing from the cultivation of such staples as sugar and, later, cotton explain both the origin and maintenace of the plantation economy that flourished on the coast of Peru.[97]

Cortez, in his Second Letter, outlined his ideas on how to maintain a proper Spanish residence in the New World; and his own later behaviour proved that for him pastoralism served an economic as well as a military function. When, after the final victory, he settled down on his princely estate, he at once "imported large numbers of merino sheep and other cattle, which found abundant pastures in the country around Tehuantepec".[98]

Cortez blazed the trail; and within a few decades "oxen, horses, sheep, and pigs multiplied in a surprising manner in all parts of New Spain".[99] Acosa, an early observer, cites excellent pasturage as the reason for the presence of an "innumerable quantity of horses, cows, sheep and other animals".[100] At the time of his arrival in America (before 1571), some individuals owned as many as 70,000 and 100,000 sheep.[101] A very small flock of imported sheep could increase to some 10,000 or more animals within two decades.[102] Wherever cattle could multiply unchecked, the size of the herds increased rapidly, not only in Central America, but also in the North American Southwest,[103] Peru,[104] and Yucatan.[105]

[94] Humboldt, op. cit., IV, pp. 369 and 378.

[95] Hussey, op. cit., p. 326; Humboldt, op. cit., IV, pp. 369, 378.

[96] Hussey, op. cit., p. 326.

[97] E. W. Middendorf, Peru, Berlin 1894, II, pp. 293 ff.

[98] Prescott, The Conquest of Mexico, p. 671.

[99] Humboldt, op. cit., III, p. 224.

[100] Cf. D. F. S. Clavigero, The History of Mexico, translated by C. Cullen. Philadelphia, 1817, III, p. 180.

[101] Op. cit., p. 235.

[102] Cf. Obragon's History, p. 151; cf. also Clavigero, op. cit., II, p. 235.

[103] Obragon's History of the 16th Century Explorations in Western America, Translated, edited and annotated by G. P. Hammond and A. Rey. Los Angeles, 1928, p. 151.

[104] Cf. C. R. Markham, A History of Peru. Chicago, 1882, p. 163; see also Clavigero, op. cit., III p. 238 and Don G. Juan and Don A. de Ulloa, A Voyage to South America. London 1806, I pp. 300 and passim.

[105] Shattuck remarks that "formerly, cattle was raised in abundance on the Spanish estates or haciendas in Yucatan". (G. C. Shattuck, The Peninsula of Yucatan. Carnegie

In the New World wool became a valuable source of revenue,[106] for in many places it was "as fine as the wool of the sheep in Spain".[107] But the real goal of the cattle-breeding was to produce hides for which the leather industries of Europe offered a profitable market. Mendoza, who visited America in 1584, gives a vivid picture of the way in which hides were obtained, often with wanton disregard for the meat. He says, "In this kingdom [Mexico] there are bred and brought up more cattell then in any other parts knowne in all the world, as wel for the good climate and temperature of the heauen, as also for the fertility of the countrie. The kine and sheepe many times bring forth twise a yeare, and goates ordinarily thrise a yeare; so that because they haue many fields in that countrie, and much people that doo giue themselves vnto that kinde of gettings (as grasiers) is the occasion that there is so great abundance, and solde for a small price; and manie times it happeneth that the bringers vp of them doo kill tenne thousand head of them onely to profite themselues with the skinnes, in sending of them into Spaine, and leaue the flesh in the fieldes to feede the foules of the ayre, without making any more account thereof".[108] On a smaller scale, the same situation existed in California, where the Spanish settlers combined a small and imperfect agriculture with the "rearing of cattle for the commerce of the hides and tallows".[109] The export of hides from the New World to Spain early reached extraordinary figures. In 1587, a single, fleet carried over 64,000 hides to Seville.[110]

The Madrid government carefully monopolized the new export trade,[111] hence it raised no basic objections to the pro-pastoral policy of New Spain. Many abuses were criticized, but few were corrected,[112] since "the first thing was to strain every nerve to send riches home to Spain".[113] Aiton, who by no means condemns the Spanish policy as a whole, nevertheless states, "In the eyes of the monarchs of Spain, colonies existed

Institution of Washington, Washington 1933, publ. no 431, p. 15). Recently the production of the sisal fibre has largely replaced the pastoral economy which still prevailed when Stephens made his famous explorations before the middle of the 19th century. (See below).

[106] Cf. Aiton, Mendoza, p. 111.

[107] Clavigero, op. cit., p. 235.

[108] J. G. de Mendoza, The History of the Great and Mighty Kingdom of China and the Situation Thereof. The Hakluyt Society, London 1854, vol. 15. II, p. 225.

[109] See F. W. Blackmar, Spanish Institutions of the Southwest. Baltimore 1891, p. 268.

[110] Clavigero, op. cit., III, p. 232.

[111] Hussey, op. cit., p. 324.

[112] Prescott, History of the Reign of Ferdinand and Isabella, III, pp. 474 ff.

[113] Markham, A History of Peru, p. 192.

chiefly for the production of revenue."[114] Consequently, "when the needs of the royal revenue and humanitarian principles clashed, the latter was inevitably the loser".[115]

The establishment of a Mesta by Cortez, patterned upon the Mesta in Castille,[116] is a symbol of the official attitude toward cattle-breeding. Owners of twenty cows or horses or three hundred small animals automatically became members.[117] A further interest in pastoral matters may be inferred from a questionnaire sent to Mexico from Madrid in 1580. Question 4 dealt with good pasturage, while problems of irrigation were relegated to question 19.

Within "the most ingeniously perverse system of laws"[118] introduced shortly after the conquest, the regulations governing land *tenure* were particularly noteworthy. The Indians were assigned only a small fraction of land around the newly built churches; the remainder became the property of the conquerors.[119] Thus "the great mass of people were left without sufficient land", while a small number of individuals became hereditary owners of immense tracts.[120] These new landowners cultivated only the best fields and used the rest for the raising of cattle.[121] Some of the estates were so large that considerable parts were not used at all, neither for plantation agriculture[122] nor for cattle-breeding.[123]

Mendoza, the first viceroy of New Spain, a member of the haughty Castillian aristocracy[124] and a son of a long line of fighters against the Moors,[125] chose as his "pet interest ... the sheep industry, which he fostered and encouraged".[126] In addition to the considerable fiefs owned by his family in the Asturias and in Castille,[127] he acquired large lands in New Spain, a ranch near Mexico, five in the vicinity of Marabatio, others near Vera Cruz, two near Tecamachalco, and "the entire valley of Ulizabal".[128] In the main the ranches "were stocked with sheep", and the valley was used as a horse-ranch.[129]

---

[114] Aiton, *Mendoza*, p. 70.
[115] *Op. cit.*, p. 85.
[116] Klein, *The Mesta*, pp. 9 and 276.
[117] Hussey, *op. cit.*, p. 320.
[118] Prescott, *Ferdinand and Isabella*, III, p. 478.
[119] Humboldt, *op. cit.*, I, p. 425.
[120] L. E. Fisher, *The Background of the Revolution for Mexican Independence.* Boston 1934, p. 154.
[121] *Op. cit.*, p. 155.
[122] Middendorf, *Peru*, II p. 294.
[123] Fisher, *op. cit.*, p. 155.
[124] Aiton, *Mendoza*, p. 4.
[125] *Op. cit.*, pp. 34 ff.
[126] *Op. cit.*, p. 111.   [127] *Op. cit.*, p. 5.
[128] *Op. cit.*, p. 48.   [129] *Loc. cit.*

Individual trees and even whole forests were cut down,[130] perhaps in part, as Humboldt assumes, because the *conquistadores* wanted to recreate in the beautiful valley of Tenochtitlan the bare Castillian landscape,[131] but in part certainly because lumber was needed for the mines and other new constructions, and because the Spanish experience suggested that such procedures aided a pastoral economy.

The laws that compelled the natives to work on the newly established estates provided their aristocratic and clerical owners with cheap labour. Cattle-breeding was one of the industries for whose benefit the *repartimiento* system of forced labour had been set up. The laws also dealt with agriculture, which provided food for the people and made it possible for them to work in the mines, on the ranches and large plantations. But, as in post-Moorish Spain, the water works were poorly maintained and acreage under tillage shrank spectacularly.

Future studies will give a fuller picture of these aspects of the agricultural development in post-conquest America. Here I shall only indicate them in a very general way. In the environs of Mexico City, "the flocks and herds ... had become a nuisance and hindered agriculture, as the crops tilled by the natives were consumed by the unfenced animals".[132] The Bishop of Oaxaca "had to be warned to cease troubling the natives with his ranches and flocks".[133]

Humboldt claims that in Mexico the Spaniards "artificially dried up huge expanses of terrain".[134] By doing so, they made the famous valley a less dangerous place to live in, but they "destroyed the source of fertility in a great part of the plateau of Tenochtitlan".[135] The change, while greatly benefitting the newcomers, seriously worsened the condition of the Indians. Humboldt concluded that "the drainage system may be considered the main cause for the misery of the natives in the valley of Mexico".[136]

In Yucatan the greater part of the magnificent Mayan system of water works was so neglected that it was some time before Dr. Stephens realized that the original reservoirs and water holes had in large part been man-made.[137] In Peru sections of the old irrigation works were preserved

---

[130] Prescott, *The Conquest of Mexico*, p. 12.
[131] Humboldt, *Essai Politique*, II, p. 128.
[132] Aiton, *Mendoza*, p. 111.
[133] *Op. cit.*, p. 113.
[134] Humboldt, *Essai Politique*, I, p. 302.
[135] *Op. cit.*, II, p. 249.
[136] *Loc. cit.*
[137] See J. L. Stephens, *Incidents of Travel in Yucatan*, New York 1843, I, p. 250 and passim.

and utilized;[138] but many of the more elaborate constructions ceased to function [139] because of neglect or wilful destruction. Humboldt, who admired the hydraulic accomplishments of the ancient Americans was appalled when he saw what was left of the long aqueducts that had carried water for irrigation from the slopes of the Andes to the arid coastal zone. "The conquerors of the sixteenth century destroyed these aqueducts; and this part of Peru, like Persia, became again a desert bare of vegetation. Such is the civilization that the Europeans carried to those people whom they pleased to call barbarians."[140]

VII

The demographic effects of all this are clear. The great and quick decrease in the native population repeated what had happened in Spain after the victory of the northern cattle-breeders. In Mexico, as already noted, mining expanded, grazing increased, and "agricultural methods took on the extensive character".[141] Answers to the official questionnaire circulated in 1580 emphasize the great population loss both shortly before and directly after the conquest.[142] Death-dealing epidemics are usually given as the causes;[143] and such epidemics did indeed occur.[144] But Humbodlt in concluding his discussion of disease in colonial Mexico remarks that in addition to illness there was also famine—and that this factor was "perhaps the most cruel of all".[145] In 1575, Zurita held the *repartimiento* responsible for the reduction of the Indian population to one-third their former number.[145] Motolina called this system of forced labour, the "sixth plague".[147]

Actually, the causes of depopulation were more complex than the writings of these early observers suggest. But there can be little doubt that it largely resulted from the economic policy pursued by the *conquistadores*. Again and again epidemics seriously reduced the populations of India and China; but such losses were recouped, and often quite quickly, because the general economy favoured repopulation. The decimation

---

[138] Cf. Prescott, *The Conquest of Peru*, p. 799.

[139] Cf. Sapper, *op. cit.*, p. 180.

[140] Humboldt, *op. cit.*, II, p. 142, note.

[141] H. J. Priestly, *The Mexican Nation, A History*, New York 1923, p. 9.

[142] See Official Reports of the Towns of Tequizistlan ... Papers of the Peabody Museum of American Archaeology and Ethnology. Harvard University. XI, 2, 1926.

[143] *Op. cit.*, pp. 54 ff.

[144] Cf. Humboldt, *Essai Politique*, I, pp. 344 ff.

[145] *Op. cit.*, I, p. 354.

[146] See *Reports on the Discovery of Peru*. The Hakluyt Society. London 1872, pp. 13, 20, 24, 80 ff., 90, 122.

[147] See *Letters of Cortez*. F.A. MacNutt, Appendix to Fourth Letter, II, p. 226.

caused by epidemics will be permanent only when the socio-economic order requires fewer people to serve its needs.

And this was the situation in Mexico after the conquest. It was also the situation in Peru and Yucatan. Pizarro and his companions were impressed by the great number of persons they found in Peru's coastal and highland regions. However, after the conquest "vast tracts [of land] were thrown out of cultivation", and not surprisingly, "the country was rapidly depopulated".[148] In Yucatan several provinces, which earlier had boasted a dense population, were left desolate after the conquest.[149] What Indians remained were dependent upon "the big Spanish plantation owners",[150] whose interest in cattle-breeding shaped the country's cultural landscape for centuries.

Later developments in Spanish America are not my concern here. The colonial period is over and considerable changes have occurred since, and continue to occur now. But for an understanding of these changes a knowledge of the economic policies of the conquest is highly desirable. For a proper analysis of America's ancient civilizations it is imperative.

[148] Markham, *A History of Peru*, p. 193. This situation still persisted at the end of the 19th century. Middendorf states that "on most estates large tracts of fertile soil lie uncultivated and unused." Middendorf, *Peru*, II, p. 294.

[149] Landa, *op. cit.*, p. 86.

[150] Gann and Thompson, *The History of the Maya*, p. 95.

18

CUBA—REVOLUTION
WITHOUT A BLUEPRINT

MAURICE ZEITLIN

THE WORLD-HISTORICAL significance of the Cuban revolution is that for the first time in the western hemisphere a revolution has been put through in the name of socialism. It is the first socialist revolution led by independent radicals throughout its most decisive phases. Even when they were to identify with the international Communist movement, and to fuse with the old Communists, they retained the clear initiative within the revolutionary leadership, and gained for Cuba a singular place among Communist states. The Cuban revolution has gone further, and has more profoundly and rapidly transfored the prerevolutionary social structure than has any other "socialist" revolution anywhere. Most of the fundamental transformation of the political economy—of property relations and of the class structure—occurred within a couple of years of the revolutionaries consolidation of power; and with the recent (March 1968) nationalization of some 55,000 small businesses, primarily in food retailing and services, virtually the entire economy is now in the public sector: In agriculture, 70 percent of the arable land is in the public sector, leaving only farms of less than 67 hectares (160 acres) to be worked by their owners.

What explains the rapidity and thoroughness of the Cuban revolution, compared not only to the other national and social revolutions in our

time, but to other "socialist" revolutions as well?—and, perhaps inseparable from this, why did it become a "socialist revolution," unlike, for
instance, the social revolutions in Mexico and Bolivia?

The Cuban, Mexican, and Bolivian revolutions have certain similarities
which are neither superficial nor unimportant. In each, there was a fundamental agrarian transformation that abolished the existing land tenure
system and destroyed the economic base of the ruling strata in the countryside. In each, the old military apparatus was smashed and replaced
with armed detachments (or militias) of peasants and workers. In each,
strategic sectors of the national economy which were foreign-owned were
nationalized. In Bolivia, the tin mines were occupied and run by the
armed miners themselves. In Mexico, though late in the revolutionary
process, the Cárdenas regime nationalized the oil industry.

These three revolutions, therefore, are unquestionably set apart from
other so-called revolutions in Latin America. Nevertheless, the similarity
between the Cuban revolution and the revolutions in Mexico and Bolivia
is far less important than the major difference: Scarcely an aspect of
the prerevolutionary social structure in Cuba has remained intact, primarily because of the expropriation of private property in the system of
production and distribution, and the establishment of a centrally-planned,
publicly-owned economy.

What were the features of the prerevolutionary social structure in Cuba
that determined the type of social structure created by the revolution?
Somewhat differently: What were the constraints and the options that were
given to the leaders of the Cuban revolution by the prerevolutionary
social structure? What did they have to put up with, what was the
social material they had to work with, in order to make this revolution—
in contrast, for instance, to those who led revolutions and came to power
in Russia, China, and Yugoslavia, or in Bolivia or Mexico? In the book
which I wrote with Robert Scheer several years ago (*Cuba: Tragedy
in Our Hemisphere*) we took the prerevolutionary social structure as
given and focused on the interaction between the United States and
Cuba and in what way the interchange between them radicalized the revolution. Of course, the two are really inseparable, and it is likely that the
interchange was itself determined by the prerevolutionary social structure. I want now to take that interchange as given, in order to search
out the relevance of the prerevolutionary social structure itself.

My leading hypothesis is: Cuba's is the first socialist revolution to
take place in a capitalist country—a country in which the owning class was
capitalist and the direct producers were wage-workers. The argument may
be stated in the following schematic working hypotheses:

Cuba's dominant economic class was capitalist—a peculiar type of capitalist class but a capitalist class nonetheless. There were no significant feudal or seignorial elements remaining in the upper economic strata. The major elements of the dominant strata were in exporting (mainly of sugar and other primary products) and its financing, importing (mainly luxury goods), and tourism, small-scale manufacture of consumer goods for the home market; and they were also agents of, and representatives and, investors in United States-owned manufacturing firms using equipment and materials imported from the United States. These elements tended to overlap and intertwine, and to be integrated by concrete economic interests and social and familial bonds. In short they formed the capitalist class. The agrarian component of this class was export-market oriented and employed wage-labour on a large scale in the sugar mills and cane fields. As a result, the revolution did not have to be anti-feudal.

Of the classes, the working class was the largest, the most cohesive, and the most politically conscious. It was an organized national class that spread throughout the country, and that had a durable revolutionary and socialist political culture set in motion by the anarcho-syndicalists and continued under the Communist leadership of the workers. This cannot be said of any other country in which revolutions in our time—whether anticolonial, nationalist, or Communist—have been put through. It cannot be said of prerevolutionary Russia certainly, where the Petrograd workers were an insignificant minority (in numbers) of the total population though decisive in the revolution. Nor certainly can it be said of pre-revolutionary China, nor of Mexico, Bolivia, Algeria, nor of Vietnam. This may come as something of a conceptual shock, since the image of pre-revolutionary Cuba held by many, whether friends or foes of the revolution, is that of a peasant society. Nor was it, in an important sense, an "underdeveloped" country. From the standpoint of an analysis of the economic system and class structure of prerevolutionary Cuba, I believe it is much more fruitful to view it as a relatively unevenly developed or misdeveloped capitalist country of a special colonial type.

In the agrarian sector, there was no subsistence peasantry, nor the nonwage tenant-labour characteristic of the *hacienda* or manorial economy. The vast majority of the economically active population employed in agriculture were wage workers. Improved working conditions and higher wages—working-class interests—rather than "land hunger" were their essential demands and aspirations, unlike the situation in other countries where revolutions calling themselves "socialist" have occurred. Moreover, what there was of a nonwage working population in Cuba's countryside was a small proprietor stratum—the *colonos*—who were integrated into the market economy and dependent on the large, economically strategic sugar "centrals" (production centres including mills, workers' housing and transportation) for credit, milling, and marketing; in the case of tobacco and coffee cultivation, there were also small proprietors and/or tenants whose overall economic significance was marginal. The agrarian sector was based on large-scale capitalist enterprises which employed both industrial and agricultural wage workers.

What strengthened the hands of the ruling class in other social revolutions in this century was a mass social base, largely in the countryside, which they could mobilize as allies to defend their own interests. A counterrevolutionary movement in these countries was possible because the rulers still had legitimacy in and social control of the rural population. It was no historical accident that a bloody civil war was required in revolutionary Russia to put down the counterrevolution, that three decades of armed warfare preceded the triumph of the Chinese Communists, or that the Mexican revolutionaries had to violently confront and overcome the combined might of the Catholic Church and *hacendados*—the large landowners. The Cuban revolutionaries (and this is not to detract from their own extraordinary abilities) did not have to confront a similar situation. The landed upper stratum had been virtually expropriated by the development of capitalism much before the revolution.

Of course, Cuban capitalism was absentee-owned, foreign-controlled, and quasi-colonial. This meant that not only did the ruling strata not have roots in the countryside but that, indeed, they had no significant independent base of economic power in the country as a whole. The so-called Cuban capitalist class was dependent on American capitalism—politically, militarily, economically. Because of this dependency they also lacked social legitimacy. The justification of their rule stood nakedly revealed as their control of the means of violence. They stayed in power because they had a military regime (and behind it the power of the United States government) to protect them, not because anyone believed that they *deserved* power or that they had the *right* to rule. They were illegitimate in the eyes of virtually the entire population because they had shown their incapacity to rule effectively.

Contrast this for a moment with the situation of the ruling strata in Chile, since it is the only other country in the western hemisphere in which a mass-based Marxian socialist movement has had relative durability—and is rooted predominantly in the working class. Despite this, Chile's ruling strata have considerable legitimacy. A coalition of owning strata which is both landed and industrial has been able to demonstrate its capacity to rule over a period of a century without either foreign control or the intervention of the military as an autonomous social force. In the countryside, the *hacendados* ruled a peasantry involved in tenant-labour, living on the great *fundos* and exploited through seignorial and paternalistic relations. Only recently has agrarian agitation and organization begun to shake this stability. This is in contrast to the instability and massive struggles that characterized the Cuban past, and in which the struggles were directed against a class that was scarcely considered (and perhaps scarcely considered itself) Cuban.

This contrast in the capacity of these classes to rule is also shown by the fact that Chilean political stability and parliamentary democracy have been inseparable. In Cuba, the forms of political democracy associated with capitalism had, so to speak, exhausted themselves. The brief interregnum of political democracy was considered to be a sham and not substantially more relevant to the needs of Cuba as a nation and to the interests of its people than military rule. Parties and politicians associated with Cuba's "Congress" were all but universally held in contempt. Parliamentary democracy as the legitimate mode of representative government and the bounds within which major conflicts ought to be resolved and government policy determined had lost legitimacy, if indeed it ever existed; a major ideological obstacle to revolutionary change had, therefore, been eroded well before the revolutionaries took power.

Eroded also had been whatever ideological dominion over the great majority of workers and "peasants" the Catholic Church may once have possessed. The Cuban upper strata, therefore, lacked the advantage of a significant ally that ruling classes confronted by revolutionary movements have usually had—an ally whose means of social control and moral suasion supported the existing social order and clothed revolutionary movements in the guise of mammon. That is not to say that the Church hierarchy did not oppose the social revolution. But because the communicants of the Church were drawn largely from the upper and upper-middle urban strata, and little from the countryside or peasantry, its weight in the struggle was not decisive. (It was neither a large land owner nor did it have church centres, schools, monasteries or nunneries scattered throughout the country—these scarcely existed.) Moreover, it was one of the peculiar benefits (or consequences) of direct United States occupation in the founding years of the Republic that Church and State were separated, and the American presence was a secularizing and rationalizing influence.

Large-scale enterprise in the countryside and the inter-mingling of industrial and agricultural workers in the sugar centrals permeated the country largely with capitalist, rationalistic, secular, antitraditional values and norms of conduct. In this sense, the country was *prepared* for development—the only thing lacking being the revolution itself which took control over the economy and the means of violence from capitalists, both foreign and domestic, and put it in the hands of a sovereign Cuban state.

Whereas the ruling strata lacked legitimacy and had no independent ideology that was expressive of their own peculiar interests and that they could impose on society at large, there was in the working class of Cuba a socialist political culture (of anarcho-syndicalist and Communist elements) born in an insurrectionary past, which had already existed for no less than three decades (and far longer in segments such as the tobacco workers). The outlook of the typical worker toward the system was impregnated by socialist ideas; what is most important, the vision of a future without capitalism was most firmly and widely held by the most decisive sectors of the working class. This is, what Max Weber would have called a "'simple historical fact" of such significance that without taking it into account one cannot understand the socialist revolution. If it was not the vision of the majority of workers in town and country, the dominant vision among them was, nonetheless anticapitalist, antiimperialist, and socialist. Even the essentially reformist and middle-class leadership of the Auténtico (and later *Ortodoxo*) party which had considerable influence among workers since the aborted revolution of the 1930s, and which was the only opposition of consequence to the Communists in the working class, also clothed its actions and programme in a quasi-socialist rhetoric. Its influence among workers, however, was not of the same order as Communist influence and was debilitated by the widespread corruption of the Auténtico leadership. Most working-class struggles, whatever the leadership and however narrow the economic demands, tended to take on the political slogans of antiimperialism and anticapitalism; it was their one consistent theme. The immediate ends of the struggle and the broader political aims—however tenuously—were linked. Thus, the historically significant impact on the workers' consciousness.

Communist Influence Among Workers

The *Report on Cuba* of the International Bank for Reconstruction and Development concluded that in the years of the most clandestine activity of the Communists about one-fourth of all workers (in 1950) "were secretly sympathetic to them"; I found, when I interviewed a national sample of workers in 1962, that some 29 percent claimed to have been partisans of the Communists before the revolution. Most important, the ideas held by workers who were non-Communist, even anti-Communist, also tended to be suffused by socialist content. As the *Report* also pointed out, "nearly all the popular education of working people on how an economic system works and what might be done to improve it came first from the anarcho-syndicalists, and most recently—and most effectively—from the Communists." It was, I believe, as naturally a part of the Cuban workers' conceptions of the system, their interests, and of the creation of a world which abolished their exploitation, as bread-and-butter unionism is "natural" to workers in the United States. Both resulted from given historical conditions in which the role of leadership (durable and institutional) was crucial. From the standpoint of the development of the socialist revolution, the importance of this simple historic fact cannot be exaggerated. Despite the vacillations, zigzags; and opportunism of the Communists, one thing occurred: the infusion in the workers of a vision that transcended the Communist leadership itself. The workers could in fact, abandon the Communists for Fidel to seek the fulfilment of the vision the Communists once represented. When the Revolutionary Government was established, it had a mass working-class base that likely was beyond its leaders in its vision of the society to be created by the revolution. This is in striking contrast to the situation in other countries in which the revolutionary leaders were far beyond their own mass base. The fact of a socialist political culture in the working class—a nationally-based, cohesive working class—combined with the force of nationalism and antiimperialism, created a potent revolutionary force waiting to be tapped by the revolutionary leaders once they took power.

Cuba, moreover, was in certain important respects a developed country. I say in important respects and emphasize at the same time the very uneven development of the country. Advanced industrial technology and primitive agricultural implements coexisted in interdependence within the same system. On the one hand, as James O'Connor has shown, economic institutions generally appearing in wealthy capitalist countries were fundamental in Cuba's prerevolutionary market structure. Production and distribution tended to be controlled by a few firms and producer's associations, and output, wages, prices, and earnings were determined within the framework of such market controls. Thus, Cuba had a vast reservoir of untapped, underutilized and misutilized resources which the revolutionary government could utilize by reordering and planning the objectives of production and distribution. A relatively developed infrastructure, obviously colonial in nature and possessing its attendant problems but nonetheless of great significance, already was established in Cuba before the revolution. Both in terms of its ability to communicate with the nation as a whole and to provide it with immediate, visible, and concrete benefits from the revolution, the revolutionaries enjoyed great advantages compared to the leaders of other social revolutions in our time. The revolutionary government could do what other revolutions' leaders could not do: They could put through an immediate and significant redistribution of the national income and improve the conditions of the masses within, so to speak, the first days of taking power. The share of the national income received by wage workers was increased by roughly one-third, according to conservative estimates (such as those by Felipe Pozos, former President of the National Bank of Cuba, in exile). This provided a cement between the regime and the masses in the early phases of the revolution which other revolutionary governments could not create in this way.

The sugar-central, wage-labour, agrarian complex also made it possible to create relatively rapidly and easily a socialist agrarian sector—virtually by shifting the locus of control wihin it and reorganizing and reordering the objectives of production. This, again, is very much in contrast to the prerevolutionary agrarian structure inherited by other revolutionaries. Most important, the labour movement in the countryside already included wage labourers within the central labour organization; industrial and agricultural workers associated naturally in the countryside and created bonds of social solidarity.   Thus, the classical revolutionary slogan of the alliance and unity of workers and peasants was already, in a very important sense, a durable social fact before the revolutionaries came to power. The factories in the field, the sugar centrals containing the sugar mills and associated lands, provided a situation in which agricultural workers living and working on the central's lands came into more or less regular contact with industrial workers. Also, the agricultural worker himself, or his brother, or friends, may have worked at one time as a cane-cutter and another in the sugar mills, providing the industrial and agricultural worker with a fund of common experiences and perceptions. Poor proprietors also often worked in similar situations.

These centrals were, in addition, not only centres of industrial production and a basis for the creation of natural social bonds between "peasants" and workers, but also centres of political agitation and education. The most important prerevolutionary political base of the Communists was here. Forty-one percent of the sugar-central workers, compared to thirty percent of urban workers who had those occupations before the revolution, said in our interviews with them in 1962 that they were prerevolutionary supporters of the Communists. Therefore, for all these reasons, the very same acts which the Revolutionary Government would have to take from the standpoint of economic rationality, that is, to spur development, were also acts that helped secure its mass social and political base.

Think for a moment of what confronted the Soviet Communists—what, from their standpoint, they found necessary to do to destroy the old agrarian structure and replace it with a modern one. The New Economic Plan, distribution of the land and then its forcible expropriation from the very same peasants upon whom the regime rested—none of this was necessary in Cuba (nor the vast chaos and destruction of civil war). On the contrary, almost the very act of taking over and nationalizing the sugar centrals cemented the already extant bonds between workers and peasants; their working conditions and living conditions were immediately and positively transformed. The immediate and long-range interests of both were identical; each needed the other in past struggles and each was affected similarly by the fluctuations in the economy. With the revolution, these common interests became even more intimately associated. Contrast this with the Mexican revolution, where the "red battalions" of Carranza's workers helped to put down peasant rebellion, or with peasants and tin miners played off against each other in Bolivia in order to maintain the *status quo.* Contrast this with the massive repression of the peasantry under Stalin, and it indicates the profound importance of the prerevolutionary social structure in determining the pace and direction of the revolution in Cuba.

The Cuban revolutionaries—whatever their extraordinary abilities, especially Fidel's—came to power in a society whose prerevolutionary social structure endowed them with vast advantages compared to the leaders of other major social revolutions in this century. Neither the capacity of the revolutionary leaders nor their actions and reaction to the United States (nor the presence of the Soviet Union as a potential ally) can be separated from the *reality* (the "real world") of the revolutionary process. However, I think that it can be shown also that the rapidity and thoroughness (as well as the humane and libertarian aspects which I have not discussed here) of the Cuban revolution, and its movement into socialism, to a great extent were the result of the prerevolutionary social structure. Once a leadership came to power in Cuba that was really committed to a national solution to her problems—once revolutionaries committed to economic development and an independent national existence took power, and would brook no interference (indeed, a highly problematic "if" provided by Fidel, Che, and their comrades), the revolution's course was profoundly influenced by the prerevolutionary social structure. Therefore, Fidel led a socialist revolution almost without knowing it and the Communists were virtually dragged into socialism by the *fidelistas* because history made this possible.

19

THE POLITICS OF
LATIN AMERICAN DEVELOPMENT

JAMES PETRAS

WHILE THE historical development of the countries of Latin America, both
in their social and economic as well as their political aspects, manifests
a specific pattern, they also share some of the overall trends found in
Latin America. Exceptionally uneven development—in relation to the
growth of regions and industries as well as in the distribution of the rewards—is one example of the common thread found in all Latin American
countries, despite obvious dissimilarities in the levels and degrees at which
unevenness manifests itself. All face the growth of political demands for consumption emerging from a multiplicity of sources (diffusion
of values from industrial centres, intense urbanization, extensive bureaucratization, etc.). None have established an economic system to meet
popular demands. Most Latin countries have experienced growing social
differentiation resulting in the proliferation of intermediary groups. These
"middle strata" include a broad variety of occupations and skills. Though
their members receive their primary source of income from salary, their
style of life resembles the traditional elites. These common trends make
it useful to examine the overall developmental process before we attempt
to analyze the specific characteristics affecting specific areas of the region.

Latin America presents the paradox of having changed greatly during
the last forty or fifty years while at the same time exhibiting a basic

437

continuity with the past. Merle Kling has accurately described both the chronic instability and political changes in Latin America and the continuity in society; political "revolutions" do not usually result in basic changes in economic or social policies.[1] This problem can best be handled by identifying and relating the forces or processes which direct social and economic change to existing institutions. We will focus on analyzing the *meaning* of social and economic change both in terms of the consequence of these processes on present and future development possibilities and on the social classes which make up the social system.[2] This approach allows us to avoid the impressionistic view that "nothing has changed", and the official view that change in Latin America is a gradual cumulative process which is radiating benefits throughout the society.

INDUSTRIAL DEVELOPMENT IN HISTORICAL PERSPECTIVE

The process of industrial development can be divided into two general periods, the stages before and after 1930. (1) *The period before the 1930's.* This was the "pre-factory" era during which (a) domestic manufactured goods were largely the products of cottage industry; (b) the demand for manufactured goods was mostly satisfied by imports; (c) the few modern factories were foreign-owned industrial islands which had few dynamic repercussions on internal development. This period of economic development prior to the depression has been referred to in Latin American economic thought as "outward directed development" (*desarrollo hacia afeura*). Economic development associated with the expansion of the primary producing sectors was the dominant feature of the pre-depression period. (2) *The period from 1930 to the present.* During this period the emphasis was on encouraging and substituting domestic manufactured goods for foreign imports. This resulted in the initiation or invigoration of the industrialization process. Three distinct phases mark the industrialization process: the development of traditional industries, basic industries, and metal transforming industries.

Traditional industries generated sizable nuclei of factory employees in place of the artisan preponderance of the pre-factory period. Domestic industries produced consumer goods like food, shoes, etc., and in general there was a substitution of domestic products for foreign imports. The

[1] Merle Kling, "Towards a Theory of Power and Political Instability in Latin America". *Political Change in Underdeveloped Countries*, ed. J. Kautsky (New York: Wiley, 1962), pp. 123-39.

[2] Osvaldo Sunkel, "Cambio Social v. Frustracion en Chile". (Institute Latinoamericano de Planificacion Economico y Social), United Nations, Santiago, Chile, 13 April 1965, p. 3.

extent to which industrialization through import substitution of consumer goods has proceeded can be gauged by comparing imports to total production. In 1929, just prior to this period, imports accounted for 20-29 percent of total production. In 1963 imports accounted for about 10 percent of total production.[3] Import substitution was one of the mainsprings of the industrialization process. The growth of the factory system is evident in the declining percentage of artisans composing the manufacturing labour force: 75 percent during the pre-factory period (1925), which dropped to 60 percent in 1940 and to less than a majority (48 percent) in 1960.

The development of basic industries (manufacture of simple equipment and capital goods) has occurred in three countries (Argentina, Brazil and Mexico). Three other countries (Chile, Peru and Colombia) have encountered difficulties in developing basic industries. The great inequalities and low mass purchasing power are major obstacles to rapid and sustained development based on traditional consumer industries. The major difficulty in developing basic industries is the higher capital intensity requirements necessary to develop each productive unit in addition to the limits imposed by the market.[4]

The industrial development effort in Latin America has been conditioned by two major historical events: (1) the world crises of the 1930's; (2) the growth of State interventionism as part of a conscious effort to industrialize. The Chilean experience illustrates the importance of these two developments.

The world depression dramatically exposed the dependence of the Chilean economy on external sources even for its most basic needs. Chile's capacity to import fell from 100 in 1929 to 40 in 1931, posing the necessity either to produce domestic substitutes or do without essential con-

---

[3] The import coefficient (ratio of imports over total domestic product) for Latin America in 1929 was 20-25 per cent in 1963, barely 10 per cent. About 36 per cent of the expansion of the industrial product was directly related to import substitution incentive between 1929/1960 (for Brazil, Argentina, Chile, Colombia, Mexico). If the comparison were confined to Argentina, Chile, and Colombia, the increase attributable to substitution would exceed 50 per cent.

United Nations, Economic and Social Council, Economic Commission for Latin America, Latin America Symposium on Industrial Development, *The Process of Industrial Development in Latin America,* Vol. I (ST/ECLA Conf. 23/L. 2, 15 December 1965) (Santiago, Chile,) March 1966, p. 37.

[4] The fourth and latest stage in the industrialization process in Latin America which is the promotion of new metal-transforming industries has only been approached by Argentina, Brazil and Mexico. In addition to facing other problems, this type of production is oriented toward the export of finished industrial products and thus must cope with competition in the international market with established industrial powers.

sumer goods. The response of the Chilean government was oriented toward the production of import substitutes in four industrial sectors— clothes and shoes, food, furniture, and metal products. Together these products accounted for between 71 percent and 75 percent of the labour force of the manufacturing industry.

Beginning in the late 1930's the Government became a conscious agent of the industrialization process. The state moved beyond the protectionist policy to playing an active role in creating and financing the establishment of several basic industries. A Government Development Corporation (CORFO) directly invested Government funds in productive units in partnership with and without private investors. With the added external catalyst of World War II the rate of growth of manufacturing production during the period of 1941-46 achieved its highest average rate—11 percent per annum. In the first five years of the post-War period the gradual exhaustion of the opportunities for import substitution of consumer goods was paralleled by a decline in industrial development to 1.8 percent per year.[5] In the following period, again, external pressures, this time the Korean War, in addition to the opening of operations of the steel industry sponsored by earlier government investments,[6] stimulated a minor recovery (1949-56 rate was 4.7 percent). Creation of a limited number of state-owned enterprises and their gradual sale to private investors has turned the State Development Corporation into a commercial-industrial loan and credit bank.[7] In the latest period, 1957-63, the industrial growth rate has dipped to 2.8 per cent.

A recent UN study of the industrialization process in Latin America has pointed to the existence of a crisis and the need for a new orientation. The study notes that:

Latin American industrialization is faced, or will be shortly, with a basic need for reorientation and reliance on stimuli other than those that have played the main part in this development. Moreover, despite the various very different levels and stages of industrial development that exist in the countries of the region, the need for reorientation seems to be arising at the same moment in most of them. The coun-

[5] *El desarrollo industrial de Chile, op. iit.,* p. 7.
[6] After the steel industry, Huachipato, showed excellent returns, it was sold to private investors and eventually became the property of Koppers Corporation, a U.S. subsidy of Anaconda Copper.
[7] Merwin Bohan and Morton Pomeranz, *Investment in Chile*, U.S. Department of Commerce (Washington: U.S. Government Printing Office, 1960), p. 220. An inventory compiled by CORFO lists at least 19 industries in which it had stock which it later sold to private investors. In addition, in eight other plants a substantial part of its stock was sold to private groups.

tries with the largest domestic market are generally those that have gone furthest with import substitution and where industrialization has reached the most advanced stage, and thus to make any further progress in existing conditions poses new problems, and could mean increasing sacrifices in terms of productivity and efficiency. In the countries with intermediate levels of population and income where the same limitations arise at less advanced stages of the process, the possibilities of import substitution have largely been exploited and at the same time there is a substantial degree of industrial diversification. The countries where the external sector is still relatively important and where consequently there would seem to be a broad field open for substitution activities are in fact those in which the size of the domestic market imposes the most severe limitations, even at the earliest stages of development through which they are now passing.[8]

We shall now discuss the type of changes and problems which the evolution of Latin American industry engendered.

INDUSTRIALIZATION AND STAGNATION

Our concern in this section is economic stagnation, a major political problem in Latin America. Stagnation of an economy is indicated by the following patterns of development: (1) the declining ability of industry to absorb the increase in the economically active population (EAP) especially in terms of urban growth; (2) the rapid mushrooming of a low-productive service sector; (3) low rates of overall per capita economic growth; (4) under-utilization of productive capacity in industry; (5) a declining or low rate of food output per inhabitant, and (6) decline in industrial exports and increase in industrial imports. Following a discussion of these indicators of economic stagnation we will consider some of the economic and social factors which may be contributing to this problem.

Between 1925 and 1960, non-agricultural employment increased by 23.5 million persons of which only 5.3 million were in industry and over three times as many (18.2 million) were employed in other urban activities.[9] The ratio of industrial employment to non-agricultural employment has fallen precipitously (see Table 1).

In contrast to what took place in the Western countries and the Soviet Union, urban growth in Latin America was not accompanied by proportionally commensurate progress on the part of modern industry (see Table

[8] *The Process of Industrial Development in Latin America,* Vol. I., *op. cit.,* p. 91.
[9] *The Process of Industrial Development,* Vol. I., *op. cit.,* p. 61.

TABLE 1

PROPORTION OF INDUSTRIAL EMPLOYMENT [10]
TO NON-AGRICULTURAL EMPLOYMENT

	1929	1960
Columbia	48/52	28/72
Chile	33/67	23/77
Venezuela	27.5/72.5	18.1/81.9

2). The quality of urban growth and development that took place especially during the period 1945-60 is quite different from that associated
with the Western pattern. In most of Latin America emigration from
agriculture has not waited upon the consolidation of urban demand for
labour but has been determined by more autonomous factors (rural unemployment or under-employment, below subsistence wages, mechanization of work, etc.). A study of nine Latin American countries showed
that during the period 1940-60 "the per capita industrial product increased
at an annual cumulative rate of 3.8 percent, while the share of manufacturing employment in all urban employment declined from 32.5 to 26.8
percent.[11]

Urban industrial development in Chile conforms to the general pattern
of Latin America.[12] There has been a steady movement from the countryside to the cities since the census of 1907. The acceleration of urbanization after 1940 and especially after 1950 can be seen in Table 3.

[10] *Ibid,* p. 63.

[11] *The Process of Industrial Development in Latin America,* Vol. I., *op. cit.,* p. 74.
The nine countries include Argentina, Brazil, Chile, Colombia, Ecuador, Honduras,
Mexico, Uruguay, and Venezuela.

[12] Noting the different patterns of development in Europe and Latin America,
Glaucio Soares stresses the impact of the diffusion of technology on the declining
ability of industry to absorb labour. "The industrializing countries of today may not
follow the same trend. Technological diffusion is new stronger than ever. Patents ...
industrial equipment and techniques are continuously borrowed and imported from
more developed countries. In general, this means going straight into an expansion of
the skilled workers' strata. But it also means less jobs available and a wider gap
between the rural migrant and the requirements of industrial occupations. Unlike the
close relation between the two factors in the advanced industrial countries, in Latin
America, especially in the period 1945-60, industrialization was at most but one of
the factors in the rapid development of the major metropolises. Urban growth,
especially in the case of the large cities, came *prior* to industry so that the emergence
of intermediate social sectors and the urban working classes dates from long before
the creation of the modern structures of production. In some countries labour and social
legislation preceded that of modern industry. The modern structure of production,
where they exist, were not the mainsprings of the urbanization processes."

TABLE 2

RELATION BETWEEN INDUSTRIALIZATION AND URBANIZATION [13]
IN SELECTED COUNTRIES
(Percentages)

Country	Census Year	Urbanization *	Industrialization **
Chile	1930	28	25‡
	1950	40	30
Cuba	1919	23	20
	1943	31	18
Mexico	1910	11†	22
	1950	24†	17
Soviet Union	1928	12	8
	1955	32	31
Sweden	1910	16	27
	1950	30	41
United States	1910	31	31
	1950	42	37

* Percentage of total population living in towns with 20,000 inhabitants or more.
** Percentage of total labour force engaged in mining and quarrying, manufacturing, construction and public utility services (electricity, gas and water).
† Percentage of total population living in towns with 100,000 inhabitants or more.
‡ Data calculated from Alieto Aldo Guadagni, "La Fuerzo de Trabajo en Chile, 1930-60" (Santiago, Chile, 1961), p. 51 (mimeographed). The somewhat higher percentage for Chile in this early period may be due to the relatively high proportion engaged in extractive industries (over 5 percent of the labour force).

TABLE 3

PERCENT OF POPULATION IN URBAN-RURAL SECTORS [14]

Year	Urban	Rural	Percent Increase in Urban Population Over Previous Date
1885	41.7	58.3	—
1907	43.2	56.8	1.5
1920	46.4	53.6	3.2
1930	49.4	50.6	3.0
1940	52.5	47.5	3.1
1950	58.7	41.3	6.2
1960	68.9	31.1	10.2

[13] "The Demographic Situation in Latin America", *Economic Bulletin for Latin America*, Vol. VI, No. 2 (Santiago, Chile: October 1961), p. 34, Table 17.
As a measure of industrialization in the earlier period, the crude index shown is inadequate. This same article argues that this is so "because industrial employment itself has a greatly variable composition. ... It would seem ... that in the countries of limited industrial development there exists a proliferation of handicrafts and dwarf industries with minimal amounts of capital, labor employed per workshop, and incomes earned which nevertheless provide some employment for relatively large numbers of persons."
[14] Compiled from Alieto Aldo Guadagni, *op. cit.*, p. 29; Bohan and Pomeranz, *op. cit.*, p. 40; *Georgrafis Economica*, *op. cit.*, p. 378.

Accelerated urbanization coincided with the economic slow-down of the 1950's and thereafter. The movement to the cities appears to be due to "push" factors forcing people to leave the rural areas rather than the "pull" factors, such as attractive remunerative urban employment. The movement to the cities did not coincide with economic growth but with the relative and absolute decline in the agricultural sector. If we look at the percentage of the EAP [15] dedicated to manufacturing in relation to the total urban population in the past 30 years we can see the historic evolution of both processes of industrialization and urbanization.

TABLE 4

PERCENT OF EAP DEDICATED TO MANUFACTURING
IN RELATION TO THE URBAN POPULATION

1930	1940	1950	1960
10.15	11.20	11.6	10.1

The result of industry's inability to employ rural migrants has been the growth of a tertiary sector. A high percentage of the under-employed and disguised unemployment is contained in the tertiary sector. In Chile, between 1940-54, while employment in industry increased from 13.2 to 16.7 percent of the EAP, personal services increased from 15.1 to 20.5 percent. Within the "service sector" as a whole, "personal services" have absorbed the largest proportion of the rural migrants in the face of industry's very limited ability to do so (see Table 5). When we analyze the components of the service sector, it is precisely the personal service group (whose per capita income is decreasing) which shows the greatest increase relative to the rest of the services (see Tables 6 and 7).

The gap between strata within the service sector indicates that "sectoral" analysis is too gross. The "service sector" includes groups with highly disparate incomes and obscures the divergent trends within it. For example, the income gap between the commercial groups and the personal servants has widened considerably between 1940 and 1960. The businessmen and public administrators who belonging primarily to the middle class achieved a 52 percent *increase* in per capita income over the twenty-year period. The per capita income of the personal services had *declined* by nearly 14 percent. For the service sector as a whole, the "deceptive" average was an 11 percent increase. The income gap that separates the commercial groups from the other services appears to be growing, not lessening, in the process of Chilean economic development.

---

[15] EAP will be used in place of "economically active population".

TABLE 5

EMPLOYMENT AND INCOME IN VARIOUS ECONOMIC SECTORS IN CHILE

Sector	Employment		Salaries and Wages	
	1940	1954	1940	1954
Agriculture	44.6	33.0	16.8	10.2
Fisheries	0.1	0.2	0.1	0.1
Mining	6.2	4.2	13.5	7.5
Industry	13.2	16.7	16.1	21.9
Construction	3.4	5.0	3.3	4.0
Electricity, gas, water	0.5	0.4	1.1	1.2
Commerce	4.1	4.6	6.2	6.5
Transportation and communication	4.3	4.9	9.3	9.1
Government services	7.6	9.7	16.3	24.2
Personal services	15.1	20.5	14.5	12.5
Finance	0.9	0.8	2.8	2.8
	100.0	100.0	100.0	100.0

TABLE 6

DISTRIBUTION OF THE LABOUR FORCE IN "SERVICES"
1930-60

Type of Service	1930	1940	1950	1960
Basic (communication, transportation, gas, energy, water, etc.)	16.2	11.3	12.5	12.3
Commercial	25.7	22.4	24.1	22.0
Personal	25.2	27.1	29.0	36.3
Professional and social welfare	8.9	9.4	11.4	11.3
Public and administrative and insurance	9.3	10.8	11.0	10.0
Not specified	14.7	19.0	12.0	8.1

TABLE 7

PER CAPITA INCOME OF EAP IN DISTINCT TYPES OF SERVICES [16]
1940-1960 (in escudos)

Service Sector	1940	1952	1960
Basic Services	1637	1589	1309
Electricity, gas, water, sanitation	1518	884	1150
Transport, warehouse, communication	1653	1742	1344
Commercial Services	2326	3228	3538
Trade	2289	3186	3623
Bank, insurance, real estate	2677	3518	2950
Personal services, professional services and social welfare	916	925	789
Public administrative services	1732	2863	2384
Per capita income for service sector as a whole	1515	1890	1688

[16] Guadagni, op. cit., p. 93.

The possibilities for dynamic growth in the future are dim, given the limited internal market. Fifty percent of the people account for less than 10 per cent of the comsumption of manufactured goods and 9 per cent of the services. The overwhelming proportion of purchases are confined to the middle and upper strata. This extremely delimited market provides little stimulus for dynamic industrial development. The absence of mass purchasing power is an outgrowth of a social system which combines rigid stratification with concentration of socio-economic power.[17]

The weakness of the Chilean industrialization effort is shown by its inability to substitute industrial exports for traditional primary goods exports. There was an absolute decline of exports of manufactured goods between 1950 and 1963. This is especially evident in the decline of exports of metal products (see Tables 8 and 9).

TABLE 8

EXPORTS OF MANUFACTURED GOODS
(Millions of Dollars)

Products	1950	1955	1960	1963
Food	3.6	3.1	3.4	13.9
Beverages and liquor	1.6	1.6	0.3	1.1
Textiles	1.2	0.4	0.2	—
Chemicals	2.3	2.5	4.7	5.1
Metals	32.2	25.2	18.4	6.0
Machinery and tools	0.5	1.6	0.4	0.6
Transport equipment	0.1	0.2	0.2	4.3
Miscellaneous	5.2	3.0	4.9	1.4
TOTALS	46.7	37.9	32.5	32.4

The decline in the value of exports and augmented dependence on manufactured imports are indicators of the sluggish nature of Chilean industrial growth.

In summary, both within the urban milieux and in the nation as a whole, economic growth has taken place, but in a highly unbalanced manner. This suggests that overall policy has been directed toward limi-

---

[17] Jorge Ahumada pointed to three conditions necessary for the promotion of economic development: continuous expansion of effective demand; expanding the source of capital goods, and creating the machinery for diffusing innovations. Jorge Ahumada, "Economic Development and Problems of Social Change in Latin America", in Social Aspects of Economic Development in Latin America, eds. Jose Medina Echavarria and Egbert de Vries (Belgium: United Nations, 1963). See also Ahumada's study, En vez de la miseria (Santiago, Chile: Editorial del Pacifico, 1958).

TABLE 9

IMPORTS OF MANUFACTURED PRODUCTS

(Millions of Dollars)

Products	1950	1955	1960	1963
Food	23.4	45.3	30.0	49.3
Beverages and liquor	0.3	0.8	1.3	0.4
Processed tobacco	0.1	0.1	0.1	—
Textiles	14.5	10.9	22.7	17.1
Chemicals	34.9	65.4	60.2	96.7
Metals	36.8	21.6	31.7	31.5
Machinery and tools	49.6	58.9	104.2	152.7
Transport equipment	20.5	52.7	77.3	74.9
Miscellaneous products	15.8	20.9	38.4	54.3
TOTALS	185.9	276.6	365.4	476.9

SOURCE: Superintendenica de Aduanas, Santago, Chile.

ted gains in industry frequently at the expense of other sectors. Policy shifts have been paralleled by decisions of economic elites to transfer their resources to the more promising areas of industry. Concentration of national resources and favourable political factors maximized industrial development and minimized the potential for other sectors.

Industrial development, rather than opening up society for the mass of the populace, has expanded access to goods from a traditional elite to a much broader strata, but still minority, of the population. Industry has not created a new "mass society" so much as it allowed the older elites to adapt to the demands of the urban middle class. Industry responded to the needs of the continued highly stratified society and supplied the goods for the limited effective demand.

DETERMINANTS OF STAGNATION

We will now examine some of the factors which may be contributing to stagnation. In most other Latin American countries fixed capital is concentrated in traditional industries. In countries which have experienced or are experiencing more dynamic growth such as Brazil, Argentina or Mexico a much greater share of investment is found in the machine producing industries.

Chile contains a greater proportion of traditional consumer industries (52 percent) than Argentina or Brazil (40 percent). Chile has a much smaller proportion of dynamic durable goods industries, 11 percent compared to 24 percent and 21 percent for the other two countries. In the US traditional industries account for only 30 percent of manufacturing. The predominance of traditional consumer industries oriented toward highly protected internal markets and geared to existing limited demand is an important contributing factor to the problem of economic stagnation. The existence, parallel to the factory system, of a large number of inefficient and unproductive artisan industries also contributes to stagnation. Though the contribution of these units to the overall output of manufacturing has been declining, they continue to employ close to half (48 percent) of the labour force action in manufacturing.[18]

In comparison with the modern metal industries the ratio of wages to value added is much lower in the traditional food, beverage and textile industries. This suggests that the economic rewards are more concentrated in the top economic groups within the industry. Thus, for example, in Chile the ratio of wages to value added in the food industry is 0.19, while in metal transforming it is almost double, 0.36.[19] The predominance of the traditional consumer industries has negative consequences from the "consumption" angle of economic development. The expansion of the metal industries could also mean higher purchasing power for the working class and a larger consumer market for durable goods.

Workers within the traditional industries earn substantially less wages than *workers* in basic industries. Chemical and metal workers make substantially higher wages than textile, shoe and furniture workers. The expansion of the modern durable goods industries tends to produce a more equal distribution of income between elite and workers. It also tends to increase the possibility for internal industrial development by increasing overall income and demand for goods. The present pattern of industrialization appears in most Latin American countries to have maintained or strengthened inequalities between top and bottom while creating a thin stratum of higher paid workers who have substantially higher income but who appear not numerically important enough to constitute a *mass* market for new products.

A recent U.N. study on industrialization and income distribution concluded that "... the shares of wages and salaries in value added by industry is very low in comparison with their share in other economies, which means that industry is also helping to some extent to preserve the gradually regressive nature of income distribution in Latin America."[20]

The owners of productive units are not adequately meeting the require-

[18] *The Process of Industrial Development, op. cit.*, p. 30.
[19] *The Process of Industrial Development*, Vol, I., *op. cit.*, p. 134.
[20] *Ibid.*, pp. 33, 134.

ments for rapid industrial development if we examine indicators such as utilization of capacity and the allocation of funds. Working capital, including inventories, credit, demand deposits and other values, absorbed 55 percent of total funds in Colombia and Venezuela, 70 percent in Argentina, Brazil and Chile, against only 32 percent in France (1953) and 37 percent in the US (1960).[21] Regarding investment in fixed capital, machinery and equipment barely represented 60 percent in Latin America compared to 70 percent in the Federal Republic of Germany.[22] The composition of industrial capital and the utilization of financial resources (high proportion of funds tied up in working capital and the low proportion of fixed capital in machinery) is unfavourable for the development of the manufacturing sector.

Latin American entrepreneurs have failed to make the fullest and most efficient use of existing productive resources. In Argentina the coefficient of utilization of industrial capacity varied from 40 percent to 82 percent in the years 1961, 1963 and 1964. For the food, manufacturing and chemical industry in Colombia the coefficient was under 40 percent. In Chile utilization was estimated to be 55.3 percent in major industries, 33 percent in medium-scale industries, and 50 percent in small industry. In Ecuador and Venezuela idle capacity amounted to about 40 percent.[23] The concentration of economic power contributes to the maintenance of a rather narrow internal market which in turn lowers the incentive for full utilization of plant.

The slowdown in industrial growth and the less than adequate performance of the entrepreneurial groups is reflected in the gradual decline in the overall growth rates in Latin America. From an annual cumulative growth rate of per capita real income of 1.9 percent for the period 1950-55 it has dropped to 1.4 percent (1955-60) and even lower in recent years (0.6 percent for 1960-63). Growing economic stagnation appears to characterize the evolution of Latin America taken as a whole in recent years. The growth rates of the gross product fell from 5 percent in 1950-55 to 3.6 percent for 1960-63 while the rate of population increased slightly from 2.8 percent to 2.9 percent.

However, industry's growth rate and contribution to national income has been somewhat higher than other economic sectors. Industry in Latin America with 14 percent of the total active population has generated over 23 percent of the Latin American gross product indicating its ability to achieve higher productivity with the factors of production than other sectors.[24] For the decade 1950-60 it has been estimated that the per capita

[21] *Ibid.*, p. 118.   [22] *Ibid.*
[23] *Ibid.*, pp. 119-21.
[24] *The Process of Industrial Development in Latin America, op. cit.*, p. 139.

industrial product for Latin America, as a whole, rose from about $80 to slightly under $110.[25] However, if we examine the increase in the per capita industrial product for the urban population, the average annual rate for the same period is only about 1.5 percent. In Latin America as a whole the proportion of industry's share of the Gross National Product has increased from 20 percent to 23.4 percent while the share of the agricultural sector has declined in the same decade from 24.6 percent to 21 percent.[26] Relative to other economic sectors the larger share contributed by industry indicates that in productive terms it is the most dynamic sector of the economy.

In summary, the problems facing many parts of Latin America are not those of backward "feudal" agrarian countries trying to create an industrial base. The problems are those of "middle-developed" countries which have not been able to attain industrial maturity. The ubiquitous social and economic problems of "stalled development" lie at the basis of the declining fortunes of the traditional Rightist parties.

The problems of economic growth and industrial expansion can be best understood in relation to the emergence of the middle strata.

INDUSTRIALIZATION AND DIFFERENTIAL SOCIO-POLITICAL CHANGE

Widespread and intense social change has taken place in Latin America— but its impact has been differentially felt. The growth of new social forces, especially new intermediary groups, was one of the most significant changes in the social structure.

These groups tend to have a high status aspiration and provide a new type of political actor—the "political entrepreneur".[27] Lacking direct economic resources in the form of property, yet possessing organizational skills, the intermediary groups provide a substantial pool of individuals who combine two roles: the traditional role as representatives of a constituency and its interests and the role of promoter of state involvement in the economy. Frequently political entrepreneurs utilize the resources of the State to promote private enterprise and private gain. One method is to convert public enterprise into private.

The bureaucratic middle strata perform several important functions in the early stages of state-promoted industrial development by: (1) providing political leadership and filling many of the organizational posi-

[25] *Ibid.*, p. 77.

[26] For a more detailed breakdown, see *Estudio Economico de America Latina 1963*, Economic Commission on Latin America, United Nations, 1964, p. 30.

[27] This concept, useful in describing the role of political leaders in the dependent countries, is borrowed from Professor David Apter.

tions; (2) opening society to new development; (3) creating the precon-
ditions for the emergence of the new urban industrial elites, and (4) "containing" social change to limited strata. Thus the bureaucratic middle
strata are politically innovative and socially and economically conservative—in the broad sense of perpetuating substantial inequalities.

The emergence and expansion of the internally highly differentiated
intermediary strata in the urban sector drew sustenance from and was
associated with the principal economic, demographic and political changes. Commonly referred to as the "middle class", these groups came to
direct the political fortunes of most Latin societies by the early forties.[28]
The political and social development of these intermediary groups passed
through several phases which paralleled similar changes in the economy.
In the process, political orientations and strategies shifted accordingly.

The political development of the middle strata can be conceived of in
terms of two phases: (1) the upward mobility phase and (2) the stabilization phase.[29] In analyzing these phases, two general behavioural concepts are useful: "manifest reformism" and "latent self-improvement". The
historical sequence which encompasses this political development began
approximately in the mid-1930's. During this early period—the upward
mobility phase of the political process—the middle strata began their rise
to power by seeking the support of the popular classes by supporting
social reform programmes. The latent meaning of these declarations and
of the institutions which emerged when they came to power consisted
rather in the expansion and betterment of the middle strata themselves.
Under their leadership the size of various component strata of the middle
class was enlarged. The extension of citizenship within urban areas, the
creation of new institutions and units of production, the pressure for
direct satisfaction of social and economic aspirations (the psychological
mainspring of the political mobilization of the middle class) all contributed
to ensuring the middle class a better life.[30] A UN study noted that in these
years of upward mobility, "systematic use was likewise made of certain
traditional institutions just as other new ones were promoted with the
aim of safeguarding and improving the status already acquired by the
rising middle class". The intermediary groups which at their boundaries
overlap or touch on both the popular classes and the traditional elites
became the "eclectic" political force which accommodated the traditional
elites and promoted an industrial-urban society. The political groups and
spokesmen of these intermediary groups played this role primarily through

[28] See J. Johnson, *Political Change in Latin America* (Stanford, California: Stanford
University Press, 1958).
[29] *Social Development of Latin America in the Post-War Period*, op. cit., p. 103.
[30] *Ibid.*

their control and manipulation of governmental machinery, distribution of "welfare", and their promotion of industrial development based on import substitution.

The "mobility phase" of political development coincides generally with the period of rapid industrial growth based on import substitution. Social mobility, politics and industrial development did not necessitate significantly altering social power or redistributing income. The rapid but short-lived expansion of industry, promoted by the middle strata, was accompanied by political changes and a number of limited social and economic reforms.[31] Universal suffrage was introduced though it did not lead to a genuine mass incorporation of the rural and urban lower class (the so-called "marginal population"). The encouragement of trade unionism had only relative success. Largely skilled urban workers amounting to less than 10 percent of the labour force were incorporated in fragmented organizations and subject to close government control and regulation. The various social security programmes were mainly geared to the needs of the dependent middle strata and organized urban workers. The lower strata benefitted on a much smaller scale if at all.

Public education was expanded but largely in the urban areas. The limitations of middle class educational reform can be measured indirectly. Since the overwhelming majority of the middle class is generally urban we can use the urban/rural distinction as a rough index to measure the degree to which educational freedom has been extended to middle strata. If we look at the distribution of illiterates in Latin America we find a systematic bias in favour of the urban population (see Table 10). Religious institutions continued to wield considerable influence even where primary schooling was concerned. School drop-out statistics suggest that educational expansion was turned to account mainly for the middle class. The benefits of the educational reforms instituted were not evenly distributed among all social strata. In Chile, a quarter of a century after the People's Front victory, 50 percent of the children of the working class still do not finish the third grade, over 85 percent drop out after six grades, and 27.5 percent finish only one year of school. This accounts for the 19 percent illiteracy rate (illiterates are also disenfranchised) which Chile has maintained for many years.[32]

The educational system, far from democratizing society or equalizing opportunity, segregates and discriminates against the lower class and becomes an obstacle to change. This becomes even clearer at the higher educational levels: less than 2 per cent of the University students come

[31] *Ibid.*, pp. 111-13.

[32] Eduardo Hamuy, et al., *Educacional elemental, analfabetismo y desarrollo economico* (Santiago, Chile: Editorial Universitaria, 1960), p 10.

TABLE 10

ILLITERATE PERSONS IN THE URBAN AND RURAL
POPULATIONS OF SELECTED COUNTRIES
1950
(percentages)

| Country | Illiterate Persons Aged 15 or Over | |
	In the Urban Population	In the Rural Population
Brazil	27	67
Chile	11	35
Costa Rica	8	28
Dominican Republic	29	67
El Salvador	35	77
Nicaragua	30	80
Panama	8	46
Paraguay	14	37
Venezuela	30	72

from working class families. Private schools, most of which are subsidized by the State, are accessible exclusively to the upper-middle and upper class.

Health conditions reflect similar differences. The high Chilean infant mortality rate, largely due to malnutrition, of 125 out of every 1,000 children born each year (one of the highest in the world) is primarily a function of the conditions of life of the lower income, especially rural groups. Comparison of the municipalities of Santiago and outlying areas reveals that predominantly middle-class areas have one-third to one-half the infant mortality rate of the lower income areas.

Income redistribution policy redounded primarily to the advantage of these middle strata that promoted it. In Chile, parallel to the decline and stagnation of production, salary and wage workers suffered a serious deterioration in income. Calculating the minimum wages of Santiago in 1950 pesos, Pinto finds a gradual decline of nearly 25 per cent between 1954 and 1961.[33] It is estimated by the same author that 46 per cent of the employees receive about the basic salary or less.

Comparing the basic salary to per capita national income, Pinto points to the growing gap between the lower strata and the upper in the period 1950-61. The ratio of the basic wage to per capita income decreases from 1 to 0.69.

Distribution of income by social classes in the same period indicates that the *lowest strata* suffered the greatest relative loss, the middle class

[33] Anibal Pinto, *Chile: un economia dificil, op. cit.*, pp. 40-42.

M-30

less so, while the owners and proprietors improved their relative position (see Table 11). The negative effects of economic slowdown have been largely absorbed by the classes which could at least afford it.

TABLE 11

PERCENT DISTRIBUTION OF INCOME BY SOCIAL CLASS [34]

	1953	1959
Workers	30.0	25.5
Middle sectors	26.4	25.2
Owner sector*	43.6	49.3

* Includes high-salary employees like executives.

Social development appears to be quite "uneven" and the pattern of economic development and industrialization appear to accentuate the disparities in income rather than reduce them.

Economic development has had a differential impact on the social structure, tending to increase the gap between social classes.[35]

The orientation of the Latin American middle class shifted from political insurgency to a concern for "stabilization". This change has four major aspects: (1) the establishment of a clientele and "patronage" political system; (2) the adoption of policies promoting upward mobility within the system; (3) the utilization of state machinery mainly to secure the benefits established earlier rather than to explore new areas for economic and social elites. The emergence of the stabilization phase coincided with a shift in the social and political orientation of the new integrated middle strata. Universal suffrage ceased to be a basic principle and military coups were supported when they were perceived as the only defence of status and economic position.[36] Demands for control over trade union activity overshadowed concern for organizing the unorganized.[37] Middle-class politicians became spokesmen for an educa-

---

[34] H. Varela, *Estratificación social de la poblacion trabajadora de Chile*, Escuela de Economica, Universidad de Chile (Santiago, Chile, 1958).

[35] Bert A. Hutchinson's study in Brazil indicates a similar pattern: "First, industrial development did not produce a dissolution of class barriers as had been anticipated. Second, the greater access to the educational system did not produce an increase in social mobility," cited by Bonilla, "The Urban Worker", in *Continuity and Change in Latin America*, ed. John J. Johnson (Stanford, California: Stanford University Press, 1964), p. 189.

[36] Jose Nun, "A Latin American Phenomenon: The Middle Class Military Coup" in James Petras and Maurice Zeitlin, *Latin America: Reform or Revolution* (Fawcett Publications: N. Y. 1968).

[37] United Nations, Economic and Social Council, Economic Commission for Latin America, *El empressario industrial en America Latina* (E/CN. 12/642, March 1963) (Mar del Plata, Argentina, May 1963), p. 17.

tional policy which gave protection to private education. Social welfare became an "organizational weapon" for undercutting demands for structural changes by representatives of the dispossessed. The initial drive for a better distribution of power, of prestige and wealth gradually lost momentum. The middle strata became much more interested in securing the relative advantages they had obtained than in striving for a new social order. The new middle class showed an increasing tendency to identify with the established social order and to grasp the opportunities it offered. The "stability oriented" political behaviour pattern of the middle strata coincides (circa 1950 onward) with the exhaustion of import-substitution as the dynamic element in industrial growth.

"Traditional society" is not closed, rigid and unresponsive to change. The new middle strata have been able to work their way into prominent positions of power, to introduce industrial development and to expand government involvement. This indicates the *flexibility* of Latin America's traditional structure, its ability to absorb new elements and to limit changes from becoming instruments for mass mobilization. While the literature on Latin America speaks of revolution and "instability", the degree to which dominant elites, institutions and hierarchies have *maintained* their position in society—even while sharing it with new groups —indicates that Latin America may be one of the most *conservative* regions in the world. Only rarely have old social elites been replaced by new ones.

The ascent and adaption of the middle strata in traditional society, one study notes, was accomplished through, "... the formation of a clientele system which was not always inimical to progress and allowed scope for more or less limited forms of reconstruction and creative capacity".[38] This "patronage political system" was based on kinship and familial ties. The same study notes that "... existing family ties and political parties with a 'prebendary' [patronage] orientation were generally based on the perpetuation of primary or personal relationships which formed a complex network extending over the public and private sector alike and affording a flexible means of maintaining and improving the status of the middle class".[39] The adaption by a modern group of traditional political practices was the converse of traditional economic elites adapting to the needs of limited modernization and industrialization. Both processes were underwritten by a control system which excluded a substantial sector of the polity from meaningful economic rewards and effective socio-political integration. The "excluded sectors" of the middle class utilized sporadic action to extend economic and social

[38] *Social Development of Latin America in the Post-War Period, op. cit.*, pp. 102-03.
[39] *Ibid.*, p. 104.

opportunity to a limited constituency. The same study notes, "... the self-promotional objectives of the nuclei interested in particular social reforms only temporarily appeared as 'ideals,' for as they were really instruments of upward mobility they were relinquished as soon as power had been achieved".[40] Latin America's pattern of political development exhibits a flexible traditional structure, as expressed in the assimilation of the middle class, and middle strata more "accommodationist" than reformist in its political and social outlook.

SUMMARY

From our brief survey of economic and social development as they relate to change and continuity in Latin America we conclude that: the strategy of "modernization from above" has tended to result in highly uneven development, confining modernization within the limits and the more immediate spheres of influence of the big cosmopolitan cities and to the middle strata and its clientele.[41]

Industrialization has been an important element in propelling social change and promoting economic development through successful efforts at import substitution. It has been less effective in replacing the external sector as the stimulant to a self-sustained growth.[42] Per capita manufacturing output, though it increased significantly, did so at rates that were very modest in relation to the increase in urban population. Although

[40] *Ibid.*, p. 105.

[41] Sunkel suggests, regarding Chile, that modernization and change has been accompanied by the extension of the traditional system of "clientele" political control to new activities and urban classes. O. Sunkel, *op. cit.*, p. 30. It would appear that clientele politics is not an attribute of traditional oligarchical societies but may serve equally well in buttressing the prerogatives of modern middle strata.

[42] Bonilla cites the lack of growth of large-scale industry and the small size of the industrial classes as a key element in limiting change. "Since total employment in industrial enterprises of five or more workers hits a peak of 13 per cent of the economically active in Argentina and Uruguay and in other countries is generally 7 per cent or less, and since most of these industrially employed are doubtless laborers and skilled workers, the percentage of middle and upper class employed in industry can only be minuscule. This helps explain why the industrial and urban revolution in Latin America remains a surface phenomenon, leaving the underlying structure of attitudes and values pretty well intact. Though the political challenge to traditionally dominant elites has been mounted in the cities and led by elements from the so-called urban middle sectors, neither the expansion of the cities nor the growth of the middle sectors necessarily implies value changes concomitant with social and political development. Conventional assumptions, assumptions about the social dynamism inevitably accompanying urban industrial growth, also bear re-examination with regard to Latin America," F. Bonilla, "The Urban Worker", in *Continuity and Change in Latin America*, ed. John J. Johnson (Stanford, California; Stanford University Press, 1964), p. 189,

there was a steady increase in the absolute number employed in manufacturing, the percentage of the total active population absorbed by
industry was rather modest while its contribution to total urban employment declined. Industrial development did not appear to have contributed much to improving income distribution or economic integration
either within the various countries or at the regional level.

The same conditions which made industrial development possible
created obstacles to further industrialization. While rapid urbanization
created new or broader markets for manufactured goods it also absorbed
a high proportion of resources that could have been mobilized for capital
formation.

Because the development process was not effectively integrated sharp
imbalances occurred between sectors. Because the rural sector lagged
far behind there was a lack of complementarity reflected in the limited
ability of the countryside to purchase manufactured goods, in agriculture's inadequate contribution to domestic capital formation, in heavy
balance of payment pressures deriving from imports of primary
commodities, in the limited growth of agricultural exports and in other
drawbacks.

The unfavourable behaviour of the external sector during the past half-
century, while it promoted and emphasized the need for industrialization, hampered the process by limiting the region's capacity to import the
machinery, equipment, raw materials and intermediate products required
for industrial development.

The Latin countries which have moved furthest along the road to
modernization are experiencing the greatest difficulty in further industrialization. The same Latin countries which have witnessed a reduction
of their rate of growth in recent years also possess the biggest middle
class with the longest and most continuous participation in political and
economic affairs.

Sharing power with traditional elites, in many cases having overlapping interests and values, the middle strata have largely ceased to be
a dynamic innovative force in society. Lacking social homogeneity and
coherence, a commitment to make sacrifices, the middle strata have been
unable to mobilize society for rapid industrial development. Their integration and participation in existing society and the interests, benefits
and values which are derived from an identification with existing
institutions and practices are major determinants of the negative role
of the middle strata.

THE POLITICS OF LATIN AMERICAN DEVELOPMENT

20

POLITICAL DEVELOPMENT
IN THE MIDDLE EAST

LEONARD BINDER

You HAVE come to listen to other peoples' troubles, and have thought, perhaps, for a fleeting moment, of the silent benediction, of the vacant litany, oft repeated during the last two decades: "Lord, blessed art Thou who hath not made me politically underdeveloped." So used are we to assuming that development was something we already have and that they are now experiencing, that we have not been prepared to find that it is we who seem to be influenced by the ideas that they have long since achieved. The goal, the end of that road which we so complacently termed political development, is, however not at all known. Far from being a reenactment of a textbook model of the American political system, with its neatly defined groups, its well-channelled processes, its adaptive mechanisms, its non-ideological pragmatism, and its safety valves, the *terminus ad quem* of the political evolution we are now witnessing defies conjecture. The idealized view of American politics which has prevailed throughout the post-war period, and the self-congratulatory way in which we have rewritten much of the history of the 1930's, assumed that the particular structures of a political system are evolved in the course of ironing out the major conflicts or contradictions in any given society. As each of the major conflicts is eliminated, and institutional adjustments are made, the system is fixed with regard to that particular, political compe-

458

tence. Barring a great upheaval, the fixing of the various parts of the system will be cumulative, until, stabilized in its ability to cope with all ordinary conflicts, and having eliminated all extraordinary conflicts, that greatest of all bourgeois utopias, equilibrium, is achieved.

This is a remarkable theory of political development—blindly ideological and ethnocentrically conservative—for it not only suggests that the more a system appears to be changing, or the more likelihood there is that it will change, the less developed is that political system. The partly developed system is changing only in some of its parts, but, manifestly, the fully developed system is no longer and can no longer change. Some theorists have grasped this problem, and have attempted to escape from the obsessive-compulsive implication of equilibrium theory by casting themselves headlong into the sea of boundless process, arguing that a truly developed political system is one that is always changing. It is difficult to know what to make of such assertions as this because it is not clear whether everything is changing or merely that something is changing in a manner which allows us to distinguish between the persisting thing and its changing attributes. The idea of constant flux defies moral definition and challenges even the most insightful efforts to discern the incidence of universal principle in the jumbling rush of boundless, endless, self-generating change. If not equilibrium, then we have the alternative of trivial change, or existential nothingness. But maybe there is another sort of answer to the dilemma of political development, maybe we have not yet achieved the highest stage of political development, maybe there is at least one other stage, the stage which some have facetiously named the stage of post-modernity.

We have more or less assumed that we knew where the underdeveloped areas were headed, and that was along the well-trodden, but not very attractive path we had only recently traversed. Our assumptions have been rooted in a kind of neo-Marxian economic determinism, wherein the central hypothesis is that material prosperity aids in reducing major conflicts to minor controversies. This hypothesis is not so much incorrect as it is inadequate to the variety, comprehensiveness, and subtlety of the problem of political development. There is no reason to assume that economic development alone will reduce Middle Eastern problems to reasonable manageability—although it is useful to keep this notion of political development in mind. We have tended to see in our own history the stages of world development. But if there is a pattern of world development into which all must inevitably fit, then even though we have solved all our major problems and produced the best of all possible political solutions, we, too, must obey the decree of history and follow the unmarked path, whereas we may find some of the developing nations, having skipped a stage or two, pressing on with the enthusiasm of the newly converted and the inexperienced.

The pessimistic social theorists of the nineteenth century, many of whom have been echoed by our own contemporaries, saw sadly the decline of the aristocratic virtues and the corruption of the natural communities out of which the political and theological fiction of society was composed. They foresaw an ever-increasing progress of urbanization, bureaucratization, isolation, and alienation. Some sorrowfully concluded that human beings could adapt to any circumstances, and others, believing firmly in the beneficence of an Hegelian destiny, predicted a great seizure of exasperation, a revolution which would once again humanize our technologized society. There is no way of ascertaining from the examination of an existing trend whether the future bears its further intensification or a sudden violent reaction which will restore some lost but ill-understood equilibrium. With these caveats, we cannot help but notice that there does seem to be a connection of a sort between the most disturbing new problems in our own country and the issues which greatly concern the political elites of the developing areas. Political development, therefore, may be linked to universal stages, and our own situation may give us some indication of what the next stage will be.

The three protest movements which have raised what have normally been limited controversies to the level of major conflicts, which might, as some exploitative journalists would have it, signal "the passing of the old order" in America, are, first, the protest against materialism, second, the protest against the position of Negroes in American society, and, third, the protest against the war in Viet Nam. Now, these are movements which are quite specific to the United States, yet it would be quite incorrect to reject the idea that these problems are simply local manifestations of similar problems which beset other peoples as we move into the postmodern stage. I believe that we share these problems with the countries of the Middle East and other parts of the underdeveloped world.

Technologism and materialism have long been targets of the critics of modern society, whether out of the stubborn attachment to the elegance and individualism of tradition or out of the perennial mystical rejection of this-worldliness. Both of these kinds of argument have been made by the victims of Western Imperialism and particularly by the Muslims. To some extent, these arguments have been borrowed, but they have also grown out of a genuine critique of Western Society and out of the natural ground of traditional Islamic thought. The great paradox has been that the Muslims of the Middle East have striven mightily to acquire all of the technological achievements and material accomplishments of the West. Some strove to transform Islamic society and some to preserve it, but nearly everyone recognized that without acquiring these Western stigmata, they could not cope with the West. But while coping and while copying, while sending young people to study in the West and while importing Western advisers, Middle Eastern intellectuals have deplored the advance of materialism and the decline of the peculiarly Islamic and traditional humane values. The Bedouin ideals of generosity, hospitality, and courage; the courtly ideals of poetry, romance, and personal justice; the peasant ideals of loyalty, stability, and community; and the folk ideals of piety, mystic devotion, honour and shame; all have been the victims of modernization in some degree. We design to define development in terms of rationality, secularism, scientism, universalism, and the like, while yet believing that nothing has been lost in the process and that progress of this sort is wholly without injury to mankind.

Westerners have experienced the disenchantment of the modern world and the emptiness of moral choice in a world without presuppositions. Many of the most revolutionary intellectuals in the Middle East are violently opposed to all of the still powerful elements of tradition. Unlike their Western counterparts, they have no disturbing pangs of nauseating nostalgia. These intellectuals can sustain traditional symbols only as employed on travel posters or on the floats which follow the largest missiles in the annual "defence" parades. Nevertheless, even such modernizers, and the traditionalists a fortiori, all too frequently justify their opposition to the West and their contempt for us because of our overwhelming materialistic concern.

These intellectuals have been led by the logic of their own circumstances to seek a way of combining the best of the old and the best of the new. They, too, have adopted the dualistic metaphysic of the dialecticians, but they have established the material West and the spiritual East as the two principles in place of the bourgeoisie and the proletariat. The materialism of the West is to be balanced with humane values by means of an adaptation of traditional values. The search for special doctrines which will provide for the middle way between tradition and modernity has found satisfaction in the idea of socialism. The particularistic thrust which motivates this kind of romantic socialism has resulted in the addition of religious or nationalist adjectives in order to describe the kind of socialism which is desired. Hence we find in the Middle East the terms Islamic Socialism, Arab Socialism, Destour Socialism, as well as Syrian National Socialism.

The Black Protest Movement in the United States would seem to have little relevance to world-wide trends, except as it may be influenced by the growing political successes of the Black People of Africa. I think this appearance is misleading. If we see this protest as one more phase in the general progress of equality in the world and as another step in

the comprehensive achievement of full cultural integration in the
United States, I fear that we may well be missing the point. That point
may be accessible to us only if we try to understand what is going on
in the United States in terms of what is going on in Africa rather than
the other way around.

There is much to protest about the treatment meted out to Negroes in
America, but what is the remedy which is being sought by the most radical
and, in particular, what can account for the exclusion of so many white
members of the most militant groups? The remedy cannot sensibly be
the eradication of all differences between whites and blacks, because
blackness will always exist. In confronting the assimilation of the Negro,
we have come to understand the ultimate impossibility or the utter ruth-
lessness of really melting down all differences in our American "pot".
It seems to me that the Black Protest Movement is, in part at least,
a protest against the discrimination against human differences. It is as
though we have admitted that we cannot abide such differences, so that,
in order to avoid practising discrimination, we have to make everyone
like ourselves. The Black Protest Movement is, therefore, a kind of
nationalism which only in its extreme form demands political independence. The West has come to look upon nationalism as irrational, romantic,
tradition-oriented, and tending to lead to war for trivial, that is non-
material reasons. But in the Middle East, as in the black ghettos of our
cities, the demand for dignity and the search for a relevant identity
leads to nationalism.

In some parts of the Middle East, this nationalism is not so problematic and it is, as a consequence, relatively easy to contain its negative
elements by the use of soundly reasoned institutional adaptations like a
parliament, or by recognizing more or less workable boundaries. To a
large extent, Persian, Turkish, and maybe even Israeli nationalism are
of this sort. The problems emerging from the fact of Arab nationalism
are more numerous, however, for aside from such local patriotisms as
Moroccan, Tunisian, Egyptian, Yemeni, and Lebanese, and the lack of
minimally desirable social cohesion in Algeria, Syria and Iraq, there is
no agreement on whether there should be one or more Arab states, and
if more than one, what their relations with one another ought to be.

As we know from our own experience, there is a tendency during times
of crisis for the more extreme position to drive the others from the field.
Such a critical situation has prevailed for some time in the Middle East
and has been intensified by the six-day war of June 1967. Doubtlessly,
were it not for the fact that Syria and Egypt as well as the Palestinian
refugees are thought to constitute one nation, the June conflict might
never have occurred. What is more to the point is that, in the absence of

any agreed answers to the questions of Arab nationalism, the possibility of a reasonable and a peaceful solution of Arab-Israeli controversy will remain dim. More significant even, in the long run, is the possibility that political development in the Middle East will depend to a large extent upon the resolution of the difficulties of Arab nationalism. Nationalism, therefore, far from being a spent force in the modern world, is an integral part of the Middle Eastern future and quite possibly a decisive aspect of the post-modern world about which we still have much to learn.

The third omen of the coming stage of political development is the protest against the Viet Nam war. This protest, too, appears to be a very parochial phenomenon with little world significance except in the strategic sense. There is a deeper implication here though, because, beyond the specifics of the Viet Nam situation itself, we are now witness to a dramatic demonstration of the difficulties popular governments have in determining and following a foreign policy which does not put all its cards on the table at the start of each hand. Most of our academic notions of political development are restricted to events within single countries, and the international dimension is rarely considered. But even a casual reading of the textbooks on international relations will quickly tell us how the age of popular government has wreaked havoc on the international legal and political order bequeathed to us by the statesmen and diplomats of the Concert of Europe.

In our case, the protest movement appears to be related simply to the question of whether we have a right to fight in either a civil or an international conflict in a particular place. But underlying this protest is the question of how much freedom for manoeuvre must or can a government have when it is simultaneously competing for superiority in secret weaponry and secret strategic deployments, and when it must also justify every major act in terms that the average voter can understand. The credibility gap which some argue has now emerged can most charitably be attributed to this dilemma. The opposition to the war has been the more vocal, but it is also apparent that the more quiescent Hawks have greatly influenced the authorities, who feel that withdrawal from our present position might lead to a severe, nationalistic, reversal toward isolationism.

In the Middle East, popular support for nationalistic and aggressive policies is the more vocal, and proponents of moderation and compromise far fewer than in the West. The popular Turkish reaction to the Cyprus situation is but one bit of graphic evidence in this regard. Even in Iran, where enthusiasm is often lacking in popular support of the Shah, his nationalistic foreign policy has received the widest approval. So great, so moving is the symbol of the solitary nation in its internal confrontations, that many governments have succumbed to the temptation of using this sort of reification as an effective means of mobilizing popular support where the population is still largely under the influence of tradition and reluctant to commit themselves to a shaky and often illegal regime. But once foreign policy rigidity has been used as a means of mobilizing the population, it becomes very hard to change the policy which served as the instrument of mobilization. It takes no great insight to realize that this rather frequent concomitant of political development has occurred with the monotonous irritation of hiccoughs in the Middle East. The post-modern stage seems to hold out the prospect of ever more rigid foreign policies based upon ever more populistic politics. The present possibility of peaceful compromise in the Arab-Israel dispute may well prove an unfortunate casualty of this third omen of post-modernity.

There is more to political development than these three trends. These three represent attacks on an elaborate system of conventions and institutional rationalizations which are fairly well established in the West and which are weak or non-existent in the Middle East. While these protests are often aimed at changing institutional structures in the United States, it is also true that we can expect to cope with these three specific protests, at least in part, by means of existing structures. For the Middle East, less can be said. Existing structures are weak, they have been changed too frequently, and there is no reason to assume, as the specialists in political development so often do, that institutional growth is automatic, inevitable, and unidirectional. To put the issue in another way, we might say that despite the severity of the protests challenging the American institutional system, our own political institutions are so well established that they will survive these pressures. Even if they do not survive intact, existing institutions will determine the pattern of political conflict. This sort of institutional development is often associated with the idea of political development. Most Middle Eastern countries lack this patterning influence of political institutions, and there is little reason to believe that they will acquire these elements of institutional strength in the near future. Let us explore this proposition.

Most of the countries of the Middle East are successor states to the Ottoman Empire. They lack the heritage of traditional institutions, the memory of responsibility for the welfare of large populations, the wisdom required in juggling the diverse interests of a poly-ethnic, poly-religious, and polyglot empire. The Ottoman sultan ruled from Istanbul in the time-honoured way of sending out governors who were to maintain order and collect taxes. The governor usually found it necessary to get along with the urban elites of his gubernatorial seat, and to hold the landlords and tribal chiefs at bay. But even the urban elites were united by little more than their common desire to get all they could out of the governor while giving the least possible. It is unlikely that the governor could have governed at all if the urban elites were better allied, so that the governors generally learned that it was unwise to upset the conditions they found when they first entered upon their duties.

After World War I, nearly all of the Arab world found itself under colonial rule of one sort or another, but the old Ottoman imperial system was smashed. In its place were found imperialists, British, French and Italian, deciding whether to favour the urban elites or to work with the tribes. Despite much ambivalence, the Western preference for order led to the choice of the urban elites, but it has been of crucial importance that these urban elites were in almost all cases without substantial influence outside of their own city and at times even beyond the limits of a single city quarter. No national elite was discovered, and in nearly all cases two or more cities were included in the newly cut up territories. The political heritage of the local elites was primarily that of opposing the government and they intensified this attitude when confronted with a government of unbelievers.

Despite the seditious tendencies of the urban elites, their fragmentation prevented them from seriously challenging alien rule. In the meantime, the interwar years, and for Egypt the years before World War I as well, were years in which an urban middle class of intellectuals and civil servants grew up to challenge the traditional urban elites while the traditional urban elite, in turn, was enabled to acquire and peacefully hold agricultural land, and the tribal sheikhs were transformed into large landholders as well. The urban traditionals usually acquired the land of dispossessed, indebted peasants, and the sheikhs often took legal title to the land traditionally enjoyed by their tribesmen collectively. The origin of the educated, professional, or government-employed middle class is more difficult to pin down, but it would appear that while some of them came from merchant and artisan families, a great many more are the sons of medium-size landholders who were born in the larger villages.

Some scholars hold the view that social cohesion may be substituted for strong institutions in political development, though few would argue this with regard to the attainment of democracy. At any rate, such social cohesion is still rare in the Middle East. The political role of the urban intelligentsia is more significant and will be more important in the long run in those countries where their rural middle class origins are more homogeneous. This is the case in Turkey, in Egypt, and in Tunisia. It is not the case in Iraq, Syria, Jordan, Lebanon, Algeria, Morocco, and Iran. Political development will take diverse paths in these two groups of countries depending upon the presence or absence of a homogeneous rural middle class with links among the urban intelligentsia. But, despite this second proposition, the presence of a potentially unifying elite does not automatically provide for the institutional prerequisites for channelling and patterning the changes which are demanded.

In all of the countries mentioned, whether the counter-elite is homogeneous or not, they succeeded in breaking the power of the landlords, weakening or destroying the traditional aristocracy, and subordinating or driving into exile the exponents of the old Ottoman bureaucracy. In many cases the result has approached explosive fragmentation and alienative centrifugality. There is no attachment to the institutions bequeathed by European imperialism and often a denial of the legitimacy of the political boundaries of the country. Many of the political ills of the Middle East emerge from the very success of the provincial elites in their struggle for autonomy. The Ottoman Empire was an important stabilizing influence, and its institutional apparatus bore a kind of traditional prescriptive legitimacy. But the West destroyed that empire, and it would have been a total anachronism anyway. Nevertheless, the negation of Ottomanism did not appear in the guise of the compelling positive of an alternative nationalism or set of nationalisms. The intensity with which the symbols of Arab nationalism are presently invoked is revelatory of no less genuineness of conviction for the fact that it is almost meant to counterbalance the lack of social integration, the lack of institutional means, and the lack of an effective identity resolution. Middle Eastern nationalism is still at the romantic level, linking individual and abstract nation by means of an imputed identity, but without any clear sense of the community to which values such as the common good might be applied.

When we look more specifically at the institutional resources of Middle Eastern countries we find that they will appear to be well equipped with bureaucratic, executive, and judicial establishments, but they are weak in the institutions of popular government. Every country has a well-defined executive branch. Iran, Morocco, Libya, Jordan, and Saudi Arabia are monarchies; Egypt, Iraq, Syria, Algeria, Sudan, and maybe Yemen are ruled by revolutionary military oligarchies although some are nominally presidential systems and some are pseudo-party systems. Lebanon, Turkey, Tunisia and Israel have constitutional presidencies, although it is well to bear in mind that Lebanon has a no-party system and Tunisia a one-party system.

In just about every one of these countries the executive branch is the most powerful, quite overshadowing the judicial, administrative, representative and popular institutions of government. All of these countries have judicial branches, but the judiciary is usually subordinated to the executive through the Minister of Justice who can appoint, transfer, or fire judges. Traditional religious influence still prevails in the courts of Lebanon, Iran, Morocco, Libya, Jordan, Israel, Sudan, Saudi-Arabia, Yemen, and Kuwait. A degree of judicial independence has been evidenced in Egypt, Turkey and Israel.

Just about all the countries of the Middle East have nominally well-organized, regulated, and responsible bureaucracies, but in point of fact really effective administrative control is found only in Egypt, Israel, Turkey, and Tunisia, with increasing improvement in Lebanon and Algeria.

Most Middle Eastern countries have parliaments, but their effective and meaningful function is limited to Lebanon, Turkey, and Israel. From time to time, the parliaments of Morocco, Libya, Jordan, Egypt, Tunisia, and Iran are active, usually in voting support of their traditional monarchies or one-party systems, but occasionally giving a hint of some opposition. In all of these countries except Egypt and Tunisia, the parliament has been suspended for long periods of time when the monarchy was threatened. Parliament is not now functioning in Syria, Iraq, Jordan, Sudan, Libya, Morocco, and Algeria.

Only Turkey, Morocco, and Israel might be said to have working multi-party systems. Otherwise, strong one-party systems prevail in Egypt and Tunisia, and weak one-party systems in Syria and Algeria. Weak and intermittent multi-party systems appear from time to time in the Sudan and Iran, but in all the rest, political parties tend to be insignificant except insofar as they are cliques of influential traditional politicians.

Effective interest groups can be found in Lebanon, Israel, Morocco, and Turkey. In Egypt and Tunisia, the two strong single-party systems, interest groups have been mobilized by the party or by the government, and they are controlled by officials.

Popular elections have been significant aspects of the political process only in Lebanon, Turkey, and Israel. Elsewhere, plebiscites pass for elections or the government gets involved in rigging the results, or the results may be upset by the executive branch if they happen to be uncongenial.

That nothing is or can be permanent is accepted doctrine here below, and in the light of such a notion, political institutions must be, by definition, at their least viable when they are oldest. Yet, at any given moment, it would seem that the older the institutional arrangement, the more likely is it to be supported by a complex of unexamined and unquestioned beliefs. It is surely unsafe to predict stability on the basis of the longevity of existing institutions, but it is as faulty to argue that political development cannot take place without institutional change. So rather than argue about the relevance of the continuity of institutions, let us see what the facts of such continuity suggest in the case of the Middle East,

In terms of the temporal continuity of their central institutional arrangements, Middle Eastern countries may be divided into three classes. The first class is comprised of those countries which have maintained various dimensions of traditional authority of a kind historically linked with the territory in question. Examples of members of this class are Morocco, where a sultan still rules, Iran where the Shah claims that his crown is 2500 years old, Saudi-Arabia which is ruled over by the descendants of a powerful clan leader who formed an alliance with a pre-modern puritanical religious reformer, Libya where the King is still associated with a similar pre-modern religious movement, and Kuwait which is ruled by a traditional sheikh.

The second class of countries has derived important elements of their present institutional arrangements from reforms which resulted from the impact of Western imperialism during the last century. In nearly all cases, the source of these institutions was administrative, but it is important to remember that the superordinate executive of the Ottoman imperial system was subsequently removed, thus strengthening regional administrative institutions, or at least leaving them with less significant rivals. Among the countries in this category are Turkey itself, where the roots of the present political system were sent down in the guise of administrative and legal reforms, the Tanzimat, during the nineteenth century; Egypt, which long enjoyed limited autonomy from the Ottoman Empire, but which centralized its administration under Muhammad Ali during the first half of the nineteenth century and which developed a parliament during the second half; Tunisia, where the foundation of the modern state is linked to the government of the beys of the last century, and particularly to the administrative reform efforts of Khair-ed-din Pasha; and finally Lebanon, where the basis of the present blend of parliamentarism and confessionalism was laid in the Mutasarrifiyyah system of the 1860's and after.

The third class of countries can trace their institutions back to the settlement following World War I, or even later. The Syrian presidential system with its unicameral legislature derives from the period of the French mandate. The Iraqi constitution is but a modification of the constitutional monarchy set up by the British. The kingdom of Jordan started out as a modest emirate in the early 1920's when it was severed from Palestine. Sudanese institutions are based on a constitutional system worked out in the last days of British rule during the mid-1950's. Algeria was first subjected to French imperialism in 1830, but its institutional set-up is better understood as developed during the much later period when Algeria was treated as a French province.

When we re-examine these three classes of countries in the light of the recent political history of the region, we cannot but come to the conclusion that the first group of traditional authoritarian regimes is faced with severe challenges. Only Morocco and Iran have some chance of sustaining their traditional institutions through the most imminent political vicissitudes. Even in these countries, it is apparent that kingship must decline and other elements become more exalted. The countries which began to develop modern institutions during the nineteenth century—that is, Turkey, Egypt, Tunisia, and Lebanon—seem most likely to be able to build on their existing foundations and create effective, comprehensive, and stable institutional systems. No such optimism can be conjured up when we attempt to peer into the obscure futures of the countries which have been floundering from *coup d'état* to constitutional suspension and back again, some of them for three decades and more.

Another possible indicator of the institutional strength of Middle Eastern governments may be the continuity of the territorial bounds which are associated with these governments. The historical legitimacy of political institutions is often associated with areas which were traditionally under their authority. The continuity of a politically defined territorial unit is also evidence of the accumulation of a bundle of attitudes which will tend toward the acceptance of the continuity of a government in that territory and possibly of the creation of a new, but traditionally linked, nationalism. In some sense, territorial continuity might supply the political vigour which is absent from the institutions themselves.

Once again we may divide our countries into three groups, the first of which has preserved the territorial legitimacy of tradition, the second of which is comprised of countries whose boundaries represent substantial adjustments of traditional arrangements, and the third of which has territorial bounds which have been contrived rather precariously in recent times. All of these countries have troublesome minorities and no boundaries are wholly legitimate or safe from objection. Despite this, the continuity of the territorial core of Morocco, Iran, Yemen, Tunisia, and Egypt, in our first group, functions to add political strength. The second group includes Turkey, the Anatolian residue of the Ottoman Empire, Iraq, made up of the three Ottoman vilayets of Mosul, Baghdad, and Basra, the Sudan, which stretches from Nubia to the Nilotic Bantu regions, and Algeria, which has been constructed out of the cities, mountains, deserts, tribal areas, and agricultural regions which lie between Tunisia and Morocco. Finally, there is the third group, which appears to be quite artificial or at least arbitrary from a territorial point of view. This group includes Libya, which was contrived out of Egypt-oriented Cyrenaica, Maghreb-oriented Tripolitania, and the Saharan Fezzan; Jordan, an arbitrary slice of the Fertile Crescent; Lebanon, which was made up

M-31

of the Christian Mountain, the Sunni coastal cities, the Shi'ite south and east, and the Druze Mountain enclaves; Syria, which includes the Alawite Coast, the Druze Mountain, the Christians of the Orontes Valley, the tribesmen and peasants of the steppeland, and the Muslims of the cities; and finally Saudi-Arabia conquered and unified by Ibn Saud in the 1920's and 1930's.

The ability to execute an effective economic policy aimed at industrialization and economic development as well as at a more egalitarian distribution of wealth is a salient performance characteristic which can also serve to strengthen support for existing institutions. There are only six Middle Eastern governments which might be said to be strengthened by the effectiveness of their economic policies. These countries are Turkey, which has an effective parliamentary government, but where the adventurous subordination of economic soundness to electoral success contributed to the *coup d'état* of 1960; Tunisia, which is lacking in capital and resources but which has provided a very fine planning apparatus for disposing of American aid; Egypt, whose socialist regime has nationalized almost all of the economy except for agriculture; Iran, where an enormous income from petroleum exports has permitted a generous programme of industrial development without the need for forced savings; Lebanon where, recently, political wisdom overcame the traditional laissez-faire attitudes of the economically dominant and has permitted a far-sighted policy of redistribution among the diverse religious communities; and finally, Israel, which continues dependent on foreign financial assistance but which has used its capital resources well enough to be faced with the problem of disappointing a public lately grown used to the idea of a constantly expanding economy. In all other Middle Eastern states, economic policy and economic conditions tend more to weaken than to strengthen existing governments.

I am sure that you will agree that what emerges from this brief survey of some of the political dimensions in the Middle East is a disturbing sense of the great tension between the drive for non-material values, for nationalism, and for popular political participation on the one hand and the need for effective institutions, stable concepts of legitimacy, ideologically and politically acceptable boundaries, and rational economic policies. From our examination of the countries of the Middle East it is possible to conclude that, for several, the prospects of development are not bad, particularly if events beyond their borders do not lead them to emphasize romantic adventurism above the building of sound institutions. For Turkey, Egypt, Iran, Israel, Lebanon, and Tunisia, there are significant possibilities for political development and for the attainment of a high level of political performance. It would be beyond the limits of responsible optimism to suggest that more than one or two of the other

Middle Eastern states have even such limited prospects. One might be willing to settle for even the meagre hopes which this formal comparative analysis allows, but the spirit of counting our blessings cannot be invoked because, in fact, it is doubtful that peace and stability can long endure in this region so long as it is half developed and half backward. Anti-rationalism, anti-materialism, traditionalism, and rampant populist nationalism are not alone the susceptibilities of the countries lacking strong institutions. They are the potential vulnerabilities of all. If we ourselves are not immune to these forces, if we ourselves run the risk of over-bureaucratization in order to cope with these forces of post-modernity, can we expect that even the strongest Middle Eastern country will long escape their influence? If, in addition, the territorial, institutional, and nationalist legitimacy of the state is constantly called into question these vulnerabilities can only be enhanced. It is this political weakness, and not the lack of wealth or training or equipment or courage which must explain the shocking defeat of the combined Arab states. It is only this political weakness which can explain why a leader of the outstanding accomplishments and personality of a Gamal Abd al-Nasser should have thought it necessary to feign a resignation, to purge the army, to beg for political support from Algeria and from Jordan, and in general to act as though he felt that all he had done for Egypt, and all his popularity among the ordinary Egyptians had been dissipated. If Nasser had been acting wisely, then it is clear that no matter what his other accomplishments, little political advance has occurred in Egypt since 1952. This conclusion holds, by the way, even if a rearmed Egyptian army is able to face and hold its own against the Israeli army in the near future. On the other hand, I have the feeling that Nasser had not acted with his usual wisdom in this case, and my thoughts are with Abd al-Hakim Amer at this juncture, because he has shown how much he distrusts the very people who have reposed and continue to repose their faith in him. Nasser had not acted irrationally, however, because the institutional arrangements in Egypt, while better than in many Middle Eastern countries, did not permit him to know more than he knew about the condition of the Egyptian body-politic. It might be going too far to argue that no government so afflicted can win a war, but it is probably not an exaggeration to say that no government so handicapped can find it easy to approach the peace table.

A small group of scholars affiliated with the Social Science Research Council has been working for some years with a sort of shorthand formula for describing what happens in the process of political development. We agreed that this process may be described in terms of six critical changes which constitute a kind of threshold between tradition and modernity. The path to modernity involves critical changes of legitimacy from God to man and from individuals to nations. It involves critical changes of identity from the religious to the ethnic and from the parochial to the societal; it involves critical changes in political participation from elite to mass and from family to group; it involves critical changes in the degree of administrative and legal penetration into the social structure and out to the remote regions of the country, and it involves critical changes in the mode of integrating diverse popular groups often entailing the breakdown of traditional compartmentalization as well as the traditional reservation of certain occupations to specific ethnic or religious groups.

If we re-examine these six areas of critical change, or these six crises of political development, the crisis of legitimacy, the crisis of identity, the crisis of participation, the crisis of distribution, the crisis of penetration, and the crisis of integration, we will find that all six types of change may occur without any concomitant strengthening of the political institutions to which we have referred. The institutions might change, but they need not become stable nor effective. Popular legitimacy may be required ideologically, but, in fact, no government may acquire such legitimacy. A national identity may become established, but it may not reflect the identity resolutions of the masses. Mass popular political participation may be attained through plebiscites without building solid party organizations. Policies of egalitarian income distribution may be pursued, but effective development planning and sound investment organizations may not be created. The modern bureaucratic and security administrations may penetrate the most private or the most remote segments of society, but they may only succeed in breaking down the traditional social compartments without constructing any substitutes. New integrative relations may develop among diverse social and occupational groups but these may not be recognized in either legitimate interest associations or in the civil administrative apparatus. Political development, according to this definition, refers to changes in the type and style of politics. It refers to the informal political process which must always be a challenge to the formal processes. And political development refers to the new requirements which are demanded of institutions if they are to maintain stability and cope responsibly with social conflict.

I cannot compel you to accept this definition of political development, but you will notice that this definition allows for a variety of particular outcomes. Each country may take a somewhat different path, but within the same general framework of meaning. To these particular outcomes we will attach our own values in accordance with our judgments. In this sense, political development is neither good nor bad in itself; it rather represents an observable and all but universal historical phenomenon. I have tried to suggest that in the Middle East the particular dimensions of the process are the need for regulatory institutions and the pull of romanticism, of nationalism, and of populism. The process of political development intersects with these forces so as to cause diverse outcomes according to the condition of each country and its political role in the region.

In conclusion, I suppose that I must at last turn to what is probably the real question I have been asked to answer for you, and that is whether or not political development in the Middle East can lead to peace. Or, more specifically, are the governments of the Middle East developing a war-making capacity more rapidly than they are developing a peace-making capacity? The answer to these questions, to my mind, depends upon whether, in the long run, Middle Eastern institutional capacities become strong enough to channel the forces of anti-materialism, anti-rationalism, nationalism, and populism into truly humane, sympathetic, and creative cultural channels. The real resolution of this issue, and that is the answer that cannot now be supplied, turns on the fundamental political fact that men and societies are not destined to be the passive victims of some unknown and unfathomable historical mechanism. Political development is not merely an extrapolation from existing trends, for, as we have seen, a trend is longest just before it ends. Political development is, therefore, the way things are actually changing and the way in which we would like them to change. The area is urgently in need of institutional restraints and of peace, but it is even more urgently in need of men of courage who can distinguish between antimaterialism and obscurantism, between nationalism and traditional reaction, and between a responsible foreign policy and one that submits to popular frenzy.

21

SOME ASPECTS OF MIGRATION AND MOBILITY IN GHANA *

MEYER FORTES

THE PROPENSITY of the species *Homo Sapiens* to move about, across seas, across deserts, over mountains, through dense jungles, is a datum more or less taken for granted among students of mankind. The archaeological record of every continent testifies to its deeply ingrained nature and sempiternal character. Historical research, wherever we turn to it, and whatever branch of human social life and its material, or intellectual or artistic products we look at, would be rendered jejune without assuming this. In ethnology and sociology, geography and economics, we have to make allowances for it all the time. Nomadic peoples offer striking examples. Spatial mobility is so built into their social and economic life that no sense can be made of their social organization or of their cultural outfit without consideration of this parameter.

However, this general propensity of *Homo Sapiens*—a propensity shared with his hominid ancestors and with large sections of the animal kingdom—is a theme more fitting for the speculative philosopher than for a working anthropologist. As an anthropologist, I am much more interested

* This paper is a revised version of a paper originally delivered in November 1967 at a Conference on Migration and Mobility at the University of Florida, Gainsville, Fla., under the joint auspices of the Center for Latin American Studies and the African Studies Program.

474

in what can be learnt from taking a close look at the facts on the ground in a limited socio-geographic region. First, however, let me say a word or two about my terminology. Two concepts are involved. I shall call them "migration" and "mobility". I propose to use "migration" for the movements of people—individually or in groups—*across* boundaries; and "mobility" for movement *within* boundaries. I speak of boundaries in this general and abstract sense; for I want the term to cover any kind of boundary recognised by the actor as a boundary—it may be geographical, or structural or ethnic or cultural. Thus the total fact of movement we encounter in a particular case can be made up of both a migration element and a mobility component. Analytically speaking we have to consider both variables in any attempt to depict what is happening.

It is obvious, of course, that I am here simply generalising what is well established practice in the conceptual and statistical procedures of the specialists who have accumulated the vast array of studies on these topics in every country of the world in the past sixty or seventy years. In my paradigmatic case, that of an African from a tribal area migrating to an urban centre, he crosses a series of boundaries, it might even be an inter-national political boundary. He crosses socio-geographical, structural, politico-jural, economic, and cultural boundaries. But once in the new environment, he is faced with a challenge of mobility; first, possibilities of economic mobility in occupation and earning capacity; then of cultural mobility in his style of living, in his skills, modes of thought, his pre-ferences, and so on, during his own life time; lastly, possibilities of laying the foundations for the so-called vertical mobility of his children, mobility which, from the observer's angle, is movement in time. For what does time signify in the context of human social existence but the dialectic of continuity and growth within a generation and succession and displace-ment of each generation by the next?

I need hardly draw the moral of this example. It is the fact that my topic confronts us with a multidimensional phenomenon about which many analytical questions can be posed and investigated. Naturally, you might well say; for what I have adumbrated is the movements of persons in and through social systems. It is to emphasize this point that I have resisted the temptation, which automatically arises in any discussion of this topic, to plunge straight into statistics or into historical narrative. The limitation of bare statistics can be seen from the following example from Great Britain, for which I am indebted to Professor Donald MacRae. In the decade 1951-61, Scotland lost—or, if you prefer, exported —about 24,000 people a year to England. In one sense this is a case of geographical mobility, for it represents a population movement within the political society of which Scots as well as English are equal citizens with freedom to live wherever they wish to. However, for the Scotsmen it was also an emigration across a cultural and economic boundary within the total social system. For certain areas in England, such boom towns as Luton, for instance, which received substantial numbers of these Scottish emigrants, it was an immigration, an accretion of a socio-cultural group which had to be physically, socially, and culturally accommodated and in due time integrated. However, if we want to understand the slope of this gradient, so to speak, why 24,000 people left Scotland for England every year and only about 3,000 moved in the reverse direction, we must consider what sort of people they were in social and cultural terms. Those who moved to places like Luton, where the automobile and other new industries were producing the boom, were skilled workers and their families. Elsewhere, the immigrants were professional men and women, mainly doctors (who were then being over-produced in Scotland) and other academically trained cadres.

It is an easily justified guess that, in the case of the skilled workers, the factor of migration was more conspicuous in the way they perceived their movement than the factor of mobility, whereas for a doctor or academic it was the other way round. The demographic statistics tell us only a small part of the story; and occupational and class data, another part; there is the complex area of motivation, as well as the more complex dimension of structural accommodation to be reckoned with, too.

The point I am making is more graphically apparent if we look at a country like Ghana. According to the 1960 *Census* of Ghana [1] (Special Report E) there are 92 so-called "tribes" in a population of about 7½ million. The term "tribe", needless to say, is not, in the Census, used in an anthropologically strict connotation but quite empirically to identify ethnic groups or local communities that distinguish themselves from others by criteria of provenance, language, culture, and social structure. This is sufficient to remind us that Ghana, taken as a whole, is now socially and culturally heterogeneous to a notable degree. On one level, this heterogeneity is inherent in the traditional geographical distribution of the culturally diverse peoples of Ghana,[2] and goes back in time as far as human memory records. But the aspect of interest in the present connection is the degree to which this heterogeneity is the product of migration and mobility in recent times.[3]

[1] I draw here on an unpublished analysis of the Census data by Dr. Polly Hill Himphries, for access to which I am indebted to her.

[2] A useful outline of this distribution is given in Bourrett, F. M., 1960. *Ghana— the Road to Independence, 1919-1957*. Stanford University Press, Ch. I.

[3] A fundamental contribution to the demographic and sociological analysis of migration and mobility in Ghana is *A Study of Contemporary Ghana*, Vol. 2. *Some Aspects of Social Structure*, edited by Walter Birmingham, I. Neustadt and E., N. Omaboe. Allen and Unwin, London, 1967, especially Ch. III by J. C. Caldwell.

On a rough estimate, something of the order of the ½ to ¾ million of
the people living and working in Ghana in 1960 were Africans from other
African states—Nigeria, Dahomey, Haute Volta, etc. But these crude
figures tell us little. We learn more when we find that there are about
100,000 Yoruba from Nigeria in Ghana, most of whom are engaged in
commerce and trade; that there are 130,000 Mossi immigrants from the
Haute Volta, the majority of whom are recorded as farm workers or
general labourers or domestic servants; that there are 5,000 or so immigrants from Gao who consist almost entirely of males and that they
all work as unskilled labourers—in fact as "carriers". Here we meet with
indications of the political, economic, structural, and cultural components
of the cross-national cross-cultural mobility that has produced the present
ethnic patchwork in Ghana.

Among much vital information necessary for a proper study of our
problem that is lacking in the Census data, one stands out. We cannot
tell from the Census how long these foreign immigrants—let us call them
exo-migrants for short—have been living in Ghana at the time of the
Census. This kind of question can be answered only by fieldwork, not by
census enumeration. A few indications are available from research that
is now in train in Ghana. What emerges is that exo-migration has a very
varied temporal range. There are Mossi, Yoruba and Hausa groups who
have lived in Ghana continuously for up to half a century, and at the
other extreme temporaries who come only for a season to work on farms
or in one of the extractive industries or to trade, and then go back home—
to marry with the bride-price they have earned and to cultivate their
fields.[4] There are many in these exo-migrant communities who have been
born and brought up and educated in Ghana and who are now, by the
process of intergenerational mobility, moving into new occupations and
professions different from those of their parents and into corresponding
shifts in their life-style.

But to get a more complete anthropological picture of spatial and
temporal mobility in Ghana, we must look at the aggregations of the
population in towns, villages, and local communities. Unfortunately we
still lack the social and historical data needed to discuss this in a systematic way. What we do know, from the sources at present available, is
that all the bigger towns have very mixed populations; and that these
include a large number of what I shall call *endo-migrants*—comparable

---

[4] A number of studies have been made of migration in Ghana, with special reference to the immigration of foreign Africans. I draw special attention to the study
by Jean Rouch, "Migration au Ghana", *Journal de la Société des Africanistes*, Vol. 26,
1956. See also Skinner, E. P., "Labour Migration and its Relationship to Socio-cultural
Change in Mossi Society", *Africa*, Vol. 30, 1960.

to the Scots who migrate to England—as well as numerous exo-migrant groups from other West African countries. And this is true nowadays not only of the major urban areas (such as Kumasi and Accra) or the industrial (e.g. mining) areas, but also of the increasing number of small urban agglomerations growing up at main crossroads, centres of administration, in the vicinity of schools and hospitals, etc.

The development of motor roads in particular has contributed to fostering and facilitating mobility and migration internally in Ghana to an extent that was undreamt of when I first went there 33 years ago.

In 1934, when I was living at Tongo among the Tallensi,[5] if I had run short of sugar, or matches, or kerosene—to say nothing of whiskey or flour or tinned meats—I might have obtained a small supply from a local store in Navrongo, 35 miles away; but the chances are that I would have had to send 100 miles to Tamale for these supplies. In the dry season the round trip would have meant a journey of at least two days by a dusty and uncomfortable dirt road. Today, a metalled, all-weather road enables one to drive to Tamale in a couple of hours and one can do the round trip in a morning. During the thirties, rainy-season travel was even more arduous, for one had to cross two fast-flowing rivers by ferry or by dugout canoe. Today concrete bridges carry the road over these rivers.

The expansion and improvement of communications by road are symbolic of the fundamental restructuring of the social space and cultural environment of the people of Ghana that has taken place in the span of time since I first went there—a span equivalent to at most two demographic generations. By 1963, an urban centre had grown up within ten miles of Tongo. A modern hospital, schools, several well-stocked stores, an imposing Catholic church, a bank, a post-office, a police station and jail, a large transport yard packed day and night with passenger lorries and goods trucks en route to the coast towns some 500 miles south or to centres of trade as far north as the Niger, and a typical open-air market, had grown up around what used to be a traditional, local market centre. An expanding suburban development was providing housing for the very considerable population of white-collar, salaried, educated clerks, teachers, clergy, government officials and traders mostly from Southern Ghana. And of course the usual excrescences on urbanisation were amply evident—beer shops with juke boxes, prostitutes, thieves and psychotics as well as a regiment of beggars and vagrants. It is today a cosmopolitan community, in which almost every one of the

[5] Cf. Fortes, M., 1936, "Culture Contact as a Dynamic Process", Africa, Vol. 9, 1 : 24-25, and Idem: 1945. The Dynamics of Clanship among the Tallensi, Oxford University Press, London.

92 ethnic groups, native and foreign, enumerated in the census, is represented. It replicates on a small scale what can be observed of the socio-economic structure and the cultural heterogeneity of the larger urban areas of Ghana. In terms of our topic, spatial mobility brings together in a single territorial aggregation persons and groups of diverse political, ethnic, social and cultural origins, of varied occupational skills and vocations, of different religious faiths and practices; an aggregation stratified by status, by income levels, by prestige rating, and by style of life.

The question that immediately arises is: what sort of community does such an agglomeration constitute? What sort of common interests bind them together? And when we try to answer this question we come up at once against the time dimension.

Heterogeneous urban aggregations have long existed in Ghana. There was a sizable foreign settlement in Kumasi in the early years of the last century.[6] It included Moslems from the bend of the Niger and even further north. Trade was the main incentive that brought them there, and though many were transients, there can be little doubt that many were more or less permanent residents there. It is difficult to determine how much these foreign sojourners influenced Ashanti material and social culture. Thus, though Islam is a proselytising religion, there is no evidence of Ashanti being converted by these foreigners on any appreciable scale. One reason is that they never ceased to be regarded as foreigners. Neither collectively nor individually were they admitted to citizenship in the Ashanti state. This was not due to xenophobia, which we can assert with certainty never existed and does not really exist now in Ghana. It was due to the impossibility of assimilating a free foreigner into the Ashanti clan structure, which was an indispensable prerequisite for citizenship. Residence alone, however long, could not serve as a credential for this. On the other hand, it is also pretty certain that the foreigners did not desire to accept Ashanti citizenship, which would have meant finally severing their bonds with their natal societies and cultures. It was not a handicap or a disgrace to be a foreigner, living in the foreign quarter, and carrying on business relations with the Ashanti from there.

The significance of this is obvious. The kind of community developed in a heterogeneous population aggregate depends in a fundamental respect on the political system—and, *ergo,* on the legal system—that applies in it. Modern urban aggregations are, of course, enormously larger and more complex than was Kumasi in 1818; and the problems of citizenship that correspond to the socio-economic and juridical institutions of con-

[6] As is described in the famous book by T. E. Bowdich, 1819, *Mission from Cape Coast Castle to Ashantee.*

temporary Ghana are much more involved. It would take a special paper to deal with these problems in any detail. Suffice it to note that citizenship, nowadays, is in effect a whole cluster of politico-jural statuses. There is the element of citizenship, or rather civil status, under the local and regional administration, citizenship in natal tribal communities, and citizenship in the national state; and each of these grades of citizenship carries its specific rights and obligations, privileges and immunities. The pertinent fact here is that spatial mobility, whether by endo-migration or by exo-migration, does not create new or extinguish natal citizenship. A Tallensi living in Accra does not stop being tribally a Tallensi either in terms of financial and other obligations due from him to his home community, or in terms of rights he has in it. Thus in 1963 I found that two recently installed Custodians of the Earth Shrines[7] had lived and worked in Southern Ghana for thirty and forty years respectively but had returned to take up these offices that fell to them by right of seniority in the lineage. The same rule applies to all immigrants in any region of Ghana. Yoruba, Hausa, Mossi, and so on, remain citizens of their countries of origin.

The significance of this is far reaching. For not only do non-natives of a town, a village, or a region, remain legally citizens of their countries and tribes of origin—they tend to remain also culturally and socially attached to their own natal communities. In geographical and economic respects they are migrants; culturally and more ambiguously, politically, they are mobiles. The repercussions of this disparity need much more investigation than has yet been devoted to them. The gross manifestations are easy to see and were indeed even clearer in 1945, when I met them in Kumasi, than they are today, for reasons I will come to in a moment. They appear in the occupational and residential ecology of the towns. In Accra and Kumasi today, immigrants from Northern Ghana tend to congregate heavily in certain residential areas and not in others. Mossi, Hausa, and Yoruba, tend to cluster in their own residential areas in the towns. This facilitates the practice of their religion among Moslems, and, in general, the trading and other specialised activities of exo-migrant groups. It facilitates mutual hospitality, commensality and marriages, as well as mutual assistance in times of crisis such as sickness or death. It facilitates the formation of associations and the emergence of leadership and political organization in each group. Most of all, it facilitates the preservation and the transmission to the next generation of critical cultural possessions, those felt to be distinctive of each group, primarily their language and their family system.

Two consequences are obvious. Ethnically and culturally diverse groups

---

[7] See Fortes, 1945, p. 20, and *passim* for a description of these functionaries.

do not fuse merely by virtue of juxtaposition in a local community and participation in the use of common instrumental amenities and provisions. This holds even when there is residential intermingling. The Ghanaian urban aggregate tends to be a "plural society" in the sense given to this concept by J. S. Furnivall.[8] Its main focus of common interest is economic, and in the realm of economics competition is far more in evidence than is cooperation. As far as political, moral and cultural interests are concerned, the tendency is towards divergence. I must add that in 1963 there was on the surface in many places a great show of political consensus in allegiance to the CPP, adulation of the then President, and a response to the political and social propaganda of press and radio. But it seemed doubtful to me if this movement was drawing any of the foreign groups into its scope; and it was not extinguishing primary tribal loyalties. There are caste-like features in the social and cultural relations of different ethnic groups in modern Ghana. But only shadowily so; for none of the classical inter-caste barriers exist. Socio-cultural compartmentalization with much circulation, inter-communication, and collaboration is a more accurate description.

But now I must draw attention to a dimension that runs athwart this picture. It is the dimension laid down by the succession of generations. I have space to consider only one component of this. Compared with the thirties, there has been, in the past ten years or so, a veritable explosion of literacy due to the great expansion of schooling and higher education at all levels. This was striking among the Tallensi. In 1937 there were no more than half a dozen literate young men and a handful of school children in Taleland. In 1963 the majority of school-age children were in schools, and there was at least one literate young man or young woman in almost every extended family. The literates, nowadays, are in occupations undreamt of by their fathers and grandfathers. They are clerks, teachers, catechists, tax collectors, civil servants, district commissioners, members of parliament, and party officials. Their style of life is in important respects different from that of their parents and grandparents, though their allegiance to their tribal community and the most important features of traditional culture remain unimpaired. But their intellectual and cultural horizons stretch far beyond the tribal culture. In residence they are children of their families; when it comes to marriage they are Tallensi to the core; in religious allegiance they are pragmatists. Many are nominal Christians but continue to be participants in the traditional ancestor worship still tenaciously maintained by their elders. In their world view, they are part western, part traditional. Transistor radios and newspapers,

[8] See, in particular, his classic analysis of the plural society as a product of colonial rule in his book, *Colonial Policy and Practice*, 1948, Cambridge University Press,

relatives at secondary schools and in the university, in urban occupations and in politics, all of these keep them informed of events in the world at large. Incipiently, they are on the way into the cultural universe of contemporary western mankind.

The same pattern of cultural and intellectual mobility in time is found, much more elaborated, among the youth of the urban immigrants. In an effort to counteract what appear to them to be the dangers of a drift away from their parental cultural moorings among the young, urban immigrants, both from within Ghana and from other countries, often send their children back to their natal homes for schooling and cultural indoctrination. Whether or not this will be effective remains to be seen. The signs everywhere are, I think, that intergenerational mobility promoted by the westernisation of Ghanaian society will have the same result as it has had in such countries as the United States. The big difference, at the present time, is that in Ghana many of the immigrant groups still maintain their links with their natal communities, both in Ghana and abroad.

Regular new arrivals from the home community, whether as traders or as seasonal workers or as aspirants to more lasting jobs, maintain the flow of information; and there is always a steady stream of people returning—if only, in old age, to finish their days in the home community. Here, again, modern transport and communications are significant. Nigerians living in Ghana can nowadays easily and expeditiously go back for short visits by air; they keep in close contact by mail and telephone. The radio and newspapers keep them up-to-date with the events in their home countries. A point of importance is that money is readily transferable—international politics permitting—through banks and the postal services. This means that immigrants can fulfil financial responsibilities to their kinsfolk and their natal community and, in addition, if they wish, build up assets at home against the time when they might wish to return. An indication of the strength of these links with the home communities is the very marked tendency for immigrants to seek wives in their home communities. Too little research has been done on this subject for me to be able to give figures, but my impression is that there is relatively little interethnic marriage among the various ethnic segments of Ghana (except in elite circles) considering their close local and social association. Here again we meet with signs of caste-like cultural segregation.

We are confronted thus with a well-known paradox of mobility. Given the right international and intra-national political conditions for freedom of movement, and the possibilities of economic absorption, modern facilities enable groups and individuals to migrate easily. These facilities enable migrants, at the same time, to keep strong links with their natal countries and communities. They are not compelled to commit themselves to citizenship, and to cultural and social assimilation, in the countries and regions to which they migrate, so long as political pressure or economic necessity or cultural discrimination is not brought to bear on them. They can participate regularly, or at least periodically in those strongest of all cultural events that keep groups and individuals loyal to their original social identity, that is to say the religious festivals and rites of passage distinctive of their home communities. At the same time these conservative opportunties and inducements are opposed by the temporal mobility between generations fostered in the immigrant environment. The children of illiterate ancestor-worshipping immigrants become literate Christians aspiring to white-collar careers and to the style of life that prevails in the society around them. The natal language of the parents which, next to religion, forms the strongest bond of separate identity for a group of immigrants, falls into the background for the children. In Ghana, unlike the United States, first generation locally born people of immigrant origin do not, as a rule, lose their family language; but it becomes more definitively the medium for family, and for ethnically distinctive and closed-off relationships, serving to segregate its speakers from the external system of social and economic relations. It is not surprising to find, in some immigrant groups that have long been settled in Ghana, a tendency to discourage their children from taking advantage of the educational, political, and social developments in the country at large.

This kind of self-sufficiency in an immigrant group is associated with a tendency for the group to close itself off, as a relatively distinct community, within the total society in which it is encapsulated. Emphasis on endogamy and on linguistic or religious or other forms of cultural separation is both an expression of this tendency and a means to its implementation. It reinforces, and is reinforced by, economic specialisation and it often influences the party allegiance of immigrants in modern national politics.

The process here at work is circular. On the one hand, self-sufficiency is strengthened by such internal forces of social and cultural continuity in immigrant groups as a distinctive language or religion and the more so if these are continually reinforced through contacts with the home communities. On the other hand, however, the greater the degree to which pluralistic values and patterns of social organisation are accepted or enforced in the total society, the more likelihood is there of self-sufficiency being emphasised and defended among immigrant groups.

And here lie the germs of the conflicts and contradictions so agonisingly exemplified by the Ibo tragedy. Pluralism in the total society and self-sufficiency in its component parts are tolerable and even viable over considerable periods of time if the structural boundaries between the parts are consistent and congruent at all levels of social and political structure,

Then pluralism can serve as a framework for a generalised social symbio-
sis. A perfect and balanced caste system would come near to this ideal
model. Conflict emerges when incongruities develop between boundary
interfaces at different levels. The Ibo immigrants were secure and were
able to maintain in-group self-sufficiency in Northern Nigeria as long as
there was consistency between their civic status as immigrants, their cultural differences from the Hausa, their occupational specialisation, and
their distinctive style of life. Conflict arose when, at the political level,
their civic status became ambiguous, and, at the economic level, claims
on a share of the occupational quasi-monopoly they had established had
become legitimate and feasible among Hausa literates. As we know from
many plural societies, leadership in the revolt of racially or culturally or
economically underprivileged communities regularly comes from individuals and groups who have the qualifications, by education or style of
life or civic status, to be equal to the privileged elements and therefore
resent and reject the inconsistency between their ethnic situation and
their legitimate aspirations. I return to this in a moment.

Similar incongruities underlie the socially and psychologically patholo-
gical manifestations of unbalanced pluralism due to spatial and temporal
mobility in a rapidly changing society. But I have not the space here to
suggest how vagrancy, prostitution, certain classes of crime and so forth,
may be related to the pluralism of mobility. It is one of the concerns in
the literature on what has come to be called "alienation".

Mobility and change appear to be so intrinsically linked that it is well
to remind ourselves that there are limits on their covariation, at any rate
in the short run. Ghana provides some striking examples of what some
would describe as structural continuity, others, perhaps, as conservative
features, or as indications of cultural lag. I refer, of course, to the extraordinary tenacity of the ideology, and the associated patterns of social
organization, of matrilineal descent. And lest this might be interpreted as
a peculiarity of Akan social structure, I might add that matrilineal ideology has shown the same sort of tenacity in the face of changes due to
occupational and class mobility in other areas of Africa and even in the
case of the classically extreme matrilineal system of the Nayar of South
India.

A nice example from Ghana is presented in the study by Polly Hill of
the early development of cocoa farming.[9] She describes how cocoa farming
was established in the early years of this century in Southern Ghana by
the incursion into areas of virgin forest of groups of farmers who migrated
from older settlements and villages. As chance would have it, two main

[9] Hill, Polly, 1963. *Migrant Cocoa Farmers of Southern Ghana*. Cambridge
University Press.

"tribal" groups were concerned in this movement. Though coming from adjacent localities, they had a number of contrasting customs, above all in their kinship system. One group had and have Akan matrilineal corporate lineages; the others have patrilineal descent groups without corporate functions. Now the interesting thing is that the former took up land and exploited it for cocoa corporately. The chief entrepreneur would enlist support from brothers, sisters, and sisters' children. The area opened up would be developed *en bloc*, bit by bit, with portions allocated in a patchwork-like distribution to each participant, not in accordance with his or her monetary contribution to the purchase price—if indeed he or she made such a contribution which they often did not do—but in proportion to his or her status in the lineage segment. Then, at the death of any member of the lineage, his or her cocoa patch would, formally, revert to the corporately owned pool. It could in theory be reallocated to any other member of the lineage segment but in practice was often taken by his or her heir, who would, however, be a member of the lineage segment anyhow. In the generation after the first migrations younger members of these lineages became educated and often moved into towns to enter white-collar or commercial occupations. They never, however, lost their rights in the cocoa land owned by the lineage segment and the practice developed of leaving the management of the plantation to the head of the lineage segment and pooling all profits for such purposes as providing education for the younger members, paying for funerals of members, and settling debts of members.

By contrast, the patrilineal groups exploited their land by forms of partnership. A number of men, not necessarily kin, would form a "company" each contributing to the purchase price of the land in accordance with his means and ambitions. The chief entrepreneur would buy the rights in a defined stretch of forest in the name of the company. Then the land would be marked out in strips, one for each of the partners, the width of each strip being proportional to the amount of the partner's contribution; and each strip-owner was responsible for growing his cocoa on it in the way he thought best. But the crucial point is this: in contrast to the practice of the matrilineal group, when a strip-owner died, his strip was inherited by his sons, who might subdivide it or arrange for one son to buy the others out. Again, in the matrilineal groups, members might own a cocoa plot for their lifetime but could not sell or mortgage their plots without the consent of the lineage assembly, a restriction which often resulted in financial assistance being provided by the lineage to prevent the use of the plot being alienated. By contrast, in the partnership arrangement every strip-owner was free to dispose of his strip as he pleased. For the matrilineal lineage segment joint exploitation of

M-32

the virgin cocoa land resulted automatically from their corporate descent group structure and the laws of property associated with it. The finance was often provided by the head of the segment himself, who acted thus because his wealth would in any case, after his death, revert to the lineage. Again, by contrast, for the partnership, the joint purchase of land was motivated partly by considerations of mutual trust based on common citizenship in their tribal community, common customs, and the wish to live and work together in the cocoa colony, and partly by the political and legal considerations that the chiefs who were selling the land had to sell it in large blocks.

Here then we have an impressive demonstration of a number of factors relevant to our enquiry. First, there is the negative evidence that ecological, technical, and economic requirements do not dictate the institutional form assumed by an organization the functions of which are primarily economic. Secondly, there is the evidence of the tenacity with which traditional family and kinship structures are preserved in the face of social and economic changes of apparently radical extent. Thirdly, there is the evidence of the adaptability of familial institutions which have been regarded—especially by economic planners—as impediments to progress. These familial institutions do not necessarily collapse when a modern market economy replaces the traditional subsistence and trading economy. Fourthly, there is the evidence that spatial, social and cultural mobility can be accommodated within the framework of traditional familial institutions and norms. Lastly, and marginally perhaps, it is most interesting to have so clear-cut a case of neighbouring tribal groups speaking each other's language and whose social and economic and political relations were formerly, and are even more now, intermeshed in innumerable ways, yet vigorously maintaining their separate cultural identities right up to the present day. The groups concerned are among the most progressive and most westernised tribal communities in Southern Ghana, largely Christianised and literate, and involved in the modern political and economic structure of Ghana. Yet they continue to hold on to their traditional family and kinship values and ideology, and to assert their separate cultural identity. And I would like to add that this picture can readily be duplicated from other parts of Africa, and elsewhere, in what are nowadays called the developing nations.

But let me go back to the Tallensi. My own enquiries in 1963 and the figures one can get from the 1960 Census show that the only immigrants in the tribal area are a couple of white missionaries and a few schoolteachers and clerks. Taleland never was and is not now a reception area for immigrants, if only because of its penurious subsistence economy. On the other side, migration from Taleland to Southern Ghana is nowadays very substantial. Up to half of the men under the age group 30-40 seem to be away at any time and a correspondingly marked proportion of the women of child-bearing age. Labour migration, principally of men who went to work in the towns, on the mines, or joined the army or the police force in Southern Ghana was significant even in the thirties. But not on this scale. In addition to older economic incentives for migration, educational qualifications, and especially literacy, harnessed to the political and social developments of the fifties and sixties, have conduced to both the quantitative increase and qualitative change in the pattern of mobility, internally as well as externally. As a result of the great development in education since the attainment of independence in Ghana, a proportion which may well be as much as 50 per cent of young men and women in the 20-30 age group are literate and are engaged in clerical and similar occupations either at home or in other parts of the country as I have previously remarked; and many people are nominally, if not wholeheartedly, members of Christian churches, as I have already implied.

What has been the effect of these quite marked cultural changes? In the thirties, if men went to work in Southern Ghana for any length of time it meant virtually cutting themselves off from home and family. Months and indeed years might pass without an absent son or brother or father being heard from or of, and remittances were rarely sent back home. As to the tribal area, the native-born literates could be counted on the fingers of one hand; there was no radio; newspapers which reached the tribal territory came to the European or Southern Ghanaian officials. The tribal society was pretty well closed and wholly traditional. Knowledge of the outside world and contacts with it were almost entirely mediated by labour migrants. At that time migration from the tribal territory was apt to be deplored by the people themselves. They regarded it as primarily a response to economic need or as due to ambitions which were linked with a search for economic opportunity or for escape from familial and lineage authority. Though emigrants did return occasionally for a short stay, this was rare. However, it was quite common for men to return to their home settlements in their old age or after a number of years abroad. They then became quickly reabsorbed into the traditional ways of life which had been hardly affected at all by alien cultural and social forces.

The picture today is very different. As I have already remarked, the literate young people are of course aware of the world outside and familiar with political, social, and cultural ideas and practices and with the public affairs of distant countries as well as of their own country. They have a notion of what it means to be a citizen of Ghana apart from being a Tallensi. Their scheme of values and their world view is, if only sketchily, infused with western ideas and theories. Their social horizon is not confined to the tribe. And through them, through the radio and the coming and going of schoolboys, clerks, and others, even the illiterate older people are significantly aware of what is going on in the world outside, though they remain tenaciously and unquestioningly Tallensi in language, in religious practices and in their general scheme of values.

This expansion of the intellectual and social horizon of the Tallensi has been accompanied by changes in their whole conception of their cultural and political environment; and this is closely bound up with the development of communications and transport in the country at large. A literate youth happily stays at home now if he can find a suitable job; for if he has a hankering to pay a visit to kin or friends in Accra it is as easy to travel down for a few days as formerly it was to visit a kinsman living five miles away. And this is typical. Old and young travel frequently back and forth to places in Southern Ghana where they have kin or friends. Letters, telegrams, money orders, etc., go back and forth. Again, emigration is not frowned upon or feared, except insofar as it removes manpower needed to keep up the farms at home. For emigrants now keep in touch with the home settlement by letter and telegram and by visits, especially at the times of the great festivals, and there is reciprocal communication in the opposite direction. Thus Tallensi now think of Ghana as a more or less unified social space and arena for their economic and social activities. There is no longer the old feeling that if a son went south he might be lost for years. Emigration is understood as a means of seeking greater opportunities without having to cast off tribal allegiance. And it is striking how in fact loyalty to the home country and culture now waxes more strongly than ever among literates and people normally living and working abroad. Political, economic, and social changes have made mobility possible where formerly only migration was the rule. To be sure this has brought new strains and tensions in its train, but these cannot be discussed in the present context.

The story of A is characteristic of modern developments. A is the son of one of my best friends and informants of the thirties. I knew him as a small boy. Venturing out of Taleland at the beginning of the war he went into the armed forces and was there taught to read and write. He early showed a shrewd head for business. Today he lives in Accra, where he is a businessman and entrepreneur of substantial wealth with a string of wives—all Tallensi—and a good deal of property. His only brother stayed at home and in due course succeeded to their father. He has remained illiterate. But A maintains very firmly his ties with his brother, his kin, and his home community. He sent some of his children home to live with his brother and to go to school in Tongo, with the aim of ensuring that they should become imbued with the proper Tallensi values. A himself periodically drives up to Tongo in one of his cars and members of his family constantly visit him. He is financing the rebuilding in modern style of his paternal dwelling house. He played a key part in the manoeuvres that were last year going on to find a successor for the late chief. And underneath all of this he remains a Tallensi, consulting diviners when his children are ill, sending home money for the purchase of sacrificial animals, paying bride price for his wives, and so on. On a smaller scale the same patterns of relations between members of a family living in Southern Ghana and those who have remained at home are found in dozens of other families.

Thus the physically and culturally expanded horizons, which have made possible a great increase in both migration from and mobility within and without the Tallensi tribal boundaries, far from causing the disintegration of the tribal society and the decay of the traditional culture, in this case forms the basis of an extension and reinforcement of tribal loyalties and a reshaping of the tribal culture to accommodate new ideas and values. It was striking to find how proud the majority of the educated Tallensi youth, at home and abroad, are of their homeland and the traditional ways of life of their parents and grandparents. My wife and I were often invited to notice the respect which the educated young people showed for their illiterate elders and the tolerance and pride of the latter towards the former. Ancestor worship and the traditional festivals and rituals flourish as of yore in the changed and changing circumstances symbolised by the universality of the bicycle and the desuetude of maidenly nudity.

Many similar instances could be cited which show how the migration and mobility made possible by some modern political and social changes enhance individual development, make opportunities for new kinds and levels of achievement and aspiration, diffuse skills and values new to Africa and in other ways conduce to advantages and desirable modifications in ways and standards of living without necessarily destroying the traditional ways and value systems. What cannot be too much emphasised is the fact that these positive developments are made possible by the expansion of the political structure and the cultural field within which migration and mobility are free and legitimate. Economic advances such as the development of modern industries and the diffusion of western skills such as literacy or western techniques for dealing, for instance, with problems of health and disease cannot by themselves thus canalise migration and mobility to personal and social advantage.

There is, however, also a negative side to migration and mobility. Thus I have explained that in certain contexts of political and social structure migrant and mobile groups and individuals hold on tenaciously over long stretches of time to the social and cultural identity that is rooted in their home communities. Now if we consider again the history of Ibo migration in Nigeria,[10] we cannot avoid concluding that persistent adherence to their home-based familial and kinship values and the retention of their loyalties to and links with their home communities played an important part in the success formerly achieved by Ibo migrants in adapting to and exploiting the socio-economic environments they moved into. We can see the same process at work among other endo-migrant groups like the Tallensi in the areas of Southern Ghana into which they migrate and also among exo-migrant groups like the Mossi. There are strong indications, to say the least, that immigrants and mobiles often succeed in their adoptive socio-economic environment, both in striking out along new paths of individual life style and activity and in promoting innovations, where the equally able "insiders" lag behind through being too closely bound up in the constraints of their own social system. I need hardly remind readers of the theories that have grown up around the concept of the "marginal" man. Now the point that strikes me is that the preservation by migrants and mobiles of their distinctive tribal and familial ties and values can serve as a social and psychological sheet anchor, so to speak, for them. For the first generation, at any rate, it may serve as a buffer against going adrift in an alien social environment. Having a home to go back to in crisis or personal disaster, a community and a culture that serves as an independent focus of their cohesion and a sanction for their mutual support, can provide a secure basis for their sense of identity and unity as a group, face to face with the long-vested interests and organised unity of the host society, as well as, often, with the solidarities of other immigrant elements. This, I suggest, may be correlated with successful adaptation of migrant groups in their adoptive social environments—provided, of course, they are permitted to adapt freely by the political and social policies of the host community.

But there is another side to this. If we take the case of the Ibo again, it is arguable that it was their very success as migrants and mobiles that eventually became their doom in Northern Nigeria. It has been claimed that it was the combination of individual success in business, professional and service occupations, with Ibo in-group or, in more modern terminology, nationalistic solidarity, that provoked the hostility which ruined them. We could go even further and speculate—remembering such parallels as the Nazi destruction of Europe's Jews—as to whether this hostility was not, in large part at least, projected on to the Ibo as an expression of suspicions and discontents generated within the host society by tensions and conflicts internal to their social system. Be this as it may,

[10] Cf. the excellent analysis in Coleman, James, S., *Nigeria: Background to Nationalism*, 1958. Chapter 16.

it is evident that where racial, cultural or economic barriers are deeply entrenched in the structure of a plural society, the more internally cohesive and socio-culturally differentiated an immigrant group is, the more chance there is of friction and xenophobia developing between it and the host society.

But there is yet one more point that I must draw attention to. To put it summarily, I would argue that migration and mobility lie at the heart of modern nationalistic movements in Africa. First, of course, there is the well known fact that elite mobility—that is, western schooling and higher education at home and abroad, residence in Europe or America, confrontation with the political and social institutions of these countries, and eventual entrance into professions and occupations in the westernised socio-economic sector of the life of their own countries—has been, to all intents, the *sine qua non* for the emergence of the political leaders of the "new nations" of Africa. The life story of Nnamdi Azikiwe, or Kwame Nkrumah,[11] or indeed of any other nationalist African leader, eloquently documents this. But what I want to emphasise is a different facet of this development. Before the colonial period peoples like the Ibo—or on a smaller scale the Tallensi (and, of course, numerous other African tribal clusters)—never thought of themselves as forming a unitary tribe or national entity. Neighbouring localities and clans were often at war with one another and there was no over-riding political framework embracing all the separate segments.[12] Colonial administrative policies often imposed some degree of formal unity on such clusters. But a real sense of tribal or national unity was never thus created. It was in the towns, among the migrant expatriates from their natal communities, that the impulse towards cross-clan and cross-segment unity arose and the idea of tribal unity took shape. It was in the towns that the Ibo immigrants, for example, formed the mutual aid associations of the common West African type described by Kenneth Little and his colleagues[13] which soon took on a political complexion and became the nuclei of wider nationalistic movements. It is in Accra and Kumasi that, nowadays, we find the literate elite of the northern Ghanaian tribes associating together and emphasising the affinities among their natal languages and cultures in contradistinction to the socially or other culturally distinct group they are in contact with. Mutual aid associations have emerged, often under the patronage of wealthy or influential men like my friend A, and it is significant that

[11] Cf. e.g. *The Autobiography of Kwame Nkrumah* by Kwame Nkrumah, 1957, Nelson and Sons, Edinburgh.

[12] This is well documented in Middleton, John and Tait, David, *Tribes Without Rulers*, 1959. Routledge, London.

[13] Little, Kenneth, *West African Urbanization*, 1964. Cambridge University Press.

these tend to include men and women of all northern Ghanaian tribes, though in A's case the Tallensi predominate. The germs of a northern nationalism are there. All that is wanting, perhaps, is for more northerners to receive some higher education (or training at military academies!) at home or abroad, to spend some time in Europe or America and to gravitate into western-type elite professions and occupations, for the ground to be ready for a northern Nkrumah. Add to this some experience of discrimination or frustration, actual or assumed, in an unbalanced plural system, and separatist demands could easily flare up.

Finally, mention should also be made of the penalties that often accompany inter-generational mobility, not only in migrant groups but also within long-established societies and communities. In Africa this may be associated with the acquisition of literacy and western education and the adoption, in consequence, of non-traditional religious allegiances and moral values, western-type styles of life and material aspirations, and western-type ideas about health and disease and the natural world. First generation elites frequently marry differently from their parents, in the top professions often cross-racially, tend to live in different kinds of houses and to eat different kinds of food, and, in general, lead a life that is very different from that of their parents and grandparents. This is not inevitably disruptive of good relationships between the generations, within families. But it cannot avoid giving rise to some strains, and already there is evidence that psychological illness may be increasing in transitional sectors of modern African society. Occupational mobility also follows upon migration when a non-literate traditional farmer or herdsman leaves his home to work as a labourer or petty trader or even a semi-skilled hand on a mine or at the docks in an area far from his home. In these cases, too, there is often a price to be paid, as is reflected in rising crime rates, increasing psychosis, and the spread of venereal and other urban diseases among this class of migrants. But I, for one, am not qualified to strike a balance sheet.

22

PROBLEMS CONNECTED WITH MODERNIZATION OF UNDERDEVELOPED SOCIETIES

EDITA VAJAS

Yugoslav Experience

I CONSIDER modernization as a process of manifold interrelated changes in the economic, social, political and cultural field, through which less developed societies acquire the characteristics of more developed societies.

According to our conception concerning socio-economic processes, modernization should be directed towards a better harmonization of productive forces with scientific and technological achievements, or, in other words, towards modernization of the means of production through the implementation of modern technology, which also involves a better training of the human factor to enable it to utilize and develop modern techology. On the other hand, within the framework of the same process, it will be necessary to adapt the already more advanced productive forces to production relations (the latter term designates the mode of ownership of the means of production and the way of utilizing them). Changes in the pattern of production relations are usually connected with the establishment of a more progressive pattern of social organization, offering a better framework for the further advance of productive forces.

493

Each country has its own assets and liabilities, and this balance sheet constitutes the point of departure in its efforts towards modernization, so that it seems pointless to insist upon a uniform model. Nevertheless, it is possible to detect some similar characteristics common to all the countries striving for modernization. Therefore, it may be useful to analyze the experience of individual countries, but only on the more general lines, paying attention to the basic trends of the modernization process.

When considering the experience gathered in Yugoslavia during the past quarter century, one must bear in mind the fact that Yugoslavia is a European country, although the level of its economic development is still substantially below the Western European level. In view of this fact, its approach to development problems, as well as its social structure in general, considerably differ from those of underdeveloped societies in other continents.

We may add to this that the modernization process which is under way in Yugoslavia advances more rapidly in some respects, while in others it is more slow, and this is bound to create some new problems connected with quantitative changes and the timing of actions and measures, showing that modernization is not a continuous and uninterrupted process.

In order to get a proper insight into the trends and dimensions of the modernization process in Yugoslavia during the past few decades, we must start from the economic, social and political situation which existed at the outset of that process.

Yugoslavia was created at the end of World War I, in 1918, as a multi-national state. Apart from differences due to the ethnical characteristics of various peoples and nations living within the borders of the new state, there were considerable differences in social and economic structure among the various parts of the country. The southern part of the country had been for more than four centuries under the yoke of the Ottoman empire, while the northern provinces constituted an integral part of the Austro-Hungarian monarchy, which, at a somewhat later time, also annexed Bosnia and Herzegovina (forming the central part of present-day Yugoslavia). In the northern parts of the country, feudalism was liquidated already in the first part of the nineteenth century, whereas in the southern parts it persisted even in the inter-war period. There were considerable differences in the level of economic development between the various parts of the country. While the northern and western parts had made some strides along capitalistic lines, having attained a certain level of industrial development, the southern and central parts were supported by a subsistence economy and handicrafts. On the eve of the Second World War Yugoslavia still possessed the characteristics of a backward agricultural country. Almost 75 per cent of her population, with a rate of increase of 1.5 per cent (being one of the highest in Europe) were active in agriculture. According to estimates, agrarian overpopulation amounted to 2 million (about 25 per cent of the total agricultural population). The annual rate of growth of national income was about 2 per cent, with a per capita income of US $115. During the 17-year period from 1921 to 1938, due to the slow advance in industrial development which, together with the handicrafts, employed less than 10 per cent of the total active population, the share of the agricultural population in the total population declined by a mere four per cent. In some parts of the country about 40 per cent of the population were illiterate and only a half of school age children were attending schools.

Being under such economic and social conditions, no wonder the country was torn by class and national antagonisms and conflicts which culminated in the National Liberation War against foreign occupation between 1941 and 1945. The liberation war was at the same time a social revolution, waged with the intention to introduce a new social order.

The first steps entailing changes in social and economic relationships were taken during the war and immediately after the war. The most important measure along these lines was the confiscation of the property of the German minority and other collaborators with the occupying power, followed by the nationalization of industrial and trade enterprise, banks and large financial houses. Under a radical land reform legislation, land was taken over from big landlords and in part was distributed among landless peasants, the remainder being allocated to agricultural cooperatives or serving to form large state farms. Later, in 1955, the ownership of land was limited to 10 hectares per holder. In contrast to the vast amount of material destruction and human casualties during the war, all these reforms were carried out without causing serious disturbances and human losses. In its very essence, this process was carried out in a humanitarian way, because the leading political forces succeeded in integrating the various strata of the population, mobilizing the human potential, awakening the desire for progress and modernization in all the domains of social and economic life—all of which made it easier for the population to bear the burden of privation rendered necessary by the first efforts towards accelerated development.

Thus, the new order was the main propelling force in promoting postwar development, both social and economic, and impressed its mark upon the modernization process. The main tendencies were towards reforming the socio-economic structures, eliminating the old and creating new institutions, and bringing about changes in the "scale of social values".

In the economic field, the fact that the means of production have passed into social ownership has contributed to a fuller and more efficient utilization of available economic resources, which is of utmost importance in efforts to accelerate eccnomic development. The new pattern of socio-economic relationships played the role of a powerful incentive stimulating physical and mental efforts without which it would have been difficult to speed up the industrialization process, which, in itself is an essential prerequisite for the creation of modern civilization.

In Yugoslavia, industrialization has enabled a more intensive transfer of surplus labour from agricultural to non-agricultural activities by making possible the introduction of new agricultural techniques based on mechanization in the rural economy, creating thereby the necessary pre-conditions for its modernization. Under the then existing circumstances economic growth depended primarily on the possibility of improving labour productivity, and this required radical changes in the pattern of production, within the framework of which it was possible to achieve a better utilization of power sources and other natural resources (non-ferrous metals, agricultural and forest resources, shipping, tourist trade, etc.). Parallel to changes in the economic structure there were important shifts in the structure of employment, this being the best way of overcoming the contradictions and difficulties that arose in the initial phase of accelerated development out of the still existing discrepancies between the new and more modern socio-economic structure, and the backwardness of material production forces. This developmental trend has contributed to strengthening the working class as the bearer of the more modern organizational forms of the society.

Concentration of efforts on industrialization and electrification projects, along with centralistic and "administrative" methods of management in the economy and in social activities resulted in the neglect of certain economic and social sectors. Also Yugoslavia could not avoid treating agriculture as a source of means for financing industrial development in the first stages of industrialization. This has engendered imbalances in the economy and led to disproportions in inter-sectoral relationships— a phenomenon also peculiar to other countries at this stage of economic development. Changes in agricultural techniques and in the organization of agricultural production could be introduced only in the second period, when people became aware of the fact that too rigid and too comprehensive planning systems inevitably lead to bureaucratic and social deformations, largely detrimental to the deployment of individual initiatives. The utmost concentration of power was inappropriate also from the viewpoint of the national and social structure, because there was in Yugoslavia a powerful drive for the national affirmation of individual nationalities. The search for new ways of development was necessary both for economic and social reasons.

After 1950 the evolution in Yugoslavia was towards replacing the functions of the state in managing the economy and social activities by a system of workers' management and social self-government. Workers' management in enterprises constitutes in fact a form of association of direct producers, and is one of the best ways for eliminating the phenomenon of alienation of the human being which, in the modern world, is increasingly becoming a matter of major concern for democratic forces outside socialist countries also.

The system of workers' management of enterprises should also be observed in connection with other characteristic traits of Yugoslav economic reality. Social ownership of the means of production, "commodity production"—a system under which the economic activities of the enterprises, which are the basic cells of economic life, are governed by their own interest (although at the same time overall social production is determined by their activities). The main instruments through which the state regulates the activities of economc units are the social plan, and financial-fiscal and monetary policies. The very fact that the enterprises dispose of two-thirds of their total revenues entirely at their own discretion places them in a position to use the fruits of production for the improvement of the living conditions of the producers, so that workers' management can be characterized as collective enterpreneurship. In this way, the economic and social interest of individuals and of the workers' staff as a whole tends to become the main propelling force of development policies.

Workers' management has given scope to the initiatives of the working people. It has opened favourable prospects for development along democratic lines and has substantially contributed to accelerating the development of productive forces. The workers' councils have become schools for the working people through which they become acquainted with modern production techniques, learn how to conduct affairs in a profitable way, and master proper methods of management. In managing production and distribution the worker becomes aware of the importance of his own position in society and of his potential influence on social development.

The whole socio-economic system based on self-government—which is today the overall system of management not only in economic enterprises, but also in other social services, in administration and in institutions of a non-economic character—confirms the affirmation of the individual as a creator and active promoter of development by placing him in a position where he may directly foster modernization.

The Yugoslav economic and socio-political system, in its present shape, possesses several specific traits. The economy is not centrally administered and planned nor is it a private capitalistic market economy, or a combination of both. The Yugoslav economy is a market economy with decentralized decision power. This pattern of organization of the economy with its system of self-government has paved the way for its modernization, and efforts in this direction have yielded substantial results which, however, in each new phase, create new tasks for the economy and give rise to new problems and difficulties which have to be overcome.

In some periods, and more particularly during the past decade, the growth rate of the Yugoslav economy was among the highest in the world. National income grew at an annual rate of 9 to 12 per cent, but this accelerated growth has not been recorded during the entire postwar period. The average growth rate of national income was about 6 to 7 per cent, and the real increase over the two postwar decades was 250 per cent. In relation to prewar figures industrial production increased 7 times, and agricultural production 1.7 times. In considering the latter figure, one should take into account the fact that, in the ownership structure of agriculture, the dominating share is that of peasant small-holdings (owning 85 per cent of the total surface); while the remaining surface belonging to the socialist sector with a share of 15 per cent in the total surface, yields 30 per cent of the total product achieved in agriculture. On the farms of the socialist sector the growth of production was four times more rapid than on the small holdings. The true nature of shifts which have taken place in the structure of the Yugoslav economy is reflected in the fact that by now the share of industry is about 33 per cent, that of agriculture about 25 per cent and that of the building industry 10 per cent. The role of the tertiary sector is still inadequate.

Rapid changes in economic structure require supplies of equipment and various materials for production at an accelerated rate, and, hence, higher domestic production of these goods. The failure to achieve higher output figures at home results in higher imports which as a rule cannot be paid for by exports, although the physical volume of the latter has grown three times. A consequence of this is instability on the market. In some years considerable fluctuations of output in agriculture and the building industry strengthened this tendency. Instability in the growth process had very unfavourable repercussions on other aspects of economic life, more particularly on price formation. Prices rose, but this phenomenon is an inevitable corollary of growth in all countries advancing rapidly.

As already outlined, accelerated industrialization has created possibilities for a rapid transfer of agricultural labour to industry, so that in the period of rapid growth overall employment grew at a rate surpassing 6 per cent (in the period between 1952 to 1964). Thus, during the entire period the increase of economically active population, and a substantial share of surplus labour (about one million of people) were transformed into wage earners and salaried employees. (In 1961 the total population of Yugoslavia numbered 18.5 million; of this number 8.3 million were economically active.) This was a substantial shift in the structure of the active population, so that the share of agricultural labour in total population declined to less than 50 per cent. Nevertheless, one cannot say that the entire increase in the number employed in non-agricultural activities was utilized efficiently. The extent to which productive capacities were activated fluctuated from one period to another, but, as a rule, manpower is not flexible enough to adjust itself immediately to changes in production. This has led to up and down movements in productivity, fluctuating between 3 and 12 per cent. Experience has shown that in the initial phases of industrialization productive capacity expands rapidly through new investments, but in less-developed countries a certain amount of time is required fully to activate these capacities. This has induced the effort for a more intensive use of resources in enterprises and for structural changes, through mechanization and modernization of production processes, which is now going on within the framework of the economic reform. Under these circumstances, no wonder that employment is stagnating. The solution of the problem of providing jobs, first of all to unskilled or semi-skilled labour, has been found in permitting free migration to Western Europe, where demand for foreign workers is constantly increasing. Through measures that are being taken in order to speed up economic growth, the absorption power of the economy for domestic labour will increase. In view of the fact that, taken as a whole, annual population increase does not exceed 1.1 per cent, the demand for working places will gradually be satisfied.

Modernization in the form of technological progress is particularly conspicuous if we consider the advance achieved during the last ten years in electrification. Both installed capacity of electric power plants and consumption of electric current have increased three times. Considerable progress has been achieved in the chemical industry which plays the major role in efforts towards the modernization of agriculture. The advance of this branch has enabled an expansion in the consumption of fertilizers (about four times) and plant protection chemicals. In a more general way, technological progress is achieved through intensive mechanization of production processes, through automation of particular branches of industry, through the introduction of new products, and through concentration processes in industry. The importance of mechanization and automation should be underlined, because the advance in these lines leads to changes in the ratio of physical to intellectual work, and to higher productivity, which today has become an economic, technical and social necessity, and the main factor in efforts to achieve fuller integration of the Yugoslav economy into the international division of labour.

Today the extent of productivity increases depends largely on technological innovations, which are the result of scientific research and of the level of education. The two latter are the basic factors in efforts to promote economic development and modernization. As regards investment in these two fields, Yugoslavia has made efforts corresponding to the level of her development, and has engaged in these tasks an adequate number of skilled personnel. So far she has not succeeded in overcoming the difficulties arising out of a too large dispersion of institutions engaged in research, or due to the fact that so far the research institutions were not fully successful in establishing close links wih economic enterprises in order to further cooperation. Investment has been particularly high in research institutions in the field of technology and mathematics.

Industrialization and rapid growth of non-agricultural activities have brought about considerable changes in the socio-economic structure of the Yuguslav population, helping to increase the number of people employed in non-agricultural activities from 750,000 to 3.5 million. At the same time, the process of stratification of the rural population progressed in two directions. First, a considerable part of the agricultural population left their holdings for non-agricultural jobs. Secondly, a number of peasants took part-time non-agricultural jobs without leaving their farms, or took such jobs from time to time, while remaining members of peasant households, working together with other members of the household in their leisure time, and sharing in the income and the produce. Thus a particular socio-economic group has been formed among the rural population which lives and works in so-called mixed households. In considering the sources of their livelihood, a fraction of these households are primarily agricultural, while some others are primarily non-agricultural. The differences in the sources of livelihood exert a direct influence on the way of living of these families, and are, first of all, reflected in their diet, particularly in the quality of food consumed. It we consider the agricultural population as a whole, we shall find that about 55 per cent of peasant households draw revenues exclusively from their work on the farm, while the remaining 45 per cent draw income steadily or from time to time also from non-agricultural activities. The fact that a large number of peasant households are in fact mixed households shows that a certain discrepancy exists between the degree of urbanization and the process of disagrarianization.

Although a large number of rural households are in fact mixed households, differences between villages and towns as regards personal incomes and the part of incomes designed for consumption have not disappeared and are estimated to be $1:2$ in favour of towns, while the ratio between per capita income of the active population working in agriculture to income earned in non-agricultural occupations is $1:3.5$, due to differences in the level of productivity.

As a consequence of the transfer of rural population to towns and the schooling of their children, a certain ageing of the rural population has been recorded. Also, as a consequence, women are saddled with work not only in livestock rearing but also in land tilling. These changes have contributed to the phenomenon that the birth rate in villages is lower than in towns.

Due to the well-developed network of roads, to the growing role of the market, and to institutional changes, modern villages are increasingly being integrated into broader territorial communities, and tend to become less self-sufficient. Yet, experience has shown that there can be no true modernization of villages if villagers are not treated as subjects of political and social processes, regardless of the objectives and results which can be expected.

The dynamism and structure of the urban population show that deep economic and social changes have occurred in the country.   Positive effects have been obtained by locating industrial enterprises in smaller towns and by the relatively even growth of towns of all sizes. Thanks to the fact that there are in Yugoslavia several centres of republican and provincial governments, it has been possible to avoid an excessive agglomeration of the population in one or a few big towns. On the other hand, the economy of urban centres has not always been capable of securing productive jobs for the entire manpower seeking work, so that many towns are overburdened with unskilled labour, and the social and municipal services cannot meet the growing needs of accommodation and public utilities. In fact urbanization lagged behind the physical growth of the towns especially owing to the speed of the industrialization process, while modernization was hampered by the inadequate level of education of the urban population.

The structure of the urban economy and the structure of employment gradually change as a result of the progressive concentration in the towns of highly accumulative branches employing skilled personnel, with much emphasis on tertiary activities.   Nevertheless, some contrasts do appear between the most developed parts of Yugoslavia, where a large process of decentralization has created many urban centres, and the less developed southern parts distinguished by too great agglomerations.

The differences between individual regions are still very important, more particularly in the level of per capita income, the ratio between incomes being 1:5. In spite of industrial progress in some underdeveloped areas, the growth rate of the economy has not been sufficiently high to level the differences in economic development. Different levels of economic development are reflected in demographic indicators (structure of the active population, birth rate, infant mortality) and in indicators showing the consumption pattern of the population, educational levels, health, and housing conditions. The period of post-war development has been too short to level out differences due to the historical background.

So far the most essential instruments of modernization have been social factors. The way in which these factors have acted upon the socio-economic system has enabled people to accept changes, and, in a more general way, has furthered the flexibility and the initiative of the human factor. In fact, both structural changes and social factors have increased flexibility, and the institutional framework characterized by the system of self-government has strengthened these tendencies. Education has played an important part as a factor furthering mobility and economic growth. The very substantial efforts of the community, resulting in high investments, have made it possible today for about 90 per cent of the total number of school-age children to attend primary schools, while secondary schools are attended by one-third of the total number of children of the respective age-group. There are about 1,000 students to every 100,000 inhabitants (almost the same proportion as in France), and this is likely to modify rapidly the structure of skills of wage earners and salaried employees. Today this structure is rather unfavourable, because about one half of the employed people are meagrely educated and without special skills. The adverse influence of historical factors responsible for the low level of education of the Yugoslavs has not yet been overcome, and this is reflected in the large number of illiterates in backward areas, and in the extent of daily newspaper circulation, which is somewhat below the level which would correspond to the level of development (measured in terms of per capita income) of about 600 dollars per head. Experience has shown that the raising of the educational level is a long-term task and that it is more difficult to achieve progress in this field than in the economic one.

Considerable results have been achieved in raising health standards. This is reflected in the increase in the expectation of life at birth (now somewhat lower than in most other European countries: 63-66 years), and in reduced infant mortality which, however, is still much higher than in developed European countries. Substantial progress has been achieved in the training of medical personnel which is now at a level corresponding to that in other European countries as well as in increasing the capacity of health institutions, which are not yet fully adequate. Practically the entire population is socially insured, although not with the same rights for villagers. As regards the tempo of construction of new dwellings, Yugoslavia is on the middle of the scale among the European countries, the average number of new dwellings completed each year ranging between 4-11 per 1000 inhabitants. The share of new dwellings in the towns in the total number of dwellings is about 50 per cent, but the supply of new dwelling is not yet satisfactory.

Access to social services is not evenly distributed among the regions of Yugoslavia owing to differences in the possibilities of financing these services in different regions.

Under the Yugoslav economic system, it is of utmost importance to provide incentives through the system of remuneration. Opinions differ widely concerning the efficiency of the existing system. In economic enterprises income differentials are 1 : 4-5, while income differentials between skilled and unskilled workers are of the order of 1 : 3. But, there still are considerable differences in personal incomes of different categories of wage-earners resulting from differences in earning possibilities of particular branches and groupings in the economy, dependent on the structure of production factors. Taken as a whole, personal incomes have increased 1.8 times in real terms during the last decade, and indirect incomes from social consumption funds have increased almost in the same proportion, unlike in other socialist countries, have increased where indirect incomes have increased more rapidly.

Comparisons between results achieved in economic as against social development (which are of particular importance for evaluating modernization trends) between Yugoslavia and countries at a similar level of economic development have shown that Yugoslavia has advanced more rapidly in certain sectors of social development such as education and certain sectors of health, while she lags behind other countries at the same stage of development in her employment structure owing to her large agricultural population, but, as already explained, there are transitional stages between agriculture and non-agricultural activities (mixed households).

Yugoslavia's experience shows that modernization is a painful process consisting in efforts to create a dynamic economy and society, and potential capabilities for steady development. Changes along these lines are interdependent and interrelated. Development is a cyclical process fraught with temporary imbalances of a longer or shorter duration, both in the economy and in non-economic fields.

If it is possible to speak of generally valid experience concerning modernization, one should, after analysis of Yugoslav developments, emphasize the importance of a broad participation of the population in the development process as one of entailing social changes without unrest and losses,

APPENDIX
INDICATORS OF THE LEVEL OF LIVING [1]

		1956	1964	1967	1968
1.	Real volume of global consumption (personal and social) per inhabitant (1,000 dinars at 1962 prices)	82.5	169.0	175.1	180.8
2.	*Personal consumption*				
2.1.	Real volume of personal consumption per inhabitant (1,000 dinars at 1962 prices)	72.5	131.0	143.8	146.9
2.2.	Caloric value of nutrition, per day	3745	3154	3200	3200
2.3.	Cereals, in kg. annually	219.40	245.20	232.6	228
2.4.	Meat kg.	24.20	27.10	31.8	33.0
2.5.	Milk, lit.	170.30	114.20	128.0	128.0
2.6.	Textiles, square meters	9.61	19.94	18.38	19.0
2.7.	Leather footwear, pairs	0.70	1.36	1.38	1.40
2.8.	Electrical power, kwh	36.36	136.88	145.5	224
2.9.	TV sets (per 1,000 inhabitants)	—	10.60	12.03	12.7
2.10.	Radio sets (per 1000 inhabitants)	7.07	20.80	17.5	18.0
2.11.	Refrigerators (per 1000 inhabitants)	0.56	6.58	9.5	10.5
2.12.	Motor cars (per 1000 inhabitants	0.02	1.34	4.0	4.5
3.	*Education*				
3.1.	Enrolment in % of the generation at school age				
	— primary	77.6	90.6	91.0	...
	— secondary	16.7	30.7	34.6	...
	— high	2.2	5.1	5.9	...
3.2.	Share of cost of education in the social product	1.8	4.3	4.5	4.6
4.	*Housing*				
	Number of new constructions (per 1,000 inhabitants)	2.1	6.3	6.6	6.4
5.	*Health*				
5.1.	Infant mortality (per 1,000)	98.3	75.8	62.6	...
5.2.	Number of physicians (per 1000 inhabitants)	4.0	7.7	8.8	...
6.	*Employment and work*				
6.1.	Wage earners in percentages of active population	27.6	41.6	38.8	38.3
6.2.	Effective number of working hours (per month)	...	180	173	...
7.	*Economic position of producers* Percentage of social product at the direct disposal of producers	...	55.0	61.2	60.2 (First semester)

[1] Dr. Berislav Sefer: *Economski razvoj Jugoslavije i privredna reforma,* Beograd 1969, str. 72 i 73 (Economic Development in Yugoslavia and the Reform).

23

MODERNIZATION AND EDUCATION

S. C. DUBE

THE COMPLEX processes of modernization assume a series of interpenetrating and interdependent transformations. On the level of personality, it is now widely recognized, they envisage characterological changes resulting in the promotion of rationality, empathy, mobility, and high participation. These attributes of the modernized personality are promoted and sustained by—and, in their turn, they also promote and sustain—institutional and value change on the social and the cultural levels. The social and cultural milieu, thus, increasingly acquires achievemental, universalistic, and specificity-oriented emphases. It accepts and produces more innovations, builds up associational capability, and sharpens its problem-solving abilities. Absence of fit between the modernized personality and the social/cultural framework would lead to an uncomfortable imbalance. For this reason harmonization and interlinking of the changes in the personality and in the cultural and the social systems is essential. In the context of modernization these transformations must be viewed as a precondition to the growth of complex organizations that can adequately and effectively exploit and manipulate energy from inanimate sources for human well-being and prosperity.

Three assumptions are basic to this conception of modernization:

1. Inanimate sources of power must be tapped increasingly to solve

505

human problems and to ensure a minimum acceptable standard of living, the ceiling of which is progressively rising.

2. This can be done best by collective rather than by individual effort: associational capability to operate through increasingly complex organizations, thus, is a prerequisite to at least the middle and the higher reaches of modernization.

3. Such complex organizations cannot be created and run without radical personality change and attendant changes in the social structure and in the cultural fabric.

No techniques are known to achieve an instant switch from the stone axe to the steam engine. Man's technological progress has been slow and tortuous: some groups progressed more because of their propitious ecological, cultural, and motivational settings, others could first assimilate and adopt the new technology only in limited doses and later made efforts to develop it independently, while still others could accept only its products without being able to master the intricacies of its organization and techniques. The third category, now an aspirant to modernized status, constitutes two-thirds of mankind. Far from being able to take the road to creative innovation, many of these societies are not ready even for transfer or adaptation of modern technology. This is accounted for partly by their attitudinal and institutional inadequacies, and partly also by a lack of associational capability in them. They have the desire to enjoy the fruits of modernization, but their institutional-organizational and ideological-motivational framework is not ready yet to adopt modern technology on a large scale. They lack also the infrastructure to adapt foreign technology to their peculiar needs and to innovate in the modern style to meet the challenge of the revolution of rising expectations.

A sound strategy for modernization would appear to include:

1. Directed change in the system of attitudes, beliefs, and values, and also in the institutional complex, to enhance the acceptability of modern technology and its organizational and operational framework;

2. Growth of the infrastructure essential to the adaptation of technology of foreign origin to specific national needs; and

3. Laying the foundations of institutions and organizations which could, in time, assume responsibility for independent innovation and technological growth to the country's needs and problems.

Undeniably, education can be a most potent instrument of modernization.

Directly, it seeks to promote knowledge and to develop skills, both of which are essential for the furtherance of the goals of modernization. At the same time some of its indirect consequences, such as value and attitude change, are also not without significance. The priority accorded to education in programmes of modernization, thus, is not misplaced: how effectively it is organized and how well it is directed is a different matter.

Some of the ways in which education is functional to the programmes of modernization can now be highlighted.

1. By enlarging the cognitive map of those exposed to it, education suggests alternatives to tradition, brings into focus the rewards implicit in them, and indicates—roughly at least—the paths through which the new goals with their attendant regards can be achieved. It broadens mental horizons, raises expectations, and predisposes people to make experiments.

2. As an instrument of socialization it can project new images and values. Purposively used, it can be a help in obliterating attitudes and behaviour patterns that are dysfunctional to programmes of modernization.

3. By providing ideological articulation it can promote the development of nation-ness and can help people see their needs and their problems in a national perspective. This can stimulate the creation of a national consensus at least on major issues.

4. Education provides a highway to elite status. It is not the only source from which personnel to the elite ranks is recruited, but there is perhaps no developing society which does not confer a special status on the educated. The educated provide a reference model to the masses, who, in imitation of the former, take the first steps away from tradition. Modernizing elites are almost always the products of modern or semi-modern school/university systems.

5. Problem-solving leadership—scientists and technicians, management experts and administrators—with the requisite knowledge and skills can only be expected to emerge out of the educational system. Large-scale programmes of modernization demand specialists of several types at different levels, and look to the educational system for a steady flow of technocrats, planners and managers to operate them.

6. Education is a mobility multiplier. Although its initial impact is on the immobility of thought-ways, in the long run it does alter rigid forms of social stratification. Modernization requires both types of mobility.

In sum, with proper planning and under efficient direction, education can make a meaningful contribution to the attainment of modernization. It can be harnessed to diffuse attitudes and ideologies required for the adoption of modern technology and its associated values and organizational premises, to provide personnel to operate and sustain the programmes of modernization, and to create capabilities for adaptation and origination of new technology.

But education is only an instrument, and an instrument, in the final analysis, is only as good as the person wielding it. The efficacy of education as an instrument of modernization would depend largely on its orientation and content as well as on those who impart and receive it. In fact, it is a two-edged weapon: it can serve the aims of traditionalists just as well as it can serve the aims of modernizers. Under certain conditions, by generating stresses and strains, it may even produce anomic disturbances that are difficult to control and that obstruct ordered movement towards modernization. Therefore, it would be useful to bear in mind some of its dysfunctional aspects also.

1. By enlarging the cognitive map education redefines and resets cultural goals. Up to a point this is necessary and is functional. But cultural goals must bear some relationship to institutional means. Education often becomes dysfunctional when it sets cultural goals way beyond the institutional means of a society. Inadequacy of the institutional setup results in anger and frustration and, later, in defiance and destruction.

2. While education can project new images and help in the inculcation of new values, it can also be turned into an instrument for the perpetuation of certain traditional values that run counter to the objectives of modernization. Education does not produce only modernizers, it produces traditionalists also. And some of these traditionalists-by-choice are incomparably more articulate and sophisticated than those who may be called "traditionalists who know nothing different". Several types of traditionalists can be identified:

i.   Those with whom tradition is a habit of mind because they know nothing better or even different, and whose naive and and simplistic traditionalism stands apart as a category by itself.

ii.   Those with a highly selective perception, who identify their culture with its past high achievement in particular fields, ignoring harsh and inconvenient empirical realities both ancient and contemporary.

iii.   The cultural narcissists with unbounded and indiscriminating nostalgia for the past, who find in tradition a compensation for what the society lacks (or is denied) today.

iv.   Those with whom traditionalism is a pose, a mask and a carefully cultivated style, and who only want to stand out from the rest.

This category includes also those to whom traditionalism is a convenient political gimmick.

v. Those who have a vested interest in tradition and who remain attached to it because of its short-term payoff.

vi. Pragmatic traditionalists, who are afraid of the uncertainties of modernization and associate it with some of the ills of the contemporary world.

Traditionalists of the last five categories can easily superimpose their value-attitude systems on education. For political reasons they may even consciously feed the irrational beliefs of the first category. Education, thus, may be promoting conflicting goals.

3. Because of the simultaneous operation of push and pull factors in education, both centrifugal and centripetal forces may be promoted at the same time. Ideological contradictions in the content of education may weaken nation-ness and consensus by lending at least partial support to parochialism.

4. Education is undeniably an avenue to status, but when it fails to maintain a proper want-get ratio it also results in status denial to many who feel entitled to, and qualified for, it. It may create status aspirations that do not take account of the society's needs and the aspirants' talents and abilities.

5. The foreign models and idiom of education often produce academic and scientific styles that fail to see problems in the perspective of national needs. International styles—including current fashions and even fads—are blindly imitated, when their relevance—if any at all—to national problems is obviously doubtful. Intellectual activity, thus, faces the danger of degenerating into barren exercises in futility. Problem-solving objectives get blurred and blunted.

6. Vested interests may often seek to utilize education to maintain and sustain traditional forms of stratification. In many cases it may actually widen the gap between classes and between categories.

7. When education gets to be viewed as an end in itself rather than as a means to certain objectives, it becomes an article of consumption, involving considerable cost. The scarce resources invested in it could be more meaningfully utilized in other sectors of economic growth.

8. Management of the educational explosion is often difficult. The stresses and strains built into the system result in the production of highly volatile and inflammable material that adds to the corpus of problems rather than contributes to their solution.

It is, thus, evident that education, if ineptly handled, can put societies in reverse motion. The dangers to be guarded against most are: education becoming an instrument of traditionalism, education raising hopes and aspirations whose fulfilment is not immediately feasible and practical, education attaining aims and purposes unrelated to modernization and often pulling in an opposite direction, and education creating pervasive discontent and anomic conditions retarding the progress towards modernization.

Strategies of educational planning for modernization are beset with several unresolved dilemmas: national need vs. "social justice" or expanded opportunity, quality vs. quantity, strategic and selective planning vs. operation of market laws of demand and supply, good education for *some* vs. *some* education for *all*, and consumption-orientation vs. production-orientation in education. All too often, scarce resources are thinly spread, the development of needed skills is subordinated to the requirements of diffused consumption-type education dictated by popular pressure, and substandard teachers working in sub-standard institutions turn out sub-standard products. The full potential of education for modernization, thus, is rarely exploited. Unless these dilemmas are satisfactorily resolved, it is doubtful whether education can make its proper contribution to modernization. It needs focus, direction and, above all, relevance.

24

CONFLICT, COMPETITION, AND
SOCIAL WELFARE

ARTHUR S. BANKS

THE PURPOSE of this paper is to examine, both for the "old" nations and the "new", patterns of relationship between domestic conflict, political competition, and social welfare for the period 1946-66. Emphasis will be placed on the question of whether correlations involving domestic conflict are as universally low as much of the recent literature would suggest (Banks, 1967; Burrowes, 1968; Rummel, 1969), particularly when the latter is employed as a "moderator" or control variable.[1]

A longitudinal format was adopted to facilitate determination as to whether there is a) interaction through time, or b) time-lag interaction between the three phenomena. The unit of analysis is the independent nation-state, thus excluding all dependent territories and sub-national political entities,—consideration of which might substantially augment the results of the present inquiry.

Construction of the Indicators

Each of the phenomena being investigated is indexed by a composite of primary variables. Their construction is as follows:

1. Domestic Conflict. In order to measure domestic conflict in a manner that would permit at least a partial check on data reliability, eight

---

[1] On "moderator" or control variables, see Saunders (1956) and Johnson (1960).

of the nine variables and variable definitions advanced by Rummel (1963) were adopted.[2] These variables are:

1. Assassinations
2. General Strikes
3. Guerrilla Wars
4. Major Government Crises
5. Purges
6. Riots
7. Demonstrations
8. Revolutions

Rummel's own data were derived from a variety of sources (*The New York Times Index, Facts on File,* etc.)[3] and covered a span of three years, 1955-57. In a subsequent inquiry, Tanter (1966) utilized the same sources in assembling data for the same variables for the period 1958-60. Thus for six of the twenty-one years in question, domestic conflict data had previously been assembled that could be compared with data assembled for the present study.

A team of six researchers extracted the relevant data from the daily files of *The New York Times* for 1946-66. Each individual consulted four non-consecutive years of the *Times*, three of the 21 thus being overlapped, i.e., read by two individuals, as a further reliability check.

The measure of inter-judge reliability employed was the Robinson Co-efficient of Agreement (A).[4] The results were highly gratifying. For the three test years, 1951, 1956, and 1961, the paired observations yielded co-efficients of agreement of .976, .957, and .989, respectively. The coefficient of agreement with the Rummel-Tanter data for 1955-60 was equally satisfactory: .952.[5]

---

[4] See Robinson (1957). The Robinson coefficient is more rigorous measure of conflict indicator, Number Killed in Domestic Violence, was dropped partly for reliability reasons, and partly because it did not easily scale with the others.

[3] *Ibid.,* p. 6.

[4] See Robinson (1957). The Robinson coefficient is a more rigorous measure of agreement than the product moment correlation coefficient, since the latter measures the degree to which paired values are *proportional*, rather than *identical*. The Robinson formula is:

$$A = 1 - \frac{\Sigma\,(X_{1j} - \bar{X}_j)^2 + \Sigma\,(X_{2j} - \bar{X}_j)^2}{\Sigma\,(X_{1j} - \bar{X})^2 + \Sigma\,(X_{2j} - \bar{X})^2}$$

[5] In order to check reliability for the three test years, 1951, 1956, and 1961, the data were summed horizontally to provide an aggregate yearly index for each country. In checking against Rummel and Tanter, the data were summed both horizontally and vertically for 1955-60.

As a means of providing suitable weighting for the composite domestic conflict indicator, its eight component variables were factor analyzed for each seven-year span using a principal component solution and an orthogonal rotation of the factor matrix. In each case, two factors emerged, with General Strikes, Government Crises, Riots, and Demonstrations loaded heavily (> .50) on the first, and with Assassinations, Guerilla Wars, Purges, and Revolutions loaded heavily (> .50) on the second. The proportion of total variance explained by each of the first factors was .49, .49, and .51 respectively; the proportion explained by each of the second was .11, .11, and .10. Since these ratios were approximately 5:1, the component variables were weighted accordingly.[6] Each had previously been scaled by grouping according to geometric progression (in accordance with the Rummel-Tanter procedure), thus obviating the need for other means of data transformation.[7]

2. *Political Competition.* For purposes of this inquiry, political competition was, in essence, equated with party competition. Five component variables (one interval-scaled and four ordinal-scaled) were employed:

1. Index of Legislative Seats Held by Largest Party
   [see below]
2. Legislature
   3 — Effective
   2 — Partly Effective
   1 — Largely Ineffective
   0 — None
3. Nominating Process
   3 — Competitive
   2 — Partially Competitive
   1 — Largely Non-Competitive
4. Coalitions
   3 — More than one party, no coalitions
   2 — More than one party, coalition with opposition
   1 — More than one party, coalition without opposition
   0 — No coalition, no opposition
5. Party Exclusion
   3 — No parties excluded

---

[6] The two factors extracted might be identified as indexing the two dimensions: "turmoil" and "revolution". Both Rummel and Tanter succeeded in extracting three factors, the difference presumably being attributable to dropping "Number Killed in Domestic Violence" from the present inquiry.

[7] The raw data and group value equivalents are as follows: 0=1, 1=1, 2-3=2, 4-7=3, 8-15=4, 16-32=5, >-32=6.

> 2 — One or more minor or "extremist" parties excluded
> 1 — Significant exclusion of parties (or groups)
> 0 — No parties, or all but dominant party and
>   satellites excluded

To obtain the index of legislative seats held by the largest party, the total number of seats in each national legislature for each year was divided by the number of seats held by the largest party. The principal reason for calculating the index in this manner (rather than as a percentage of seats held) was that the indices for a country with no parties (or no legislature) and a country with a one-party system would be adjacent, rather than at opposite extremes of the array.[8]

The indices of legislative seats were averaged for each seven-year period for each country, while the ordinal scores for the other four variables were summed horizontally for each year and vertically for each seven-year period for each country. Since the two resultant indicators proved to be highly intercorrelated (at .77, .69, and .82) for each of the three periods in question, each was weighted 50 per cent in calculating the overall competition index.[9]

3. *Social Welfare.* For the purpose of indexing social welfare, four interval-scaled variables were employed:

1. Inhabitants Per Physician
2. Per Cent Literate
3. Gross Domestic Product Per Capita
4. Energy Consumption Per Capita

While additional or alternative indicators might well have been utilized, the four listed above seemed to represent the best "mix" in terms of both theoretical relevance and data accessibility. Indeed, they were virtually the *only* seemingly relevant indicators for which near-100 per cent data, for the time-period and case-span in question, could be obtained.

In order to make the direction of the first variable comparable with that of the others, its reciprocal (physicians per inhabitant) was calcula-

---

[8] Thus a country with no parties would have a score of 0.00, a one-party system would have a score of 1.00, a system with 40 out of 100 seats held by the majority party would have a score of 2.50, etc. There are, of course, more sophisticated ways of calculating "legislative fractionalization" indices. See, for example, Rae (1968).

[9] Since Variable 1 and the aggregate of Variables 2-5 were, of course, scaled differently, both sets were converted into standard, or Z-scores, to achieve comparability. The resultant distributions were then averaged to form the aggregate competition index. For a discussion of Z-scoring, see Edwards (1954), p. 101, ff.

ted. The four variables were then factor analyzed for insight as to proper weighting.

As in the case of the conflict variable components, two factors were extracted, on the first of which Physicians and Literacy were heavily loaded ($>$ .85) and on the second of which GDP/Capita and Energy/Capita were heavily loaded ($>$ .70). The proportion of total variance explained by each of the first factors was .68, .76, and .75, respectively, while the proportion explained by each of the second was .18, .15, and .12. Since these ratios were also approximately 5:1, the component variables were weighted accordingly.

Variable Transformation

In order to permit a more meaningful analysis of the statistical interaction of the aggregated conflict, competition, and social welfare indicators, each of the two latter was tested for normality of distribution.[10] The social welfare indicator proved to be skewed to the right and a logarithmic transformation substantially improved the normality of its distribution. In other words, its distribution was approximately lognormal, and was treated as such in the subsequent analysis. The distribution of the competition index, on the other hand, proved to be somewhat bimodal, but the improvement realized by the application of an arcsin transformation proved to be so slight that the variable was retained in its original form.[11]

---

[10] The specific test employed was the BIMD-15 Data Screening programme, in which deciles of the normal curve are fitted to the sample data and the X^2 test of goodness of fit applied. An alternative test, in which certain functions of the moments of the sample are calculated and the significance of their departure from the expected values for a normal population examined, is contained in Geary and Pearson (n.d.). For an application of the latter test, see Naroll (1967).

[11] The reduction in X^2 for the competition index by arcsin transformation was from 25.9 to 20.7. Comparable reduction in X^2 by applying logarithmic transformation to the social welfare indicator was from 69.7 to 27.8. In addition, one outlier $>$ 3.0 S.S. for social welfare was eliminated. There were no outliers at $>$ 3.0 S.S. for the untransformed competition data.

The purpose of data transformation is to approximate, with due regard to capacity to interpret one's data after transformation, the assumption of distributional normality imposed by most correlational procedures. Since transformation is designed to improve normality, a heightened correlation coefficient (and thereby a larger proportion of explained variation) will usually result,—at least for correlation (such as the Pearsonian r) based in the linear model.

It is, of course, possible to employ a procedure such as T-scoring to transform any given distribution into one that is perfectly normal. While such procedures are often utilized (see, for example, Cutright, 1963 and Neubauer, 1967), it is impossible to interpret the nature of their impact on one's data. This difficulty is not present in the case of a "describable" transformation such as the calculation of a log or a square root. For a discussion of T-scoring, see Edwards (1954), pp. 11-113.

TABLE 1

CORRELATION COEFFICIENTS [1]

	1	2	3	4	5	6	7	8	9
1. ConF$_{49}$				04 -03	08 01	07 02	09 13	01 08	-02 07
2. ConF$_{56}$				03 01	03 03			04 01	01 01
3. ConF$_{63}$						-02 05			-03 09
4. SW$_{49}$	04 -03	04 -01	00 01				66 77	64 77	65 80
5. SW$_{56}$		03 01	00 03					63 77	65 81
6. SW$_{63}$			-02 05						63 80
7. ComP$_{49}$	09 13	06 02	05 -04	66 77	65 76	63 75			
8. ComP$_{56}$		04 01	01 08		63 77	55 75			
9. ComP$_{63}$			-03 09			63 80			

[1] Coefficients multiplied by 100 and rounded to 2 significant figures.
Top figures in each set: N = 65
Bottom figures in each set: N = 52 (Communist nations excluded)

TABLE 2

CORRELATION COEFFICIENTS BY HIGH, MEDIUM, AND
LOW CONFLICT STATUS [1]

	1	2	3	4	5	6	7	8	9
1. ConF$_{49}$				43 38 08	41 40 11	44 41 10	42 40 08	44 48 12	56 36 15
2. ConF$_{56}$					36 14 07	34 16 08		28 30 11	20 28 11
3. ConF$_{63}$						55 29 -29			35 17 -29
4. SW$_{49}$	43 38 08	35 13 10	59 35 -27				55 69 96	60 65 96	65 67 95
5. SW$_{56}$		36 14 07	53. -21 -12					56 67 96	66 68 95
6. SW$_{63}$			55 29 -29						69 74 95
7. ComP$_{49}$	42 40 08	23 21 16	26 26 -32	55 69 96	49 70 96	44 68 96			
8. ComP$_{56}$		28 30 11	32 26 -29		56 67 96	52 65 96			
9. ComP$_{63}$			35 17 -29			69 74 95			

[1] High N = 18
Medium N = 17
Low N = 18

M-34

TABLE 3

CORRELATION COEFFICIENTS BY HIGH, MEDIUM, AND
LOW COMPETITION STATUS [1]

	1	2	3	4	5	6	7	8	9
1. ConF_{49}				-47 -15 52	-42 -15 53	-36 -15 55	15 18 40	24 -04 37	-20 -04 41
2. ConF_{56}					-59 -04 64	-54 -04 65		32 04 38	-14 -07 44
3. ConF_{63}						-43 09 41			-31 -20 48
4. SW_{49}	-47 -15 52	-59 -05 63	-48 09 42				-20 49 54	-29 62 71	-00 50 65
5. SW_{56}		-59 -04 64	-49 10 42					-30 58 69	-01 58 62
6. SW_{63}			-43 09 41						-06 60 61
7. ComP_{49}	15 18 40	23 12 58	10 -06 46	-20 49 54	-15 44 54	-12 45 51			
8. ComP_{56}		32 04 38	19 -11 31		-30 58 69	-28 59 67			
9. ComP_{63}			-31 -20 48			-06 60 61			

[1] High N = 18
Medium N = 17
Low N = 18

TABLE 4

CORRELATION COEFFICIENTS BY HIGH, MEDIUM, AND LOW SOCIAL WELFARE STATUS [1]

	1	2	3	4	5	6	7	8	9
1. $ConF_{49}$				-22 12 40	-14 11 44	-10 11 47	-28 12 38	-28 -05 36	-49 11 21
2. $ConF_{56}$					-31 03 31	-12 -03 30		-40 -08 16	-55 -06 08
3. $ConF_{63}$						-32 05 57			-50 31 36
4. SW_{49}	-22 12 40	-34 05 25	-49 06 50				33 48 55	22 36 71	42 55 66
5. SW_{56}		-31 03 31	-42 10 53					28 35 77	27 34 75
6. SW_{63}			-32 05 57						24 27 75
7. $ComP_{49}$	-28 12 38	-36 -08 47	-21 19 49	33 48 55	24 33 58	26 34 51			
8. $ComP_{56}$		-40 -08 16	-22 19 43		28 35 77	32 35 60			
9. $ComP_{63}$			-50 31 36			24 27 75			

[1] High N = 18
Medium N = 17
Low N = 18

Correlation Analysis

Tables 1-4 contain the relevant portions of linear correlation matrices involving the conflict, competition, and social welfare indicators. The matrices were designed so as to reveal any "time-lag" effect between indicators and, for this reason, the case size remains constant, at n = 65 for the upper rows of Table 1, and at n = 53 for the remainder. In other words, the coefficients exhibited in Tables 1-4 are based on observations limited to nations that were independent in 1946 and remained so throughout the 21-year period embraced by the present study.

The coefficients in the upper row of each set of Table 1 are for *all* independent nations, while the coefficients in the lower row of each set of Table 1 and in all rows of the remaining tables are for all *non-Communist* independent nations.

Three facts clearly emerge from an examination of Table 1. First, the only significant correlations involve the competition and social welfare indicators. Second, these correlations are quite stable through time, offering no evidence of "time-lag" effect. Third, correlations for the non-Communist group are substantially higher than for the total group. Alternatively, for the group as a whole, approximately 42 per cent of the variation in social welfare status is "explained" by variation in political competition (and vice versa) while this figure rises to approximately 61 per cent with the Communist nations excluded.

One might assume from an examination of Table 1 that variation in domestic conflict is completely unrelated to variation in either political competition or social welfare status. Tables 2-4 indicate quite clearly, however, that this is by no means the case. The evidence of these tables may be summarized in a number of ways. It may be asserted, for example, (reading ←→ as "tends to vary with") that for:

Hi ConF	SW ←→ ComP (POS)
Lo ConF	SW ←→ ComP (POS)
Hi ComP	ConF ←→ SW (NEG)
Lo ComP	ConF ←→ SW (POS)
Hi SW	ConF ←→ ComP (NEG)
Lo SW	ConF ←→ ComP (POS)

In other words, the basic relationship between competition and social welfare (a positive correlation) is unaffected by changes in conflict status. But the relationships between conflict and social welfare, on the one hand, and conflict and competition, on the other *reverse* (moving from negative to positive correlations) as one moves from high to low along the competition and social welfare continua, thus explicating the apparent lack of relationship between the two pairs of variables in Table 1. Conflict/social welfare and conflict/competition *do* vary systematically, but both co-variations are complex rather than simple.

Correlations Involving Nations Becoming Independent Since 1946

Tables 1-4 involve only nations that have been independent for the entire period, 1946-66. What differences, if any, emerge for the 1956 (1953-59) and 1963 (1960-66) data points if countries becoming independent between 1947 and 1960 are included? What results are obtained if these countries are considered independently of the group which was continuously independent from 1946-66?

The overall case size for the 1949 data point (as previously noted) is .65. Comparable case sizes for 1956 and 1963, respectively, are 79 and 107. Overall correlations for 1956 (n = 79) and 1963 (n = 107) turn out to be remarkably similar to those for 1956 (n =65) and 1963 (n = 65). Again, correlations involving the conflict/social welfare and conflict/competition indicators fall well below the level of statistical significance, while those involving social welfare and competition *are* significant (at .001), with coefficients of r = .59 for 1956 and r = .62 for 1963. Furthermore, the patterns exhibited in Tables 2-4 are also exhibited in comparable matrices for 1956 and of 1963, based on the larger case sizes.

Because of the relatively small case size, no analysis was attempted involving only nations achieving independence during 1947-52. A separate analysis was, however, undertaken for the 1963 data point, embracing 39 of the 42 nations becoming independent during 1947-60.[12]

On an overall basis, relatively weak correlations of .14 between conflict and social welfare and of .19 between conflict and competition were obtained, while a relatively strong correlation of .56 between social welfare and competition was obtained. Only the latter is, however, significant at the .001 level, while the first two are not significant, even at .01 level.

Correlations based on trichotomized conflict, competition and social welfare status (equivalent to Tables 2-4) were also calculated, though with somewhat less conclusive results. Again, a number of significant correlations involving the competition and social welfare indicators emerged. Correlational *patterns*, similar to those reported above for high and low competition and social welfare, respectively, also emerged, but most of the coefficients fell below the level of statistical significance.

[12] East Germany, North Korea, and North Vietnam were excluded.

Conclusions

The evidence of this paper indicates a relatively strong relationship between political competition and social welfare,—a relationship which holds through time and which exists not only for the older nations, but for the newer (and presumably "less developed") nations as well. The one categoric group for which no such relationship appears to obtain is that made up of highly authoritarian or dictatorial regimes, particularly the Communist nations. There is, at the same time, no evidence (in either direction) of a time-lag relationship between these two variables, nor should causal impact of either variable upon the other be inferred. In addition, with the sole exception of nations of low social welfare status where the explained variation is approximately 91 per cent, a substantial amount of unexplained variation remains, at least some of which might be accounted for by the multiple regression of variables not considered in this paper.

The relationship of conflict to the other two variables is more difficult to assess. As previously noted, for nations of high social welfare status the relationship of conflict and competition is negative, while for those of low social welfare status the relationship is positive. Similarly, the relationship between conflict and social welfare is negative for nations of high competition status and positive for nations of low competition status.

Of greater theoretical interest, however, is an additional finding, viz., that social welfare and conflict are *negatively* correlated for nations of high social welfare (and presumably more "developed") status, but positively correlated for nations of low social welfare (and presumably less "developed") status. Not all of the coefficients supporting this finding are significant (even at the .05 level), hence the least that can be said is that major components of variation in social welfare are unexplained in the context of the present inquiry. Nonetheless, there is sufficient evidence to support the *hypothesis* that conflict is functional (in the social welfare sense) for the less developed nations and dysfunctional (in the same sense) for the more developed. While the strongest evidence in support of this hypothesis stems from an analysis of nations independent since 1946, there is similar evidence—admittedly weaker— stemming from a separate analysis of nations *becoming* independent during 1947-60. Collaterally, in accordance with the most pronounced finding of this paper, there is no evidence to support the widely-entertained hypothesis that *competition* is dysfunctional for an underdeveloped nation. Moving from description to prescription can be dangerous. But if one accepts James S. Coleman's assertion that "competitiveness is an essential aspect of political modernity",[13] it might also be argued that competitiveness is vital to the *achievement* of modernity.

[13] Almond and Coleman (1960), p. 533.

REFERENCES

Almond, Gabriel A., and Coleman, James S., *The Politics of the Developing Areas*. Princeton: Princeton University Press, 1960.

Banks, Arthur S., *Multivariate Analysis of A Cross-Polity Survey*. Washington: The George Washington University, 1967.

Burrowes, Robert, "The Strength and Direction of Relationships Between Domestic Conflict and External Politics: Syria, 1961-67." Paper delivered at tde Annual Meeting of the Middle Eastern Studies Association, Austin, Texas, November 15-17, 1968.

Cutright, Phillips, "National Political Development: Social and Economic Correlates", in Polsby, N. W., Dentler, R A., and Smith, P. A., *Politics and Social Life*. Boston: Houghton Mifflin Co., 1963, 569-82.

Edwards, Allen L., *Statistical Methods for the Behavioral Sciences*. New York: Holt, Rinehart and Winston, 1954.

Geary, R. C., and Pearson, E. S., *Tests of Normality*. London: Biometrika Office, n.d.

Johnson, Cecil D., "The Population Control or Moderator Variable in Personnel Research", *Proceedings, Tri-Service Conference on Selective Research*. Pensakola, Florida, May, 1960. Washington: Office of Naval Research, Department of the Navy, 1960, 125-34.

Naroll, Raoul, "Imperial Cycles and World Order", *Peace Research Society Papers*, VII (1967), 83-101.

Neubauer, Deane E., "Some Conditions of Democracy", *American Political Science Review*, LXI (December, 1967), 1002-9.

Rae, Douglas, "A Note on the Fractionalization of Some European Party Systems", *Comparative Political Studies*, I (October, 1968), 413-18.

Robinson, W. S., "The Statistical Measurement of Agreement", *American Sociological Review*, XXII (February, 1957), 17-25.

Rummel, Rudolph, J., "Dimensions of Conflict Behavior Within and Between Nations", *General Systems Yearbook*, VIII (1963), 1-50.

————, "Some Empirical Findings on Nations and Their Behavior", *World Politics*, XX (January, 1969), 226-41.

Saunders, David R., "Moderator Variables in Prediction", *Educational and Psychological Measurement*, XVI (Summer 1956), 209-22.

Tanter, Raymond, "Dimensions of Conflict Behavior Within and Between Nations, 1958-60", *Journal of Conflict Resolution*, X (March, 1966), 41-64.

25

THE IMPACT OF ZIONIST COLONIZATION ON PALESTINIAN ARAB SOCIETY

NATHAN WEINSTOCK

ALTHOUGH the Palestine war of 1948 and the debacle that ensued, resulting in the majority of the Palestinian people being reduced to the state of helpless refugees, can hardly be disconnected from the subject of the present paper, and although these tragic events repeated themselves in an almost identical form during the war of June 1967, the study of the effect of Zionist colonization in Palestine on the indigenous population prior to 1948 is not lacking in interest.[1] One frequently comes across statements by authorities who can by no means be considered as mere propagandists —wherever their sympathies may lie as regards the Palestine problem— which tend to stress the benefits which the Arab population is alleged to have derived from Jewish settlement in the mandatory period, i.e. before 1948.[2]

In this respect the following quotation from A. Dorra's assessment of the impact of Zionism on Palestine and on the neighbouring countries may

[1] Unless stated otherwise the factual material is fully documented in my book *Le sionisme contre Israël*, Editions François Maspero, Paris 1969.

[2] D. Horowitz, "Arab Economy in Palestine", in J. B. Hobman (ed.), *Palestine's Economic Future*, London 1946, pp. 55-65; A. Dorra, "Palestine and the Economic Development of the Middle East", *Ibid.*, pp. 98-104; Robert Misrahi, "Les Israéliens, les Arabes at la terre", *Les Temps Modernes*, No. 147-148, June 1958, pp. 2182-2209, etc.

be regarded as typical:[3]

Zionism is one of the major factors that have determined the economic evolution of the Middle East since the end of the last war. . . . The result in every field affected by Jewish colonization has been very great, especially if measured by the scale of development in the surrounding countries during the same time. Arid land and malarial swamps were turned into blossoming fields and groves, barren slopes were covered with fruit trees and forests. . . By applying capital and science, and by judiciously selecting profitable crops and choosing the right methods of farming, the Jews were able to increase appreciably the productivity of Palestine agriculture, though only after years of hard pioneering exertions. Their Arab neighbours gradually learnt from their improved methods, greatly assisted by the large amounts of Jewish imported capital that flowed into their hands through land purchase, internal trade, and through Government services paid for by taxes collected from the Jews. . . . In many respects the expansion in Palestine of Jewish immigration and the development of Jewish economy can only bring advantages to the Middle East. Not only will Jewish capital flowing on to the Palestinian Arabs help them raise their own economic standard to the level reached by the Jews, but the Jewish economy itself will be an ever-growing consumer of foodstuffs and raw materials supplied by the neighbouring states. Moreover, the growing capital goods and quality goods industries of Palestine will also be in a position to help accelerate the industrial equipment of the Middle East countries. . . .

One might add that this sounds quite plausible. After all, even if one categorically rejects Zionism and takes an absolutely negative view of the manner in which its aims have been implemented, this should not preclude us from recognizing its achievements. It is a matter of common knowledge that the despicable apartheid regime in South Africa affords the oppressed indigenous coloured population a higher standard of living than the neighbouring independent states. To admit facts such as these does not imply that one approves or condones apartheid. It could actually easily be shown that the very dynamics of the segregated South African society have been instrumental in bringing about this at first sight paradoxical situation. In contemporary Israel, the Arab labour force enjoys a standard of life far more favourable than in the Arab countries. Needless to say, this does not contradict the reality of national oppression of the Palestinian population in the Jewish state.

[3] Dorra, *op. cit.*, pp. 98-104.

The aim then of this research is to verify the statements regarding the alleged benefits Zionism is presumed to have held for the Palestinian Arabs before the war of 1948. Our thesis is that the Zionist enterprise represents a *deviant pattern of colonization* in comparison with the usual schema (exploitation of the indigenous labour force by the settlers). Zionism has some unique features implied by its particular ideology. However, these did not ripen until the second wave of Jewish immigration (roughly from 1903 onwards). Before this date, the Jewish settlements in Palestine did not evolve any characteristics at variance with the prevalent colonial pattern. So much so in fact that many disillusioned idealistic Zionists broke off their relationship with the movement because they considered that the Jewish settlers had become mere "planters".

To understand how this peculiar situation arose, a concise description of the Zionist movement is required. Initially Zionism (from Mount Zion in Jerusalem) was the creed of the Jews who aspired to return to the Holy Land in order to settle there. As long as it retained this primitive form, it remained a romantic ideology of a pre-political nature, reflecting the anguish of the oppressed Jewish masses in Eastern Europe still permeated by the spirit of the ghetto and conveying their yearning for a national revival. During the last quarter of the nineteenth century—the era of modern Imperialist expansion—the current took a new turn under the impulse of Theodor Herzl who had developed a new brand of Jewish Nationalism in his pamphlet *Der Judenstaat* (The Jewish State) and convened the first Zionist Congress at Basle in 1897 on the basis of his programme. The assembly described its aim as being the establishment for the Jewish people of a home in Palestine secured by public law. This modernized version of the original Zionist mystique, now stripped of its initial religious and quasi-messianic content, and remoulded in the spirit of contemporary Nationalism is commonly called "policical Zionism". It carried obvious implications for the inhabitants of Palestine since they were scheduled to become aliens in their own country—assuming they were to be allowed to remain where they were—without even being consulted.

But the unique characteristics of Jewish colonization in Palestine eventually appeared as a consequence of an ironical development in its history, namely the growth of a powerful Socialist wing within the Zionist movement. This current especially prevailed in Eastern Europe—the main reservoir of prospective immigrants—under the influence of Tolstoy's doctrines and the general popularity of Socialism among the Jewish youth during the years preceding the first Russian Revolution of 1905. The defeat of this first major attempt to revolutionize the Tsarist Empire, following in the wake of a fearful wave of pogroms, strengthened the left-wing Zionist current tremendously: the future of the revolutionary movement in Russia seemed very dim indeed and many disappointed Jewish revolutionists switched over their allegiance to Zionism. These people sought to combine their former socialist commitment with their desire to build a Jewish State in Palestine. The result of this new blend of Zionism was a socialistic doctrine that was to have a lasting effect on Zionist ideology and practice. It is hardly an exaggeration to claim that the distinctive pattern of Zionist colonization in Palestine (the growth of the collective kibbutzim and co-operative settlements, the unique importance of the trade-union Leviathan, the Histadruth, the foremost employer of the country) can be traced back entirely to the left-wing Zionist currents. In fact, the majority of the immigrants who belonged to the third wave of colonists (in the beginning of the 1920's) were left-wing Zionist pioneers. The leading theoretician of this movement was Ber Borochov.

Under the influence of these Labour Zionists, Jewish settlement in Palestine was to take on a new form, conveniently yet sincerely rationalized by the use of Marxian terminology. Now, the first Jewish settlers, aided by Baron Rothschild, had bought land from the feudal owners (the Effendis), exploiting the fellaheen who had formerly tilled the land in a typical colonial fashion. But the left-wing Zionists meant to create a Jewish working-class in Palestine: this was achieved by implementing the slogan of exclusive Jewish labour which in effect prohibited the native population from being employed on Jewish farms or factories. The Jewish National Fund was especially adamant about this in its policy of leasing land to prospective colonists. Strangely enough this outspoken racialist attitude, motivated by the need to suppress the competition of cheap local labour, which was obviously strikingly similar to the stand taken by Australian or American reactionary trade unions on the immigration of workers from the colonial countries, was actually explained away as signifying a rejection of colonial practice. To tolerate Arab labour on Jewish farms, these Zionist pioneers were fond to point out, was tantamount to colonialism. Thus they construed their advocacy of a Jewish labour policy as a necessary consequence of their socialist outlook.

This attitude was the root of the "economic separateness"[4] that struck all the observers of the Palestinian scene. Clearly this philosophy had to lead to some type of partition of the country in the long run. In fact the subsequent development of the Zionist experiment rested entirely on the twin principles of (exclusive) "Jewish labour"—i.e. the boycott of the landless fellaheen—and "Jewish produce"—i.e. the boycott of Arab produce.[5] This was required in order to guarantee the viability of

---

[4] Report to the General Assembly by the U.N. Special Committee on Palestine, Geneva, 31 August 1947, p. 19, No. 25.

[5] Rony Gabbay, A Political History of the Arab-Jewish Conflict, Geneva, 1959, and Abraham Revusky, Les Juifs en Palestine, Paris, 1936, p. 85.

Jewish enterprise and the comparatively high wage level of the Jewish worker. Ultimately, the implementation of this segregationist policy led to the development of a quasi-autarchic Jewish economy organized on rigidly national lines (nationalistic trade-unions, militia, schools and social and political institutions), embodying the embryo of the future Jewsh state.

The interesting point about Zionist colonization in Palestine is that it cannot be explained by the mechanisms that generally apply to colonialism. Palestine hardly represented an important market or a vital source of cheap labour in view of its modest population. Its raw materials were scarcely worth mentioning. The land was abysmally poor. Surely, this was not the ideal place to export vast amounts of capital in the hope of reaping huge profits! An expert on the agriculture of the Middle Eastern countries [6] has pointed out that in Palestine "the most modern and intensive methods achieve only the some wheat yields as the Balkan peasant, with his primitive and extensive cultivation". So much for the legend of "the land of milk and honey". And the authors of a standard textbook on the industrialization of the Middle East stress the psychological background which is the only logical explanation for the large-scale Jewish investments in the Palestine industry.[7] These remarks are sufficient proof of the specific features of Zionist colonization, prompted as it was by sentimental considerations rather than by economic motives. Yet the application of colonial techniques to Palestine ultimately gave rise to a typically colonial, though markedly original, pattern of dispossession of the native population.

Christopher Sykes has summarized the nature of the Palestinian problem, resulting as we have seen from the Zionist programme of a Jewish state based on its own working-class and thriving on a separate economy, in the following words: [8]

The land problem of Palestine came primarily from ... the sales, often of very large tracts of country, by absentee landlords to Zionist individuals and syndicates. A usual condition of such sales was that the tenants should be evicted, for of what interest to Zionists was the possession of Arab-tenanted land? The wretched people who had earned a living, sometimes for many generations, on the land in question, found themselves forced out of their homes and deprived without compensation of their only means of earning bread. .... Evicted tenants, the real sufferers by Jewish immigration, were the essence of the Palestine problem.

---

[6] Doreen Warriner, *Land and Poverty in the Middle East,* London, 1948, p. 52.

[7] Kurt Grunwald and Joachim O. Ronall, *Industrialization in the Middle East,* New York, 1960, p. 259.

[8] Christopher Sykes, *Orde Wingate,* London 1959, p. 106.

The testimony of an Israeli historian is especially valuable in this respect because he illustrates the reaction of local Arab opinion to the implementation of the Labour-Zionist ideology with its apartheid-like implications.[9] This is how he describes the attitude of the fellaheen before the first world war:

The local Arab fellaheen occasionally reacted—from the earliest days of the new Yishuv [Jewish community, N.W.]—by perpetrating physical violence. These outbreaks were not the results of the actual purchase by Jews of land in Palestine—since most of the fellaheen themselves were not landowners—but its implementation. Hitherto the proprietors had been chiefly absentee landowners to whom a percentage of the crops had to be paid but who did not interfere with the traditional rights of pasture, or with other aspects of everyday life that gave rise to bad feeling and sometimes conflict when the Jewish colonists came to settle on the land they purchased. In the course of time the neighbouring Arabs of each village or colony also manifested their dissatisfaction with the attempts to introduce Jewish labour.

With regard to the arrival of the wave of Socialist-Zionist settlers, he comments:

These Russian Jewish labourers, together with the principle of exclusive Jewish labour, were considered by a number of Zionist and members of the Yishuv to constitute a major factor in arousing the hostility of the Palestine Arabs.

And, finally, he sketches the ideology of the left-wing Zionists as far as the "natives" were concerned:

They preached that the international brotherhood of workers applied only to workers who were already secure in their employment; it did not apply to a potential proletariat that had to struggle to find employment and could not refrain from conflict with those workers whose place of work they must take for themselves.

This brief introduction will enable us to investigate the problem we set out to study in this paper—to assess the impact of Zionism on Palestinian Arab society.

When the first Zionist settlers established themselves in Palestine (from 1882 onwards), the country was a small underdeveloped corner of the Ottoman Empire. The existing subsistence economy was already

[9] Yaacov Ro'i, "The Zionist Attitude to the Arabs, 1908-1914", *Middle Eastern Studies*, Vol. 4, No. 3, April 1968, pp. 201-02, 223 and 233.

engaged in a process of distingeration as a result of the gradual absorption of the Turkish Empire in the capitalist orbit. This trend was accelerated by the acquisition of large tracts of land and real estate by the Greek Orthodox Church which resulted in the injection of considerable amounts of money in the country. One should also mention the activities of the German Templar sect and the effect of the financial contributions sent to the Levant by Lebanese and Syrian émigrés and, lastly, as far as the Palestine Jewry—approximately one tenth of the indigenous population—was concerned, the remittances sent by Jewish communities abroad to sustain the scholars residing in the Holy Land.[10]

On the whole, the country still remained semi-feudal and the small trickle of trade was confined to the larger towns. Eventually, Jewish colonization gave the final impetus to capitalist penetration in Palestine, hastening the ruin of the subsistence economy. The social pyramid was dominated by the small aristocracy of landowners admitted to the *effendi* or governing class, a mere handful of families.[11] A numerically unimportant middle class, composed of professional men, shopkeepers and prosperous owner-cultivators was in fact structurally dependent on this elite. At the lowest rung of the ladder came the vast majority of the population, the fellaheen, tenant-farmers or tillers of the communal grounds held collectively in mesha'a tenure or, more and more, landless peasants.* Although small ownership was increasing as a result of the breakdown of communal ownership (one of the objects of the Ottoman Land Code of 1858), rural indebtedness was assuming such tremendous proportions that a growing number of cultivators were forced to sell their holdings to wealthy merchants, becoming share-tenants.[12] The general situation is reflected in the following statistic: 91.8 per cent of the land plots in the 1930's were inferior to 100 dunams (1 dunam = 0.247 acre) and yet they covered only 36.7 per cent of the cultivated area. On the other hand, the 13 estates of more than 5,000 dunams— 0.01 percent of the total number of plots—amounted to 19.2 percent of the cultivated area.[13]

Now we can endeavour to assess the results of Zionist colonization on the various facets of Palestinian society. As the reader will notice, this analysis brings out in a striking fashion the importance of the dual nature of the Palestinian economy in which a modern Jewish capitalist

[10] Weinstock, *op. cit.*, pp. 62-75, and Robert Szereszewski, "Palestine on the Eve of Jewish Colonization" in *Essays on the Structure of the Jewish Economy in Palestine and Israel*, Jerusalem, 1968, pp. 88-92.
[11] *Palestine Royal Commission Report* ("Peel Report"), Cmd. 5479, p. 44.
* The Beduins being nomads, were not considered part of settled society.
[12] Warriner, *op. cit.*, p. 22.
[13] A. Granott, *The Land System in Palestine*, London, 1952, pp. 34-35.

economy was "projected on to a backward Arab economy, yet hermetically sealed and segregated from it".[14]

(a) Demography

The demographic mutation of the Palestinian society has obviously been the most apparent change wrought by Zionist immigration. The Jewish community, which amounted to some 24,000 people in 1882, had already expanded to 85,000 in 1914. Palestine Jewry suffered considerably under the rule of Djamal Pasha, the military governor of Syria during the first world war, and its numbers declined sharply. By 1922, however, the Jewish population once again amounted to 84,000 persons, the total number of inhabitants being 752,000. During the following years, as result of immigration, the Jewish minority steadily increased: 175,000 Jews in 1931 out of a total population of 1,033,000. The rise of Fascism in Europe gave a considerable impulse to immigration and by 1940 the Jewish community was estimated to number no less than 464,000. At the end of the second world war the 583,000 Jews represented roughly one third of the Palestinian population which was estimated at 1,033,000 souls.[15]

Initially only a small minority of loosely related congregations living a marginal life dedicated mainly to religious pursuits, the Jewish community had been transformed into a tightly knit unit, increasingly aware of its national characteristics which had developed on the basis of a quasi-autarchic economy and been considerably enhanced by the practice of self-government and the generalization of the Hebrew language. The indigenous Jewish community had been completely estranged from the Palestinian society they initially belonged to as a result of the segregated development of Zionist society.

On the other hand, Arab society too had acquired a distinct degree of cohesion. The Palestinian Arabs, especially the Muslims who constituted the vast majority of the villagers, were increasing at an extraordinarily fast rate—their birth-rate (47.8 per cent duding the years 1927-39) was believed to be one of the highest of the world while their death-rate had fallen from an average of 28.6 per cent in 1925-27 to 20.3 per cent during the period 1927-39.[16] This improvement was largely due to the effect of Jewish immigration on health and hygienic

[14] Horowitz, op. cit., p. 55.
[15] I.N.S., "Mémento Economique", La Palestine, Paris, 1948, p. 38.
[16] Warriner, op. cit., p. 64 and Horowitz, op. cit., p. 55.

standards. Even such an uncompromising foe of Zionism as Abcarius [17] grudgingly admits that "no one, however, can cavil at the moderate statement in the Peel Report that the measures carried out by the Jews have benefitted the Arabs incidentally." The trend towards urbanization should also be stressed: by 1942 27.0 per cent of the Muslim population —compared to 76.0 per cent of the Jews—lived in urban areas. [18]

(b) *Land*

It is of course in this field that the transformation was most acute. Jewish-owned land increased from 25,000 dunams in 1882 to 420,700 in 1914. [19] Thanks to the acquisition of large tracts of land by the Jewish National Fund and other Zionist private or public agencies it amounted to 594,000 dunams in 1922, 1,058,500 in 1939 and 1,604,800 in 1941. [20] The land was bought mainly from large landowners, mostly absentee landlords, and the transfer of property usually resulted in the eviction of the tenants. According to Granott's computations, [21] only 3.8 per cent of the land acquired by Zionist settlers' organizations, especially the J.N.F. and its agencies, was sold by the fellaheen themselves during the years 1920-22 and only 1.6 per cent from 1923 to 1927. It is difficult to estimate the number of peasants evicted as a result of these sales effected by the Arab landowners. "The number of landless agricultural workers was estimated at 30,000 families or 22 per cent out of a total of 120,000 families dependent on agriculture, according to the census of 1931. Their numbers are now certainly larger," stated Doreen Warriner in 1948. [22] In addition to the agricultural workers, countless families drifted to the towns. Naturally, the sales increased the high pressure on the land which was aggravated besides by the primitive and wasteful exploitation of the land in Arab agriculture, the high birth-rate and the lack of opportunities for employment in industry. [23]

Undoubtedly, these sales led to the settlement of the Jewish agriculturists in the most fertile areas of the country. A rough assessment of this trend can be deduced from the fact that only 19.7 per cent of the Jews lived in the hill districts (as opposed to the fertile plains) in 1943

---

[17] M. F. Abcarius, *Palestine through the Fog of Propaganda*, London, n.d. (1946?), p. 118.

[18] Nathan, Gass and Creamer, quoted by Shlomo Sitton, *Israël, Immigration et croissance, 1948-1958*, Paris 1963, p. 70.

[19] *La Palestine*, p. 57.

[20] *A Survey of Palestine*, I, Jerusalem, 1946, p. 372.

[21] Granott, *op. cit.*, p. 277.

[22] Warriner, *op. cit.*, p. 63.

[23] *Ibid.*, p. 58.

compared to 56.7 per cent of the Arabs.[24]

However, the tremendous inflow of capital in the hands of the Arab landowners who sold their estates contributed to the development of cash-crop farming and to increased productivity in the Arab countryside. Arab citrus plantations, for instance, increased from 22,000 dunams in 1922 to 144,000 in 1937.[25] During the years 1925-34, it was estimated that the productivity of Palestinian Arab agriculture amounted to 15 per cent of that of neighbouring Syria.[26] This trend was stimulated by the boom experienced by the Palestinian economy during the second world war.

Nonetheless, although the inflow of capital was an answer to the *technical* problems of Arab agriculture, i.e. mainly the process of introducing irrigation and changing over from the production of energy producing foodstuffs to that of protective foodstuffs—the cultivator's standard of living increased by 17 per cent through irrigation alone, it could not solve the *structural .and social* problems of Arab farming, namely the twin problems of indebtedness and land tenure.[27] "In 1930 it was estimated that the average indebtedness of a fellah family was £P 27 on which interest at an average rate of 30 per cent was being paid, while the average income of a fellah family was between £P 25—30 per annum. Thus it was virtually impossible for any farmer to repay more than a fraction of his debt, and a debt once incurred could never be cancelled, but had to be renewed at intervals at exorbitant rates of interest."[28] One need hardly add that under these circumstances only the privileged stratum of rich landowners could think of investing capital in agriculture (if they did not prefer the quick gains of speculation in real estate).

The dramatic situation of the fellaheen and the pressure on the land, aggravated by the continuing land sales of the Effendi class to Zionist organizations, was the backcloth to the Palestinian revolt of 1936.

(c) *Industrialization*

The structural factors which impeded the progress of Arab agriculture were felt even more sharply in the industrial sphere. In 1942—at a moment when the war effort was affording an extraordinary stimulus to the economy—Arab industry in Palestine consisted in 1,558 establishments engaging 8,804 persons, overwhelmingly concentrated in light industry. It

[24] Nathan *et al.*, according to Sitton, *op. cit.*, p. 68.
[25] Horowitz, *op. cit.*, p. 59.
[26] Misrahi, *op. cit.*, p. 2192.
[27] Horowitz, *op. cit.*, p. 59.
[28] Warriner, *op. cit.*, p. 62,

534 MODERNIZATION OF UNDERDEVELOPED SOCIETIES

is apparent from the ratio between the number of establishments and the number of employees that the vast majority of these firms were ludicrously small.[29] The Arab industrial sector amounted at most to 10 per cent of the total Palestinian industrial produce [30] and the invested capital did not exceed £P 2,000,000. The structural weakness of Arab industry was reflected in the fact that its produce amounted to £P 1,545,000 in 1935 compared to 6,046,000 for Jewish industry. During the same year the Jewish capital invested in industry amounted to more than six times as much as the Arab counterpart (the foreign concessions had actually invested eight times as much).[31] Some idea of the backwardness of the native industry can be gained by comparing the above figures with the statistics for Syria and Lebanon where, out of a combined population of 3,650,000 in 1938, there were 203,900 workers employed in industry, of whom more than 33,000 were in modern industry alone (respectively 175,000 and 18,600 if one subtracts non-indigenous occupations).[32]

So, even allowing for the traditional reluctance of the landowning class in underdeveloped countries to invest in industry, these results show that Arab Palestine has been quite exceptional in its backwardness. The explanation is simple:

Possessing technological and financial advantages, the Zionist capitalist economy blocked the emergence of an Arab capitalist class. Having clashed with the Arab peasants by driving them off their land, Zionism also prevented them from becoming a proletariat in the Jewish sector of the economy. Since the Arab sector's capitalist development was retarded and hindered, the peasants (as well as the Arab intelligentsia) found it hard to get any employment at all except in the British Mandate administration and the public services.[33]

The social structure of the Arab population and the nature of the nationalist and working-class movements likewise reflect this deformation of the social and economic background.

(d) Social Structure

The typically semi-feudal occupational distribution of the Palestinian population illustrates its structural distortion and is brought into prominence in the Table below by a comparison with the Jewish population.[34]

[29] Horowitz, op. cit., p. 62.
[30] Sitton, op. cit., p. 69.
[31] A Survey of Palestine, I, p. 507.
[32] Grunwald and Ronall, op. cit.. p. 298.
[33] The Other Israel, Tel-Aviv, 1968, p. 2.
[34] Horowitz, op. cit., p. 61.

OCCUPATIONAL DISTRIBUTION OF THE POPULATON (%)

	Arabs	Jews
Agriculture	59.0	19.1
Construction, Industry, Mining	12.9	30.6
Transport	6.0	5.1
Commerce	8.4	13.8
Administration	1.3	2.0
Liberal Professions	2.3	11.6
Domestic Service	3.2	5.3
Miscellaneous	6.9	12.5

The paradoxical result of this situation was that the landowning class was able to retain the leadership of the Arab population although it had in fact liquidated its social basis by selling its land. So no urban movement was able to compete with them or to wrest the hegemony in the national movement out of their hands. And when the Arab revolt broke out in 1936, the feudal élite was able to orient it (incidentally preventing the peasants from undermining their social position by carrying out a pro- gramme of radical land reforms) through the absence of a powerful bour- geois or working-class leadership. It is highly significant that with the solitary exception of the Arab wing of the Communist Party, *all* the Palestinian political parties were led by scions of wealthy landowning families. In fact, they hardly deserved the name of parties at all as they were mere cliques centered on a few powerful families of the effendi class: the Husseini's, the Nashashibi's, the Abdul Hadi's, the Dajani's, etc. As Warriner has pointed out,[35] "the young effendi feels no link with his father's tenants . . . there is . . . no sense of responsibility attaching to landownership. The Arab national movement, therefore, lacks any real conception of reforming peasant life."

(e) *Nationalism*

The anachronic Arab leadership led to dramatic consequences. We are already acquainted with the spontaneous protests against Zionist colo- nization which had broken out before the first world war. The hostility increased markedly from 1908 onwards and expressed itself in the cam- paign against Zionism fought in such papers as *Filastin* (Jaffa) and *Al- Karmal* (Haifa). Incidentally, there were about 31 newspapers in Palestine on the eve of the war. These press campaigns, the foundation of anti- Zionist societies, and the issuing of anti-Zionist propaganda and election programmes, were evidence of the swift growth of a specifically Palesti- nian brand of Arab nationalism called to life by the very implementation

---

[35] Warriner, *op. cit.*, p. 24.

of the Zionist enterprise. They also indicate that around 1910 the spontaneous opposition expressed by the fellaheen had been superseded by a political protest movement against Zionism supported by the urban population. "Already in 1913," states Neville Mandel,[36] "Albert Antébi had noted that popular feeling was such in Jerusalem that no responsible Arab notable wished to compromise his political position by openly favouring the Zionists." The failure of the attempts to arrive at an Arab-Zionist understanding in 1913-1914 revealed that "by 1914 popular feeling in Palestine was too hostile to the Zionists to have allowed such an entente to stand".[37]

During the first world war, Palestine notables figured among the Arab nationalists hanged on the orders of the notorious Djamal Pasha. When the Balfour Declaration was issued, popular indignation in Palestine expressed itself in attacks against Jewish settlements in Gallilee, and outbreaks in Jerusalem (1920) and Jaffa (1921). These anti-Jewish outbursts were still of an obviously primitive sort and consisted in wild assaults on Jews or on symbols of Zionist immigration. There was yet nothing like a political platform. The worst incidents of this type occurred in 1929.

Meanwhile strikes and boycotts such as those of 1925, 1926 and 1933 revealed that new political forms of action were appearing. These culminated in the general strike and boycott of 1936, following the Syrian model, which lasted more than six months and was followed by intensive guerilla warfare in the Arab countryside. The new maturity of the masses was reflected in the objectives of these protests which were now clearly directed against the British colonial authorities. However, under the pressure of the foreign Arab feudal leaders, the strike was called off and the outcome of the peasent revolt—mercilessly crushed by the British aided by Zionist militiamen after the rebels had been abandoned by the urban petty-bourgeoisie—pointed towards the fundamental weakness of Palestinian Arab Nationalism: the absence of a high calibre cadre. This explains why such doubtful characters as the Mufti and Fawzi al-Kawukji were able to appear as the leaders of the revolt. The Palestinians lacked a dynamic bourgeoisie or a powerful working-class, either of which would have been able to provide a genuine leadership for the struggle (this should not be construed as an attempt to gloss over the notorious halfheartedness of the bourgeoisie in the colonial countries). For the want of this social base, they had to make good with corrupt feudal demagogues, the very same people who were actually selling out their land to the Zionists.

[36] Neville Mandel, "Attempts at Arab-Zionist Entente: 1913-1914", *Middle Eastern Studies*, Vol. 1, No. 3, April 1965, p. 263.
[37] *Ibid.*, p. 264.

After the rebellion had been stamped out (thousands died on the battlefield; dozens were hanged; many villages were summarily destroyed or bombed out of existence by the R.A.F.), seventeen infantry battalions finally succeeded in "pacifying" the countryside. This was a crushing defeat for the Palestinians, and their passivity after the second world war and during the war of 1948 can be traced back to its effects: it takes more than a generation to overcome the total annihilation of the militant vanguard.

The persistence of the feudal structure of the Arab community also explains why so many thousands of villagers and townsmen fled in panic in 1948 and why the deliberate campaign of terror of the Israeli Army, and especially of its irregular units, succeeded so well. It is perhaps significant that the inhabitants of Nazareth who stayed where they were happened to be Christians and consequently much less subservient to the traditional Muslim leadership.

From a Marxist point of view one should underscore that only a revolutionary socialist leadership—i.e. a working-class party—would have been able to lead the Palestinians to victory. But the point we wish to emphasize here is that in contradistinction to the neighbouring countries, the Palestinian population did not even succeed in giving life to a genuine bourgeois nationalist current, and this in spite of the obvious pugnacity of the masses. What a difference to Egypt where powerful mass movements arose from 1919 onwards, spearheaded by the Wafd, with Syria where the cities were the hub of Nationalist movements! Palestine never saw the equivalent of a Mustapha Kamil, a Saad Zaghlul, of a Shukri al-Kuwatli. Nor did the radical petty-bourgeoisie or the Communist nuclei ever manage to play anything approximating a leading role in the national or social struggle.

This anomalous situation was the result of the distortion of the Palestinian social structure by the apartheid-like principles of Zionism. The low calibre of the leadership and its propensity to confuse the anti-Imperialist objectives with straight antisemitic propaganda, (such as the Mufti liked to indulge in under the influence of his German associates) reflected, in the final analysis, the successful attempts of the Zionist leaders to block the emergence of an Arab middle class and bourgeoisie and, similarly, at least until the development of the Haifa bay area (refineries, etc.), of an Arab urban proletariat.

(f) Labour and Class-consciousness

Obviously, the very fact that the Jewish working-class and labour movement were based on the specifically Zionist segregationalist principles represented a formidable obtacle to the endeavour to unite Jewish and

Arab workers in a common struggle. The fact that the Histadruth trade-union was committed to Zionism and to the policy of boycott of Arab labour prohibited cooperation except in marginal areas such as the Government services (where both Arabs and Jews were engaged) or in the Army (where identical wages were paid to Jews and Arabs). Elsewhere the double wage standard prevailed. In fact, the existence of this discrimination was the very rationale of Zionist segregation: the creation of a Jewish economy that would afford the (Jewish) working-class a standard of life similar to that of Europe despite the fact that Palestine belonged to the colonial world. General labourers, for instance, were paid £P 0.07-0.20 if they were Arabs, £P 0.12-0.40 if they were Jews (or at least European Jews. Oriental Jews were counted among the Arabs and the officially computed tables of comparative wages classify them as *Asiatic* labour).[38] In 1944, the average income of the workers employed in the building trade was £P 145 for the Arabs and £P 300 for the Jews.[39]

A noteworthy evolution seemed to be taking place in the Haifa area where the Arab workers organized an independent trade-union federation. It was also here that the Arab Communists exerted the most influence. At the end of 1942 nearly 130,000 Arabs were being employed as workers or salaried employees. For the first time in Palestinian history the embryo of an Arab workers' vanguard appeared to be developing and proving itself capable of wresting the control of the urban masses from the feudal Nationalists.

The Zionist movement intended to *replace* the Palestinian population, rather than to exploit it according to the classical colonial pattern. Knowing the ultimate results of this policy, one can hardly consider this course to have been a lesser form of injustice and alienation imposed on the inhabitants of the country. Zionist colonization, while unquestionably exerting a favourable effect on the cultural and hygienic standard of the country, built a new society in which Hebrew capitalists exploited a Hebrew proletariat by implementing specific segregationist principles—at the expense of the Palestinians. The apartheid-like ideology of Zionism precluded it from fulfilling the historically progressive function of colonialism—the generalization of the capitalist mode of production. Nor were the victims of the Zionist enterprise able to lead a consequent struggle for self-determination since the underlying principles of the Jewish colonization led to

[38] *The Political History of Palestine under British Administration,* Jerusalem, 1947, republished, New York, n.d., p. 16, No. 66.
[39] *La Palestine,* p. 166.

the distortion of the Palestinian social structure and the obstruction of the development of the Palestinian bourgeoisie and working-class which should normally have followed each other up as standard-bearers of the struggle for national liberation.

Yet, by a strange paradox, the pauperized and wretched Palestinian refugees now appear to be spearheading the new upsurge of the Arab revolution. And, in the last instance, this too is a result of Zionism, albeit an unexpected one. Paraphrasing the comments of Marx on the British rule in India one might comment that "whatever may have been the crimes of Israel it was the unconscious tool of history in bringing about that revolution".[40] It is doubtful whether the founders of the Zionist movement would have relished this prospect.

---

[40] Karl Marx, "The British Rule in India", Karl Marx and Frederick Engels, *Selected Works*, Vol. 1, Moscow 1950, p. 317.

26

REFLECTIONS ON LEADERSHIP IN THE THIRD WORLD

MANY ASPECTS of the last decades have lent new potency to the contention both that the great man, the Hero (to draw upon Carlyle's term), plays a creative role of dramatic significance in history and that events would have taken a quite different course if other leaders had chanced to take their place. It is asserted at the moment that lesser and more routine figures, such as Prime Minister Wilson and President Nixon, have now largely replaced the striking and colourful figures who, for good or evil, dominated the recent past. The memory of these personalities—such as Lenin, Stalin, Gandhi, Nehru, Hitler, Mussolini, Roosevelt, Churchill—is, however, still fresh and vivid, and others—such as de Gaulle and Mao, Castro and Nasser—are still with us. Particularly in the "new countries" of the third world the great man—great at least for a brief span within the orbit of his own domain—has been a commanding figure in determining by which paths his country should advance or retreat, although it has also become increasingly evident that the leader's innovations, notably those aiming at a forced draft modernization, have often found sharp limits in the resistance of the traditional society to change. The assurance that the leader leads and that the followers do in fact follow has become somewhat less confident than it was a few years ago, but it is still usually

540

the leader who sets the course which the country is publicly committed to follow.

The basic issue, representing a controversy of ancient standing in which historians, philosophers, and many others have participated, has been well stated by Sidney Hook. When we assert that an event-making man has had a decisive influence on a historical period, we are asserting, he claimed,

> that in such situations the great man is a relatively independent historical influence—*independent of the conditions that determine the alternatives*—and that on these occasions the influence of all other relevant factors is of subordinate weight in enabling us to understand or predict which one of the possible alternatives will be actualized. In such situations, we should also be able to say, and to present the grounds for saying, that if the great man had *not* existed, the course of events would in all likelihood have taken a *different* turn.[1]

Let me at the outset dispose of one aspect of the subject which need thereafter trouble us no more. The role of the great man as himself a creative force in history, as opposed to a determinist position, or say, a reliance on broader social forces or cycles, has been a constant matter of dispute, and I assume that it will continue to be one, both because it is a question of inexhaustible fascination and because it has no possible definitive answer. This essay does not attempt to prove the unprovable, which, for the present purpose, is the conviction that the great man can give history a certain distinctive turn and determine significant phases of the destiny of the people whose lives he touches and whose destiny would otherwise have been different. No matter how persuasive a case can be made for this conviction, or, for that matter, for alternative versions of the nature of history, it and they can be neither proved nor disproved for the simple reason that we can only speculatively, but never actually, reverse the course of history and play out a different scenario than that which has already taken place. In different circumstances history might indeed have been different, but we cannot rerun it to see what the differences would have been. While I am prepared to assert that, if Z had come to power instead of A, a quite different set of events would have taken place; I am well aware that I can never overwhelm the skeptic with proof which he must acknowledge as indisputable. The "if" involved in endowing Z with power under the identical circumstances which accompanied A's accession to leadership can only be a hypothetical enterprise, not to be translated into the unimpeachable stuff of history. It

[1] Sidney Hook, *The Hero in History* (Boston, 1955), p. 166.

endows the great man thesis with a certain air of authenticity to point out that, in many actual cases, Z later ousted A, and, representing the other end of the alphabet, reversed A's course, thus indicating the malleability of history in the making. But the ready answer is surely that it was necessary that A should precede Z in order to establish the particular conditions which made Z's rise possible.

Because it inevitably runs into the stone wall created by the impossibility of subjecting it to any empirical tests, the great man theory, if pursued with undue diligence, soon becomes a fruitless enterprise, but if its wholly hypothetical character is realized, it can be drawn upon to throw a revealing speculative light on the course of history and the alternatives which might have been.

One thing which should at all events not be allowed to obscure the argument is the fact that journalists, historians, and others have written brilliant works to demonstrate the inevitability of what has happened. We may be quite confident that if some different historical tapestry had been unrolled, the justifications which it would have evoked from the same writers would have been no less brilliant and convincing. Is there any reason to assume, for instance, that if Sékou Touré had been over- thrown in the last half-dozen years by a conservative or middle-of-the- road military or civil regime, this event would not have found an array of commentators to demonstrate that it was an inevitable outcome of the forces at work in the Guinean scene?

Mention should perhaps here be made of the peculiar circumstance, although it is as far as ever removed from scientific proof, that mankind is inescapably endowed with a sense of freedom of the will; indeed, of the absolute necessity of making choices. To give a mundane and trivial example, it may be wholly predetermined whether I put on my black or my brown shoes, or no shoes at all, but I cannot overcome the belief that this is a choice which I must make and which might go the other way. The Indian voter feels that he is free to decide between the Congress and its rivals, with a sense that it makes a difference which one wins, and Prime Minister Gandhi believes she must make a choice between launch- ing India on a nuclear weapons programme or abstaining from it.

One other preliminary point of controversy must be examined: to what extent is the great man, assuming him to have some measure of autono- mous freedom, free from or bound by the environment within which he acts? It is self-evident that the limits within which even the greatest of men can successfully operate impose severe restraints upon him. How severe these restraints may be can presumably never be stated with more than the most approximate precision, and, furthermore, I see every reason to assume that they vary in different cases and circumstances. It need scarcely be said that Gandhi's creed of non-violence would have scant appeal to Muslim Arabs bent upon a *jihad* or upon tht destruction ot Israel nor would Napoleon make much headway in Hindu or Buddhist communities. But to what extent was Gandhi an innovator, bringing a new doctrine to India, or was he essentially only expressing what the *Zeitgeist* and the Indian heritage already demanded and contained? It is my own opinion that Gandhi released old resources and tapped new forces which no one else in fact could reach as he could but to those who look askance at great man theories he is in much greater degree to be absorbed within or attributed to his environment.

Citing William James to the effect that "If anything is humanly certain it is that the great man's society, properly so called, does not make him before he can remake it," Morris R. Cohen has contended that the controversy between the great-man historian and the social-force historian is based upon a false dichotomy. He saw the great men of any age as likely to be precisely those who embody the aspirations of a large number of their fellowmen or who are fitted to manage the particular society into which they are born. Suggesting that great men are precisely the point of intersection of great social forces, he concluded that:

> The appearance of outstanding human capacities at any moment may be an unpredictable accident but the causes and endeavors to which those capacities can be directed are found in a setting of social forces. In this limited sense the production of great personalities is a social phenomenon.[2]

William James himself, a firm believer in the creative role of the great man, saw the men of genius laying out alternative ways for their societies, ways to a large extent indeterminate in advance and any one of which could lead to prosperity, "just as a man may enter either of many businesses". The relation of the environment to the great man he saw was in the main exactly what it is to the "variation" in the Darwinian philosophy.

> It chiefly adopts or rejects, preserves or destroys, in short *selects* him. And whenever it adopts and preserves the great man, it becomes modified by his influence in an entirely original and peculiar way.[3]

In brief, the fruitful and suggestive version which William James put forward was that as evolution proceeds through the selection of varia-

[2] Morris R. Cohen, *The Meaning of Human History* (La Salle, Illinois, 1961) pp. 220-21.

[3] William James, "Great Men and Their Environment", *Selected Papers on Philosophy* (London and New York, 1961), p. 173.

tions which appear in nature, so human society changes by its adoption or adaptation of innovations selected from those offered to it by its men of genius. The source of innovation is the great man, but the survival of the variations or mutations which he introduces is dependent upon their acceptance or rejection by the society at large.

The great man is inevitably a product of his own society, and the creed which he preaches, the path and the policy which he advocates, must be intimately related to his environment and the experience and aspirations of his people; but he may also open new doors to them and start them off in new directions.

I I

It is in periods of crisis, birth, or basic transformation that the role of the inspired servants, the prophets of the people, takes on full importance.[4]

The relation of the great man to periods of crisis which Jacques Maritain has thus pointed out is one which has frequently been noted. "In rebellious ages, when Kingship itself seems dead and abolished," wrote Carlyle in his *On Heroes and Hero-Worship,* "Cromwell, Napoleon step forth again as Kings"; and while Carlyle found a King indispensable in all movements of men, it was in times of upheaval that he found him most necessary.

It is obviously not inevitable that a crisis should produce the "heroic" leader, but it does enhance the need for him and renders the populace more ready to accept him than in untroubled times. Put in other terms, it might be said that a time of crisis lowers the threshold beyond which some measure of charisma is both looked for and acknowledged in the leader. Furthermore, I believe that crises, and particularly those involving the "birth or basic transformation" of the Third World countries, very substantially widen the limits within which the leader can act freely, imposing upon the society certain courses of action which it would otherwise not have taken. A country in transition from colonialism to independence and from its traditional structure and way of life to development and modernization has in many respects a much greater diversity and fluidity than a country which is more firmly set upon an established course. The gaps between the modernized elite, the transitional middle strata, and the mass leave open the possibility that quite different sets of policies might be adopted; but the same gaps, of course, also leave open the possibility that policies adopted at the centre may

---

[4] Jacques Maritain, *Man and the State* (Chicago, 1951), p. 140.

trickle off and disappear into the sand long before they reach the general populace whose life they are supposed to transform and determine.

It has often been pointed out with what striking regularity colonial nationalist movements and the new countries have brought forth a single leader who was both the symbol and the flesh-and-blood personification of national identity and the wielder of central power. Of such leaders K. R. Minogue has written:

In states where the identity of the nation was fluid and indeterminate, their acts and pronouncements incarnated the national spirit, and gave to politics just the flamboyance needed to sustain the attention of populations in the process of emerging from the narrow preoccupations of the village.[5]

A countervailing theme, deserving more attention than it can be given here, is the recent trend among commentators and analysts to examine with a much more skeptical eye than a few years ago the assumption that Third World leaders deserved to be seen as charismatic and as truly embodying and speaking for the great mass of their people, usually through the instrumentality of the single or dominant party. The series of attacks upon leaders such as Ben Bella, Nkrumah, and Sukarno, their overthrow by the military or by civilian rivals, and the acclaim which greeted their self-appointed successors, all worked to tarnish the notion of charisma and to downgrade the earlier estimates of their strength and significance. One writer saw the emergence of charismatic leaders in the struggle for national independence as "sometimes almost inflicting charisma on some very improbable persons",[6] and W. Arthur Lewis warned in the same vein that almost any charming rogue in West Africa could have charisma bestowed upon him by the political journals of the Western world:

Actually only a minority of the West African Presidents or Premiers have a wide charismatic appeal in their own countries. . . . Charismatic figures do not need the oppressive tactics which so many Presidents use. One is always hearing about the popularity of these great men— yet, when they fall, hardly anybody crosses the street, even for a good man like Olympio.[7]

[5] K. R. Minogue, *Nationalism* (London, 1967), p. 129. "Charismatic leadership is a form of crisis leadership." Dankwart Rustow, "Ataturk as Founder of a State", *Daedalus* (Summer, 1968), p. 794.

[6] Frederick W. Frey, *The Turkish Political Elite* (Cambridge, Mass., 1965), p. 410.

[7] W. Arthur Lewis, *Politics in West Africa* (London, 1965), p. 32. A decade ear-- lier Sidney Hook protested that today, more than ever before, belief in "the hero"

These sober revisions of the over-enthusiastic acclaim with which the "great men" of the nationalist movements and new countries were greeted are a salutary corrective to earlier views, but they tell only part of the story. For all the skepticism one may display, surely some of the Third World leaders must still be accepted as both great and charismatic; and no one could have a more indisputable claim to these titles than Gandhi and Nehru. Furthermore, even if both titles must be denied to other Third World leaders, it would still remain the fact that during their span of office they spoke authoritatively for their communities, however inadequately their pronouncements may have been implemented. When others succeeded to the post which these men held, their policies were almost certain to be changed and perhaps reversed. In a sense all that the skeptical re-examination has achieved is to demonstrate that it was not necessary to be a great man endowed with charisma in order to be acclaimed as authoritarian leader of a Third World country and even to have the label of charisma attached to your name and fame. Power at the centre was formally vested in such leaders, but detailed inquiry on the spot was necessary to determine whether the power actually extended much beyond the capital and out into the countryside. An extreme example, no doubt, would be the Congo in the first years of its independent existence when the writ of its central government often barely reached to the outskirts of Leopoldville.

III

No other example of the role of leadership in transforming a country and a people can be more striking than that of India from 1919 to 1964— the era of Gandhi and Nehru, although their share in that dramatic era of the subcontinent's development was, of course, supplemented by the contributions of many others, great and small. The inevitable question arises as to how deeply and lastingly the new ideas they brought penetrated into India's age-old masses, and here one cannot expect to do much better than, on the basis of William James's formulation, await the verdict of time: will the Indian people adopt as their own the "variations" which their great men sought to present to them? Whatever the ultimate answer, it is hard to conceive of India in the latter part of the twentieth century without an immediate conviction that, however strong

is a synthetic product. "Whoever controls the microphones and printing presses can make or unmake belief overnight." If public acclaim for greatness is not thrust upon the modern dictator, he can easily arrange for it. *The Hero in History*, p. 10. For a generally skeptical appraisal of charismatic leadership, with special reference to the Third World, see K. J. Ratnam, "Charisma and Political Leadership", *Political Studies* (Vol. XII, no. 3; October 1964), pp. 341-54.

antiquity and tradition may be, this is a country shaped in large measure by its two great leaders. Yet for all their hold upon the people of India they were unable to prevent what they abhorred: the victory of the two-nation theory and the breaking away of Pakistan in the midst of mass murder and hatred.

Tributes to Gandhi as the man who inspired his people and, indeed much of the rest of the world, who organized the mass party which still rules the country, and achieved freedom for India from British rule are so numerous and universal as to make it superfluous to cite them. In place of many, let me cite only two. André Malraux has recently written that after his murder Gandhi was still present in the Indian Parliament and Capital:

> But the policies of India were no more fashioned in the Congress or in Parliament than the policies of Hitler's Germany were fashioned in the Reichstag: the policies of India were the legacy of the little man in a loincloth who had taken it into his head to lead millions of Indians off to glean salt from the Indian Ocean as a protest against the salt tax, and to find freedom there.[8]

It was Nehru's conclusion in 1940 that while Gandhi had aged,

> Yet the old spell is there, the old charm works, and his personality and greatness tower over others. Let no one imagine that his influence over India's millions is any the less. He has been the architect of India's destiny for twenty years or more, and his work is not completed.[9]

Nehru saw Gandhi as not descending from the top: "he seemed to emerge from the millions of India",[10] and he brought an amazing psychological change not only to his followers but also to his opponents and the neutrals who could not make up their minds.

> The time was ripe for it, of course, circumstances and world conditions worked for this change. But a great leader is necessary to take advantage of circumstances and conditions. Gandhi was that leader ... Gandhi has played a revolutionary role in India of the greatest importance because he knew how to make the most of the objective conditions and could reach the heart of the masses.[11]

[8] Andre Malraux, *Anti-Memoirs* (New York, 1968), p. 129.
[9] See the "Final Epilogue" to Nehru's *An Autobiography* (Bombay, 1962), p. 610.
[10] J. Nehru, *Discovery of India* (New York, 1946), p. 361.
[11] Jawaharlal Nehru in *Gandhi, Maker of Modern India?*, edited by Martin Deming Lewis (Boston, 1965), pp. 7-8. Nehru also spoke of Gandhi as a demon of energy and action, driving himself and others, and doing more than anyone else to change the characteristic quietism of the Indian people, *Ibid.*, p. 6,

It might be argued that essentially all that Gandhi did was to refurbish the ancient creed of Hinduism and appeal to the masses through that medium, but to say this is to take no account of his revolutionary impact, to which Nehru bears witness as do any number of others. In his attack upon the status of the Harijan and upon other elements of what he regarded as abuses in Hinduism, drawing in part on other great religions and ethical principles, he was regarded as an enemy by the orthodox and drew many millions of Indians, high and low, including many Muslims, into an unprecedented participation in the affairs of their country. As Nehru put it.

> Reactionary or revolutionary, he has changed the face of India, given pride and character to a cringing and demoralized people, built up strength and consciousness in the masses, and made the Indian problem a world problem.[12]

Reaching far beyond India to make an impact in many parts of the world, his doctrine of non-violent non-cooperation or civil resistance was itself a revolutionary contribution of the first order, even though to his intense grief it was often beyond the ability of his own people to live up to. At once saint and shrewd political leader, he had a command over India's elites and masses which no rival could challenge during his lifetime, but his way of thought and life and leadership was distinctively and uniquely his own, both deriving from the ancient Indian soil and introducing new elements and ideas. His political style, which was inextricably intermixed with his social, religious, and ethical outlook, provided a vital link between the modernist and the traditional approaches.

It has occasionally been contended that putting forward his creed of non-violence, to take only a single aspect of his work and teachings, he was doing little more than tapping an old-established segment of Hinduism, but whatever the proper doctrinal position may be, it seems clear on the record that India throughout its history has experienced more or less as much violence as other parts of the world, and the nationalist movement, before Gandhi took command of it, had been marked by much violence and terrorism. At the end of World War I and in the immediate postwar period violence broke out at many points in India. Given both what had been going on in the Indian setting and what

---

[12] Nehru, *An Autobiography*, p. 406. Two recent writers on India have contended that "a great leader may mobilize in his followers unsuspected strengths and virtues, superego strivings not previously lived up to, which are made active by his moral challenge. ... Gandhi evoked in himself and those who 'heard' him responses that transcended the routine of ordinary life, producing extraordinary events and effects on character which, metaphorically, can be described as 'magical'." L. I. & S. H. Rudolph, *The Modernity of Tradition* (Chicago, 1967), pp. 199-200.

was characteristic of nationalist and anti-colonial movements elsewhere, it was only common sense to expect rising violence in the subcontinent in response to Britain's repressive measures and particularly the Amritsar massacre of 1919 in which hundreds of Indians were killed and thousands wounded by British forces. Yet Gandhi imposed on the nationalist movement his faith in non-violent civil disobedience, whatever the shortcomings of his people in living up to it, and made the Congress a model for similar movements throughout the world. As with so much of his creed and activity, non-violence represented both lofty ethical-religious principles and eminently sound political strategy, given the British readiness to play the political game according to certain rules.

The revolution which Gandhi brought to pass in India was uniquely and distinctively his own. The alternative leaderships which were available would in all probability have chosen different courses, perhaps drastically different ones. The extent to which India's political outlook and development were, in a sense, arbitrary and imposed by the special and peculiar attributes of Gandhi is evident in the changes wrought by his chosen successor, Jawaharlal Nehru. Nehru, during Gandhi's lifetime, on the whole, followed in Gandhi's footsteps, acknowledging his supremacy, but it was apparent that the two were very different kinds of men and that Nehru only reluctantly went along with some of the Mahatma's basic beliefs and political decisions. Aside from impressive and significant differences in political style, involving the kind of relationships which each had with his associates and with the people at large, perhaps the most important differences related to non-violence, which Nehru appears to have viewed with substantially less devotion than Gandhi, and a far greater readiness on Nehru's part to bring India into the modern rationalized industrialized world. Where Gandhi looked to the Indian villager as the embodiment of the best of India and to small-scale village production as the proper economic centre, Nehru sought the kind of development which would make it possible for India to take its place among the great modern nations of the world.

In a challenging comment on Nehru, Walter Crocker held that

The supreme irony was that most of Nehru's values were nearer to the British, whose *raj* he had been bent on destroying, than to the Indians, whose subjection to the *raj* he wept over.[13]

Although Gandhi also had been strongly influenced by Britain, his involvement in the spiritual traditions of India was far too profound to make it possible for anyone to make a similar estimate of his relation to

[13] Walter Crocker, *Nehru* (London, 1966), pp. 164-65.

M-36

British values. Here were two men, intimately associated with each other for many years of immense importance to themselves and to their country, and one the chosen successor of the other, whose views of their role and of the proper destiny of their country differed greatly. Yet each had an overwhelming hold on the Indian people—Crocker believed that Nehru's relationship to the Indian crowd was unique, "not rivalled even by Gandhi's" [14] —and each led India in the direction which he was convinced the country should go; but the directions were different and even ultimately incompatible.

If Gandhi was a leader who shaped the destiny of his country, Nehru was surely not far behind him:

> For Nehru is a giant, both as man and statesman. If political greatness be measured by the capacity to direct events, to rise above the crest of the waves, to guide his people, and to serve as a catalyst of progress, then Nehru surely qualifies for greatness.[15]

Whether or not the leaders are followed in the long run is for the ultimate inchoate wisdom of the people to decide, but that the leaders can for the time being impose very different courses upon their countries seems beyond question.

I V

Elsewhere in Asia and Africa, and in other parts of the world as well, masses of evidence point in the same direction. As has already been noted, it is a familar fact that the trend in the bulk of the countries concerned has been toward authoritarian one-man rule, often superseded by a military take-over. Within the kind of limits which have been suggested, power at the centre over both the party and the governmental apparatus has been vested in the leader who finds his authoritarian centrality justified by the assumption that he personifies the nation, that he maintains national unity as against the many centrifugal forces, and that he represents the necessary consolidation of power and forward movement in a period marked by major crises. Furthermore, given the great gaps existing within each of the societies, the uses to which the leader can put his power are less circumscribed, the limits within which he can operate with relative freedom are less tightly drawn than in the developed countries

---

[14] Crocker, *Nehru*, p. 24. The author added that Nehru's "prestige with the Indian people had something of the magical about it. Here was why over a dozen years or so he could have been a dictator if he had so desired, without guns or propaganda."

[15] Michael Brecher, *Nehru, A Political Biography* (Boston, 1962), p. 245.

which have already made the essential transition from earlier worlds to modernity. Seen from another angle, this implies that the leader may within a broad range arbitrarily impose one course of policy and action on his country, whereas if the accidents of history had brought another "great man" to the fore a quite different course would have been followed.

The examples which might be cited are almost without end. No attempt will be made here to do more than cite a few which seem particularly striking or illustrative.

Two leaders in different corners of the globe who have attracted much attention and who have not infrequently been bracketed together for one or another purpose are Sukarno of Indonesia and Nkrumah of Ghana. Both in their different fashions have been flamboyant rulers of their countries and both have lent themselves to the charge of megalo-mania. Both have sought to play a distinctive role on the international scene; both have flirted with the extreme left with a greater or less degree of seriousness; and both have been ousted by their military who in each instance have turned back to a more middle-of-the-road posi-tion, adopting a neutralist stance benevolent to the West rather than the East. In each instance the position which the new military rulers have taken is sharply at variance with that of the civilian leader whom they ousted, but they appear in both countries to have been accepted by the populace and to have had as large a measure of freedom to follow the lines which they thought appropriate as did their predecessors. In nei-ther instance do I see anything approaching a compelling reason why the particular Sukarno should have come to power at the time that he did —save, of course, the fact that he had already established his leader-ship of the nationalist movement.

Harry Benda contended in 1964 that Sukarno's regime was to be properly interpreted as "the agonizing, difficult adjustment of Indonesia to its own identity". In Benda's opinion, the Indonesian river, including Guided Democracy, was flowing more and more in an Indonesian bed:

If Indonesia's charismatic President has shed constitutional restraints and surrounded himself with a glittering palace entourage in the midst of accelerating poverty, if he is seeking ideological, magical for-mulas to restore the realm to harmony and balance, he is surely less Machiavellian than Javanese.[16]

This is an appealing characterization of Sukarno's reign, but it was not long after it was written that the military leaders, no less Indonesian

[16] Harry Benda, cited in *Nations by Design*, edited by Arnold Rivkin (New York, 1968), pp. 46-47.

than the man whom they replaced by cautious gradual stages, reversed the direction which Sukarno had given the Indonesian river and moved it into another stream bed. Sukarano was unquestionably a political leader of immense skill and charm and the degree of national unity which Indonesia has achieved may well be attributed to his leadership; but was it a necessity that a man so meagrely endowed with administrative ability and so devoid of sound economic sense should have come to power in a country potentially so rich? That the Indonesian economy should continuously have declined under his management and that the country should increasingly have linked its destiny with communism in its Chinese guise, despite the old-standing disaffection with the Chinese in Indonesia, were surely personal idiosyncracies of Sukarno rather than necessities inherent in the Indonesian situation.

The leftward swing of Nkrumah and his insistence on an international role for Ghana may be examined in much the same terms, although at a superficial glance it appears that his relation to his country's economy was a more positive one than that of Sukarno despite the ruinous deficits and the morass of corruption which he left behind him. But was there anything inherent in Ghana's situation which forced the leftward swing? Here was, at least in African terms, a relatively well-to-do country with a tidy accumulated surplus to draw on and a prosperous cocoa industry as well as other economic resources. Indeed, the existence of these conditions and of a stable middle class of cocoa farmers was often cited as justification for the early grant of independence to Ghana.

To draw in another country and leader, is there any sufficient reason why Nkrumah should have headed in one direction (or in several divergent ones) while his neighbor, Houphouet-Boigny, whose Ivory Coast could have been described in roughly similar terms, should have led his country in a quite contrary direction? The rightward turn of Houphouet, seeking intimate collaboration with France and French capital and entrepreneurs, is in a way all the more surprising when it is remembered that it was under his auspices that the R.D.A., the most significant of the French African parties, was affiliated in Paris with the Communists for parliamentary purposes in the immediate postwar years.

If one more country and leader may be added, I would suggest that the sharp leftward inclination of Sékou Touré had no necessary basis in the socio-economic structure of Guinea. What was important was not the special circumstance of Guinea, but the fact that Sékou Touré had established himself as the national leader, operating through a party largely of his own creation, and that these were *his* views. *West Africa,* indeed, in an editorial comment of 28 September 1968, remarked that

Before independence, Guinea was always reckoned one of the most economically favoured of France's African colonies, with a sound agricultural economy and plentiful minerals.

Would it be wholly implausible to speculate that the policies of Nkrumah, Houphouet, and Touré, despite the fact that each differed markedly from the other, might have been interchangeable from country to country, and that the fact they turned up in one country rather than another was more an accident of personal history than an inescapable adaptation of policy to the necessities of a particular country?

Another approach to the problem—still inevitably dwelling in a realm of unrealizable if's—might be to glance at cases in which the leadership which has actually emerged exhibits qualities out of keeping with what the history and experience of the country might have led one to expect. Three which can be briefly mentioned are Jomo Kenyatta, Tunku Abdul Rahman, and Lee Kuan Yew —each of whom has given his country a more moderate and conciliatory regime than the country's circumstances might have been held to imply.

Kenyatta was regarded by the British as the evil genius of the Mau Mau movement, and was denounced by Governor Renison in 1960, in an often quoted phrase, as "the African leader to darkness and death". For years he was banned from all political activity by the colonial authorities. Given the racial tensions of Kenya it seemed reasonable to predict that if he were to come to power, the White Highlands and all that they implied for the social, political, and economic structure of the country would come tumbling down in ruins. In reality, under Kenyatta's leadership racial peace and collaboration have been maintained at an unusually high level, at least as far as relations between Europeans and Africans are concerned, and the contribution of Europeans to Kenya's economy has continued to be substantial. The bitter opposition of some of the more ardent Kenya nationalists, among whom Kenyatta would certainly have been numbered in the past, has not swayed him from the path which he has laid out for his country.

Malaya in the postwar decades might also very plausibly have been seen as more likely to be afflicted by racial conflict than to be something of a model of multi-racial concord. The bitter experiences of the war and the Emergency, each of which tended to set race against race, enhanced the likelihood that the strains of independence would intensify the rivalry between Malays and Chinese, perhaps drawing in the Indians as well. The emergence of rival racial leaders violently struggling for control of the state as independence approached could have come as no great surprise to anyone; and yet the actual development within the framework of the Alliance produced a high degree of racial tolerance and accommodation. For this achievement a large debt is undoubtedly owed to the Prime

Minister, Tunku Abdul Rahman, whose political good sense and discretion have enabled his counterparts in the Chinese and Indian communities to accept a considerable measure of Malay political ascendancy. Not a charismatic leader, perhaps not even a "great man", the Tunku has left a strong imprint on his country.

The Tunku also, it has been asserted, almost singlehanded, without other significant pressures or debate, took the decision to join Singapore to Malaya as part of the new Malaysian federation;[17] but it must also have been in good part the Tunku who decided before long that Singapore was more of an irritant in the federation than out of it. The man with whom he had to deal in both instances was Lee Kuan Yew, Prime Minister of Singapore, who, while he may be accused of having tried to carve out too large a role for himself and his party in Malaya, has been an important moderating influence in Singapore itself. Given the proximity and vast weight of mainland China and the strength of leftist sentiment among the Chinese of Singapore, it is extraordinary that Lee Kuan Yew has been able to maintain as even a balance as he has.

A last example involving a still different method of approach: What difference might it have made for Pakistan if Jinnah had not died so early in the life of the new state for whose creation he was so largely responsible, and what might have been Burma's course if Aung San and six of his principal associates had not been murdered in 1947? Such questions have no answer, and yet they reflect accidents of such historical magnitude as to have a great bearing on the fate of nations.

V

Any effort to predict the role and nature of leadership in even the future which lies immediately ahead is a hazardous venture. De Gaulle, now again withdrawn from power, is quoted as having said at some earlier time that the age of giants is over. For the moment, as was mentioned at the beginning of this essay, this appears to be true, particularly for the more developed countries, but it is a dangerous realm for prophesy since the emergence of "giants" is singularly unpredictable and the recurrence of crises, surely not unlikely in so divided and rapidly changing a world, might thrust forward strong leaders whose full talents had not yet been called upon.

In the countries of the third world some of the leaders who organized the nationalist movements and led them to victory have survived in power,

---

[17] Bernard K. Gordon, "Problems of Regional Cooperation in Southeast Asia", *World Politics* (January, 1964), p. 245.

but a number have already vanished from the scene, either through the normal operations of time or, all too frequently, because they were pushed aside by violent means. While the evidence is still too scanty to build much on, it appears that they are generally being replaced by men who loom less large in the public eye and do not lay as vigorous and highly publicized a claim to heroic stature. It is a rare event that leadership passes from one great man to another as in Nehru's succession to Gandhi; and it might be added that equally striking and rare is the continued governmental succession in India by peaceful and constitutional means as contrasted with the pattern of coups, imprisonments, and assassinations in so many countries. Instead of greatness following upon greatness, the more common sequence was set in the case of Ataturk, the brilliant prototype of the modernizing Third World leader, who was succeeded by lesser figures in Turkey, as have been many of his later counterparts elsewhere.

It may be that in some instances at least a part of the explanation is to be found precisely in the fact that the prior exorbitantly heralded charismatic leadership led to a depreciation of the idolatrous coinage, large segments of the concerned populace turning away in disgust from the public spectacles to which they were constantly exposed. When this was combined not only with a sense of widespread corruption on the part of the political leaders but also with their failure to make much headway toward development, their repudiation and the temporary repudiation of politics and politicians in general followed naturally enough. It should go without saying that even politicians who have been tossed aside may come to be more valued again when their successors demonstrate much the same vices and incapacities as those whom they have replaced—do Nkrumah and his former entourage perhaps rise again in esteem in Ghana?—but the speedy repetition of a regime based on the greatness and infallibility of the leader seems unlikely for present purposes.

Another relevant aspect is presumably that (apparent) freedom of the leader to impose his own personal ideology and inclinations on his country inevitably comes to be limited as time goes by. That that freedom is in large part only apparent comes to be more keenly appreciated when it is recognized that development is a slow and intricate process, often blocked by the relative inertness of the mass which must be carried along. In addition, as the new countries become more firmly and stably established, they develop institutions and commitments which make arbitrary swings at the behest of the leader both more difficult and more unlikely. The apparent freedom, for example, to interpret the almost universally accepted slogan of socialism, capitalism being seen as the imperialistic creed of the exploiter, as falling at almost any point in the spectrum from free enterprise to communism begins to be much more restricted as the new order, however it may be defined, takes concrete shape. The options effectively open to the leader tend to narrow down as time goes by, although it must also be seen as the measure of the greatness of the leader that he can lead a society to decisions which lesser men could not approach. Gandhi could call a halt to revolutionary disobedience movements which were in full swing and de Gaulle could bring about the independence of Algeria.

The other side of the coin, confusing the issue further, derives from the intimate relationship between crises and the rise to dominance of great men. For almost all Third World countries the first set of crises of nationalism, of independence, and of a surge toward development have been, or are being, passed. The adjustments which still need to be made, however, in almost every country as it moves into the modern world are terrifyingly large. In particular, the overturn of the existing order and the way of life of the bulk of their people implies a series of crises through which the developed countries have already for the most part passed, although it is all too evident that more of the same variety may lie ahead of them.

More or less routine governance by civil servants acting with rank-and-file political leaders or a military junta does not seem likely to meet the public demand for both stability and change or to contain the growing pressure of dissident elements. All things considered, it seems more probable than not that many of the Third World countries will again turn for salvation to the man, military or civilian, who gives the appearance of greatness, allowing the mantle of charisma to be wrapped around the leader who promises to guide them through the crisis to harmony and well-being.

27

URBANIZATION AND WORLD VIEW
IN THE MIDDLE EAST *

WILLIAM McCORD & ABDULLA LUTFIYYA

"The city is the teacher of man," Plutarch once commented. And indeed no one who passes through the developing cities of today could deny his observation. In Cairo, flowing *galbiyas* mingle with Western clothes, camels compete with buses, 100,000 students flock to the universities. In New Delhi, jets fly overhead while beggars sleep in the streets, snake-charmers practise their art in front of air-conditioned hotels, bars flourish while men fast to protest the slaughter of sacred cows. In Jakarta, gourmets dine on the cuisine of the Hotel Indonesia, bicycles block the streets, trucks full of military men drive back and forth—while a few miles away religious instructors teach children the ancient method of reciting the Koran in classical Arabic.

The cities and all their accompanying appurtenances—most importantly, their factories—do in fact teach significant lessons. Today, one might expand Plutarch's observation by also noting that the machine—in all of its manifestations from a tiny radio to a giant coke oven—is

* This research was conducted under the auspices of the Center for Research in Social Change and Economic Development at Rice University, Houston, Texas. This Center-sponsored research was supported by the Advanced Research Projects Agency under ARPA Order No. 738 and monitored by the Office of Naval Research, Group Psychology Branch, under Contract Number N00014-67-A-0145-0001, NR 177-909 and National Institute of Mental Health grant 11838-01.

also a potent teacher of men. Yet, what is learned? Despair or hope? Frustration or a belief in progress? Tolerance or confusion? New concepts of time, progress, health, human relations? These are vital questions for the political and economic development of emerging nations, since every observer agrees that these nations are engaged in a sweeping transformation from rural to urban societies.

As Gideon Sjoberg's book, *The Pre-Industrial City*,[1] amply demonstrates, urban centres have existed since the beginning of recorded history.* Obviously, however, cities in developing areas differ from ancient Babylon or Timbuctu in several significant ways. First, they are (to a greater or lesser degree) industrialized. Second, supporting services— water supply, transportation, lighting—have become highly technical. Third, the mass media pervade the city environment. Fourth, contemporary migrants often come from a countryside close to the city and frequently return to their peasant environments. Thus, as Denis McElrath has observed:

> This means that in a very real sense many of these migrants are perpetual newcomers to the cities. . . . They are not yet urban men. For a long time these future urbanites will be oriented away from the cities, sometimes to a tribal village, often to a rural community which no longer exists, to a way of life which is being displaced by industrializing agriculture. . . . They will see the city with peasant eyes, unaware of the requirements of time, money, and urban skills.[2]

Most significantly, the pace of migration to cities has accelerated vastly since World War II. United Nations' reports indicate that urban populations have increased by 100 per cent or even 200 per cent a decade. Cairo has doubled its population in the last twenty years. At its present rate of growth, Calcutta will have some 70 million people by the year 2000. Ankara increased from 23,000 people in 1923 to over 1 million in 1968.

Much of this urban explosion concentrates in one or two urban centres within each developing nation. A United Nation's survey has shown that in Latin America, 16 of 22 nations crowded 50 per cent of their urban population into a single city.[3]

---

[1] See References at the end of the paper.

* In defining a city, we are using the very loose concept of a densely populated region whose people engage in non-agricultural activities to earn their livings. We are fully aware there are vast differences between various cities and that urbanization cannot be viewed as an homogeneous process. For practical purposes in our research, we have defined a *city* as a *metropolitan area* containing 50,000 or more dwellers within its borders.

Historically, urbanization has accompanied industrialization. In the contemporary underdeveloped world, however, it is all too evident that industrialization has lagged behind the pace of urbanization. Increasing population pressures, among other factors, have pushed people to the cities in the futile hope of finding employment. Consequently, a large class of transitional men has been produced: people who have been exposed to the ambitions and titillation of an urban environment but who have not been accommodated within an industrial complex. Exact figures are unavailable. Some of these men are simply unemployed, others eke out a living as street peddlers, still others provide minor services to the more affluent. It is this group of urban pilgrims whom we have labelled "transitionals".

The basic question which we ask in this article is how does the world view of these transitional urbanites differ from the view of the fully urbanized person, as well as from the folk whom they have left behind in the fields, the mountains or the desert. We have confined our research to two Middle Eastern countries, Jordan and Lebanon, but we hope our findings may have relevance to other developing areas. Our essential concern has been to illuminate—but by no means resolve—an issue which has engrossed scholars of social change: Do industrialization and urbanization, once they have come about, entail fundamental changes in beliefs and values?

VALUES AS THE EFFECT OF URBANIZATION

Two groups of scholars—the classic European inventors of sociology and American social scientists who emerged from the so-called "Chicago School" —have concerned themselves with the impact of city life. In many ways their work converged, since they often viewed urbanization as a negative influence on the human condition.

The classic scholars—most importantly Weber, Tönnies, Simmel, and Durkheim—conceptualized social change on a rural-urban continuum. Tönnies viewed the *Gemeinschaft* (typically a village community) as an organic unit, undifferentiated, and strongly integrated, in which individuals shared the same values and beliefs. In contrast, he conceptualized the *Gesellschaft* as a modern, differentiated, utilitarian unit ruled by rational laws which were formulated as a result of compromises between conflicting private interests.[4] Simmel saw the historic trend as the disintegration of the *Gemeinschaft*. Durkheim, too, thought of society as originating in a "horde", a homogeneous group with common customs and beliefs. Tradition ruled society and the group itself was held sacred. As the division of labour increased, a modern society emerged ruled by laws rather than by tradition. The group was no longer sacred, individuals

gained more freedom (for good or ill), and people became more oppor-
tunistic. In his classic *Peasant Society and Culture,* anthropologist Robert
Redfield largely confirmed the speculations of prior scholars with his
empirical observations of village life.[5]

Waves of foreign migration to American cities prompted some of the
most sophisticated investigations of urban life, the works of the Chicago
School. Men like Louis Wirth, Robert E. Park, W. I. Thomas and Florian
Znaniecki thoroughly investigated the impact of an urban environment
upon recent migrants.[6] While some inconsistencies flawed their work,
these scholars presented a fairly uniform point of view. They regarded
the city as an impersonal, anonymous environment which sharply con-
flicted with (and eventually destroyed) the traditional peasant cultures
from which the migrants emerged. The extended family distintegrated and,
especially among second generation Americans, personal disorganization
became widespread. Temporarily, a high rate of crime, alcoholism,
mental alienation, and familial conflicts resulted. Communal solidarity
decreased. While the Chicago sociologists deplored some of the results
of urbanization, they regarded them as a necessary price to be paid for
liberation from the oppressive atmosphere of peasant societies. Once
migrants could become assimilated, they would find greater freedom and
greater opportunities in the American urban setting.

Subsequent scholars have criticized the traditional theories. Is there
truly a rural-urban dichotomy in the present world? Have technical innovations, such as the spread of mass media, made previous distinctions
irrelevant? Is industrialization rather than urbanization the real instrument in transforming man? Is there in fact such a creature as "modern
man"?

Is There A Modern Man?

Among contemporary sociologists, Alex Inkeles (and his collaborators) have
given the most thoughtful consideration to the "modernization" of man.*
Inkeles believes that, "Indeed, in the end, the idea of development requires the very transformation of the nature of man—a transformation
that is both a *means* to the end of yet greater growth and at the same
time one of the great *ends* itself of the development process."[7] While
Inkeles argues that certain new forces—urbanization, education, exposure
to the mass media, industrialization, and "politicization"—contribute to
the creation of modern men, he adheres to the hope that these influences

* We wish to acknowledge with gratitude the thoughtful assistance of Alex Inkeles in this research, particularly for permission to use parts of a questionnaire which
he invented.

will not necessarily conflict with "what is best in the cultural tradition and spiritual heritage" of developing nations.

Specifically, Inkeles conceives of modern men as exhibiting nine qualities:

(1) They are open to innovation, to change, to risk-taking, and to new ideas.

(2) They are "empathetic" and able to form opinions about complex issues which go beyond the confines of their immediate environment.[8]

(3) The modern man is more "democratic", in the sense that he will acknowledge and tolerate differences of opinion.

(4) Such individuals develop a sophisticated sense of time, oriented to the present and future, rather than the past. They can learn punctuality, and thus adjust to the industrial process.

(5) The modern man learns how to plan, to visualize and organize his future.

(6) He abandons fatalism and assumes that events in this world are calculable and open to reasonable human control.

(7) He recognizes the dignity of others, despite their traditional status, and consequently changes his view about the role of women and children.

(8) The modern person evinces greater faith in science and technology as a means of controlling nature.

(9) He holds to the view that men should be rewarded for their contribution to society, rather than their particular status.

Inkeles does not believe that these qualities are limited to particular historical periods. Indeed, he sees the same configuration exhibited in ancient Greece or Elizabethan England. Yet, he does postulate that the traits of modern man are "intimately related to the individual's successful adjustment as a citizen of a modern industrial nation".[9]

Inkeles contends that a number of forces at work in developing nations can transform traditional man into modern man. He assigns pre-eminence to education as to the revolutionary factor. He further suggests that urbanization, with its exposure of the individual to a variety of new influences, can also effect the transformation. He gives important roles, too, to the growth in mass communications, the emergence of the national state, and to the factory environment itself.[10]

Inkeles' portrait of modern man is undoubtedly the most systematic and provocative description of the relation between modernization and values. Currently, Inkeles is conducting research in six nations to confirm his hypothesis (and, of course, our own research reflects directly upon Inkeles' conceptions).

The intention of the research reported here is to illuminate the question of the relation of urbanism and a "modern" outlook on life. In broadest outline, the goal of the study was to question a large number of men from differentially modern segments of the Middle East concerning their basic values. In all, we interviewed 3066 men drawn from desert settlements, peasant villages, and cities. They ranged from sophisticated professionals to illiterate wanderers. Originally, we had hoped to investigate four countries (Jordan, Lebanon, Egypt, and Libya), but the events of the 1967 Arab-Israeli conflict forced us to limit ourselves to Jordan and Lebanon. In significant respects, these two nations differed. Lebanon is, perhaps, the most commercialized and urbanized nation in the Middle East, and one of the richest. It has the largest Christian population and, because of its trading tradition and population structure, has long been exposed to European influences. Jordan has yet to undergo extensive industrialization, although an urban culture has been well established and per capita income has risen substantially in recent years. Jordan is unique, too, in having a large Palestinian refugee population as well as a high proportion of desert Bedouins.

Within each nation, we selected four social groups which differed in the degree to which they had been exposed to an industrial-urban milieu:

(1) *Traditional-Rural Environment*: A sample of men in each country was drawn from that part of the population which lives in an isolated rural area and engages primarily in agricultural work. In each nation, our sample conformed to the cultural configuration of the country: in Lebanon, for example, six traditional samples were selected ranging from Muslims living in the Bekaa valley to Maronite Catholics in the hilly area above Beirut.

(2) *Transitional-Rural Environment*: A sample of men in each nation was selected from villages which had more than the usual exposure to urban influences but had not yet become fully engaged in an industrial process. In Jordan, for example, we found men who worked in urban occupations and yet lived in a rural village.

(3) *Transitional-Urban Environment*: An additional sample of men was drawn from cities such as Amman and Beirut. These individuals had been directly exposed to an urban environment but had not yet been integrated into the industrial process. They were unemployed, or peddlers, or servants to the more affluent.

(4) *Modern-Urban Environment*: Finally, we selected a sample of men from each country who lived in an urban environment and, in addition, currently participated in an industrial or professional occupations. According to present theories, these men should have the most "modern"

set of values. They were selected from such industries as oil refining, cement, canning, and textile factories.

A final word on sampling: because of the very nature of population statistics in the Middle East (Lebanon, for example, does not even attempt to take a census), we cannot claim that our sample is representative in the strictest sense. Rather, we were forced to rely upon our knowledge and our experience in the Middle East to make up what seemed to us the closest replica of a representative sample. Anyone with the slightest knowledge of Jordan, for example, knows of the great differences in background which distinguish Palestinian refugees from desert Bedouins. Consequently, we attempted to get a fair representation of each group. We believe that most Middle Eastern scholars would agree on the standards we used for choosing samples of different regions.

Between 1965 and 1968, we administered a long questionnaire to the various samples. We excluded women from the interviews for two reasons: the great difficulties involved in a stranger talking with women in the Middle East, and, more importantly, the preponderant influence of men in Islamic culture. The questionnaire was administered in the colloquial Arabic of each nation and took approximately five hours to complete. Regional adaptations had to be made (e.g., certain religious practices in Jordan do not exist in Lebanon).

Sections of the questionnaire (on family relationships, birth control, the role of women, and awareness of the outside world) had already been used on small urban and rural samples in Egypt. Other questions (e.g. on psychosomatic ailments) have been used by Alex Inkeles and his colleagues in several comparative studies.

As in all social research, various methodological problems plagued us. It would be ideal, for example, to conduct an extended longitudinal study of peasants who have just arrived in the city and examine the changes which occur. Neither time nor money permitted such an undertaking. Further, one might well expect that those people who migrate to an urban area may well differ in their original characteristics from those who remain in the village; we will attempt, in future articles, to examine this possibility by analyzing the reasons city-dwellers gave for their migration. In the Middle East, the pace of urbanization has been much more rapid than that of industrialization. It seemed probable that city life in itself produced certain changes in attitudes, even for people who could not secure work in an industrial environment. To avoid confusing the influence of industrialism with that of urbanization, we have, therefore, been concerned with analyzing that part of our sample which has been exposed to an urban environment but not to industrial activity. Finally, we would have liked to touch on political attitudes but the delicate nature of the subject prohibited such a venture.

Despite both practical and theoretical obstacles, we hope we have produced the most extensive empirical survey of changes in basic values in the Middle East. We further hope that some of our generalizations can be substantiated in other developing regions of the globe. We recognize, however, that we are dealing with a unique cultural area and that the reader should have some awareness of the peculiar, elusive "Arab identity" which may affect our findings.

VALUES IN THE MIDDLE EAST

Three distinguished scholars—Daniel Lerner in *The Passing of Traditional Society*, Morroe Berger in *The Arab World Today*, and Jacques Berque in *Les Arabes D'Hier à Demain*—have independently produced a comprehensive portrait of Middle Eastern values. None of them, of course, believes that one can describe a single Arab personality that characterizes all people in the Middle East. Nonetheless, Arabs are exposed to a common religious experience, a similar set of institutions, and a historical background which tends to produce a more or less universal set of values.

All commentators on the Middle East have observed the pervasive influence of Islam, a religion which supposedly governs all aspects of life. While Islam certainly has elements receptive to modernization—witness the early scientific discoveries of Moslems—it can also be interpreted as a faith which has prescribed an impermeable form of knowledge, a way of behaving, and a set of beliefs. Seen in this fashion, Islam has often produced a profound fatalism. For many of the rural masses, God has ordained their fate and there is no point (and indeed, real danger) in questioning one's lot in life. As Berger has observed:

> Until quite recently, there was no questioning of this prescribed order of things. Popular belief has held ... that heredity fixes human character in such a way as to make it useless to try to change it; one's nature is fully determined before birth and merely plays out its appointed roles in life.[11]

This fatalism can serve as a serious impediment to technological, economic, or political change. Yet most Middle Eastern scholars are convinced that waves of secularization, unleashed by exposure to modern life, have seriously eroded the bastion of fatalistic religion. Secularism has challenged the old faith and, in the opinion of many, triumphed over religion—particularly among the urban, educated group. The very fact that airplanes now transport pilgrims to Mecca symbolizes the invasion of a new technology into the heart of Islam.

Authoritarianism—in politics, religion, the family, and education—has also long been a companion to fatalistic attitudes. The subjugation entailed by colonial rule undoubtedly encouraged authoritarian attitudes. Many facets of Middle Eastern life testify to the authoritarian trend: the autocratic nature of most governments, the utter submission of students to their professors, the (supposed) absolutism of the father, and the completely secluded role of women in rural areas.

Conservatism, particularly an aversion to risk-taking, has also been noted as a characteristic of the Middle Easterner. True, Arabs have historically been involved in great religious, military and trading endeavors, but the average villager, as Berque has observed, has been ruled by the "heroes of the rural drama: land, water, animal and plant".[12] The peasants have seldom been inclined to alter their relationship with these grand "heroes". According to Berque: "To the Westerner, nature rules but can be mastered if understood; to the Oriental, nature simply rules."[13] The quietude of the peasant has historically engendered contempt among his rulers. In 1865, for example, Muhammad Ali, the ruler of Egypt, commented "The Fellah [peasant] is an animal—kind, docile, laborious: a higher sort of dog."[14]

This conservatism is reinforced by a strong need for security—a desire to feel familiar and comfortable in what is, after all, a threatening, unpredictable world. "The society resists forays into the unknown", as Berger has commented.[15] The Koran itself rejects various forms of risk-taking Even the Arabic language provides conventional phrases, formal and rigid in tone, which can be used to cope with almost any situation. The desire for security results in unusually mannered and polite relationships, designed presumably to reduce the uncertainty of life.

Hospitality has always been a symbol of Arab life. Even today, a stranger must not express admiration for another person's property—for fear that the other may literally "give him the shirt off his back". The kindness and hospitality are all very real, yet some observers believe that fear and hostility motivate a great deal of the politeness. One Arab historian, viewing Syrians and Lebanese, has commented: "Suspicion, fear, restlessness, lack of confidence in the future, lack of social balance and stability are characteristics which the people display."[16] Some of this suspicion becomes manifest in what Berger calls "negative individualism" —a tendency to revolt against any authority, an egotism which prohibits a sense of social responsibility, and an aversion to any form of civic cooperation.

All of these presumed Arab traits—fatalism, authoritarianism, acquiescence to nature, the failure to take risks, the ballet of hospitality and hostility—seem to be undergoing change. The authority of the older generation, the isolated role of women, the supremacy of Islam, have

M-37

been altered by new influences ranging from the mass media to nationalistic movements. As Lerner has summed up the current situation: "The underlying tensions are everywhere much the same—village *versus* town, land *versus* cash, illiteracy *versus* enlightenment, resignation *versus* ambition, piety *versus* excitement." [17]

Because of the pace of change and the sheer diversity of the Arab world, few would attempt to define "Arab" values—or even embark on the kind of research which we have, in the hope that it may have relevance beyond the Middle East. Yet, as Berger has commented, "People interested in the Arab world today want to know simply: what kind of person is the Arab? To the social scientist, such a plain question is exasperating and forbidding." [18] But, Berger adds, "The simple question has a nagging relevance; is it really unwarranted? Unanswerable, perhaps, in a definitive way, but not unwarranted. For that is what anyone, social scientist or not, wants to know about any social group: what kind of people are they?" [19] In the next section, we will present a few of our empirical results concerning the Middle Eastern *Weltanschauung*.

VIEWS OF THE WORLD IN URBAN AND RURAL AREAS

Many of our results bear out the customary theories concerning the relation between one's world view and one's exposure to city life, but in some cases the research produced findings which point to certain unique values held by almost everyone in an Islamic culture. And, in a few instances, certain puzzling results contradict not only the prevailing theories but commonsense itself. Perhaps our clearest conclusion is that secularization and a decline in superstition accompanies urbanization.

Secularization: On every relevant question, urbanized Jordanians and Lebanese indicated less adherence to their religion, although many still practised traditional observances. Moslems are, of course, expected to pray five times a day and also to fast during the period of Ramadan. As the charts indicate, a majority of the most remote peasants do pray (perhaps because of immediate social pressures within their tribe or village) while most urbanites do not. Fasting continues to be a practice of most people, but many urbanites admitted to abandoning this heritage (charts 1 and 2).

A common superstition in the Middle East involves a belief that certain people possess the "evil eye" and can destroy you if you do not take precaution against its force, usually by wearing an amulet. In addition, some people believe that dreams can foretell your future. Both of these beliefs appear to be much less firmly imbedded in the fully urbanized people than in any of the other groups (charts 3 and 4).

CHART 1

HOW OFTEN DO YOU PRAY IN A DAY?

		Traditional Rural (N : 667)	Transitional Rural (N : 815)	Transitional Urban (N : 948)	Urban (N : 1180)
1.	Not at all	10%	10%	10%	50%
2.	One to four times	2	15	4	2
3.	Five times	75	45	35	24
4.	Don't know/no anwer	12	30	51*	24

* The high proportion of transitional urban people who did not answer possibly reflects either indecision or a hesitancy to admit their failure to pray.

CHART 2

HOW MANY DAYS WERE YOU ABLE TO FAST LAST RAMAZAN?

		Traditional Rural (N : 667)	Transitional Rural (N : 815)	Transitional Urban (N : 948)	Urban (N : 1180)
1.	Every day	98%	79%	60%	57%
2.	One to 25	1	10	10	11
3.	None	.05	10	10	20
4.	Don't know/no answer	.05	1	20	12

CHART 3

SHOULD YOU TAKE PRECAUTION AGAINST THE EVIL EYE?

		Traditional Rural (N : 667)	Transitional Rural (N : 815)	Transitional Urban (N : 948)	Urban (N : 1180)
1.	Yes	49%	51%	50%	25%
2.	No	50	49	49	60
3.	Don't know/no answer	1	1	1	15

CHART 4

DO DREAMS FORETELL THE FUTURE?

		Traditional Rural (N : 667)	Transitional Rural (N : 815)	Transitional Urban (N : 948)	Urban (N : 1180)
1.	Yes	20%	15%	10%	9%
2.	No	70	75	80	90
3.	Don't know/no answer	10	10	10	1

It is somewhat surprising to note that every group rejects the traditional superstition about dreams. Nonetheless, one can see from the response to these questions (and others which will be reported in later publications) a clear decrease in religious practice and in superstition as urbanization increases. One can, of course, interpret this finding in a number of ways: perhaps less religious people venture into the city, perhaps the city itself exerts an influence, and perhaps the village puts tighter control over religious practices. Whatever the reason, urbanites seem clearly less interested in the supernatural world than are peasants or Bedouins. As a corollary, one would expect that urbanites would believe that they personally (or the technology invented by man) could influence this world, despite any supernatural forces at work.

Worldly Efficacy: We did indeed find that more urbanites either believed in the efficacy of science in solving world problems or were, at least, unsure on the issue. In one question, for example, we posed these alternatives:

Which statement do you agree with more?

1. Some people say that man will some day fully understand what causes floods, drought, etc.
2. Other people say that such things can never be fully understood by man.

Rural people generally chose the second, more pessimistic response while urbanites either evinced greater optimism or indicated more confusion over the subject (chart 5).

CHART 5

EFFICACY OF SCIENCE

	Traditional Rural (N : 667)	Transitional Rural (N : 815)	Transitional Urban (N : 948)	Urban (N : 1180)
1. Science will be effective	37%	42%	50%	49%
2. Science will not be effective	60	50	20	39
3. Don't know/no answer	3	8	30	12

It became evident, too, that urbanites had a more pronounced sense of their own effectiveness in changing the world or in changing what destiny had supposedly ordained for them (charts 6 and 7).

CHART 6

WILL YOU HAVE ANY INFLUENCE IN THE CHANGES THAT ARE TAKING
PLACE IN THE WORLD NOWADAYS (IN DAILY LIFE AND SOCIETY)?

		Traditional Rural (N:667)	Transitional Rural (N:815)	Transitional Urban (N:948)	Urban (N:1180)
1.	Some/Much	41%	44%	45%	64%
2.	None	30	39	30	22
3.	Don't know/no answer	20	17	25	14

CHART 7

CAN MAN CHANGE HIS DESTINY?

		Traditional Rural (N:667)	Transitional Rural (N:815)	Transitional Urban (N:948)	Urban (N:1180)
1.	Yes	26%	26%	35%	44%
2.	No	70	70	57	44
3.	Don't know/no answer	4	4	8	12

In Arabic, these questions have somewhat different meanings. It would
be possible, for example, for someone to respond that a person can change
the world but still believe that this was his ordained destiny. It is surprising to find that *any* of the traditional rural people believe that they
can be efficacious or that man can change his destiny. These are, however,
rather abstract issues. When one comes down to a more concrete level, such
as a projective question about how hard a man should work, a somewhat
different pattern emerges. In one question, for example, we asked people
to make a complete sentence out of the phrase "The man who works
hard ...." Some people responded with a positive attitude toward work:
"... makes more money," "... gains more," "... is appreciated," etc. Others
regarded the effects of hard work as harmful: "... gets tired," "... gains
nothing," "... dies quickly." Fitting the stereotype of the lethargic peasant,
most of the traditional rural people did not relish the effects of hard
work (chart 8).

Obviously, within our sample, one cannot find a majority of any group
that definitely believes that hard work is useful. Thus, even the urbanites
who believe that they will influence the course of world events, do not
take easily to the concept of working for their goal. The traditional rural
people, on the other hand, definitely oppose the presumed virtues associat-

CHART 8

EFFECTS OF HARD WORK

		Traditional Rural (N : 667)	Transitional Rural (N : 815)	Transitional Urban (N : 948)	Urban (N : 1180)
1.	Positive	28%	43%	44%	47%
2.	Harmful	60	49	54	31
3.	Don't know/no answer	12	8	2	22

ed with the "Protestant ethic". Perhaps, we believed, this aversion to hard work might be associated with fatalism. After all, why should one choose to work an extra amount if one cannot expect unusual rewards?

Fatalism: We have already indicated that many urbanites believe that a man can change his destiny, while a majority of the rural people dis-agree: a finding indicative of a decline in fatalism as people become urbanized. *Other questions* suggested a similar relationship between urbanization and a change in beliefs about fatalism. We asked, for ex-ample, "To be successful in life, what do you need most?" We presumed that the rural samples would assign more importance to luck, fate, or mere chance than to conscious planning for the future. This assumption was confirmed but not as strongly as we had presumed (chart 9).

CHART 9

WHAT DETERMINES SUCCESS?

		Traditional Rural (N : 667)	Transitional Rural (N : 815)	Transitional Urban (N : 948)	Urban (N : 1180)
1.	Luck is all important	21%	12%	10%	1%
2.	Luck is a little more important than planning	28	24	27	35
3.	Planning is more impor-tant than luck	41	50	35	60
4.	Don't know/no answer	10	14	28	4

Clearly, more of the most urbanized people put their faith in planning, but so did a surprisingly high proportion of the most remote, supposedly traditional rural people. Apparently, then, the stereotype of Islamic fatalism is either false or it applied to other peoples at other times.*

* Luck and fate, while often considered as opposites by some people (e.g., the ancient Greeks) are traditionally regarded as synonymous by the Muslims.

Answers to several other questions lend credence to this opinion. We asked whether or not human nature could be changed, on the hypothesis that the more traditional people would regard man's basic qualities as externally fixed. The specific question was: "People sometimes disagree about whether human nature can be changed or not. What is your opinion?" The results contradicted our expectation (chart 10).

CHART 10

CAN HUMAN NATURE CHANGE?

		Traditional Rural (N : 667)	Transitional Rural (N : 815)	Transitional Urban (N : 948)	Urban (N : 1180)
1.	Yes, for the better	80%	72%	69%	50%
2.	Yes, for the worse	0	0	1	1
3.	No	9	11	10	10
4.	Depends on circumstances	5	14	10	10
3.	Don't know/no answer	6	13	10	19

Only a minority of every group believed that human nature cannot change; one more sign that fatalism is not a prevalent characteristic of the Middle East.* Oddly, the traditional rural people appeared most optimistic about the possibility of man changing for the better. Conceivably, the modern urbanites had, in fact, seen more change in people than the rural sample and, as a result, had become somewhat more confused about the results.

One other question bore on the apathy which one usually associates with fatalism. In an attempt to examine the material aspirations of the people, we asked, "Suppose an ordinary man has a good house and can feed and clothe his family well enough. Some people would say that this is enough. Other people would say that a man should always strive for more material goods. Which statement do you agree with more?" (chart 11)

While the most urbanized people exhibit a greater tendency to strive for material goods, it is quite clear that the "revolution in expectations"

* Although fatalism is a common attitude of Islam, one also finds many pronouncements in the *Qur'an* (Koran) and in the *Hadith* (sayings attributed to the Prophet) suggesting that hard work leads to success in worldly affairs. One *Hadith* in particular indicates that the working man is more religious than the non-working man, and that work and achievement are essential parts of the Muslim's faith. The Muslim is indeed expected to labour hard, to achieve, to improve his lot and to be prudent with his money. It is also believed that the Almighty may alter the world for the better if the faithful would offer sincere and continuous prayers requesting such change.

CHART 11

MATERIAL STRIVING

		Traditional Rural (N: 667)	Transitional Rural (N: 815)	Transitional Urban (N: 948)	Urban (N: 1180)
1.	Greater striving is bad	20%	15%	10%	10%
2.	Greater striving is good	71	80	81	84
3.	Don't know/no answer	9	5	9	6

has swept both the rural and the urban areas.* All of our results point to the conclusion that fatalism, if it ever existed, is now dead in Jordan and Lebanon.

Since fatalism implies a certain concept of time—living in the present and accepting it—we hypothesized that the more urbanized group would put greater emphasis upon planning for the future. In addition, we expected that the urbanites would have developed a concept of punctuality which would distinguish them from the rural sample.

Sense of Time: Without planning, without an orientation to the future, and without a careful calculation of time, no nation can embark upon a path of "modernization" or industrialization. Consequently, we thought it important to investigate the relation between urbanization and the concept of time. At first glance, it appears that people in rural and urban areas harbour the same concept of planning and time. As one question, we asked, "People are different in how much they like to plan and arrange their affairs (lives) in advance. Would you say what you yourself prefer?" (chart 12).

CHART 12

PLANNING

		Traditional Rural (N: 667)	Transitional Rural (N: 815)	Transitional Urban (N: 948)	Urban (N: 1180)
1.	To plan ahead carefully in most matters	68%	66%	49%	58%
2.	To plan ahead only in a few matters	13	17	18	10
3.	To let things come without working	15	13	18	9
4.	Don't know/no answer	4	4	15	23

* These results may appear to contradict the previous finding that many people in all areas regarded hard work as harmful. We think, however, that a person may very well aspire to more material goods but quite naturally dislike the hard work which may be necessary to achieve these benefits.

Clearly, the only pattern which emerged was that most people, regard-less of where they fell on a rural-urban continuum, had some abstract concept that planning was desirable.

In their concept of the utility of a timetable for their work, the rural and urban people again did not differ strikingly. We asked urban people, "Some people think that a factory should be run with a strict time schedule of work (fixed time for everything; fixed timetable). Others think there should be less concern with time in a factory. What do you think?" The same question was also asked of rural people except that we substituted the word "farm" for "factory". In general, the various groups agreed that a strict timetable was necessary either on a farm or in a factory. Among urbanites, 66 per cent of the transitional urbanites and 52 per cent of the completely urbanized people believed that a strict timetable was "good and necessary". Among rural dwellers, 70 per cent of the traditional peo-ple and 56 per cent of the transitional ones agreed that farms should also be worked on a planned schedule.

In the abstract, therefore, most people have apparently assumed a "Westernized" concept of time and planning. Yet, we knew from our own and other ethnographic studies that rural people in the Middle East often do not behave in accordance with the views they express.[20] There-fore, we asked a more indirect question concerning the concept of time which, we believe, reveals more about the actual thought processes and behaviour of Middle Easterners than the abstract questions. A rural-urban difference did appear when people were asked, "How long would it be before you would consider a friend who is late in meeting you to be a *little* late?" (chart 13)

CHART 13

CONCEPT OF "LATENESS"

		Traditional Rural (N:667)	Transitional Rural (N:815)	Transitional Urban (N:948)	Urban (N:1180)
1.	15 minutes	15%	30%	37%	55
2.	16 to 60 minutes	51	61	44	37
3.	Over an hour or never	19	8	17	8
4.	Don't know/no anwer	15	1	2	0

Clearly, in viewing their personal relationships with other people, only a handful of the rural traditional people have a concept of punctuality while a majority of the most urbanized people have a highly developed sense of time. On balance, therefore, it would appear that most Middle Easterners have accepted an ideal that people, factories, or farms should be planned "on time". In fact, however, in their personal relationships, only the urbanites adhere to the ideal. The sense of time is clearly related to "risk-taking", for only if one is oriented to the future is it possible to conceive of sacrificing past or present goods in the hope of achieving a better future.

Risk-Taking: Almost all theories of economic development postulate the need for entrepreneurs or "high-achievers" who are willing to take risks as the central impetus for change. And many theorists, such as Hagen, have conceived of the traditional peasantry as unwilling to take risks. Our results, while confusing, do not support this assumption. In general, we found almost all segments of the population willing to take risks.

On a number of questions dealing with responsibility and initiative, the rural people did not differ strikingly from the urbanites. On three of these questions, we asked people to complete unfinished sentences. The results can be seen in charts 14, 15 and 16.

CHART 14

WHEN THE MACHINE WOULD NOT WORK THE MAN

	Traditional Rural (N : 670)	*Transitional Rural* (N : 815)	*Transitional Urban* (N : 947)	*Urban* (N : 1180)
1. Fixed it	53%	47%	54%	49%
2. Stops working	30	35	33	38
3. Others/don't know	17	18	13	13

CHART 15

WHEN OFFERED MORE RESPONSIBLE WORK THE MAN ...

	Traditional Rural (N : 670)	*Transitional Rural* (N : 815)	*Transitional Urban* (N : 947)	*Urban* (N : 1180)
1. Did it	47%	48%	47%	50%
2. Refused it/Got tired	29	31	26	27
3. Others/don't know	24	21	27	23

The general conclusion from these charts is clear: many people both in the countryside and the city say they are willing to assume responsibility and take initiative. To the degree that these responses can be trusted, they lend credence to the belief that a pool of entrepreneurs exists anywhere in the Middle East.

CHART 16

WHEN A WORKER THINKS OF A NEW AND BETTER WAY OF DOING THE WORK

	Traditional Rural (N:670)	Transitional Rural (N:815)	Transitional Urban (N:947)	Urban (N:1180)
1. He does it the new way. ...	40%	33%	32%	35%
2. It is good/should tell the boss	33	46	56	55
3. Other/no answer	27	24	12	10

Another question indicated the willingness of rural people to adapt to innovations. Indeed, traditional rural people seemed even more willing than transitionals, in this case, to use a new type of plough (chart 17).

CHART 17

WHEN THE CULTIVATOR GOT A NEW TYPE OF PLOUGH. ...

	Rural Traditional (N:672)	Rural Transitional (N:915)
1. He uses it/production increases	82%	67%
2. Don't know/other	18	33

Another question, put in the form of a story, indicated the willingness of all segments of the population to accept change (and, incidentally, a rather equalitarian concept of the father-son relationship). The story was this:

Two twelve-year old boys took time out from their work in the cotton fields. They were trying to figure out a way to grow the same amount of cotton with fewer hours of work.

1. The father of one boy said, "That is a good thing to think about. Tell me your thoughts about how we should change our ways of growing cotton."

2. The father of the other boy said, "The way to grow cotton is the way we have always done it. Talk about change will waste time but not help."

Which father said the wiser words?

The results are set out in Chart 18.

CHART 18

CHART 18

	Traditional Rural (N : 675)	Transitional Rural (N : 814)	Transitional Urban (N : 995)	Urban (N : 1182)
1. The first father	86%	87%	70%	74%
2. The second father	12	10	14	16
3. Don't know/other	2	3	16	10

Human Relationships: Many of our questions implicitly dealt with human relationships, but two findings in particular have relevance to understanding the world view of Middle Easterners. In order to ascertain the people's concept of cooperation, we asked: "If you saw that a job needed to be done at your work which someone else should have done, would you do it?" A majority of every group responded affirmatively, although the most urbanized people appeared more reluctant to give aid:

PERCENT WILLING TO DO SOMEONE ELSE'S JOB

Traditional Rural	81%
Transitional Rural	87%
Transitional Urban	82%
Urban	65%

The reasons which people offered for helping someone else indicated a wide gulf between rural and urban people. The rural folk most often cited a "particularistic" reason, such as helping a fellow worker, for their cooperation. Urban people, on the other hand, most often cited reasons of self-interest or called upon an abstract concept such as "cooperation is necessary for the success of the enterprise" as their justification (chart 19).

CHART 19
REASONS FOR COOPERATION

	Traditional Rural (N : 575)	Transitional Rural (N : 712)	Transitional Urban (N : 771)	Urban (N : 775)
1. Help a fellow worker	85%	55%	49%	39%
2. Self-interest (e.g., "please the boss")	9	29	22	34
3. Cooperation is good	0	11	19	17
4. Don't know/other	6	5	10	10

Clearly, friendship does not create a cooperative attitude among urbanites while it is a paramount motivation among traditional rural people.

One other finding should be reported: distrust of strangers permeates our sample, regardless of whether the interviewees come from rural or urban areas. When we asked, "When you meet someone for the first time, what should you do?" The vast majority of every group said they would distrust him (chart 20).

CHART 20

TRUST OF STRANGERS

		Traditional Rural (N:667)	Transitional Rural (N:815)	Transitional Urban (N:948)	Urban (N:1180)
1.	Trust him until he proves untrustworthy	9%	8%	9%	9%
2.	Distrust him	90	90	89	90
3.	Don't know/other	1	2	2	1

This nearly universal distrust of newcomers is, in our experience, a common cultural characteristic of the Middle East. A critic could justifiably comment that this pervasive distrust undermines all of our findings, for why should one trust a strange interviewer by revealing one's actual views? We recognize that distrust may well bias our findings. Yet, we still have confidence in our general results. First, the distrust is apparently so common, it can be regarded as a "constant factor"—nonetheless, certain differences in opinion did distinguish rural from urban people. Second, since the respondents could not possibly know our ultimate goal, it would be impossible for their distrust to bias the findings in a consistent direction. Third, in the most sensitive area of inquiry—such as religious practices—one would expect the most lying. Undoubtedly, some people did lie, but it was exactly in these delicate areas of questioning that the greatest urban-rural differences appeared, and made sense in terms of prevailing sociological theory. Consequently, while we have found that distrust permeates the Middle Eastern atmosphere, we do not believe that this pervasive caution about strangers has consistently, in an understandable way, invalidated our findings.

CONCLUSIONS

From our findings, a variegated picture of the Middle Easterner emerges; a portrait which, in some ways, contradicts the usual stereotypes about the nature of Arabs and the effects of urbanization. In some respects, urbanites do seem to adhere to a different view of the world than rural, more traditional people:

Urbanites are more secularized and less superstitious.

Urbanites more often put their faith in the ultimate efficacy of science and technology.

Urbanites believe that they can influence the course of events.

Urbanites more often believe that man can change his destiny.

Urbanites more often said they believed in hard work—but a majority of neither urban nor rural people appeared convinced of the utility of hard work.

Urbanites seemed more future-oriented and more convinced that planning rather than luck would determine their future. Nonetheless, all groups believed that planning would be useful in their personal lives.

Urbanites were least willing to do the job of a fellow worker. If they did help someone else with a job, they seemed motivated by self-interest or abstract considerations about the welfare of the enterprise. Traditional-rural people, in contrast, overwhelmingly cited friendship as their justification.

Transitional urbanites, on many issues, seemed the most confused in their orientation.

Thus, urbanism does coincide with new ways of looking at the universe, at oneself, and at others. Yet, regardless of the rural-urban continuum, a majority of our sample apparently agreed on certain opinions. Every group believed that human nature could change, everyone aspired to better material conditions, and almost all demonstrated a willingness to assume initiative, accept responsibility, and adapt to changing conditions. On a theoretical level, the rural as well as the urban people had a similar concept of time (although in their personal relationships, urbanites put much greater emphasis on punctuality). In two significant ways, therefore, our entire sample contradicted two stereotypes which prevail about Middle Easterners: First, they do not, as an entire group, seem resigned to a fatalistic approach to life; second, they expound a number of attitudes which many theorists regard as prerequisite to modernization. These are, on the whole, hopeful findings. One must admit, however, that the distrust which seems to permeate the desert, the village and the city may well hinder civic cooperation and respect for the rights of others.

Our conclusions must, of course, be regarded as tentative. We have not in this article explored the possible relationships of age, education, social class, exposure to the mass media, or national origin to the person's world view. It is quite conceivable that any one of these variables would have a greater effect than urbanization itself. In future publications, we will examine the influence of these variables in detail. Nonetheless, we already know that urbanization has a high correlation with these factors: urbanites tend to be younger, better educated, richer, and more exposed to the mass media than traditional rural people. Consequently, on a provisional basis, we may conclude that a new world view does accompany the process of urbanization but that many of the opinions held in the Arab countryside do not, in themselves, militate against the modernization process.

REFERENCES

[1] Gideon Sjoberg, *The Pre-industrial City*, Free Press, New York, 1960.

[2] Dennis McElrath, "Introduction: The New Urbanization", in *The New Urbanization*, edited by Scott Greer, Dennis McElrath, David Miner and Pater Orleans, St. Martin's Press, New York, 1968, p. 6.

[3] John Duand and Caesar Palaez, "Pattern of Urbanization in Latin America", *Millibank Memorial Fund Quarterly*, 1965, 43, 4, Part 2.

[4] See, for a classic example of their writings, F. Tönnies, *Community and Society*, Michigan State University Press, East Lansing, 1957.

[5] Robert Redfield, *Peasant Society and Culture*, University of Chicago Press. Chicago, 1956.

[6] For diverse examples of their writings, see Louis Wirth, "Urbanism as a Way of Life", *American Journal of Sociology*, 44, July, 1938; Robert E. Park and Herbert Miller, *Old World Traits Transplanted*, University of Chicago Press, Chicago, 1925; and W. I. Thomas and Florian Znaniecki, *The Polish Peasant in Europe and America*, Dover Publications, New York, 1958.

[7] Alex Inkeles, "The Modernization of Man", Chapter 10 in *Modernization*, edited by Myron Weiner, Basic Books, New York, 1966, p. 138.

[8] This particular quality is well investigated in the excellent work of Daniel Lenner, *The Passing of Traditional Society*, The Free Press, Glencoe, Illinois, 1958.

[9] Inkeles, *op. cit.*, p. 150.

[10] *Ibid.*, p. 144.

[11] Morroe Berger, *The Arab World Today*, Doubleday, New York, 1962, p. 176.

[12] Jacques Berque, *Histoire Sociale d'un Village Egyptian XXéme Siécle*, Mouton, Paris, 1957, p. 9.

[13] Jacques Berque, *Leçon Inaugurale*, 1 December 1956, College de France, Paris, pp. 14-15.

[14] Nassau William Senior, *Conversations and Journals in Egypt and Malta*, ed. M. C. M. Simpson, Sampson Low, Matston, Searle, and Rivington, London, 1882, Vol. 1, p. 273.

[15] Berger, *op. cit.*, p. 175.

[16] Nicola Ziadeh, *Syria and Lebanon*, Benn, London, 1957, p. 237.

[17] Lerner, *op. cit.*, pp. 44, 83.

[18] Berger, *op. cit.*, p. 154.

[19] Berger, *Ibid.*

[20] See Abdulla Lutfiyya, *Baytin: A Jordanian Village*, Mouton, The Hague, The Netherlands, 1966,

28

POLITICAL THEORIES AND
POLITICAL REALITIES

Institutionalization and Participation—Their
Contribution to Democracy in the New States

HUGH TINKER

THE VOCABULARY of political science has recently acquired a cluster of terms in consequence of the coming into fashion of the concept of modernization/political development. We have all ceased to speak of westernization: meaning the transplantation of "western" political concepts in Asia and Africa, such as parliament, an independent judiciary, press and political parties. In part the change arises from a very proper recognition that within a brief period of time the idea or the institution becomes "nationalized" so that to compare the Indian Parliament with Westminster, and assess its performance by reference to the Westminster model is now quite irrelevant. But our preference for modernization instead of westernization also comes from an acknowledgement that the "western" (i.e. Anglo-American) political pattern of the first half of the twentieth century can no longer be regarded as the ultimate form of the evolution of democracy. The so-called "two party system", for example, has obviously fossilized and shrivelled democracy in both the United States and Britain the realignment of parties and programmes in terms of social and economic change has failed to occur in both these countries because both

580

are held within the two-party system straitjacket, and political protest has been compelled to find expression outside the established party network. The rise to supreme power of the USSR and the emergence of political structures quite different from the Anglo-American model in the other major countries—India, China, Pakistan, Indonesia, Brazil, Japan —make it obvious that the modern world has rejected westernization. And so we have substituted the word modernization: but without attempting to reassess our fundamental terms of reference as western-trained political scientists. We are still stuck in the old grooves: we think in terms of "competitive politics" or the "multi-party system" or "the dominant party system". We haven't really revised our basic Anglo-American belief in political institutions expressed in terms of competing ideologies and competing parties.

Moreover, modernization has its own traps as a term of art. Modernization: from what? We may have escaped from the crude dichotomy, colonialism/independence, but we appear to have fallen into another false dichotomy: tradition/modernity. Tradition is what is old. Modernity is what is new. Modernization consists in replacing the former by the latter. This form of thinking still appears to satisfy the economists, though political scientists confronted by the inescapable continuance of the power of the past in the most revolutionary situations are compelled to recognize the falsity of the dichotomy, and some have now evolved the concept of "the modernity of tradition". Even these revisionists continue to argue in the context of political development: the umbrella term under which so many take shelter.

What is political development? The plain answer seems to be that it is the political equivalent of economic development. If we ask the economists for their definition of that term we shall receive a hundred answers. Perhaps some might settle for "raising the standard of living: not merely absolutely, but by comparison with all the other countries of the world". How do we relate this definition to political development? One popular index seems to be that of *participation*, which might also be called political productivity. The more people in general that play a significant role in the political process, the more it is developed. But how do we measure the process? One example of an attempt to demonstrate a scientific scale of measurement is presented in *State Politics in India*, edited by Myron Weiner (Princeton, 1968), and to this we shall shortly turn. Another indicator of development is termed *mobilization*. The military derivation of the term may be implied in the idea of the drafting of people from a rural, traditional organic society into an urban, industrial, mechanized structure under direction, or under control or policy-planning from the centre. A third index is that of *institutionalization*. Traditional society is supposed to be non-specialized, with leadership exerted either on an ascriptive basis (squire, lord, prince) or from leadership which has multiple functions (the priest as teacher, scribe, lawgiver; or the soldier as policeman, tax-collector, or administrator). In a modern situation, leadership is supposed to crystallize within specialized structures, the politician in his party, the bureaucrat in his department, the journalist on his newspaper. The more developed and specialized these structures become, the more is a system institutionalized and modernized.

Now, these terms of art have not really provided us with a new, scientific technique of political analysis. And acceptance of any one implies acceptance of the others. They exhibit an obvious osmosis. Political development/modernization/mobilization/participation/institutionalization: all are siblings of the now defunct sire of westernization. But it is much easier to dissect and dissolve the new techniques of political science which emerge from North America than to suggest a more appropriate system of analysis. The purpose of this essay is confined to establishing a more exact understanding of the two key concepts, *participation* and *institutionalization*; with the suggestion that modern Indian social and political philosophy may have a significant contribution to make towards determining what constitutes development, and what regression in terms of these concepts.

First we may identify contemporary American application of the two concepts, participation and institutionalization. It is the conclusion of the authors of *State Politics in India* that development of either feature hinges upon development of the other: the two are complementary. First, participation is identified "as an act of selecting and influencing governmental personnel" (p. 32) which in effect means taking part in elections. A high poll is equated with high participation. In distinguishing why certain states of the Indian Union score high voting levels, the authors point to urbanization, literacy, and "high indices of communication" (that is, a higher circulation of newspapers, more roads, and more radios, than in the low-voting states). In addition to these factors amenable to quantitative assessment, the states of high participation are also identified as areas where the "freedom struggle" was particularly important during the British period: on the assumption that this involved the mobilization of the masses into the political process.[1]

Myron Weiner and his associates measure participation, political development and mobilization by rather simplistic determinants. Their assessment of the institutionalization is even more simplified. They write:

---

[1] The authors do not explain why Uttar Pradesh, the epicentre of the national movement, together with Bihar, also an area of strong nationalist activity, are almost at the bottom of the table of states if participation is measured by voting, literacy and urbanization (see p. 33).

If we view the number of candidates who failed to retain their deposits (indicating the number of individuals [i.e. minority, or independent candidates] unable to judge their capacity to translate personal influence into electoral votes) as one measure of institutionalization, then we can rank states along this simple index. Using these criteria, Uttar Pradesh was the least institutionalized state and Kerala the most institutionalized. (p. 41)[2]

The rationale of this deduction seems to be that where several candidates stand, party politics must be at a primitive level, whereas if only one, two or three parties put up candidates, the political process has attained a high level of sophistication, or institutionalization. This reasoning has too may flaws to be convincing. There is a mass of evidence from many countries to show that when election by popular choice is first introduced, parties are too poorly organized to contest more than a limited number of seats. Thus candidates will be returned unopposed: no election, no forfeiting of deposits. When political parties have attained an advanced level of organization they may still avoid elections in backward, reactionary areas (e.g. the British Labour Party seldom contests seats in Northern Ireland), while in areas of greatest activity, the marginal constituencies, there will be a concentration of all the political parties and multiple contests. Under the British—and Indian—systems, where there are more than three candidates *one* is almost certain to lose his deposit. But keen competition is usually a sign of high politicization, not the reverse.

However, *State Politics in India* is untroubled by any doubts about the method of measurement of institutionalization, and the authors feel confident enough to assert that

The institutionalization of political participation through political parties seems most pronounced in states with large-scale participation, least in those with least participation.... India is one of the few developing countries in which political participation at the constituency level is institutionalized into a party system. (p. 43)

While this equation of participation with institutionalization remains the most fashionable view among American political scientists, the opposite case has been stated by Samuel Huntington in "Political Development and Political Decay" (*World Politics*, April 1965). He insists that partici-

---

[2] In India (as in Britain) anyone wishing to stand as a parliamentary candidate must deposit a sum of money with the returning officer. If he fails to obtain one-eighth of the total vote he forfeits his deposit. This is intended to deter frivolous candidates.

pation has outpaced institutionalization. It is the latter, he claims, which provides the framework of modernity: he will categorically "identify political development with the institutionalization of political organization and procedures" (p. 386). He also states that "Participation distinguishes modern politics from traditional politics" and quotes Almond and Verba (*The Civic Culture*) who wrote: "If there is a political revolution going on throughout the world it is what might be called the participation explosion." (p. 388) However, this kind of venture into modernity may breed not political development but decay: with an echo of the military derivation of mobilization he warns: "people can be demobilized out of politics". The remedy is a concentration on building up central political institutions. In the United States, when the President is active, this works for the good; when passive, for bad: "Institutional interest coincides with public interest. The power of the presidency is identified with the good of the polity." (p. 413) The next step is to declare that "The existence of political institutions (such as the [US] presidency and the [Soviet] Presidium) capable of giving substance to public interest distinguishes politically developed societies from underdeveloped ones" (p. 415), and finally "Modernizing states with multiparty systems are much more unstable and prone to military intervention than modernizing states with one party, one dominant party, or with two parties." (p. 247)

Thus, Huntington's concept of political institutionalization is of the Party in Power. The public interest is identified with strong government. The success of a system may be judged by its capacity to rule effectively. Huntington agrees with Weiner that institutionalization may be equated with the simplification or rationalization of party politics; the refinement of free competition into oligopoly (once again the parallel with economic theory is obvious). But Huntington is barely concerned with the electoral process as a basic element in modernization, whereas the Weiner school feel able to base their assessment of performance (productivity) on high levels of voting at elections.

How far does either the Huntington formula—the creation of efficient engines of government (institutionalization), or the Weiner formula—the mobilization of the public to vote by means of efficient party organization (participation), help us to understand how democracy works? John Bright observed in 1876: "Many persons are shut out from any participation in political power." But the extension of the franchise, which he expected to remedy this situation, ended in mass alienation. Today, in Britain, there is a sudden realization that a mood of cynicism has entered the national life because the over-development of political institutions ("big government") has left the ordinary voter feeling excluded and impotent. Richard Crossman, Labour Cabinet Minister and erstwhile Oxford politics teacher, examined the problem in the 1968

Granada Lecture. He distinguished "participatory democracy ... of which the constitutional form is parliamentary government, and plebiscitory democracy, of which the constitutional form is presidential government". Crossman went on to indicate that the institution of parliament was failing at the present time: "The basic aim of participatory democracy is to develop the individual's power of decision and choice.... Participatory democracy was intensely alive, argumentative, awkward —in fact, a drag on strong government." In Britain today, plebiscitory government has assimilated the parliamentary system: popular participation, limited to general elections, is inadequate: "Parliament ceases to be an active mediator between government and people and becomes the forum where government and shadow government do propaganda and counter propaganda." Crossman draws the conclusion that "The public's reaction to our democracy today is ... a growing alienation through the feeling that people are mattering less and less."

Much the same unease is expressed among British Conservatives. A party policy paper, *Make Life Better* (1968) includes this passage: "We in Britain are rightly proud of our system of parliamentary democracy. But democracy in many countries has collapsed. Because the politicians did not trust the people, and did not involve them in the process of decision-making. Or because the people did not trust the politicians and became alienated from them." And finally here is Enoch Powell, speaking as Tribune of the Plebs: "Whole sections of the population ... are treated with contempt as incapable of understanding great issues of politics. It is sufficient for them to know that their betters have these complicated matters well in hand. Their own part is just to pay up and shut up: in short to be governed." (Speech 23 October 1968)

If British politicians of the Left and the Right are united in concluding that institutionalization has diminished participation and produced an alienation of the electorate which could lead—even in Britain—to total disillusionment with parliamentary government, they are less specific on the necessary remedies. Crossman observes rather sweepingly: "I believe it is vital that this sense of alienation [among the public] is removed ... by reviving active participation at all levels." The Conservative manifesto, *Make Life Better*, merely suggests that participation can be encouraged "By bringing back honest and competent government. By not overloading the Houses of Parliament with legislation." There is little original thinking here; and for an honest acknowledgement of the difficulty of achieving participation in the face of institutionalization we must go to a work by the former leader of the Liberal Party, Jo Grimond. In *The Liberal Challenge* (London, 1963), subtitled "Democracy Through Participation", he observes:

Today, one of the main tasks of the Left is to widen the area of participation. It is difficult to achieve this in the old ways when the scale of government and industry has grown so big, when populations have increased and so much of the old group life in villages or crafts has disappeared. If we are to have more participation by more people we have to think in new patterns. (p. 26)

What, in my view, is required from political activists and political theorists alike is a revolution in our conception of representative government. Because of institutionalization, and the stratification of politics, with the parties forming a quite distinct segment of the polity, and the public yet another, we have accepted a one-way traffic system in which the sole function of the electorate is to make a very limited choice (the two-party system is only one step away from the one-party system) at fixed intervals of time. Having given a *mandate* to a set of rulers, the electorate's function is then to be ruled. There is no traffic the other way, with the representatives coming back to the electorate to report and consult. The necessity for a new relationship was well expressed by Eugene McCarthy in his campaign manifesto *First Things First* (1968). This was his estimate of the power excercised by the President of the United States:

He should understand that this nation does not really have so great a need for the imposition of power from the top, because the potential for excellence and leadership exists in every American. The President must be a channel for the desires and aspirations of the people. He must never impose the weight of his office upon the nation, but rather guide it to the goals its people seek, largely by way of setting people free.

While the Western politicians laboriously search for means to realize the ideal of participation—without which democracy loses its fundamental meaning—Indian political and social philosphers have provided us with the key to the dilemma.

The greatest of India's modern thinkers have realized how hollow is the whole notion of development or progress. Here is Rabindranath Tagore:

You have to judge progress according to its aim. A railway train makes its progress towards the terminus station—it is a movement. But a full-grown tree has no definite movement of that kind, its progress is the inward progress of life. It lives, with its aspiration towards light tingling in its leaves and creeping in its silent sap.

A belief in organic growth, in the community, in humanity—and a suspicion of mechanical expansion, aggregated in organization and order, is found in the most profound modern Indian thinkers. The whole of Gandhi's life and teaching was directed to showing that politics is about people, not power. He insisted that Indians would only govern their country (in any meaningful sense) when they had learned how to govern themselves: "Self-government is self-rule, which is self-control." His political strategy rested upon the belief that not only leaders but led would be involved in a mutual movement. Hence that insistence upon manual labour—spinning and weaving, and sometimes sanitary work —in which the privileged would share with the deprived. Hence also Gandhi's pilgrimages into the depths of the countryside. Above all. the philosophy of *satyagraha*, emphasizing the truth as the foundation of politics and sacrifice as the means whereby men could attain political goals. Words were only a guide to a politics of *action*: not the mindless mass action of totalitarian movements, but action by individual decision. Gandhi's style—combining austerity, self-discipline, dignity, and an immense awareness of human relationships, was an essential part of the philosophy.

Gandhi began by thinking that his vision could be realized—could achieve success—within measurable time. His first campaign in South Africa probably came near to the ideal of *satyagraha* more completely than any later campaign. His followers were mainly the poor labourers, artisans, who had nothing to lose but their chains. They understood, almost instinctively, that they had to make their sacrifices for the good of the community; giving, not expecting to receive. Gandhi, despite his Western veneer, was always an Indian of the Indians, and he achieved complete rapport with these simple folk. The South Africa campaign was successful, in that uneasy consciences were stirred, and a settlement was negotiated. Gandhi returned to India, expecting a similar response. He even announced "Swaraj within one year": but increasingly he discovered that the sophisticated lawyer-politicians, and the urban middle classes with their itch to get ahead of the others were an imperfect vehicle for his experiments with truth. He was complled to become an example through his own fasts, in order to influence the British rulers and his own followers alike. Before his death, Gandhi knew that contemporary India had failed to understand the meaning of *satyagraha*. At the end he condemned the Congress leaders, running after power: "Such is our bankruptcy", he said. His last testatment emerged as a cry from amid the encircling gloom:

What should we do then? If we would see our dream of panchayat raj, that is true democracy, realized, we would regard the humblest and the lowest Indian as being equally the rulers of India with the tallest in the land. This presupposes that all are pure, or will become pure, if they are not. And purity must go hand in hand with wisdom. ... Everybody would regard all as equal with oneself and would hold them together in the silken net of love.... Everybody would know how to make an honest living by the sweat of one's brow and make no distinction between the intellectual and physical labour.[3]

The thinking of M. N. Roy, which began from an opposed position to that of Gandhi (conceived in strictly politicized terms of Party and State), attained the same conclusion: that politics is made for man, and not man for politics. When Roy designed a constitition for free India (1945) he called it 'Organized Democracy' and founded it in local people's committees: he named the local unit the 'co-operative commonwealth': the same term Gandhi employed for village government. But he looked for the ulterior solution to the problem of democarcy in the creation of personal freedom, in order to achieve 'the unfolding of man's rational, moral and creative potentialities'. He rejects an economic solution; likewise he rejects a party solution:

Having reduced man to impotence, politics degenerated into a scramble for power between groups of people calling themselves parties. Though the party system is believed to be the essence of democracy, it has done more harm to democracy than anything else. It has reduced democracy to demagogy.... In all probability, those who make the big promises may really want to do good things. But engaged in the game of power they must play it according to the rules.... Degraded to the formality of counting heads, democracy does not bother what is in the heads. If the heads are empty of sense, the party getting the largest number of votes will have the largest amount of ignorance as its sanction.[4]

Having thus exposed the pretensions of those who believe that institutionalization is a creative element in democratization, Roy acknowledges that the politicians are unlikely to heed his warning: "People engaged in party and power politics cannot take a long view. Laying foundations is too long a process for them. They want a short cut." He therefore sees the future of democracy reposing in the hands of those outside of party politics, prepared to carry out the long, unrewarding task of political education among the ordinary people. However, Roy believes that they do achieve a positive end:

[3] *Mahatma: Life of Mohandas Karamchand Gandhi*, by D. G. Tendulkar, Delhi (1960-63), Vol. VIII, pp 253-54.
[4] M. N. Roy, *New Humanism: A Manifesto*, Calcutta, 1947 (2nd ed. 1961), p. 38.

When a man really wants freedom and to live in a democratic society he may be able to free the whole world ... but he can to *a large extent at least* free himself by behaving as a rational and moral being. and if he can do this others around him can do the same and these again will spread freedom by their example.[5]

The ideas of Gandhi and of Roy have been restated and interpreted by Jayaprakash Narayan. Again, he insists that institutionalization represents a blind alley:

> Democracy does not merely consist in its formal institutions. It lives, really and truly, in the life of the people. ... It is not only through the representative assemblies and elected governments that democracy works, but in an equally true sense through the voluntary associations and actions of the citizens.... Professor Harold Laski, when asked how he would judge the worth of a democracy replied that he would do so by the amount of voluntary activity in it.[6]

JP sees the contemporary dilemma as "how to recreate the human community". At present the polity (in India and elsewhere) is represented by "an inverted pyramid": it is top-heavy, with a swelling bureaucracy aggregating power at the top and the people denied the opportunity to express themselves at their own level. JP does not deny the need for organization encompassing all India; but he insists that authority must flow upward. This includes the all-important planning function which has been so excessively centralized in India.

In portraying the polity which will help India to recreate a "communitarian society", JP uses Indian terms. He wants to see the transformation of the politics of power and of the state (*rajniti*) into the politics of humanity (*lokniti*) under the law of the community (*gram dharma*). "The function of *dharma* is to hold together harmoniously the social order," he says; but not the social order of the past, based upon status and heredity, condemning some to perpetual inferiority, but a classless, casteless society embracing *sarvodaya*, "the uplift of all".

The system of *Panchayati Raj* which now covers India does not really answer JP's needs. It has brought the party into the village through the elections for representatives contested on party lines; and the new party lines have intensified old lines of division on the basis of faction. Unless local democracy attempts to function through harmony, true con-

---

[5] M.N. Roy, *Politics, Power and Parties*, Calcutta, 1960, p. 196.
[6] Jayaprakash Narayan, *A Plea for Reconstruction of Indian Polity*, Kashi, 1959, p. 8.

sensus, based on equality and brotherhood, it will contribute towards the total breakdown of democracy :

> Self-government through faction-fighting will not be self-government but self-ruination. . . . If this state of affairs continues there is danger that in a few years everyone would become so sick of the very word panchayat that government from above through bureaucratic civil servants would be welcomed with open arms and people's democracy would have been declared a total failure and a chimera.

Here then, is a brief and inadequate account of modern India's great contribution to political theory and the actual functioning of politics: an exposure of the falsity of institutionalization as a pathway to democracy and a revelation of the real meaning of participation as a continuous process fructuating within society. Why, then, it will be asked, has political India been influenced so little by this philosophy? And has not India demonstrated a major achievement in the field of institutionalization by the dominance of the Congress Party, the drive of centralized planning, and the control of a technically highly developed administrative pyramid?

It would be the argument of the present writer that political India has functioned in two different spheres: the formal and the informal. In the formal sphere, the procedures, the regulations, the rules of institutionalization have been followed. Informally, the structure has functioned and adapted because it has to a large extent assimilated itself to the social network. For a long time the Congress party was able to straddle the political stage because it provided a market-place for trading between all the interests of Indian society. The Congress never represented a "dominant party system"; it did represent a "reconciliation system". Now the arena of politics has been enlarged, and the Congress is merely the most important element among many elements. If we accept the model of institutionalization, we shall look for the emergence of one or perhaps two strong competing parties; perhaps the Jan Sangh on the Right and the Communists on the Left, to provide a firm institutional framework. Instead, we are seeing a proliferation of parties. The Congress, which has mothered several new parties, is giving birth to more. The Communists, so monolithic in other lands, are fracturing into half a dozen sects. Individual politicians, and groups are "floor-crossing", defecting and returning and defecting again. All this must fill the institutionalists with dread. But if we dare to take Gandhi and Roy and JP seriously, then we shall be less worried. All this may be some way from the goal of partyless democracy, which they have cherished. But it certainly represents participation. Here are people making individual choices, and asserting that parties are for politicians. not politicians for parties. *Rajniti* is giving way to *lokniti*. The motives of these men may be far from those of truth and sacrifice. But in most cases their actions arise from a sense of membership of a living community and not of subordination to a lifeless power-structure. Can India recognize that the post-1967 political situation represents a stirring of the pot by authentic Indian ladles? Localism and communalism may have their dark implications: but they also represent the genius of the Indian people. If India can forget the stereotypes of Westminster and Washington, then the fluidities of contemporary politics may flow into their own courses.

But can Indian leaders tear themselves free from the stereotypes of modernization and development which seem to enslave them in what is the real neo-colonialism: an acceptance of other people's fashions as the only respectable and legitimate fashions to follow. I will end with some thoughts by an Indian writer which appeared in the community development journal *Kurukshetra*:

> The common needs of environment and the sharing of problems of living are the essence of community development: and the mechanical age is breaking through it. Our country has not gone as far as the West. Individual and social happiness, with all the things it involves, is the ultimate goal. Social desires will have to be created which will result in small, self-managing communities. It seems as though it could still be achieved in India, and her "backwardness" is one definite advantage from this point of view.[7]

Can Indian leaders have the courage to be non-Western, and therefore "backward"? Previous passages in this essay tried to demonstrate that there is a growing awareness among British political leaders that "modernization" achieved through institutionalization has diminished our capacity to be, fully, ourselves. India has an immense potential resource in the philosophy of Gandhi, Tagore and others who understand what participation really means. More might be attained by realizing this resource than by turning to the knowhow of the West.

in India, R. Braibanti & J. J. Spengler, Eds, Duke University Press, 1963, p. 131.

[7] The author is K. S. V. Raman: cited in "The Village in the Framework of Development" by the present writer in *Administration and Economic Development*

29

POLITICAL MODERNIZATION IN INDIA: CONCEPTS AND PROCESSES

YOGENDRA SINGH

THE STUDY of political modernization has become quite an attractive theme for social scientists these days. Specially in the "new nations" there is a spate of such studies both by social scientists belonging to these nations and those from abroad. One could not, however, be sure that in the conceptual frameworks and underlying pre-suppositions in the study by these two types of scholars, there is always common outlook. There are many obvious reasons for this probable difference. These range from historical to existential. There has been no attempt to categorize the variations in the conceptual orientation of modernization studies so that the perspective of these studies could be analyzed. In that light probably it would also be possible to place the process of political modernization in a more comprehensive and historically relevant frame of reference.

In this paper we have first tried to categorize the types of methodological and conceptual orientations that underlie most studies of political modernization as revealed by the contemporary literature on this subject. Of course, examples have been chosen selectively for methodological individuality and representative character. These approaches have been further examined in terms of their relevance for study of political modernization in India. The analysis of selected issues in the substantive realm of modernization has been attempted following this conceptual analysis. The focus is mainly on the examination of the process of political modernization in terms of the bearing that social structure and cultural traditions in India have on this process.

APPROACHES TO POLITICAL MODERNIZATION

We can review the literature on political modernization on the basis of two types of theoretical considerations: first, in regard to formulations concerning the nature and direction of this process emerging in different societal situations, and secondly, in terms of the conceptual components or variables that are used to determine the direction and process of modernization. In the first sense (nature and direction), the formulations concerning political modernization could either be "evolutionary" or "relativistic". The evolutionary approach is based on the presuppositions that all societies will ultimately evolve a similar structural and cultural form of modernization, despite their historical dissimilarities, and that the historical factors will only determine the sequence of the evolutionary stages rather than their direction. The "relativistic" approach on the other hand recognizes the possibility of divergent patterns in modernization owing to diversity of historical traditions.

On a conceptual basis or in terms of variables the treatment of political modernization can be classified as being "systematic" or "componental": the former being oriented to analysis of modernization in terms of macro-structural variables and the latter trying to analyze this process with the help of isolated micro-level variables often selected for reasons of operational feasibility rather than architectonic coverage. The systematic approach may utilize groups, classes or even large-scale social systems such as national societies as units for analysis in modernization; or political modernization may be analyzed even in global perspective. The essential element in this type of analysis is the presupposition that modernization proceeds through transformations in the system as a whole and that the process operates teleologically towards its goal. On the other hand, the componental approach is usually focused on studying the interaction between selected variables that operationally define the process called "political modernization" and which are arrived at by a process of abstraction from case histories of political modernization in various societies. Here too the unit of analysis may be a single society or a set of societies, but this is not relevant. What is relevant is the extent to which interdependence of variables is demonstrated to be generating or thwarting political modernization.

When we combine the above two sets of approaches to the analysis of modernization into a single paradigm we get four types of orientation in the study of political modernization; these are: "evolutionary-systematic", "evolutionary-componental", "relativistic-systematic" and "relativistic-componental".

The evolutionary-systematic approach is to be found mainly in the writings of the Marxist and neo-Marxist analysts of modernization. It postulates a single and uniform ultimate destiny for all societies, irrespective of their divergent historicities. The political modernization that it attributes to society is characterized by rational anarchy, classlessness, and equality and freedom in all spheres of life. It also postulates a state of "real democracy" and "true liberty", but the means through which it is to be realized are intermittent revolutions until the final stage of evolution has been realized. The treatment of political modernization by such thinkers has a world-system perspective and the main analytical concept used is that of economic force which, being the social substructure, is supposed to determine the whole superstructure—the social, cultural and political institutions of society. The process of evolutionary modernization is, however, governed by the progression of social conflict at the global level between nations and at the national level between classes. The conflict is resolved only when the ultimate societal destiny that embodies the value-frame of modernization is realized.

The evolutionary-componental approach to political modernization is on the other hand non-Messianic but this too assumes certain universal sequences in the growth pattern of all societies towards modernization. This is believed to happen through a series of stages, and although the sequence of these stages might be arrested in the time dimension in different societies, yet the direction does not change and the sequence is not reversed without also creating structural conflict. Talcott Parsons' "evolutionary universals" are a good example of this kind of formulation (Cf. Parsons, 1964). In his formulation we find that structural universals of modernization emerge from primordial and pre-modern universals. The primordial universals are: "religion, communication with language, social organization through kinship, and technology"; the pre-modern universals being, social stratification and cultural legitimation, and, from these, modern universals such as, "bureaucratic organization", "money and the market complex", "generalized universalistic norms" and "the democratic association" evolve in stages. Parsons grants unevenness in the process of growth of these universals but the structural attributes of modernization he assumes to be universal. Political modernization, according to him, finds its highest symbolization in the democratic association "with elective leadership and fully enfranchized membership".

A significant difference between the evolutionary-systematic and evolutionary-componental approaches to political modernization is that the former emphasizes the process of conflict or revolution through which structural changes occur and growth is realized; these processes being located not only within the social system concerned but also outside, as often the contradictions might emerge from inter-system economic inequalities and hierarchies. Even when contradictions originate mainly within the system these have aggregative or collective properties based on group conflict. The Parsonian model, on the other hand, does not assume such conflicts as being the prime mover of modernization. The causal importance is given by Parsons to biological and demographic compulsives for the survival of the human species which lead to evolutionary adaptations and these tend to be selective, syncretic and universal.

The third, the relativistic-componental approach may be found in the writings of most contemporary political scientists belonging to the behavioural and comparative-developmental schools in political science (Cf. Almond and Coleman, 1960; Almond and Powell, 1966; Almond and Verba, 1963; Pye, 1966; Riggs, 1964 and R. Bendix, 1964 etc.). The analysis of political modernization as attempted by these scholars tends to focus on selected components. Almond and his associates have formulated nine such functional components such as socialization, recruitment, interest articulation, interest aggregation, political communication, rule making, rule application, and rule adjudication. For each component, functional properties of modernization are postulated in structural and cultural terms. Political modernization is thus associated with progressive differentiation of structural forms and functions related to these variables. It is, however, granted that the specific manner in which these variables affect the political system is different in each society owing to the historicity of the sequence in which these components are articulated and institutionalized. For instance, Lucian W. Pye postulated six types of crises through which political modernization begins in the developing countries. These are the crises of identity, legitimacy, penetration, participation, integration and, finally, distribution. His contention is that the sequence in which these crises develop in different societies may not always be uniform and to that extent the historicity of political modernization could differ from society to society. Similarly, other sets of components have been formulated by other political scientists.

Finally, the fourth typology is of the relativistic-systematic approach. Here, the attempt is to "explain" and not only demonstrate the functions of the processes of political modernization; it is said that "the study of functions is not a study of causes, and a theory of Political Development must be a theory of causation" (Myron Weiner, 1965). The treatment thus begins with the analysis of a system as a whole, and the inter-relationship between systems is analyzed in the context of historical forces. The analysts here assume the relevance of historicity called "initial conditions", or "inheritance situation" of different societies in the process of political modernization. These conditions tend to determine the process of political modernization with the help of the pre-existing institutional forces which are different in each society so that universal uniformity in the form of modernization is not always achieved. Moreover, in this approach, the treatment of the process of modernization is such that the role of conflict, revolution and indigenous political movements towards modernization of political structures is accepted (Cf. Myrdal, 1968; Weiner, 1965; Levy, 1966; Horowitz, 1966; Nettle and Robertson, 1968). The system orientation in the analytic framework is thus maintained without a presupposition of a universal evolutionary direction in modernization.

A Conceptual Model for Political Modernization in India

In the light of the above four approaches, it may be possible for us to evaluate which conceptual formulation is most relevant for analyzing the Indian phenomenon of political modernization. To our mind, the historical-relativistic formulation tends to be the most appropriate. In contradistinction with Western modernization, modern political institutions and norms established in India have not been entirely or even mainly a contribution of its orthogenetic tradition. They are, on the contrary, a matter of historical inheritance from the colonial past. The contingency in their growth was not evolutionary but historical, and this fact should materially alter the frame of reference in which the process of political modernization is analyzed in the Indian context.

Political modernization in the accepted sense of the term assumes universality of a political consensus based on political individualism or citizenship role. The organization of the political system through governmental and party administration, the communication of political values and ideologies, and the interplay between various political groups—such as national and regional political elites, their followers etc.—are expected to be rationally constituted in bureaucracies through wider structural differentiation of political roles and statuses. Hence, a modern political structure is supposed to be not fused but differentiated, not holistic but individualistic, and not hierarchical but corporate. The question that arises is: how far is this conceptual model of modernization relevant for an analysis of political modernization in India? Is the implicit dichotomous formulation of structural differentiation a universal sociological reality? Social scientists have increasingly pointed out the simplistic assumption that may be involved in such a view of modern structure. Here we may quote from Nettle and Robertson on modernization:

Objectively speaking, the stipulations of the structural differentiation model are inadequate in terms of the societies to which it can be applied. In the use of the theory of structural differentiation in the conventional manner we find one of the main reasons for the equation of modernity with Western liberal democracies. The idea of structural differentiation owes much in its evolution to the economic concept of the division of labour in capitalist or neo-capitalist societies. In fact, culture-boundedness in conceptualization and classical economistic tendencies are both prominent features of the intellectual uses to which the structural differentiation concept has been put. For one thing it has not lent itself readily to the analysis of authoritarian and totalitarian societies. Using the degree of structural differentiation (in terms of the specialized and interdependent separation of major institutional sectors and particularly their respective collectivities and role complexes) as an "'index" of modernity, analysts have designated authoritarian and totalitarian societies as pre-modern on the grounds that the manifested degree of differentiation is low in relation to that of many Western societies. Sometimes the adoption of authoritarian or totalitarian patterns has been interpreted under the concept of de-differentiation (or structural homogenization), a process which logically involves the fusion of collectivities and roles previously separated on a specialized basis. Whilst not denying that this is an empirically discoverable occurrence, we would prefer to speak of compressed structural differentiation, notably in reference to Communist societies. By compressed structural differentiation we mean the process whereby differentiation (particularly in the economic and political spheres) occurs under intensive and extensive elite surveillance. In such a process the elite "compresses both time and the social order". In other words, whilst the members of the political elite assume and/or indirectly control (or at least attempt and claim to control) strategic, frequently multirole, positions in all "key" areas of society, this does not mean the proliferation of specialized and separated political and economic tasks does not continue apace. Nor does it mean that concrete organizations cease to multiply on interdependent-specialized (as well as segmented) bases. It may well be argued that in accordance with such a definition of compressed structural differentiation, contemporary Britain and France are certainly in some respects more akin to the Soviet Union, as a matter of degree, than conventional wisdom suggests. (*Op. cit.*, pp. 45-46)

This leads us to an important issue in conceptualization of political modernization. What is being attacked is the prevalent one-sided or unilinear formulation of modernization of political structures. Modernization may not only involve progressive differentiation but also "de-differentiation" or fusion of roles at certain level of growth. But the more important bearing of this formulation lies in the corollary that it may not be necessary for all social systems to attempt to achieve the same degree of individualism, rationalism and specialization of roles in the political and other structures in order to realize the goal of political modernization. The authors refer to the Maoist approach in China where the very basis of specialization of roles is being systematically challenged to reduce the paradox of over-bureaucratization in the process of modernization. And does not bureaucracy introduce through specialization a trained incapacity among incumbents which may be exploited? Does it not lead to impersonalization and through that to alienation? How can we achieve political modernization without also thereby institutionalizing inqualities, this time not based on birth but on the theory of relativity of reason and skill?

The question assumes added significance for Asian societies which suffer a good deal from lack of material resources and are over-populated. In these societies institutions of political modernization borrowed from Western societies create structural and emotional disbalances which have all the potentiality to push the system towards radical breakdown or in the absence of that to a protracted state of conflict and decadence. They may also have another dangerous consequence, that of political fragmentation or forced unity based on some kind of totalitarianism. It might be useful to analyze the trends of political modernization in India in the light of these structural hazards.

Our purpose, however, in highlighting this point is different. We intend to draw attention to a significant historical episode in Indian political life which, to our mind, did recognize the need for developing an alternative model for political modernization in conformity with the orthogenetic limitations of Indian society. This episode was the emergence of Gandhi on the Indian political horizon and his alternative to modernization.

We will, therefore, analyze some important aspects of political modernization in India, taking into account the above consideration. First, we shall analyze the structure and process of political modernization in the contemporary Indian situation and its emerging contradictions. We shall particularly refer to structural and cultural contradictions. Then we will also hypothesize how different and probably more effective would have been the extent of political modernization in our country had we seriously either followed the Gandhian alternative or at least had faithfully integrated some of the salient elements of his model into the model of political modernization which we have adopted.

POLITICAL MODERNIZATION IN INDIA

The process of political modernization in India should be analyzed in two stages, before and after Independence. Overarching these stages is the cultural and political encounter of India with the West which laid down most of the basic themes and values of political modernization. Thus emerged the foundation of civic rights, an equalitarian legal system, courts and administrative structures, the concept of nationhood and parliamentary government, the party system, a series of constitutional Acts, rational bureaucracy, army and legal profession and educational institutions which today form the basis of India's modernity. The growth of these institutions was historically determined and uneven in magnitude and significance. During the pre-Independence period it was highly localized, persisting only in a subcultural and substructural form. During this period too the major contemporary ideologies such as those of secularism, militant nationalism, communalism, liberal democracy, Marxism and Gandhism came to fruition and established the historical contingency of cultural forces which even to this day overshadows the processes of political modernization in India. Outstanding among these several currents was the contribution of Gandhi, on the one hand, and, on the other, the challenge it faced from the Western ideology of democratic liberalism and its cultural manifestation—Westernization.

The conflict and the contingency of these two ideologies formed an element in the "inheritance situation" for political modernization following Independence. Gandhism, which was never rationally accepted by the majority leadership in the Congress party, including Nehru, was disowned by free India. It persisted only as a peripheral movement. On the other hand, the liberal-democratic tradition was further consolidated: its salient features were the establishment of a federal constitution, a parliamentary democratic system, the creation of linguistic states, the integration of numerous princely states in the Union and rationalization of the judicial-administrative structure in conformity with the new political idiom.

Latent in this process was the ideological legacy of socialist and democratic liberalism which envisaged a transformed social structure for India, based on economic and social equality, freedom, secularism, and social justice. In a society which was mainly rural, ridden by caste, tribal and regional loyalties, this was an uphill task, but the objective was set, to be realized through economic planning. The three major sectors to be mobilized for this purpose were, *human, industrial* and *agricultural.* For human development an educational policy was adopted by most states aimed at the abolition of illiteracy and widening of educational opportunnities. Industrial policy resolutions formulated a controlled mixed economy, and agricultural improvements were sought to be realized in two stages: first, through the abolition of vested interests in the rural social structure through land reforms and, secondly, through the Community Development Programme and Panchayati Raj. As soon as planning was launched the factors which were contingent to it emerged in sharp relief; these were: dependence on developed nations and foreign aid, dependence on bureaucracy, both developmental and administrative-technical, to keep the process of planning going and dependence on political leadership and party mobilization to communicate the new ideology of welfarism and social justice. All these levels of dependence would have rendered the process of political modernization ridden with tension right from the beginning but for some major historical factors: these were, (a) single-party rule in the country; (b) homogeneity of the political and bureaucratic elites in the cultural and economic structure; (c) the cold war between the USA and USSR which accentuated the process of courting the third world nations for their support, and finally, (d) the collective euphoria of the Indian elites on Independence, reinforced by the compliments of the Western democratic nations on India being the first new nation in Asia to follow the liberal-democratic path to social transformation. These factors reinforced the subsequent process of political modernization which were actively pursued in India and which slowly led to the structural-cultural contradictions which India encounters today.

STRUCTURAL ASPECTS OF POLITICAL MODERNIZATION

An important structural change in India's political modernization which took place following Independence was the shift of emphasis from the mass-politics of Gandhi to the elite politics of Nehru. This elitism persisted purely as a result of structural constraints under which the political system had to function right from the village panchayats to parliament. It will be our purpose to analyze some of its ramifications and their bearing on the contemporary political process in India. For this, important structural isolates would be: (a) social structure and political party system; (b) social stratification and concentration of power and political resources at the levels of (i) caste, class and party, and (ii) elites and bureaucrats; (c) the growth of regionalism and regional disbalances; and finally, (d) structural compulsives of future trends in political modernization.

SOCIAL STRUCTURE AND PARTY

The unique historical situation in India in respect of the growth of political parties is their development without the disintegration of the status principle in social structure. In the West, parties emerged as political interest groups (as distinguished from political factions) following the breakdown of estates and the acceleration of the industrial revolution. With the breakdown of estates, the nexes of primordial loyalties were replaced by secular-rational ones and this helped in modernization through the growth of parties. The other distinctive features in the West were the more extensive utilization of the press and higher levels of literacy. These circumstances have been absent in the case of the growth of parties in India. Here, the social structure took one long jump from status direct to party, without any intervening class transformation. Consequently, the growth of political parties was more dictated by historicity than by the dialectic of social forces. This historicity can mainly be identified with the progressive disintegration of the Indian National Congress. Prior to Independence, the Congress was not a political party in the technical sense of the term, but a platform for collective mobilization. This is why it could become the source of so many new political parties emerging from within its fold in the changing contingency of historical circumstances.

Another important feature of the Congress and also of other parties in India was their subcultural-substructural representation. The members of the middle-class professions, urban traders, lawyers, landlords and doctors, mainly constituted these parties; incidentally, most of them belonged to the upper and intermediate castes as well. Hence, membership of a political party far from cutting across social stratification, fully conformed to it. The only exception in this regard was once again the Gandhian viewpoint, but Gandhi did not believe in the system of political parties. Hence, as the process of political modernization began with these parties in the arena, led mainly by the Congress, contradictions slowly began to emerge.

These contradictions can be briefly indicated by pointing out some of the major trends in party formation in contemporary India: (a) progressive disintegration of the Congress; (b) formation of political parties of a purely regional character; (c) a continued process of internal schism within each party based on primordial loyalties but rationalized in terms of ideologies; (d) a shift in the ideology of parties from urban to rural class interests owing to the progressive articulation of the rural sector in political life, and, finally, (e) the lack of an all-India perspective in the ideology of newly emerging political parties.

In time sequence these developments took place gradually as the extent of politicalization of the social structure increased through the spread of modernizing networks, developmental ideologies, the adverse demonstration effects of affluence of some sections in the rural and urban areas and the heightened sense of regional political identity articulated by the panchayats and the Community Development Programme.

In our opinion, the main reason for these contradictions lies in the defective approach to economic planning and measures of structural reform. Paradoxically, the proposed socialistic goal of planning in India never rid itself of the theory of economic voluntarism of the early nineteenth century Western ideology. The result was that planning in India could not root out social and economic inequality; land reforms were undertaken half-heartedly and the concentration of economic resources among certain classes increased instead of decreasing. This economic contradiction coincided with the status versus class contradiction in the Indian polity.

In contemporary India it appears as if the contradiction of status-party overlap in political articulation is running full cycle after the loss of many states by the Congress in the elections of 1967 and the break up of the Congress Party. These processes, to our mind, are not accidental but are an articulation of the trends which were latent in the political organism of the Congress party. The serious consequence, however, of these developments to the political modernization in India is quite evident It puts new pressures on the unity and the federal structure of the nation; it highlights the possible instability of the system or even the probability of its breakdown. It may, however, also test the capacity of the inherited political institutions for newer adjustments to work out an equilibrium. It is here that the relationship between social stratification and politics assumes added significance.

SOCIAL STRATIFICATION AND POLITY

Social stratification articulates the inequality in the distribution of power and sharing of norms. The caste system has been the main embodiment of the Indian system of social stratification, and recent studies have shown that this institution has not withered but has actively responded to political demands of social stratification through the formation of caste associations.

The manner in which caste in Indian politics is transformed into caste association is indicative of the response of the Indian social structure to emerging structural contradictions of political modernization. If we analyze this transformation in terms of the emerging structural contradictions of political modernization in India we find that the caste system offers a very apt means through which the entire gamut of the relationship between social structure and modernization can be studied. Many studies of relationship (cf. Weiner: 1962; Bailey: 1963; Srinivas: 1964; Brass: 1965; Beteille: 1966; Rudolph and Rudolph: 1970; Kothari: 1970) have brought out diverse patterns. On the basic question, the extent to which the caste system enters into the political process in India as an integrative or segmental force, there is no unanimity of opinion.

There is one trend, however, that has been widely noted. Castes have been increasingly mobilized for obtaining political support both at the state and national levels of political participation. This could be indicative of political modernization, depending upon the value frame with which modernization is defined. If we define modernization in terms of the classical liberal-rationalistic value frame derived from the West, we may not find in the contemporary mobilization of caste in Indian politics fuller correspondence with that ideology, caste being rooted in a segmental and particularistic universe of social intercourse and social relationship. But, should this value frame in the definition hold true for all societies irrespective of their historicity? Here, opinions may differ. In our view, the process of modernization, as also its form, will differ from culture to culture depending upon the structural individuality of each society. It is for this reason again that increasing consolidation of caste organization following its political articulation should not be taken as an indication of increasing casteism, a non-modernizing phenomenon. Kothari (*op. cit.*) rightly observes:

Politics is a competitive enterprise, its purpose is the acquisition of power for the realization of certain goals, and its process is one of identifying and manipulating existing and emerging allegiances in order to mobilize and consolidate positions. The important thing is organisation and articulation of support and where politics is mass-based the point is to articulate support through the organisations in which the masses are to be found. It follows that where the caste structure provides one of the principal organisational clusters along which the bulk of the population is found to live, politics must strive to organise through such a structure. The alleged "casteism of politics" is thus no more and no less than politicisation of caste. It is something in which both the forms of the caste and the forms of politics are brought nearer each other, in the process changing both. By drawing the caste system into its web of organisation, politics finds material for its own design. In making politics their sphere of activity, caste and kin groups on the other hand get a chance to assert their identity and to strive for positions.

Assuming such a process in the mobilization of caste, the tradition-modernity conceptual dichotomy loses its significance except as a purely heuristic device. Through politicization the structure of caste undergoes only marginal changes as corporate organizational mechanisms emerge. Within the system both fusion and fission continually go on as the interaction of principles of status (birth), class (economic position), and power within the caste system keep on changing the balance of inter-caste and intra-caste relationships. Accordingly, caste as a unified social structure sometimes enters and sometimes withdraws from political participation (Paul Brass: 1965; Hardgrave, Jr.: 1969). The process does not involve a neat transformation of caste into class but highlights variations in the transformation pattern for which caste and class only provide a boundary situation.

As a component of social stratification caste influences politics in India through the functioning and emergence of dominant castes. We find two stages in which the modernization process has been influenced. In the first stage, political modernization remained confined to the traditionally dominant castes, such as Brahmins in the South and Peninsular India, and Kshatriyas, Brahmins, Bhumihars, Kayasthas and other upper castes in Northern India. At this stage, political modernization kept its purely sub-structural form; it was the Politics of the "entrenched" castes as Kothari aptly describes it. In the second phase, these entrenched castes or dominant castes began to be challenged by lower-middle castes through a slow process of political mobilization and increasing political consciousness among them. This took almost a decade to happen even after India's independence. In the second phase, non-Brahmin castes in the South, the Marathas in Maharashtra, the Patidars in Gujarat, the Kurmis and Ahirs in Uttar Pradesh and Bihar, the Jats in Rajasthan and Haryana, etc., slowly emerged as new contenders for power. These "ascendant" castes, in the language of Kothari, tend to introduce a new dynamic element in the political modernization of the country. An important result is that, with these changes, the mass character of Indian politics which was lost in the early years of freedom has slowly again begun to assert itself. The elitist nature of politics is being not so much changed as transformed.

The ascendant castes operate through a new type of elite which identifies with the rural cultural symbols, language and style of life, and works its way upward in the political network of the national levels through exploitation of regional and local identities. In this process, a series of political middlemen or political brokers emerge (cf. Mayer, 1966) who serve to keep the political linkages between the local, regional and national levels of interaction alive and articulate. In this process the mass-support and influence-base of these regional elites occasionally gets widened, as in the process of political competition or movement when some local leader champions causes that have a wider affective involvement of the public, such as formation of new states, protection of linguistic identity, allocation of resources and industries, etc. On these occasions, mass feelings are articulated and heightened to such a pitch that a success realized on such issues, even though championed by a regional elite, might add charisma to his political status and calling. This is how charisma works in politics, through political mobilization on issues thrown up by historicity as well as by design. The elites of the "ascendant" castes who generally occupy lower positions in the traditionally strong political parties, tend to break away from the older organizations and form new political parties as arenas for their own status ascendance in political leadership. Thus, social stratification also influences stratification of political elites and through variant patterns of mobilization engenders as well as institutionalizes political charisma.

Social stratification has been helpful in making political modernization possible in India without conflict between "entrenched" and "ascendant" caste groups and their leadership, only up to a point; that is, during the early phases of sub-cultural, sub-structural modernization. Since caste had a good deal of structural autonomy, tensions did not appear when one segment of it (the upper-middle castes who first Westernized) took to modernization. Its pluralism helped in modernization only as long as political values and aspirations had not reached all the caste strata; but now, when this has happened, structural contradictions have had to emerge as they do at present. Today, the ideology of modernization has become a diffuse phenomenon through the length and breadth of the social structure and its peculiar historical characteristic is such that it promotes fission as well as fusion in the segment of social stratification.

Another structural contradiction which stratification has brought into being through political modernization is the progressive dissociation and conflict among the various types of elites, especially political elites on the one hand and bureaucratic (either business, military or administrative) elites on the other. Some scholars have, of course, disputed any such dissociation (Cf. Beteille 1967; Bottomore, 1967), but we would suggest that the problem needs further investigation. With increasing emphasis on primordial-regional symbolisms in political articulation, political elites increasingly come under pressure to reflect the regional norms and identities from which they derive support. Under these pressures, the echelon of political leadership might put forward demands for "committed" bureaucracy and "committed" judiciary etc. and seek in this guise to carry ideology to the bureaucrat's desk. Pressures for radical stances generated by local circumstances might thus engender new conflict situations between the political and the bureaucratic elites. There is evidence in India that such a process has already started. This trend should, however, be scrutinized with great care since it is pregnant with radical and unforeseen consequences.

REGIONAL DISBALANCE

The differential rates of economic growth in various regions too might have an impact upon the process of political modernization. But the extent to which economic growth may really enter into the political process would depend upon the manner in which other sociological variables combine with it to render it politically more effective. Sociological studies have shown that actual deprivation, economic or social, does not matter as much in people's evaluation of the betterment of their life chances as does their *perception* or *evaluation* of deprivation. Education, political mobilization and communication may be such important variables. In this respect communication holds an important position. If the rate of economic growth in a region is slow but the communication multiplier is high, there may develop radical political movements, depending upon a suitable combination of other variables.

Now, in the light of this a complicated problem for political modernization arises. On the one hand regionalism engenders primordially motivated parties, and on the other regional disbalances of economic growth cannot be removed without significant central aid and intervention. How can this dilemma be resolved if the political leadership tends more and more to veer towards regional interests? The same problem holds with regard to the removal of economic inequalities among various groups. The solution of these problems demands structural elasticity in Centre-State relations but not to the point of the emaciation of the power of the Centre. Institutional mechanisms which maintain the superiority of the Centre should not be given up in a huff or in the face of regional pressures as far as the mediating and balancing role is concerned. This is necessary purely in the interest of distributive justice among regions, communities and classes.

From the above analysis the salient structural compulsions for political modernization in India that emerge are mainly distributive justice and economic growth. Other factors follow from these two. The twenty-two years of planning have certainly contributed to an increase in industrial resources and national income. Recently, a break-through in agriculture in terms of high productivity through new seeds and use of fertilizers has followed, and it appears that in the aggregate the growth rate may be further increased. But how do these patterns of growth affect social stratification, distribution of opportunities and sharing in political power? Here the picture is sadly discouraging. With every increase in national productivity, concentration of economic power in certain sections and classes has increased; the poor man has become poorer and the opportunities for him remain closed in structural terms. Industrialization has created some occupational mobility, new role structures and job opportunities, but only a small segment of the population has benefited from this and this does not include the poorer and the most needy ones.

CULTURAL ASPECTS OF POLITICAL MODERNIZATION

The relationship between the Indian cultural tradition and political

modernization can be understood through the extent to which established cultural institutions in India are concomitant with the political culture of modernization. The question immediately arises: how shall we
define a modern political culture? In the contemporary literature on this
subject we find that modern political culture is equated with "civic culture", to borrow the term from Sydney Verba and G. Almond, or it is
equated with institutionalization of the universalistic norms of democratic associations. In both formulations, the notions of individual cit-
zenship and civic rights and privileges based on constitutional guarantees
are implicit. The enfranchisement of the citizens is only an extension of
this principle of civic freedom. It is then postulated that, as traditional
societies move towards political modernization, this concept of individual and citizenship roles emerges from the traditional background of
communal and group-based solidarities and identities. The normative
base of the culture of political modernity thus lies in the citizenship
idea.

Postulated in these terms, the relationship between traditional culture
in India and the political culture of modernity assumes significance. It
is particularly so because since Max Weber an array of Western social
scientists has denied that the concept of the individual existed in the
normative framework of the Indian culture. Louis Dumont has recently
offered analytical confirmation of this well-established standpoint. His
view is that the only equivalent to the concept of the individual in the
Indian tradition is that of the "sanyasim" or the renouncer. The question
thus arises: how shall we reconcile the democratic political system of India
which is founded upon the idea of the individual citizen as the unit with
the denial of this role in the traditional Indian society?

The question is to our mind wrongly posed. All traditional societies
laid emphasis upon collectivity and the idea of individual rights and
responsibilities slowly emerged in the normative structure of these societies in the process of differentiation through modernization. It is quite
possible that societies that are in the transitional stage of the modernization process might well be using traditional collectivities such as
caste, family and other communal group-identities for political participation. Studies conducted in India by social scientists do confirm this
phenomenon. Moreover, right from the beginning of political modernization in India and the freedom struggle there existed an alternative political ideology concomitant with the normative attributes of the traditional
Indian culture.

As we have mentioned above, democratic-liberalism, Marxism and
Gandhism were the three most important cultural ideologies. The first
two were of Western origin and the last was an orthogenetic response.
In course of time, other lower-order normative developments took place

owing to forces of history. These were the growth of values of secularism, communalism, and tribalism as political sub-ideologies. The growth
of these cultural values also coincided in India with the general process
of cultural change through Sanskritization and Westernization. Sankritiza-
tion reflected the urge for cultural and social mobility in the caste structure. Westernization, however, was a cultural movement of heterogenetic
origin.

Gandhism was, however, inclusive of all the three cultural processes.
It was a composite approach and should be treated as an alternative
model for political and general modernization of Indian society. It took
notice of both types of Western cultural challenges, the Marxist and
liberal-democratic, and tried to offer a model independent of these, in
harmony with the traditional ethos of Indian society. Its chief elements, forming a value system, were: asceticism, egalitarianism, activism, mass
participation or populism, along with theism and non-individualism in
political life. Gandhi did not believe in the parliamentary form of democracy, individualistic constitutionalism and welfare socialism, but in
ethical egalitarianism through collective mobilization, radical economic
changes, total alteration of the structure of social and economic relationships, and decentralization of political and economic power along
with the creation of pluralistic functional institutions. Gandhi did not
accept the theory of progressive structural and cultural differentiation
as a unilinear universal of modernization. Very much like Mao, Gandhi
believed in modernization through creation of such structures as would
have fully utilized collective-communal social structures pre-existing in
the Indian social system. And is it not true that despite the failure of
Gandhi in India, and the growth of parliamentary democracy, the political
culture of India continues to be that of castes, communities and tribes
rather than of individual citizens or their aggregates—classes?

However, the political culture which caught the imagination of the
political elites in India was not the one suggested by Gandhi but one
which was obtained as a legacy of colonialism with trimmings from the
constitutional history of the Western nations. Its key values were wel-
fare-socialism, secularism, individualism and rationalism. It was thus
totally Western in idiom and ethos. Even secularism, which otherwise
is older in Indian tradition than in the West, was acknowledged in its
Western form of religious neutrality rather than transcendance and fusion
of religions at a higher level.

Moreover, owing to the historicity of India's partition and the trauma
of the preceding Islamic conquest of Hindu India, secularism in Independent India has become a symbol which evokes mixed feelings and
emotional anxieties in all communities. It thus fails to evoke the response
for which it has been idealised. In the meantime, militant and orthodox

Islamization (*tabiligue*) proceeds as a counter process to tre growth of the Hindu militancy of the RSS variety.

In what direction then has political culture developed in India? We find that it has fully corresponded with structural changes and its tendencies; in other words, liberal democratic culture (in the Western sense) even today exists only in a subcultural form, and the wider political spectrum has evolved an altogether different equation of modernity with tradition which is rooted in the status principle of stratification. We have mentioned how this creates formidable structural problems for political modernization in India.

CONCLUSION

We may observe that the structural and cultural contradictions which have emerged in India's process of political modernization call for serious thought and corrective measures. The choice now no longer is between the mobilization system of Gandhi and constitutional democracy. But historically the emerging contradictions do indicate that, if constitutional democracy is not rendered more effectively socialistic and the precepts of socialism, equality and freedom are not translated into practice, there will definitely emerge forces of political radicalism which will be hard to counter. What is needed, therefore, is not palliative reform but effective measures for structural change. How rationally these can be phased is a matter for more specific discussion and deliberation.

Moreover, modernization should not be identified with the symbolism of "universal redemption" of the fallen. It is a composite process and a structurally (in terms of power, distributive justice and differentiation of social forms) neutral agent as far as the theory of change is concerned. No one particular model of modernization should, therefore, be held sacred and, particularly, the people of Asia whose historical contingency in political and economic development is rather special, if not unique, must keep an open mind about this form of change, much more than others, and much more than has hitherto obtained.

BIBLIOGRAPHY AND REFERENCES

Andre Beteille: "Elites, Status Groups and Castes in Modern India", *India and Ceylon: Unity and Diversity*, Philip Mason ed. (Bombay: Oxford University Press, 1967).

————*Caste, Class and Power* (Bombay: Oxford University Press, 1968).

F. G. Bailey: *Politics and Social Change—Orissa in 1959* (Bombay: Oxford University Press, 1963)

F. W. Riggs: *Administration in Developing Countries* (Boston: Houghton Mifflin Co. 1964)

G. A. Almond & James S. Coleman (eds): *The Politics of Developing Areas* (Princeton: Princeton University Press, 1960).

G. A. Almond and G. B. Powell Jr.: *Comparative Politics: A Developmental Approach* (Boston: Little Brown & Co., 1966)

G. A. Almond & S. Verba: *Civic Culture* (Princeton: Princeton University Press, 1963)

Guner Myrdal: *Asian Drama* (Penguin Books, 1968)

R. L. Hardgrave, Jr.: "Caste Fission and Fusion" (*Economic and Political Weekly*, July, 1968)

Rajni Kothari (ed.): *Caste in Indian Politics* (Delhi: Orient Longmans, 1970)

Irving L. Horowits: *Three Worlds of Development* (New York: Oxford University Press, 1958)

Lucian W. Pye, *Aspects of Political Development* (Boston: Little Brown & Co., 1966)

Myron Weiner: "Political Modernization and Evolutionary Theory" in *Social Change in Developing Areas*, eds. Hr. Barringer, George I. Blanksten and Raymond W. Mack (Massachusetts: Schenkman Publishing Co., 1965)

————*Politics of Scarcity* (Chicago: University Press, 1962)

A. C. Mayer: "The Significance of Quasi-Group in the Study of Complex Societies" in *The Social Anthropology of Complex Societies*, Michael Banton (ed.) London: Tavistock Publications, 1966)

M. J. Levy: "Contrasting Factors in the Modernization of China and Japan", eds. Simon Kuznets, Wilbert E. Moore and Joseph J. Spengler (Durham, N. C.: Duke University Press, 1955)

J. P. Nettl and Robertson Roland: *International System and the Modernisation of Societies* (London: Faber & Faber, 1968)

Paul Brass: *Factional Politics in an Indian State: The Congress Party in Uttar Pradesh* (Berkeley: University of California Press, 1965)

R. Bendix: *Nation-Building and Citizenship* (New York: John Wiley and Sons, Inc, 1964)

L. Rudolph & S. H. Rudolph: "The Modernity of Tradition: The Democratic Incarnation of Caste in India", *American Political Science Review*, LIX, 4 December, 1965.

Srinivas M. N.: *Caste in Modern India and Other Essays* (Bombay: Asia Publishing House, 1964)

Talcott Parsons: "Evolutionary Universals in Society", *American Sociological Review*, Vol. 29, No. 3, June 1964

T. B. Bottomore: "Cohesion and Division in Indian Elites", ed. Philip Mason, *op. cit.*,

30

HIGHER EDUCATION
AND SOCIAL DEVELOPMENT

JAN SZCZEPANSKI

WHOEVER WRITES about higher education usually begins by invoking the universities of the middle-ages and the proud tradition of those times. Much has been written about the function of higher education in the history of European culture, but there are few empirical studies attempting to estimate the contribution of these institutions in the development of European societies. It is only recently that more detailed studies have been initiated on the problem of what the Universities have in fact been and what in their written history is only a lovely legend stemming from the self-adoration of university men. It is often stressed that the universities have been centres of knowledge and scientific progress, but the history of knowledge tells us that many great scientific discoveries were achieved outside the Universities and many social and philosophical ideas, inspiring whole epochs, were also born outside the scholarly societies. Eric Ashby has shown convincingly[1] that the industrial revolution in England was achieved without any contribution from the universities, and that academic circles fought bitterly against the introduction of technical sciences into higher education. Some authors hold that educa-

[1] E. Ashby, "On Universities and the Scientific Revolution", ed. *Education, Economy and Society*, 1961.

tion imparted in a certain way can even be a barrier to progress;[2] a statement quite obvious for Poles who remember vividly the conservative influence of the backward schools of the eighteenth century in our country. It is quite clear that the part higher education plays in social development does not result from the very nature of these schools, but from some of their organizational features, from the attitudes of their personnel, and the characteristics of the students and the graduates. This is why research is being done to determine the organizational characteristics of the higher schools—their programme and methods, the characteristics of their teachers, students and graduates—so as to determine how best the institutions of higher learning could contribute to social progress as well as to economic and political development. This paper is devoted to discussing these problems.

I

Although planning the development of economy, culture and politics came into vogue only in the 'twenties of our century and became widespread only about 1950, the nineteenth century laid a strong base for this phenomenon. It is only now that we realize the full importance of the Humboldt reforms, and of his conception of higher education, a conception which made of the German universities an important factor in the development of Germany in the last century. These reforms, achieved immediately after the defeats of Jena and Auerstaedt, which destroyed the two essential instruments of power of the Prussian State— the army and the bureaucracy organized on the pattern of the army— were aimed at finding new leading ideas for higher education in order to train the new managing class which society increasingly required. Humboldt foresaw that knowledge would be the new directing power of nineteenth century societies. He therefore based his university reform on the principle "Erziehung durch die Wiessenschaft". Even today, in all discussions on the subject of higher education in Poland, this principle is still considered an unalterable criterion, separating secondary education from higher education. By introducing the principle that higher education consists in the activity of the professor initiating the student into scientific research and teaching him, above all, *methods* of solving scientific problems; and, further, by stating the idea of "Lehrfreiheit" for the professor as well as for the student, Humboldt created a type of higher school which proved to be a powerful factor of modernization in German society, and an exam-

---

[2] T. Belough, The Economics of Educational Planning: Sense and Nonsense— *Problems and Strategies of Educational Planning in Latin America*, UNESCO, Paris 1964.

ple for Europe and the United States.[3] It thus appears that knowledge was a factor of technical development in the nineteenth century in all fields of the economy, and the German universities, being the centres of scientific research in all departments, such as technics, medicine, agriculture and so on (unlike the English universities of the eighteenth century), were a leading force in this development, educating the directing elite in all domains of social life. Thus the question arises: Is it possible for the institutions of higher learning, in this second half of the twentieth century, to find such leading ideas which would be as imporant for the future as the principle "Erziehung durch die Wiessenschaft" was for the nineteenth century? In other words, what should be done with higher education to make it the most efficient factor of social progress?

II

And what do we call progress? We shall not enter into the long arguments concerning this very controversial subject. We shall simplify our task by bringing it down to earth and limiting our consideration to that part of social progress called modernization. We shall also put aside the arguments of those who remind us that the price of scientific and technical progress, measured in human suffering, considerably darkens the aura surrounding the idea of progress in the eyes of the enthusiasts.[4] We realize that modernization is only one part of progress; that it is not a complete entity; but such a limitation of our discussion will enable us to keep to facts.

Modernization is often considered to be the key to social development; measured in terms of economic expansion—a higher standard of living, expanding opportunities, such as access to education, medical help, employment and good working conditions. Progress can also be measured in terms of extension of civil liberties, and expanding participation in political and economic decisions concerning society. In order to achieve these conditions of modernization, it is necessary for a society to possess institutions for scientific research which will make continuous technical progress in all the fields of the economy possible. It is also necessary to have highly qualified managers, economic as well as political, possessing the qualities of foresight and adaptability to changing conditions. It is necessary, as well, to have an appropriately qualified working force, ready for efficient effort. And, last but not least, it is necessary to have a network of well-organized planning and directing institutions, and an organizational

[3] E. Ashby, "The Future of the Nineteenth Century Idea of a University", *Minerva*, 1968, No. 1.
[4] Bertrand Russell, *The Impact of Science on Society*, 1953.

level of economy, politics and other departments of public life which does not hinder progress.

With this view of modernization and the conditions of conquering it, we can now proceed to consider the part of higher education in securing definite aims. From this point of view, the higher schools fulfil, in general, the following duties: (a) conducting scientific research in all fields of knowledge; (b) training highly qualified personnel and, by educating teachers, influencing indirectly the education of the working force; (c) educating the leaders of economic, political and social life; (d) forming the local cultural centres and influencing indirectly the advancement of the culture of the surrounding society. Of course, these are not all the functions of the higher schools. Every individual has a constitutional right to education, and therefore the higher schools are the institutions, where this right can be realized in the highest degree. Higher education gives to the individual the opportunities for the fullest development of his capacities. From this point of view, we can consider all the derivative functions as resulting, in a large degree, from the realization of this right.

However, we are interested rather in the functioning of institutions of higher learning from the point of view of the needs of the whole society and its interests, or, in a narrower sense, from the point of view of modernization. The problem is a very complicated one, and therefore we shall consider only some of its aspects: the planning of higher education so as to make it correspond to the actual demands of modernization; recruitment from the point of view of modernization; the teaching organization and programmes judged from the point of view of modernization.

There can be found in our society, and more particularly in its directing group, the disastrous view that the higher seats of learning are some kind of institutions working for their own sake and having little influence on the development of the society. Is this true, and what role do the institutions of higher learning really play in the progress of the society as a whole? We shall try and examine this question.

III

The planning of higher education derives from economic planning, in the same way as economic planning derives from the theory of economic growth, considered as the basis of planning in general. The planning of higher education can be done in different ways, but all of them may be reduced to two principal methods discussed below:

(a) The method of social demand, issuing from the principle of the right of every individual to higher education; trying to determine how many people of the particular class will apply in future to be accepted in the institutions of higher learning and, therefore, how many places should be made available in the lecture rooms, the libraries, the laboratories, the hostels and canteens to meet this demand. In this case the anticipated flow of students is the basis of the planning of investments in higher education, the education of university teachers and so on. The difficulty of such planning consists in the fact that it is very difficult to foresee for which departments of study the students will apply in largest numbers, and in what numbers; how they are going to be distributed from the territorial point of view; etc. There exists a large literature dedicated to the problems of planning from the point of view of social demand.[5]

(b) The second basic type of planning in higher education is based on the prediction of the demand for qualified workers from the point of view of the needs of the economy and social life. In this case, the basis of planning is the general economic plan and other plans of social development elaborated by central planning institutions, and the anticipated demand for workers possessing higher education. This type of planning, developed at first in the Soviet Union, also has a large literature.[6] It is also applied in Poland; and although not all of its theoretical implications are commonly known, nevertheless the principles to be followed in determining the number of free places in different departments of study are now part of the current way of thinking. This kind of planning also has its difficulties. It does not exclude the freedom of the individual to select his profession and line of study, but only tries to direct this selection into existing channels and to control it. This sort of planning makes it impossible that forty per cent of school graduates should apply to be accepted for the study of the history of art, or psychology, as happens in some western countries. There are, however, other difficulties: the economic plan can be subject to radical changes during its realization, and the development of some departments of study can thus be severely limited. As the plan of recruitment has been determined to meet the needs of the initial economic plan, under a revised plan, for some years, the higher schools will be educating workers for "non-existent" institutions and demands. Such plans should also foresee technical changes, modifying in a radical way, the social situation in relation to anticipations.

It is not my purpose to discuss here the methods and techniques of securing the efficiency of the planning of education through the method

[5] Among others: *Economic and Social Aspects of Educational Plannning*, UNESCO, Paris 1964; H. S. Parnes: *Manpower Forecasting in Educational Planning*, OECD, Paris 1957; *Handbook of Statistical Needs for Educational Investment Planning*, OECD, Paris 1966; *Educational Planning*, Geneva, UNESCO, 1962.

[6] K. G. Nozko, *Methods of Estimating the Demand for Specialists and of Planning Specialized Training within the USSR*, UNESCO, Paris, 1964.

of estimating the demand for manpower of various kinds. I will only note some of the conditions which should be fulfilled to ensure that the planning does not defeat its purpose. What is essential is quantitative planning, foreseeing and formulating the demand in numbers, but accepting, at the same time, a series of implicit assumptions, conscious or unconscious, concerning the level of the education, the characteristics of the graduates and so on. The planning of recruitment is only one part of the problem. The other part is the planning of the organization of higher education, its programme, its equipment and its level, if the graduates of the higher schools are to fulfil all the functions they are expected to for the purpose of social development.

It must be stressed that the value of higher schools, from the point of view of their part in social development, is not judged by the quality of their students, but by the ability of the graduates to solve particular problems in social life and in all the departments of the economy. The capacities of the students, their ability to learn, and self-dependence in this respect, determine the atmosphere of the schools, and the amount of material which can be transmitted by the professors to their students; but only the results of scientific work executed in the higher schools, and the results obtained by their graduates have an influence on social development. These results are judged by different criteria than the results of students' work. A student is judged by his ability to learn, the graduate by his ability to cope with practical problems. The difference between these two kinds of abilities can be very great.

Thus, in order to be able to plan with greater assurance that the graduates of the higher schools will really be able to cope with the particular problems, situations and people they will meet in their work, educational planning should comprise not only a complex of efforts directed to foresee how many workers will be needed in the respective fields of social life after so many years, but should also be concerned with a number of activities tending to ensure that the candidates admitted will not only be good students, but also, above all, be successful graduates. Moreover, if the higher schools are to realize also the other conditions required by their part in social development, then the planning of the number of students received should be complemented by several other measures aimed at ensuring that the candidates selected will make successful graduates.

I V

Among the measures having particular importance, two should be mentioned in the first place: *first*—educational and vocational guidance organized in a proper way; *second*—proper methods of selecting candidates for admission to courses.

The tasks of educational guidance are somewhat different from those of vocational guidance. The first, after recognizing the capacities, interests and individual characteristics of the student, advises him in what kind of school he would probably achieve maximum success. Vocational guidance attempts to determine the profession best suited to the abilities, interests and individual characterisics of the particular student. It is essential that these two types of guidance be coordinated, because only then is it possible to direct properly the choice of school and profession in cases in which professional interests and capacities are not in accord with physical abilities: for example when his health does not permit the selection of a profession corresponding best to his capacity.

Over-simplifying, it may be said that guidance is an indispensable complement of educational planning. If the plan for education states that so many students should be accepted in a particular department of study, then it is the task of guidance to "provide" candidates who can "guarantee" that, on graduation they will be able to cope with the problems arising in that field in the execution of the economic plan.

Guidance in a secondary school is expected to lead the pupil to the line of learning best suited to his faculties and individual characteristics, save him disappointment and distress, as well as secure his success in school-work. This kind of guidance, as well as vocational consulting, is based upon psychological investigations, and it should be stressed that the scientific value of these investigations is a deciding factor of the success of the guidance.

However, vocational guidance should not take into consideration only the individual characteristics of the students, it advices on the choice of a line of study. It should also consider the demand for a working force. For this reason, some of the theoreticians of educational guidance stress that, in this kind of activity, we have a meeting of two basic methods of educational planning: planning based on the needs of the individual, and planning based on social demand. If educational planning is to be successful and if pupils are not to be directed to "dead ends", it should consider the actual state and the anticipated development of the economy.

Educational and vocational guidance should influence the access to higher schools in different ways. In the first place it should build the element of "pedagogical efficiency" by directing the students to schools and learning departments where their chances for success in learning are the best, and the probability of having to be screened out on their dropping out the smallest. Further, by directing students to such professions where their chances for professional success are highest, a factor which raises the efficiency of their professional work, it ensures their economic efficiency.

Professional success has been widely discussed, and the difficulty of measuring the degree of such success has been shown in Polish literature by the researches of Z. Grzelak.[7] However, let us stress that by professional success, important as it is for economic development, we understand an activity of efficiently solving situations met in professional work and introducing in these solutions innovations increasing the efficiency of work and the productivity of investments.

The possibility of forecasting the future professional usefulness of the youth is the most important problem of guidance. The reliability of such foresight depends on the general level of the methods of investigating the abilities of the students. It is obvious that along with great successes in directing the youth to some particular professions, for example such as piloting and special types of mechanical duties, we also have reported in the literature cases of serious failures and mistakes.[8]

In connection with the problem of guidance, a few words should be said about the subject of early recognition and special care for particularly gifted children. After the second world war, in some countries this problem has been considered crucial for scientific and technical progress, and a great effort has been made to elaborate methods of early recognition of talents, their development, special education and making the best use of them after the completion of studies. Some pedagogues, such as J. Petzold, suggested the organization of schools for specially gifted children as early as in 1905. In recent years, such schools have been organized in the Soviet Union and in other countries. However, it is generally considered that the results obtained have not been satisfactory. In any case, the phenomenon of the so-called "nivelation", meaning the adaptation of gifted children to the general level of their class, by lowering their abilities and learning possibilities, is well known to the pedagogues. Hence the efforts to eliminate such waste of abilities, which can prove to be creative abilities of a high quality. If, therefore, educational planning is to be comprehensive, it should be concerned not only with ensuring school and professional success, but should also anticipate the part of youth in the expansion of the creative potential of the society, i.e. the provision of the largest possible number of people capable of providing creative solutions to problems and giving them scope for action.

---

[7] Z. Grzelak, *Zaleznosè miedzy studiami, a praca absolwetnów szkólwyzszych* (Dependence between the studies and the work of the graduates of Higher Schools), Institute for Research on Higher Education, Warzawa 1965.

[8] Jacques Dubosson, *Le problème de l'Orientation Scholaire*, Neuchâtel, 1957, pp. 24-28.

V

Here we are coming upon the problem of selection. In many countries this problem is being solved by the free action of social and economic forces determining what part of the youth will come to the threshold of instruction of higher learning and be accepted. In other countries, everybody applying for reception to higher school is accepted without any selection, and all selection is forbidden by law. However, in a planned economy, such as ours, the students must be selected according to the number of places anticipated by the planning institutions for the particular lines of study.

There are in our scholar system some factors which undermine seriously the rationality of our planning: (a) A weak development of vocational and educational guidance, and a very feeble effort to improve the methods of this guidance and, therefore, a big percentage of screening-out among the students resulting from accidental and unconsidered choice of line of study. (b) A double examination: a final examination in the secondary school, and an entrance examination at the university, both giving access to higher education, conducted by different methods and setting different requirements. It is well known that the entrance examinations are often based upon the prejudices of the examining professors, testing and classifying the amount of knowledge in a field close to their interest, considering their own line the most important, without regard to its usefulness for further success in study. (c) The entrance examination can tell very little about the usefulness of the candidate after his graduation.

But, after all, the problem of initial selection is the fundamental factor in the rational planning of education, considering that improper methods of selection can change the whole of educational planning into a useless game, if the methods of recruitment for a limited amount of free places cannot be corrected in a spontaneous way. If the number of free places and the demands of the economy are both planned, the selection cannot be left to the free play of forces. If educational planning is to be logical, it should be complemented by a strong institution of guidance which ensures the rational selection of candidates for free places and gives hope that the graduates will be of the kind needed for the realization of the economic plan.

The mechanical assignment of particular professions was, however, known only in the history of the Inca empire. In our planned system the individual is free to choose the department of his study and his profession, as well as to change one line of study for another one, and far-reaching administrative limitations cannot be introduced in order to make the choice of the line of study rational. The institutions guiding the proper choice of the line of study should, therefore, be developed and should work not only with the students but also with their parents.

As can be seen, educational planning is only one of the elements necessary for improving the contribution of higher education accelerating social development and it should naturally be complemented by guidance and the elaboration of selection methods more effective than entrance examinations.

VI

The part of the higher schools in the acceleration of social development depends also on other factors, such as: (a) the organization of higher schools, (b) the teaching programme, (c) the quality of the teachers and their pedagogic ability, (d) the equipment of higher schools with teaching material such as research apparatus and so on. These four factors are complicated by a series of phenomena. The rapid increase in the number of students should be mentioned in the first place. The rapidly growing professionalization of learning and a purely professional disposition is a second factor. At the same time, big changes are occurring in the structure of the particular professions themselves, considered as systems of series of functions (for example the workers rebuilding Warsaw in 1950, and those active in the building trade at present, are specialized professionally in quite different ways). The rapid technological progress in the research apparatus, and the "electronization" of research techniques in all learning departments, even the humanities and social sciences, is the third factor. Further, the growing demand for teaching personnel diminishes constantly the level of their qualifications. In 1963, in the American higher schools [colleges], only 40 per cent of the teaching professors possessed the doctor's degree. It is anticipated that in 1970 this percentage will be only 20. In Polish higher schools also, the main weight of teaching falls on the shoulders of assistant professors with master's degrees.

All these processes and factors completely upset traditional forms of organization of higher schools, which all over the world are in the state of permanent reform. The adaptation of the organization of higher schools—their chairs, sections, departments and all the other units—is done in different ways, according to the number of students, the professionalization of education, the research equipment of the laboratories, and the new methods of the libraries, using more and more film and electronic techniques etc., according to the level of the teaching personnel and the necessity of closely directing the educational activity. The development of research institutions outside of the higher schools is also an important factor changing the functioning of these schools and the teaching and research done in them.

The teaching programmes and the requirements from the students are also changing under the influence of the demands of the economy, new working techniques and so on. The biggest danger for social progress consists, in this respect, in losing the necessary attitude of being "before one's time". It is a well-known situation consisting in the fact that professional education is preparing the students to work in technical conditions quite different from those actually existing. Therefore the technical backwardness of higher schools can result in the backwardness of their graduates in regard to the actual state of the techniques in all domains of life. They will also not have the necessary ability of adjustment, and their education will be devoid of the elasticity that will enable them to get acquainted with changing conditions during the thirty years of their future professional life. Therefore, all over the world, lively discussions are being led, and research work being done, in order to devise programmes and teaching methods most efficient from the point of view of economic growth and social development. It is a problem of the highest importance, especially for the countries of the Third World.

The problem of the qualifications of the teaching personnel, the methods of their education and selection, is closely connected with the organization of study and its programme. The time of Humboldt's conception of the professor as a master, initiating his students into the mysteries of knowledge by means of common research, belongs to a never-returning past. The development of the research institutions *outside* of the higher schools and the mass influx of students into these schools is the reason why modern research methods, elaborated in the huge laboratories of industry and the army, are losing their educational usefulness. Further, the number of professors is too small to be able to direct the research of their students in mass departments of study. Therefore, the higher schools [colleges] are becoming purely teaching institutions, where assistant professors introduce students into their new professions, and the contact with the professors is growing very loose. In the light of these tendencies, the setting up before the candidate professors of very high requirements during the examination for the right to teach at higher schools seems a tendency towards dividing the teaching personnel in two groups, those who are teaching, and those attaining high qualifications, but having little contact with the students.

Therefore, the view that scientific research should be concentrated outside of the higher schools, in departmental research institutes, and the higher schools should be limited to teaching activity, seems understandable. This of course is "ostrich policy" because, after all, higher schools deprived of the possibility of scientific research will be so sterilized of scientific talent and the contact with scientific progress that

M-41

they will educate people in a manner that will not prepare them for work in the research institutes, thus lowering their scientific level. In this way, by a boomerang effect, the concentration of scientific research outside of the higher schools will result in lowering the scientific level, not only of the higher schools themselves, but also of the scientific institutions all over the country.

All these problems are an inseparable part of the problem of educational planning for social development. The anticipation and determination of the number of students in different departments of study is only one, and not the most important, aspect of this process.

VII

Among the theoreticians of social progress and politicians responsible for this progress, there is a common understanding of the fact that higher education, the level and quality of the teaching personnel of the higher schools, are the crucial determinants of the speed of economic progress and the development of other factors determining social progress. The best indication of this understanding is the growing expenditure on higher education, and the growing means dedicated to scientific research in the higher schools. These are staggering sums! Data could be mentioned here about the budgets of some American Universities reaching 150 million dollars a year or milliards of dollars which American schools [colleges] are getting for scientific research from the federal or state governments. This, however, is not the point, and the part of higher education in planned social development does not depend only on the amount of money spent. The point is that the planning of a complex activity and its different elements should be harmonized. Not only such obvious elements as the fact that the increase of the number of students requires a still larger increase of the expenditure on higher education; but also that the planning of higher education should mean the planning of its organization, programmes, quality of the teaching personnel, equipment, and teaching methods, needs constantly to be borne in mind. The higher schools are not means of progress by themselves. They are becoming such means only in precisely defined conditions. If these conditions are not fulfilled, the higher schools can become institutions vegetating on the margin of the society—or even obstacles to progress. It is not the institutions themselves that decide on whether or not they will be factors of development but the entire economic and cultural policy and the degree to which this policy is willing to make use of the potential of the higher schools.

INDEX

623